# The Routledge International Handbook of Lifelong Learning

As lifelong learning grows in popularity, few comprehensive pictures of the phenomenon have emerged. *The Routledge International Handbook of Lifelong Learning* provides a disciplined and complete overview of lifelong learning internationally.

The theoretical structure puts the learner at the centre and the book emanates from there, pointing to the social context beyond the learner. Up-to-the-minute syntheses from many of the leading international experts in the field give vital snapshots of this rapidly evolving subject from wide-ranging perspectives including:

- learning throughout life
- sites of lifelong learning
- modes of learning
- policies
- social movements
- issues in lifelong learning
- geographical dimensions.

This authoritative volume, essential reading for academics in the field of lifelong learning, examines the complexities of the subject within a systematic global framework and places it in its socio-historic context.

**Peter Jarvis** is an internationally renowned expert in the fields of lifelong learning, adult and continuing education and is founding editor of *The International Journal of Lifelong Education* (Taylor & Francis). He is Professor of Continuing Education at the University of Surrey, UK, honorary Visiting Professor at City University and Professor of the University of Pécs, Hungary (honoris causa).

# The Routledge International Handbook of Lifelong Learning

Edited by
Peter Jarvis

Routledge
Taylor & Francis Group

LONDON AND NEW YORK

First published 2009
by Routledge
2 Park Square, Milton Park, Abingdon, Oxon., OX14 4RN

Simultaneously published in the USA and Canada
by Routledge
270 Madison Avenue, New York, NY 10016

*Routledge is an imprint of the Taylor & Francis Group*

© 2009 Selection and editorial matter, Peter Jarvis;
individual chapters, the contributors

Typeset in Bembo by
Florence Production Ltd, Stoodleigh, Devon
Printed and bound in Great Britain by
The Cromwell Press, Trowbridge, Wiltshire

*British Library Cataloguing in Publication Data*
A catalogue record for this book is available from the British Library

*Library of Congress Cataloging in Publication Data*
The Routledge international handbook of lifelong learning/edited by Peter Jarvis.
    p.cm.
    Includes bibliographical references and index.
    1. Adult learning—Handbooks, manuals, etc.   2. Adult education—Handbooks,
manuals, etc.   I. Jarvis, Peter, 1937–.   II. Title: International handbook of
lifelong learning.
    LC5225.L42R68 2008
    374–dc22                                              2008008939

ISBN10: 0–415–41904–2 (hbk)

ISBN13: 978–0–415–41904–8 (hbk)

# Contents

# CONTENTS

# Illustrations

## Figures

## Tables

# Contributors

**Paul Bélanger** After directing research centres on education and work in Québec, Canada, Paul Bélanger became Director (1989–2000) of the UNESCO Institute for Education in Hamburg, Germany and, in 1997, the General Secretary of CONFINTEA V. He is now Professor at the UQAM Montreal University and director of the Interdisciplinary Research Center on Lifelong Learning (CIRDEP). He is author and co-author, in particular, of *Lifelong Learning* (1995), *Shifting Patterns in Adult Education Participation* (1997), *Transitions Toward LLL: Social indicators* (1998), *Transnational Analysis of Adult Learning Policies* (1999) and *Participation à l'éducation des adultes* (2004). He is currently President of ICAE, the International Council for Adult Education.

**Stephen Brookfield** Since the beginning of his career in 1970, Stephen Brookfield has worked in England, Canada, Australia and the United States, teaching in a variety of college settings. He has written and edited ten books on adult learning, teaching and critical thinking, four of which have won the Cyril O. Houle World Award for Literature in Adult Education (1986, 1989, 1996 and 2005). He also won the 1996 Imogene Oakes Award for Outstanding Research in Adult Education. He has authored over 75 chapters in edited books, published over 70 papers in refereed journals and delivered 40 papers that were published in juried conference proceedings. His work has been translated into German, Finnish and Chinese. He has been awarded two honorary Doctor of Letters degrees, from the University System of New Hampshire (1991) and Concordia University St Paul (2003), for his contributions to understanding adult learning and shaping adult education. In 2001, he received the Leadership Award from the Association of Continuing Higher Education (ACHE) for 'extraordinary contributions to the general field of continuing education on a national and international level'. He currently serves on the editorial boards of educational journals in Britain, Canada and Australia, as well as in the United States. During 2002, he was Visiting Professor of Education at Harvard University. He is currently Distinguished University Professor of the University of St Thomas in Minneapolis-St Paul, where in 2008 he won the University's Diversity in Teaching and Research Award and the John Ireland Teaching and Scholarship Award.

**Rachel Brooks** Rachel Brooks is a Senior Lecturer in Social Policy at the University of Surrey, UK, and co-convenor of the British Sociological Association's Youth Study Group. She was awarded a Ph.D. from the University of Southampton for her work on young people's higher education choices (subsequently published as *Friendship and Educational Choice: Peer influence and planning for the future*, 2005). Since completing her doctoral research, she has explored the interface between higher education and lifelong learning through an Economic and Social Research Council (ESRC)-funded project on 'Young Graduates and Lifelong Learning' and is currently working on a British Academy-funded project on international higher education (with Johanna Waters at Liverpool University).

**Jacira Câmara** Jacira Câmara is a founder and Professor of Education at Brasília Catholic University, former director of the graduate programme and former dean of the postgraduate programme. As a curriculum specialist, she has wide experience of all levels of education. She was a postdoctoral fellow at the University of London and has extensive experience ranging from that of a rural and urban periphery school teacher to participation in postgraduate programmes. She has published widely both in Brazil and abroad and was Secretary-General of the Brazilian Comparative Education Society. She has contributed to the World Council of Comparative Education Societies.

**Clélia Capanema** Clélia Capanema is a founder and Professor of Education at Brasília Catholic University, with a wide experience of educational policies, particularly as Secretary of Education and Chair of the Federal District Board of Education. She has published widely both in Brazil and abroad. She has been a postdoctoral fellow at the University of London and President of the Brazilian Comparative Education Society, and has served on the World Council of Comparative Education Societies.

**C. P. S. Chauhan** Professor Chauhan is currently working as National Fellow at the National University of Educational Planning and Administration, New Delhi (India). He has previously worked in the National Council of Educational Research and Training, New Delhi, and Banaras Hindu University. He also worked as Professor and Chairman, Department of Education, Aligarh Muslim University, Aligarh. He has published over forty research papers and articles in national and international journals. His email address is cps_chauhan@yahoo.com.

**John Daniel** Sir John Daniel is President and Chief Executive Officer of the Commonwealth of Learning. A graduate of the universities of Oxford and Paris, he has worked in ten universities in five jurisdictions. He was President of Laurentian University, Canada (1984–90); Vice-Chancellor of the Open University, UK (1990–2001) and Assistant Director-General for Education at UNESCO, Paris (2001–4). Among his 250 publications, the best known is his book, *Mega-universities and Knowledge Media: Technology strategies for higher education*, which established his reputation as a leading thinker on how technology can improve academe. He was knighted by Queen Elizabeth II for services to higher education in 1994 and has received 30 honorary doctorates, fellowships and professorships from universities in 15 countries.

**Cornelia Dragne** Cornelia Dragne is a doctoral candidate in Leadership Studies in the Department of Education, University of Victoria, Canada. She holds an MSc in Computer Systems and a BSc in Engineering. Her research interests focus on adult and continuing education, lifelong learning and higher education.

**Kim Duckett** Kim Duckett is the Principal Librarian for Digital Technologies and Learning at North Carolina State University, USA. She takes a lead in the library's efforts to incorporate library resources, services and instruction into teaching and learning environments and serves as the primary distance education librarian.

**Chris Duke** Chris Duke is Honorary Professor of Lifelong Learning at the Universities of Leicester and Stirling and Visiting Professor of Regional Learning at the RMIT University of Melbourne. He was a Jesus College Major Scholar with a first-class honours degree in History from the University of Cambridge and a PGCE; he also holds a Ph.D. from the University of London and an Hon. D.Litt. from Keimyung University, Republic of Korea.

He has worked for 45 years in higher education institutions, mainly in the UK and Australia, across the spectrum from polytechnics to ancient and modern universities, including Auckland, Greenwich (as Woolwich Polytechnic), Leeds, RMIT, Warwick and Western Sydney Nepean. He has held such positions as Foundation Director and Professor of Continuing Education or Lifelong Learning at ANU, Auckland, UWS Nepean and Warwick, Pro-Vice Chancellor at Warwick and RMIT, and President at UWS Nepean. From 2002 to 2005 he was Director of Higher Education for the National Institute of Adult Continuing Education (NIACE), and from 2003 to 2005 he was Associate Director, Adult Learning for Action on Access.

Other leadership positions have included the Asian South Pacific Bureau of Adult Education (ASPBAE) (Secretary-General and Life Member); the International Council for Adult Education (ICAE) (Associate Secretary-General and Life Member); and the UK Universities Association for Lifelong Learning (formerly UACE) (Secretary, Vice-President and Life Member). He is currently the Secretary-General of Pascal, the International Observatory of Place Management, Social Capital and Learning Regions.

**John Field** John Field is Professor of Lifelong Learning at the University of Stirling, Scotland. His research interests include adult learning, social capital and the history of adult education and training. He has published widely, and has served as an expert adviser to various policy bodies, including the UK Government, the Northern Ireland Assembly and the Organization for Economic Cooperation and Development (OECD). He is a Visiting Professor at Birkbeck College, University of London.

**Candido Gomes** Candido Gomes is a founder and Professor of Education and Sociology at Brasília Catholic University. He has been adviser to the Federal Senate and the Constituent Assembly, seeking to build bridges between educational research and policy, President of the Brazilian Comparative Education Society and Chairman of the Research Committee of the World Council of Comparative Education Societies. He has acted as an consultant for international organisations on the re-democratisation of Brazil.

**Stephen Gorard** Stephen Gorard holds the centrally funded Chair in Education Research at the University of Birmingham, UK. His research is focused on issues of equity, especially in educational opportunities and outcomes, and on the effectiveness of educational systems. Recent project topics include widening participation in learning (*Overcoming the Barriers to Higher Education*, 2007), the role of technology in lifelong learning (*Adult Learning in the Digital Age*, 2006), informal learning, 14–19 provision, the role of targets, the impact of market forces on schools, underachievement, teacher supply and retention (*Teacher Supply: The key issues*, 2006) and developing international indicators of inequality. He is also interested in the process and quality of research (*Quantitative Research in Education*, 2008).

**Colin Griffin** Colin Griffin worked for many years in the Department of Educational Studies, University of Surrey, UK, where he is now a Visiting Senior Fellow. He has published widely in adult education and lifelong learning, especially in the fields of curriculum and policy analysis. Among his more recent publications are *Adult and Continuing Education: Major themes* (5 vols;

ed. Peter Jarvis with Colin Griffin) (2003), *Theory and Practice of Learning* (2nd edn; with Peter Jarvis and John Holford) (2003) and *Training to Teach in Further and Adult Education* (2nd edn; with David Gray and Tony Nasta) (2005).

**Budd L. Hall** Budd L. Hall is the founding director of the Office of Community-based Research at the University of Victoria, British Columbia. He is a former Dean of Education at the same university and previously he served as Chair of Adult Education at the University of Toronto and Secretary-General of the International Council of Adult Education (ICAE). Budd is a scholar-activist who has worked with Julius Nyerere, Paulo Freire, Dame Nita Barrow and others over the years in building adult education frameworks for large-scale social change efforts. He has been involved in peace movements, environmental movements, anti-apartheid movements, indigenous rights movements, the right to learn and adult literacy movements throughout his adult life. He is also a poet.

**Soonghee Han** Soonghee Han is Professor of Lifelong Learning in the Department of Education at Seoul National University, S. Korea. He earned his Bachelor's and Master's degree from Seoul National University and Doctorate from the State University of New York at Buffalo. His academic work has focused mainly on studies of the learning society and learning ecology, comparative and global studies of lifelong learning, and critical theories in adult education. He is also deeply involved in studies of popular education and human rights education in the Korean context. Currently he is leading a government-funded research project, BK21, which mainly investigates the agenda of Competency-based Education Change (http://competency.snu.ac.kr).

**Heribert Hinzen** Heribert Hinzen is the Director of *dvv international*, the Institute for International Cooperation of the German Adult Education Association (formerly IIZ/DVV), Bonn, Germany. His doctoral dissertation was on Adult Education in Tanzania at the University of Heidelberg. He joined the Institute in 1977, and has worked on a number of projects, serving for several years in Sierra Leone and Hungary, and is the editor of the journals, *Adult Education and Development* and *International Perspectives on Adult Education*. He is currently a Vice-President of both the European Association for the Education of Adults (EAEA) and the International Council for Adult Education (ICAE), and is a member of the CONFINTEA VI Consultative Group and of the UN Literacy Decade Expert Group. As an Honorary Professor he teaches at the Universities of Pecs and Iasi, Romania. In 2006 he was elected to the International Adult and Continuing Education Hall of Fame.

**John Holford** John Holford is Robert Peers Professor of Adult Education at the University of Nottingham, UK. He is the author of *Union Education in Britain* (1993), and has written widely on the history of adult and workers' education. His recent research has focused on life-long learning, citizenship and social cohesion, particularly in the European Union. He is joint editor of the *International Journal of Lifelong Education*, an Honorary Professor at the University of Hong Kong, and a Fellow of the Royal Historical Society.

**Susan Imel** Susan Imel is an Adjunct Instructor at Ohio State University and North Carolina State University, USA, and co-editor-in-chief of *New Directions for Adult and Continuing Education*. Previously, she directed the Educational Resources Information Center (ERIC) Clearinghouse on Adult, Career and Vocational Education and, from 1997 to 2006, served on the ALADIN Task Force.

**Knud Illeris** Knud Illeris is Professor of Lifelong Learning at the Danish University of Education in Copenhagen. He is also the author of *How We Learn: Learning and non-learning in school and beyond* (2007), *Adult Education and Adult Learning* (2004) and *Learning in Working Life* (2004). He was elected to the International Hall of Fame for Adult Education in 2006 and was Adjunct Professor of Educational Learning and Leadership at Teachers College, Columbia University, New York in 2004. Recently Illeris has edited *Contemporary Theories of Learning*, to be published by Routledge in 2009.

**Peter Jarvis** Peter Jarvis left school without sufficient qualifications to go to university and so he served for three years in the ranks in the Royal Air Force. Later he entered the Methodist ministry and during his training was able to study for his first degree. During his pastoral ministry he studied for a second first degree. On leaving the pastoral ministry he became a teacher trainer and then lecturer in adult education at the University of Surrey, UK. During these years he researched for his Masters degree and his Ph.D. None of his qualifications is in education. During his time at Surrey, he served as Head of Department of Educational Studies for a period, but for over ten years has been Professor of Continuing Education – now part-time.

He has published over 200 papers and written or edited over 35 books. He is the founding editor of the *International Journal of Lifelong Education* and has served on many other editorial boards throughout the world, including being Chairman of the Board of *Comparative Education*. He was awarded a higher doctorate (D.Litt.) by the University of Surrey for his publications in many branches of education for adults. He has many awards for his work, including five honorary doctorates, the Cyril O. Houle Award and the Comenius Award, and was elected as an individual member to the Standing Conference of University Teachers and Researchers on the Education of Adults (SCUTREA) and to the International Hall of Fame for Adult Education. He is also a Fellow of the Royal Society of Arts. He has been Visiting and Guest Professor in many countries of the world, having lectured in over 40 countries, and has been an Adjunct Professor at the University of Georgia, USA, and Noted Scholar at the University of British Columbia, Canada. He is currently Honorary Visiting Professor at City University, UK, and Professor of the University (honoris causa) at Pecs University, Hungary.

His latest books are a trilogy for Routledge on lifelong learning and the learning society: *Towards a Comprehensive Theory of Human Learning* (2006), *Globalisation, Lifelong Learning and the Learning Society: Sociological perspectives* (2007) and *Democracy, Lifelong Learning and the Learning Society: Active citizenship in an age of late modernity* (2008).

**Victoria J. Marsick** Victoria J. Marsick, Ph.D., is Co-Director of the J.M. Huber Institute for Learning in Organizations and Professor of Adult and Organizational Learning, Department of Organization and Leadership, Teachers College, Columbia University, New York. Victoria's research is on informal learning at the individual, team and organisational levels, action learning and organisational learning assessment.

**Roger Morris** Roger Morris was, until he retired, an Associate Professor in Adult Education at the University of Technology, Sydney, Australia. He retains an ongoing relationship with the University as an Honorary Associate. He is the long-term National Secretary of Adult Learning Australia. Roger has been inducted into the International Adult and Continuing Education Hall of Fame and has been appointed as a Member of the Order of Australia for services to adult and continuing education.

**Michael Omolewa** Michael Omolewa is a Professor of the History of Adult Education at the Department of Adult Education, University of Ibadan, Nigeria. He is currently Ambassador and Permanent Delegate of Nigeria to UNESCO and member of the Governing Board of the Commonwealth of Learning. He is also a recipient of the Fellowship of the Commonwealth of Learning (FCOL) and elected to the International Hall of Fame for Adult Education.

He was Dean of the Faculty of Education, Chairman of the Committee of Deans of Faculties of Education of Nigerian Universities and for two terms was Head of the Department of Adult Education at the University of Ibadan. He has also served as a member of the Executive Board of the International Standing Conference of the History of Education (ISCHE), President of the 32nd session of the General Conference and Chair of the Education Commission of the 31st session of the General Conference of the organization.

He has published widely in the areas of the history of formal, non-formal and informal education and he is a leading historian of adult education, member of several editorial boards of leading learned journals in education including the *International Review of Education*, the *Journal of African American History* and the *International Journal of Lifelong Education*. His most recent book is *Cross Over Unto the Other Side: The mission of adult education* (2006), a Valedictory Lecture delivered at the University of Ibadan.

**Adama Ouane**   Adama Ouane is currently Director of the UNESCO Institute for Lifelong Learning (UIL) in Hamburg, Germany. In 1976, he received his Ph.D. in applied linguistics from the Institute of Linguistics at the Moscow Academy of Sciences.

From 1977 to 1982 he was the Deputy National Director-General for Literacy and applied Linguistics in Mali, Professor at the École Normale Supérieure (ENS) in Bamako and Consultant to UNICEF, the United Nations Development Programme (UNDP), the Agence de la Francophonie and the World Bank. He directed the overall linguistic development plan of Mali and launched the first programme of the use of local languages in schools. He was a founding member of the Regional Council for Literacy and Adult Education in Africa (CREAA), and created a doctoral on-the-job training course in literacy and adult education in Mali, within the Department of Psychology and Pedagogy of the ENS and with support from external visiting professors.

Adama has a very long association with the UNESCO Institute for Education (UIE), where he served as a Senior Research Specialist from 1982 to 1995. His responsibilities included research, capacity building and technical support to Member States, NGOs and CSOs in the areas of literacy, post-literacy, curriculum development, monitoring and evaluation. He also designed and implemented a large number of inter-regional programmes in these areas and conducted cooperation action and policy-oriented research on learning strategies, monitoring and evaluation and innovative content areas.

Adama has published many books and papers dealing with literacy, post-literacy and continuing education, adult and lifelong learning, mother tongue and multilingual education. He was Executive Editor of the world's longest-running comparative international education journal, the *International Review of Education* (IRE) from 1985 to 1987 and is Chairperson of the Editorial Board. He was the Director of the UNESCO Institute for Education in Hamburg from 2000 until its closure in June 2006 and spearheaded all the complex processes in its transformation into the UNESCO Institute for Lifelong Learning.

From 1995 to 1999 he was a Senior Programme Specialist as well as a leading specialist responsible for literacy, adult education, non-formal and basic education at the UNESCO Headquarters in Paris. He was coordinator of the UNESCO NGO/Civil Society Consultation on Literacy and Adult Education and organised major events in many developing countries to promote adult education at policy and professional levels. He was the main author of the major education papers and reports prepared by UNESCO and one of the key organisers of the Fifth

International Conference on Adult Education (CONFINTEA V). He has full responsibility for preparing and conducting the forthcoming CONFINTEA VI, scheduled to be held in Brazil in May 2009.

Besides speaking many African languages, he is fluent in English, French, Russian and German, and has delivered keynote addresses on literacy, adult learning, non-formal education, lifelong learning and multilingualism in many universities and at conferences in all the world's regions.

**Santosh Panda** Santosh Panda has a Ph.D. in Education, Certificate in Educational Television (BBC, UK), and is a Professor of Distance Education and Director of the Staff Training and Research Institute of Distance Education, Indira Gandhi National Open University (IGNOU), India. Santosh has taught in the faculty of education at campus-based universities; has been Director of Policy and Research at the Association of Indian Universities; founding Director of the Inter-university Consortium for Technology-enabled Education at IGNOU; a senior Fulbright scholar at the University of New Mexico, Albuquerque; Visiting Professor at Manchester Metropolitan University and the University of London, UK; and an Adjunct Professor at the University of Maryland, USA and the University of Oldenburg, Germany. His books include *Planning and Management in Distance Education* (2003) and, with William Bramble, *Economics of Distance and Online Learning* (2008).

**Otto Peters** Otto Peters is Professor Emeritus at the FernUniversität in Hagen, Germany. He studied education, psychology and philosophy at the Humboldt Universität and the Free University in Berlin and earned his doctorate at the University of Tübingen. He has been active in describing and interpreting distance education since 1965 for purely academic reasons, first at the Education Centre in Berlin, then at the German Institute for Distance Education Research in Tübingen and then as Professor of Education in Berlin. In 1975 he became the Founding Rector of FernUniversität in Hagen and served in this position for nearly ten years. After this he devoted his time exclusively to distance education research. He has visited many distance teaching institutions on all continents and has written a number of books, the most important of which are *Learning and Teaching in Distance Education* 4th edn (2004) and *Distance Education in Transition* (1998). For eight years he served as Vice-President of the International Council of Distance Education. Otto has received four honorary doctorates, from the Open University, UK; Deakin University, Australia; Empire State College, New York; and the Open University, Hong Kong. Since 1991 he has been Professor Emeritus at the Fern Universität, dealing mainly with pedagogical problems in distance education. In 1999 he was awarded the ICDE Prize for Excellence for lifelong contributions to the field of open and distance education. In 2008 he was elected to the International Hall of Fame for Adult and Continuing Education.

**Julia Preece** Julia Preece is Professor of Adult Education at the National University of Lesotho, and Honorary Senior Research Fellow at the University of Glasgow, UK, where she was formerly Professor of Adult and Lifelong Education. Prior to that she worked at the University of Botswana and, in the UK, at the Universities of Surrey and Lancaster, following a 13-year career in community education and development in the inner-city areas of Birmingham. She has published extensively on issues to do with social exclusion, gender, citizenship and lifelong learning. Her most recent publications include a co-authored book, *Research Methods for Adult Educators in Africa* (2005), and a co-edited book, *Adult Education and Poverty Reduction: Issues for policy, research and practice* (2007).

**William M. Rivera** William M. Rivera has published widely. His research centres on interpretive and explanatory modes of investigation, and much of his work has been at the cutting edge of agricultural development and extension reform. He has edited three texts that are well known in his field: *Agricultural Extension Worldwide: Issues, practices and emerging policies* (1987), *Agricultural Extension: Worldwide institutional evolution and forces for change* (1991) and *Contracting for Agricultural Extension* (2002). The latter was described by Professor Emeritus Carl Eicher as a major contribution to the field and a seminal work for graduate studies. In a co-edited five-volume work compiled for the World Bank (2003), he organised case studies of agricultural extension reform experiences in more than 40 countries. More recently, in 2007, he completed research for a manual to be used by the Food and Agriculture Organization (FAO) of the UN in training senior-level government officials and practitioners on *Agricultural Extension in Transition Worldwide: Policy, strategies and reform*.

**Kjell Rubenson** Kjell Rubenson held the first Chair of Adult Education in Sweden before moving to Canada, where he is Professor of Education at the University of British Columbia and co-director of the Centre for Policy Studies in Higher Education and Training. He has been the research supervisor for several large national and international projects that have addressed the structures, policies and outcomes of adult education and lifelong learning. He is the founding president of the European Society for the Study of the Education of Adults.

**Henning Salling Olesen** Henning Salling Olesen is Professor of Education and Pro-Rector of Roskilde University, Denmark, and Director of the Graduate School of Lifelong Learning there, where he runs the Ph.D. programme for interdisciplinary learning and education research. He was a founding member of the school in 1973, following his graduation in Literature from the University of Copenhagen. He has been engaged in ground-breaking collaborative research with trade unions and work life since the 1970s and his research areas include adult learning, work-related learning, life history and psycho-societal methodology and lifelong learning policies. He has been Chair of the European Society for Research in the Education of Adults since 1998. He is a founding member of the International Research Group for Psycho-societal Research and Advisory Professor for doctoral studies at East China Normal University, Shanghai. He has published books, articles and research papers in Danish, English, German and several other languages.

**Tom Schuller** Tom Schuller, MA (Oxford), PGCE (London), Ph.D. (Bremen) is Head of the Centre for Educational Research and Innovation (CERI), OECD, Paris. Formerly Dean of the Faculty of Continuing Education and Professor of Lifelong Learning at Birkbeck College, University of London from 1999 to 2003, he was also co-director of the Centre for Research on the Wider Benefits of Learning. He worked previously in the UK at the Universities of Edinburgh, Glasgow and Warwick, at the Institute for Community Studies and for four years in the 1970s at the OECD. He is the author or editor of some 15 books, and his research history covers many areas of lifelong learning, but also fields such as employee participation, social capital and the social study of time. He has been an adviser to governments on numerous issues, especially on lifelong learning. From February 2008 he took up the post of Director of an independent inquiry into the future of lifelong learning, sponsored by the National Institute of Adult and Continuing Education (NIACE).

His major publications include: *The Benefits of Learning: The impact of education on health, family life and social capital* (with John Preston *et al.*, 2004), *International Perspectives on Lifelong Learning* (ed. with David Istance and Hans Schuetze, 2002), *Social Capital: Critical perspectives* (ed. with Stephen Baron and John Field, 2000), *Part-time Higher Education in Scotland* (with David Raffe *et al.*, 1998) and *Life After Work* (with Michael Young, 1991).

**Hans G. Schuetze** Hans G. Schuetze, LL.M (UC Berkeley), Doctor Juris (Göttingen) is Professor Emeritus and former Director, Centre for Policy Studies in Higher Education and Training, University of British Columbia (UBC), Vancouver, Canada. He is also an attorney-at-law, specialising in legal issues in education.

He studied law, economics, history and education in Göttingen and Bonn, Germany, Grenoble, France, and at the University of California at Berkeley, USA. Before the appointment as Professor of Higher Education at UBC in 1991, he worked as a lawyer, policy analyst and researcher in Germany (private law practice and two levels of government), France (Centre for Educational Research and Innovation at OECD) and the USA (research associate and private law practice). He has been a Visiting Professor in Austria, France, Germany, Japan and Mexico, and Honorary Senior Research Fellow at the University of Glasgow, UK since 1994.

His areas of interest and expertise include educational policy and legal and economic issues in education. He has published several works, especially in the fields of higher and adult education, lifelong learning and work and learning, most of them from a comparative perspective.

**Richard Taylor** Richard Taylor is Professor and Director of Continuing Education and Lifelong Learning at the University of Cambridge, UK, and a Professorial Fellow of Wolfson College. He was previously Professor of Continuing Education at the University of Leeds, where he had been Head of Department and, subsequently, Dean of the Faculty of Business, Law, Education and Social Studies.

His first degree was in philosophy, politics and economics (PPE) at Oxford and his Ph.D. was on the history and politics of the British Peace Movement in the 1950s and 1960s. He has published widely in politics and peace studies. He has worked in university adult education for many years and has published several books and journal articles on adult education and higher education, and comparative studies on the politics of post-compulsory education in North America and India. His most recent book is *For a Radical Higher Education: After postmodernism* (with Jean Barr and Tom Steele, 2002). He is currently engaged in researching and publishing on the evolution of the Labour Party's higher education policy since 1945.

He has had a long involvement in adult education teaching and development, with a particular focus upon trade union studies teaching, developing community education with educationally and socially disadvantaged adults, and continuing professional development programmes.

He was Secretary of the Universities Association for Continuing Education (UACE) from 1994–8, was Chair of the National Institute of Adult Continuing Education (NIACE) from 2001–6 and became the Chair of the Board of Trustees of the Workers' Educational Association (WEA) in 2006.

**Mark Tennant** Mark Tennant is Professor of Education and Dean of the Graduate School at the University of Technology, Sydney, Australia. His academic focus has been on developing a critical focus on psychology in its application to pedagogy, with emphasis on adult education contexts. He received the Cyril O. Houle Award for Literature in Adult Education for his book *Psychology and Adult Learning* (2006). His other well-known books are *Learning and Change in the Adult Years* (1995) and a collaborative book, *Reconstructing the Lifelong Learner* (2003). Mark has been a Visiting Professor at a number of universities in Japan, the USA, the UK and Canada.

**Janos Szigeti Toth** Janos Szigeti Toth is the President of the European Association for the Education of Adults (EAEA) and he has served on its Executive Board since 1998. He is also Managing President of the Hungarian Folk High School Society (HFHSS) and has been Head of the Adult Education Department at the Faculty of Esztergom of the Pazmany Catholic University, Budapest-Esztergom, Hungary, since 2006. He holds a doctorate in adult education and his research was on folk high schools. Among his honours are the Award for Culture from the Ministry of Education in 1993 and the Golden Cross of Merit of the Hungarian Republic, awarded by the President of the State in 1998. He also received the Appreciation Diploma of the Minister of Employment Policy and Labour of Hungary in 2003 and was elected to the International Adult and Continuing Hall of Fame. He also serves on the International Council of Adult Education (ICAE) Executive.

He has undertaken many consultations as an expert in adult education and has made presentations in many countries of the world. He was also a member of the editorial board of the *Socrates* magazine, Hungary, in 2001 and a Board member of Danube Television's public channel in 2000. He has published widely both internationally and nationally.

**Alan Tuckett** Alan Tuckett, OBE is Director of the National Institute of Adult Continuing Education (NIACE), having worked previously as an adult education organiser in Brighton, UK, and as a Principal in inner London. He started Adult Learners' Week in the UK in 1992, and supported its adoption by UNESCO, and then its spread to more than 50 countries. He is a Special Professor in Continuing Education at the University of Nottingham and an Honorary Professor at the Institute of Lifelong Learning at Leicester University. He is Treasurer of the International Council for Adult Education (ICAE).

He was Vice-Chair of the National Advisory Group for Continuing Education and Lifelong Learning from 1997 to 1999 and advises UNESCO on adult learning. He was President of the International League for Social Commitment in Adult Education in 1986–7, and President of the Pre-School Learning Alliance from 1999 to 2003.

Alan was a member of the Adult Learning Committee of the Learning and Skills Council from 2000 to 2007, and of the Government's Skills Alliance from 1997 to 2003.

He has seven honorary doctorates, is a Fellow of City & Guilds, and was inducted into the International Hall of Fame for Adult Education in 2006. He was awarded the OBE in 1995.

**Jean-Louis Vignuda** Jean-Louis Vignuda works with the United Nations Economic and Social Commission for Asia and the Pacific (UNESCAP) in Bangkok, Thailand, and is attached to the Transport Policy and Tourism Division within the Transport and Tourism Division.

**Kenneth Wain** Kenneth Wain is Professor of Education at the University of Malta, where he has served as Head of the Department of Foundations in Education and as Dean of the Faculty of Education. He currently teaches philosophy of education in the Faculty's B.Ed. (Hons) and M.Ed. courses and also moral and political philosophy to Arts students. Before taking up his first appointment at the University as lecturer, he taught in state primary and secondary schools for several years. He received his Ph.D. from the University of London. Over the years he has published numerous articles in academic journals as well as chapters in books. He has also authored the following books: *Philosophy of Lifelong Education* (1987), *The Maltese National Curriculum: A critical evaluation* (1991), *Theories of Teaching* (1992), *The Value Crisis: An introduction to ethics* (1995) and, most recently, *The Learning Society in a Postmodern World* (2004).

**Shirley Walters** Shirley Walters in Professor of Adult and Continuing Education at the University of Western Cape, South Africa. She is the founding director of the Division of Lifelong Learning, which is concerned with helping the university realise its lifelong learning mission. She is Chair of the South African Qualifications Authority and has been involved in many civil organisations, including being the Chair of the Cape Festival Steering Committee for four years.

**Karen E. Watkins**  Karen E. Watkins is the Associate Dean for Research and External Affairs and Professor of Human Resource and Organisational Development in the College of Education at the University of Georgia, USA. Previously, Dr Watkins was an Associate Professor of Educational Administration at the University of Texas at Austin, where she directed the graduate programme in Adult and Human Resource Development Leadership. Research foci for Dr Watkins have been in the areas of human resource and organisational development. She has consulted with numerous businesses and industries and is the author or co-author of over 70 articles and chapters, and six books. With Victoria Marsick she also developed and validated the organisational survey, *Dimensions of the Learning Organization*, which was the focus of a recent issue of *Advances in Developing Human Resources* entitled 'Making learning count: demonstrating the value of a learning culture'. She was voted Scholar of the Year by the Academy of Human Resource Development and served as President of the Academy from 1994 to 1996; was named a distinguished graduate by the University of Texas at Austin, Community College Leadership Program; and was inducted into the International Adult and Continuing Education Hall of Fame in 2003.

**David Watson**  Sir David Watson is an historian and Professor of Higher Education Management at the Institute of Education, University of London. He was Vice-Chancellor of the University of Brighton (formerly Brighton Polytechnic) between 1990 and 2005. His academic interests are in the history of American ideas and in higher education policy. His most recent books are *Lifelong Learning and the University* (1998), *Managing Strategy* (2000), *New Directions in Professional Higher Education* (2000), *Higher Education and the Lifecourse* (2003), *Managing Institutional Self-Study* (2005), *Managing Civic and Community Engagement* (2007) and *The Dearing Report: Ten years on* (2007).

He has contributed widely to developments in UK higher education, including as a member (from 1977 to 1993) of Boards and Committees of the Council for National Academic Awards. In 1988 he was appointed to the CNAA Council and the Polytechnics and Colleges Funding Council, and in 1992 to the Higher Education Funding Council (England). He chaired the HEFCE Quality Assessment Committee until his retirement from the Council in May 1996 and was a member of its Learning and Teaching Committee between 1998 and 2003. He was a member of the Paul Hamlyn Foundation's National Commission on Education (whose report *Learning to Succeed* was published in 1993), of the National Committee of Inquiry into Higher Education chaired by Sir Ron Dearing (whose report *Higher Education in the Learning Society* was published in 1997), and of the Roberts Review of Research Assessment in 2002–3. He was the elected Chair of the Universities Association for Continuing Education between 1994 and 1998, and chaired the Longer Term Strategy Group of Universities UK between 1999 and 2005. He is a Trustee of the Nuffield Foundation and a Companion of the Institute of Management. He is chair of the Commission undertaking the *Inquiry into the Future for Lifelong Learning*, supported by NIACE. He was knighted in 1998 for services to higher education.

**Linden West**  Dr Linden West is Reader in Education in the Department of Educational Research at Canterbury Christ Church University, UK, and Co-Director of the Centre for International Studies of Diversity and Participation. He was formerly Senior Lecturer in Continuing Education at the University of Kent and a researcher at the Universities of Keele and East London. He has been employed by the Workers' Educational Association (WEA), by Local Education Authorities, including heading an Adult Basic Education Unit, and in broadcasting. His books include the widely acclaimed *Beyond Fragments* (1996) and *Doctors on the Edge* (2001). He is lead editor of *Using Life History and Biographical Approaches in the Study* *of Adult and Lifelong Learning: European perspectives* (2007) and has a chapter in the book on families and their learning. Linden coordinates the Life History and Biographical Research Network of the European Society for Research on the Education of Adults (ESREA) and is a member of the Society's Steering Committee. He is also an Honorary Life Member of the Standing Conference of University Teachers and Researchers on the Education of Adults (SCUTREA) and a Fellow of the Royal Society for the Encouragement of Arts, Manufactures and Commerce (RSA). He is presently working on a new book, with Dr Barbara Merrill of the University of Warwick, on the use of biographical methods in social science, to be published in 2008. Linden is also a qualified psychoanalytic psychotherapist.

**Arthur L. Wilson** Arthur L. Wilson is Professor and Chair of the Department of Education at Cornell University, USA. He earned his Masters in adult education from Virginia Polytechnic Institute and State University and his doctoral degree from the University of Georgia. He worked as a practitioner for nearly two decades in adult basic education, staff development and continuing education for the professions. His research has focused on adult education philosophy and history, programme planning and cultural studies/critical discourse analysis. Overriding research concern in all of these areas is with the politics of education. His 2006 book, *Working the Planning Table: Negotiating democratically for adult, continuing, and workplace education*, was awarded the Cyril O. Houle World Award for Literature in Adult Education. He has also co-authored *Planning Responsibly for Adult Education: A guide to negotiating power and interests* (1994) and was co-editor of *Power in Practice: Adult education and the struggle for knowledge and power in society* (2001). He was co-editor of the 2000 *Handbook for Adult and Continuing Education* and is a past editor of the *Adult Education Quarterly*. He has received the Imogene Okes Award for Research twice from the American Association for Adult and Continuing Education for his research into the politics of education.

**Mary Alice Wolf** Mary Alice Wolf, EdD, is Professor of Human Development and Gerontology and Director of the Institute in Gerontology at Saint Joseph College, Connecticut. She is a graduate of Boston University, and of the Sorbonne, University of Paris, and holds a Master's degree from Columbia University, New York. Her doctorate is from the University of Massachusetts, where her research was in the process of life review and the older learner. She is the author of over 80 journal articles and several books, including *Connecting with Older Adults: Educational responses and approaches* (with P.T. Beatty, 1996), *Adults in Transition* (with M. Leahy, 1998), *Using Learning to Meet the Challenges of Older Adulthood* (with J.C. Fisher, 1998) and *Adulthood: New Terrain* (2005). She is the Book Editor of *Educational Gerontology, An International Journal*, a Charter Fellow of the Association for Gerontology in Higher Education, and a Fellow of the Gerontological Society of America. She is interested in areas of lifespan development, learning and gerontological issues. Currently she has been working on methods for the study of life course narratives and moments of transition in adulthood.

**Weiyuan Zhang** Weiyuan Zhang is Head and Chief Researcher at the Centre for Research in Continuing Education and Lifelong Learning, School of Professional and Continuing Education at the University of Hong Kong. He is an adjunct Professor at Beijing Normal University, Advisory Professor at East China Normal University, and Visiting Professor at China Central Radio and Television University, Shanghai Television University, Guangzhou Normal University, and Jiangsu Radio and Television University. He has over twenty years combined experience in educational research at East China Normal University, the University of Victoria, the University of Edinburgh, the Open University of Hong Kong, and the University of Hong Kong.

He is the recipient of eleven institutional, national, regional, and international awards in education, and has written or edited eleven books and published over 200 articles in scholarly journals and conference proceedings. He is a Chief Editor of the *International Journal of Continuing Education and Lifelong Learning* (in both English and Chinese versions) and has been on the editorial board of a number of journals, including the *International Journal of Lifelong Education*, the *International Review of Research in Open and Distance Education*, the *Asian Journal of Distance Education*, the *Malaysian Journal of Educational Technology*, the *Turkish Online Journal of Distance Education*, *China Distance Education*, *Open Education Research* and the *Journal of Distance Education*.

**Henrik Zipsane** Henrik Zipsane obtained an MA in History from the University of Copenhagen in 1985 and a Ph.D. in History and Pedagogy from the Danish University of Education, Copenhagen, in 1996. He has been a Director for the Local Archives and Museums in the Municipality of Farum, near Copenhagen, including the Immigrants Museum, from 1987 to 2001, an external lecturer in local and immigrant history, University of Copenhagen, from 1997 to 2001, and Chair of the Association for the History of Migration in Denmark from 1999 to 2001. He has been a Director of Jamtli – the County Museum of Jämtland in Östersund, Sweden – since 2001, co-founder and Chair of the European Network LLOAM (Lifelong Learning in Open Air Museums) since 2002, and co-founder and co-director of the Nordic Centre for Heritage Learning in Östersund, Sweden, since 2005. He has been a Pascal Observatory associate since 2007.

# Abbreviations

| | |
|---|---|
| AAES | Australian Army Education Service |
| AAHM | Asian Academy of Heritage Management |
| AALAE | African Association for Literacy and Adult Education |
| AAM | American Association of Museums |
| AAMD | Association of Art Museum Directors |
| ABCA | Army Bureau of Current Affairs |
| ABET | adult basic education and training |
| ABLE | adult basic learning and education |
| ACACE | Advisory Council for Adult and Continuing Education |
| ACAS | Advisory, Conciliation and Arbitration Service |
| ACE | adult and continuing education |
| ACHE | Association of Continuing Higher Education |
| ACS | Australian Correspondence Schools |
| ADB | Asian Development Bank |
| AED | *Adult Education and Development* |
| AGI | Adolf Grimme Institute |
| AGS | Social Improvement Network |
| AiDA | Accessible Information on Development Activities |
| AIOU | Allama Iqbal Open University |
| AIR | All India Radio |
| ALADIN | Adult Learning Documentation and Information Network |
| ALL | Adult Literacy and Life Skills Survey |
| ALRA | Adult Literacy Resource Agency |
| AMES | Adult Migrant Education Service |
| ANC | African National Congress |
| ANLAE | Arab Network for Literacy and Adult Education |
| APETIT | Network of Asia-Pacific Education and Training Institutes in Tourism |
| APOU | Andhra Pradesh Open University |
| ARLO | Arab League Literacy Organization |
| ASPBAE | Asian South Pacific Bureau of Adult Education |

| | |
|---|---|
| ASTD | American Society for Training and Development |
| ATP | Anti-Terrorism Package |
| BBC | British Broadcasting Corporation |
| BE | basic education |
| BFI | British Film Institute |
| BIAE | British Institute of Adult Education |
| BIDE | Bangladesh Institute of Distance Education |
| BLN | basic learning needs |
| BMBF | Federal Ministry of Education and Science |
| BMZ | Federal Ministry for Economic Cooperation and Development |
| BMZ | Federal Ministry of Economic Cooperation and Development |
| BOU | Bangladesh Open University |
| BPA | Federal Government Press and Information Service |
| CACE | Centre for Adult and Continuing Education |
| CARCAE | Caribbean Regional Council for Adult Education |
| CCI | Correspondence Course Institution |
| CCIC | Canadian Council for International Co-operation |
| CDP | Community Development Project |
| CEAAL | Latin American Council for Adult Education |
| CEC | Commission of the European Communities |
| CEDAW | Convention on the Elimination of all forms of Discrimination Against Women |
| CEEAL | Consejo de Educación de Adultos de América Latina |
| CERI | Centre for Educational Research and Innovation |
| CFTC | Commonwealth Fund for Technical Cooperation |
| CIDA | Canadian International Development Agency |
| CIRDEP | Interdisciplinary Research Center on Lifelong Learning |
| CIS | Commonwealth of Independent States |
| CLD | community learning and development |
| COL | Commonwealth of Learning |
| CONFINTEA | International Conference on Adult Education |
| CPD | continuing professional development |
| CPE | continuing professional education |
| CREAA | Regional Council for Literacy and Adult Education in Africa |
| CRS | Creditor Reporting System |
| DAC | Development Assistance Committee |
| DEC | Distance Education Council |
| DED | Department of Economic Development |
| DFA | Dakar Framework for Action |
| DfEE | Department for Education and Employment |
| DfES | Department for Education and Skills |
| DFID | Department for International Development |
| DLL | Division for Lifelong Learning |
| DPEP | District Primary Education Programme |
| DUK | German UNESCO Commission |
| DVV | Deutsche Volkshochschule Verband (German Association of Folk high schools; German Adult Education Association) |
| EAEA | European Association for the Education of Adults |

| | |
|---|---|
| EBAE | European Bureau of Adult Education |
| EBiS | Adult Education in South Eastern Europe |
| EC | European Commission |
| ECCE | Early Childhood Care and Education |
| EFA | Education for All |
| EGREES | European Group for Research on Equity in Educational Systems |
| EOTO | each one teach one |
| EPA | Educational Priority Area |
| ERT | European Round Table of Industrialists |
| ESL | English as a Second Language |
| ESRC | Economic and Social Research Council |
| ESREA | European Society for Research on the Education of Adults |
| ESSU | Education Sector Strategy Update |
| ETP | Education and Training Policy Division |
| EU | European Union |
| FAO | Food and Agriculture Organization |
| FDI | foreign direct investment |
| FLOSS | Free/Libre Open Source Software |
| FTIs | Fast Track Initiatives |
| GCAP | Global Campaign Against Poverty |
| GCSE | General Certificate of Secondary Education |
| GDP | gross domestic product |
| GER | gross enrolment ratio |
| GLO | generic learning outcome |
| GMS | Greater Mekong sub-region |
| GNI | gross national income |
| GNP | gross national product |
| GNVQ | General National Vocational Qualification |
| GPEX | Gross Public Expenditure on Development |
| GTZ | Agency for Technical Cooperation |
| HDI | Human Development Index |
| HE | higher education |
| HECS | Higher Education Contribution System |
| HEFCE | Higher Education Funding Council for England |
| HEI | higher education institution |
| HEPI | Higher Education Policy Institute |
| HESA | Higher Education Statistics Agency |
| HRM | human resource management |
| HTML | HyperText Markup Language |
| HTTP | HyperText Transfer Protocol |
| IALLA | International Academy for Lifelong Learning Advocates |
| IALS | International Adult Literacy Survey |
| IBE | UNESCO International Bureau of Education |
| ICAE | International Council for Adult Education |
| ICCE | International Council of Correspondence Education |
| ICCROM | International Centre for the Study of the Preservation and Restoration of Cultural Property |
| ICECU | Central American Institute of Popular Education |

| | |
|---|---|
| ICFTU | International Confederation of Free Trade Unions |
| ICT | information and communication technology |
| IDS | International Development Statistics |
| IFLA | International Federation of Library Associations |
| IFT | Institute for Tourism Studies |
| IGNOU | Indira Gandhi National Open University |
| IIEP | UNESCO Institute for Educational Planning |
| IIZ/DVV | Institute for International Cooperation of the German Adult Education Association |
| IIZ/DVV | Institute for International Cooperation of the DVV |
| IJLE | *International Journal of Lifelong Education* |
| ILA | Individual Learning Account |
| ILO | International Labour Organization |
| IMF | International Monetary Fund |
| IMHE | Institutional Management in Higher Education |
| INGO | international non-governmental organisation |
| IP | Internet Protocol |
| ISCED | International Standard Classification of Education |
| IT | information technology |
| ITE | Institute of Technical Education |
| ITS | intelligent tutoring system |
| ITU | International Telecommunications Union |
| JSN | Jan Shikshan Nilayam (People's Learning Centre) |
| KFW | Bank for Reconstruction |
| LCSA | Local Community Services Association |
| LIFE | Literacy Initiative for Empowerment |
| LLC | local learning centre |
| LLL | literacy and lifelong learning |
| LLP | local learning partnership |
| MDG | Millennium Development Goal |
| MLAC | Museums, Libraries and Archives Council |
| MOEHRD | Ministry of Education and Human Resource Development |
| MPFL | Mass Programme of Functional Literacy |
| NAAPAE | North-American Alliance for Popular and Adult Education |
| NAEP | National Adult Education Programme |
| NARSIS | Natural Resources Information System |
| NCCR | National Center for Creative Retirement |
| NCERT | National Council of Educational Research and Training |
| NCLC | National Council of Labour Colleges |
| NESS | National Evaluation of Sure Start |
| NFE | non-formal education |
| NFIL | National Forum on Information Literacy |
| NGO | non-governmental organisation |
| NIACE | National Institute of Adult Continuing Education |
| NIAE | National Institute of Adult Education |
| NIC | newly industrialised country |
| NIEPA | National Institute of Educational Planning and Administration |
| NIOS | National Institute for Open Schooling |

| | |
|---|---|
| NLM | National Literacy Mission |
| NPA | National Plan of Action |
| NPE | National Policy on Education |
| NPO | non-profit organisation |
| NQF | National Qualification Framework |
| NTEC | new technologies of education and communication |
| NTO | National Tourism Organizations |
| NUPE | National Union of Public Employees |
| NWFP | North Western Frontier Province |
| OA | official assistance |
| ODA | Official Development Assistance; or Overseas Development Agency; or Organisation Development Africa |
| ODL | open and distance learning |
| OECD | Organization for Economic Cooperation and Development |
| OER | Open Education Resources |
| OWL | Web Ontology Language |
| PAALAE | Pan-African Association for Literacy and Adult Education |
| PACES | Professional and Continuing Education School |
| PAWC | Provincial Administration of the Western Cape |
| PEB | Programme on Educational Building |
| PEL | paid educational leave |
| PFA | Programme for Action |
| PIAAC | Programme for the International Assessment of Adult Competences |
| PISA | Programme for International Student Assessment |
| PLCE | post-literacy and continuing education |
| PNDPC | Philippine National Development Plan for Children |
| PULMAN | Public Libraries Mobilising Advanced Networks |
| QAA | Quality Assurance Agency |
| QCA | Qualifications and Curriculum Authority |
| RAE | Research Assessment Exercise |
| RB | Responsible Bodies |
| RDF | Resource Description Framework |
| RDFS | RDF Schema |
| REFLECT | Regenerated Freirean Literacy through Empowerment Community Technique |
| REPEM | Red de Educacion Popular Entre Mujeres de America Latina y el Caribe |
| RLM | Real Literacy Materials |
| SALP | Scottish Adult Learning Partnership |
| SASEC | South Asia Sub-regional Economic Cooperation |
| SCONUL | Society of College, National and University Libraries |
| SCUTREA | Standing Conference of University Teachers and Researchers on the Education of Adults |
| SDP | Social Democratic Party |
| SIDA | Swedish International Development Cooperation Agency |
| SSA | Sarva Shiksha Abhiyan (Education for All Movement) |
| SW | Semantic Web |
| TAFE | Technical and Further Education |
| T&V | training and visit |

| | |
|---|---|
| TLC | Total Literacy Campaign |
| TUC | Trades Union Congress |
| TUTA | Trade Union Training Authority |
| TVET | technical and vocational education and training |
| UACE | Universities Association for Continuing Education (now the UK Universities Association for Lifelong Learning) |
| UBE | Universal Basic Education |
| UEE | universalisation of elementary education |
| UfI | University for Industry |
| UIE | UNESCO Institute for Education |
| UIL | UNESCO Institute for Lifelong Learning |
| ULF | Union Learning Fund |
| UN | United Nations |
| UNDP | United Nations Development Programme |
| UNESCAP | United Nations Economic Social Commission for Asia and the Pacific |
| UNESCO | United Nations Educational, Scientific and Cultural Organization |
| UNIVA | University Village Association |
| UNLD | United Nations Literacy Decade |
| UNWTO | United Nations World Tourism Organization |
| URI | Uniformer Resource Identifier |
| URL | Uniform Resource Locators |
| US/USA | United States of America |
| USAID | United States Agency for International Development |
| USD | US dollars |
| VENRO | Association for Development Policy |
| VET | vocational education and training |
| VHS | Volkshochschule (folk high school) |
| VUSSC | Virtual University for Small States of the Commonwealth |
| WBL | Wider Benefits of Learning |
| WCEFA | World Conference on Education for All |
| WCL | World Confederation of Labour |
| WEA | Workers' Educational Association |
| WETUC | Workers' Educational Trade Union Committee |
| WHO | World Health Organization |
| WTTC | World Travel and Tourism Council |
| WWW | World Wide Web |

# Introduction

*Peter Jarvis*

Lifelong learning has become a 'buzz word' in the educational vocabulary in recent years but it has not always been as widely accepted as it is now. Indeed, we do not have to go back many years to find the time when it was widely thought that adults could not learn a great deal new – indeed, 'you cannot teach an old dog new tricks!' – and that intelligence gradually declined with age. But in some countries, such as Denmark, there was a wide acceptance that adults could learn and, from 1812, there was a ruling that allowed schools to be used by adults in out-of-school hours. However, the general expectation was that education was for the young and so a front-end model of education emerged. Education became defined in terms of transmitting knowledge to the young – Durkheim (1956: 71) defined it as 'the influence exercised by older generations on those who are not yet ready for social life', and it was distinguished from training during which skills as opposed to knowledge were transmitted from the skilful to the apprentice. At the same time, teaching and learning were regarded as synonymous, although from early in the twentieth century the idea that adults should be given educational opportunities was emerging with Dewey claiming that schooling was designed to help continued human growth and development thereafter:

> the purpose of school organization is to insure the continuance of education by organizing the powers that insure growth. The inclination to learn from life itself and to make the condition of life such that all will learn in the process of living is the finest product of schooling.
>
> (1916: 51)

Perhaps the most influential statement about the place of adult education during this period came with the famous 1919 Report in Britain when the chair of the committee was to write these words:

> That the necessary condition is that adult education must not be regarded as a luxury for the few exceptional persons here and there, nor as a thing which concerns only a short span of early manhood, but that adult education is a permanent national necessity, an inseparable aspects of citizenship, and therefore should be universal and lifelong.
>
> (Smith, 1919, introductory letter: para. xi: 5)

It was not long after that one member of the 1919 report committee was to write the first book on lifelong education (Yeaxlee, 1929) – long before it was adopted by UNESCO or any other agency. Yeaxlee (1929: 31) claimed that:

> the case for lifelong education rests upon the nature and needs of the human personality in such a way that no individual can rightly be regarded as outside its scope, the social reasons for fostering it are as powerful as the personal.

However, the growth and gradual acceptance of adult education and then lifelong education was to span many decades. After the Second World War we began to see the spread of adult education and then lifelong education. UNESCO was to play a large part in this with the Faure Report (1972) and the work of Paul Lengrand (1975), but other concepts were also to play their part in its development, including continuing education and recurrent education – the latter being adopted by the Organization for Economic Cooperation and Development (OECD) for a while in the 1970s as a strategy for lifelong education (OECD, 1973).

In the USA there was a similar concern during the 1970s that led to the Mondale Lifelong Learning Act, which authorised the expenditure of $40 million annually between 1977 and 1982 on lifelong learning. But this money was never forthcoming and Peterson et al. (1979: 295) were forced to conclude that 'lifelong learning policies are gaining favour in numerous foreign countries, notably Scandinavia, [but] there are signs of slackening progress [in America]'. It will be noted that Arthur Wilson, in the final chapter of this book, also catches this lack of enthusiasm in the USA for lifelong learning – but it would certainly be true to say that, in some ways, America has led the world of adult education throughout this period, such as innovative vocational education, the education of older adults and so on. Hence, we cannot agree totally with this pessimism.

However, there is one other way in which adult education differed between English-speaking Europeans and Americans. From the outset the Americans confused education and learning and so many adult education books in the USA were described as being about adult learning. But it is the term 'learning' that was to prevail when prefixed by 'lifelong'. 'Lifelong education' was the term adopted by UNESCO, but by the mid-1990s it was 'lifelong learning' that was to prevail. There were many reasons for this, such as the fact that 'adult education' was regarded as liberal in the UK, whereas 'adult learning' included vocational education in the USA and, towards the end of the twentieth century, there was a deliberate policy designed to unite liberal and vocational education into a single entity. So, by the time the European Union (EU) began issuing its policy statements on the education of adults, they were about lifelong learning. But the EU was both confused and idealistic in its use of language: idealistic because it treated the term as about all learning, from the cradle to the grave, but confused as it had three different policy units: one concerned with education and training (initial education) a second concerned with higher education and the third directed towards the education of adults, which it called lifelong learning. Only in 2006, when it issued a policy statement on adult learning, did it untangle this confusion.

However, learning is a human process and this is not to be confused with learning in adult learning and lifelong learning – in these latter usages, learning is used as a gerund and in, in a sense, institutionalised learning. In this sense, this is precisely what education is, but the use of the term 'learning' does overcome some of the difficulties contained in the term 'education', although, as we see, it causes others! It is mainly in the institutionalised sense, rather than the human process sense, that lifelong learning is used in the following chapters, although it is hard to separate the two at all times.

This book has been written by some of the leading and most influential experts in the world of lifelong learning and I am very grateful to them for contributing their chapters. None needed to write and many were constantly pursued by me to write their pieces: some few authors dropped out and this was mostly due to illness or to the illness of family – rarely was it because of overwork! However, a couple of chapters that I would like to have included were necessarily omitted because of these problems.

The book itself falls into eight parts: the first two chapters build upon this opening introduction and were written by me. The first reflects the social ambiguities that this problematic concept generates and the second reflects the human process of learning in everyday life. In a sense, they, together with this introduction, form the basis of this book. The second section contains three chapters – on youth, middle age and old age. I seriously considered including a chapter on learning in very early life, since modern brain research has raised some significant issues about lifelong learning:

> As early as the first trimester of pregnancy, the fetus already possesses centers of balance and motion that respond to the mother's own movements. At the halfway point of gestation a fetus can hear. Sight remains severely muted though, unlike the sense of hearing there are few external stimuli in the uterus. By the seventh month the eyelids are open and the fetus can see diffused light coming through the abdominal wall. Taste too is working as the fetus takes in amniotic fluid. In addition to these basic functions of sense and motor control, there is also clear evidence that the human brain is busy *learning* in the womb . . . Numerous . . . experiments confirm that before birth individual brains are already attentive and actively engaged with the surrounding world, however limited.
>
> (Tremlin, 2006: 51)

This confirms the type of folk knowledge of the North American Indians – one pregnant mother in Alaska told me how her people teach that babies should be spoken to in the womb. Such research as this calls into question even the most basic definition of lifelong learning as something that happens from the cradle to the grave. In my own research (Jarvis, 1987) I called this pre-conscious learning and it clearly begins before the cradle. While I did not include this topic in this book, it is a subject that needs to be grasped firmly by those who are involved in lifelong learning.

The third part of the book focuses upon sites for learning and there is a sense in which these form a basis for a book in itself: each site of human activity is a place of learning, but we have tended to overemphasise the workplace as a site of learning and neglect some of the others. This overemphasis reflects the, what I feel is misplaced, concern with vocationalism in education. Of course there is a vital place for it, but we see its power in the way that it defines lifelong learning and how employability has become a fundamental aim of lifelong learning – rather than living itself! I have deliberately extended the sites for learning here so that we grasp some of the new and important ones, such as tourism. Indeed, tour guides are becoming a major sector in adult learning and Vignuda shows this in Chapter 17.

In the fourth part we have looked at five modes of learning and, having started this book, I was asked to supervise a dissertation for a masters degree in m-learning (mobile learning). M-learning is a new mode and there are a number of projects that are investigating this as yet another approach to lifelong learning and one that might develop in significance in the coming years. However, I deliberately omitted it as I do not feel that there is sufficient research to include it at this stage.

In the fifth part we look at policies and lifelong learning. I felt that it would have been possible to put in a number of national policy statements since they all differ in their emphasis. For instance, the UK's policy perspective is much more vocational than Finland's, and so on. However, it would have been problematic to do this, although I think that there is a place for comparative lifelong learning policy analysis in future studies. In this section the clearest policy differences may be seen between the World Bank and OECD, on the one hand, and UNESCO on the other. I have also, at the risk of a little overlap, inserted the EU in this section as well as having Europe in the geographical section, but the overlap is surprisingly small. Once we enter this field, we also have to examine issues of globalisation and power. See Jarvis (2007, 2008) in which I have begun to unravel some of the complexities of this in a late modern age. Perhaps it is natural to follow this section with a sixth part that examines non-governmental organisations (NGOs), so leading exponents on NGOs have written about the work that they do within the field of lifelong learning. Initially I was tempted to put the Commonwealth of Learning in this section but, since it was established by the Commonwealth countries as an aid agency, I thought that it belonged in the previous section. The authors of these chapters have focused on some of the major agencies, although the US Agency for International Development (AID) is not discussed.

In the seventh part I have included some other academic disciplines that are relevant to the study of lifelong learning, including economics, sociology and psychology. The chapter on philosophy also has a political orientation and it was for this reason that I decided to omit a chapter specifically on politics, although I concede that, with the work of scholars such as Habermas (deliberative politics) and Rawls (public reason) there would have been a major place for this. I included both feminism and religion in this section as well and I also considered topics such as health education; so it can be seen that the parameters of not only this section, but the whole book, could have been expanded considerably.

Finally, in the eighth part, we have chapters from each of the continents and, in India's case, the subcontinent. Any macro-geographical study necessarily omits some countries and so there are no specific mentions of many of the major countries providing lifelong learning. Nevertheless, this has already been undertaken much more thoroughly in books devoted to these individual countries or to comparative studies and thus I considered this to be an unnecessary concern. One of the other topics that I have deliberately omitted is the relationship between lifelong learning and war and oppression, but we have seen international and civil wars in recent years and those who participate in them undergo traumatic learning experiences; thus, another aspect of lifelong learning untouched here is the relationship between learning and trauma.

The book has been designed to offer a broader perspective on lifelong learning than is normally assumed. In this sense, it seeks to capture some of the ambiguities of the opening chapter while also pointing to the complexity of the topic. Indeed, this complexity reflects that of contemporary society, so it can be hoped that this book begins to open a number of doors that have not fully been opened.

In concluding, I must thank the two people who assisted me at the outset of the project: Dr John Peters from the University of Tennessee and Dr Weiyuan Zhang from Hong Kong University. My thanks also go to the many people, including the contributors, who have supported this enterprise and especially to Philip Mudd – my publisher – from Routledge who entrusted me with it. Without his constant support I do not think that the work would have seen the light of day so quickly. Finally, I am grateful to all who read these pages and I hope that the book will prove both enlightening and useful.

# References

Dewey, J. (1916) *Education and Democracy*, New York: The Free Press.

Durkheim, E. (1956) *Education and Sociology* (trans. S.D. Fox), New York: The Free Press.

Faure, E. (Chair) (1972) *Learning to Be*, Paris: UNESCO.

Jarvis, P. (1987) *Adult Learning in the Social Context*, London: Croom Helm.

—— (2007) *Globalisation, Lifelong Learning and the Learning Society: Sociological perspectives*, London: Routledge.

—— (2008) *Democracy, Lifelong Learning and the Learning Society: Active citizenship in an age of late modernity*, London: Routledge.

Lengrand, P. (1975) *An Introduction to Lifelong Education*, London: Croom Helm.

Organisation for Economic Cooperation and Development (OECD) (1973) *Recurrent Education: A strategy for lifelong learning*, Paris: OECD.

Peterson, R.E. (ed.) (1979) *Lifelong Learning in America*, San Francisco, CA: Jossey Bass.

Smith, A.L. (1919) 'Adult Education Committee Final Report', reprinted in University of Nottingham (eds) *The 1919 Report*, Nottingham: Department of Adult Education, University of Nottingham.

Tremlin, T. (2006) *Minds and Gods*, Oxford: Oxford University Press.

Yeaxlee, B. (1929) *Lifelong Education*, London: Cassell.

# Part 1
## Setting the scene

# 1

# Lifelong learning
## A social ambiguity

*Peter Jarvis*

This book is about lifelong learning: every chapter analyses it from a different perspective and this opening chapter raises some of the issues that surround the concept. It does not seek to provide answers, only to set the scene for some of the ensuing discussions.

Lifelong learning is now a common, taken-for-granted concept in the educational and business worlds: it is a term whose meaning has just been assumed but rarely questioned. On the surface its meaning seems self-evident – learning from 'cradle to grave' – but beyond that self-evidency there are a number of issues lurking that suggest that the concept and the implementation of lifelong learning are much more problematic. I have called lifelong learning ambiguous for a number of reasons; for example, it is not a single phenomenon – it is both individual and institutional; it appears to be both a social movement and a commodity; it carries value connotations that are sometimes misleading; in one form it is a Western idea that we have tried to universalise in the light of globalisation; it is both a policy and a practice; it might be a gloss on social change or something more permanent. Naturally, in this chapter it is impossible to explore all of these ideas in depth, although I want to open up the discussion about some of them here.

## Individual and institutional

Field and Leicester (2000: xvi–xix) pose this issue quite nicely when they ask the question about whether we are dealing with the question of lifelong learning or permanent schooling. However, they do not go on to develop the ambiguity that they focus upon in the title of their chapter. But, it is a question hidden from the debate by the traditional definition of the concept, such as the one given by the European Commission:

> all learning activity undertaken throughout life, with the aim of improving knowledge, skills and competences within a personal, civic, social and/or employment-related perspective.
>
> (EC, 2001: 9)

This in an individualistic definition that is open to question on its instrumental perspective; it suggests that lifelong learning must have an aim. However, I have argued elsewhere (Jarvis, 2006) that learning is an existential phenomenon that is co-terminal with conscious living, that is, learning is lifelong because it occurs whenever we are conscious and it needs have no objective in itself, although it frequently does have a purpose. In a sense, lifelong learning is neither incidental to living nor instrumental in itself – it is an intrinsic part of the process of living that I have defined as:

> The combination of processes throughout a life time whereby the whole person – body (genetic, physical and biological) and mind (knowledge, skills, attitudes, values, emotions, beliefs and senses) – experiences social situations, the perceived content of which is then transformed cognitively, emotively or practically (or through any combination) and integrated into the individual person's biography resulting in a continually changing (or more experienced) person.
>
> (Jarvis, 2006: 134)

Since we all live within time in society, there are times when we can take our life-world for granted and act almost unthinkingly within it for so long as we respond to the familiar, but once we are confronted with novel situations we can no longer take that world for granted. It is in this state of disjuncture that we become conscious of the situation and are forced to think about it or adapt to it in some way – that is learning. Disjuncture, itself, is a complicated phenomenon, discussion about which lies beyond the scope of this chapter, but briefly it is the gap that occurs between our experience of a situation and our biography, which provides us with the knowledge and skill that enable us to act meaningfully. When this gap occurs, we are not able to cope with the experience and so we are forced to ask: What do I do now? What does this mean?, and so on. The ambiguity of disjuncture is that it is when we know that we do not know that we are in a position to start learning and, in order to cope with the disjunctural situation, we have to learn something new. Moreover, in a rapidly changing world we can take fewer things for granted and so disjuncture becomes a more common phenomenon; thus, throughout our life time, we are forced to keep on learning – lifelong learning – and it is only when we disengage from social living that the rate at which we learn may slow down.

Traditionally, learning has been regarded as the preserve of psychology, but it is a humanistic phenomenon and we have to recognise the wide range of academic disciplines that examine learning (Jarvis and Parker, 2005). But learning is both individualistic and lifelong, so it is an existential phenomenon: there is no way that it can be anything else since it is one of the driving forces of human living. But, when we read much of the literature on lifelong learning, we are certainly not confronted with an existential phenomenon but a social one, so that we have to recognise that the term is used in a totally different manner. This is the point implicit in Field's and Leicester's title – just how is it related to lifelong education, or even to education itself. While Field and Leicester recognise that lifelong learning transcends schooling, they do not discuss the idea that the term has come to imply attending formal learning sessions for a specific educational purpose, just as that contained in the EC's definition. In this sense, the intermittent attendance at educational institutions throughout one's life time – albeit in policy documents this usually means the duration of the work life until the most recent one (EC, 2006) – indicates that the term is used in a different manner to the learning process but that it also includes that process. In this sense, the non-existential approach to lifelong learning also embodies a form of recurrent education – a concept that was popular with the OECD and other institutions in the 1970s, but it also goes beyond it by including initial education. Lifelong learning, therefore, includes formal and non-formal, as well as informal, learning. In addition, senior citizens' learning should be included, although it is frequently omitted in policy documents (but see EC, 2006). Consequently, in a recent book (Jarvis, 2007: 99), I also regard lifelong learning as a social and institutional phenomenon:

> Every opportunity made available by any social institution for, and every process by which, an individual can acquire knowledge, skills, attitudes, values, emotions, beliefs and senses within global society.

Both of the definitions refer to different approaches to lifelong learning. In this sense, the second definition might also be indicative of the so-called learning society, or the institutionalisation of the learning process. We are not faced with one term but two, not totally different, but overlapping phenomena – one human and individual and the other both individual and social – or at least institutional; one more likely to be studied by the philosopher and psychologist, although not entirely, as Jarvis and Parker (2005) show, and the other to be studied by both of these and also by the economist, the policy theorist and the sociologist. Certainly, the study of lifelong learning requires a multidisciplinary approach.

## New social movement and commodity

In our contemporary society people are frequently urged to return to learning, to get qualifications, and so on. It has become a new social movement, and yet some of the institutions that are urging us to return to learning seem to have totally different motives – they are trying to sell their wares. In some ways this relates back to the two definitions that we have just discussed. It is the first way of viewing lifelong learning that lends itself to being regarded as a new social movement, while the second approach allows for it to be seen as a commodity.

### A new social movement

The existential definition of lifelong learning is about the process of transforming experience into knowledge and skills, etc., resulting in a changed person – one who has grown and developed as a result of the learning. In this sense, learning is essential; indeed, just as food and water are essential to the growth and development of the body, learning is an essential ingredient to the growth and development of the human person – it is one of the driving forces of human becoming and enriches human living. In this sense, learning assumes value – it is something that is apparently self-evidently good, and something that human beings must engage in if they are going to grow and develop and, as a result, be useful members of society. Learning, then, is a valuable human process and, the more that we learn, the richer we will be as human beings, and the recognition of this has led to many campaigns to encourage learning. However, the main motivator of these campaigns has not always been a concern only to enrich the human person, so much as to ensure that society's needs are met in this knowledge economy. Learning is necessary to ensure that individuals are employable and enable European societies to achieve the Lisbon goals of making Europe a global leader by 2010 – something it now acknowledges it will not achieve. But some who have espoused this more humanistic and individualistic approach to learning have also embedded it in the social context, especially for those who are responsive to the EU's aspirations embodied in the Lisbon Declaration. 'Learning pays!' claims

Ball (1998). Here we see a pragmatic and instrumental approach to learning and the learning society – it pays to learn, but Ball actually produces no empirical evidence to support his claims, although there is clear evidence to show a correlation between the level of education and the amount of money earned.

But this rather evangelistic approach to lifelong learning, echoed by the writings of Longworth and Davies (1996), reflects more than an academic approach to analysing the process; it has become an ideology and a vision for the future. This same but more measured approach is to be found in Ranson (1994), where he maps out what a learning society should be like. There are also, in the UK, a variety of groups that fervently encourage learning, such as The Royal Society of Arts' project on Learning, the British Institute of Learning, the European Lifelong Learning Institute, and so on, and their existence suggests that lifelong learning has become a new social movement. This is a different approach to that adopted by Crowther (2006), who asks how lifelong learning should be associated with social movements rather than seeing it as a social movement. We read the same enthusiasm for lifelong learning in the learning city network, which has its own aims, means of action and organisation (DfEE, 1998). In addition, there are frequent media advertisements to persuade people to return to learning and many slogans such as 'Learning is Fun' are publicised. New social movements differ from traditional social movements since they are not class-based interest groups agitating for political change. They tend to be broad movements seeking to change society through the political processes. Abercrombie *et al.* (2000) suggest that new social movements have four main features: aims, social base, means of action and organisation.

## Aims

The aims of the lifelong learning movement are to create a culture of learning, or intended learning, as learning per se occurs naturally in the process of living, but intended learning is basically vocational, although in learning cities and regions there is a greater emphasis on the non-vocational than there is in learning organisations. The second purpose of learning cities and regions, according to the then Department for Education and Employment (DfEE, 1998) document, is 'to support lifelong learning' and 'to promote social and economic regeneration' (p.1) through partnerships, participation and performance.

## Social base

Unlike traditional social movements, the social base of new social movements is not social class, but, in this case, appears to be professional educators, often from an adult education background, who have embraced lifelong learning, and the leadership can stem from one organisation – not necessarily an educational one. For instance, in Hull 'City Vision Ltd is the public/private partnership charged with taking this ambition forward' (DfEE, 1998: 15).

## Means of action

Those who propagate the ideas of learning cities do not now need action in the forms of social protest so much as lobbying those who are influential in their the various layers of society in which they function, through international and national conferences, publications and public lectures. In addition, we find that advertising and other ways of spreading the 'good news' of lifelong learning are also employed.

## Organisation

Lifelong learning per se has a variety of organisations, as we have already noted, and, in addition, there are learning city partnerships of educational and other service providers, which includes business and industry. Each organisation acts as a coordinator, having its committee and, maybe, part-time or full-time staff.

Part of what these organisations are doing is trying to create a greater awareness of the advantages of learning and to get educational establishments to provide more opportunities for adults to learn, so that the social movement has social aims that, in an interesting manner, actually coincide with those of the educational organisations and the government. Consequently, one major difference between this new social movement and many other social movements is that it is pushing against an already opened door, whereas most traditional social movements seem to push against closed, and even locked, doors because they oppose the dominant sectors of society, as was the experience of many adult educators until the early 1960s.

### *Lifelong learning as a commodity*

As governmental funding for the education of adults is increasingly being decreased in many countries, so it has become important that educational institutions continue to recruit fee-paying students, and this has changed the ethos of many of these institutions. They now have to market their courses in order to recruit customers rather than students – I make this difference because an employer can pay for an employee to attend a course and then the employer is actually the customer. However, this changing ethos is one that many academics do not like and it has been attacked in many publications: in higher education, for example, we get such titles from the USA as *The Knowledge Factory* (Aronowitz, 2000); *Universities in the Market Place* (Bok, 2003); *Academic Capitalism* (Slaughter and Leslie, 1997) and, in adult and continuing education, works such as that by Tuckett (2005), amongst others. Each of these titles reflects precisely the same thing – universities are being forced to market their courses, through a variety of means, in order to gain financial income. In other words, lifelong learning has become both a commodity to be sold in the market place of learning and a process of consumption.

Once we see lifelong learning as a process of consumption, we have to recognise the power of the consumers: they will only purchase what they want or what they need, and the more lifelong learning becomes vocational, the more likely it is that only certain teaching and learning commodities will be purchased. Stehr (1994) makes the point very clearly when he points out that the learning society utilises only scientific knowledge, so we can also say that his approach to lifelong learning is generally not a process of learning a very broad range of knowledge – it tends to be instrumental and narrow, which is an impression that the concept of lifelong learning does not in any manner convey. Once it is recognised that the learning society only emphasises certain types of knowledge, then the question must be raised about those who want or need to learn those forms of knowledge that are not emphasised. By contrast, there are those who may not benefit from these emphases. In addition, this raises questions about the idea of social inclusion – included into this form of society and learning knowledge that is only relevant to this type of society? We will return to these questions below.

Significantly, both government and those who espouse lifelong learning as a new social movement want to know who is actually learning and so there are many surveys seeking to show who is enrolling on courses. In the UK, for example, there have been National Learning Surveys (Beinart and Smith, 1997; LaValle and Blake, 2001) and the National Institute of Adult and Continuing Education (NIACE) has also conducted surveys of the amount of learning undertaken by the population (Sargant, 1991; Sargant *et al.*, 1997; Sargant and Aldridge, 2003; Aldridge and Tuckett, 2004, among others). These surveys provide information for the adherents to the movement and for the policy makers, but for those who are marketing learning materials as a commodity they provide excellent market research.

## The value of lifelong learning

Existentially, learning is a driving force in human living, it is one of the major means by which we become ourselves, and it is a stimulus enriching our lives and making us truly human. In this sense lifelong learning is good. It is impossible to conceptualise a human being who does not learn. Hence both theorists of learning and those who espouse the social movement encouraging learning have a moral foundation to their beliefs and practices. Learning is self-evidently good.

This self-evident goodness of learning has also permeated the other aspects of lifelong learning, often without a great deal of consideration, so that the commodity approach to lifelong learning 'trades' on the value intrinsic to the first approach . There are at least two ways in which we might illustrate that the second approach to lifelong learning is not self-evidently good: the first is the market and the second is seeing lifelong learning as a means of control. First, the learning market is not driven by concern for the learner but concern for the provider and even the provider's profit and own interest. This is the nature of the market system, but the profit's profit is not a self-evidently good concept. Increasingly, however, we are finding profit and loss accounts of educational providers being presented to governors' meetings and university courts, although not to the general public. Second, employers are in a position to expect their employees to learn and to keep abreast of changes as work becomes increasingly knowledge-based. This expectation might entail employees attending continuing education courses at their own expense and at times that are detrimental to other aspects of their and their families' lives. For instance, in the research of Hewison *et al.* (2000), it is recorded that:

> Less than half the sample (42%) said that they thought the course was fitting reasonably well with home and family life. Forty-eight percent (n=43) thought that the course was a strain and 10% of the participants (n=9) thought that the course was causing serious detrimental effect to their home and personal lives.
>
> (p. 186)

The authors go on to state:

> The rhetoric of the *learning society* is upbeat and positive. It is about 'opportunities' and the benefits that learning can bring. Lifelong learning promises that there will be many such opportunities, following one after another, throughout an individual's career.
>
> To many of the participants in our study, such a prospect would be a threat not a promise. It is not that they lacked the motivation to learn, but rather that learning opportunities were often offered on very disadvantageous terms.
>
> (p. 193; italics in original)

Since Hewison's sample consists of health service employees, many were probably women, so this suggests that, in this still male-dominated world, even lifelong learning is not always attractive to everybody and that an element of this value orientation may be male-dominated, which calls for a feminist perspective on lifelong learning to be undertaken. There is a whole element of social control in the way that lifelong learning opportunities are presented in some work situations and, as might be seen from these quotations, lifelong learning is no longer self-evidently good. The value of the phenomenon depends on what aspects of lifelong learning are being analysed and the perspective that is being adopted in the analysis.

## Globalisation and lifelong learning

In the first definition of lifelong learning, we recognised that learning is an individual process that happens in a social context. Consequently, if we seek to study lifelong learning in different social contexts, we will see that different forms of knowledge are necessary. The first definition of learning is applicable to every social context and to every type of social living, whether it occurs in the North or the South, in sophisticated urban or traditional and primitive society. Since lifelong learning is almost co-terminal with conscious life itself, it embodies all learning. We continue to learn throughout our lives, but in less rapidly changing societies there may be less to learn, or there may be other things to learn at greater depth, which we have been unable to explore.

But, fundamentally, lifelong learning, as we have currently formulated it in the second definition, is a Western concept, based on formal learning, literacy, individual responsibility for learning, scientific knowledge, and so on. Those who have learned in informal and non-formal situations but have no certificates to prove it and those who are not literate are considered to be uneducated and in need of 'literacy for all', which, in itself, is another aspect of the social movement. It almost assumes that those who are illiterate do not know and have not learned but, as we have already pointed out, knowledge societies tend to emphasise certain forms of scientific knowledge and omit others and so the illiterate may not be unlearned since they have such forms as traditional and indigenous knowledge. Clearly, contemporary Western knowledge has produced a high standard of living for those of us who enjoy it – but it may not have made us a happier people! But one of the main dangers of globalisation is that of homogenisation, in which indigenous knowledge and cultural diversity are neither recognised nor respected. Yet those people who live in traditional societies have their own indigenous knowledge, which is functional to their own context, but which the second definition of lifelong learning might be too narrow to recognise. The UNESCO (2005) study of knowledge societies states:

> As we have seen, the information revolution reinforces the supremacy of technological and scientific knowledge over other kinds of knowledge such as know-how, indigenous knowledge, local knowledge, oral traditions, daily knowledge and so on. Oral and written abilities correspond to different written systems, and this plurality mainly accounts for the diversity of cultures.
>
> (p. 148)

The report goes on to note that the 'simple substitution of scientific knowledge for local knowledge would have disastrous consequences for humanity' (p. 148). Indigenous knowledge is extremely functional in its own context and its loss would contribute to the destruction of local cultures and lifestyles. However, the social conditions that have given rise to the idea of lifelong learning are Western and there is an assumption that all peoples on the earth should be like us – but lifelong learning is not such a simplistic concept as this.

## Policy and practice

In one sense, there can be no policy for lifelong learning because it is an existential phenomenon; it occurs wherever we are, provided that we are conscious of the world in which we live. It occurs because we are alive and it is essential to human living. This is one of the reasons why it is perceived to be good – another being that opportunities can be provided for education and training across the lifespan so that individuals can respond to the needs of society, or perhaps more accurately the needs of the capitalist system that is wrongly often equated with society. This brings us once again to our second definition of lifelong learning – that opportunities for learning are provided across the lifespan. At this level it is possible to formulate a policy for lifelong learning, or perhaps better to see lifelong learning as a guide for policy for education and training (Hasan, 1999). It is significant, however, that when Hasan discusses policy he is actually writing about education and he uses this term rather than lifelong learning. It is interesting to recognise that this confusion of education and learning in this way did not begin with lifelong learning – in the American adult education literature there is almost a synonymous use of adult education and adult learning – see for instance, Long's (1983) study *Adult Learning*, which is actually a study of adult education in America. But the change in term from education to learning is much more profound than just illustrating the linguistic dominance of America; it points to issues of responsibility – the lifelong learner's responsibility for learning is their own but it may be the state or the employer that has the responsibility for providing education. Yet Hasan is right – the ideal of providing as many opportunities for individuals to learn as they need or desire does form a baseline for policy, but the provision of the opportunities, whether it is formal, non-formal or informal, which does form a base-line for policy, does not actually constitute the learning itself.

## Lifelong learning and social change

For many years adult educators campaigned for more opportunities to be provided for adults to learn. In the UK there is that well-known statement by Arthur Smith, chairman of the committee that produced the famous 1919 Report:

> [t]hat the necessary conclusion is that adult education must not be regarded as a luxury for a few exceptional persons here and there, nor as a thing which concerns only a short span of early manhood, but that adult education is a permanent necessity, an inseparable aspect of citizenship, and therefore should be both universal and lifelong.
>
> (Ministry of Reconstruction, 1919: 5)

Adult educators certainly campaigned throughout the twentieth century to achieve this aim – adult education was certainly a social movement in the more traditional sense. Throughout almost the whole of that period the door appeared to be closed and only limited opportunities were provided for it. But towards the latter half of the century the door seemed to be opening, as business and industry needed a more knowledgeable workforce. Suddenly lifelong learning became important – a new social movement – but it was not the adult educators who forced open the door, because in many ways they have been left behind with the rapidity of the transition. Kett (1994), commenting on this rapid change, writes: 'Today, no one can plausibly describe adult learning as a marginal activity, but professional adult educators have become increasingly marginal to the education of adults' (p. xviii).

When lifelong learning was growing in significance, usually through the development of professional continuing education and human resource development, adult educators did not recognise the change. It was not education that was causing the change but the social and economic conditions, which we now call globalisation, that were demanding a knowledge economy, and thus rapid social change ensued. In that situation, people were confronted with changing social conditions and were forced to learn (Jarvis, 2007).

In my own understanding of learning, the learning process commences at the point of disjuncture – that is, when I am confronted with an unknown or a novel situation; when I am forced to ask: Why? How? What for?, and so on. At these points my biographical memory no longer provides the answers and I cannot take my existence for granted – I am consciously aware of the social situation in which I find myself and I begin to learn from the experience. The more rapid the social change, the more frequently I learn. This might be called incidental learning – but it is happening all the time with rapid social change; in other words I am continually learning. Our awareness of lifelong learning is an awareness of rapid social change and the fact that, in order to exist, we need to learn. The social conditions have given rise to lifelong learning – following our first definition of lifelong learning.

But the capitalist system upon which our Western society is built is now based upon knowledge – we live in a knowledge economy. In order for capitalism to survive, it needs to produce new commodities to sell and produce older ones more efficiently: both require new knowledge and when the commodities are sold on the market they introduce new ways of living. In order for these commodities to be produced a knowledgeable workforce is necessary – and so individuals have to be given more opportunities either to keep abreast of the changes that are occurring or to prepare themselves to join the workforce. It is essential, therefore, that more opportunities are provided and so we need policies and a culture of lifelong learning – and this fits our second approach.

It is perhaps interesting to note that the second definition of lifelong learning is one that is social – it is one that can suggest that learning can contribute to change, although it is still a response to global imperatives, whereas the first definition, the existential one, is a response to change.

## Conclusions

Lifelong learning is certainly an ambiguous concept: both a causal factor in change and a response to social change; a policy and a practice; something that can sustain and enrich the lives of many and yet undermine and contribute to the decline of other societies and the break-up of families; at the same time valuable, threatening and controlling; both societal and existential. It is a linguistic ambiguity – one with which the English-speaking world has to live but, more significantly, it is one with which the globalising world is confronted and, until our lifelong learning takes a different policy direction and we learn to place value on other forms of knowledge and lifestyles, its self-evident goodness lies only with the existential approach to learning, while the societal emphasis raises as many existential questions as it answers and its value lies open to debate. The ambiguity lies in the fact that, in the first definition of learning, we place value in the learning itself because it is existential and fundamental to our living but, in the second definition, we place value on some of the perceived outcomes of learning but we have not yet learned to place social value on learning itself.

# References

Abercrombie, N., Hill, S. and Turner, B. (2000) *Dictionary of Sociology*, 4th edn, Harmondsworth: Penguin.

Aldridge, F. and Tuckett, F. (2004) *Business as Usual. . .?*, Leicester: NIACE.

Aronowitz, S. (2000) *The Knowledge Factory*, Boston, MA: Beacon Press.

Ball, C. (1998) 'Learning pays', in S. Ranson (ed.) *Inside the Learning Society*, London: Cassell, pp. 36–41.

Beinart, S. and Smith, P. (1997) *National Adult Learning Survey 1997*, London: Department for Education and Science.

Bok, D. (2003) *Universities in the Market Place*, Princeton, NJ: Princeton University Press.

Crowther, J. (2006) 'Social movements, praxis and the profane side of lifelong learning', in P. Sutherland and J. Crowther (eds) *Lifelong Learning: Concepts and contexts*, pp. 171–81.

Department for Education and Employment (DfEE) (1998) *Learning City Network: Practice, progress and value*, London: DfEE.

European Commission (EC) (2001) *Making a European Area of Lifelong Learning a Reality*, COM (2001) 678 final, Brussels: European Commission.

—— (2006) *Adult Learning: It's never too late to learn*, (COM 2006) 614 final, Brussels: European Commission.

Field, J. and Leicester, M. (2000) 'Lifelong learning or permanent schooling', in J. Field and M. Leicester (eds) *Lifelong Learning: Education across the lifespan*, London: RoutledgeFalmer.

Hasan, A. (1999) 'Lifelong learning: implications for education policy', in A. Tuijnman and T. Schuller (eds) *Lifelong Learning: Policy and research*, London: Portland, pp. 51–62.

Hewison, J., Dowswell, T. and Millar, B. (2000) ' Changing patterns of training provision in the National Health Service: an overview', in F. Coffield (ed.) *Differing Visions of a Learning Society*, vol. 1, Bristol: Policy Press, pp. 167–97.

Jarvis, P. (2006) *Towards a Comprehensive Theory of Human Learning*, London: Routledge.

—— (2007) *Globalisation, Lifelong Learning and the Learning Society: Sociological perspectives*, London: Routledge.

—— and Parker, S. (eds) (2005) *Human Learning: An holistic perspective*, London: Routledge.

Kett, J. (1994) *The Pursuit of Knowledge Under Difficulties*, Stanford, CA: Stanford University Press.

LaValle, I. and Blake, M. (2001) *National Adult Learning Survey 2001*, London: Department for Education and Skills.

Long, H. (1983) *Adult Learning: Research and practice*, New York: Cambridge.

Longworth, N. and Davies, K. (1996) *Lifelong Learning*, London: Kogan Page.

Ministry of Reconstruction (1919) *Adult Education Committee: Final report*, London: HMSO (reprinted as *The 1919 Report*, Nottingham: University of Nottingham, Department of Adult Education, 1980).

Ranson, S. (1994) *Towards the Learning Society*, London: Cassell.

—— (ed.) (1998) *Inside the Learning Society*, London: Cassell.

Sargant, N. (1991) *Learning and Leisure*, Leicester: NIACE.

—— and Aldridge, F. (2003) *Adult Learning: A persistent pattern*, Leicester: NIACE.

——, Field, J., Francis, H., Schuller, T. and Tuckett, A. (1997) *The Learning Divide*, Leicester: NIACE.

Slaughter, S. and Leslie, L. (1997) *Academic Capitalism*, Baltimore, MD: Johns Hopkins University Press.

Stehr, N. (1994) *Knowledge Societies*, London: Sage Press.

Tuckett, A. (2005) 'Enough is enough', *Adults Learning* 17(1): 6–7.

UNESCO (2005) *Towards Knowledge Societies*, Paris: UNESCO.

2

# Learning from everyday life

*Peter Jarvis*

When my grandson comes home from school we often ask him, 'What have you learned at school today?' And we expect a response! But if we ask adults, 'What have you learned from life recently?', we might well get little or no response. This is precisely what I find when I conduct research into learning and when I run workshops on the topic of human learning. Many an adult, when asked to write down a learning event, finds it extremely difficult and this is because a great deal of our everyday learning is incidental, preconscious and unplanned. In a sense, we respond to events in a living manner – but then learning is about life. Indeed, for most people it is, or should be, lifelong. We all live in a social context (life-world) in which we learn (Jarvis, 1987).

Everyday life is a strangely under-researched subject when it comes to human learning (but see de Certeau, 1984; Heller, 1984; and Gardiner, 2000) and, while we will not delve deeply into these studies, we do need to recognise their significance if we are to really understand lifelong learning. Fundamentally, there are two states in this life-world – one in which we are in harmony with it and the other in which we are in disjuncture. Schutz and Luckmann (1974) describe this state thus:

> I trust that the world as it has been known to me up until now will continue further and consequently the stock of knowledge obtained from my fellow men and obtained from my own experiences will continue to preserve its fundamental validity. We would designate this (in accordance with Husserl) the 'and so forth' idealization. From this assumption follows the further and fundamental one: that I can repeat my past successful acts. So long as the structure of the world can be taken as constant, and as long as my previous experience is valid, my ability to operate on the world in this and that manner is in principle preserved. As Husserl has shown, the further ideality of the 'I can always do it again' is developed correlative of the ideality of the 'and so forth'.
>
> (p. 6)

In other words, we can take our world for granted because we are in harmony with it. But the world is not a constant and unchanging place and so there are times when we cannot take it for granted and we are forced to ask questions: Why? How? What does it mean? What do I do? and so forth. This is disjuncture; we have to find new explanations, new knowledge, new ways of doing things – in other words, we must learn. These are the questions with which every parent and teacher is familiar, as children keep asking questions but they also adjust their behaviour to fit into that of their group, family, and so on. But often, as we grow older, we do not ask the questions so openly and we merely adjust our behaviour or our knowledge base, although there are times when we may not even notice that we are doing it. We actually take this process for granted and so much of our learning is not only incidental, it is unrecognised. In this sense, learning is both experiential and existential – the philosophical and human basis of learning is often missed in theoretical discussions about learning. But, then, so is its opposite – non-learning. Because we do not always want to change our behaviour, we sometimes want to change the world! I discussed non-learning many years ago (Jarvis, 1987) but, at that time, I failed to recognise that non-learning can also be a major strength when we are committed to a cause and do not want to change: but the inflexibility of fundamentalism – both religious and political – can be extremely dangerous in a world that demands degrees of tolerance and a level of deliberative politics (Habermas, 2006). It was the breadth of human questioning and the recognition of the need to understand the learning process that led Jarvis and Parker (2005) to edit a volume analysing learning from a number of different academic disciplinary perspectives.

In more recent years the significance of learning from experience has been widely recognised, although it has mostly been seen in terms of experiences that are created by teachers so that learners can learn the practical side of some theoretical propositions. It has been less frequently used from the perspective of recognising learning from everyday life. There is a sense in which this form of learning from everyday life comes close to the ideas of instinct and even intuition – both of which are important concepts as we endeavour to understand human learning at greater depth. I want to maintain here that, despite the considerable significance of genetics and issues of human evolution, human beings do not have instincts in the sense of species-based innate patterns of behaviour, but that we have to learn these and the patterns occur through routinisation, whereas intuition is itself most frequently a learned phenomenon – as we will discuss below.

Learning, then, is a complex process about human living and, while now is not the place to discuss it conceptually (see Jarvis, 2006, 2008; Illeris, 2007, among others) I will offer an existential definition here:

> the combination of processes throughout a lifetime whereby the whole person – body (genetic, physical and biological) and mind (knowledge, skills, attitudes, values, emotions, beliefs and senses) – experiences social situations, the perceived content of which is then transformed cognitively, emotively or practically (or through any combination) and integrated into the individual person's biography resulting in a continually changing (or more experienced) person.
>
> (Jarvis, 2006: 134)

In the remainder of this chapter, we will explore the process of human learning in greater detail; second, we will look at the social conditions of learning; third, we will suggest some of the basic aspects of learning from everyday life; and, finally, we will explore some of the conceptual implications of this discussion, such as preconscious learning, tacit knowledge and pragmatic behaviour.

## Understanding the learning processes

What becomes clear from the above discussion is that, while it is individuals who learn, and never groups as a whole, we always learn in a social context. Consequently, when more than one individual is in the same place at the same time and subject to the same external phenomena, then their experiences are similar but not identical. We can, therefore, pursue this argument using a single learner as the basis of our discussion, although we can be sure that the processes are almost universal within a similar culture – although there may be some differences between people of different cultures, as studies on the Chinese learner (Watkins and Biggs, 1996) illustrate.

### *The social context*

We can, therefore, begin our discussion on the learning process by looking at the social context, or the subculture, within which the learners function. For heuristic purposes only, we will depict this culture as if it is objectified, although in practice it is more individualistic and carried by individual members of that social group.

In Figure 2.1, Ego is the individual learner. The arc represents the objectified culture of the learner's life-world, although in reality it is not a static phenomenon. The larger inward arrows represent the process of internalising that culture, while the smaller external ones represent the process of externalising. The two arrows together represent social interaction. The culture is internalised and carried by individuals so that, when people meet, the commonality of their cultures enables meaningful exchange to occur. Social interaction is always an arena for sub-cultural negotiation: there is always an exchange of subcultural differences and individuals adjust in response to those differences – in other words learning takes place although it is not always recognised. With young children, and in all forms of didactic teaching, the large inward arrows

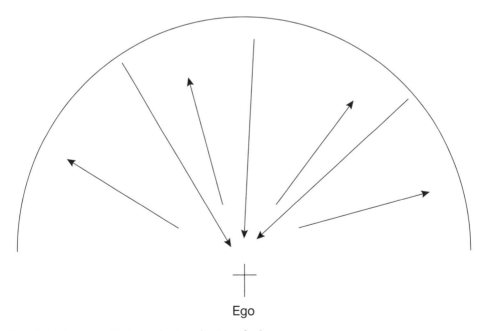

Ego

*Figure 2.1* The internalisation and externalisation of culture.

21

predominate, whereas in normal interaction there is an exchange of subcultural differences. It is here that incidental learning occurs – it is often unrecognised and it is also preconscious, when we are not fully conscious of the extent of the stimulus that we have received, and this is often the case in a cognitive world with sense experiences.

### Sense experience

Children are much more aware of sense experience in many ways than adults, since linguistic cognition results in our being more concerned with meaning in the interaction than we are with sounds, or with the environment, and so on. Indeed, the environment only intervenes when we might say, 'It is hot in here – shall we open the window?' and so forth. Yet we are having these sense experiences all the time and children, often being less aware of the cognitive dimension, may be more aware of the senses. Figure 2.2 represents this process.

In Figure 2.2, we see that the disjuncture is caused by an inability to take the sensation for granted: we cannot give it meaning or we are unsure about the meaning we give it. In other words, there is no connecting arrow from the subculture to the individual or vice versa, as in Figure 2.1. Thus we need to resolve the dilemma caused by the experience (box 2). When we have an answer to our problem – that is we can give meaning to the sensation, as a result of self-directed learning, teaching, and so on (box 3) – we are able to practise it in a social situation. If our answer is acceptable inasmuch as the people upon whom we practise our answer do not contradict us in some way, then we can assume it to be socially correct even though it may not be technically correct. As we continue to practise it, we are able to universalise it and take it for granted, until the next time that a disjunctural situation occurs. Kolb (1984) actually includes generalisation in his learning cycle, but my research does not suggest that generalisation occurs immediately following a new learning experience but only after we have tried out the resolution to our disjuncture on several occasions. If we do not resolve the dilemma, then we revert to box 2 and try again, so that the arrows between boxes 2 and 3, and between 3 and 4, are not uni-directional, illustrating that there is a process of trial-and-error learning at both stages. At the point of taking our sensations for granted, we move to the next phase – when

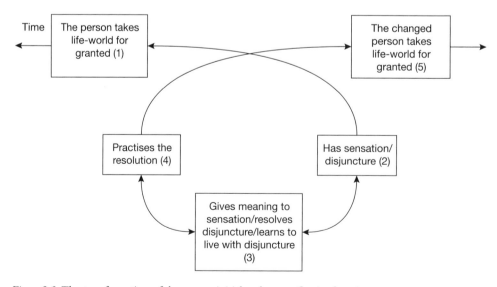

*Figure 2.2* The transformation of the senses: initial and non-reflective learning.

we discuss meaning itself rather than the sensation. Adults and older children are more likely than young children to experience disjuncture in the cognitive domain, but a similar process actually occurs in that domain, only in this instance the disjuncture is caused by not knowing the meaning of the event or of some aspect of the experience.

## The learning processes

As we put these two diagrams together and recognise that disjuncture can occur not only with the sense and the cognitions but with the emotions as well, we can begin to see something of the complexity of the learning processes through which we all go in everyday life – the point being that, in formal situations, the disjuncture is created by the teaching, which is often didactic, whereas in everyday life it occurs naturally in interaction. But it also occurs naturally in the environment; we may see beauty, etc. and be amazed by it – all forms of aesthetic and religious experience may be seen in this light. We are now, therefore, in a position to look at the complexities of the learning processes as a whole (Figure 2.3).

Box 1.1 depicts the situation of people in their life-worlds, and concerns Figure 2.1 above, which we have already examined in greater detail. I would argue that learning stems from social experience, but recognise that that type of experience is determined to some extent by the nature of both the body and the mind in relation to each other and the external world. However, we continue to live in a taken-for-granted situation until such time as a situation causes us to question this taken-for-grantedness. Hence the arrow from box 1 – pointing forwards in time – that merely depicts the unquestioning process of much daily living. It is in the social situation that people are most likely to experience disjuncture (box 1), although this state can occur when people are alone, reflect on previous events, or even when they have an experience in interacting with the natural world, so that not all disjunctural experiences occur as a result of language and inter-action as some social constructivists hold (see Archer, 2000: 86–117). The state of disjuncture occurs when we can no longer presume upon our world and act upon it in an almost unthink-ing manner; it is at this point that we have an experience (box 2) and it need not be contained within the bounds of language. Indeed, it can and does precede language in small children and in inexplicable situations (Jarvis, 1987, 1997). Experience can be transformed by thought, emotion or action (boxes 3–5), or any combination of them: the precise mechanisms of these transformations constitute considerable studies in their own right and these have not been undertaken here. Box 6 is included to underline the fact that the outcome of the transformation is that people actually learn or fail to resolve their disjuncture, but this process itself always results in a changed person, even when there is apparently no learning, since the experience still affects the self of the learner (box 7). When people fail to resolve their disjuncture they can either learn to live in ignorance or with an awareness that they need to learn in order to resolve their disjuncture, or they can start the whole process off again. But even then they have learned the process of living is ongoing and so, then, is the process of learning as box $1_2$ indicates.

In the above diagrams I have tried to depict the outcome of many years of researching the processes of human learning and they also summarise a great deal of the previous discussion about human learning. One of the major issues in this discussion, which cannot be treated here (see Jarvis, 2006), is the nature of experience and interaction, and another is the nature of the person. Nevertheless, it is necessary to highlight one of the major conceptual confusions in the educa-tional vocabulary here: there is no difference in the human process in different forms of learning, so that we do not have formal learning, non-formal learning and informal learning, but we do have formal interaction, and so on. It is the nature of the interaction that provides for different learning experiences and it is these that affect emotion, motivation to learn, and so on.

## Conditions of learning

There are a number of conditions that are fundamental for learning to occur and that are basic to everyday living. Two of these are social interaction and disjuncture.

### Social interaction

The first thing that we need to note about everyday life and about Figure 2.1 is that the arrows are in both directions and that this signifies interaction. This is the basis of social living: we nearly all live in families and are members of organisations, and so forth. Unless we are meeting

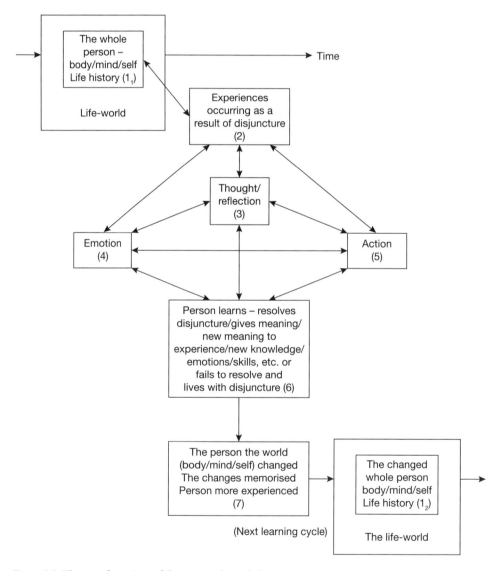

*Figure 2.3* The transformation of the person through learning.

with people whom we know intimately, it is hard to take for granted the whole of a process of interaction in which all our senses are operative. Even our nearest and dearest change as a result of their own learning and, as the old maxim tells us, the same water does not flow under the same bridge twice – situations never repeat themselves precisely. It is in meeting with others both within our life-world and beyond it that makes us aware of difference. Social interaction involves exploring difference and adjusting our behaviour to enable the interaction to proceed smoothly. People are different and during interaction we learn to respond to those differences, accommodate them and even to learn from them. Disjuncture, then, is a normal experience in social interaction.

## *Disjuncture*

The first thing that we need to note here is the complex nature of disjuncture itself: it is as complex as human living in a social context and it may best be seen as a continuum from a short instant of disjuncture to a lifetime of recognising that there are some things in our lives that we can never take for granted. For instance, I am prepared to acknowledge that I will live in a disjunctural experience with regard to the knowledge of theoretical mathematics and nuclear physics – in other words, in this complex world I acknowledge that I have to live in ignorance and leave that knowledge to specialists. Hence, we can accept that, in some aspects of human living, ignorance is an acceptable response to disjuncture. But disjuncture is still a complex phenomenon. Significantly, we can see that, once we discuss the whole person, disjuncture can occur and cause dissonance in any aspect – knowledge, skills, sense, emotions, beliefs, and so on:

- It can occur as a slight gap between our biography and our perception of the situation, to which we can respond by slight adjustments in our daily living – a gap we hardly notice since it occurs within the flow of time.
- It can also occur with larger gaps that demand considerable learning, even to the extent of studying courses and disciplines and embarking on self-directed projects.
- In the meeting of strangers, the disjuncture might not only occur in the discourse between them, but it might actually occur between them as persons and their cultures, and it takes time for the stranger to be received and a relationship, or harmony, to be established.
- In addition, some disjunctural situations – often emotive in nature – just cause us to wonder at the beauty, pleasure and so forth that we are experiencing. In these situations, it is sometimes impossible to incorporate our learning from them into our biography and our 'taken-for-granted'. These are what we might call 'magic moments' to which we look forward in the hope of repeating them in some way or other but upon which we might often reflect.

Disjuncture, then, is a varied and complex experience, but it is from within the disjunctural that we have experiences that, among other things, start our learning processes. There is a sense in which learning occurs whenever the harmony between us and our world has been broken, so that the relationship between our present understanding and our experience of the 'now' needs to be established, or re-established. In other words, learning begins when we recognise that we are in a state of ignorance, but a great deal of our everyday learning occurs when the disjuncture is so slight that we barely notice it. A rather interesting speculation is about when there is no disjuncture and whether there was ever a time when humankind existed in perfect harmony with the world.

## Theories of learning involved in these processes

There are a number of fundamental learning processes that form the basis of learning from everyday life, e.g. copying, trial and error, instruction and demonstration, thinking/reflecting/musing/planning, and doing, exploring and investigating.

### *Copying*

Imitation is fundamental to our everyday learning: we all recognise that, when we go into new situations, we watch other people's behaviour carefully and then we copy it so that we feel that we fit into our situation. This is part of the process of socialisation – when we can imitate and feel part of the whole. In other words, a great deal of everyday learning is conformist, but it is natural for us to do it since we have evolved to live in groups (Tremlin, 2006). The fact that it is natural displays something of the cooperative or societal nature of human living: it is unnatural to live alone or, therefore, to learn alone. The emphasis on individuality, however, has led many schoolteachers to condemn copying, rather than see it as a fundamental element in everyday living and learning and use it in their teaching to the advantage of all the students.

### *Trial and error*

Answers to our questions are not always forthcoming in social situations and so we have to think through some of the problems and try out our solutions until we discover one that works for us in whatever domain we are functioning in – cognitive, affective or connative. Often, however, our learning occurs in more than one domain at the same time and through self-directed learning we can work out many of our own solutions but, when we cannot, we can often discover the answers either by asking others or by being told by someone else who knows – who may be a teacher or a parent. Not always knowing 'the' answer is something that we learn to take for granted in our everyday life and so we learn to be innovative and imaginative and to some extent this adds to our own individuality. Many of our individual solutions to our everyday problems are not new and we merely rediscover what others who have been in similar situations have discovered before us and, sometimes, these acts of discovery are hardly treated as learning experiences since we tend to assume that this is the way that life is lived.

In this sense, we return to the fundamentals of behaviourism and at this point we can see the validity of such theories, but we can also see their weakness when they are treated as blueprints for the only way to learn, or when a correct answer to a teaching and learning process is expected – the one provided by the teacher, which then becomes both a matter of teacher-power and also raises questions about the morality of such teacher–learner interactions.

### *Instruction and demonstration*

We are often passive recipients of information provided by word of mouth or by written instructions. In didactic teaching it is the school or university teacher who transmits new knowledge or demonstrates new skills. Learners merely copy a more formalised presentation from someone who is expected to have the 'correct' knowledge, rather than copying from a fellow learner who may not have such acceptable credentials. In a sense this might be non-reflective learning (Jarvis, 1987) and often it is what teachers expect, but much of our learning is reflective.

## *Thinking/reflecting/musing/planning*

We all spend a great deal of our conscious lives thinking – from those forms that we refer to as reflection to the everyday musing, and to the day-dreaming. Indeed, Schön's (1983) well-known discussion of the 'reflective practitioner' is most frequently applied to the work situation, but life itself is reflective practice. Heller (1984: 168–70) recognises that, in our thinking and planning in everyday life, we do take into consideration probability. Thinking is a major part of the learning process, as we saw from Figure 2.3 above, and there have been a number of very influential studies about thinking (for example, Ryle (1979) and Gilhooly (1996) among others). Gilhooly (1996: 1) defines thinking as 'a set of processes whereby people assemble, use and revise internal symbolic models'. Thinking occurs not only as reflective processes upon events past but also when we are planning actions into the future. All forms of thinking are learning processes and so the question must be asked as to whether learning is synonymous with thinking, which is a very complex question. But we have already seen that we learn through certain forms of action, so we can safely conclude that they are not the same, although there are times when the thinking process is synonymous with the processes of learning even though both are also very closely related to consciousness. However, we have to acknowledge that some theorists, such as Ryle (1949), would argue that only one action has taken place. All the different forms of thinking may be regarded as learning and many of them occur in the natural processes of everyday living.

## *Doing, exploring and investigating*

This is also called problem solving or discovery learning, depending on the age group to which it is applied, but at its most fundamental it occurs when we try to respond to disjuncture by seeking to find out the causes of a phenomenon or experience that we do not understand. It can result in self-directed learning but it also typifies Schön's (1983) 'reflective practitioner'.

In all of these situations we learn to memorise the outcome of the process so that we can repeat past successful acts. We know that the more that we perform the same action, the more that we will learn to take it for granted and then we will do what Kolb (1984) suggests when he regards generalising as part of the learning process. Often, it is the mere repetition of the process that helps implant the 'answers' in our memories and failure to repeat them that leads to forgetfulness. But the fact that these are everyday occurrences means that they are not necessarily regarded as learning or anything out of the ordinary and it is for this reason that learning is regarded here as an existential process as well as an experiential one.

## Theoretical considerations of learning from everyday life

The above discussion gives rise to a number of theoretical issues and in this section we shall look briefly at ten of these, although it must be recognised that it is impossible to do justice to any of them in this brief chapter (see Jarvis, forthcoming): motivation, preconscious/conscious learning, attitude formation, value formation, belief formation, meaning creation, tacit knowledge, identity, pragmatism and the aging process. Since none of these can be treated in depth in a short chapter, we will actually combine some in the following discussion. There is also a sense in which they are not exclusively related to learning in everyday life although they all occur within everyday living.

## Motivation

At the heart of many studies of learning lies the concept of motivation, although intentionality might be a better concept to use. Human beings rarely act in a mindless and aimless manner – it is regarded as almost unnatural for this to occur – at least until old age. There are very broadly two types of motivation. One is to remove the uncomfortableness of disjuncture, since we mostly prefer to live in harmony with our environment and social group, although we recognise that this uncomfortable feeling is a penalty of rapid social change and individuality; nevertheless, it has always been part of the human condition. The second is seeking to satisfy our desires, hopes and aspirations, and so on. Desire is something that is not only self-created but other-created by such things as watching others who possess those things that we desire, advertising and hoping for a better life, better world, and so on. Naturally there are many studies on motivation, although it will be noted here that it does not occur as a separate concept in Figure 2.3 and this is because the disjuncture is central to the idea of learning in the social context as Figure 2.2 demonstrates.

## Preconscious/conscious learning

All learning is conscious, although we might repress or suppress some of it, but in our everyday life we are not fully conscious of all the things that occur within our purview at any one time and so our minds take in and acquire many sense experiences without necessarily being conscious of them. When I first discussed preconscious learning (Jarvis, 1987) I equated it with incidental learning, although now I would differentiate them. Preconscious learning is the type that occurs incidentally but is also unrecognised, so that in the first instance it would be problematic to call it learning at all. We only recognise it when a subsequent experience brings it to our consciousness and we become aware that we have actually internalised an experience previously that is significant in the new experience and that affects either our perception or our interpretation thereafter. Perhaps the most common situation where this occurs is in speed-reading, when we scan columns of words and take in much more of the meaning than the actual words upon which we focus.

## Formation of attitudes, beliefs and values

None of us is conscious of every experience that leads to us holding the attitudes, beliefs and values that we do. At the same time, we are all aware that there are other times when we concentrate on each of these and spend a great deal of time and energy pondering them. It is clear, therefore, that the formation of these aspects of our personality is a complex process of both conscious and preconscious learning in everyday life. The recognition of this complexity is significant for learning theory – even experiential learning theory, which has tended to regard experience always as a conscious phenomenon.

## Meaning creation

In discussing sense experience in Figure 2.2, we go through a process of trying to give meaning (make sense) of these experiences and in doing this we go through the process that Ricoeur (1995) refers to as the 'logic of meaning'. It is as if we feel that in every experience there is a meaning that we have to discover. In this we can make meaning or take meaning. Living in social communities it is easy to associate our experiences with the meanings given by the life world and so the meaning-making process is often implicit.

## Tacit knowing

Another factor associated with learning in everyday life is tacit knowing. Polanyi's (1967: 4) well-known example – that we can recognise a face in a crowd yet we cannot tell how we do this – is central to this idea. We have knowledge but we cannot put it into words, although through 'identikit' photographs we can often recognise the face through the picture. In the same way we recognise many of our sense experiences, such as smell, taste, and so on. More recently, Baumard (1999) has employed the idea of tacit knowing in organisational settings in examining managers' knowledge. Clearly, not only managers but all experts incorporate a great deal of tacit knowing in their everyday practice, since they have learned incidentally from the practice of work itself – but a great deal of this expert knowledge has been lost as mechanisation has replaced expertise. What is clear about the tacit dimension is that, in cooperative enterprises and discussion between experts, a great deal of their incidental learning is brought into consciousness. It may be that this process also helps explain Argyris and Schön's (1974) distinction between 'theory in use' and 'espoused theory' since it can be explained in part by incidental and unrecognised learning and tacit knowledge.

## Identity

From Figure 2.1 we can see that our first identity is a social one given to us by those who transmit the culture of the life-world. Through all the everyday learning processes that we have described above we eventually also develop a personal identity, but this is part of the process of development. Thereafter it is through reflecting upon our experiences that we change or reinforce our personal identity.

## Pragmatism

In everyday life we tend to respond to situations by doing things rather than by considering the theory underlying them and, in this sense, we do things and learn by our doing. In this sense, learning is pragmatic. All our knowledge, learning, comes from experience as our understanding of learning above makes clear, so that theory itself is learned from experience and practice: it is part of our everyday learning about life and so practitioner research (Jarvis, 1999) is also based upon this understanding of learning. This is diametrically opposed to the traditional, but now dying, idea that theory always preceded practice. Theory may precede practice in the pure sciences but in everyday life it is often the reverse.

## Aging

The wisdom of the elders was to a great extent the result of incidental and preconscious learning throughout a great deal of a lifetime. These preconscious experiences were brought to consciousness as older people discussed what they had learned in their lifetime. But in a rapidly changing world many of these experiences are now dated and older people's learning from life has been devalued by many people, since it appears to have come from a different world. But much of it is not about the technologies of contemporary living but about the lessons of human relationships and interaction and these still have some validity. However, these modern technologies actually cause many people to learn that they cannot learn: it is not uncommon to hear older people (and sometimes younger ones) exclaim, 'I don't know what this world is coming to these days!' Their lives' experiences seem far removed from the demands of the present day and they experience considerable disjuncture – in this case they learn that they cannot necessarily cope, might be considered to be ignorant by the younger generation, and so on. When this happens they may seek to disengage and this can be a dangerous situation since, as we pointed out, learning is an existential phenomenon.

## Conclusion

This brief chapter has only scratched the surface of a major dimension of learning that certainly needs a great deal more research than it is currently receiving since it actually helps us to understand the human processes of becoming a person much more clearly.

## References

Archer, M. (2000) *Being Human: The problem of agency*, Cambridge: Cambridge University Press.

Argyris, C. and Schön, D. (1974) *Theory in Practice: Increasing professional effectiveness*, San Francisco, CA: Jossey-Bass.

Baumard, P. (1999) *Tacit Knowledge in Organizations*, London: Sage.

de Certeau, M. (1984) *The Practice of Everyday Life*, Berkeley, CA: University of California Press.

Gardiner, M. (2000) *Critiques of Everyday Life*, London: Routledge.

Gilhooly, K. (1996) *Thinking*, 3rd edn, Amsterdam: Academic Press.

Habermas, J. (2006) *Time of Transition*, Cambridge: Polity Press.

Heller, A. (1984) *Everyday Life*, London: Routledge and Kegan Paul.

Illeris, K. (2007) *How We Learn*, London: Routledge.

Jarvis, P. (1987) *Adult Learning in the Social Context*, London: Croom Helm.

—— (1997) *Ethics and the Education of Adults in Late Modern Society*, Leicester: NIACE.

—— (1999) *The Practitioner Researcher*, San Francisco, CA: Jossey-Bass.

—— (2006) *Towards a Comprehensive Theory of Human Learning*, London: Routledge.

—— (2008) *Democracy, Lifelong Learning and the Learning Society: Active citizenship in a late modern era*, London: Routledge (in press).

—— (forthcoming) *Learning to Be a Person in Contemporary Society*, London: Routledge.

—— and Parker, S. (eds) (2005) *Human Learning: A holistic perspective*, London: Routledge.

Kolb, D. (1984) *Experiential Learning*, Englewood Cliffs, NJ: Prentice Hall.

Polanyi, M. (1967) *The Tacit Dimension*, London: Routledge and Kegan Paul.

Ricoeur, P. (1995) *Figuring the Sacred*, Minneapolis, MN: Fortress Press.

Ryle, G. (1963) *The Concept of Mind*, Harmondsworth: Penguin (first published by Hutchinson, London, 1949).

—— (1979) *On Thinking*, Oxford: Basil Blackwell.

Schön, D. (1983) *The Reflective Practitioner*, New York: Basic Books.

Schutz, A. and Luckmann, T. (1974) *The Structures of the Lifeworld*, London: Heinemann.

Tremlin, T. (2006) *Minds and Gods*, Oxford: Oxford University Press.

Watkins, D. and Biggs, J. (eds) (1996) *The Chinese Learner: Cultural, psychological and contextual influences*, Hong Kong: CERC, and Victoria: ACER.

# Part 2
## Learning throughout life

# 3

# Youth and lifelong learning

*Rachel Brooks*

Experiences during the period of 'youth' or adolescence have always been important in helping to explain adults' attitudes towards (and take up of) lifelong learning. Indeed, there is a large literature exploring the impact of young people's experiences of compulsory schooling on their attitudes towards subsequent learning (e.g. Gambetta, 1987; Taylor and Spencer, 1994; Gorard and Rees, 2002). However, it seems timely to subject this relationship (between youth and lifelong learning) to a renewed scrutiny for two main reasons. First, as will be argued below, within the UK and across Europe more generally, young people have come to assume an increasingly important place within lifelong learning policy. Second, there have been a number of significant changes to the way in which 'youth' is understood and experienced over recent years, many of which have, or are likely to have, considerable bearing on young people's experiences of lifelong learning. Thus, this chapter sets out to explore the impact of learning (and learning policy) on young people's lives. It also considers the way in which broader changes to the period between childhood and adulthood (such as the increasingly individualized nature of youth transitions and the rise of youth consumerism) may themselves exert a reciprocal influence on the nature of lifelong learning.

For the purposes of this chapter, a relatively broad definition of 'youth' will be employed. As Holdsworth and Morgan (2005) have noted, adulthood is an uncertain status, with little clarity about when it begins and what it entails. Moreover, as a result of some of the changes that will be discussed in more detail below, such as labour market restructuring, mass expansion of higher education and the globalized development of youth culture, transitions from youth to adulthood have become extended and, in some cases, reversible and non-linear. Indeed, Manuela du Bois Reymond, whose work has been particularly influential in this area, has argued that:

> It is impossible to define an age limit after which one is not post-adolescent any more, but an adult. This is because objective and subjective definitions of life compound with individual elements which can no longer be isolated. Concepts of life, formerly determined by the dominant norms of values of social institutions such as the church(es), family traditions and neighbourhood cultures, have become individualized concepts.
>
> (1998: 65)

Whether or not society has really become as individualized as du Bois Reymond suggests will be discussed further below. However, her broader point – about the difficulty of identifying an upper age limit to the period of 'youth' – is generally accepted by researchers in this area who refer variously to 'young adults', 'post-adolescents', 'over-aged young adults' as well as to the more traditional 'young men' and 'young women'. Reflecting this wider literature, the young people referred to in the studies discussed below do not all fit into the 'adolescent' age category (of 14 to 19), but the broader mid-teens to mid-twenties age bracket.

## Policy changes

The increasing importance of young people to debates about lifelong learning is evident within both the academic literature and policy texts. Within the UK, at least, lifelong learning policy under the current Labour administration has foregrounded the experiences of young learners. In his analysis of lifelong learning policy, Taylor (2005) has argued that three major themes have underpinned initiatives in this area since Labour was elected to power in 1997: a focus on the 'skills agenda'; a commitment to 'widening participation' (particularly in higher education); and an emphasis on the civic or social purpose of education. In two of these three areas, young people play an important role. First, while the 'skills agenda' has focused on developing the skill levels of adults, particularly those for whom poor basic skills act as a barrier to employment (DfES, 2003, 2005), it has also identified those who currently leave school at the age of 16 as particularly in need of further training and skill development. This has been articulated with notable clarity in the plans, announced in 2007, to ensure that all young people receive some education and/or training until at least the age of 18 (DfES, 2007). Second, in relation to widening participation to higher education, the policy focus is on younger learners (the under-30s) and, more specifically, those of a 'traditional age' (i.e. 18–21) enrolled on full-time programmes. Taylor argues that this emphasis (despite the fact that older learners constitute almost half of the higher education student population) can be explained by policymakers' emphasis on 'human capital' and the assumption that, in focusing on younger learners, they will receive a greater return on their investment, as young people are likely to have a longer working life ahead of them than those who take up degree-level study at a later point in life. Taylor also suggests that this emphasis may, in part, be driven by various cultural assumptions about the nature of university study: most policymakers experienced higher education at a 'standard age' and their assumptions about the sector are often conditioned accordingly. This increasing focus on young people also reflects the strong emphasis on children and young people within lifelong learning policy at European level, as articulated within the relevant sections of the Maastricht Treaty (1992) and the Lisbon Strategy (2000), which outlined plans to develop Europe's knowledge-based economy. This emphasis is also evident within the mission statement of the European Commission's Directorate-General for Education and Culture, which states that its purpose is 'to reinforce and promote lifelong learning, linguistic and cultural diversity, mobility and the engagement of European citizens, *in particular the young*' (italics added) (EC, 2007).

The evident blurring of boundaries between what has, in the UK, traditionally been referred to as the 'schools sector' and lifelong learning may also have a part to play in the foregrounding of young people within lifelong learning agendas. Indeed, as Taylor (2005) has argued, until Labour came to power in 1997, the schools sector had dominated education policy within all main political parties. However, over recent years, the profile of lifelong learning has been raised considerably, as it has been assigned a central role in maintaining national competitiveness within a globalized economy. Indeed, it seems that much education policy within the compulsory sector has focused on creating a well-educated workforce for the future and, as a result, been subsumed under the banner of lifelong learning (France, 2007). Moreover, at the same time, the boundary or end point of the 'front-loaded' education system has been extended considerably such that, for many, formal learning has continued well into early adulthood – part of the 'academic drift' witnessed across the globe. Further questioning of the boundaries between school-based education and lifelong learning has come from those who have explored the nature of learning undertaken in different locations (Colley *et al.*, 2003). Indeed, Hodkinson (2005) problematizes certain assumptions that college-based and workplace learning are inherently different, highlighting important similarities between the two. For example, he argues that, in both locations: learning is related to the particular practices found there, which are, in turn, part of a wider culture that is rooted in the past as well as the future; learning entails elements of formality and informality; and learners and tutors/supervisors influence and are influenced by the culture, value and practices of the site where they participate.

## Individualization

The shifting relationship between young people and lifelong learning has also been influenced by changes in the wider lives of adolescents and young adults. Within the youth studies literature, theories of individualization have been particularly influential in teasing out the nature of some of these changes. Proponents of individualization (Beck, 1992; Giddens, 1991) argue that, as a result of global forces of production and consumption, industrial society is being replaced by a new modernity in which old certainties are threatened and a new set of risks and opportunities are brought into existence. Central to arguments about individualization are notions of 'self-reflexivity', in which individuals take more responsibility for the ordering of their lives. Instead of being socially conditioned (through social characteristics such as class, gender and ethnicity), as life-courses and 'biographies' tended to be in the past, they are now much more variable or 'destandardized'. Tradition and old, collective ways of managing are, it is argued, no longer able to help us navigate the new risks and opportunities and thus we have to rely on our own biographies and personal skills. In this way, individuals have more input into organizing their lives and more responsibility to make the 'right' decisions. As Furlong and Cartmel have noted, such changes have had a considerable impact on young people, in particular:

> Despite the maintenance of traditional lines of inequality, subjectively young people are forced to reflexively negotiate a complex set of routes into the labour market and, in doing so, develop a sense that they alone are responsible for their labour market outcomes . . . Young people are forced to negotiate a complex maze of potential routes and tend to perceive outcomes as dependent upon their individual skills, even when the objective risks of failure are slim. In turn, the perception of risk can lead to subjective discomfort.
>
> (1997: 39)

Within this new 'destandardized' context, lifelong learning is believed by many to assume particular importance. Allat and Dixon (2005), for example, contend that the transformations in many young people's lives are predicated on an adult model of the lifelong learner, in which work and learning are combined from an early age (through engaging in part-time employment while in full-time education) and that both are then maintained throughout the rest of the life-course, partially as a means of ensuring that one remains employable within a competitive and globalized economy.

Du Bois Reymond (2004) has taken this argument further by arguing that young people are particularly important in generating new forms of learning under the conditions of late modernity. Thus, she suggests that, for some young people in contemporary society, individualization has brought about not the 'subjective discomfort' discussed by Furlong and Cartmel, but a more creative and productive engagement with education, training and learning more broadly. On the basis of detailed empirical work in several European countries, she argues that many young people have come to 'blend' areas of their lives in innovative ways – combining learning and work, and work and leisure. Indeed, she claims that 'active investment in one's professional future means activating one's leisure time for it, without wanting to sacrifice the fun involved' (du Bois Reymond, 1998: 67). For these young adults, even periods of unemployment are often viewed positively, offering extra time for learning and living during which they are able to continue their education and development. It is, however, important to recognize some of the significant cleavages and social divisions between young people across Europe: du Bois Reymond is not suggesting that this pattern of blending different aspects of one's life is evident across all social groups. Indeed, she distinguishes clearly between those more privileged young people who have the necessary resources to follow a 'choice' biography (characterized by a wide range of choice about future options, but also a requirement to reflect upon and justify all decisions), and those who tend to follow more traditional 'normal' biographies.

In relation to lifelong learning, specifically, du Bois Reymond's focus is primarily on more privileged groups of young people who, she contends, are the ones who are developing new 'life and learning' strategies and creating different types of learning. These 'trendsetter learners', as she describes them, tend not to rely on formal education but blend different types of learning (such as formal, informal, non-formal and peer learning) and, as a result, she argues, they have better opportunities within knowledge societies. They prefer to learn from their peers rather than adults, and often have a strong dislike of learning from 'official people'. For these young people, learning, work and leisure are combined in creative ways – such as through marketing one's hobbies. In extending her argument, she maintains that this approach allows trendsetter learners to acquire 'youth cultural capital' that helps to realize 'self-determined ways of learning and living which are not as dependent on cultural inheritance from the family as was the case with former generations' (p.195). In this way, learning is understood as a key means of achieving relative independence from traditional family resources.

Proponents of the individualization thesis have also suggested that late modernity has witnessed a transformation in the relationship between men and women, presenting this as both evidence for and explanation of some of the changes they discuss (e.g. Beck and Beck-Gernsheim, 1995). However, while the 'trendsetter learners' discussed above include both young men and young women, other studies have pointed to a more complex picture of the ways in which gender is implicated in newly emerging patterns of transition to adulthood. With respect to learning, in particular, Thomson and Holland (2002) argue that, on the basis of their longitudinal study of young people's movement from compulsory education into other forms of learning and work, the analysis presented by some individualization theorists is overly simplistic. Indeed, they suggest that choices about learning (as well as work, leisure and family), while more fluid than for many previous generations, continue to be structured by social class, race and locality. Moreover, 'they are also constrained by a resilient model of adulthood anchored in heteronormative notions of "settling down"' (p. 348). Thus, decisions about post-school learning continue to be influenced by considerations about relationships, marriage and establishing a family. Further questions about the individualization thesis are raised in later parts of this chapter.

## Changing labour markets

The new emphasis on lifelong learning within the lives of young people can also be explained by changes to the labour market. Indeed, as France (2007) argues, major restructuring of labour markets around the world has brought about transformations in how young people move from school into work. First, in many countries, the youth labour market has been stagnant for a considerable period of time, offering very limited opportunities to those who choose to leave school on completion of their compulsory education. Second, post-16 education has expanded significantly in many countries across the globe while, third, the 'training state' has become a major pathway for young people leaving school, as a means of both managing youth unemployment and addressing particular skills shortages. Alongside these changes to transitions from education into work are other, broader changes to the labour market, which have also had an impact on how young people understand the options available to them. For example, as part of his wider theorization of individualization and the 'risk society', Beck (2000) has drawn attention to the fragmentation and casualization of work, with people often having to string together a series of short-term packages of work in order to make a living. It is worth noting, however, that this analysis is not shared by all. On the basis of their work with young adults in Bristol in the UK, Fenton and Dermott (2006) have argued that the trends outlined by Beck and others are concentrated largely among those with less education and in lower-status, lower-paid occupations; it seems that their data do not support a generalized picture of uncertainty and discontinuity among young people.

While there is some debate about the extent to which Beck's analysis can be applied generally, within the education literature there does appear to be more of a consensus that the relationship between educational credentials and labour market position has undergone significant change over recent years. Indeed, research into the lives of young people in a variety of different social positions has shown how, despite localized variations in perceptions of the labour market, this relationship has largely broken down. For example, McDonald and Marsh (2005) argue that, in some areas of the UK, the collapse of both the youth labour market and regional employment opportunities (in many cases brought about by global restructuring) transmits strong messages to young people about what they are likely to achieve and, in depressed communities in particular, this reinforces the notion that education is not what gets you a 'good job'. (This is not necessarily a new development: a similar argument was made by Wallace (1987) 20 years ago.) At the other end of the social spectrum, Brown and Hesketh (2004) have shown how, as a result of the expansion of higher education and the increasing marketization of the education system more generally, a good degree is no longer sufficient to obtain secure professional employment on graduation. They go on to argue that, to be successful in the graduate labour market, the 'hard currency' of educational qualifications and relevant work experience has to be combined with the softer currency of interpersonal skills and charisma, which together constitute one's 'personal capital'. On the basis of their work in Australia, Dwyer and Wyn (2001) have pursued a similar argument, maintaining that, on completion of their degrees, young people often experience labour market uncertainties that, in previous decades, were associated primarily with the end of compulsory schooling.

Although it is possible that this increasingly uncertain relationship between education and labour market success may cause young people to reject further learning, empirical studies have suggested that there is little evidence to support this hypothesis. Indeed, among more privileged learners, in particular, lifelong learning seems to assume an important role within young adults' responses to labour market change. While Brown et al. (2000: 118) contend that 'it is no longer a question of gaining credentials in order to climb bureaucratic ladders', they go on to argue that externally validated credentials and in-house training programmes both have a central role to play in maintaining one's employability and 'keeping fit in both the internal and external market for jobs'. Furthermore, Brooks and Everett (2008) and Bowman (2005) have argued that one reason why increasing numbers of young adults go on to postgraduate study is to seek distinction – through further learning – in a congested graduate labour market. It also seems that learning opportunities often constitute what Lewis *et al.* (2002) term 'a new transactional contract' between young adults and their employers. They suggest that, for many young people across Europe, training and development opportunities are an important part of the 'employment package' that they expect to receive in return for working long hours. Moreover, it is evident that further learning is frequently promoted by policymakers as a response to problems within both the labour market and the formal education system. In her analysis of learning across Europe, du Bois Reymond (2004) argues that non-formal learning, in particular, is often put forward by European Union (EU) policymakers as a general panacea for young people, to: prepare them for new labour market challenges; compensate for deficiencies in apprenticeships and training schemes; lead to more equal opportunities; and help to develop European citizens.

These various trends suggest that, while the relationship between educational credentials and labour market position may be less predictable than for previous generations, this has not discouraged young people from pursuing further learning. Indeed, young adults' motivations for engaging in lifelong learning as well as the type of learning offered to them by policymakers both seem to be strongly influenced by labour market conditions.

## Consumption

It has been argued above that the increasing importance of lifelong learning to young people (as well as the heightened profile of young people within lifelong learning policy) has been driven by the individualized nature of contemporary society and changes to the labour market, as well as specific policy responses to what is perceived to be a highly interdependent and competitive global economy. A further influence on the relationship between young people and lifelong learning is youth consumption. Over the past 50 years, the populations of most industrialized countries of the world have experienced an increase in wealth. As a result, a smaller proportion of an individual's income has to be spent on basic necessities, and a larger proportion can be spent on consumer goods. This has facilitated the growth of what has been called a 'consumer culture'. As this culture has grown, many writers have argued that consumer behaviour has taken on new meanings, with the consumption of particular goods and services being linked to specific social positions (Featherstone, 1987).

Such arguments have been made particularly forcefully in relation to young people. Indeed, there is broad agreement that, in the post-war period, young people have, to a large extent, driven consumption and consumer culture as both purchasers and creators of fashion, style and related cultural practices, and that consumption has come to play an important role in the construction of youth identities (Miles, 2000). A large market has developed, targeted at the teenager and his or her relatively large disposable income. Within the youth literature there is, however, considerable debate about the extent to which young people are able to operate agency within such markets. On one hand, some argue that young people are creative innovators – and thus far from passive purchasers – in their use of consumer goods. Writers pursuing this line of argument point to the creativity with which young people manipulate music and new technologies, and the innovative ways in which commodities are used, often having little to do with the 'original' role of the good (Willis, 1990). On the other hand, others (e.g. Griffin, 1993) have argued that this is merely a chimera and that, in reality, young people continue to be subordinated to the market, facing pressures from advertisers and peers to keep pace with the demands of consumer culture.

In light of these debates, young people's engagement with education and other forms of learning can, in some ways, be viewed as part of wider processes of consumption. Indeed, Field (1996) has suggested that many forms of learning can be understood, in part, as key components of consumer culture, while Usher *et al.* have argued that:

> Educational activities have become consumer goods in themselves, purchased as the result of choice, by free agents within a marketplace where educational products compete with leisure and entertainment products . . . the boundaries of leisure, entertainment and adult education activities blur as, for example, people increasingly learn from television programmes aimed at entertaining, and educational activities geared to consumer satisfaction produce outcomes previously associated only with leisure and entertainment.
>
> (1997: 17)

Although the majority of studies in this area have focused on consumption patterns among families choosing schools (Allat, 1996) or older adults pursuing lifelong learning (Usher *et al.*, 1997), a similar analysis can be extended to the activities of younger learners as they engage with various learning markets. Indeed, such an analysis allows us to explore the impact of consumption on: the delivery of learning; the relative prioritization of learning; and the meanings attached to learning within young people's lives. These are now each explored in turn.

First, it has been argued that a consumer culture affects the way in which learning is delivered to young people. Discussing lifelong learning, in general, Field (1996) has noted that growing consumerism has led to: increased use of private (as opposed to state) forms of educational provision; growth of provision that is directed towards self-development; and an increasing tendency for learners to insist upon attention to physical comfort and well-being in the service they have paid for. In relation to young people, more specifically, we can see similar trends emerging – particularly in the range of learning providers used by young adults to maximize their advantage within congested labour markets (Brown *et al.*, 2000) and the increasingly hierarchical way in which such providers are positioned by learners (Brooks, 2006b). Within the UK, there is also growing evidence that the shift to a more market-driven higher education system has resulted in more consumerist attitudes on the part of younger learners (e.g. Naidoo and Jamieson, 2005) – a trend that has been evident within the compulsory sector for some time (Ball *et al.*, 1997).

Second, there has been some concern, expressed by policymakers and teachers, as well as academics, that the importance attributed to consumption has had a significant and deleterious effect on young people's commitment to learning and, in particular, to formal education. Indeed, numerous studies have pointed to: the increased participation of young people in paid employment during compulsory education, 16–18 education and on into university (Broadbridge and Swanson, 2005); the adverse impact of such work on academic achievement (Hunt *et al.*, 2004); and the role of youth consumption in driving these patterns. However, again, this analysis is contested, with other writers highlighting a more complex range of factors that may underpin a decision to work during full-time education (Hodgson and Spours, 2001), and some of the ways in which labour market participation – even during a period of full-time education – may, in some circumstances, actually promote learning (Brooks, 2006a).

Finally, there is evidence to suggest that, as part of the shift towards a consumer society, the *meanings* that young people attach to learning change. Again, there is considerable debate here, with some arguing that consumption (of education, among other things) has been used to signal an individual's distinctiveness from his or her peers:

> When consumption becomes a matter of meaning, those with the necessary cultural and economic capital no longer consume for the sake of utility or need alone but to signify difference, to say something about themselves and to identify themselves in relation to others. A desirable lifestyle is no longer about consuming in order to be the same as others but rather about consuming in order to be different. In other words, it is difference, rather than goods or services per se, that is consumed.
>
> (Usher *et al.*, 1997: 5)

However, this analysis is not shared by all. Indeed, it has been suggested by others that the consumption of education, training and other forms of 'learning' can be seen as a process of social differentiation – choosing particular kinds of courses, qualifications or forms of learning as a way of signalling one's membership of a particular social group. For example, in their study of young people's higher education choices, Reay *et al.* (2005) argue that, across the social spectrum, choices are underpinned by assumptions about what is appropriate for 'a person like me'. Furthermore, Furlong and Cartmel (1997) argue that even those young people who understand their own decisions about the take-up and consumption of learning in fairly individualized terms are influenced by the resources upon which they have to draw (what they term 'structured individualism'). Thus, in their analysis, a shift to a more consumer-orientated society has had relatively little impact on the ways in which the learning opportunities available to young people are structured.

## Social divisions

Continuities in structural inequalities and the ensuing social divisions are both important themes in the literature on young people and lifelong learning. Indeed, although many of the changes outlined above (in terms of both policy and broader social change) have affected the lives of numerous young people and the ways in which they engage with lifelong learning, it is important to recognize that they have not affected all equally. In her insightful analysis of the European Union's policies on young adults and lifelong learning, Brine (2006a: 659) argues that two different types of learner are constructed by the discourse. The first of these is the high knowledge-skilled graduate and postgraduate learner, who 'is only ever referred to in terms of educational status and whose particular learning needs are never identified'. In contrast, the second type of lifelong learner is the low knowledge-skilled worker; it is this group that is most frequently targeted by EU policy. As Brine (2006b: 39) notes: 'they are the learners with the most prescriptive curricula in terms of (new) basic skills and vocational training; they are the learners who, without easily recognisable qualifications, must gather, record and attempt to gain accreditation for non-formal and informal learning'. These learners, Brine goes on to suggest, are constructed as at risk within a knowledge society, but also as a risk in themselves. Developing a similar argument in relation to UK policy, Burke (2006) contends that lifelong learning policy, particularly with respect to how it relates to young people, is too narrowly focused on simplistic notions of 'raising aspirations' among learners who are constructed through policy discourses as inferior. It thus fails to address wider questions about the way in which concepts of individualism and meritocracy, upon which current lifelong learning policies are built, may themselves serve to further disadvantage young learners.

Similar types of binary distinction emerge from empirical studies. As noted above, in her research across Europe, du Bois Reymond (1998) distinguishes between those more privileged young people able to pursue 'choice' biographies and their less privileged peers who follow more traditional 'normal' biographies. With respect to learning, more specifically, she also distinguishes between 'trendsetter learners' and their 'disengaged' counterparts (discussed above), acknowledging that one's capacity to become a trendsetter is, to a considerable extent, linked to structural factors:

> Trendsetters strive to redefine the constraints created by flexibilisation and rationalisation of labour and the requirements of lifelong learning; they aim to incorporate their personal lifestyles into their working lives. On the other hand, disadvantaged young people may be unable to take advantage of the benefits of modernisation and the areas of leisure and work tend to get separated from one another.
>
> (2004: 67)

Thus, while 'trendsetting learning' does enable some young people to develop their own 'youth cultural capital', an individual's ability to engage in such learning depends, at least to some extent, on the familial resources to which he or she has access. Recent studies of young people's engagement with lifelong learning have also pointed to social divisions within (what would traditionally be seen as) more privileged groups of learners. For example, even among graduates in the UK, social class continues to have a bearing on the take-up of postgraduate study (Wakeling, 2005), through the cost of such study (Bowl, 2003) and also class-related dispositions that students bring with them that influence their perceptions of the particular options open to them (Bowman, 2005).

Social class is also cross-cut by gender and 'race'/ethnicity in many analyses of these structural inequalities. Beck et al.'s (2006) study of vocational training is a good example of the way in which some forms of lifelong learning can work to reproduce disadvantage among young people. They show how the 'Apprenticeships'[1] programme, operating in England, was segregated by both gender and ethnicity. Moreover, it offered young people no formal opportunities to discuss gender or ethnic stereotyping within the labour market, and no information about the consequences of following particular occupational pathways. This, the authors argue, disadvantages all young people, but is particularly problematic for young women who populate apprenticeships in sectors with low pay and low completion rates. Other writers have suggested that some young people are facing particular barriers to lifelong learning because of the narrow way in which learning is understood on the part of policymakers. For example, in their research on young, white, working-class males, Quinn et al. (2006) argue that formal educational institutions – particularly universities – do not offer sufficient flexibility to accommodate the preferences of many young men. Indeed, in exploring the views of those who dropped out of university, they contend that what these ex-students really wanted was a flexible system, which allowed them to change course, go part-time or withdraw and return, without being penalized or vilified. They argue that, to understand these young men properly, policymakers have to pay much more attention to the role of informal learning in their lives:

> Instead of focussing on the inadequacy of male learning dispositions we need to use their informal learning as a route into high-status accredited study . . . there is much more that universities could be doing to foster the applied and participative learning that many of these men found most engaging and rewarding.
>
> (p. 747).

## Conclusion

This chapter has explored some of the ways in which changes to young people's lives over recent years have influenced their engagement with lifelong learning. It has argued that processes of individualization, while perhaps not as pronounced and widespread as Beck and other theorists suggest, have, nevertheless, had an important influence on the way in which learning is often combined with paid work and leisure in the lives of many young people, a pattern that often extends into later life. Individualization may also be responsible for the emergence of more creative lifelong learners – the 'trendsetters' in du Bois Reymond's analysis – among more privileged groups of young people. The chapter has also argued that changes to the labour market have affected the nature of the learning pursued by young adults. It has suggested that, while the relationship between education credentials and labour market outcomes may have become less predictable, this has not resulted in a widespread disillusionment with learning. Indeed, lifelong learning appears to be seen by many young adults as one way in which they can try to secure their position relative to others in a competitive and, at times, insecure jobs market. Lifelong learning can also be seen as being bound up with the increasingly consumerist nature of youth culture. Although the nature of this influence is contested, some writers have argued that consumption has affected the ways in which learning is delivered, as well as the meanings attached to it by young people.

Despite these changes to the relationship between 'youth' and learning in late modernity, important social differences remain; these have also been highlighted in this chapter. Indeed, even those youth researchers who have been most sympathetic to the individualization thesis have pointed out the enduring nature of inequalities (by class, gender, 'race'/ethnicity and other variables) in access to formal and non-formal learning. This remains a challenge for policymakers at both the national and regional level. While this chapter has shown how young people have come to occupy an increasingly important place in lifelong learning policies, such policies have also tended to reproduce divisions between young learners. Perhaps it is now high time for educationalists and youth researchers to take up du Bois Reymond's (1998: 77) invitation to 'combine their knowledge . . . taking into account lifelong learning, changing labour markets and new life concepts of modern youth'.

## Note

1    'Apprenticeships' refer to a government-supported programme in the UK for 16–25-year-olds. 'Advanced Apprenticeships' lead to level 3 qualifications (intermediate/technical skills) and 'Apprenticeships' lead to level 2 qualifications (a level that is expected to be reached by the end of compulsory schooling).

## References

Allat, P. (1996) 'Consuming schooling: choice, commodity, gift and systems of exchange', in S. Edgell, K. Hetherington and A. Warde (eds) *Consumption Matters*, Oxford: Blackwell.
—— and Dixon, C. (2005) 'Fashioning flexibility: dissolving boundaries between employment, education and the family among A Level students engaged in full-time schooling and part-time jobs', in C. Pole, J. Pilcher and J. Williams (eds) *Young People in Transition: Becoming citizens?*, Basingstoke: Palgrave, pp. 74–96.

Ball, S., Bowe, R. and Gewirtz, S. (1997) 'Circuits of schooling: a sociological exploration of parental choice of school in social-class contexts', in A. Halsey, H. Lauder, P. Brown and A.S. Wells (eds) *Education: Culture, economy, society*, Oxford: Oxford University Press, pp. 409–21.

Beck, U. (1992) *Risk Society: Towards a new modernity*, London: Sage.

—— (2000) *The Brave New World of Work*, Cambridge: Polity Press.

—— and Beck-Gernsheim, E. (1995) *The Normal Chaos of Love*, Cambridge: Polity Press.

Beck, V., Fuller, A. and Unwin, L. (2006) 'Safety in stereotypes? The impact of gender and 'race' on young people's perceptions of their post-compulsory education and labour market opportunities', *British Educational Research Journal* 32(5): 667–86.

Bowl, M. (2003) *Non-traditional Entrants to Higher Education*, London: Trentham Books.

Bowman, H. (2005) '"It's a year and then that's me": masters students' decision-making', *Journal of Further and Higher Education* 29(3): 233–49.

Brine, J. (2006a) 'Lifelong learning and the knowledge economy: those that know and those that don't – the discourse of the European Union', *British Educational Research Journal* 32(5): 649–65.

—— (2006b) 'Locating the learner within EU policy', in C. Leathwood and B. Francis (eds) *Gender and Lifelong Learning: Critical feminist perspectives*, London: Routledge.

Broadbridge, A. and Swanson, V. (2005) 'Earning and learning: how term-time employment impacts on students' adjustments to university life', *Journal of Education and Work* 18(2): 235–49.

Brooks, R. (2006a) 'Education and work in the lives of young adults', *International Journal of Lifelong Education* 25(3) (Special issue: *Beyond the Learning Society*): 271–89.

—— (2006b) 'Young graduates and lifelong learning: the impact of institutional stratification', *Sociology* 40(6): 1019–37.

—— and Everett, G. (2008) 'The impact of higher education on lifelong learning', *International Journal of Lifelong Education* 27(3): 239–54.

Brown, P. and Hesketh, A. (2004) *The Mismanagement of Talent: Employability and jobs in the knowledge economy*, Oxford: Oxford University Press.

——, —— and Williams, S. (2000) 'Employability in a knowledge economy', *Journal of Education and Work* 16(2): 107–26.

Burke, P.-J. (2006) 'Men accessing education: gendered perspectives', *British Educational Research Journal* 32(5): 719–33.

Colley, H., Hodkinson, P. and Malcolm, J. (2003) *Informality and Formality in Learning: A report for the Learning and Skills Research Centre*, London: Learning and Skills Research Centre.

Department for Education and Skills (DfES) (2003) *21st Century Skills: Releasing our potential* (Cm. 5810), London: The Stationery Office.

—— (2005) *Skills: Getting on in business, getting on at work* (Cm. 6483), London: The Stationery Office.

—— (2007) *Raising Expectations: Staying in education and training post-16* (Cm. 7065), London: The Stationery Office.

du Bois Reymond, M. (1998) '"I don't want to commit myself yet": young people's life concepts', *Journal of Youth Studies* 1(1): 63–79.

—— (2004) 'Youth – learning – Europe. Ménage à trois?' *Young: Nordic Journal of Youth Research* 12(3): 187–204.

Dwyer, P. and Wyn, J. (2001) *Youth, Education and Risk: Facing the future*, London: Routledge.

European Commission (EC) (2007) *Our Mission*, Directorate for Education and Culture. Available online at http://ec.europa.eu/dgs/education_culture/index_en.html (accessed 29 October 2007).

Featherstone, M. (1987) 'Lifestyle and consumer culture', *Theory, Culture and Society* 4(1): 55–70.

Fenton, S. and Dermott, E. (2006) 'Fragmented careers? Winners and losers in young adult labour markets', *Work, Employment and Society* 20(2): 205–21.

Field, J. (1996) 'Open learning and consumer culture', in P. Raggat, R. Edwards and N. Small (eds) *The Learning Society: Challenges and trends*, London: RoutledgeFalmer, pp. 136–49.

France, A. (2007) *Understanding Youth in Late Modernity*, Maidenhead: Open University Press.

Furlong, A. and Cartmel, F. (1997) *Young People and Social Change: Individualisation and risk in late modernity*, Milton Keynes: Open University Press.

Gambetta, D. (1987) *Were They Pushed Or Did They Jump?*, Cambridge: Cambridge University Press.

Giddens, A. (1991) *Modernity and Self-Identity: Self and society in the late modern age*, Cambridge: Polity Press.

Gorard, S. and Rees, G. (2002) *Creating a Learning Society? Learning careers and policies for lifelong learning*, Bristol: Policy Press.

Griffin, C. (1993) *Representations of Youth: The study of youth and adolescence in Britain and America*, Cambridge: Polity Press.

Hodgson, A. and Spours, K. (2001) 'Part-time work and full-time education in the UK: the emergence of a curriculum and policy issue', *Journal of Education and Work* 14(3): 373–88.

Hodkinson, P. (2005) 'Reconceptualising the relations between college-based and workplace learning', *Journal of Workplace Learning* 17(8): 521–32.

Holdsworth, C. and Morgan, D. (2005) *Transitions in Context: Leaving home, independence and adulthood*, Maidenhead: Open University Press.

Hunt, A., Lincoln, I. and Walker, A. (2004) 'Term-time employment and academic attainment: evidence from a large-scale survey of undergraduates at Northumbria University', *Journal of Further and Higher Education* 28(1): 3–18.

Lewis, S., Smithson, J. and Kugelberg, C. (2002) 'Into work: job insecurity and changing psychological contracts', in J. Brannen, S. Lewis, A. Nilsen and J. Smithson (eds) *Young Europeans, Work and Family: Futures in transition*, London: Routledge.

McDonald, R. and Marsh, J. (2005) *Disconnected Youth*, Basingstoke: Palgrave.

Miles, S. (2000) *Youth Lifestyles in a Changing World*, Buckingham: Open University Press.

Naidoo, R. and Jamieson, I. (2005) 'Empowering participants or corroding learning? Towards a research agenda on the impact of student consumerism in higher education', *Journal of Education Policy* 20(3): 267–81.

Quinn, J., Thomas, L., Slack, K., Casey, L., Thexton, W. and Noble, J. (2006) 'Lifting the hood: lifelong learning and young, white, provincial working class masculinities', *British Educational Research Journal* 32(5): 735–50.

Reay, D., David, M. and Ball, S. (2005) *Degrees of Choice: Social class, race and gender in higher education*, London: Trentham Books.

Taylor, R. (2005) 'Lifelong learning and the Labour governments 1997–2004', *Oxford Review of Education* 31(1): 101–18.

Taylor, S. and Spencer, L. (1994) *Individual Commitment to Lifelong Learning: Individuals' attitudes*, London: Department of Employment.

Thomson, R. and Holland, J. (2002) 'Imagined adulthood: resources, plans and contradiction', *Gender and Education* 14(4): 337–50.

Usher, R., Bryant, I. and Johnston, R. (1997) *Adult Education and the Postmodern Challenge: Learning beyond the limits*, London: Routledge.

Wakeling, P. (2005) '*La noblesse d'état anglaise?* Social class and progression to postgraduate study', *British Journal of the Sociology of Education* 26(4): 523–38.

Wallace, C. (1987) *For Richer, For Poorer*, London: Tavistock.

Willis, P. (1990) *Common Culture*, Milton Keynes: Open University Press.

# 4

# Middle age

*Mary Alice Wolf*

> In the middle of the journey of our life, I came to myself within a dark wood where the straight way was lost. Oh, how hard it is to tell of that wood, savage and harsh and dense, the thought of which renews my fear. So bitter is it that death is hardly more.
>
> Dante Alighieri

Middle age is a chronological, physical, social and psychological state. It is more than just an age; it is the transition from young to older adulthood. As a transitional life experience, it may begin with a "discovery" process, self-awareness, mourning for the end of previous times, grieving for lost opportunities, and moving on. This chapter explores the history of "middle age" in developmentalism, its significance to the culture, and changing parameters. It looks at the process of learning at midlife and suggests ways that adult educators might enhance this transition and provide environments for creative growth and development. Further, it examines the newest midlife cohorts, the Baby Boomers, and asks what specific learning opportunities might support their transition into older adulthood.

Of the life course, *The Talmud* observes:

- 20 for seeking a livelihood;
- 30 for attaining full strength;
- 40 for understanding;
- 50 for giving counsel;
- 60 for becoming an elder;
- 70 for white hair;
- 80 for Gevurah [new, special strength of age];
- 90 for being bent under the weight of the years.

If middle age comes in the middle of the lifespan, we can expect the tasks to be universal: new understandings (both affective and cognitive), generativity and mentorship, and the beginning of a new status as community elder. These tasks form the foundation for understanding the world of the middle-aged.

# First inclinations of middle age as a phase of adulthood

Carl Gustav Jung was the first developmentalist to talk about the second half of life. He observed that young adults (twenties and thirties) are involved in freeing themselves from their childhood conflicts and establishing themselves with new families and careers. Around 40 there is a significant opportunity for psychological change and growth. He called 40 the "noon of life" and stated that there is continued personality individuation during the second half of the life cycle. His metaphor was the daily course of the sun:

> A sun is endowed with human feeling and man's limited consciousness. In morning it arises from the nocturnal sea of unconsciousness and looks upon the wide, bright world which lies before it in an expanse that steadily widens the higher it climbs in the firmament. In this extension of its field of action caused by its own rising, the sun will discover its significance, it will see the attainment of the greatest possible height—the widest possible dissemination of its blessing—as its goal. In this conviction, the sun pursues its unforeseen course to the zenith; unforeseen, because its career is unique and individual, and its culminating point could not be calculated in advance. At the stroke of noon the descent begins. And the descent means the reversal of all the ideals and values that were cherished in the morning. The sun falls into contradiction with itself. It is as though it should draw in its rays, instead of emitting them. Light and warmth decline and are at last distinguished.
>
> (Jung, 1933: 108)

Jung believed that during the first half of life important aspects of a man or woman's self are neglected or suppressed. At midlife significant features of thought, feeling, intuition and sensation can be developed and integrated. These include young (puer) and old (senex), anima (feminine) and animus (masculine). For Jung, development is continuous throughout life. Thus, Jung introduced us to the concept of a flip in meaning-making at midlife. We see and interpret our life experiences in new ways. The second half of life, according to Jung, is a period of individuation and greater intuition. The task of middle age is for the individual to get in touch with his or her psychic energy, or, in the parlance of our times, to discover who we are. Thus, midlife can be viewed as a "second adolescence" (Jung, 1933: 106–7).

Bernice Neugarten and Nancy Datan (1974) identified tasks of the middle years as:

- reaching the peak of one's occupation;
- launching children from the home;
- the death of parents;
- the climacteric (menopause for women);
- grandparenthood;
- the advent of chronic illness;
- retirement.

Obviously, the ages vary for the tasks above and many of them do not occur until much later. A recent *New York Times* article featured two stories about men in their sixties who have very young children to raise (Vinciguerra, 2007; *New York Times*, April 14, 2007). Social status is also a determining factor in midlife task setting: frequently a blue-collar worker experiences aging sooner. Women who have children earlier will become grandparents sooner, etc. Middle age, however, is a combination of biological and historical events, often determined by peers and social cues. In my experience as a professor of adults, men and women in their forties, fifties, and sixties return to school to begin new careers.

Further, Neugarten and Datan (1974: 593) found the following characteristics in samples of midlife adults:

- enthusiasm and heightened awareness;
- reassessment of self, termed "greater interiority";
- sense of "executive" abilities;
- becoming a mentor.

When timing themselves, the middle-aged look at their positions (body, family, career) within different contexts rather than chronological age (for example, they might say, "When the children are gone from the house, I will go back to school . . .). Neugarten and Datan continue:

- women feel more freedom;
- men are concerned with health; they experience a decrease in sexual vigor and fear of performance can cause impotence;
- women begin "body monitoring," especially of their husbands.

Neugarten and Datan also described the "rehearsal" heart attack: Where the man goes into the hospital ER with symptoms of a heart attack but there is no actual infarction. Both men and women experience a difference in time perception: "Life is restructured in terms of time left to live rather than time since birth" (p. 593). Finally, Neugarten and Datan's last point:

- the concept of death is personalized.

Thus, despite the "changing boundaries of middle age" (p. 592)—whether it is seen as ages 35 to 60 or 40 to 65, individuals conceive of themselves as entering new terrain. Their interests begin to change, marked shifts in gender roles occur, social and family networks undergo development, and, depending on the cohort, new opportunities are explored.

## Current perspectives of middle-age development

Today's midlife cohort has even more dimensions to explore. The famous "Boomer" generations have somewhat different values. They have invented new "lifestyles" for middle age. More highly educated than earlier cohorts, they perceive of a longer transition into older adulthood and participate in greater numbers in work and social pursuits. In recent research I have found the following characteristics of middle age:

- a re-evaluation of roles, particularly traditional gender roles;
- a re-evaluation of relationships;
- dreams are more realistic;
- adjustments to physical changes are required;
- the "sandwich generation" phenomenon exists (where the adult is between her children and her parents and has responsibilities for both);

- the adult feels new responsibilities;
- the adult feels more in control of things (this is what Neugarten called the "executive processes of middle age," mentioned above);
- there is new emphasis on the partner;
- Erikson's generativity vs. stagnation is evidenced;
- there is a sense of "time left" rather than "time past";
- the middle-aged become learners.

Price (1991) studied a group of midlife women in a classroom setting. Through several methods, including in-depth interviews, she concluded: "Midlife women learners are determined to achieve. They are assertive, enterprising, and confident of attaining their goals" (p. 173). She found the women (mean age 42) to be purposeful copers and cited Neugarten and Datan's earlier statement: "The events of middle age may produce new stresses for the individual, but they also being occasions to demonstrate an enriched sense of self and new capacities for coping with complexity" (p. 167).

Judith Viorst, in a book of poetry aptly called *How Did I Get To Be 40 & Other Atrocities* (1976), described the sadness and surprise that comes in finding oneself further down the track than previously thought. In one poem, Mid-Life Crisis (p. 17), she touches on the physical awareness of the loss of youth and eloquently observes that this comes as a shock. She touches on the symbols of aging: the quick passage of time from acne to sagging kneecaps, the boys she knew once who are now losing their hair, and the sense that she *still* has plenty of poetry left in her. Kegan (2006) refers to this phenomenon as "an emerging reality" which precipitates a transition. Adult learners often discover that they need to transform their self-image as they grapple with changing times. Although the "aha" may feel sudden to the individual, it is usually a process begun earlier and only now acknowledged: this stage, after all, represents an end as well as a beginning. And the beginning is the doorway to old age. A biology student observed her own transition in the following way:

It is like the first frost on a window pane—all of a sudden *it* is. But, the long period of the cooling of the earth and the collection of moisture in the environment were necessary precursors.

Yet, other mid-life learners prefer to take even more time "maturing." Often, they find they belong in a cohort of "older people," despite their own identity as "youthful", and this is profound. In middle age, there is a constant shift into new visions and what is referred to as "meaning making" (Kegan, 1998, 2006; Merriam, 2005; Price, 1991; Wolf, 2006). In a recent class, I asked the learners to divide into groups based on cohort tasks (20 to 29; 30 to 39; 40 to 49; 50 to 59). A gentleman, clearly in the eldest category said that he would join the youngest group because he "thinks like a young person." Self-deception aside, middle-aged persons are often caught in a personal identity crisis: "Who is that person in the mirror?"

Henri Bergon (in Kegan, 2006) observed:

To exist is to change;
To change is to mature;
To mature is to create oneself endlessly.

Identity is central to the "developing self in midlife" (Whitbourne and Connolly, 1999; Whitbourne and Willis, 2006). Assimilation and accommodation occur for the individuation, just as they do at all stages of life. Relationships, work-related experiences, parenting, and community experiences all contribute to new demands and the need to blend and rebalance the everyday demands of modern life. Further, we know that midlife is a time of serious transitions and that the tasks of adulthood are fully operant. However, do we actually have a "crisis," where we run off with the handsome gypsy and take the collection plate? Bjorklund and Bee (2008) state:

> A recent survey of over 700 adults between 28 and 78 years of age showed that 26 percent of the respondents (both male and female in equal numbers) claimed they had experienced a midlife crisis. When questioned more closely, the events they described were not crises, nor had they occurred at midlife. Instead, the term 'midlife crisis' seems to have come to mean coping successfully with some threatening situation in one's adult life and making personal changes as a result . . . Longitudinal evidence . . . found no indication of a widespread upheaval in midlife. Those who experience a genuine upheaval at this period of life, and perhaps 5 percent of the population do, are likely to be people who have experienced upheavals at other times as well. That is, the midlife crisis (along with its cousin, the empty-nest syndrome) is, to some extent, an aspect of individual personality rather than a characteristic of this particular age period.
>
> (pp. 354–5)

The stereotype of "midlife crisis" is just that: an invention of the media and television situation comedies.

Nonetheless, we know that serious internal shifts in meaning-making and transitional movement occur during this period. Vaillant and Koury (1993) observe: "If mankind does not truly experience a life cycle in the caterpillar-to-butterfly sense, we believe that adult personality is changed from within as well as from without" (p. 1). Levinson and colleagues (Levinson et al., 1978; Levinson and Levinson, 1996) explored transitions at midlife (ages 40 to 45) and at middle adulthood (ages 40 to 65). They found that at midlife the individual—man and woman—becomes "more compassionate, reflective, judicious, and less tyrannized by inner conflicts and external demands" (Levinson, 1997). They propose that the central components of the life structure at midlife are marriage and occupation. Vaillant has amended Erikson's (1963) eight-stage model to add two new levels of meaning at midlife: "career consolidation" and "keepers of the meaning" (Vaillant and Koury, 1993; Vaillant 2002). It is relevant for adult educators to acquaint themselves with developmental structures in research and theory to understand that the underlying pattern or design of a person's life at a given time is not permanent, but reflects the roles and relationships of a particular moment in the life cycle (Erikson, 1963, 1982; Levinson, 1997; Levinson and Levinson, 1996; Levinson et al., 1978; Vaillant and Koury, 1993; Vaillant, 2002; Wolf, 2005). Educators would do well to examine how learning environments can support the work-lives and help direct the inner tensions of middle-aged persons.

## Midlife learners

Learning journals of midlife adults touch on the multiple demands and enthusiasms of this growing population. In a largely middle-class American population, some midlife learners made the following self-observations:

49

Middle age seems to be the time when you realize that life is finite, that you have limitations in terms of years and accomplishments. At the same time, you can look back and see youth as a time when you had different hopes and aspirations.

. . .

We are all very busy, but we are all going in different directions. Some are busy studying, some are going off to seminars and In-services and many are trying to get promoted. We rarely call in sick and are usually on time for work. We dress conservatively and professionally most of the time and don't discuss certain consciousness-raising issues in public. We are tired! The women seem to be working on "self" or what one visualizes as "self." Men are working for "the corporation" which they have incorporated into the "self".

## Review of the literature

The current literature of adult education encompasses several threads of theory that describe how learners differentiate, deconstruct, and reintegrate knowledge into their meaning systems. One thread posits that learners "see" content from subjective perspectives, often recycling their own personal narratives to better understand new concepts (Belenky *et al.*, 1997; Grabinski, 2005; Merriam, 2005; Wolf, 2005, 2006; Kegan, 2006). Others suggest that learners engage in a "meaning perspective transformation" (Mezirow, 1991) through a "disorienting dilemma, engaging in self and reintegrating" (Maciuika *et al.*, 1994: 259). In ethnographic and phenomenological research midlife adults describe how this transition takes place.

Midlife adults recognize that there is a phasic process in the life cycle. They may not name it per se, but they can intuit the shift in meaning-making. For example, a 41-year-old observed:

As I started to think about the seasons and our preparations for them, I began to think about the seasons of life and how we prepare for each—sometimes also being caught off-guard by an unexpected happening. Life rolls from day to day and all of a sudden one finds that he has passed from one stage into another sometimes having made plans and at other times slipping into a stage without thought or notice. Just as it is hard to be caught off-guard by a freak snowstorm, so it is hard to be caught off-balance by a life-crisis. At times we can over-plan and plans can fall apart, but in general, I think it is important to understand where one is and plan for whatever can be done at the time. It is important to understand the different stages so that we can anticipate what may happen and plan accordingly. We have paid a price for not being ready for winter—the roof on our gazebo collapsed from the weight of the snow, all shrubs were bent over, some broken, and the oak leaves are covered and molding on the ground under the snow. A lesson can be learned from this and hopefully in life we will think ahead and be prepared for the unexpected.

The middle-aged learner is in a stage of preparation for changes that will come. Often he or she is ready to replace a former job situation, hoping for the opportunity to meet personal goals before it becomes too late. There is an urgency to move ahead. The following excerpts from learners' journals express this phenomenon:

The idea of transitions in a person's life seems so eminently sensible to me. I look at all of the things that I have done in the past year and I realize that something is going on in me. More accurately, something has gone on in me. It's not all of the new ingredients that have "changed" me. Something changed inside me, and all of these outward manifestations are nothing more than a reflection of something that's already happened.

But the point at which the change occurs is what fascinates me. What is it that we do to prepare for these life changes? How is it that we get ready to move into the next place? The hardest part about learning to do the next thing is that we're very often in the middle of doing it before we realize that it's our job to do. There's a "lag time" that leaves us working, sometimes, on old work when we've already been moved into new.

I think when we're finally ready to go on to the new place, then there will be all kinds of "signs and symptoms" of that readiness. Those are the periods when generativity is possible—the times when we have achieved, however briefly, a "good fit" with ourselves.

Levinson and colleagues (Levinson *et al.*, 1978; Levinson and Levinson, 1996; Levinson, 1997) described this phenomenon as "changing life structure" and found it occurred in both men and women at times of transition. Adults progress through stages: stable periods lasting six to eight years and transitional periods of four to five years. During the transitional periods midlife adults reappraise their situations and look at the possibilities for change and renewed adaptation. Contrary to the Neugarten and Datan (1974) findings, midlife adults do not experience themselves as reaching their occupational peak: many are only now focusing on true vocational goals. They may not be launching their children, but welcoming new family members into their lives or making room for returning adult children. And retirement—especially early retirement—is no longer the ultimate goal of late adulthood. Late midlife adults are returning to education for retraining and voluntary engagements for fulfillment and remuneration.

## Strategies for working with middle-aged learners

The first strategy is to honor the code of adult educators: focus on the learner's own perspective and recognize that meaning-making is fluid. Learning results in a myriad of ways. Robert Kegan (1998) suggests that the true role of education is to enable the learner to achieve a "new order of consciousness," rather than simply to provide information. Learning involves critical reflection that begins with one's reorganization of previously held assumptions. In a classroom with mixed cohorts, this can be a challenge: each individual may be "locked" into a view of how the world operates. In a recent class in which gender roles were discussed, younger cohorts did not agree that women and men see the world differently, whereas the midlife learners were richly vocal about the many stresses that gender roles have created in their lives. It was a perplexing discourse: "Is it true," I wondered, "that all the inequities in workplace and family roles had been ended?" I did not share my own perspective but, after the class, a 52-year-old woman approached me. "I so enjoy the twenty-somethings' point of view," she remarked. "I wonder how they'll deal when they hit the wall . . .." Ah, the wisdom, the Talmudic understanding!

In cognitive dimensions, Schaie and Zanjani (2006) observe that primary mental abilities remain in place during the first years of middle age (that is, from ages 39 to 60). In the Seattle Longitudinal Study, Schaie and his colleagues have examined age-related changes in intellectual aging over the past 45 years. They observe that, in the primary mental abilities, "inductive reasoning, spatial orientation, perceptual speed, numeric facility, verbal comprehension, and verbal memory" (p. 102) there is little change. They go on to say:

On average, there is gain until the late thirties until the mid-fifties or early sixties . . . Because of modest gains from young adulthood to middle age, longitudinal comparisons from a young adult base (age 25) show significant cumulative decline only by the mid-seventies. (p. 102)

. . .

The phenomenon has been explained by increased educational opportunities and improved lifestyles. Nutrition and mastery over childhood diseases have enabled successive generations to reach ever higher ability.

(p. 105)

We can anticipate, therefore, that future cohorts of midlife adults will be able to maintain their intellectual abilities well into their seventies. They will experience a rise in verbal meaning.

Grabinski (2005) explores the nature of barriers to learning by midlife students and approaches the environment for learning using Kegan *et al.*'s (2001) concept of the "holding environment." She suggests that the functions of a good classroom as holding environment—support, challenge, and maintaining—be related to developmental transitions. Affording opportunities for complex and reflective analysis, even in the most pragmatic of curricula, helps to prepare the midlife learner for the inevitable challenges of future aging.

## Cohort issues: the Baby Boom phenomenon

The understanding of middle age has been slow in coming due to the small quantity of longitudinal research. However, several concurrent studies of midlife individuals are under way, tracking how they display changes in psychological and behavioral abilities well into their sixties. The University of Wisconsin has been engaged in a longitudinal study of the personal lives of a group of aging graduates (N=10,317) of the high school class of 1957 in the state of Wisconsin, in order to explore the shifting social and psychological events of their lives. A MacArthur Foundation grant (MIDMAC) has also examined midlife development and has made available a wide selection of bulletins dealing with changing family and work life, menopausal transitions, and psychological well-being at midlife (MIDMAC, 2006).

The demographic phenomenon that we call the Baby Boom refers to a large post-World War II upsurge in births in the United States and other countries, those born between 1946 and 1964 representing several cohorts of middle aged adults (Eggebeen and Sturgeon, 2006):

What happened was that more individuals married, married sooner, had children sooner, had children tightly spaced, and more likely had two or three children. This historically unprecedented growth in housing, education, transportation, and manufacturing created jobs—lots of jobs. Incomes grew at a rapid rate; prosperity was widespread. However, this extra income, as some have noted, was not expended on consumer goods or luxury items, but on extra children.

(p. 5)

Consequently, these individuals now represent the largest birth cohort born in the United States to reach midlife. The first of the Baby Boomers are now in their sixties and represent a new aging population. The learning needs of the Baby Boomers are related to employment, personal identity, and planning for the later years. However, we must be careful not to overgeneralize about this population, which is actually quite diverse. While they may have achieved higher educations than their parents:

One of the most fundamental axes of differentiation is race. Differences between the races, most notably black/white differences, in marriage, education, labor force participation, and income are so stark as to make broad generalizations about Baby Boomers as a whole erroneous.

(Eggebeen and Sturgeon, 2006: 17)

Nonetheless, we can observe that the workforce is aging, companies are downsizing (Vlasic, 2008), and pensions may not be available for this large cohort now nearing the end of their economic productivity. These midlife workers will be required to stay longer in the workplace, take on part-time employment in retirement, and face crucial social and personal dilemmas with scant national support. Policy debates about health care and national social security and entitlements are under way in seats of government across the world.

Many midlife workers are faced with caring for elderly parents. It is estimated that 25 percent of Baby Boomers are currently involved in parent care (ABC News, 2007). Scientific research now indicates that early interventions with persons affected by Alzheimer's disease can dramatically curtail its devastating effects. Midlife persons are confronted with their future—aging—and they are seeking and will seek gerontological expertise. Many will train in this area as a second, third, or even fourth career. Surely, it is a growth industry.

Baby Boomers will seek learning in the following areas:

- training in technology;
- to enter de-gendered work roles; this may include more men seeking caregiving expertise, or training as teachers or daycare workers, or learning Army-transferable skills such as cooking;
- pastoral work, counseling, and bereavement training;
- general continuing education;
- knowledge of health care (for both personal and professional application);
- policy related to health care, insurance (such as long-term care insurance), or workplace environments for leadership and management;
- political impact on policy and economic issues;
- planning for civic engagement, housing options and financial independence.

## Summary

This chapter has explored emotional mandates for learning, developmentally appropriate environments, cognitive functioning, and lifestyle issues related to current midlife Baby Boomers. It touches on their strengths and several of their most pressing real-world needs. What must be remembered is that the experience of a large portion of the population—middle age—is a relatively recent adventure. Just 100 years ago, middle age would have been at around 22 years of age! Our current elongated life course and the growth of a large worldwide adult population is the product of good public health and powerful economic circumstances. We are exploring new terrain.

Interestingly, Jung also wrote of the realm of subjective meaning at midlife and observed:

Wholly unprepared, they embark upon the second half of life. Or are there perhaps colleges for forty-year-olds which prepare them for their coming of life and its demands as the ordinary colleges introduce our young people to a knowledge of the world and of life? No, there are none. Thoroughly unprepared we take the step into the afternoon of life.

(1933: 108)

## References

ABC News (2007) "Role reversal: the high cost of elder care," June 23.

Belenky, M.F., Clinchy, B.M., Goldberger, N.R., and Tarule, J.M. (1997) *Women's Ways of Knowing*, New York: Basic Books.

Bjorklund, B.R. and Bee, H.L. (2008) *The Journey of Adulthood*, 6th edn, Upper Saddle River, NJ: Pearson and Prentice Hall.

Eggebeen, D.J. and Sturgeon, S. (2006) "Demography of the Baby Boomers," in S.K. Whitbourne and S.L. Willis (eds) *The Baby Boomers Grow Up: Contemporary perspectives on midlife*, Mahwah, NJ: Lawrence Erlbaum, pp. 3–21.

Erikson, E.H. (1963) *Childhood and Society*, 3rd edn, New York: W.W. Norton.

—— (1982) *The Life Cycle Completed*, New York: W.W. Norton.

Grabinski, C.J. (2005) "Environments for development," in M.A. Wolf (ed.) *Adulthood, New Terrain*, New Directions for Adult and Continuing Education, no. 108, San Francisco, CA: Jossey-Bass, pp. 79–89.

Jung, C.G. (1933) "The stages of life," in *Modern Man in Search of a Soul* (trans. W.S. Dell and C.F. Baynes), London: Harcourt Brace Jovanovich, pp. 106–7.

Kegan, R. (1998) *In Over Our Heads: The mental demands of modern life*, Cambridge, MA: Harvard University Press.

—— (2006) *The Evolving Self*, Cambridge, MA: Harvard University Press.

——, Broderick, M., Drago-Severson, E., Helsing, D., Popp, N., and Portnow, K. (2001) *Toward a New Pluralism in AGE/ESOL Classrooms: Teaching to multiple "cultures of mind,"* Cambridge, MA: Harvard University Graduate School of Education, National Center for the Study of Adult Learning and Literacy. Available online at http://gse.harvard.edu/research/reports.htm (accessed May 19, 2008).

Levinson, D.J. (1997) *The Seasons of a Woman's Life*, Workshop, Northampton, MA.

—— and Levinson, J.D. (1996) *The Seasons of a Woman's Life*, New York: Ballantine Books.

——, Darrow, C.N., Klein, E.B., Levinson, M.H., and McKee, B. (1978) *The Seasons of a Man's Life*, New York: Ballantine Books.

Maciuika, I.V., Basseches, M. and Lipson, A. (1994) "Exploring adult learning from learners' perspectives," in J.D. Sinnott (ed.) *Interdisciplinary Handbook of Adult Lifespan Learning*, Westport, CT: Greenwood Press, pp. 249–69.

Merriam, S.B. (2005) "How adult life transitions foster learning and development," in M.A. Wolf (ed.) *Adulthood, New Terrain*, New Directions for Adult and Continuing Education, no. 108, San Francisco, CA: Jossey-Bass, pp. 3–13.

MIDMAC (2006) *Bulletin Index*. MacArthur Foundation Research Network on Successful Midlife Development. Available online at www.midmac.med.harvard.edu (accessed May 19, 2008).

Neugarten, B.L. and Datan, N. (1974) "The middle years," in S. Arieti (ed.) *American Handbook of Psychiatry*, 2nd edn, vol. 1, New York: Basic Books, pp. 592–608.

*New York Times* (2007) "Older fathers are a joy and a blessing," April 14, p. 14.

Price, J.G. (1991) "Great expectations: hallmark of the midlife woman learner," *Educational Gerontology* 17: 167–74.

Schaie, K.W. and Zanjani, F.A.K. (2006) "Intellectual development across adulthood," in C. Hoare (ed.) *Handbook of Adult Development and Learning*, New York: Oxford University Press, pp. 99–122.

Vaillant, G.E. (2002) *Aging Well*, Boston, MA: Little, Brown and Company.

—— and Koury, S.H. (1993) "Late midlife development," in G.H. Pollock and S. Greenspan (eds) *The Course of Life*, vol. VI, Madison, CT: International Universities Press, pp. 1–22.

Vinciguerra, T. (2007) "He's not my grandpa. He's my dad," *New York Times*, April 12, p. 1.

Viorst, J. (1976) *How Did I Get To Be 40 & other atrocities*, New York: Simon and Schuster.

Vlasic, B. (2008) "Ford is pushing buyouts to workers," *New York Times*, Business section, February 26.

Whitbourne, S.K. and Connolly, L.A. (1999) "The developing self in midlife," in S.L. Willis and J.D. Reid (eds) *Life in the Middle: Psychological and social development in middle age*, New York: Academic Press, pp. 25–45.

—— and Willis, S.L. (eds) (2006) *The Baby Boomers Grow Up: Contemporary perspectives on midlife*, Mahwah, NJ: Lawrence Erlbaum.

—— and Schaie, K.W. (2006) "Cognitive functioning in the Baby Boomers: longitudinal and cohort effects," in S.K. Whitbourne and S.L. Willis (eds) *The Baby Boomers Grow Up: Contemporary perspectives on midlife*, Mahwah, NJ: Lawrence Erlbaum, pp. 205–34.

Wolf, M.A. (ed.) (2005) *Adulthood: New terrain*, New Directions for Adult and Continuing Education, no. 108, San Francisco, CA: Jossey-Bass.

—— (2006) *Developmental Perspectives in the Classroom and Later*, Presentation to the 32nd Annual Meeting of the Association for Gerontology in Higher Education, Indianapolis, IN.

# 5

# Older adulthood

*Mary Alice Wolf*

> There is never a moment when the new dawn is not breaking over the earth, and never
> a moment when the sunset ceases to die. It is well to greet serenely even the first glimmer
> of the dawn when we see it, not hastening toward it with undue speed, nor leaving the
> sunset without gratitude for the dying light that was once dawn.
>
> Adapted from *Havelock Ellis* by Howard Y. McClusky

It comes as a surprise to many people that older adults engage in learning activities. Why are we so surprised? Perhaps there is a general assumption that older persons are fading, disinterested in anything but chatting about the past, beyond learning and changing. That is the first lesson about aging: Older adults are no different from other age groups when it comes to a dislike of boredom. They are often highly motivated to learn new things and respond to education with enthusiasm and vigor. In a recent discussion in my gerontology classroom, an elder care manager described with amazement that several of her 80 and 90-something Russian émigré clients were attending English as a Second Language classes at the town Adult Education Center with great success. Even among these highly prepared graduate gerontology students, there was wonderment: Could this actually be true? Could 80 and 90-somethings be conquering the English language? Of course, the answer was yes.

This chapter explores the phenomenon of late-life learning. It presents an underpinning of learning theory, a brief overview of the field of older adult learning, a rationale for learning in older adulthood, and research on cognition, lifestyle and cohort differentiation. It presents the past and present of the field and speculates about its future. We know only snippets of what learning opportunities will exist for elders of the future, but we do know there will be many sunsets ahead with glimmering lights.

## Learning as a way of life

### Isn't there a pill for that?

Learning involves several processes: differentiation, dissonance, deconstruction, and reconstruction. The process of differentiation is part of a cognitive and affective continuum by which we adapt to environmental changes. When 75-year-old Hazel D. heard that she had to adapt to another nutritional plan, she was initially a disbeliever. Why should she change the way she had eaten all her life? Yet, when shown the statistics for women in their seventies who die when they do not address their diabetes, she understood. She needed to learn and she needed to change (Wolf, 2005a). Differentiation is noticing that something is new. When we differentiate, we "make object" of information and feelings that have always made sense to us, seemed right and natural—our "truths." But now we are alerted to a need to understand in a new way, perhaps create new truths.

Dissonance is connected to that confusion as we realize things are illusive and contradictory. Hazel D. spent weeks calling friends, hearing conflicting advice from chums at the Senior Center, the Mahjong club, the family barbecue (where, incidentally, she ate plenty of fatty pork barbecue), the pharmacy, her online chat group, her uppity granddaughter, and the newly minted nurse ("She doesn't even know enough to hem her own skirts! Imagine her telling *me* how to eat!"). Finally, barraged by advice from all sides, listening to a tape left on her sewing table and wearing a "magic bracelet" she had picked up along the way, Hazel deconstructed her previous way of thinking about meals. ("I still think there should be a pill," she continued to mumble.)

Deconstruction is literally the taking apart of a previous understanding of our reality. We deconstruct the way we understood something and *re*construct it to match the new reality (Kegan, 1994, 1999; Piaget, 1968; Piaget and Inhelder, 1969; Wolf, 1994). That is the stage of "aha!" So Hazel D. changed: she accommodated; she assimilated; and she adapted. She bought a cookbook and set out to be the next know-it-all among her cohorts. Now she could tell everyone she knew how to redesign his or her eating habits to avoid diabetes. Hazel D. now sees things differently and is ready to convert the world. That is learning.

Older people are no different from learners of any age. They are curious, able, and constantly in need of adaptation and assimilation. As a principle of learning and development, Beatty and Wolf (1996) observed: "Learning capacity is adequate for meeting life challenges" (p. 47). There is no question that the average 75-year-old is capable of adapting; he or she has had a lifetime of adaptation, accommodation, and assimilation (Schaie and Zanjani, 2006). Indeed, the 95-year-old can still do it! When motivated, the older adult will develop digital photographs of grandchildren, program a cell phone, and email a joke. In fact, one retired gerontologist recently commented on the amount of time her husband spent on the computer. "He has exchanged jokes with every high school classmate and is now blogging with his Army buddies," she observed.

There is great social exchange in learning centers designed for older persons. George Vaillant (2002), in his longitudinal studies of aging, found that learning was one of the prime activities in a rewarding retirement. "Retirees should continue lifelong learning," he wrote, "The challenge in retirement is to combine the fruits of maturity with the recovery of childlike wonder" (p. 224). Gusto for education in late life is highly correlated with psychological health. The capacity to take a fresh look at things makes a young person out of an old person. Indeed, in ancient Greece the word scholar meant leisure, underscoring that what you did with free time in Athens was to learn new things (p. 246).

We have witnessed a remarkable surge of interest in learning activities, educational centers, programs, and curricula designed to enhance the lives of older adults. It is a time of rich experimentation and the shattering of old myths, i.e. "You can't learn in old age"; "You can't teach an old dog new tricks." And now we are preparing to welcome the largest populations of over-65-year-olds ever into our learning centers.

## History of the field

Surely, the "father" of older adult education in the United States was Howard Y. McClusky (1974, 1990) who addressed learning needs in older adults and connected those needs to practice in adult environments. He opened our eyes to the myths of aging and demonstrated the potential for older people to grow, develop, enlighten, and contribute. Other major contributors to the field include, among others: Paulette T. Beatty, James Birren, E. Michael Brady, Bradley C. Courtenay, James E. Fisher, Roger Hiemstra, Peter Jarvis, JoAnn Luckie, D. Barry Lumsden, R.J. Manheimer, H.R. Moody, and David A. Peterson. In the past 30 years, there has been a growing body of gerontological theory and research, practice and analysis, and participation of older learners. These adult educators have explored cognitive and affective dimensions of development through research and theory defining the need to learn and the pragmatics for practitioners and curriculum development. Several journals focus entirely on learning theory and research, as well as applied curricula and interventions designed for late life learners. These include: *Educational Gerontology; Geriatrics and Gerontology Education; Older Learners; The LLI Review: The Annual Journal of the Osher Lifelong Learning Institutes; and The International Journal of Lifelong Learning;* as well as *The Older Learner,* a newsletter of the American Society on Aging. In the United States, the Libraries of the Future (Americans for Libraries Council, 2007) has begun training librarians across the country to develop outreach for older persons, particularly that behemoth: the Boomer generation.

However, no one theorist has influenced our work as much as has Erik Erikson (1968, 1978, 1982, 2001, and 1986 with Erikson and Kivnick). Erikson focused on understanding the inner life of older people. In his eight-stage theory of psychosocial development, he pointed out that older adults also have mandated "tasks" to achieve fullness and to grow as human beings. "Integrality" was his term for the wisdom and perceptions that are uniquely available to older people (1982). He wrote:

> This we have described as a kind of "informed and detached concern with life itself in the face of death itself," as expressed in age-old adages and yet also potentially present in the simplest references to concrete and daily matters.
>
> (p. 62)

We can well use his assertion of growth in old age as a rationale for advances in education for elders. Erikson asked:

> What is the last ritualization built into the style of old age? I think it is *philo-sophical*: for in maintaining some order and meaning in the dis-integration of body and mind, it can also advocate a durable hope in wisdom.
>
> (pp. 62–64)

In light of Erikson's ontological model of development, we might assert that education for older persons is *essential* for the civilization. For those who seek it, the learning process enables the older adult to develop to "integrality" and achieve well-being, as well as make genuine contributions to the culture. Older adults can be fully integrated into the everyday changes that other cohorts experience. They will not be isolated, marginalized, or "fogies" to be tolerated. Learning for lifelong development and a recognition that all human beings change, grow, and develop will be the international educational perspective. Education can be the hallmark of the search for hope, meaning, and connection for all other generations. Elders can experience themselves as conduits of appreciation of life and joy.

Fisher and Wolf (2000) cited several needs for education in the *Handbook of Adult Education*: these continue to drive older learners into educational experiences. Today they would include learning as meaning-making, and for employment, inclusion, self-efficacy, spiritual development, leisure and travel, the desire for intellectual maintenance, caregiving, health, and wellness.

Programs for older learners have proliferated during the past 20 years. In the United States, they include The Third Age Initiative, Civic Engagement, Encore Careers (Reserve), New Chapters Centers, The Osher Lifelong Learning Institutes, The University without Walls, Transitional Keys, The Elderhostel, Roads Scholars, and National Centers for Creative Retirement (NCCR). Of this movement, Manheimer (2007a) observes:

> Older Adult Education, a field within adult education that emerged during the middle of the twentieth century, is generally of the non-formal type. Conditions that encouraged older adult education to flower include: lengthening of the life course, improved health and economic status among retirement-aged adults, higher rates of prior education among those reaching later life, the rising popularity of the notion of lifelong learning (whether formal or non-formal) as both a personal and public good, developmental and neurological theories advancing the appropriateness and the benefits of continued learning, and greater opportunities for learning and teaching in mid and later life through such diverse organizations as colleges and universities, churches, synagogues and mosques, senior centers, public libraries, day health centers, hospitals, unions and residential housing groups.
>
> (p. 2)

Many creative groups have formed in local communities to tap the learning potential of older adults. Luckie (2005) found a unique setting for creative work by older persons in a church project; Eisen (2005) reported on a successful program designed to involve retired persons in focused civic projects; and Collins (2006) examined the potential for increased mastery in a population of low-income housing and senior centers in urban and rural areas and found significant decrease in loneliness and stress. Brady and Sky (2003) employed journal writing as a prime activity with older learners; Butler (2005) found a need for increased enrollments in college settings; and Henkin (2007) developed intergenerational communities with Native American traditionalists instructing youngsters in ancient arts. Hori and Cusack (2006) compared the learning needs of Canadian and Japanese "Third-agers" and found significant government support for learning centers. Young and Rosenberg (2006) identified a multitude of opportunities for education for the elderly throughout Japanese elementary and secondary schools. These are just a sample of the wide assortment of opportunities aimed at learning for older adults: there is no one model, no one economic level targeted, no one notion of success. There is abundant evidence that educational outreach to older adults has come of age (Fisher and Wolf, 1998, 2000; Grams, 2001; Hendricks, 2001; Henkin, 2007; Manheimer, 2007a, b; Rowe and Kahn 1998; Sherman, 2006).

## New visions of late-life learning

### *Leisure and work*

Traditionally, adulthood was divided into neat boxes containing education, work, retirement, and leisure. Today, life course studies indicate that this arrangement is in flux (Settersten, 2006).

Our life course now mixes leisure, more education, work, new work, retirement, other work, etc., in flexible modules rather than linear boxes. This is true of the 70-year-old cohort and it is becoming clearer that the coming cohorts will continue to reinvent the life course schedule (Cullinane, 2006; Czaja, 2006; Eggebeen and Sturgeon, 2006).

## Self-efficacy

Locus of control—whether a decision is made by choice (internal locus of control) or by fiat (external locus of control)—is a central factor throughout the life span (Beatty and Wolf, 1996). It is a highly motivating principle of human development and of learning; it allows the learner to construct the future. It is aligned with self-efficacy. Cervone *et al.* (2006) observe that "self–efficacy refers to our sense of confidence and competence" (p. 171). Models of successful aging and research on positive aging appear with increasing regularity. In an effort to ensure and enhance quality of life in late adulthood and senescence, investigators aim to enable older adults to live engaged, purposeful, and meaningful lives as free from mental and physical debilities as possible (pp. 169–170).

## Intellectual stability and maintenance

There is increasing evidence that older adults who are stimulated mentally experience less decline in memory and continued growth in verbal knowledge well into their late seventies (Cavanaugh and Blanchard-Fields, 2006; Cohen, 2001, 2006; Hooyman and Kiyak, 2008; Hoyer and Verhaeghen, 2006; McFadden and Atchley, 2001; Rowe and Kahn, 1998; Schaie, 2005; Schaie and Willis, 2002; Schaie and Zagani, 2006; Sherman, 2006; Snowden, 2001).

## Socialization

Older persons benefit from maintaining social connections in many ways (Baltes and Carstensen, 2000). They tend to be healthier (Krause, 2006), have a wider range of social supports, and enjoy higher levels of self-satisfaction (Perls and Silver, 1999; Vaillant, 2002). However, it has often been stated that we age as we are (Costa and McCrae, 1994; Mroczek and Little, 2006; Neugarten, 1977); we do not suddenly find ourselves to be craving social groups at the age of 65. Older adults who participate in formal learning activities are frequently long-term learners (University of Wisconsin, 2007).

## Integration and meaning making

Older adults have emotional needs, including coming to terms with their stories, resolving issues of dissatisfaction in their life histories, and exploring the connections they have with the relationships in their worlds (Birren and Schroots, 2006; Grams, 2001; Gubrium and Holstein, 2003; Jung, 1933; Kenyon *et al.*, 1999; McClusky, 1990; Peck, 1956; Rowe and Kahn, 1998; Setterson, 2006; Tennant, 2000; Vaillant, 2002). As Kaufman wrote:

> The key here is integration; this is the heart of the creative, symbolic process of self-formulation in late life. If we can find the sources of meaning held by the elderly and see how individuals put it all together, we will go a long way toward appreciating the complexity of human aging and the ultimate reality of coming to terms with one's whole life.
> (1986: 188)

## The cohort factor

A cohort is, "in life course analysis, a group of people who are roughly the same age during a particular historical period" (Newman and Newman, 2006: G-4). We need to ask: Who are our learners? Who will they be in the next ten years? The next twenty years? We know that numbers will increase exponentially. But how will they differ from our current population of over-65 adults?

## Research and assessment

Enlightened research tapping into the inner lives and meaning-making required of new elders will provide guidance into the nature of development in the future (Berger and Luckmann, 1967; Gubrium and Holstein, 2003; Jarvis and Parker, 2005; Moody, 2000; Rowe and Kahn, 1998). In addition, longitudinal research on life course habits will inform practitioners of shifts in social, family, and work and leisure patterns (University of Wisconsin, 2007).

Hazel D.'s son, Michael D., is 55 years old. Michael is a successful educator in an adult evening program in a large urban community. At this point, however, after 25 years in the school system, he is considering becoming a specialist in programs and curricula for older adults. He believes he could make a nice contribution to this area of education before his own actual retirement in a few years. (It has not yet dawned on Michael that he will be an "older adult" himself in a mere ten years, and that he will not even be able to *think* of retirement before the age of 70, if then.) He imagines a learning environment in which late-life adults will want to learn about computers, history, and Shakespeare, perhaps upgrading their language skills for travel abroad. His mother's life was enhanced by studying nutrition and health in her seventies.

Welcome, Michael, to learning as a way of life! You will now need to undergo several processes: differentiation, dissonance, deconstruction, and reconstruction. You will need to explore the new terrain of adulthood: what you knew is now gone. You will want to prepare settings for the diverse needs of some billion Baby Boomers who represent three distinct cohorts in and of themselves. Eggebeen and Sturgeon (2006) state that Baby Boomers consist of three birth cohorts: Leading (1947–9), Middle (1953–5), and Trailing (1960–2). Levels of education vary greatly for each cohort depending on race, ethnicity, and economic status. Each cohort has experienced a unique childhood, historic perspective, health environment, social and family relationships, labor history, cultural expectations, and economic background. Michael will learn to create projects for changing environments, perhaps build new learning centers and intergenerational work programs. He will deconstruct his perception of aging and reconstruct it using research resources, longitudinal data, and much optimism (Wolf, 2005a, b, 2007). He may answer the pivotal question we asked a few years ago:

> As this population increases in size and proportion of the larger population, questions emerge as to when education and learning will be viewed as legitimate responses to heterogeneous needs of significant portions of this population in addition to their use of leisure time, and when it will be employed to help this population address the substantive needs of the society of which they are integral parts.
>
> (Fisher and Wolf, 2000)

## Conclusion

At a recent meeting of housing officials, a gerontologist asked what preparations had been put in place for the coming cohorts of elders who may not want to live in our current "assisted living" accommodations. The panel of housing experts simply stared. Then one said, "We will put in a sushi bar." Oh my, what a lot of learning will have to accompany this parade of aging persons!

We are now in uncharted territory. Never before has the adult education movement been so challenged to organize around a growing demographic surge: with 420 million people aged 65 and over in 2000, we can anticipate that, by 2050, there will be 1.5 billion people over 65 (Population Resource Center, 2007). How many of these individuals will seek learning for work or leisure? We must begin. For, as Howard McClusky reminded us, "There is never a moment when the new dawn is not breaking over the earth, and never a moment when the sunset ceases to die."

## References

Americans for Libraries Council (2007) *Lifelong Access Libraries*, Chapel Hill, NC: Lifelong Access Libraries Leadership Institute, July 29–August 3, 2007.

Baltes, M.M. and Carstensen, L.L. (2000) "The process of successful aging," in E.W. Markson and L.A. Hollis-Sawyer (eds) *Intersections of Aging*, Los Angeles, CA: Roxbury Publishing Company, pp. 65–81.

Beatty, P.T. and Wolf, M.A. (1996) *Connecting with Older Adults: Educational responses and approaches*, Malabar, FL: Krieger Publishers.

Berger, P.L. and Luckmann, T. (1967) *The Social Construction of Reality*, New York: Doubleday.

Birren, J.E. and Schroots, J.J.F. (2006) *Telling the Stories of Life Through Guided Autobiography Groups*, Baltimore, MD: Johns Hopkins University Press.

Brady, E.M. and Sky, H.Z. (2003) "Journal writing among older learners," *Educational Gerontology* 29: 151–63.

Butler, C.B. (2005) "Age-related paradigms," in M.A. Wolf (ed.) *Adulthood: New terrain*, New Directions for Adult and Continuing Education, no. 108, San Francisco, CA: Jossey-Bass, pp. 61–8.

Cavanaugh, J.C. and Blanchard-Fields, J.C. (2006) *Adult Development and Aging*, 5th edn, Belmont, CA: Wadsworth, Thomson Learning.

Cervone, D., Artistico, D., and Berry, J.M. (2006) "Self-efficacy and adult development," in C. Hoare (ed.) *Handbook of Adult Development and Learning*, New York: Oxford University Press, pp. 169–218.

Cohen, G.D. (2001) *The Creative Age: Awakening human potential in the second half of life*, New York: Basic Books.

—— (2006) *The Mature Mind: The positive power of the aging brain*, New York: Basic Books.

Collins, C.C. (2006) "Seniors CAN: community-based education to promote independence for older adults," *The LLI Review: The Annual Journal of the Osher Lifelong Learning Institutes* 1: 60–9.

Costa, P.T. and McCrae, R.R. (1994) "Set like plaster? Evidence for the stability of adult personality," in T.F. Heatherton and J.L. Weinberger (eds) *Can Personality Change?*, Washington, DC: Academic Psychological Association, pp. 21–40.

Cullinane, P. (2006) "Late-life civic engagement enhances health for individuals and communities, *The Journal of Active Aging* 5 (November/December): 66–73.

Czaja, S.J. (2006) "Employment and the Baby Boomers: what can we expect in the future?," in S.K. Whitbourne and S.L. Willis (eds) *The Baby Boomers Grow Up: Contemporary perspectives on midlife*, Mahwah, NJ: Lawrence Erlbaum Associates, pp. 283–98.

Eggebeen, D.J. and Sturgeon S. (2006) "Demography of the Baby Boomers," in S.K. Whitbourne and S.L. Willis (eds) *The Baby Boomers Grow Up: Contemporary perspectives on midlife*, Mahwah, NJ: Lawrence Erlbaum, pp. 3–21.

Eisen, M.J. (2005) "Shifts in the landscape of learning: new challenges," in M.A. Wolf (ed.) *Adulthood: New terrain*, New Directions for Adult and Continuing Education, no. 108, San Francisco, CA: Jossey-Bass, pp. 15–26.

Erikson, E.H. (1968) *Identity: Youth and crisis*, New York: W.W. Norton.

—— (ed.) (1978) *Adulthood*, New York: W.W. Norton.

—— (1982) *The Life Cycle Completed*, 2nd edn, New York: W.W. Norton.

—— (2001) "Reflections on the last stage—and the first," in R. Diessner and J. Tieggs (eds) *Notable Selections in Human Development*, 2nd edn, Guilford, CT: McGraw Hill, pp. 340–7.

——, Erikson, J.M., and Kivnick, H. (1986) *Vital Involvement in Old Age*, New York: W.W. Norton.

Fisher, J.C. and Wolf, M.A. (eds) (1998) *Using Learning to Meet the Challenges of Older Adulthood*, San Francisco, CA: Jossey-Bass.

—— and —— (2000) "Older adult learning," in A.L. Wilson and E.R. Hayes (eds) *Handbook of Adult and Continuing Education*, San Francisco, CA: Jossey-Bass, pp. 480–92.

Grams, A. (2001) "Learning, aging, and other predicaments," in S.H. McFadden and R.C. Atchley (eds) *Aging and the Meaning of Time: A multidisciplinary exploration*, New York: Springer, pp. 99–111.

Gubrium, J.F. and Holstein, J.A. (2003) *Ways of Aging*, Malden, MA: Blackwell.

Hendricks, J. (2001) "It's about time," in S.H. McFadden and R.C. Atchley (eds) *Aging and the Meaning of Time: A multidisciplinary exploration*, New York: Springer, pp. 21–50.

Henkin, N. (2007) *Communities for All Ages: Lifelong learning and civic engagement*, Chapel Hill, NC: Lifelong Access Libraries Leadership Institute.

Hooyman, N.R. and Kiyak, H.A. (2008) *Social Gerontology: A multidisciplinary perspective*, 8th edn, New York: Pearson.

Hori, S. and Cusack, S. (2006) "Third-age education in Canada and Japan: attitudes toward aging and participation in learning," *Educational Gerontology* 32(6): 462–81.

Hoyer, W.J. and Verhaeghen, P. (2006) "Memory aging," in J.E. Birren and K.W. Schaie (eds) *Handbook of the Psychology of Aging*, 6th edn, New York: Academic Press, pp. 209–32.

Jarvis, P. and Parker, S. (eds) (2005) *Human Learning: An holistic approach*, New York: Routledge.

Jung, C.G. (1933) *Modern Man in Search of a Soul* (trans. W.S. Dell and C.F. Baynes), New York: Harcourt Brace Jovanovich.

Kaufman, S. (1986) *The Ageless Self: Sources of meaning in late life*, Madison, WI: University of Wisconsin Press.

Kegan, R. (1999) *The Evolving Self*, Cambridge, MA: Harvard University Press.

—— (1994) *In Over Our Heads: The mental demands of modern life*, Cambridge, MA: Harvard University Press.

Krause, N. (2006) "Social relationships in late life," in R.H. Binstock and L.K. George (eds) *Handbook of Aging and the Social Sciences*, 6th edn, New York: Academic Press, pp. 181–200.

Kenyon, G.M., Ruth, J.-E., and Mader, W. (1999) "Elements of a narrative gerontology," in V. Bengston and W. Schaie (eds) *Handbook of Theories of Aging*, New York: Springer, pp. 40–58.

Luckie, J.A.C. (2005) "Life journeys: awakenings and learning experiences," in M.A. Wolf (ed.) *Adulthood: New terrain*, New Directions for Adult and Continuing Education, no. 108, San Francisco, CA: Jossey-Bass, pp. 69–78.

McClusky, H.Y. (1971) *Education: Background*, Report prepared for the 1971 White House Conference on Aging, Washington, DC.

—— (1990) "The community of generations: a proposed goal and context for the education of persons in the later years," in R.H. Sherron and D.B. Lumsden (eds) *Introduction to Educational Gerontology*, 3rd edn, Washington: Hemisphere, pp. 324–55.

McFadden, S.H. and Atchley, R.C. (eds) (2001) *Learning, Aging, and Other Predicaments*, New York: Springer Publishing Company.

Manheimer, R. (2007a) "Adult education," in J. Birren (ed.) *Encyclopedia of Gerontology*, 2nd edn, New York: Academic Press.

—— (2007b) "Allocating resources for lifelong learning for older adults," in R.A. Pruchno and M.A. Smyer (eds) *Challenges of an Aging Society*, Baltimore, MD: Johns Hopkins University Press, pp. 217–37.

63

Merriam, S.B., Caffarella, R.S., and Baumgartner, L.M. (2006) *Learning in Adulthood: A comprehensive guide*, San Francisco, CA: Jossey-Bass Higher and Adult Education.

Moody, H.R. (2000) *Structure and Agency in Late-life Learning*, Harry R. Moody website. Available online at www.hrmoody.com (accessed September 23, 2007).

Mroczek, D.K. and Little, T.D. (eds) (2006) *Handbook of Personality Development*, Mahwah, NJ: Lawrence Erlbaum Associates.

Neugarten, B.L. (1977) "Personality and aging," in J.E. Birren and K.W. Schaie (eds) *Handbook of the Psychology of Aging*, New York: Van Nostrand Reinhold.

Newman, B.M. and Newman, P.R. (2006) *Development Through Life: A psychological approach*, 9th edn, London: Thomson Learning.

Peck, R. (1956) "Psychological developments in the second half of life," in J.E. Anderson (ed.) *Psychological Aspects of Aging*, Washington, DC: American Psychological Association, pp. 88–92.

Perls, T.T. and Silver, M.H. (1999) *Living to 100*, New York: Basic Books.

Piaget, J. (1968) *Six Psychological Studies*, New York: Vintage Books.

—— and Inhelder, B. (1969) *The Psychology of the Child* (trans. H. Weaver), New York: Basic Books.

Population Resource Center (2007) *Rethinking Global Population: The aging of America*. Available online at www.prcdc.org/summaries/worldpop/worldpop.html (accessed May 20, 2008).

Rowe, J.W. and Kahn, R.L. (1998) *Successful Aging*, New York: Pantheon Books.

Schaie, K.W. (2005) *Developmental Influences on Adult Intelligence: The Seattle Longitudinal Study*, New York: Cambridge University Press.

—— and Willis, S.L. (2002) *Adult Development and Aging*, 5th edn, Upper Saddle River, NJ: Prentice Hall.

—— and Zanjani, A.K. (2006) "Intellectual development across adulthood," in C. Hoare (ed.) *Handbook of Adult Development and Learning*, New York: Oxford University Press, pp. 99–122.

Settersten, R.A. (2006) "Aging and the life course," in R.H. Binstock and L.K. George (eds) *Handbook of Aging and the Social Sciences*, 6th edn, New York: Academic Press, pp. 3–19.

Sherman, A. (2006) "Toward a creative culture: lifelong learning through the arts," *Generations* 30(1) (Spring): 42–6.

Snowden, D. (2001) *Aging with Grace: What the nun study teaches us about how to lead longer, healthier, and more meaningful lives*, New York: Bantam.

Tennant, M. (2000) "Adult learning for self-development and change," in A.L. Wilson and E.R. Hayes (eds) *Handbook of Adult and Continuing Education*, San Francisco, CA: Jossey-Bass, pp. 87–100.

Vaillant, G.E. (2002) *Aging Well*, Boston, MA: Little, Brown and Company.

University of Wisconsin (2007) *Wisconsin Longitudinal Study*, Madison, WI: The University of Wisconsin. Available online at www.ssc.wisc.edu/wlsresearch/ (accessed June 24, 2007).

Wolf, M.A. (1994) *Older Adults: Learning in the Third Age*, Information Series No. 357, ERIC Clearinghouse on Adult, Career and Vocational Education.

—— (2005a) "Life cycle development and human learning," in P. Jarvis and S. Parker (eds) *Human Learning: From the biological to the spiritual*, London: Routledge, pp. 183–93.

—— (ed.) (2005b) *Adulthood: New terrain*, New Directions for Adult and Continuing Education, no. 108, San Francisco, CA: Jossey-Bass.

—— (2007) *Profiles in Older Adult Learners for 2010*, Presentation to the 2nd Annual Lifelong Access Libraries Leadership Institute, Chapel Hill, NC.

Young, K. and Rosenberg, E. (2006) "Lifelong learning in the United States and Japan," *The LLI Review: The Annual Journal of the Osher Lifelong Learning Institutes* 1: 69–85.

# Part 3
## Sites of lifelong learning

# 6

# Lifelong learning and the family
## An auto/biographical imagination

*Linden West*

Considering families in the context of a book on lifelong learning leads us to ask some potentially profound questions: about, for instance, the relationship between experiences of 'learning' in earliest and subsequent experience; or about learning in private as well as public space, and the dynamics between these. It forces us too to ask what learning actually is and whose purposes it serves. Doing auto/biographical research, over many years, among families and professionals involved in what are termed family 'support and learning programmes', has prompted these sorts of questions. We enter, in fact, when working auto/biographically on such a topic, a complex lifelong but also lifewide learning territory that reminds us, perhaps, of the indivisibility of learning and experience, wherever and whenever these find expression. And certainly of the danger of equating learning simply with what transpires in schools or other formal institutions. Or the equivalent danger of separating, arbitrarily – under the banner of andragogy, for instance – processes of adult learning from early years learning (Knowles, 1973). Auto/biographical research on families and learning challenges narrowness and reductionism of many kinds just as it demands interdisciplinary and what I term 'psychosocial' understanding of the interplay between inner and outer worlds, self and other, the psychological and sociological, past and present, in learning lives.

Remembering, always, that lifelong learning is contested territory, and that the main discursive thrust tends to be narrowly economistic (Field, 2006). Lifelong learning is easily reduced to worklong training and the perpetual even frenetic updating of knowledge and skills. Emphasis is given to individuals' capacity to adjust (under the impact of globalisation, and technological and scientific innovation, for instance) to a constantly changing work environment. This has to do with adaptability rather than human agency and the need, in effect, at the bottom line, for people to invent, or reinvent themselves as marketable products. Frank Coffield (1999), an enthusiastic proponent of lifelong learning, questions the concept, and its associated values, when it entails shifting responsibility for learning on to individuals, simply to ensure employability; or when the modernisation of education becomes primarily a matter of servicing employer needs. In the context of the recent mushrooming of 'family learning programmes', at least in the Anglo-Saxon world (under labels like Best, Sure or Head Start), the rhetoric, at least from on high, can similarly be one of making parents employable, in a pervasive neo-liberal mantra. The spirit of learning for more humanistic, personal and social ends – as part of a struggle for human agency, well-being and for building a just world – can sometimes get lost in policy pronouncements. Yet, as will be illustrated, the position on the ground is far more complex and various agendas can be in play (West, 2007).

## A wider, more humanistic perspective

Other stories can be told of lifelong learning, including in families: broader, more humanistic, holistic and even democratic in scope. Underlying this, in part, is a growing perception of the crucial role of learning, or what social scientists call reflexivity, in a constantly changing culture in which biographies have, more consciously, to be composed and recomposed many times over the life course. There may be new opportunities for self-definition here in a kaleidoscope of choice but this can take place in conditions of frightening economic instability, cultural discontinuity and existential anxiety (Field, 2006; Alheit and Dausien, 2007). This is a culture in which inherited familial and local templates have often fractured (in processes of deindustrialisation, for instance) and individuals are forced, like it or not, to make choices without confident points of reference or inherited certainties. Choices can range, perhaps, from the most banal (which fashion trend to follow, in the relentless pressure of consumerism) to the most profound, for instance to do with what it means to be a man or woman or how to raise children; or, at another level, whether to allow a child to have the MMR innoculation,[1] against a backcloth of conflicting scientific prescription. There are no unassailable authorities to turn to, no uncontested body of knowledge in which to find easy comfort while the cultures of the so-called developed world have become more individualistic and fractured (often accompanied by the break-up or dispersal of extended family structures) and parents may feel existentially more on their own.

There is a further, more psychological aspect when thinking about lifelong learning, the subject called the learner and families. Orientations to learning, in the basic sense of openness to experience and curiosity towards the world (rather than paranoia, at the other extreme), alongside the feeling that the world is, in some way, sufficiently good and nourishing – or its antithesis – are forged in the crucible of earliest relationships with significant others. It is suggested that these primitive emotional processes exist in adult learning too, although they are sometimes disguised, neglected or treated suspiciously by adult educators, for fear of over-psychologising or pathologising human experience (West, 2004). Yet interactions with a tutor or a subject in an adult learning group can mirror earlier experience as we may resist taking in anything new or resent a potential dependence, for fear, perhaps, of rejection or of not being good enough.

Moreover, learning, from a psychosocial perspective, is no simplistic linear progression towards self-actualisation but rather, at times, a troubling, anxiety-provoking, back and forward, unpredictable as well as potentially exhilarating and liberating process. All of us, on occasions, feel lost, uncertain, messy and confused – at times of illness, redundancy, divorce or existential crisis, for example – and need others, and some attentive, even loving care, to manage this and to learn from experience. This is not to pathologise people or learning, rather to avoid sanitising what it means to be human and to learn. Anxiety, for instance, drawing on psychoanalytic insights, can be considered fundamental to the human condition, reaching back to earliest experience and our complete vulnerability and dependence on others (Klein, 1997). It can be triggered, to greater or lesser extents, across a life, at times of change and difficult encounters with learning. There is, I suggest, always and inevitably an infant at the heart of the adult, fragility at the core of change, the past in the learning present.

## The context

Such a perspective is partly shaped by having done 'auto/biographical' research, over many years, among diverse groups of parents and children (as well as professionals) in 'family support and learning programmes' located in marginalised communities in the United Kingdom (West and Carlson, 2006; West, 2007). We sought, in the research, to chronicle and illuminate the meaning and impact of particular interventions by professionals and various agencies – including the provision of adult and family learning – through the eyes of the families concerned, in what, as noted, is deeply contested territory. Do these programmes, to repeat, represent a means to empowerment, individually and collectively, or are they overly intrusive and even a form of social control and disciplining for the labour market (Ecclestone, 2004)? In a related way, Coffield (1999) detects a morally authoritarian tone in the dominant discourse of lifelong, including family, learning: learn or face reductions in welfare benefits; constantly update yourself or face exclusion from the labour market. Learn, in short, or be socially and materially damned.

I want to use case studies from two family projects to explore the meaning and parameters of lifelong learning, which includes the interplay of past and present, self and other, informal and more formal experience, over time. We note, in the material, the role of anxiety in learning, rooted in biographies, and how this can be made manageable and to an extent overcome. The narratives, similarly, enable us to appreciate the potentially sustaining role of informal and non-formal learning (non-certificated and taking place outside educational settings), but also how informal and non-formal processes may create important transitional and transactional space. Transitional spaces lie between people: in an informal group, a seminar, a playgroup or an artistic activity, for instance. They are a mix of the subjectively experienced, the objectively perceived and the relational. When the quality of space is good enough and we feel enabled to take risks, to play, imagine, think and perceive differently and claim space for self, then we and our perceptions can begin to change in potentially transforming ways, mirroring transitional processes in early experience (Winnicott, 1971). But the difficult questions that flow from this are what is it that makes the difference and how can we best theorise it?

I suggest, drawing on psychodynamic insights as well as the research, that part of the answer lies in thinking more about intersubjective processes: in particular the extent to which others, tutors or facilitators, are able to be alongside in caring, attentive yet also challenging ways. The nature of symbolic activity itself provides a further potential answer – like art or creative writing – because it can provide what amounts to a container in which we project and process sometimes deeply painful, messy aspects of our inner world, work on them symbolically and begin to understand them in different, less threatening ways; and over time re-introject them, in psychological language, as good objects (Hunt and West, 2006). Transactional space, in a related way, enables people to question and challenge dominant agendas and how others may script us in demeaning ways; to become, in other words, a subject in history rather than an object. Spaces can be both transitional and transactional at one and the same time as people begin to conceive themselves as learners, artists and even questioning political activists, perhaps for the first time in a life. The practice of democracy and citizenship is itself refigured in this perspective: from notions of deficit and ignorance to a dynamic, relational, learning process, forged in the actual practices that make up people's lives (Wyn and Dwyer, 1999).

## The family

But, first, some background to the current preoccupation with families and the state of the family, at least in the Anglo-Saxon world, particularly those living in marginalised communities.

If, as the British Home Office (1998) maintains, the family, for a range of reasons, is an institution under stress – because of high levels of divorce, for instance – this seems greatest among families living in economically fragile spaces. Neo-liberal economic policies and ideology, including the retreat of the welfare state, and structural changes in patterns of employment, can impact most strongly on the poorer sections of society, while divorce rates for unskilled manual workers are double the rate for the average and over half of lone parents in the UK live in poverty (Ranson and Rutledge, 2005). Alongside this is growing evidence of increased mental health problems, across society, with, according to one estimate, one in six families affected, rising to one in three in marginalised communities (LSE, 2006). Some see the rise in health problems of this kind to be related to the increasing inequalities of Anglo-Saxon countries (Wilkinson, 1996). It should be noted that families living in poorer communities are the target for myriad social and educational initiatives, including education for employability, no doubt derived, as suggested, from fear of the marginal other as well as the 'efficiency' imperatives in welfare provision (Ecclestone, 2004).

The preoccupation with families is, of course, nothing new. Delinquency, domestic violence, child abuse, mental illness, illegitimacy and family instability are long-standing concerns, which have characterised many cultures and historical times. But there is evidence of growing preoccupation with the state of the family (Furedi, 2001) and concern from 'on high' about the well-being of young children living in run down, materially poor and socially fragmented public housing estates. Governments argue that a range of measures is needed, including parenting and literacy classes. Educational success – for young children but also their parents – is thought to be essential in challenging deprivation as well as what is often called a 'dependency' culture.

Programmes such as Sure Start, building on the American Head Start programme (there are similar programmes in Australia) (Eisenstadt, 2002) are designed to break cycles of disadvantage and exclusion. Sure Start (along with associated Children's Centres) is now established in over 1,000 areas in England identified as having high levels of deprivation. It is a multi-agency initiative involving diverse professionals working collaboratively to support 'vulnerable' families and to tackle 'disadvantage', so that every child can go to school more able to learn, while parents themselves are encouraged to participate in various forms of adult learning. Sure Start and Children's Centres can vary but may offer diverse services: child support, crèche, access to specialist services such as speech and language therapy or child and mental health. There can also be varied opportunities for informal and non-formal adult and family learning, ranging from 'training' to broader notions. But getting parents into paid work – as a means to tackle poverty and social exclusion – is, as observed, a powerful driving force in the funding of such initiatives and one that project organisers have to take note of (Ranson and Rutledge, 2005).

Yet, government rhetoric can vary while the lived experience of parental support programmes (and many other community initiatives) is not simply shaped from on high. There are a number of players as well as agendas occupying the space represented by these initiatives: including diverse professionals who may bring their own distinct values and practices into play, despite pressures from on high. They may exploit government rhetoric – on the need to strengthen community capacity building, or improve service delivery via partnership arrangements, or to nourish new forms of sustainable local development (Home Office, 2004) – to justify more participatory approaches to project management and community regeneration alongside more diverse and questioning forms of learning (Coare and Johnston, 2003).

## The research

Our studies of family support programmes are in fact unique in their longitudinal, auto/biographical, in-depth design. They are quite different, for instance, from the design and methodological assumptions of the national evaluation of Sure Start in the UK (NESS, 2005). Our opportunistic sample of 100 parents in a Sure Start programme was small and there were only ten parents in a second and organisationally different project in East London. But we spent many hours with individual families (as well as staff), and the auto/biographical design of our research enabled us to explore the meaning of experience, narratively, in depth and over time, in ways that other kinds of research can barely get near (West and Carlson 2006; West, 2007). We spent time too visiting a range of courses and meetings – formal and informal – across a number of years.

We sought to build rapport and deeper forms of listening in the research, building on feminist epistemology (Fine, 1992; Hartsock, 1987) as well as psychodynamic insights (Hunt and West, 2006). Our capacity, as researchers, to feel, identify and empathise with our subjects is crucial, which includes the ability to contain anxieties generated in the process and to maintain an open, reflexive stance towards material (rather than seeming judgemental) and to feed back what is said, and interpretations, in digestible form, paralleling processes in psychotherapeutic contexts (Hunt and West, 2006). We touched, frequently, on painful experience, including psychological problems and abusive relationships in families, but also in interactions with authority and institutions such as schools. The research was shaped too by values of social justice and the importance of giving voice to marginalised peoples, however problematic notions of 'voice' might be. The intention was to create a kind of transitional space in the research itself: for storytelling and reflexivity; one relatively free from what may be the normalising, disciplinary gaze of government and its agendas or even the project managers (Foucault, 1977, 1988). Working collaboratively with our research subjects also derived from the constructivist idea that the social is not simply internalised but is actively experienced and given meaning to, which can sometimes help change it. It is important, in other words, to chronicle how people themselves make sense of their experience but may also come to question their assumptions (Chamberlayne *et al.*, 2004).

Our understanding and use of the term 'auto/biography' (with a '/', or slash) draws attention to the interrelationship between the constructions of one's own life though autobiography and the construction of the life of another through biography. The implication is that we do not write stories about ourselves without making reference to and hence, in some sense, constructing others' lives and selves, and that the constructions made of others in writing their life histories contain and reflect our own histories, social and cultural locations as well as psychological histories (Stanley, 1992; Miller, 2007). We were in fact provoked in the work to consider, very frequently, our own family histories, both as parents and children, as well as any assumptions we were making about 'the other'. The resilience of particular parents in keeping on in the face of what could be horrific experience quickly earned our respect and disabused us of any lingering deficit models (West and Carlson, 2006). We engaged with our own struggles and imperfections as parents and the impact of painful experience in our learning life histories, as we listened to others and thought about what they had said. How much had significant others, like parents, encouraged in us a desire for learning; or something more complicated and confused? The qualities of interaction between parents and a child can induce behaviour that has more to do with a need to please, appease or perform; or, perhaps intense feelings of desperation and vulnerability born of the emotional unavailability of a prime caregiver. This in turn may generate the need to bring order, control and intelligibility in highly individualistic ways in what might seem a very chaotic and scary world. Such dynamics can have a lifelong vitality and be played out in a range of educational and other settings (West, 1996; Hunt and West, 2006).

Auto/biographical research also encourages researchers to be open, explicit and reflexive about all aspects of the process – paying attention to the workings of power and what may be unconscious dimensions in research – and to question the notion of detached biographers of others' histories, in the name of 'objective' science (Stanley, 1992; West, 2001; Miller, 2007). As Roper (2003) notes, research is not simply a matter of generating words but involves a relationship, which, as well as producing evidence of life outside itself, is, in its own right, a dynamic process, shaping, consciously and unconsciously, the enquiry and the development of understanding. It can be a space for learning and telling new stories in its own right, contrasting with the kind of research in which people will give the answers, however unconsciously, they think the researchers want to hear – not least to get rid of them – or respond with what is considered respectable or safe. Moreover, as stated, if other people's stories of family life evoke strong, even disturbing feelings in researchers, this can be seen as a resource rather than a problem (West, 2001; West and Carlson, 2006). Contrary to the conventional objectivist idea of keeping the researcher's subjectivity at bay – representing as this does a source of bias or contamination – our own responses and feelings can, reflexively, in what psychologists call the counter-transference, provide resources for learning and empathy, even if this asks a great deal of the researcher.

## Learning as a sustaining space

The meaning of particular programmes could change for parents, especially for the women in our samples: from uncertain, even threatening spaces to more sustaining ones. Parents could initially be suspicious and in some cases paranoid: 'Was this social workers checking up on us?' Yet most in our samples came to see projects, over time, as important resources. Joe, Heidi, (all names are pseudonyms) and their children were involved in a local Sure Start project. Heidi participated in different ways, such as attending parent support sessions, a playgroup (with the children) and adult classes. She was given access to specialist psychological services. She and Joe were understandably cautious about seeing us, as researchers, but shared experiences, over time, and in some depth. The two of them had known each other since childhood. They had been abandoned by parents (Heidi was abandoned by her mother at birth), and went into residential homes, followed by periods in foster care. The material poured out as Heidi described being moved from one foster family to another. She had never been able to talk to anyone about her life history before, she said. It was hard to explain, and she did 'not really under-stand myself why the things that had happened had happened, and not knowing how or where to start'.

She told us that some of the adult courses 'gave me more confidence to know what to do with my two children'. She suffered from mental health problems, she explained, and began to talk about being upset with her children, 'when they laugh at me'. Sure Start had been very threatening, at first: they were afraid that people might be 'checking' on them and 'that was going through our heads all the time'. They were frightened of their children being put into care, as they themselves were. They would frantically fill the fridge with food and buy new clothes for the children, whenever a Sure Start worker came near, even if they could ill afford to do so. Yet the quality of Heidi's relationship to Sure Start shifted, however contingently – as did her relationship to the research – from suspicion to some trust.

Heidi talked about the importance of contact with other mothers and the physical relief at getting out of the house, of having access to adult conversations and of the positive effects of realising that other mums struggled with their children too, in controlling them or dealing with their own irritation and anger. Being involved in a range of activities – including adult education – as Tom Schuller *et al.* (2007) have noted, can provide a crucial 'sustaining' effect for mothers like Heidi. Schuller *et al.* observed, like us, how taking part gave mothers a temporal structure and a new rhythm to the week, access to adult conversations, new friendships and senses of purpose. These processes are not to be judged simply in individualistic terms: self-confidence was being built on a collective basis and the social fabric was being strengthened in small but important ways. For Heidi, 'Sure Start was like one big family really, one I never had'.

We asked Joe and Heidi, at the end of a second interview, about the research and they said it was 'good' to be able to share their stories and to weave strands together, in ways they had not done previously, as they linked their own histories of abandonment with intense suspicions of authority at all levels. And they felt listened to and valued by us – as they did by particular project workers – even when talking about disturbing things. The research became, however briefly, a lifelong learning, meaning-making and even therapeutic space, in its own right, although we were also concerned to maintain a boundary between the research and therapy. We chose to ignore or pass over some aspects of their narratives, or what was not being said, because we considered it inappropriate in a research setting. But there are issues to consider in the border country between auto/biographical research and therapy, when engaging with potentially painful issues, such as learning and education. On the other hand, feeling listened to in attentive ways can be therapeutic and such processes are ubiquitous in caring, whether in families or even educational settings, if frequently undervalued or even unnoticed, because of the low status of emotional labour in the culture (West, 2001; Hunt and West, 2006).

## *Learning to play*

East London was a setting for another parenting project, designed to support young single mothers who lived on a run-down public housing estate, suffering badly from deindustrialisation, demoralisation and poverty. A family support programme provided the base for a university and a community arts collaboration to use the visual arts to stimulate creativity and confidence among hard-pressed single young mothers. The project was located in a youth centre and the disaffected young mothers were to be recruited via outreach. The arts, it was hoped, would boost participants' confidence, 'planning and parenting skills' as well as broaden horizons. The young mothers would be encouraged to progress towards 'structured educational achievement' or into work (West, 2007).

Shazir was living in bed and breakfast accommodation when she began attending the centre. Her social worker wanted her to take her son 'somewhere and do things'. The social workers thought her incapable of looking after the baby properly, she said angrily. She had 'split up with his dad', because he was 'cheating' on her. The police were involved and the baby was sick 'with meningitis and loads of other problems'. Eventually she 'escaped' bed and breakfast and 'was moved' into a one-bedroom flat.

Shazir was initially wary of other group members and the whole process, including the research. She did not like talking to people, including me. They only had 'to say the slightest or do the wrong thing . . . and I would blow up about it'. Eventually, she settled down. She liked it when everyone got together, for a period of a week, in an adult education centre, in a rural location, which gave her some space because the crèche workers had the children all day. People took turns in cooking and washing up but, on her own admission, she resisted becoming part of the group at times, and disparaged the whole parenting project. She could be vengeful and destructive as well as dismissive of others, including her tutors.

Shazir talked, over a period of time, of her learning life history. She wanted educational qualifications, she said, because she needed 'a job, office work, or whatever'. She had thought about computing but nothing was clear for her. She never gained qualifications at school and she ran away from home. And then she 'fell pregnant'. The school 'didn't want me there', in any case, and she hated some of the teachers, she said. She ran away aged 12 and 'carried on running' until 15. She moved in and out of foster homes and never really settled anywhere, 'until now'. She had not seen her parents for three and a half years, while she and her dad 'never got on'. He used to hit her, she said.

She lived with a friend and started to take heroin: 'it would start off with a little bit of weed, think nothing of it, and just went a bit further than we should have done'. Her Dad thought her baby was 'evil because he is a white man's baby and he would kill him if he saw him, but he knows that I would never let him do it'. Her mother, she felt, was never really available because of an illness and in any case always took her father's side. Shazir eventually joined a church, via an organisation called Lifeline. The vicar and his wife helped her with her baby, when she needed it most. They were 'there when he has been sick, and the hospital when I need them, and stuff like that. They come up to the flat and make sure he is OK. They have been like surrogate parents to me'.

Stability, among significant others, and feeling cared for, were precious commodities for Shazir. Schooling, like home, was somewhere to escape from. Yet Shazir came to think of the arts project as 'fun' and her group as like a family. She had learned to play in new ways and liked 'experimenting like a five-year-old again'. She felt:

> a kid again, messing about with paint. You really think about doing it now. Except when you do it with your little boy or girl. And it is quite weird because you sit there and just splash paint around and that is nice, just do a little bit more here and there. So here it has been quite like a therapy.

It had made her more aware, she said, of her son's need to play and experiment, 'instead of thinking he is going to get dirty all the time'. She bought crayons and paints and he can 'splash paint around and make it more exciting for him'. She was changing:

> You see more things in perspective when you are doing art, because you see more colours and stuff and you think this would look better in his room, this would make him more cheerful. Stuff like that, yes it does. And you make more things for him too.

Shazir smiled as she talked: she rarely mentioned 'family stuff' because it made her feel 'like jelly', but she could talk to me. Sometimes in the group someone would burst into tears, but they went outside 'for a fag and talk about it and cuss our boyfriends off, or babies' fathers off'. It was 'nice' to have people who could say, 'I know what it feels like', or just listened. The centre, she said, had been a lifeline, 'more like a family, one big family we are, quite good'. She had also been encouraged to get involved in advocacy work for single parents – which she enjoyed – and she participated in a peer sex education programme in local schools, which emerged out of the project. The youth leader encouraged her and she learned, working collaboratively with other mums, how to make a case to the local authority over housing. She learned to compose an argument, with supporting evidence. She had never ever imagined herself being political in that kind of way. But it was all of a piece with the art, nourished by the centre, and the people at its heart, however precariously.

## Gina and the transitional space of art

Gina provides a third example. She is black and living on her own with her young baby. She has a past riddled with pain, rejection and hard drugs. I interviewed her early in the project and towards the end, and spent much time with her in the group, over many weeks. Her relationship to the research, rather like the project itself, evolved from suspicion to a more open, committed participation. She told me she felt pressurised to participate in education and to get a job but that a sympathetic Health Visitor had introduced her to the project. She was suffering from depression at the time. At first she was upset at leaving her daughter in the crèche and resisted involvement. But she changed as a result of the programme, in different ways, she said, including in her relationship with her daughter (Gina talked of learning to play for the first time in her own life). Moreover, she too became an advocate for young single mums with a local housing authority as well as, like Shazir, getting involved in the peer sex education programmes. There was a time when she would never have imagined herself doing such things, just as she could not tolerate mess in the home or anywhere else. Everything had to be kept in order, she said. She had never let her baby play on the floor, in case she got dirty, just as she, Gina, resisted letting herself go in creative ways. She changed, over time, although resisting the process too, often aggressively.

Gina was working on a sculpture, when we talked, near the end of the research:

> When I was pregnant and I didn't really get very big, I made myself a little pregnant belly from a washing basket to put your washing in. I used chicken wire and plaster of Paris and painted it up funny colours. They kind of expressed my mood when I was pregnant, bit dark, dull colours, bit cold. Yes . . . I don't know people who are looking at it probably won't get it, but to me it's a hangover for anger.

Her pregnancy was hard and troubling and she felt unreal, she said, since she did not look pregnant and sought to deny it. She was depressed and 'really ill throughout'. Her mood was translated into the sculpture. She was trying, she said, 'to get across that, the darkness.' There was no head on the sculpture, which was 'deliberate', since she felt disconnected from her bodily experience. Gina found sculpting to be therapeutic and moved, in effect, from the edge of a community of practice into beginning to think of herself as an artist for the first time in her life. She was perpetually anxious and uncertain but took risks, mainly because, as she put it, she felt understood and supported by particular youth leaders and tutors while her art had been a powerful experience.

A young woman like Gina could continue to act out, on her own admission, in highly destructive ways. She could retreat defiantly to the edge of the group. In Melanie Klein's depth psychology there is a never fully resolved struggle between our capacity for love (that is to give ourselves openly and fully to another or to symbolic activity) and also for hate, resistance and even destruction of new possibility; alongside the capacity for reparation – to try again – and to make good the damage we do (Klein, 1997; Froggett, 2002). Art provided some transitional, partly reparative space for Gina, as messy feelings were projected into the sculpture, worked on and, to an extent, transformed, via new narrative understanding. The idea of transitional space, as noted, depends on the quality of interactions between people and the extent someone like Gina felt encouraged and able to play, imagine, think and perceive herself differently, as a learner, mother and person, and to relate to her toddler in new ways too (Winnicott, 1971). Gina entered and claimed some space in these terms. She was doing biographical work and, if the past constantly intrudes into the present, the present and a belief in another kind of future can help reshape the past. Notions of linear time unravel in the biographical work that lies somewhere near the heart of lifelong learning.

## Transactional space

Yet these programmes were operating at far more than an individualistic level. The workers in them were committed to creating space for parents, collectively, to talk back to power, including to some of the agencies represented in projects. There was passionate conviction among key project staff in one Sure Start programme – derived from their commitment to social justice – that top-down models of service delivery and decision-making alienated local people while parents had much to offer, if the space provided was good enough. The aim was to celebrate parents' skills and strengths rather than identify their deficiencies. There was careful attention to detail and support, in highly sensitive and dialogical ways, in this project where, for example, parents were included in interview panels, on the management board, in debating policies with professionals (in relation to child abuse, for instance), in running crèche and nursery programmes as well as in devising opportunities for early and adult learning. In fact the entire exercise was a laboratory for informal yet deeply significant collective forms of learning and community development (West and Carlson, 2006).

We asked these parents once more about the factors enabling them to take risks in such ways. Relationships and the role and personalities of particular workers were essential, we were told, time and again: 'like good parents really'. These projects enabled nervous, diffident, poorly educated and often self-disparaging people to challenge, collectively, others' agendas and take on new roles, as well as find individual sustenance. If local people initially entered this space on others' terms, some, at least, made it more their own (Coare and Johnston, 2003). They had learned, however provisionally, a new grammar of learning and community activism. Space was created for what Zygmund Bauman terms the 'agora': a transactional place in which people learn to translate private problems into a more collective language of public issues and potential solutions, and where ways forward are sought and negotiated and the social and even democratic fabric is correspondingly strengthened (Bauman, 2000).

## Only connect

Auto/biographical research enables us to understand lifelong learning in families and more widely, in such holistic ways. We can chronicle its personal, social, liberatory and even democratic dimensions, over time, and the intimate connections between past and present experience. Such research requires us to compose new forms of psychosocial understanding too, connecting the interplay of inner and outer worlds, the social and psychological. Auto/biographies – like those of Gina, Heidi and Shazir – force us to question and transcend narrow disciplinary boundaries. Their struggles to learn, to play and become more active subjects are to be understood as historical as well as psychosocial, echoing Wright Mills' interdisciplinary, sociological imagination (Wright Mills, 1970). They are to be located within the histories of whole communities as well as the potentially demeaning scripts of class, gender and/or ethnicity, which can be projected on to marginalised parents like them.

Also, thinking sociologically, learning does not take place exclusively 'inside' the heads of such individuals, or any of us. It depends on communication and interaction with others and in relation to a social and cultural context. We are all enmeshed in relationships, which encourage or stifle. The social spaces created by particular family projects enabled some oppressive and demeaning scripts to be questioned. Yet building new forms of social space – for parents, children and communities – requires understanding of the inner world and of the making of subjectivity too. The capacity to resist abuse, to struggle for new ways of being, and to question and change oppressive scripts, depends on becoming a more confident 'I', a desiring subject who may be in tension with a 'me', who may well have been the object of others' frequently demeaning prescriptions. From a psychosocial perspective, there is a defended as well as a social subject, in lifelong learning and elsewhere. Anxiety, as noted, is ubiquitous, to greater or lesser extents, grounded in our initial vulnerability and dependence on others, and we can spend our time avoiding others or new opportunities as a form of self-preservation.

Lifelong learning can evoke potentially crippling anxiety for many people. Drawing on psychodynamic insights, Isca Salzberger-Wittenberg (Salzberger-Wittenberg *et al.*, 1999) notes how even very confident people can feel helpless and overcome in demanding situations, such as entering a new course in higher or adult education. None of us is immune: there was never a perfect family or learning history. Such moments may link back to earlier feelings of inadequacy or failure, as past and present elide. Melanie Klein (1997) termed this 'memory in feeling', expressed in bodily and emotional states, rather than conscious thought. Such embodied memory may, however, be especially intense for those 'taught', from earliest times, that they are of little consequence or inadequate or that authority cannot be trusted (Salzberger-Wittenberg *et al.*, 1999). A range of psychological defences may come into play, including withdrawal or denial of needs (that something may be important or desirable). There were clear glimpses of all this in the research. But these mothers stayed mainly because they felt wanted, cared for and listened to; challenged as well as supported, despite their hostility and rejections. The programmes served, in effect, as good enough surrogate families, in which the 'parent' figures, represented by some of the workers, had sufficient resilience themselves to survive attacks and to remain alongside in fundamentally loving ways. And, like all good families, they facilitated active forms of citizenship, not so much by talking about it but doing it in the lived experience of the programme. The political was made personal, and the personal political in such ways. If our resistance to learning and being a subject is forged in the crucible of early family experience, there are ways, even in the most difficult of biographies, to re-experience ourselves in other kinds of 'families', differently, and to become more confident lifelong learners in the process.

## Note

1  The MMR (measles, mumps and rubella) vaccine is a three-part vaccine, given by injection, which is to protect (immunise) against measles, mumps and German measles (rubella). In the UK, it is given to children at 12 to 15 months, with a reinforcing dose (a booster) before school, usually between 3 and 5 years. The possible effects of the combined vaccine are contested, even if the majority scientific option may be in favour of its use.

## References

Alheit, P. and Dausien, B. (2007) 'Lifelong learning and biography: a competitive dynamic between the macro- and micro level of education', in L. West, P. Alheit, A.S. Anderson and B. Merrill (eds)

*The Uses of Biographical and Life History Methods in the Study of Adult and Lifelong Learning: European perspectives*, Munich and New York: Peter Lang, pp. 57–70.

Bauman, Z. (2000) *Liquid Modernity*, Bristol: The Policy Press.

Chamberlayne, P., Bornat, J. and Apitzsch, U. (2004) (eds) *Biographical Methods and Professional Practice*, Bristol: The Policy Press.

Coare, P. and Johnston, R. (2003) *Adult Learning, Citizenship and Community Learning*, Leicester: NIACE

Coffield, F. (1999) 'Breaking the consensus: lifelong learning as social control', *British Journal of Educational Research* 25(4) (September): 479–99.

Ecclestone, K. (2004) 'Therapeutic stories in adult education: the demoralisation of critical pedagogy', in C. Hunt (ed.) *Whose Story Now? (Re)generating research in adult learning and teaching: Proceedings of the 34th SCUTREA Conference*, Exeter: SCUTREA, pp. 55–62.

Eisenstadt, N. (2002) 'Sure Start: key principles and ethos', *Child Care, Health and Development* 28(1): 3–4.

Field, J. (2006) *Lifelong Learning and the New Educational Order*, Stoke-on-Trent: Trentham Books.

Fine, M. (1992) 'Passion, politics and power', in M. Fine (ed.) *Disruptive Voices: The possibilities of feminist research*, Michigan: Michigan University Press, pp. 205–32.

Foucault, M. (1977) *Discipline and Punish: The birth of the prison*, London: Penguin.

—— (1988) 'Technologies of the self', in L. Martin, H. Gutman and P. Hutton (eds) *Technologies of the Self: A seminar with Michel Foucault*, Armhurst, MA: University of Massachusetts Press, pp. 16–49.

Froggett, L. (2002) *Love, Hate and Welfare*, Bristol: The Policy Press.

Furedi, F. (2001) *Paranoid Parenting*, London: Penguin Books.

Hartsock, N. (1987) 'The feminist standpoint: developing the ground for a specifically feminist historical materialism', in S. Harding (ed.) *Feminism and Methodology: Social science issues*, Bloomington, IN: Indiana University Press, 157–80.

Home Office (1998) *Supporting Families: A consultation document*, London: HMSO.

—— (2004) *Firm Foundations*, London: HMSO.

Hunt, C. and West, L. (2006) 'Learning in a border country: using psychodynamic ideas in teaching and research', *Studies in the Education of Adults* 38(2): 160–77.

Klein, M. (1997) *Love, Gratitude and Other Works, 1921–1945*, London: Virago.

Knowles, M. (1973) *The Adult Learner: A neglected species*, Houston, TX: Gulf.

London School of Economics (LSE) (2006) *The Depression Report: A new deal for depression and anxiety disorders*, Report by the Centre for Economic Performance's mental health policy group, chaired by Lord Layard, London: LSE.

Miller, N. (2007) 'Developing an auto/biographical imagination', in L. West, P. Alheit, A. Anderson and B. Merrill (eds) *Using Biographical and Life History Methods in the Study of Adult and Lifelong Learning: European perspectives*, Hamburg: Peter Lang/ESREA, pp. 167–86.

National Evaluation of Sure Start (NESS) (2005) *Early Impacts of Sure Start Programmes on Children and Families*, Research report NESS/2005/FR/013, London: HMSO.

Ranson, S. and Rutledge, H. (2005) *Including Families in the Learning Community: Family centres and the expansion of learning*, York: Joseph Rowntree Foundation.

Roper, M. (2003) 'Analysing the analysed: transference and counter-transference in the oral history encounter', *Oral History* 21 (Autumn): 20–32.

Salzberger-Wittenberg, I., Williams, G. and Osborne, E. (1999) *The Emotional Experience of Learning and Teaching*, London: Karnac.

Schuller, T., Preston, J. and Hammond, C. (2007) 'Mixing methods to measure learning benefits', in L. West, P. Alheit, A.S. Anderson and B. Merrill (eds) *The Uses of Biographical and Life History Methods in the Study of Adult and Lifelong Learning: European perspectives*, Munich and New York: Peter Lang, pp. 255–78.

Stanley, L. (1992) *The Auto/biographical I*, Manchester: Manchester University Press.

West, L. (2004) 'Re-generating our stories: psychoanalytic perspectives, learning and the subject called the learner', in C. Hunt (ed.) *Whose Story Now? (Re)generating research in adult learning and teaching: Proceedings of the 34th SCUTREA Conference*, Exeter, pp. 303–10.

—— (1996) *Beyond Fragments: Adults, motivation and higher education: A biographical analysis*, London: Taylor and Francis.

—— (2001) *Doctors on the Edge: General practitioners, health and learning in the inner-city*, London: FABooks.

—— (2007) 'An auto/biographical imagination and the radical challenge of families and their learning, in L. West, P. Alheit, A.S. Anderson and B. Merrill (eds) *The Uses of Biographical and Life History Methods in the Study of Adult and Lifelong Learning: European perspectives*, Munich and New York: Peter Lang, pp. 221–39.

—— and Carlson, A. (2006) 'Claiming and sustaining space? Sure Start and the auto/biographical imagination', *Auto/Biography* 14(2): 359–80.

Wilkinson, R. (1996) *Unhealthy Societies: The afflictions of inequality*, London: Routledge.

Winnicott, D. (1971) *Playing and Reality*, London: Routledge.

Wright Mills, C. (1970) *The Sociological Imagination*, London: Penguin.

Wyn, J. and Dwyer, P. (1999) 'New directions in research on youth in transition', *Journal of Youth Studies* 2(1): 5–21.

# 7

# Literacy and lifelong learning

*Paul Bélanger*

As revealed by its history, literacy is a paradoxical reality. In the 1950s and 1960s, at the time of the national liberation movement, the newly independent countries took immediate action to organize literacy programs or campaigns. Such efforts were undertaken as a symbolic gesture toward the "new citizens" and as an economic tool to construct the new nation. Following these golden years, literacy lost its momentum for more than a decade. It only became again a real priority in developing countries when, in 1990 at Jomtien, the United Nations agencies and 155 Member States adopted the *Education For All* (EFA) declaration and plan of action.

In the industrialized countries, once the goal of universal primary schooling was achieved, adult literacy disappeared from most national policy agendas. Since "the problem was solved," efforts were concentrated on extending schooling beyond primary education. Umbrage was even taken at questions concerning the basic competencies of adults. Literacy rates disappeared early on from official statistics, as in Germany in 1912. Adult literacy was only taken up again in these countries, first slowly in the 1980s and much more strongly in the following two decades, with the creation of national agencies and the insertion of literacy as a new priority in adult education and lifelong learning policies.

Today, literacy is clearly a global issue and a universal concern in all regions of the world. Yet, literacy suffers many definitions and is being characterized under different visions. Literacy is an area of intervention—we speak of literacy education; it is also the learning experience of adults who, later in life, attempt to master basic skills and mobilize knowledge; it is furthermore a national policy concerned with increasing people's capacity of action and communication in all areas of activities. However, the intimacy and thus the personal meaning of such learning experiences, as well as their social significance in different areas of activities, are still to be fully grasped. This may be explained by the difficult history of literacy policies and the ambiguous integration, in the North and in the South, of literacy in lifelong learning perspectives.

## Literacy: definitions

### *An expanded definition*

Traditionally, literacy was defined as the ability to read, write, and compute ("aRithmetic"): the 3 Rs. However, the reality is much more multifaceted than technical competence in the use of a script (Olson, 1996). The mobilization of new skills, knowledge, and practice by people as they strive to become more active in their changing environments is much more complex. "Learning does not just take place in classroom and is not just concerned with methods"(Hamilton 2000). The tendency today is to look for a broader notion that takes into account the various contexts in which youth and adults live and participate (Askov, 2000). The definition adopted by UNESCO (2004) is a good example of such an expanded vision. It characterizes literacy as:

> the ability to identify, understand, interpret, create, communicate and compute, using printed and written materials associated with varying contexts. Literacy involves a continuum of learning to enable an individual to achieve his or her goals, to develop his or her knowledge and potential, and to participate fully in the wider society.
>
> (UNESCO/Lamp, 2004)

### *A plural reality: different cultural models and different domains*

Considered as a social practice, and not primarily as acquisition of skills, literacy becomes necessarily a plural reality "varying according to time and space, but also contested in relations of power" (Street, 2003; Quickley *et al.*, 2006). When one refers to a practice or a program, one has to ask which cultural model of literacy we are dealing with in this context, and which model is marginalized. For example, some historians have even argued that the introduction of formal schooling could have been, in part, an effort, in some countries, "to temper and control literacy, not spread it" (Graff, 1986). Uncontrolled reading and study circles outside of formal settings could have been seen and can be seen today as threatening prevailing culture. Literacy is, indeed, determined by the various cultural, political, and economic contexts of the community in which it is developed. In that perspective, authors of "New Literacy Studies" (Gee, 2000; Street, 1995) refer to multiple literacies.

Literacy is also a plural reality through its increasing social significance in different areas of activities. Media literacy, computer literacy, health literacy, and environment literacy are all new literacies. For example, the promotion of a health-literate society, enabling people to understand and act more autonomously, is becoming a critical component of successful curative and preventive health policies (Institute of Medicine, 2004).

## A multidimensional reality

The intervention and practices to enhance people's cognitive and conative skills, indeed, cannot be understood, nor can they lead to the real improvement of living or working conditions, without considering the cultural, social, and economic contexts. Moreover, it is necessary to take into account the "landing" of this educational event in people's individual biographies and in the different life transitions.

The relation between the key words often used equivalently in literacy discourse is also more complex. As Torres (2004) explains, knowledge society, information society, learning society

81

and literate society refer to very different dimensions. A knowledge-intensive society, for that purpose, is not necessarily a learning society. More precisely, it is not necessarily one that harnesses and integrates its economic, political, educational, and cultural resources, nor is it one that is structured toward developing the human potential of all its citizens (Belanger and Federighi, 2000). Moreover, if a literate environment that requires written communication skills from all its participants may be a supportive milieu for new learners, such a technically literate society does not necessarily imply free diffusion of information. Nor does it imply that the conditions for the full exercise of rights to information will be fulfilled.

## A multi-level notion: literacy and meta-literacy

As noted earlier, literacy is more than the acquisition of basic competencies; it involves metacognitive abilities (Cromley, 2000; Schraw, 1998). Reading is more than decoding and sounding out words and numeracy goes beyond adding skills. The full mastery of literacy involves the ability of a subject to mobilize, in his or her daily activities and context, these skills and to transform them as an integrated reflexive practice in increasingly literate environments. Meta-literacy is the ability of people to validate their uses of literacy and transfer their learning from one area to another. The individual subject, then, is able to monitor spontaneously the relevance of what he is reading and to make inferences; he knows when he really knows and, as a result, can play around and choose among the arbitrary elements of acquired knowledge; he can integrate these elements with past experiences and master them in the course of his own activities. He reads an article for his immediate work and realizes that it has relevance to other areas of his work (Mikulecky and Lloyd, 1993), as well as outside his work. Meta-literacy means consequently the ability to demystify the infallible truth of printed words; to take distance from written communication or published works.

Such meta-literacy is achieved when adults can, in their environment, share and experience various uses of literacy; when they reconstruct in written words their formerly informal expertise; when they activate prior learning into their new communication skills; or when they have the opportunity to relate new abstract digitalized information, now common at workplace and in daily life, to visual and tactile perception, and the expertise that they have developed and used for years.

In brief, literacy is more than the ability to read and write, it is the person's practice of thinking and reflecting upon her current reading and writing; it is the literacy requirements of the competent citizen at her workplace or in her daily living (Venezky, 2000). Unfortunately, the personal meaning of such learning experiences and practices is an understudied dimension of literacy.

## The intimacy and the social meaning of literacy

Literacy is both an intimate and a social reality. Lack of articulation between these two dimensions may hamper expression of the social demand for literacy in all areas of activity.

### The intimacy of literacy

Literacy, from the perspective of learners, is a subjective learning experience that involves beliefs and values about the literate worlds in which the individual has lived and is now living. For often stigmatized unschooled individuals, it also means the personal experience of exclusion and symbolic violence (Bourdieu, 1978); of being socialized to blame themselves for their limited school achievement; of seeing the success of others as the result of their own personal talents and hence of their own setbacks as the effect of limited personal ability. It means to be blind to the unequal distribution of cultural capital and, consequently, to suffer, in silence throughout life, constructed disgrace and despair.

It is then no surprise if most literacy evaluation studies indicate that the enhancement of learners' self-esteem, self-confidence, and self-image is the main impact and the main reported change by participants of programmes (Beder, 1999; Wikelung *et al.*, 1992). If literacy, under appropriate conditions, tends to build self-esteem, which helps participants form new identities as active learners and as individuals, we cannot understand such advantages accrued from participation in adult literacy without referring to the prior traumatizing subjective experiences through which negative identities have been interiorized.

Literacy must also be seen and analyzed as the relatively autonomous action of learners attempting to gain more autonomy of action (empowerment), to become more confident in their own ability, and to improve their employment opportunities and incomes. To learn and, for that matter, to unlearn are, indeed, intimate experiences through which the individual, at a situated point or transitional moment in life, explores and actualizes his potential, and increases his capacity for action. In short, the subject/individual produces and transforms his personal and social identity (Crossan *et al.*, 2003; Gallacher *et al.*, 2002).

## *The social significance or dimension of literacy*

In the literacy experience, concomitant with change in the inner identity, new patterns of participation are acquired and new social identities are formed (Barton and Hamilton, 2000). The immediate social uses of literacy through an increased ability to communicate and act in private life, at work and in the community, may produce larger social benefits, such as the transformation of society and of civil society through community capacity-building, improved school results of children through more active parental support, economic benefits through skill upgrading, etc.

Of course, literacy and basic education, as such, will not solve the problems of poverty, unemployment, discrimination, violation of human rights, HIV/Aids, exclusion, etc. They require other conditions and social and economic policy changes, as well as immediate supportive contexts. Literacy is only a means to cope with basic learning needs (Lind, 2002), to enable creative participation, to extend the voice of people, to facilitate workers' participation in education and training activities, and to facilitate the communication process in health care and health promotion.

The historical relation between literacy and democracy is far from being congruous. Historians have documented cases where leading forces have used literacy discrimination policies as a means to determine whether one had the right to vote, as a mechanism to prevent popular classes from joining the electorate, and as a means to maintain the status quo (Graff, 1979, 1986; Resnick, 1983; Resnick and Resnick, 1977). One has to remember, in 1964 in Brazil, when Paulo Freire was arrested and exiled because of his work in helping Brazilian peasants to read and write.

Research on democracy and citizenship has shed light on the relationship between the use of written communication and the functioning of contemporary society, where the demand for literacy is increasingly felt (Roche, 1992). The environment of written communications needed for political life in contemporary society is too often taken for granted. The very notion of citizenship is based on the fact that each citizen, although unable to personally contact all their fellow citizens, remains in contact with them by means of the media. Indeed, the massive use of written forms of communication and the democratization of basic education are implicit conditions for the development of democratic states.

Hence, the question is not whether literacy inherently leads to democracy. Posing this question in the abstract, without distinction between different types of literacy, has no meaning. The question is whether democracy is possible in mass societies without the technologies that allow for social communication that have developed continuously since Gutenberg in 1457, and, consequently, without universal access to active models of literacy practices. Urbanization has created communities in which oral communication among people no longer suffices to create a feeling of belonging between fellow strangers and to generate structures needed to express and negotiate conflicts among social groups. The real question, then, is whether democracy is possible without a social contract between state and civil society ensuring that every citizen can exercise their right to acquire basic competencies and be able to participate fully and creatively.

As a "catalyst for participation in social, cultural, political and economic activities, and for learning throughout life" (UNESCO 1997, *CONFINTEA Hamburg Declaration*, §11), literacy is a necessary condition for democracy. However, not all literacies lead in that direction.

## The difficult history of literacy policies

### *Short history of literacy policies*

Adult literacy and basic education policy, as noted earlier, are not recent developments in education history. However, we have to wait until the second half of the twentieth century for literacy to occupy its place again in national agendas. The decade of the 1960s was a very active period. In 1961, Cuba[1] launched its literacy campaign, which dramatically changed the nation's literacy situation, while China had already initiated, in 1950, its own vast literacy program. Racing to consolidate their national independence, newly liberated countries, such as Ethiopia, Ivory Coast, and Kenya, started, in the early 1960s, to organize "fighting illiteracy" movements, events, programs, and campaigns. Meanwhile, the Arab League created, in 1965, ARLO, the Arab League Literacy Organization. Tanzania declared 1970 the year of adult education to help step up the program it had started several years earlier. During the same period, popular adult education movements, both in Latin America and in the resistance struggles in Southern Africa, developed new participatory approaches inspired by Paulo Freire (Lind, 2002). At the continental level, African ministers of education held, between 1961 and 1982, five regional conferences[2] to develop basic education and literacy.

By the early 1980s, however, the economic recession following the petrol crisis, and the request of the World Bank's Structural Adjustment Programs to cut public education and social public spending in order to facilitate debt repayment, had relegated literacy to a low priority. Using selected evaluation reports and ignoring other literature reviews also from its own services, the Bank insisted on limited results of adult basic education. At this point, "an ideology that the state should limit its service to formal education was globalised" (Lind, 2002). In many countries of sub-Saharan Africa, as well as of southern and eastern Africa, and the Arab region, literacy was then taken off national policy agendas, while non-formal literacy departments and services were dismantled.

Despite this erosion of priority given to literacy, public UNESCO discourse continued during these pre-1990 decades, as it announced routinely the total elimination of illiteracy in the years to come and proclaimed repeatedly that the "scourge would be stamped out" in the next ten years.

It was only in 1990, with the Jomtien EFA world conference, that literacy was brought back to international and national debates, and reinstated as a priority. This new policy orientation was reinforced within "an enlarged vision of adult learning" adopted in Hamburg at CONFINTEA V in 1997 and confirmed again in the EFA Dakar framework in 2000. Since then, however, in most developing countries, with the exception of some states such as Brazil, literacy either remained a discourse with very limited action or was completely eliminated from global and national policy frameworks, such as in the Millennium Development Goals (MDGs) and the Fast Track Initiatives (FTIs).

Yet, during the same decade and already earlier in industrial countries, adult literacy, following well-publicized national inquiries (OECD, 1995), became an important political and economic issue (Benton and Noyelle, 1992): national literacy secretariats or bureaus were created in Belgium, Canada, France, and the UK, and initiatives with special programs and sustained new approaches were taken in Australia, Ireland, the Netherlands, Spain, Sweden, Switzerland, and the USA.

## *The historical dynamics of literacy policies*

This history of literacy in both industrial and developing countries is well known; it is one of shifting priorities. Notably, these changes were due to the interplay of different cultural, social, and economic factors, and not merely school factors (Cipolla, 1969; Furet and Ozouf, 1977; Graff, 1979; Havelock, 1976; Verhaagen, 1999). And the advocacy strategies for literacy, as well as the struggle for the right to learn, are reflecting this ambiguity.

The entire history of literacy, as well as of adult learning, can be seen as a balancing act between two tendencies: the expression of the demand for literacy as a means to empower people in various areas of human activities, and the movement to professionalize and institutionalize literacy. In some periods of this history, one can see the prevalence of a centrifugal logic characterized by efforts to promote transversal meanings and uses of literacy. Meanwhile, in other periods, the leading logic has been more centripetal, with efforts to organize the field of literacy as a genuine area of expertise. This has been done by creating special units in education ministries, by setting up specific curriculum to train specialists, and by requiring that literacy be recognized as a specific field of research.

The vocabulary reflects this duality of visions and logics. The centripetal trend is expressed through the vocabulary of literacy expertise, such as adult basic education, andragogy, informal basic education policy, literacy campaign, literacy history, literacy program, literacy training, literacy worker, etc. The logic behind the expression of demand for basic skills and greater autonomy of action in different areas tends to have a centrifugal effect and has found expression in various discourses, including the explicit or overt literacy field. However, it goes far beyond and refers to the learning demand for "essential skills" in social movements, in industry and social economy, in health, for the autonomy of aging population, against discrimination, and in facilitating communication at distance within dispersed family members. One speaks then of popular education, of technical basic education and training, health prevention education and communication, educational gerontology, community development and intercultural education, agricultural extension work, consumer education, scientific popularization and vulgarization, etc. In each of these contexts of intervention, concern for enhancing basic skills is increasingly present and functionally integrated within the specific action of the sector.

In all the UN summits of the 1990s, from Rio in 1992 on environment, to Cairo on population, Copenhagen on social development, Beijing on women, and to Istanbul in 1996 on habitat, half of the recommendations were related to the necessity to increase the capacity of action, to raise the interest of adult citizens, and to develop people's know-how in order to deal with the risk societies of today, including ecological risk, but also economic, health, intercultural, and increasing poverty risks. The Hamburg UNESCO CONFINTEA V conference in 1997 was an attempt to encompass these dimensions within an enlarged vision of adult learning.

Later, with the MDGs adopted in 2000, the adult education networks did not succeed in including adult literacy in this new MDG world agenda. Instead of criticizing the fact that here again decision-makers refused to recognize adult literacy and instead of trying desperately to reintroduce it within the MDGs, the movement took, significantly, another advocacy approach. Having in mind the potential contribution in health and environment, for the alleviation of poverty and initial education of children, as well as for gender justice, the movement, under the leadership of the International Council for Adult Education (ICAE), began to demonstrate, in the various UN theaters of action and in the Global Campaign Against Poverty (GCAP), that the MDGs could not be reached without the active and informed participation of the adult-aged public and their increased know-how. They refer, for example, to preventive action against the progress of the Aids pandemic or to parental education as a way to improve children's achievements in school. Their advocacy practice for adult literacy was not advocacy for a profession or reinforcement of existing institutions; it was a demonstration of the transversal necessity of literacy and hence for a cross-sectorial approach.

Historically, literacy tends to become a national priority when social demand for basic education is supported horizontally by all government ministries and, vertically, through the active involvement of civil society. Indeed, literacy can only become a national issue, when "other" ministries (Planning, Agriculture, Fisheries, Industry, Youth, Defence, etc.) recognize explicitly the necessity for a general enhancement of the population's basic qualifications to achieve their own goals and when literacy education agencies take into account the expectations of those "other" ministries. As can be observed, in many countries in the national EFA forums from the end of the 1990s until today, the prioritization of literacy tends also to be related to the active involvement of civil society: parent–teacher associations, churches or mosques, community and village organizations, unions, women's groups, rural associations, community economic corporations, etc. The active role of endogenous NGOs—both upstream, in expressing the literacy demand, and downstream, in implementing a literacy component within various actions—is often a major factor.

However, this logic, precisely because of its centrifugal implications, is ambiguous and, by increasing demand, may weaken the capacity to develop the expertise required. A dialectical dynamics might be observed. By insisting on the expression of a demand for literacy across different sectors of activity, one tends to forget the expertise and specialization needed for efficient provision of learning opportunities in different activities. Strangely enough, by establishing literacy everywhere, one runs the risk of it being recognized nowhere and of achieving a Pyrrhic victory. The result could be that, by gaining so much, literacy competency could become a vital but nevertheless hidden and unarticulated dimension of activities. Similarly, by working only on specific capacity-building in literacy and autonomous literacy programs, one risks seeing literacy structured as an unconnected domain of learning; unconnected with health issues, with poverty issues, with agricultural issues, with population issues. Literacy would thus receive less attention and lose its societal relevance.

Looking at the recent difficult history of literacy policy, a critical issue for the future is certainly the articulation between these two trends. That is, whether actors will be able to develop specific expertise through research and training with a view to offering efficient literacy diagnosis and learning approaches for ensuring significant learning opportunities in diverse settings.

Such a genuine contribution of literacy specialists in health promotion, at the workplace, for autonomous ageing, or for second language learning among immigrant communities is a new trend across all continents. The emerging dynamics for the development of literacy may also require, beyond the acknowledgment of complementarity between both trends, the capacity of literacy specialists to work across institutional boundaries and intervene upstream in the expression of the demand for literacy across areas of activity. The demand for literacy is always the result of a more or less formal mediation process between the demands of organizations, on one side, and, on the other, the aspirations, fears, hopes, curiosity, interests, and inner drives of people—a negotiation that can be facilitated or hindered.

An adult educator today is, of course, a specialist in the organization and facilitation of significant learning opportunities, as well as a guidance counsellor able to relate pre-school education, initial education and the complex reality of learning across the adult life course. However, becoming an adult educator or literacy specialist in the future will require much more. It may mean the ability to capture this balancing act in the history of the field. It may also mean avoiding both the risk of the loss of relevance in an effort for institutional recognition or the danger of Pyrrhic victory, which is of being institutionally everywhere, but nowhere.

In order to develop expertise to make literacy a relevant input in various fields of human activities, literacy specialists will also have to become cultural translators (Bonaventura, 2004). They will have to build mutual intelligibility among experiences and subcultures in order to interpret the specific literacy demands in each context and transpose or reconstruct literacy expertise and practices accordingly. They will be required to become the architects of stimulating and enabling literate environments in these milieus (Hautecoeur, 1997), of developing appropriate plain language communication, and of fostering cooperation between formal and informal literacy resources. In short, both ability to work across boundaries and special expertise in literacy learning may compose the professional identity of tomorrow's literacy specialists.

While such lifewide reconstructions of the field lead to a revised vision of literacy in a lifelong learning perspective, this development also suffers major contradictions.

## Literacy and lifelong learning

The insertion of literacy in people's educational biographies is diverse. In literate societies, most people become literate during the institutionalized period of universal initial education. A minority of people, and at times quite a large one, as revealed partially by the direct assessment literacy survey (OECD, 1995), will not acquire the increased level of basic skills required to participate in the economy or in society as a whole. For them literacy could be both a past traumatic experience during their school years and, later in their adult life, a new gratifying learning experience.

In societies where the majority of people do not have access to school, literacy is a larger societal challenge. In sub-Saharan Africa, for example, only a minority of children complete primary education and adults, in spite of public commitments to that effect, have few opportunities to have their education aspirations met.

Literacy experiences in the life course are far from being linear for all people in the North as well as in the South. The sociocultural practices associated with reading and writing are much more multidimensional; they are closely linked to changing work and life environments. Literacy practices change over one's lifetime due to the alteration of social roles and the changing aspirations for more autonomy of action, as well as with the conditions and constraints involved in using such skills and in interacting with others through writing and reading. The various levels and forms of the 3 Rs are resources that people use in specific contexts, in response to the practical needs that emerge at the different phases or transition moments in their biographies. Literacy practices constitute a neverending process of personal development and enlarged communication with other people, networks, and cultures. They have also become a prerequisite to current prevailing forms of continuing education. In that sense, literacy takes its full meaning within a lifelong learning perspective.

The relation between literacy and lifelong learning (LLL) leads us directly to policy issues. That is, it leads us to the kind of literacies and lifelong learning aspirations and projects that are valued and supported by national and international agencies and institutions, as well as to the kind educational biographies that people could pursue.

Lifelong learning is obviously becoming an organizing principle of national educational policies, or at least at the level of discourse. However, this trend has evolved ambiguously, with an expanded vision of lifelong and lifewide learning in some regions and with a narrowly defined notion of basic education in other. In that perspective, according to Rosa Maria Torres (2004), the uneven development of lifelong learning policies may very well become the symbol of a new North–South social division in education, a trend running counter to the emancipatory global vision of lifelong learning proposed in the Delors Report *Learning: The treasure within* (1996). Torres shows that a dual standard and educational agenda is being shaped in which the lifelong learning paradigm becomes central in advanced industrial countries, while the education goals ascribed to in developing countries tend to be restricted to a limited provision of basic initial education, confined practically to children.

This can be observed, for example, in the discourse of the *European Memorandum on Lifelong Learning* (European Commission, 2000), on one hand, and in the MDGs discourse on the other. In fact, basic learning needs, within the current EFA management in the South, tend too often to be interpreted as minimum learning needs (Torres, 2004).

This "widening of the gap between North and South in terms of education and learning" goes much beyond the issue of accessibility to education opportunities along the life course; it also concerns the "double face of lifelong learning" (Alheit and Dausien, 2002). There is a risk of a new learning divide articulated along the lines of different possibilities to pursue one's educational biography in all its dimensions; a divide related to people's various learning aspirations; a divide based on the chances of people, whatever their location on the planet, to get support and resources to explore the potential of a life not yet lived; a divide based on the possibility to enhance the "biographicity" of social learning processes (Alheit and Dausien, 2002).

Will the dominant perspective of continuous and repetitive re-adaptation of employees to the changing work context prevail or will the demand for adaptation be interpreted within a broader perspective leading to more autonomy? The issue is not to recognize or disregard the need for recurrent short-term general or technical competency improvement along the professional life course. The real question is the way this growing social demand will be negotiated with the people involved and whether this demand will be met in ways to enhance autonomy, curiosity, and creativity, propelling the educational biographies of people further.

## Conclusion

In the North, as well as in the South, the literacy debate is growing. As noted at the beginning of this article, literacy today is a universal issue. Neither in the North, nor in the South, can contemporary conflicting visions of lifelong learning affecting the future of literacy be avoided.

Beyond the growth of leaning opportunities throughout life, a crucial issue for literacy policies will be their cultural orientation and the social practices publicly sustained or constrained.

The competing visions between the demand for adapting people's skills and the demand to unfold human potential will become increasingly central in the literacy and lifelong learning debate. This is a debate that, beyond the current international cooperation forces leading to a global divide, is taking place in all hemispheres.

## Notes

1   A similar campaign will be conducted in Namibia, Nicaragua, and Ecuador.
2   In Addis Ababa (1961), Abidjan (1964), Nairobi (1968), Lagos (1976), and Harare (1982).

## References

Alheit, P. and Dausien, B. (2002) "The 'double face' of lifelong learning: two analytical perspectives on a 'silent revolution,'" *Studies in the Education of Adults* 34(1): 3–22.

Askov, E. (2000) "Adult literacy," in A.L. Wilson and E.R. Hayes (eds) *Handbook of Adult and Continuing Education*, San Francisco, CA: Jossey-Bass, pp. 247–62.

Barton, D. and Hamilton, M. (eds) (2000) *Situated Literacies: Reading and writing in context*, London: Routledge.

Beder, H. (1999) *The Outcomes and Impacts of Adult Literacy Education in the United States*, Cambridge, MA: National Center for the Study of Adult Learning and Literacy.

Bélanger, P. and Federighi, P. (2000) *Unlocking People's Creative Forces: A transnational study of adult learning policies*, Hamburg: UNESCO Institute for Education.

Benton L. and Noyelle, T. (1992) *Adult Illiteracy and Economic Performance*, Paris: OECD.

Bonaventura de Sousa Santos (2004) *The World Social Forum: A user's manual*, Madison, WI: University of Wisconsin.

Bourdieu, P., Passeron, J.C., Bottomore, T., and Nice, R. (1978) *Reproduction*, London: SAGE publications.

Cipolla, C.M. (1969) *Literacy and Development in the West*, Baltimore, MD: Penguin Books.

Cromley, J.G. (2000) *Learning to Think, Learning to Learn: What the science of thinking and learning has to offer adult education*, Washington, DC: National Institute for Literacy.

Crossan, B., Field, J., Gallacher, J., and Merril, B. (2003) "Understanding participation in learning for non-traditional adult learners: learning careers and the construction of learning identities," in *British Journal of Sociology of Education* 24(1): 55–67.

Delors, J. (Chair) (1996) *Learning: The treasure within*, Paris: UNESCO.

European Commission (EC) (2000) *European Memorandum on Lifelong Learning*, Brussels: European Commission.

Furet, F. and Ozouf, J. (1982) *Reading and Writing: Literacy in France from Calvin to Jules Ferry*, Cambridge: Cambridge University Press.

Gallacher, J., Crossan, B., Field, J., and Merrill, B. (2002) "Learning careers and the social space: exploring the fragile identities of adult returners," *International Journal of Lifelong Education* 21(6) (November): 493–509.

Gee, J.P. (2000) "The new literacy studies: from 'socially situated' to the work of the social," in D. Barton, M. Hamilton, and R. Ivanic (eds) *Situated Literacies: Reading and writing in context*, London: Routledge, pp. 180–96.

Graff, H.J. (1979) *The Literacy Myth: Literacy and social structure in the nineteenth-century city*, London: Academic Press.

—— (1986) *The Legacies of Literacy: Continuities and contradictions in western culture and society*, Bloomington, IN: Indiana University Press.

Hamilton, M. (2000) *Sustainable Literacies and the Ecology of Lifelong Learning*, Working Papers of the Global Colloquium on Supporting Lifelong Learning, Milton Keynes: Open University Press.

Hautecoeur, J.P. (1997) *Alpha 97: Basic education and institutional environments*, Hamburg: UIE.

Havelock, E.A. (1976) *Origins of Western Literacy: Four lectures delivered at the Ontario Institute for Studies*, Toronto: OISE.

Institute of Medicine of the National Academies (2004) *Health Literacy: A prescription to end confusion*, Washington, DC: The National Academic Press.

Lind, A. (2002) *ABLE Policy in a International Perspective*, Paper given at the international conference on ASBLE in the SADC countries, Natal University/Centre for Adult Education, Pietersmaritzburg.

Mikulecky, L. and Lloyd, P. (1993) *The Impact of Workplace Literacy Programs*, Philadelphia, PA: NCAL.

Olson, D.R. (1996) "Literacy," in A. Tuijnman (ed.) *International Encyclopedia of Adult Education and Training*, Oxford: Pergamon, pp. 75–81.

Organization for Economic Cooperation and Development (OECD) (1995) *Literacy, Economy and Society: Results of the first International Adult Literacy Survey*, Paris: OECD.

Quickley, A., Folinsbee, S., and Kraglung-Gauthier, W.L. (2006) *State of the Field Report*, Nova Scotia: St Francis Xavier University.

Resnick, D.P. (ed.) (1983) *Literacy in Historical Perspective*, Washington, DC: Library of Congress.

—— and Resnick, L.B. (1977) "The nature of literacy: an historical exploration," *Harvard Educational Review* 47(3): 370–85.

Roche, M. (1992) *Rethinking Citizenship*, Cambridge: Polity Press.

Schraw, G. (1998) "On the development of adult metacognition," in M.C. Smith and T. Pourchot (eds) *Adult Learning and Development: Perspectives from educational psychology*, Mahwah, NJ: Lawrence Erlbaum Associates, pp. 89–106.

Street, B. (1995) *Social Literacies*, London and New York: Longman.

—— (2003) "What's 'new' in new literacy studies? Critical approaches to literacy in theory and practice," *Current Issues in Comparative Education* 5(2): 77.

Torres, R.M. (2004) "Lifelong learning: a new momentum and a new opportunity for adult basic learning and education (ABLE) in the South," *Convergence* 37(3): 15–25.

UNESCO (1997) *CONFINTEA Hamburg Declaration*, Paris: UNESCO.

UNESCO/Lamp (2004) *International Planning Report*, Montreal: UNESCO Institute for Statistics.

Venezky, R. (2000) "The origins of the present-day chasm between adult literacy needs and school literacy instruction," *Scientific Studies of Reading* 4(1): 19–39.

Verhaagen, A. (1999) *Alphabétisation 1919–1999. Mais . . . que sont devenues nos campagnes?* Hamburg: UIE.

Wikelund, K., Reder, S., and Hart-Landsberg, S. (1992) *Expanding Theories of Adult Literacy Participation: A literature review*, Technical Report TR92–1), Philadelphia, PA: NCAL.

# 8

# The potential lifelong impact of schooling

*Stephen Gorard*

Taking post-compulsory education and training as a totality, there are, in theory, opportunities of some sort available to the entire adult population. The opportunities for adult learning include the more traditional formal episodes as well as library drop-in centres, free basic-skills provision, job-seeker training, liberal education evening classes, and courses delivered entirely by technologies such as television or computer. In many cases, these opportunities require no prior qualification or experience, are free at point-of-delivery, and are conveniently available in the home or the local community. Why, then, is participation in these objectively open episodes stratified along the lines of residence, social class, sex, ethnicity and other background variables (Gorard *et al.*, 2003)? Put another way, why are some social and economic groups continuously under-represented in lifelong learning?

This chapter presents an argument, based on the findings of a number of related research projects, that one of the key determinants of a foundation for lifelong learning is initial schooling. The point being made is not simply that learning can become a habit, or that knowledge is cumulative, or even that basic skills such as literacy learnt at school are helpful for the potential lifelong learner. The chapter focuses instead on the impact of who goes to school with whom on patterns of post-compulsory participation.

## Patterns of participation

Participation in post-compulsory education and training opportunities has long been markedly differentiated in terms of socio-economic groups in the UK, with significant minorities routinely excluded (Beinart and Smith, 1998; Marsh and Blackburn, 1992; Pettigrew *et al.*, 1989). Of course, many people obtain much of their adult education through private reading, informal sources such as friends, and cultural institutions such as museums and art galleries, and have long done so (European Commission, 2001; Lowe, 1970). But research shows that, with some notable exceptions, informal learning tends to have the same social and economic patterning as formal learning (Gorard *et al.*, 1999a). Over a third of the adult population have not participated in any formal episodes of learning at all since reaching school-leaving age (NIACE, 2003). The individuals participating in post-compulsory education are heavily patterned by 'pre-adult' social, geographic and historical factors such as socio-economic status, year of birth and type of school attended. Sargant (2000) points out that a number of large-scale studies, such as those from Glass (1954) to Gorard et al. (1999b), have shown these patterns and that the determinants of participation, far from being easily fixable, are long-term and rooted in family, locality and history.

We know from these repeated studies that individuals currently 'disenfranchised' from formal and non-formal adult education and training (the non-learners) are more frequently not employed, and older, with lower literacy skills or with negative attitudes to institutional learning. In general, individuals from families with less prestigious occupational backgrounds, with lower incomes, the unemployed or economically inactive, the elderly, severely disabled people and ex-offenders are less likely than average to participate in any episodes of formal education or training after the age of 16. Why is this? A traditional answer would be that these groups tend to face greater barriers to participation.

## The role of barriers

If participation in lifelong learning opportunities depends upon the actions of individuals, it seems reasonable that a key issue to address is the removal of the impediments, or 'barriers', that prevent people from participating in education who would benefit from doing so. This idea underpins official policy, and the point has been made repeatedly in a succession of official and semi-official reports (Dearing, 1997; DTI, 1998; Fryer, 1997; Kennedy, 1997; National Audit Office, 2002).

Several barriers faced by potential learners have been identified, and research has suggested that to widen post-compulsory participation these barriers need to be recognised and addressed (Burchardt et al., 1999; Calder, 1993). To a large extent the barriers proposed are presaged by the patterning of adult learning, such as buildings not being adaptable to handle disability, or lack of transport for people in rural areas (Hudson, 2005). There are institutional barriers, created by the structure of available opportunities, and dispositional barriers in the form of individuals' motivation and attitudes to learning. However, the most obvious barriers are situational, stemming chiefly from the life and lifestyle of the prospective learner (Harrison, 1993). This metaphor of 'barriers' to participation is an attractive one that apparently explains differences in patterns of participation between socio-economic groups, and also contains its own solution – removal of the barriers. So, if it is observed that participation in education tends to be costly and that potential students from lower-income families have lower rates of participation, then it can be hypothesised that cost is a barrier, and removal of cost a solution, to widening participation (McGivney, 1992).

The cost of continuing in education can be of the direct kind, such as fees, or indirect, such as the costs of transport, childcare and foregone income (Hand et al., 1994). Payment of fees to institutions by instalments is not generally allowable, and many new learners are surprised by the level of other expenses, such as examination fees and stationery costs. Benefit entitlement has traditionally been incompatible with formal learning episodes, even when all of the costs of training are met by the individual (Maguire et al., 1993). During the last two decades, until the time of writing, the costs of post-compulsory education in the UK have, according to many breakdowns, gradually been shifting from the general taxpayers to the learners or their families (Gorard et al., 2007). In higher education (HE), for example, the recent redistribution of the costs might affect potential students from low-income families and non-traditional students with a high aversion to debt, facing relatively low expected post-graduation earnings (Education and Employment Committee, 2001; Metcalf 2005).

However, well-conducted studies in post-compulsory education generally do not find that finance is a key barrier. Whatever those *participating* in education may say about finance (and it obviously has not totally prevented them from accessing education), non-participants usually cite non-financial reasons for not continuing with formal education (Selwyn *et al.*, 2006). A recent survey by the Adult Learning Inspectorate shows that the widespread provision of free tuition for adults previously without prior qualifications in key skills did not increase the numbers participating in courses. Rather, it merely changed where and how existing participants went about participation (Lee, 2006). This attraction or redirection of the 'usual suspects' is common. Dearden *et al.* (2004), using the 1970 cohort British Childhood Study, found a very small gap in staying-on rates between individuals coming from families in the top income quartile and those from the bottom income quartile, and no gap between them in terms of acccess to HE. HE in Wales shows a steady long-term rise in the number of first degree undergraduates from 1995 to 2003, despite the introduction of up-front tuition fees in 1999 (Gorard and Taylor, 2001), and the same is true of the increase in student numbers in Wales both before and after the reintroduction of Assembly Learning Grants in 2001/02 and the Financial Contingency Fund in 2002/03 (Taylor and Gorard, 2005).

There is no way of telling from such official statistics how many potential students are deterred from studying by the costs involved. The proportion of students leaving or completing their course who report finance as the problem is very low (less than 3 per cent in England). This is in relation to what is reputedly one of the lowest drop-out rates in the world (second only to HE in Japan). A study of local area participation rates between 1994 and 2000 (HEFCE, 2005) also found no evidence that the introduction of tuition fees and the replacement of grants with loans had significantly affected entrant behaviour or patterns. One explanation for this is that there does not exist a large body of socio-economically disadvantaged people who are currently eligible for entry to HE but who do not participate (although financial considerations might influence their choice of subject, expected length of course and institution). At the time of writing it is becoming clear that institutions offering the largest bursaries to new students are actually falling behind in terms of applications. Finance is neither a particularly important barrier nor a complete solution to stratified participation.

It seems that finance alone is unlikely to be an important factor in generating stratified access to post-compulsory education. Examination of other potential barriers such as time constraints or travel problems leads to similar conclusions (Gorard *et al.*, 2007). Overall, the idea of barriers to learning is elegant, both as an explanation for the differences in participation and as a suggestion for their amelioration. However, there is little clear evidence of their impact in creating stratified access, and a consequent danger that they tend towards becoming tautological non-explanations. The relatively low level of participation from lower-income groups, for example, gives rise to the explanation that cost is a barrier. If this is so, then removal or reduction of the cost should lead to increased participation from lower-income groups. This is the logic underlying grants, fees remission and means-tested bursaries, but there is little direct evidence that these approaches work differentially well for the groups for whom they are intended. Removing the apparent barriers to participation is not as easy as it sounds (Selwyn *et al.*, 2006), and this casts doubt on the value of the concept of barriers as an explanation for non-participation. An alternative conceptualisation of the determinants of participation lies in individual learning trajectories.

## Learning trajectories

The early life of each individual is closely related to early educational attainment, which is related to staying-on rates at age 16, and so to patterns of traditional-age participation in HE, and so on (Gorard *et al.*, 1999c; San-Segundo and Valiente, 2003). There is a pattern of typical learning 'trajectories' that can effectively encapsulate the complexity of individual education and training biographies. Some people leave formal education at the earliest opportunity. Some of these leavers return to formal learning at some time as adults, but a high proportion do not. Other people continue into extended initial education, but never return to formal learning once this is over. Others remain in contact with formal learning for a large proportion of their lives. Which of these 'trajectories', from lifelong non-participation to lifelong learning, an individual takes can be accurately predicted on the basis of characteristics that are known by the time an individual reaches school-leaving age. Gorard and Rees (2002) entered variables measuring five determinants – time, place, sex, family and initial schooling – into a logistic regression function in the order in which they occur in real life. Those characteristics that are set very early in an individual's life, such as age, gender and family background, predict later learning trajectories with 75 per cent accuracy. Adding the variables representing initial schooling increases the accuracy of prediction to 90 per cent. Replicated analyses, conducted with several different datasets totalling 10,000 adults across the entire UK, have shown that the same determinants of post-compulsory participation appear each time (Gorard *et al.*, 2003).

One possible explanation for this finding is that family poverty, lack of role models and a sense of 'not for us', coupled with poor experiences of initial schooling, can act to create a kind of lifelong attitude to learning – a negative learner identity. In this case, the obvious barriers such as cost, time and travel will be largely irrelevant. In the same way that most of the population is not deterred from HE by lack of finance (largely because most young people with the requisite entry qualifications already attend HE), so most non-participants in basic skills training are not put off by 'barriers' but by their lack of interest in something that now seems alien and imposed. This does not imply, of course, that people do not have choices, or that life crises have little impact, but rather that, to a large extent, these choices and crises occur within a framework of opportunities, influences and social expectations that are determined by the resources that they derive from their background and upbringing. More importantly, an individual's capacity to take up whatever learning opportunities are actually available can be constrained by their previous history. Their 'trajectories' reflect more than the objective structure of access to learning opportunities. The selection of individual educational experiences reflects 'learner identities' built up over the life of the individual. To deal with this, we have first to understand it. In the relative social and economic situation for any individual, the choice not to participate could be completely rational. We need to revise any complacency that the existing set-up for learning is appropriate for all, and that the reluctant learner need only be lured back 'on track'.

Such results offer important correctives to the conventional view of participation in lifelong learning – the 'accumulation thesis' – which prioritises the determining influence of earlier adult behaviour on what education and training individuals undertake later in their lives. As Tuijnman (1991) puts it, the best single predictor of later participation in education and training is earlier participation. Nevertheless, it is important to note that the correlations are low. Therefore, 'the lifelong education cycle cannot be comprehended without the inclusion and analysis of other factors influencing the accumulation of educational experiences' (p. 283). These other factors include area of residence (representing perhaps local economic conditions), gender and parental occupation, as well as parental education (Gerber and Hout, 1995; Zhou *et al.*, 1998). The 'accumulation thesis' now appears much weaker and the role of an individual's background appears much stronger than has been argued conventionally. The reasons why early learners are more often lifelong learners could be the same as the reason for their early participation, and based on family background, gender and regional conditions. This would be as convincing an explanation as the accumulation model. For example, while initial educational success may be a good indicator of later participation according to some accounts, the success itself can be at least partly predicted by social and family background in the model of trajectories proposed here.

Precisely the same inequalities as occur in post-compulsory participation are already apparent in patterns of initial education, and they recur in succeeding generations of the same family. So pervasive are these inequalities that it might be misleading to think of them as 'educational' problems at all. At an aggregated level, Gorard et al. (2004) conducted an exploratory factor analysis, for the Basic Skills Agency, with a basket of indicators of areal disadvantage and found that nearly all of them were expressing the same underlying factor. These indicators included attainment in Maths, Science and English from ages 7 to 14, the GCSE benchmark of five or more grades A★–C, the number of school leavers with no qualifications, the number of adults of working age and of all ages with no recognised qualification, indicators of childhood disadvantage, eligibility for free school meals at primary and secondary school, child poverty, children living in households on benefit, protected and registered children, where people were born, local economic activity rates, the proportion of those on benefit, unemployment rates at age 16, long-term and overall unemployment, social housing, household income, health scores, poor health, life expectancy, child mortality, total absences from school (sickness), all indicators of teenage pregnancy, and the proportion of abortions. What role can schools play then in helping to overcome disadvantage and so widen subsequent participation?

## Absence of school effect on attainment

In the UK, the school-leaving age was raised in 1972 from age 15 to 16, producing an inevitable but not total increase in staying on in education past age 15. A very similar growth in post-16 participation took place in the 1990s despite the lack of further legal compulsion. The Youth Cohort Study shows a steep growth in full-time education post-16 after 1989 (Payne, 1998). However, this is largely a question of robbing Peter to pay Paul, because government-funded training showed an almost equivalent drop over the same period (from 24 per cent of 16-year-olds in 1989 to 12 per cent in 1994). Other commentators have observed the same, and even today increases in staying-on rates in further education often replace work-based training, and full-time takes from part-time participation, and so on (Denholm and Macleod, 2003). The total proportion of the 16-year-old cohort remaining in education, government schemes and employment-based training combined has remained almost constant for decades, even though the balance between the three routes varies according to the local history of funding and availability. And the proportion remaining in education and training continues to be stratified in terms of social class, ethnicity and region.

Research into post-16 choice suggests that the majority of students at any level report wanting to remain in education to the next level. This is partly because of the inherent bias in UK education research towards researching the best educated (Moor et al., 2004). The likelihood of remaining in education post-16 depends, to a large extent, on prior GCSE/GNVQ performance (Raffe et al., 2001). Those returning are generally the best qualified, with the highest level of parental education and support (Hammer, 2003). And those who are the least likely to participate in any phase also appear to become the most likely to drop out (Walker et al., 2004). The level of qualification at 16+ predicts very well a student's educational pathway and later employment status (Croll and Moses, 2003; Howieson and Iannelli, 2003; McIntosh, 2004). To what extent is this the product of the school attended?

State-funded compulsory education for all children is an intervention intended to equalise life opportunities and remedy inequalities such as the number of books at home or the reading ability of parents. However, because this intervention is universal in the UK and is now so mature, it is very hard to decide what effect it has had on educational differentiation and mobility. We cannot conduct research that involves the same pupil going to two different schools and then seeing the difference in their results. So, as researchers, we are left with the far less satisfactory task of trying to match pupils in terms of their relative advantages and then seeing how well they do in different schools. One result is clear and undisputed. The vast majority of the difference between schools in terms of exam results can be explained by the expected attainment of their pupil intake, taking into account prior attainment and background characteristics such as class, ethnicity and gender.

Less clear is the meaning, if any, of the small remaining differences (residuals) between schools once the results have been statistically adjusted for their pupil intake. Some commentators believe that these residuals are evidence of a peer group effect. However, large international studies show no clear pattern of relationship between test scores and the extent to which similar pupils are clustered in the same schools (Haahr et al., 2005). Some commentators believe that the remaining differences between school outcomes represent a so-called 'school effect' created by better teaching, ethos, leadership and so on. However, what is left over is mostly the product of errors, created by imperfections in testing, measuring, recording, matching equivalent pupils and analysing the data (Gorard, 2006). The larger the study, the more information available about each pupil, and the more reliable the measures are, the stronger the link between school intake and outcomes. Thus, to a very large extent it does not matter, in exam terms, who goes to school with whom.

## School organisation effect

If attainment at school really is the key predictor of post-compulsory participation, and an individual's attainment is largely unaffected by the specific school they attend, is there a role for schools in promoting lifelong learning? Unsurprisingly perhaps, the evidence on this matter suggests that the impact of schools on non-compulsory participation is more direct than one channelled indirectly through attainment and qualification. In fact, genuine lifelong (i.e. from birth) analyses of participation suggest that an individual's level of qualification (at age 16 for example) is as predictable as educational participation from early life characteristics and events. These early life factors include time, place, gender, family and socio-economic origin and also early schooling (Gorard and Rees, 2002). In this model, early schooling appears to be one element in the creation of a sense of what is appropriate in terms of later educational participation – a kind of learner identity.

There are differences between varying national systems of allocating pupils to secondary schools and the ensuing clustered nature of the intake to each school (EGREES, 2005). For example, countries such as Germany, with a system of allocating school places by ability, at the time of writing have much higher segregation of rich and poor pupils between schools than countries such as Finland that have no such selection by ability. Countries with selective school systems, whether by academic ability, ability to pay or religious belief, have the most clustered schools in terms of test scores and various measures of socio-economic status such as parental qualification, parental education and occupation. Overall, the Scandinavian countries of Sweden, Finland and Denmark show less clustering on most indicators of pupil disadvantage, while Germany, Greece and Belgium show the most. Unsurprisingly, policies for allocating school places seem to make a difference to school intakes (Eurydice, 2007). Comprehensive systems of schools based on parental preference rather than selection or geographical criteria such as zoning tend to produce narrower social differences in both intake and outcomes. Countries such as New Zealand that have experimented with allocating places at popular schools via a lottery have experienced sudden drops in social segregation.

Segregation, whether by ability or otherwise, matters because the experiences gained during initial schooling appear to be an important factor in shaping long-term orientations towards learning. 'Success' or 'failure' at school affects the choice of what to do post-16 – and there even appears to be a school effect on that choice (Pustjens *et al.*, 2004). Experience of school lays the foundation for what could be an enduring 'learner identity'. It is striking, for example, how those who experienced the 11-plus examination testified to its major and often traumatic effects (Gorard and Rees, 2002). For respondents too young to have gone through the tripartite system, although 'success' and 'failure' are less starkly defined, it remains the case that they identify positive experiences of schooling as crucial determinants of enduring attitudes towards subsequent learning. In contrast, those who 'failed' at school often come to see post-school learning of all kinds as irrelevant to their needs and capacities. Participation in further, higher and continuing education is not perceived to be a realistic possibility, and even work-based learning is viewed as unnecessary. This view is not confined to those whose school careers were less 'successful' in conventional terms (Selwyn *et al.*, 2006).

One effect of who goes to school with whom is directly related to the relative attainment levels of different school mixes. In one LEA for example, the school with the highest mean level of attainment at age 16 might see 80 per cent of its pupils continue directly into some form of education or training (mostly sixth-form courses in the same school). These 80 per cent would have a much higher average attainment than the other 20 per cent. In the school with the lowest mean level of attainment at age 16, only 20 per cent of the pupils might continue directly into some form of education or training. Again, these 20 per cent would tend to have higher attainment than the other 80 per cent. However, in an area with considerable diversity it has been observed that the 20 per cent who remain in education from the low-attaining school actually have lower attainment than the 20 per cent who leave education from the high-attaining school. Staying on is not simply a matter of qualification. As with the 11-plus 'failures', students are learning to see themselves as successes or failures in terms of their peers (their school composition), and this appears to affect their decisions about subsequent educational participation (Lumby *et al.*, 2006).

Sometimes the influence of schooling can be as simple as the highest age of the students. For example, in some educational authorities there are schools for pupils aged 11 to 18 and schools catering for ages 11 to 16 (Lumby *et al.*, 2004). The immediate post-compulsory participation rate of pupils in 11–16 schools is much lower than in 11–18 schools. The attainment of pupils in 11–16 schools in the areas studied also tends to be lower than those in 11–18 schools, but not to the extent that it can explain the larger difference in the proportions transferring to college or a sixth-form in an 11–18 school. The key element appears to be the 'transfer'. Most pupils who continue post-16 in 11–18 schools do so in the same school. For many of them the transfer is seamless, and for some the key decision is what to study next year rather than whether to study at all. Pupils in 11–16 schools, on the other hand, face a more explicit choice that necessarily involves an abrupt change. This alone could explain much of the differential transfer rate.

Another reason why it matters who goes to school with whom concerns the role of schools in building an inclusive society. Even if the school mix is not a clear factor in enhancing exam scores, it may still be important in helping to enhance a sense of what is just and appropriate for pupils. From 1996, the Council of Europe expressed concern over the dangers of intolerance within each country towards elements of society deemed different, such as recent in-migrants and local ethnic minorities. In England, this concern led to the introduction of the compulsory National Curriculum for citizenship studies. Citizenship education has been presented by the government as the means by which many societal problems can be tackled, by developing pupils' perceptions about what it is to be part of a fair and democratic society (QCA, 1998). The fundamental influence on pupils in developing their perceptions of what constitutes a fair society is probably their experience of school. The intake to a school may matter because it provides the context for creating pupils' awareness of equity.

The level of ethnic, and other, segregation in schools can affect racial attitudes, subsequent social and economic outcomes, and patterns of residential segregation. The experience of Northern Ireland suggests that separate schools can be a force for even greater societal segregation, and that teachers then become unwilling even to discuss issues of sectarianism with their (segregated) pupils. So, in divided societies, citizenship education can actually generate negative results. In general, attitudes to school, and a feeling of belonging to society, are somewhat worse in countries with school systems in which pupils tend to go to school with others like them (rather than a social mix). International studies suggest that such socially segregated school systems endanger pupils' sense of belonging, and give no clear gain in exam scores (Gorard, 2007). Inclusive schools are generally more socially and racially tolerant, and this can have a long-term effect on pupils' aspirations (Casey *et al.*, 2006) and their attitudes to and expectations of society (Massey and Denton, 1998).

## Conclusion

In summary, the potential determinants of lifelong patterns of participation in education and training are several and varied. The most stable and important of these occur early in the life of each individual, and one of these determinants is their experience of compulsory schooling. The most successful students, in conventional attainment terms, are more likely to continue into formal episodes of post-compulsory education and to have the opportunities to return to education throughout their lives. Thus, if schools are differentially effective in assisting the qualification of their pupils, and especially if part of this effectiveness is a peer effect, then it would seem clear that the school attended forms one basis for differing patterns of lifelong learning. However, the extent to which schools are differently effective is doubtful, as is the extent to which it is the qualifications themselves that matter for subsequent participation. It is perhaps more likely that the real impact of schooling lies in helping create a relatively stable opinion of the value of formal episodes of learning to the individual, and the subjective appropriateness of the individual to such episodes. Both the national and international evidence suggests that the school mix – who goes to school with whom – is important here.

## References

Beinhart, S. and Smith, P. (1998) *National Adult Learning Survey 1997*, Sudbury: DfEE Publications.
Burchardt, R., Le Grand, J. and Piachaud, D. (1999) 'Social exclusion in Britain 1991–1995', *Social Policy and Administration* 33(3): 227–44.
Calder J. (1993) *Disaffection and Diversity: Overcoming barriers to adult learning*, London: Falmer.

Casey, L., Davies, P., Kalambouka, A., Nelson, N. and Boyle, B. (2006) 'The influence of schooling on the aspirations of young people with special educational needs', *British Educational Research Journal* 32(2): 273–90.

Croll, P. and Moses, D. (2003) 'Young people's trajectories into post-compulsory education and training: a preliminary analysis of data from the British Household Panel Survey', Paper presented at the Annual Conference of the British Educational Research Association, Heriot-Watt University, Edinburgh, 10–13 September.

Dearden, L., McGranahan, L. and Sianesi, B. (2004) *The Role of Credit Constraints in Educational Choices: Evidence from NCDS and BCS70*, Discussion Paper No. 48, London: London School of Economics and Political Science, Centre for the Economics of Education.

Dearing R. (1997) *Higher Education in the Learning Society*, Report of the Committee under the Chairmanship of Sir Ron Dearing, London: The Stationery Office.

Denholm, J. and Macleod, D. (2003) *Prospects for Growth in Further Education*, Wellington: Learning and Skills Research Centre.

Department for Trade and Industry (DTI) (1998) *Our Competitive Future: Building the knowledge driven economy*, White Paper, December 1998, London: The Stationery Office.

Education and Employment Committee (2001) *Higher Education Access*, Fourth Report, HC 124, London: House of Commons.

European Commission (2001) *Making a European Area of Lifelong Learning a Reality*, DG Education and Culture, European Commission Communication.

European Group for Research on Equity in Educational Systems (EGREES) (2005) *Equity in European Educational Systems: A set of indicators*. Available online at www.om.hu/doc/upload/200507/tout_eng17_05.pdf (accessed 25 April 2008).

Eurydice (2007) *The Information Network on Education in Europe*. Available online at www.eurydice.org/portal/page/portal/Eurydice (accessed January 2007).

Fryer, R. (1997) *Learning for the Twenty-first Century*, London: Department of Education and Employment.

Gerber, T. and Hout, M. (1995) 'Educational stratification in Russia during the Soviet period', *American Journal of Sociology* 101: 611–60.

Glass, D. (1954) *Social Mobility in Britain*, London: Routledge.

Gorard, S. (2006) 'Value-added is of little value', *Journal of Educational Policy* 21(2): 233–41.

—— (2007) 'Justice et équité à l'école: ce qu'en dissent les élèves dans les études internationales', *Revue Internationale d'Education Sevres* 44: 79–84.

—— and Rees, G. (2002) *Creating a Learning Society?*, Bristol: Policy Press.

—— and Taylor, C. (2001) *Student Funding and Hardship in Wales: A statistical summary*, Report to the National Assembly Investigation Group on Student Hardship, Cardiff: National Assembly for Wales.

——, Fevre, R. and Rees, G. (1999a) 'The apparent decline of informal learning', *Oxford Review of Education* 25(4): 437–54.

——, Rees, G. and Fevre, R. (1999b) 'Two dimensions of time: the changing social context of lifelong learning', *Studies in the Education of Adults* 31(1): 35–48.

——, —— and —— (1999c) 'Patterns of participation in lifelong learning: do families make a difference?', *British Educational Research Journal* 25(4): 517–32.

——, Selwyn, N. and Madden, L. (2003) 'Logged on to learning? Assessing the impact of technology on participation in lifelong learning', *International Journal of Lifelong Education* 22(3): 281–96.

——, Lewis, J. and Smith, E. (2004) 'Disengagement in Wales: educational, social and economic issues', *Welsh Journal of Education* 13(1): 118–47.

——, with Adnett, N., May, H., Slack, K., Smith, E. and Thomas, L. (2007) *Overcoming Barriers to HE*, Stoke-on-Trent: Trentham Books.

Haahr, J., with Nielsen, T, Hansen, E. and Jakobsen, S. (2005) *Explaining Pupil Performance: Evidence from the international PISA, TIMSS and PIRLS surveys*, Danish Technological Institute. Available online at www.danishtechnology.dk (accessed 25 April 2008).

Hammer, T. (2003) 'The probability for unemployed young people to re-enter education or employment: a comparative study in six Northern European countries, *British Journal of Sociology of Education* 24(2): 209–23.

Hand, A., Gambles, J. and Cooper, E. (1994) *Individual Commitment to Learning: Individuals' decision-making about lifelong learning*, Sheffield: Employment Department.

Harrison R. (1993) 'Disaffection and access', in J. Calder (ed.) *Disaffection and Diversity: Overcoming barriers to adult learning*, London: Falmer, pp. 2–18.

Higher Education Funding Council for England (HEFCE) (2005) *Young Participation in Higher Education*, Bristol: HEFCE.

Howieson, C. and Iannelli, C. (2003) *The Effects of Low Attainment on Young People's Outcomes at Age 22–23 in Scotland*, Paper presented at the British Educational Research Association Annual Conference, Heriot-Watt University, Edinburgh, 11–13 September.

Hudson, C. (2005) *Widening Participation in Higher Education Art and Design: Part 2 Questionnaire report*, Winchester: Council for Higher Education in Art and Design.

Kennedy, H. (1997) *Learning Works: Widening participation in further education*, Coventry: Further Education Funding Council.

Lee, J. (2006) 'Free courses failed to reel in adult learners', *Times Educational Supplement FE Focus*, 23 June, p. 1.

Lowe, J. (1970) *Adult Education in England and Wales: A critical survey*, London: Michael Joseph.

Lumby, J., Gorard, S., Morrison, M. and Rose, A. (2004) *Review of Level Three Provision in North Torfaen*, Cwmbran: Torfaen LEA.

——, Gorard, S., Morrison, M., Smith, E., Lewis, G. and Middlewood, D. (2006) *14–19 Arrangements in Cardiff: Review and recommendations*, Cardiff: Cardiff LEA.

McGivney, V. (1992) *Motivating Unemployed Adults to Undertake Education and Training*, Leicester: National Institute of Adult Continuing Education.

McIntosh, S. (2004) *Further Analysis of the Returns to Academic and Vocational Qualification*, Research Report No. 370, Norwich: Department for Education and Skills/HMSO.

Maguire, M., Maguire, S. and Felstead, A. (1993) *Factors Influencing Individual Commitment to Lifelong Learning*, Research Series No. 20, Sheffield: Employment Department.

Marsh, C. and Blackburn, R. (1992) 'Class differences in access to higher education in Britain', in R. Burrows and C. Marsh (eds) *Consumption and Class: Divisions and change*, London: Macmillan, pp. 184–211.

Massey, D. and Denton, N. (1998) *American Apartheid: Segregation and the making of the underclass*, Boston, MA: Harvard University Press.

Metcalf, H. (2005) 'Paying for university: the impact of increasing costs on student employment, debt and satisfaction', *National Institute Economic Review* 191 (January): 106–17.

Moor, H., Bedford, N., Johnson, A., Hall, M. and Harland, J. (2004) *Moving Forward – Thinking Back: Young people's post-16 paths and perspectives on education, training and employment*, The Post-16 Phase of the Northern Ireland Curriculum Cohort Study: Full Report, Slough: NFER.

National Audit Office (2002) *Widening Participation in Higher Education in England*, London: The Stationery Office.

NIACE (2003) *Adults Learning Survey – 2003*, Leicester: National Institute for Adult and Continuing Education.

Payne, J. (1998) *Routes at Sixteen: Trends and choices in the nineties*, Research Brief No. 55, London: DfES.

Pettigrew, A., Hendry, C. and Sparrow, P. (1989) *Training in Britain: A study of funding, activity and attitudes. Employers perspectives on human resources*, London: HMSO.

Pustjens, H., Van de gaer, E., Van Damme, J. and Onghena, P. (2004) 'Effect of secondary schools on academic choices and on success in higher education', *School Effectiveness and School Improvement* 15(3/4): 281–311.

Qualifications and Curriculum Authority (QCA) (1998) *Education for Citizenship and the Teaching of Democracy in Schools*, Final report of the Advisory Group on Citizenship, London: QCA.

Raffe, D., Fairgrieve, K. and Martin, C. (2001) Participation, inclusiveness, academic drift and parity of esteem: a comparison of post-compulsory education and training in England, Wales, Scotland and Northern Ireland, *Oxford Review of Education* 27(2): 173–203.

San-Segundo, M. and Valiente, A. (2003) 'Family background and returns to schooling in Spain', *Education Economics* 11(1): 39–52.

Sargant, N. (2000) *The Learning Divide Revisited*, Leicester: NIACE.

Selwyn, N., Gorard, S. and Furlong, J. (2006) *Adult Learning in the Digital Age*, London: Routledge.

Taylor, C. and Gorard, S. (2005) *Participation in Higher Education: Wales*, Report for independent study into devolution of the student support system: The Rees Review, Cardiff: National Assembly for Wales.

Tuijnman, A. (1991) 'Lifelong education: a test of the accumulation hypothesis', *International Journal of Lifelong Learning* 10: 275–85.

Walker, L., Matthew, B. and Black, F. (2004) 'Widening access and student non-completion: an inevitable link?', *International Journal of Lifelong Education* 23(1): 43–59.

Zhou, X., Moen, P. and Tuma, N. (1998) 'Educational stratification in Urban China', *Sociology of Education* 71: 199–222.

# 9

# Universities and lifelong learning

*David Watson*

Universities, as individual institutions and as contributors to national systems of higher education (HE), have always had a complex and multi-faceted relationship to the world of lifelong learning. This chapter explores this relationship initially from an historical point of view (from the 'inside out') and then from the perspective of other varieties of lifelong learning provision (from the 'outside in'). It proceeds to examine implications for *participation* in HE of various types, for *practice* in learning and teaching, and for *policy* on the part of institutions and those who control them. It concludes with some reflections on HE, lifelong learning and social justice.

The epigraphs throughout are from the classic literary expression of unfulfilled lifelong learning, Thomas Hardy's *Jude the Obscure* (1895). *Jude* – the relentlessly grim story of a poor stone-mason, whose ambitions to become first a classical scholar and then a theologian are thwarted at every turn – presents just a snapshot of some of the issues raised by the university and lifelong learning, at a particular point in time (between about 1880 and 1884) and in a special place. The attack on an unreformed – or very slowly reforming – Oxford is as brutal as the evocation of the dreaming spires is romantic. It is also important to remember that Jude was (in the terms set out in the final section below) a pure autodidact; he never set foot in another classroom or situation of formal learning after his village school. But Hardy does capture, with all the benefits of poetic licence, some of the ways of thinking about universities and lifelong learning that continue to pose contemporary dilemmas. Most importantly, as E.P. Thompson established in a landmark lecture in 1968, in which he also ruminated upon Jude:

> to strike the balance between intellectual rigour and respect for experience is always difficult . . . if I have redressed it a little, by reminding us that universities engage in adult education not only to teach but to learn, then my purpose is fulfilled.
>
> (1968: 23)

Some way within the limits of the stretch of landscape, points of light like topaz gleamed. The air increased in transparency with the lapse of minutes, till the topaz points showed themselves to be vanes, windows, wet roof slates, and other shining spots upon the spires, domes, free-stone work, and varied outlines that were faintly revealed. It was Christminster, unquestionably, either directly seen, or miraged in the peculiar atmosphere.

(Hardy, 1895: 21)

It seemed impossible that modern thought could house itself in such decrepit and superseded chambers.

(p. 791)

## Historical perspectives

Much of the complexity arises from the history of the university as an institution in modern society. The story that follows is essentially about Great Britain, but several of the themes have recurred in other developed systems of HE, and often in the same order.

Most university foundations had an immediate element of service to the community in their agreed mission and purpose. While this did not necessarily presuppose a commitment to lifelong learning, the idea of responsiveness to social priorities was much more central to the founding goals of their institutions than many subsequent generations of university leaders and members have been led to believe. There is a pattern here, as set out in the following stages of university 'inventions' (for a rapid overview of these institutional developments see Lay, 2004):

- early foundations such as the late medieval colleges for poor scholars in England (Oxford and Cambridge), or for urban professionals (such as Bologna and Paris in continental Europe); several centuries later this trajectory was followed by the American colonial seminaries (many of which subsequently became expensive private schools in the USA, including the heart of the 'Ivy League');
- mid- and late nineteenth-century foundations growing directly out of perceived social and economic needs (such as the great Victorian and Edwardian 'civics' in the UK and the Morrill Act-inspired 'Land Grant' universities of the American West and Midwest, leavened by specific, primarily research-based institutions on the Humboldtian model, such as Johns Hopkins);
- mid-twentieth-century establishments of a local authority 'public system' of HE (as in the English Polytechnics, the Scottish Central Institutions and American state systems, of which the archetypes are Wisconsin and the Californian 'Master Plan');
- late twentieth-century experiments in curriculum, pedagogy and above all accessibility (such as, notably, the pioneering of open access, or admission of adults without formal qualification by the UK's Open University and New York's City College system, and their imitators around the world); and finally
- 'frontier' activity between compulsory education, voluntary 'tertiary' provision and the initial rungs of HE (as in the phenomenon of UK 'higher education in further education'

and the vitally important American 'community college' network – especially in the provision of 'intermediate' qualifications such the UK's Higher National Certificates and Diplomas and Foundation Degrees, and the USA's Associate Degrees; the latest descriptor of activity in this borderland is that of 'dual sector' provision).

Collectively, such institutional types illustrate the many ways in which HE can use lifelong learning to connect with the wider society. The term of art for this is 'diversity,' and it raises the question (returned to under 'Implications for policy' below) whether a diverse student body requires a diverse set of institutions.

> 'You are one of the very men Christminster was intended for when the colleges were founded; a man with a passion for learning, but no money or opportunities or friends. But you were elbowed off the pavement by the millionaire's sons.' (Sue [his second wife] to Jude.)
>
> (Hardy, 1895: 151)

From the late Victorian period onwards the notions of accessibility, service and hence of lifelong learning came to cohere, notably in the University Extension Movement (as at Cambridge in 1873 and Oxford 1878). Another outcome was the University Settlement Movement, as groups of dons and students attempted to take the benefits of their learning (and their social conscience) into deprived communities. The archetypes were Oxford's Toynbee Hall and Chicago's Hull House.

> 'There are schemes afoot for making the University less exclusive and extending its influence.' (Jude to Arabella [his first – and third – wife.])
>
> (Hardy, 1895: 379)

In the early twentieth century the synergy continued apace. Historians of British adult and continuing HE, such as Richard Taylor and Roger Fieldhouse, have noticed the particular force-field created between 'liberal academics, Anglicans, high-tory Conservatives, and middle-class women's lobbyists', subsequently reinforced by trade unions and groups like the Workers Education Association (WEA, founded in 1903). From this emerged the structures (from 1919) and the funding (from 1924) of 'Responsible Bodies' (RB). These were essentially directly funded university departments, often with titles emphasising their separate identity, such as 'extra-mural' (see Taylor et al., 1985 and Fieldhouse, 1996).

The resulting achievements of university adult and continuing education (ACE) have been considerable, persuading individuals and groups that, despite Christminster-style snobbery and indifference, HE was indeed for them. The literature is full of personal testimony to this effect. It confirms the strength of an honourably radical tradition of theorists, practitioners and participants (as set out by Thompson above, and eloquently revived in Taylor et al., 2002). It also produced its own literature in figures such as John Dewey in the USA and Richard Hoggart in the UK.

However, such achievements were distinctly 'of their time'. With the advent of mass, then universal HE, critics would say that there was a temptation to take an exclusive, even a patronising view of the 'new new' students (those who would not have matriculated in a more restrictive, exclusive age) and allow ACE to retreat into a enclave within the university, often serving the repeat business of older students on subsidised routes with staff and students colluding to remain outside the framework of funding and accountability for a larger, differently democratic system. In particular, an insistence that adult education was essentially nonvocational came to jar with an increasingly instrumental view of post-compulsory education.

In this sense the nature of the 'founding' of ACE could be argued to have incorporated an endemic weakness. From its early years until the Conservative reforms of the late 1980s (creating formulaic funding regimes for all higher education institutions (HEIs)), ACE subsisted as an 'alternative' stream, regulated, funded (and more than often taught) separately from the mainstream of award-bearing HE. The RB status itself came to an end in 1989. Since then the process of 'mainstreaming' ACE has continued apace, with its concomitants of requiring not only formal registration of students on 'award-bearing' courses but also assessment and completion as conditions of government funding. For some the sense of loss is extreme. In 2006 the editors of the *International Journal of Lifelong Education* lamented:

> [r]adical adult education is a form of active citizenship – it is part of lifelong learning, but it is being lost within the more institutionally based discussions on lifelong learning but also in the practice of those institutions which used to nurture it.
>
> (IJLE, 2006: 546)

## Universities and dimensions of lifelong learning

Universities relate to other parts of the educational life-course in differing ways.

They are both simultaneous formative influences upon and passive respondents to systems of compulsory education and training. The relationship between universities and school systems is symptomatic of an even wider relationship between HE and the institutions of the public service; not only education, but also medicine and health, government, and such varied organs of the state as the police, probation, social work and librarianship. Universities also have a role within various work-based routes of training, which in the UK at least overlap with the years of traditional schooling.

In this process, they have played a key role in the definition and development of some professions, while remaining aloof from and indeed hostile to others. Law and divinity (theology) were there at the beginning. The broader aspects of public administration joined in later, not least when meritocratic civil services began to be the order of the day.

They have had a love–hate relationship with the world of work and its demands for 'skills' and human capital, not least through the relentless march of 'credentialism' and the contemporary preoccupation with employment-related skills. The latest UK intervention along these lines is the Leitch Report, which would like to see the proportion of the workforce with graduate-level qualifications rise from its current level of 29 per cent to 40 per cent by 2020 (Leitch Review of Skills, 2006: 137).

Putting the two domains (public and private) together, we can track the evolution and development of two types of market: that where state sponsorship (or even direct purchase of places) is critical (with a resulting strong emphasis on the 'supply' side) and that where individual learners and their immediate employers make the decision to 'purchase' training and accreditation (a less adulterated form of 'demand'). Figure 9.1 shows how both types of market have affected the activity of UK HE over the past decade: the 'managed' increases in health and medical courses (as essentially the government has purchased places), and the 'demand-led' decline in popularity of some traditional subjects and professions (notably engineering and technology) as students impose their own view of where the employment and career enhancements lie (not least in the – for the previous generation – contentious areas of 'media

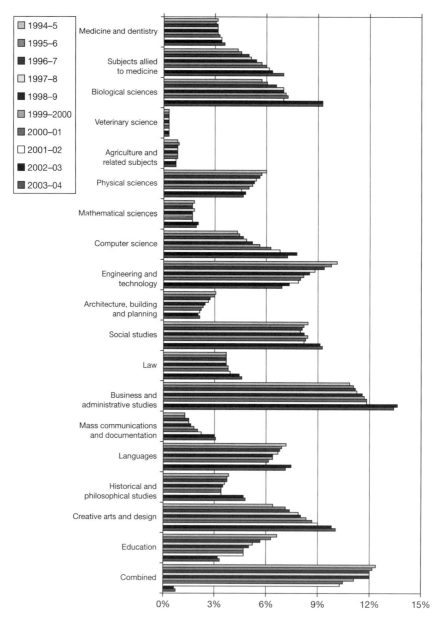

*Figure 9.1* Percentages of full-time first degree students in each subject area, 1994–2003.

Source: Watson (2006).

studies' [included here in 'mass communications and documentation']). The dramatic reduction in the 'combined' category shows the effect of disaggregating Open University students by the (subject-based) names of the awards they now aim for.

The implications here for lifelong learning are about the increased intimacy of the relationship of the academy with life beyond its walls: not just the world of work, but also the (in some cases forced) responsiveness to the ways in which students in a mass HE system will wish to mould their experience of it.

> For a moment there fell on Jude a true illumination; that here in the stone-yard was a centre of effort as worthy as that dignified by the name of scholarly study within the noblest of the colleges.
>
> (Hardy, 1895: 84–5)

Finally, universities have provided both a haven and an unattainable aspiration for aspects of adult education and learning later in life. In this sense the role of HEIs as supporters of both informal learning (by providing cultural resources such as libraries, galleries, museums and related events) and the 'recreational learning' hit hardest by the phenomenon of 'mainstreaming' must not be forgotten.

## Implications for participation

A lifelong learning mission for HE implies that the HE community should look more like, and respond more regularly to, the community as a whole. How, in enrolling and developing students from across the current groups in society, can the university or college seek to change that community for the better?

In the USA, elite universities compete for excellent students from minorities and from disadvantaged communities because they are trying to construct a 'class' that will be representative of the best and brightest that American society can offer in the future (there is an element of self-interest here too) (Bowen et al., 2005). In Great Britain the discourse is structured much more around a 'deficit' model, agonising about the 'under-representation' of lower socio-economic groups in particular in the system as a whole, and especially in the more prestigious institutions.

In both countries this has become a contentious issue, as American institutions move their financial aid resources away from 'need' and towards 'merit' (scholarly and athletic), and as UK institutions tackle the unwelcome fact that the conventionally qualified students from poorer backgrounds are just not there in sufficient numbers to satisfy the political critics.

> He began to see that town life was a book of humanity infinitely more palpitating, varied and compendious than the gown-life.
>
> (Hardy, 1895: 118)

To whom should the university be accessible? A survey of the fate of what might be regarded as 'under-represented groups' around the world illuminates the dilemma. Turn the question on its head, and look at local cultural and political preoccupations. Who, in fact, is meant to be left outside? The experience of other countries is that targeted positive discrimination invariably has unintended knock-on effects. Examples have included the physically disabled in China, the Chinese ethnic minority in Pacific Rim countries, Israeli Arabs, Hungarian Romanies and the relatives of terrorists in Japan (see Watson, 2005: 137).

All around the world there is a growing perception that improving the class base of young university participation is a long-haul proposition. It relies, in particular, on the performance of compulsory schooling (and, in advance of that, the reduction in child poverty and improvement in conditions for early years education and acculturation). However, most importantly, universities as the apex of the education system (and an informed critic and supporter of other public services) should not be allowed to use this fact as an excuse for reducing their own efforts at improving access and reducing disadvantage. This is particularly sensitive during the period of rapid expansion through which most developed university systems are now working. To achieve greater fairness will require further expansion, but at the same time it risks increasingly disadvantaging those who do not participate. So there are difficulties in working out how to help the disadvantaged without further advantaging the advantaged.

> '. . . it was my poverty and not my will that consented to be beaten. It takes two or three generations to do what I tried to do in one.' (Jude)
>
> (Hardy, 1895: 326)

## Implications for practice

The lifelong learning dimension of HE has generally been associated with terms such as 'non-standard provision', where the 'standard' is associated with undergraduate education, usually full-time and (in the UK) usually based on residence away from home. As Figure 9.2 demonstrates, the UK has had for some considerable time a system of HE in which patterns of provision associated with lifelong learning have predominated. Key indicators are the average age of participants, the proportion of part-time study, participation by those with declared disabilities and the types of provision that are designed to support those either in work or preparing for career changes. A further consideration is the tendency of full-time students to study from 'home', or at least not to travel to the other end of the country for residential HE (Slowey and Watson, 2003: 3–19).

These considerations – of mode and level, of qualification and subject selection, and of support and motivation – all have profound implications for the organisation and practice of the university. A model of the 'student experience' that is other than the highly selective (and expensive) 'gift of an interval' envisaged by Michael Oakeshott in a earlier, less pressured era requires flexible, responsive and imaginative action by the institutions. The relevant areas include credit accumulation and transfer, accreditation of prior learning, timetabling and student support across a wide field (not just academic services, but also access to libraries, to computer networks and to technical and personal support). In particular, for the promise of lifelong learning to be realised requires credit earned by students to be not only recognised but also positively

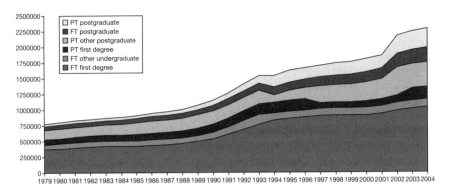

*Figure 9.2* UK student enrolments by level and mode 1979–2004.

Source: Higher Education Statistics Agency (HESA) Red Books on student numbers.

used by institutions (perhaps from different parts of the educational pecking order) for the purposes of admission and advanced standing. The Higher Education Policy Institute (HEPI) found that, in 2002–3, over 11,000 of 300,000 students entered UK HEIs having been at a different institution in the previous two years; most received no credit at all for their previous study (HEPI, 2004: para. 7).

## Implications for policy

'Can we be equal and excellent too?' asked the House of Commons Select Committee on Education and Employment in February 2001 (Majority Report of the Committee, Fourth Report, *Higher Education: Access*: para. 2001). These twin poles bedevil much thinking about the purposes and performance of universities by politicians and political commentators more generally (the Committee's answer to its own question was 'a resounding 'yes').

> 'I venture to think that you will have a much better chance of success in life by remaining in your own sphere.' (Master of Biblioll [Balliol] College to Jude.)
>
> (Hardy, 1895: 117)

In the UK a test case can be supplied by the responses of the various parties – government, funding councils and the institutions to the National Committee of Inquiry into Higher Education (the Dearing Committee) in 1997. One of the Committee's firm priorities, in a report called *Higher Education: The learning society*, was:

> the contribution of higher education to lifelong learning, as embedded particularly in the qualifications framework, views on articulation and collaboration between education sectors, and especially fairer and more effective support for all types of learners in HE.
>
> (Watson and Taylor, 1998: 151–2)

109

In responding to Dearing in their Green Paper, *The Learning Age*, the UK government expressed a broad, emancipatory hope for lifelong learning, including the role of the universities:

As well as securing our economic future, learning has a wider contribution. It helps make ours a civilised society, develops the spiritual side of our lives and promotes active citizenship. Learning enables people to play a full part in their community. It strengthens the family, the neighbourhood and consequently the nation. It helps us fulfill our potential and opens doors to a love of music, art and literature. That is why we value learning for its own sake, as well as for the equality of opportunity it brings.

(DfEE, 1998: foreword)

Against such bold objectives, how do we sensibly measure progress? In the UK the funding councils selectively support 'widening participation' (focusing particularly on the 'retention' of non-standard students), sponsor special initiatives such as 'AimHigher' and 'Lifelong Learning Networks', publish relevant 'benchmark' data and generally exhort the system to do better. The difficulty is that measuring performance in this area is both difficult and generally ignored by the composite league tables that cement relative institutional reputations in the public mind.

An eloquent example is the drive for 'world-class' status for leading national universities. The following attributes of the 'world-class university' appear to be ubiquitous, probably in declining order of importance:

- what it does in research (especially Nobel prizes and the like);
- how it is regarded by its host society, including in the popular media;
- where its graduates are (especially in government and as captains of industry; leadership in other branches of the 'public service' is much less highly regarded);
- an attractive physical presence, including some prestigious buildings and other infrastructure (for example, libraries and other collections);
- international recruitment at postgraduate level (high-volume undergraduate recruitment from overseas can, in contrast, be seen as a 'non-selective' weakness).

And, curiously, not much more. Many of the 'common-sense' elements of high performance by comprehensive universities – such as teaching quality, widening participation and social mobility, services to business and the community, support of rural in addition to metropolitan communities, as well as contributions to other public services – are conspicuously absent. Most of this alternative list is vital for the effective support of lifelong learning (see Watson, 2007: 34–46).

This is where mission differentiation, together with issues of complementarity of institutional goals and achievements, comes in. All over the world, governments would like to secure rational mission distribution (and hence – they think – ease funding pressures); all over the world HEIs (above a certain level of scope and activity) seek similar measures of esteem. This is why governments endlessly tinker with frameworks: those with 'binary systems' think they should be dissolved; those without them think they should be created.

Hans Schuetze and Maria Slowey have demonstrated that the resulting reinforcement of institutional hierarchies around traditional patterns of provision is almost universal, as they set out in Figure 9.3 below. The coincidence of formal, or 'closed', structures and high status with traditional provision, and of all of the reciprocals with the kinds of interventions that are more likely to make lifelong learning in HE actually happen, is palpable.

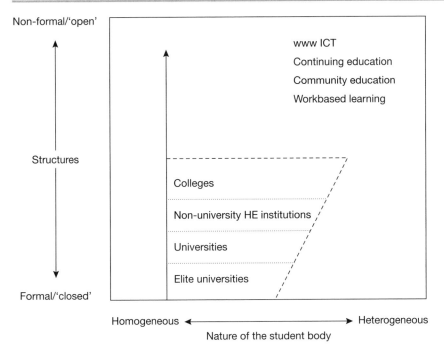

Non-formal/'open'

www ICT

Continuing education

Community education

Workbased learning

Structures

Colleges

Non-university HE institutions

Universities

Elite universities

Formal/'closed'

Homogeneous ←——————→ Heterogeneous

Nature of the student body

*Figure 9.3* Higher education and lifelong learning: a framework of change.

Source: Schuetz and Slowey (2000).

Nor is this solely an issue of policy at the national level. In 1973 the Organization for Economic Cooperation and Development (OECD) instituted its programme of 'recurrent education' and thus drew HE firmly into the web of international policy analysis. The European Union has subsequently used its lifelong learning powers to involve HE (not originally a treaty function) in a range of policies, initiatives and activities. The year 1996 was designated European Year of Lifelong Learning, while a decade later the UNESCO Institute for Education changed its name to the UNESCO Institute for Lifelong Learning (UNESCO press announcement, 20 June 2006). Meanwhile the national governments have signed up for harmonisation of credit recognition and specifications for qualifications at particular levels included in the Bologna Declaration of June 1999. This refers explicitly to credits being 'obtainable in non-HE contexts such as life-long learning' (HEPI, 2004). On the international scene, at least as much as the national, institutional conservatism means that structures for flexibility and progress are likely to precede practice.

## The question of social justice

Theories of lifelong learning have generally cohered around two models, which for the purposes of this chapter might be regarded as Weberian 'ideal-types'.

The 'programmatic' tendency has a view of lifelong learning literally from the 'cradle to the grave', commencing with 'early-years' provision (for which the British government has come close to prescribing a national curriculum), and ending with the in-retirement choices of what are called in political terms 'grey panthers'. In between are the phases of compulsory education and of semi-compulsory credentialism and continuing professional development (CPD), the stakes for which are heightened by a job market combining historically high levels of volatility (the so-called 'portfolio career' – necessitating periodic re-starts) and pressures to maintain good professional standing (often resulting in compulsory CPD). In this context it is also important to remember the role of HEIs as sources of lifelong learning for their own staff.

The 'opportunistic' tendency in its most extreme form is the domain of the autodidact (celebrated, for example, by Jonathan Rée in his study of *Proletarian Philosophers*), of the heroic second or third chancer, and of those whose primary purpose (at whatever stage in life) is either personal self-fulfilment or a role in the collective transformation of society (Rée, 1984).

---

'I love the place . . . although I know how it hates all men like me – the so-called Self-taught – how it scorns our laboured acquisitions, when it should be the first to respect them; how it sneers at our false quantities and mispronunciations, when it should say, I see you want help my poor friends . . . Perhaps it will soon wake up and be generous. I pray so!' (Jude to Arabella.)

(Hardy, 1895: 320)

---

Intriguingly, each tendency, in its own way, stresses the role of lifelong learning in human emancipation. Meanwhile, more general advocates of a liberal HE have identified its role in improving the chances of experiencing a happy, healthy and democratically tolerant postgraduate life. Substantial longitudinal studies, such as those conducted by the Wider Benefits of Learning (WBL) Group, have apparently established a scientific warrant for such claims (Bynner *et al.*, 2003). Graduates, for example, not only read to their children, they also have high and demanding aspirations for them.

---

'What I couldn't accomplish in my own person perhaps I can carry out through him. They are making it easier for poor students now you know.' (Jude to Sue about his son [her stepson].)

(Hardy, 1895: 278)

---

Critics of the tendency for the former process to overshadow the latter have developed a powerful argument that the combination of human capital and instrumental priorities summed up in the skills agenda and a naive official view of education as the key stimulus to citizenship amounts to 'social control' of the crudest kind (see, for example, Coffield, 1999). Other voices are more nuanced. For example, John Field's *Lifelong Learning and the New Educational Order* argues that, despite the problems of polarised participation alluded to above, lifelong learning can inculcate a valuable sense of reflexivity: '[a]s individuals come to rely less on traditional institutional and the authority figures associated with them – church leaders, parents, aristocracy – to guide their behaviour, so they become more self-directed' (Field, 2000: 57).

The main history lesson incorporated in this chapter is that, for such emancipatory powers for lifelong learning through HE, we have now to look beyond the radical intent and influence of ACE towards the liberating effect of mass, potentially even in Martin Trow's terms 'universal', HE, in which at least 40 per cent of the population will participate during their lifetimes. In other words the relationship between lifelong learning and universities is now inescapably 'programmatic' and less 'opportunistic'. For some teachers and students there will be an understandable sense of loss. However, as HE systems expand all around the world, in the early twenty-first century the potential contribution to social justice is significantly wider.

## References

Bowen, W.G., Kurzweill, M.A. and Tobin, E.M. (2005) *Equity and Excellence in American Higher Education*, Charlottesville, VA: University of Virginia Press.

Bynner, J., Dolton, P., Feinstein L., Makepiece, G., Malmberg, L. and Woods, L. (2003) *Revisiting the Benefits of Higher Education: A report by the Bedford Group for Lifecourse and Statistical Studies, Institute of Education*, Bristol: HEFCE.

Coffield, F. (ed.) (1999) *Speaking Truth to Power: Research and policy on lifelong learning*, Bristol: Policy Press.

Department for Education and Employment (DfEE) (1988) *The Learning Age: A renaissance for a new Britain*, London: HMSO.

Field, J. (2000) *Lifelong Learning and the New Educational Order*, Stoke on Trent: Trentham Books.

Fieldhouse, R. (1996) *A History of Modern British Adult Education*, Leicester: NIACE.

Hardy, Thomas (1895) *Jude the Obscure*, Harmondsworth: Penguin Classic edition, with introduction and notes by Dennis Taylor, 2006.

Higher Education Policy Institute (HEPI) (2004) *Credit Accumulation and Transfer and the Bologna Process: An overview*, Oxford: HEPI.

Higher Education Statistics Agency (HESA) (1979–2004) Red Books on student numbers. Available online at www.hesa.ac.uk/index.php/content/vuew/600/239/ (accessed 25 March 2008).

*International Journal of Lifelong Education* (IJLE) (2006) 'Editorial: is lifelong learning adult education?', *International Journal of Lifelong Education* 25(6) (November/December): 545–46.

Lay, S. (2004) *The Interpretation of the Magna Charta Universitatum and its Principles*, Bologna: Bononia University Press.

Leitch Review of Skills (2006) *Prosperity for All in the Global Economy: World class skills*, London: HM Treasury.

Rée, J. (1984) *Proletarian Philosophers: Problems in socialist culture in Britain, 1900–1940*, Oxford: Oxford University Press.

Schuetze, H.G. and Slowey, M. (eds) (2000) *Higher Education and Lifelong Learners*, London and New York: RoutledgeFalmer.

Slowey, M. and Watson, D. (2003) *Higher Education and the Lifecourse*, Maidenhead: SRHE and Open University Press.

Taylor, R., Rockhill, K. and Fieldhouse, R. (1985) *University Adult Education in England and the USA: A reappraisal of the liberal tradition*, London: Croom Helm.

——, Barr, J. and Steele, T. (2002) *For a Radical Higher Education: After post-modernism*, Buckingham: SRHE and Open University Press.

Thompson, E.P. (1968) *Education and Experience: The fifth Mansbridge Memorial Lecture*, Leeds: Leeds University Press.

Watson, D. (2005) 'What I think I know and don't know about widening participation in HE', in C. Duke and G. Layer (eds) *Widening Participation: Which way forward for English higher education?*, Leicester: NIACE, pp. 133–45.

—— (2006) 'UK HE: the truth about the market', *Higher Education Review* 38(3): 3–16.

—— (2007) *Managing Civic and Community Engagement*, Maidenhead: Open University Press.

—— and Taylor, R. (1998) *Lifelong Learning and the University: A post-Dearing agenda*, London: Falmer Press.

# 10

# Workplace learning

*Henning Salling Olesen*

This chapter has four main steps. The first section introduces the emergence of the theme 'workplace learning' and its usual meaning. The second section elaborates by means of examples of the complex interplay between work, learner and society. The third and fourth sections problematise the stereotypical meaning of the theme, first by pointing out the multiplicity of work types and learning contexts, and then by bringing in (women's) housework and work in the periphery of global capitalism. The fifth and sixth sections deal with the theorizing of workplace learning – first by considering some of the most important recent theoretical approaches, then by outlining a theoretical conception of workplace learning as a subjective experience process.

## Workplace learning: an emerging theme

Workplace learning is an emerging theme that has gained substantial attention in political life, in management and in education and training (Boud and Garrick, 1999; Garrick, 1998; Rainbird *et al.*, 2004). The phenomenon itself is not an absolute novelty. As long as it has made sense to speak of 'work' – intentional and systematic activity in order to provide a material product or an immaterial effect – we can also speak of learning, meaning individual adaptation to perform already known work procedures, as well as individual and collective development of new procedures. But it has obviously had a very different significance. To research the relation between work and learning and to distinguish between work and non-work is actually a modern phenomenon – a consequence of new historical conditions. In traditional societies – for most people – work was simply for maintaining life. Learning was part of work in everyday life. Learning happened by participation in fixed practices, that were gradually defined as specific working procedures. It was a broad and comprehensive technical, social and cultural education – e.g. in a society of hunting and fishing, the learning of specific techniques and, at the same time, the acquisition of basic gender roles and cultural standards.

During the historical modernisation process in the last couple of centuries, however, learning has become increasingly institutional in the form of general schooling and vocational training – it has increasingly been attempted to speed up learning and to assume that the individual enters working life with an already prepacked capacity to work without having to learn at work. In industrial capitalism the division of labour between those who do the thinking and those who conduct the work has materialised in machinery and other artefacts. Even direct workplace-related skills, e.g. to operate a new machine, have increasingly become separate training activities to a substantial extent. The modern architecture of knowledge and work has reduced learning opportunities and learning challenges in the work process to a minimum for many people.

However, the last few decades have witnessed a recurring interest in the workplace as a learning arena in itself. It is probably a double dynamic: on the one hand, there is an increasing awareness among direct actors of working life (managers as well as some groups of workers) of the significance of skills and competences and the new qualities of competences that are becoming decisive. The old saying of Karl Marx that competition does not take place in the market but in the production itself has materialised in the focus on human resources. On the other hand, there is a growing recognition that formal education and training does not fulfil the (high) expectations put on them.

However, the awareness of the need for workplace learning is not the same as an insight into the whats and the hows of learning.

## Workplace, work process, learning and the learner

Workplace learning is not just an attribute of the workplace and the work itself. It is primarily a subjective process of individual workers and groups of workers investing their body and soul, i.e. their knowledge, skills and emotional commitment, in a workplace, building experiences and learning new skills and knowledge from it. Workers do so against the background of their individual life history and the wider cultural and institutional resources available for them in their community. In the first place we tend to understand workplace learning as the process in which individual workers learn by participating in work as a specific activity – its content, technology, organisation and management, but this plastic and concrete process turns out to be deeply influenced by the societal organisation of work in any given historical and cultural context. By the same token, learning taking place somewhere other than a specific workplace – in a school or even a university – is strongly influenced by working life. So the theme of this chapter may best be seen as an umbrella comprising learning that takes place in the workplace, learning that aims at work, or learning that is informed and shaped by work.

The different levels and perspectives are indicated in the simple matrix below.

| Work process: technology and knowledge; crafts; professions; business branches | Learning in a specific location – a workplace with a specific organisation | Each worker is an individual with a specific life history experience |
| --- | --- | --- |
| Work as a societally organised relation: division of labour and socio-economic structure | Learning for or from work in general, taking place in families, schools, etc. | Workforce as a population with a subjective and cultural potential (class, gender) for engaging in work in specific forms |

*Figure 10.1* Relations of learning to work.

115

Any specific workplace situation involves learning or learning potential, i.e. challenges of workers' practices and understanding, which can in principle be traced back to those factors indicated in the left-hand column, and workers' actual learning processes (or not learning) can be related to the individual and collective experience indicated in the right-hand column – each situation forming a specific constellation of factors that involve all the dimensions. Needless to say, the matrix blurs the fact that there is a close interrelation between those societal relations that are for simplicity separated out into the right- and left-hand columns.

We might illuminate the specific contents of these categories by looking at some examples.

An electrician who completed his apprenticeship some 20 years ago and has been working in an entrepreneurial construction company ever since is facing some major technical changes in electrical installations. More and more work is related to low-voltage electronic equipment (alarms, regulation systems, communication). Even ordinary houses increasingly have such devices. There is still much work such as the simple wiring of lamps, and the installation of cookers, washing machines, etc., but the electrician also feels that this work is becoming less and less interesting because new houses are pre-manufactured for wiring, and repairing old houses is only occasional and a bit solitary. The employer offers him the opportunity to take some courses in electronics, but he refuses, slightly offended. He is a good worker, he knows he is not very good at physics and maths and, on the whole, he does not really want to go to school again, so he manages to talk to young colleagues who have learned about these new technologies in their apprenticeship school. They explain the most common devices, and he reads the instructions (he is English speaking so he manages to understand the mechanical translation from Chinese even though it is not so easy). After a while he understands most of the functions of relay switches, alarm systems and remote control regulation. However, he realises that he needs to work in teams with people who have a better background in electronics than he has.

A 35-year-old woman takes up a job as a cleaner after having worked at home for some years raising her children. She is employed in a big service-company, Group 4, and her first cleaning job is in a school. But before starting she attends an introductory course held by the service company. She finds it a bit amusing since she is an experienced housewife with a husband and three children so she feels she has all the cleaning experience in the world. But she soon realises that professional cleaning is somewhat different. She learns about hygiene and health risks, about efficient cleaning, from the best way to twist a cloth to how to operate a cleaning machine for large floors, and about chemicals that can assist in cleaning. She also learns about the risks of infections and about personal protection against chemicals (gloves, eye protection and so on). And she learns about the classification of cleaning tasks according to the type of dirt that can be expected, but also about the time allocated for each task according to the cleaning standard paid for. In the beginning she finds it a bit ridiculous but gradually she realises that cleaning is not just an unskilled home-based job. She is now a skilled cleaner, and in retrospect she senses the way her work at home has been underestimated by others. Starting to work in the school is a shocking experience. There is not enough time allocated, and for the first few days she is perspiring and not able to complete in time. She is a novice, and her colleagues tell her how she can do things more easily and save time. In some cases, however, this means dropping some of the daily tasks every second day, leaving tasks unattended to – and gradually she manages to keep to the time. But she is embarrassed about some of the work, and her newly won feeling of craftsmanship is shrinking. But she sets her own priorities – some things are more important than others – the toilets of course, but also something that is not often inspected, for example the ventilation channels – the children need clean air. The hygiene teaching and the tight working schedule come together in a mature, yet pragmatic setting of standards.

These cases are intended to illustrate preliminarily and in unjust briefness the complexity of workplace learning processes – the interaction between different aspects of the context, and the fact that they are also personal and cultural stories of specific people.

### Workplace as a metaphor and the real workplaces where learning takes place

The standard connotation of a workplace is probably a specific location of organised labour – a workshop where sweating and oil-dripping men do heavy work with tools and machines to produce physical artefacts or make specific services; or a factory where women on an assembly line conduct a few tasks as their small contribution to an ever ongoing mass production. For very many people this is a lifelong experience. But used as a general reference it becomes a stereotype that does not take account of real variation. Its symbolic connotation may not even apply to a majority of people in the developed part of the capitalist world. In order to avoid the stereotype we must think of a range of different forms of work and learning. But, still, the workplace is a powerful metaphor hovering over the reference to these particular types of work, hinting at a specific spatial and sensual workplace, as well as being a general representation of work and workers organised by capitalist modernisation.

The meaning of 'workplace learning' is to a large extent derived from the notion of workplace and is a similar amalgamation, on the one hand referring in general to the workplace as societal institution, and, on the other hand persuasively indicating a spatial and sensual reality that can only be understood in specific cases. There are still huge numbers of industrial workplaces that fit into the stereotypical image. Most of them have very little space for learning, and mostly learning is adaptation to prescribed operations and intensive training. Innovations in products or technology may very well be seen as just disturbances, requiring further adaptation. But even these one-sided repetitive work operations have their mental aspects. Management strategies of quality assurance draw the attention to certain critical aspects and extract the experience of workers for the fine-tuning of technologies and procedures. Now and then major changes in the process may strongly affect single jobs, even making people redundant or requiring entirely new job designs. Automation and digitalisation show a great many such changes, which for the individual worker mean total retraining or reorientation of fundamental roles and operations (Sawchuk, 2003; Tietel and Löchel, 1990). Such situations, of course, display great challenges – and in the case of a good organisation they also offer learning opportunities.

The concrete reality of many workplaces is, however, dramatically different from the stereotype. Industrial workplaces are developing rapidly. Most have much more space for agency, discretion and improvement for individuals or groups. A good deal of industrial work has turned into planning, control and adjustment, as well as communication and logistical tasks. Reporting has become an integrated aspect of manufacturing and service work. In this context of changing work processes, trade union policy as well as participative management have established new strategies of work process improvement, with the aim of offering learning opportunities and improving the content of work (Aagaard Nielsen and Svensson, 2004; Ellström, 2006; Gustavsen 1992).

Other types of jobs and workplaces are growing quantitatively. The proportion of office work and different types of business services is increasing, while the difference from manufacturing is becoming less obvious. Office work is undergoing many processes of industrial reorganisation similar to those that took place in manufacturing. Automation and semi-automation by means of information technology are shaping data processing, accounting and text processing in a way that shows similarities to industrial development. The learning needs and learning opportunities following on from this development for those workers employed

117

in direct operations are increasingly similar to those in manufacturing, but at the same time the new bifurcations of work – in the form of new divisions of labour between professional and technological work on the one hand and direct operational work on the other – offer new learning opportunities for those workers employed in the development of technology. The term 'professional work' is problematic, especially in an international context, since the term 'professional' is used in quite different ways in different language communities, and with a reference to significantly different societal organisations of professional work. But with a wide definition 'professional work' – referring to knowledge-based work – is increasing. And the entire labour market dynamic mediates between the development of knowledge and technology on the one hand and the development of work tasks on the other.

One area of professional and semi-professional work is of quite another kind: work with people – human services – is characterised by a direct personal relation between worker and the 'work objects', who are human beings themselves. Care and human services require the direct personal engagement of the workers in the field. In some cases it is more difficult to develop generalised procedures, independent of context, clients and professional workers. To some extent this means the application of competences developed in workers' 'private' lives, in relation to family members, friends and neighbours, to their professional work (Hollway, 2006; Salling Olesen, 2004a; Weber and Dybbroe, 2003; Weber and Salling Olesen, 2002).

This broad variety of the qualitative requirements of work situations as well as of the relation between work task, worker and the skills and competences of the workers must be kept in mind in the following discussion. The stereotypical meaning of workplace learning will mislead us to construct an overly simple and uniform relation between work and learners. But as indicated above, changing work conditions are received in the context of individual life experiences and cultural context. Learning is part of a subjective relation to work and is based on knowledge and culturally mediated competences.

Based on a number of empirical studies into professional learning I have developed a heuristic model (Salling Olesen, 2003, 2004a), which may help to organise this complexity into a handy set of factors that need to be taken into consideration to understand workplace learning (Figure 10.2). This figure does not provide any general model of workplace learning. It suggests that learning in the workplace occurs in a specific interplay of experiences and practices, identifications and defensive responses. It also suggests that learning in the workplace is not a response to technical and organisational conditions only; it mediates the specific relation between three relatively independent dynamics: the societal work process, the knowledge available and subjective experiences of the worker(s). Based on professions, the model pays particular attention to the cultural nature of the knowledge and skills with which a worker approaches a work task, whether they come from a scientific discipline, a craft, or just as the established knowledge in the field. It is the assumption that this model can be helpful as a heuristic device for examining the dynamics of workplace learning situations in general.

## Work – labour – wage labour

Workplace learning is defined by work. This chapter is written in the context of the modernised capitalist society of our time. Even though we have distinguished between different types of work – industrial production, business services, professional work, management, care, etc. – and have pointed out that work does not necessarily have a place in its most obvious sense, we have referred to the societal organisation of work as wage labour – being the societally dominant format – and we have referred to working people assuming that they are generally wage labourers.

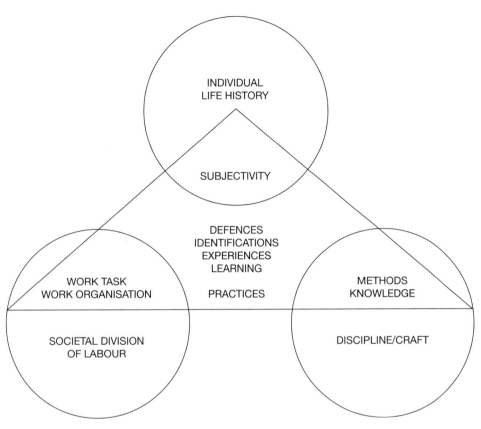

*Figure 10.2* Work, knowledge and learners.

We have pointed out some particular qualities of some types of work that make workplace learning different or even make the notion obsolete. And we have noticed that learning workers are not just wage labour, they are human beings with a life before, outside and after work.

In this part we want to focus more explicitly on work and work-related learning, which falls beyond our delimitation so far, but which ought to be treated in its own right.

One category is work that is carried out in a place that is not defined as a workplace. In the first instance we can mention the home, where substantial and necessary work is carried out in a place that is normally defined as the opposite of the workplace. But nobody – at least no woman – will deny that it actually is a place where work is being done. And, of course, a lot of learning also takes place here. In some respects this learning may be of a more challenging and comprehensive nature, e.g. the learning of parents related to childbirth and raising children, and innumerable everyday life changes. The association between wage labour and home work is most clearly experienced by women – the latter as an extra workload but also as an ambiguous relation to work that may, apart from stress, also develop specific competences. In some empirical studies we have seen a substantial shift in the work identities of women who completed vocational training and gained access to new segments of the labour market that are more comfortable or more demanding, but we have also seen a continuous ambivalence related to the double engagement in home and workplace (Salling Olesen, 2004a). We developed the hypothesis that the very handling of this ambivalence was a very basic competence in relation to workplace learning.

This is not just an individual experience, it is a societal construction of work relations in modern societies. Regina Becker-Schmidt (2004) developed the concept of 'gender relations' in the societal sense, not between individuals, but between the two sexes, which is mirrored in the work organisation of society at large. Becker-Schmidt, taking the point of departure in women's work, sees the latter as an 'ensemble' of engagements that are equally necessary and mutually complementary. Her argument runs that wage labour (carried out by men or women) is only possible on the basis of the reproductive and relational work carried out in the family and the close community (predominantly female work). This gender relation has developed historically with modernisation, from the large family households of landowners and craft workshops, and the more or less pragmatic survival units of the poor, to the nuclear family of modern society. The family on the individual level appears as a love relation as well as one of exploitation and domination, but it is still also a functional work unit. The family and the closer community are, in the perspective of this wider concept of work, also workplaces where learning takes place. The gender relation secures not only physical reproduction but also, by means of historical female socialisation, the learning and transfer of competences and dispositions that are necessary for human survival and thriving. This may seem to be playing with words, but it is not.

First of all, it illuminates the historical nature of work and the workplace. The societal division of labour in relation to gender has illustrated this clearly in modern times. Much of the work within 'female domains', which used to be private, female 'non-work', has been transformed into wage labour in caring institutions and hospitals. The skills and competences that women used to develop and display in family relations are being transformed, with more or less difficulty, into wage labour skills, as briefly indicated in the example of the cleaner earlier in the chapter. However, against the background of changing competence profiles, this type of transformation may be relevant for a wide range of work processes – e.g. competence for care is not only relevant to the caring professions.

Second, it draws attention to a wider competence range as well as to the deeper and more complex significance of work-related learning than a narrow outlook on learning in formal wage labour workplaces might provide. In a particularly significant way, the gendered nature of work shows how experiences and social learning are based on embodied dispositions, and thereby illustrates better than most other aspects that workplace learning is always part of the identity processes of workers.

The other expansion of the notion of workplace learning beyond the modernised capitalist wage labour context concerns, of course, all those work situations at the margins of global capitalism. As mentioned above, the learning systems of pre-modern cultures based on agriculture, fishing and hunting, and the elementary urban division of labour are not limited to the workplace, but involves the wider social setting, reminding us of the invisible relations that are also active in the workplaces of a formal modern economy.

But globalisation mostly transforms these cultural settings, creating and transforming workplaces and working relations that are neither simple and holistic nor modern and well defined. I would like to mention particularly those workplaces in the informal economy that are very characteristic of developing economies. The informal economy in different variations forms an alternative form of societal organisation of labour to that of the formal economy. It may in some cases be rather similar, mainly based on tax evasion, but most often it forms a different type of organisation where family relations, trust, clientelism and friendships are interwoven with strictly economic exchange in ways that would be deemed illegitimate in a formal capitalist market economy. The informal economy is not a local phenomenon, but assumes a global significance when looking into the effects of family bonds on worker migration and the economic effects of the financial transfers related to it.

These expansions or alternative notions of work might help to understand what seems natural to us in a historical and relative perspective. Work and workplaces could be something different; work may develop new qualities, and workplace learning is just as much related to individual and collective identities, and to cultural frameworks of knowledge and skills, as it is to the specific work process in question and the physical workplace. Such an consideration may enrich our understanding of workplace learning in its most simple form.

## Recent approaches to theorising workplace learning

Workplace learning has traditionally been seen in an instrumental way, described only by its supposed aim, namely to adapt to requirements of a specific work process, excluding the subjective and creative moments of learning, and mostly also reducing the complexity of work to already existing, fixed practice. More recent learning discourse, on the contrary, is very abstract, talking about individuals and general process qualities such as 'creativity' and 'innovation' without specification, and about the workplaces in similar general terms such as 'organisations', 'tools', 'knowledge' and 'practices'. But we need to look for theorising that recognises the specific quality of learning and its relation to particular workplaces, i.e. all the cells in the matrix (see Figure 10.1, p. 115).

The new interest in learning in the workplace and for work has also advanced a number of new theoretical approaches to learning that pay particular attention to the dialectic between learner and work environment. First of all, this has exposed the significance of the social context of learning and the fact that workers are not just individual learners, but are involved in an organised social environment.

Some of this thinking has been inspired by anthropological theory and research into cultural transmissions of work practices and habits to new members of a community, whereby learning is seen as conditioned by gradual inclusion in a community of practice, i.e. the group of people whose shared practice also forms a cultural framework and meaning making (Lave and Wenger, 1991). This is a useful way of thinking because it emphasises the fact that learning is embedded in social and cultural contexts, and sees work process and workplace as environments of everyday life, meaningful agency and engagement of workers. Later these approaches have been influenced by cultural psychology and cultural theory, transformed into activity theory. In this theoretical framework, work is seen as social activity and learning as the cultural transfer of knowledge and skills that take place within activities (Engeström et al., 1999). Together these anthropological and cultural theories seem to form the most influential reference of learning in a social context in recent years, also outside their own tradition (e.g. Hodkinson and Hodkinson, 2003). But they have – rightly, I think – been criticised for a conservative bias, because they tend to see learning as a process of adaptation to an already established practice or organisation under consideration, i.e. a particular workplace. Relating to the matrix (see Figure 10.1, p. 115), the societal dimension of work and learning may be especially downplayed. The social outlook is pretty narrow. Later versions of these theories (Wenger, 1998) seem to go beyond this problem by generalising the notion of 'community of practice', so that it is not in this sense necessarily a concrete social context. In this model, learning is connected with the trajectory of the learning individual across and between a number of communities in which he or she participates and negotiates meaning and identity. But it remains very vague as to how

121

community of practice relates to all the interesting – and conflicting – social affiliations of the worker in, and in relation to, the workplace: formal organisation of a company, informal organisation(s) at the workplace, professional affiliations, trade unions, family situation and so on. Also the rooting of the subjective engagement remains vague. Practical analytical application of the concepts tend to identify the subjective meaning making with the 'negotiation of meaning' in one specific context defined by task in the organisation, by work process similarity, or by location. Wenger's point of the trajectory across, and the potential conflicts between, different communities of practice is mostly lost in this application. In a more systems theory-oriented approach of cultural learning theory the dialectic between particular (individual) perspectives and meaning making is left behind, while the interest is on generalised relations and the organisational totality of systems functionality (or dysfunctionality). The important innovation that anthropological or cultural theory brought into learning theory is fading when the workplace is not a 'place', whereas a new conception of the relation between location and learning is emerging (Engeström et al., 1999).

Anthropological and cultural theory has given important help in seeing learning as a social process. But it does not provide good answers to the other important question in relation to a theory of learning: what are the driving forces and dynamics of the way in which the learning individual makes meaning of and 'negotiates' his or her identity in social communities that already exist, and when can we say that this ongoing modification of identity and meaning making has the quality of learning and not just of change? To create a theory of learning requires the theorising of the learner as a subject in its own right, and of the processes that he or she is undergoing. Whereas the subjective meaning of the immediate workplace seems obvious, the fact that 'work ' and 'being a worker' are societal life conditions, and the meanings and conflicts related to this fact, are conceptually edited out.

Until now it seems difficult to connect the attention to social context in work-related learning theory with the concepts of the individual learner and learning potential that are available in learning psychology and cognitive science, but it has been attempted and some contributions are more rewarding than others. Billett (2001), in his book on workplace learning, refers – critically, though – to the concept of 'situated learning' to frame the learning within the workplace, and combines this with constructivist learning psychology (Piaget and onwards), seeing learning as the result of practical problem solving in the work process in analysis of specific cases. This brings out important insights: first, attention to the agency of the learner and, second, the socially embedded and material nature of learning.

In this approach the particular workplace 'materiality' is characterised by its 'affordance' of learning opportunities. This abstraction may have to do with the strategic, practical development perspective, and limits the theorising of the social context. But I also see some limitations in the understanding of the subjective aspects of learning.

Learning processes are understood as the cognitive aspect of problem solving (and knowledge building). This is eye-opening in the context of the theme of promoting learning in the workplace, because it emphasises the fact that workers are learning all the time, and that there are endless possibilities to create workplaces that are more supporting and stimulating for workers' learning. The generalising distinction between routine and non-routine work does define work situations in relation to the experience of the learner subject, and hence their subjective status as problems to be solved or not. This distinction organises the possible meanings embedded in the materiality of work processes around the dichotomy of routine or challenge. Though thought-provoking, this dichotomy also seems to be a simplification. It seems equally interesting that work means more than being a routine or a challenge to specific workers, related to his or her subjective experience. It also seems likely that the possible learning outcome (or no outcome) of the meeting between the task or problem and the worker depends on much more complicated relations between worker and the perceived challenges.

Eraut (1994) has analysed professional knowledge and competences in terms of the ways of knowing and using knowledge in work situations. He provides interesting and distinctive discussions of theories of knowledge and knowledge use, and relates them to the features of the work situation and the type of work tasks being performed. In this way he provides a useful corrective to the generalising theories of knowledge and professions, and especially emphasises the process-based and contextual nature of knowledge use. Indirectly, this is also a way of theorising learning, in principle within a similar model as in Billett's analyses, namely by theorising how knowledge is being used and how knowledge resources are being modified in problem-solving processes of work.

The point of departure in this contribution to learning theory is restricted to (or at least strongly prioritises) the cognitive dimensions. Eraut's mission is to study the development of knowledge and competence. The subjective meaning of work and knowledge for the professional (Salling Olesen, 2001a, b) – the personal experiences of the learner, the specific nature of the work – appear only as ad hoc analytic observations and distinctions.

These approaches refer to different types of work, from manual low-skilled to professional work, and jointly they contribute a great deal to a general understanding of working life as social practice, of work tasks and knowledge use, and also of some aspects of learning. But they share the tendency to operate with abstract learner subjects, individuals without history – both in the sense of an individual life history and in the sense of societal and cultural attributes, e.g. gender. The ambition to theorise the subjectivity of work and learning as subjective process would not deny these insights but would in some respects reinterpret them and in some respects complement them.

Referring to the elementary context of learning in the social setting of the workplace, you can see workers learning new skills and different insights, and neglecting or resisting others. Both the differences and the contents and directions of learning may be understood in the context of a concept of subjectivity, which is sensitive to individual life history and social experience.

## Theorising workplace learning as subjective experience

Learning is a subjective process, characterised by intention, agency and engaging interaction with something outside yourself and this also applies to workplace learning. This section will outline a conceptual framework for studying workplace learning from this perspective. Subjectivity is the way of relating to the world that is. Subjectivity is a relation; individuals constitute themselves as subjects by making the world an object of reflection and action, and build experience, i.e. the type of consciousness that reflects one's own interaction with, and presence in, the world (Dewey, 1938; Negt, 1999; Salling Olesen 1989, 2006b). In social philosophy and theory terms workplace learning can be seen as a subject–object dialectic between societal work and individual identity (Negt 2001; Salling Olesen, 1999, 2004a). Human subjectivity is a product of socialisation, in which a specific version of cultural and social experience – our work society – is embodied in the individual, becoming a complex of conscious and unconscious preconditions for subjective agency and experience. Opposite liberal ideas of the independent, free and rational subject, a dialectical notion of subjectivity assumes that it is a historical and dynamic entity, which is only gradually constituted in a (learning) relation to biological and historical reality. Individual workers carry their specific social history with them into the workplace, and they embody the experiences learned in the workplace in their subjectivity. In conceptual terms this notion assumes a psycho-societal approach to the relation between individual and society (Salling Olesen, 2002, 2007).

Recently, life history and biographical approaches (Salling Olesen, 2004c; Weber, 1998, 2001) have been used to understand the subjective aspects of workplace learning (Hodkinson *et al.* 2004; Salling Olesen 2006b), both in basic research and in practical application to support learning processes. Some versions focus on the individual biographical account of the significance of work and career, while others seek to elaborate the conceptual framework to be sensitive to the social and cultural backgrounds of subjective orientations (such as gender, ethnicity and work identities; such as the identification potential in specific qualities of work processes). In order to understand this constitution process, life history research may draw on insights into the embodied and symbolic forms of psychodynamic processes, characterised by contradictions and tensions. It interprets individual subjective reactions and consciousness in the context of culture. Culture exists in socially articulated practices, meanings and symbols, which are sometimes attached to artefacts (e.g. a machine) or stabilised in social institutions (e.g. a work organisation), but which are also embodied in the agents of the culture, and (re)produced in their agency and consciousness.

The concept of experience can help us to understand the consequences for learning. This notion connects the immediate experience in everyday life with its societal as well as its individual psychic dimensions. Three aspects or modalities of experience, three relatively independent dynamics, which are mediated through each other in every agency and learning process, can be distinguished: learning in everyday life, life (history) experience and cultural knowledge. Social practice in everyday life builds a situated and embodied experience, that is structurally determined as societal history (in this case by the development of societal labour). We can speak of an industrial experience, or an urban experience, or a female experience of double work. But it is based on the consciousness informed by collective cultural experience in the form of knowledge, symbols and norms (institutions). Crafts or professions build on collective experiences that have been tried out and stabilised, but in principle we can also see general subjects and skills such as literacy and mathematical modelling in this perspective.

The use of cultural knowledge in particular everyday life is mediated in an individual life history, with interference between cognitive and emotional aspects, which comes in a specific version in every individual. Every individual has a specific emotional and social experience that has embodied a general view of the world and ways of seeing him- or herself in specific relations, e.g. to certain work operations, certain people, etc.

For learning we are particularly interested in the interference between cognitive and emotional aspects of the individual building experience in specific social contexts. Clearly the subjective handling of the social context in everyday life is not only a cognitive phenomenon. Consciousness in practical interaction incorporates all its meanings for the experiencing subject(s), the emotions connected with this situation, the perception of oneself and the situation. Learning is activated and influenced by emotional involvement, comprising moments of learning as well as moments of defence. The relation to routines is a good example.

Everyday life in work is characterised by collective and habitual routines. New phenomena are perceived as well-known phenomena – a basic mechanism of recognition and complexity reduction – but this cognitive process is also guided by the social and relational emotions attached to these well-known categories, to the situation and to projected expectations within it. The observation and systematisation of deviations and novelties – be they new phenomena or new contextual factors – are processes of cognitive as well as emotional and social change of the learner. Change may be challenging, it overloads the learner, and in some cases it is particularly threatening, because it activates life historical experiences or emotional relations in an anxiety-provoking way. In a life situation flooded with impulses and demands, individual and collective mechanisms of consciousness building preserve the individual from anxieties and ambivalences.

The maintenance of a routine is therefore not as passive as the notion seems to suggest; it is most often an active editing of perceptions and knowledge in accordance with possible practices – a defence mechanism. I call this form of consciousness 'everyday life consciousness', with a concept (*Altagsbewusstsein*) borrowed from Leithäuser and others (Leithäuser, 1976; Leithäuser and Volmerg, 1989). The selection and interpretation of perceptions is part of an active, psychic and cultural acquisition that defines the situation in a practicable way – i.e. through active, partly collective defence mechanisms.

For the individual subject, knowledge has the status of cultural resources of understanding. Professions and well-defined occupations (crafts) can be used as simple cases with a well-defined body of knowledge. Let me give another example from my own empirical research into General Practitioners (GPs). I studied the subjective handling of everyday work situations with the use of a professional biomedical knowledge base (Salling Olesen, 2006a). Sometimes this knowledge will allow the GP to understand and take action in a relatively unproblematic way, while in other cases it does not provide a very helpful framework. There is an ongoing dynamic tension between collective societal experience (the biomedical knowledge) and the clinical problem-defining and solving experience of the GP. It is handled by an individual who is strongly subjectively involved (by the professional obligation to omnipotent agency, as well as by being in immediate relation to another human being with a problem, anxieties, etc.). Since it is incumbent upon the professional, for the patient and for his profession, to be able to take action, it sometimes means that the situation must be defined (by biomedical knowledge) in a way that allows action (e.g. write a prescription) that is a defensive process, whereas it may also at the same time lead to learning (recognising a specific problem of the patient or a high frequency of particular symptoms). The interpretation of the specific situation is, on the one hand, informed by his or her personal life experience and will, on the other hand, piece by piece, contribute to his or her life experience as well as to the clinical collective experience – although this is an extremely slow process.

I think professions exhibit an exemplary case for the interplay between societal knowledge and subjective learning in work situations, because professional knowledge is, so to say, societally assigned to the work situation, and the professional worker is subjectively involved in a complex practice in which he or she is responsible for a knowledge-based agency – which is in the end morally and politically related to the quality of the work product or the service provided. I think this point can be generalised to the situation of workers in general, although some situations may be less subjectively engaging and the relevant knowledge resources may be less well defined and so on.

The example from professional work and learning also highlights the pivotal role of language use in learning. In line with Wittgenstein's concept of language games we can see the meanings of language as defined in a social interaction, and being in continuous renegotiation, containing the ongoing experience process of the participants in the language game and their communication. Problem solving in a work situation is in this perspective a combined application of language resources to define, and react to or deliberate, the task, and an impulse that a person can bring into the language game. We have already seen how this language use will involve not only the cognitive operation of the task and the situation, but a complex of emotional investments that may heavily influence the cognitive operation.

It may be necessary to state that, in addition, the elements in the psychic dynamic are socialised. This does not mean to install a social determination instead of a biological. Alfred

125

Lorenzer's materialist theory of language socialisation (1972) offers an essential link between individual subjectivity (the embodying of psyche) and culture and language (the codifying of knowledge and collective experience in disciplines or discourses). Combining these theoretical elements we can develop a holistic endogenous framework of understanding subjectivity and learning. Learning can be seen as a situated adoption of language games, as signification of experiences of the learner subject. It should be emphasised that language is not just the one discursive language. Any social symbol system that enables communication and shared meaning can be seen as a language. Different languages may have different features, and especially they may relate differently to the societal institutions of communication and work on the one hand, and to the sensual and embodied experience of the language user on the other.

Embodied life experience conditions experience building throughout life – and hence also a condition for learning. The defensive and reality-oriented aspects are dialectically connected in a way of knowing about the situation and the world, and learning takes place in this dialectic. The emotional dynamics of consciousness and knowledge can be conceptualised by the psychoanalytic concepts of the conscious, the preconscious and the unconscious. On the individual level of learning this is the dynamics of knowledge construction. In social practice the cognitive activity is conditioned in subjective dynamics, for example, the GP in his or her consultation.

## Conclusion

Every work situation has elements of subjective engagement, cognitive construction and social interaction. Social meanings established in language use are always surrounded by a 'halo' of surplus meaning, referring to the amount of experience that is very societally structured, but not culturally recognised, remaining at the boundary of socialisable meaning. The materiality of work, which is reflected in the space between bodily and conscious experiences and their linguistic articulation, between the individual and cultural meanings, and the multitude and transformations of cultural meanings (e.g. academic knowledge), are the terrains in which subjective meaning making and learning takes place.

## References

Aagaard Nielsen, K. and Svensson, L. (eds) (2006) *Action Research and Interactive Research*, Maastricht: Shaker Publishers.

Becker-Schmidt, R. (2004) 'The transformation of gender relations as a learning project', in H. Salling Olesen *et al.* (eds) *Shaping an Emerging Reality: Researching lifelong learning*, Copenhagen: Roskilde University, Graduate School in Lifelong Learning, pp. 49–66.

Billett, S. (2001) *Learning in the Workplace: Strategies for effective practice*, Crows Nest, NSW: Allen & Unwin.

Boud, D. and Garrick, J. (1999) *Understanding Learning at Work*, London: Routledge.

Eraut, M. (1994) *Developing Professional Knowledge and Competences*, London/Washington: The Falmer Press.

Garrick, J. (1998) *Informal Learning in the Workplace: Unmasking human resource development*, London: Routledge.

Gustavsen, B. (1992) *Dialogue and Development: Social science for social action*, Stockholm: Arbetslivscentrum.

Hodkinson, P. and Hodkinson, H. (2003) 'Individuals, communities of practice and the policy context', *Studies in Continuing Education*, 25(1): 3–21.

——, ——, Evans, K. and Kersh, N. with Fuller, A., Unwin, L. and Senker, P. (2004) 'The significance of individual biography in workplace learning', *Studies in the Education of Adults* 36(1): 6–26.

Hollway, W. (2006) *The Capacity for Care*, London: Routledge.

Lave, J. and Wenger, E. (1991) *Situated Learning: Legitimate peripheral participation*, Cambridge: Cambridge University Press.

Leithäuser, T. (1976) *Formen des Alltagsbewusstseins*, Frankfurt: Campus.

—— and Volmerg, B. (1989) *Psychoanalyse in der Sozialforschung*, Opladen: Westdeutscher Verlag.

Leledakis, K. (1995) *Society and Psyche: Social theory and the unconscious dimension of the social*, Oxford: Berg Publishers.

Lorenzer, A. (1972) *Zur Begründung einer Materialistischen Sozialisationstheorie*, Frankfurt: Suhrkamp.

Negt, Oskar (1999) *Adorno's Begriff der Erfahrung: Das Argument Sonderbd 229*, Main: Zweitausendeins. Reprinted in Der unterschätzte Mensch (2001).

—— (2001) *Arbeit und meschliche Würde*, Göttingen: Steidl.

Rainbird, H., Fuller, A. and Munro, A. (eds) (2004) *Workplace Learning in Context*, London: Routledge.

Salling Olesen, H. (1989) *Adult Education and Everyday Life*, Roskilde: Adult Education Research Group 1/1989.

—— (1996) 'Experience, life history and biography', in H. Salling Olesen and P. Rasmussen (eds) *Theoretical Issues in Adult Education: Danish research and experiences*, Copenhagen: Roskilde University Press, pp. 65–86.

—— (1999) 'Experience, work and learning: theorizing the subjective side of work', Keynote speech at the First Researching Work and Learning Conference at Leeds University, published in an extended form, in H. Salling Olesen and K. Weber (eds) (2001) 'Space for experience and learning: theorizing the subjective side of work', in K. Weber (ed.) *Experience and Discourse*, Frederiksberg: Roskilde University Press, pp. 27–58.

—— (2000) *Professional Identities as Learning Processes in Life Histories*, Papers from the Life History Project 12, Copenhagen: Roskilde University, Department of Educational Studies.

—— (2001a) *Professional Identities as Learning Processes in Life Histories*, Paper for the ESREA conference on Biography and Life History Research, Roskilde. (Also published in K. Weber (2001) *Experience and Discourse*, Frederiksburg: Roskilde University Press, pp. 59–84.)

—— (2001b) 'Professional identities as learning processes in life histories, *Journal for Workplace Learning* 13(7–8): 290–7.

—— (2002) 'Experience, language and subjectivity in life history approaches: biography research as a bridge between the humanities and the social sciences?', Paper presented at the International Sociology Association conference, Brisbane, in *Working Papers from the Life History Project 14*, Roskilde, pp. 5–44.

—— (2003) *Regenerating Professional Identity? Knowledge, Work and Gender*, Paper presented at the Third Researching Work and Learning Conference, Tampere.

—— (2004a) 'Work related learning, identity and culture: New work – new genders? New genders – new work?, Paper published in E. Kurantowicz, A. Bron, H. Salling Olesen and L. West (eds) *Old and New Worlds of Learning*, Wroclaw: Wydawnictwo Naukowe, 2005, pp. 25–39.

—— (ed.) (2004b) *Shaping an Emerging Reality: Researching lifelong learning*, Copenhagen: Roskilde University, Graduate School in Lifelong Learning.

—— (2004c) 'The learning subject in life history: a qualitative research approach to learning', in M. H. Menne and A. Barreto (eds) *A Aventura (Auto)Biographico: Teoria & Empiria*, Porto Alegre: EDIPUCRS.

—— (2006a) 'Be(com)ing a General Practitioner: professoinal identities, subjectivity and learning', in L. West, P. Alheit, A. Siig Andersen and B. Merrill (eds) *Using Biographical and Life History Approaches in the Study of Adult and Lifelong Learning*, Frankfurt am Main: Peter Lang Verlag, pp. 125–42.

—— (2006b) 'Experience and Learning', in S. Billett, T. Fenwick and M. Somersville (eds) *Work, Subjectivity and Learning*, Zürich: Springer.

—— (2007) 'Theorising learning in life history: a psycho-societal approach', in NIACE (eds) *Studies in the Education of Adults* 2: 38–53.

—— and Weber, K. (2001) 'Space for experience and learning: theorizing the subjective side of work', in K. Weber (ed.) *Experience and Discourse*, Copenhagen: Roskilde University Press, pp. 27–58.

Sawchuk, P. (2003) *Adult Learning and Technology in Working Class Life*, New York: Cambridge University Press.

Tietel, E. and Löchel, E. (1990) 'Der computer als evokatorisches objekt', *Psychosozial* 13: 92–102.

Weber, K. (ed.) (1998) *Life History, Gender and Experience: Theoretical approaches to adult life and learning*, Copenhagen: Roskilde University, Adult Education Research Group.

—— (ed.) (2001) *Experience and Discourse*, Frederiksberg: Roskilde University Press.

—— and Dybbroe, B. (2003) *She Was Really Out of Control: Aggression and Identification in Social Work*. Paper presented at the ESREA Biography and Life History Research Network Conference, Canterbury Christ Church College.

—— and Salling Olesen, H. (2002) 'Chasing potentials for lifelong learning', *Zeitschrift für Qualitative Bildungs-, Beratungs- und Sozialforschung (ZBBS)* 2, Leverkusen: Leske+Budrich, pp. 283–300.

Wenger, E. (1998) *Communities of Practice*, Cambridge: Cambridge University Press.

# 11

# Trends in lifelong learning in the US workplace

*Karen E. Watkins and Victoria J. Marsick*

Lifelong learning, a concept Faure *et al.* made more visible in 1972, was heralded as a vision of the future for adult education. How is lifelong learning taking on form and substance in the US workplace? To answer that question, we first highlight key interactive forces that are shaping lifelong learning, in combination with rapidly changing technology, especially changing demographics, globalization and the rise of new forms of organizing and working. Framed by earlier work on informal and incidental learning (Marsick and Watkins, 1990) and the learning organization (Marsick and Watkins, 1999; Watkins and Marsick, 1993), we discuss emerging learning practices and look at tensions that arise as the vision of lifelong learning becomes reality.

## Environmental trends

### Changing demographics

The US workforce is growing at a slower rate than in the past and is richer in diversity. The Rand Corporation (2004) describes a trend in "workforce composition . . . toward a more balanced distribution by age, sex, and race/ethnicity" due to declines in male labor force participation, increases in female participation rates, and an inflow of immigration "with Hispanics and Asians being the fastest-growing such groups in the workforce." A shrinking workforce in industrialized nations is not unique. But it does pose challenges, given competition for talent and educated workers, a mix of generations at work, and the brain drain posed by the loss of experienced workers (Gandossy *et al.*, 2006).

The Committee on Prospering in the Global Economy of the 21st Century (2005) elaborated economic implications of changing demographics. "The Organization for Economic Cooperation and Development (OECD) projects that the shrinking workforce will hamper economic growth rates between 2025 and 2050 for Europe, Japan, and the United States" (p. 9). Especially impacted is US leadership in science and technology, for example:

- Aging and a decreasing "supply of new scientists and engineers who are US citizens" means that "Immigration will continue to be critical to filling our science and engineering needs" (p. 9).
- And "rapidly increasing costs of caring for the aging population will further strain government budgets," pressure expenses of industry, and "make it more difficult to allocate resources to R&D or education" (p. 9).

The report adds, "More than 70 million US baby boomers will retire by 2020, but only 40 million new workers will enter the workforce. Europe is expected to face the greatest period of depopulation since the Black Death," while "East Asia (including China) is experiencing the most rapid aging in the world." While the workforce in industrialized countries is shrinking, it is rapidly growing elsewhere. For example, "India's working-age population is projected to grow by 335 million people by 2030—almost equivalent to the entire workforce of Europe and the United States today" (p. 9).

A key challenge is the loss of specialized knowledge and skills through retirement. A United Nations seminar entitled, "Learning in the 50+ years," considered ways to keep older workers connected to the workforce long enough to prevent a significant disruption of global economies. Nevertheless, a brain drain is predicted within the next decade as baby boomers retire and generation X workers move into mid-life transition career changes. A critical skill will be to create a culture of knowledge sharing—particularly difficult in many cultures where protecting one's knowledge is a source of power (Salopek, 2005). Salopek describes Delta Airlines' strategy for debriefing retirees and sharing knowledge via video-based learning systems. Other organizations have adopted similar practices.

Aging will not be the only challenge facing the US. In *America's Perfect Storm* (Educational Testing Service, 2007), the interaction of three forces will have a significant impact on our future—divergent skill distributions, a changing economy, and demographic trends. The authors point to falling graduation and literacy rates such that the US now has one of the highest gaps between best and least proficient among OECD countries. A knowledge economy demands high levels of skill and education, making competition for skilled workers intense but opportunities for a growing population of lower-skilled individuals grim. Large numbers of new workers come from immigrant populations, many with low English language proficiency. These forces increase the divide between the skilled and unskilled, and attenuate the economic opportunities of large segments of the US population. Both education and employer-sponsored training are fundamental tools to narrow this gap but significant shifts are needed in the allocation of resources both by government and by corporations to ensure that these individuals will not be lost in a new economy.

### Globalization

Immigration will continue to increase. "Over the past 40 years, in fact, global migration of both less skilled and highly skilled workers has doubled. Among developed nations, the United States is by far the biggest recipient of labor inflows " (Gandossy *et al.*, 2006: xiii). Globalization affects organizations in many more ways than immigration. Combined with technology, globalization means a 24/7 virtual workplace in which projects are shared across many different time zones so that, literally, employees wake up to discover the changes made in products, services, and other work tasks by their counterparts somewhere else around the globe. Globalization has given rise to many new forms of organizing and working, including the practice of moving "the work itself around the globe in search of lower operating costs . . . This controversial practice, known as offshoring or strategic sourcing, is primarily an American phenomenon with three-fourths of offshored jobs currently originating in the United States" (2006: xiv).

With more and more companies employing a global workforce, workplace learning must transcend an increasingly diverse, remote, and contingent workforce. Scully (2006: 28), who is researching emergent structures of work, observes that labor market changes "include a shift from stable and rigidly defined, firm bounded jobs to contingent, project based work linked to flexible production networks that extend across and beyond single firms and occupations" (Benner, 2002; Campbell, 2004; Cappelli, 1999; Osterman, 1999).

### Implications for work and learning

A key implication of these shifts is competition for the best talent (Gandossy *et al.*, 2006). Diversity and globalization require transformed human resource practices to align with multiple cultural norms. Organizations must accommodate an aging workforce, workers with elder care responsibility, dual career couples, and younger workers, and learn how to help these very different kinds of employees work well together.

The Rand Corporation forecasts:

> Employees will work in more decentralized, specialized firms; slower labor growth will encourage employers to recruit groups with relatively low labor participation; greater emphasis will be placed on retraining and lifelong learning; and future productivity growth will support higher wages and may affect the wage distribution.
>
> (2004: 2, para. 3)

The Society for Human Resource Management (2005) notes that global competition puts pressure on training and education systems linked to constant pressure for up-skilling, in part to combat the impact of off-shoring domestically, but also to respond to rapid technological development.

As organizations build global operating capabilities, workers must learn and perform "without walls" (Chang, 2006), often having to adapt to working virtually, across cultures and time zones. Chang notes that this requires greater knowledge of the organization and its market context, as well as process management skills. These trends, along with some negative responses to learning through technology and an attitude of entitlement among generation Y workers, will lead to a growing decline in loyalty of the workforce. This will make it more difficult to determine how to leverage learning for the long term.

## Trends in workplace learning

As workplaces, employees, and the nature of work change, so too have learning needs and preferences, which in turn has driven changes in the way in which support for lifelong learning is conceptualized, delivered, assessed, and certified.

### Increased importance of both training and informal learning

> As companies come to see innovation as the key to revenue growth and profitability, as nations come to see innovation as the key to economic growth and a rising standard of living, and as the planet faces new challenges that can be solved only through science and technology, the ability to innovate will be perhaps the most important factor in the success or failure of any organization or nation.
>
> *Committee on Prospering in the Global Economy of the 21st Century*, 2005: 9–8

131

The Institute of Management and Administration (2004) argues that there is a renewed emphasis on training in today's organizations because learning is central to innovation, which in turn drives the growth that many organizations pursue. They cite reports from the training field that correlate expenditures on training with financial performance, hours of training provided with satisfaction with the organization as a place to work, and reports by human resource professionals that they are investing more in raising employee skill levels.

Investments in workplace learning are as important to individuals as to organizations. Organizations expect employees to be self-directed and, reciprocally, many employees seek jobs that enable them to fulfill their own talents and goals. "Empowered by technological and economic forces, today's workers, especially those with critical knowledge and skills, have taken the driver's seat when it comes to controlling the direction and substance of their professional lives" (Gandossy *et al.*, 2006: xvii). The concept of a free agent worker, who moves from job to job to enrich his or her opportunities, stands side by side with unemployed jobseekers whose skills and talents do not match the jobs at hand.

Demand for highly educated, skilled workers and competition for top talent has led to the positioning of "career development opportunities (or the absence thereof) as a primary determinant of their decision to stay with (or leave) their current employer" (Bassi *et al.*, 1998: 60). Long-term employability requires currency in skills, and leads to demand for training and development as a benefit of employment. This trend can inadvertently increase the gap in access to knowledge for non-privileged employees who receive little or no training, or must seek out their own education and training using their limited time and resources.

There are discrepancies in whose learning gets supported. Organizations prioritize learning for top management, high potential employees, and knowledge workers. The manpower development focus of society is on unemployed, low-skilled workers. This leaves many workers in charge of their own development, a trend reinforced by many organizations that explicitly expect employees to take charge of their own learning. Self-directed learning, learning to learn skills, and access to online learning options are all responses that human resource developers must be able to structure and deliver.

Informal learning has also become a major modality for knowledge and skill acquisition in organizations (Dale and Bell, 1999; Malcolm *et al.*, 2003; Marsick and Volpe, 1999; Marsick and Watkins, 1990; Marsick *et al.*, forthcoming). Bruce *et al.* (1998) suggested that as much as 70 percent of all workplace learning is informal. Organizations have accordingly increased their interest in informal learning (Cross, 2007) and reorganized the way they provide formal education and training as a smaller part of a package of ongoing learning services and expectations that employees will learn continuously. Bassi *et al.* note that knowledge-intensive work requires the development of "new skills sets . . . to encourage learning through informal, natural means and to direct that learning in ways that help organizations meet their business goals" (1998: 56). Increased emphasis on informal learning approaches that develop skill in solving problems and in making judgment calls require group and individual strategies that use an individual's work as a starting point for learning. Good examples of learning integrated with work can be found in leadership development strategies.

Leadership development is, according to Bassi *et al.*, "arguably, the most critical issue faced by organizations today" (1998: 57). They also note that corporations are investing more in internal executive education programs than university-based education programs, and that many such initiatives are built around action learning. Action learning (Marsick and Watkins, 1999; O'Neil and Marsick, 2007; Revans, 1982) is an approach to learning that begins with real problems, brings together individuals to address the problems, and teaches them the tools of critical reflection and creative problem solving in order to learn and find better solutions.

Underlying this work is a view that learning should make a direct contribution to increased success.

A major mode of leadership development is executive coaching for leaders identified as high potential or top-level managers. No longer a remedial strategy, coaching provides one-on-one learning tailored to unique needs in the turbulent, complex, often lonely context in which most executives find themselves. Coaching focuses learning on real needs and organizationally defined objectives, and avoids challenges of otherwise having to transfer what is learned back into one's work context. As Bassi *et al.* (1998) note, measuring effectiveness is a significant challenge for this type of learning.

## Technology-enabled learning

Revolutions in technology have enabled learners to access what they want to know, when they want to know it, in the way in which they would like to learn it. Course delivery is increasingly technology-based, or blended with face-to-face formats, but even more importantly, technology enhances the ability to integrate learning into work practices and workflow. E-learning strategies escalate daily. Desktop learning, electronic performance support systems, podcasts, and voice recognition systems are changing the location and capacity for delivering learning to individuals across time and space divides. Despite access and design problems, technology-mediated learning is often used to make learning available to more and more employees of varying levels and at dispersed locations. Rossett (2007) notes that the percentage of courses delivered via technology increased from 9 percent in 2000 to 15 percent in 2002 to 28 percent in 2004. Rossett adds that, for companies receiving *best* awards from the American Society for Training and Development (ASTD) in 2005, 32 percent of all learning content was delivered via technology. But what is more interesting than sheer increases in volume is that "Technology is changing the how, where, and when of learning" (p. 50).

Bassi *et al.* (1998) underscore the way in which technology shifts the control and design of learning from providers to learners themselves. The evolution of electronic performance support and intelligent tutoring systems (ITS) enables employees to learn what they need when the demand arises because expertise and feedback are built into these systems. This also represents considerable savings. According to Bassi *et al.*, for example, the US Air Force Research Center achieved "a 50 percent reduction in the amount of time to train to the same criteria" using ITS and "saw a 34 percent increase in student performance over a given amount of training time" (1998: 68). These increases were attributed to the fact that, unlike other computer-based learning systems, ITS assesses where the learner is and presents the information based on those needs. ITS also critiques performance in real time, responding to the learner's actions and answering questions. The system may provide a remedial brush-up on a given task based on performance. Like executive coaching, these systems work one-on-one, adapting to unique learning needs. Instructional designers envision a world where learning objects—byte-sized independent, reusable modules of content—can be combined to quickly compile training programs.

In many ways these trends reflect a return to the former reliance on personalized, contextualized "Go Sit By Nellie" approaches to on-the-job training. The practices often rely on informal and incidental learning strategies, mediated by technology, that enable organizations to target learning to individual needs without the abstractness or complexities of fixed time, fixed place, trainer, or SME-reliant approaches. An extended example is IBM Learning Solutions' (2005) emerging Learning on Demand system, consisting of Work Apart Learning, Work Embedded Learning, and Work Enabled Learning. Work Apart Learning is enhanced formal training linked to just-in-time learning that is increasingly self-directed. For example, modules are available online to enable self-study when new capabilities are needed. Work Embedded Learning embeds knowledge in work roles and makes it available during action. For example, sales professionals can access databases of information, short tutorials linked to job tasks, or experts who can help with non-routine questions as they negotiate sales with customers through an enhanced electronic performance support system linked to electronic work tools. Work Enabled Learning involves coaching and self-initiated learning reviews.

## Knowledge communities

An alternative to individually sought and directed learning is reliance on knowledge communities and communities of practice, which grow out of collaborative problem solving. Communities of practice are naturally occurring, emergent groups at whose core are interdependent, usually practical interests (Wenger, 1998). Lave and Wenger (1991) refer to sharing knowledge of practice through stories—a repertoire of tacit know-how, an evolving "database" passed on over the water cooler, through blogs, through professional groups, both at and away from work. Knowing communities (Cahondet, 2005) are an evolution of the idea of communities of practice. "A knowing community can be defined as a gathering within the organization of individuals who accept to exchange voluntarily and on a regular basis about a common interest or objective in a given field of knowledge" (p. 1). Knowing communities are distinguishable from other organizational structures:

- They have no clear boundaries nor hierarchy that controls their work.
- They are bound by their common passion and commitment.
- Their interactions are governed by trust grounded in respect for common norms.
- Knowledge is validated, interpreted, and vetted by the community.

## Democratization of knowledge

An exponential change in the accessibility of knowledge has been coupled with a hunger for ideas in their infancy so that ideas can be used in many ways and for many purposes. According to von Hippel:

> The trend toward democratization of innovation . . . is being driven by two related technical trends: (1) the steadily improving *design capabilities* (innovation toolkits) that advances in computer hardware and software make possible for users; (2) the steadily improving ability of individual users to *combine and coordinate* their innovation-related efforts via new communication media such as the Internet.
>
> (2005: 2; italics in original)

These trends also impact design and delivery of workplace learning. Baldwin and Clark (2005) argue that knowledge does not directly translate into economic value but rather must first be translated through a design or a set of instructions that turn knowledge into marketable products, activities, or artifacts.

Design architecture, especially option-rich modular-design architecture, leads to enhanced economic potential. Illustrative of this is open-source coding through which communities of user designers create highly effective products that defy and compete against traditional closed-source coding. This represents a fundamental shift in thinking about innovation and who controls inventions. The modularity of the design architecture permits innovation and collaborative knowledge creation.

These toolkit designs change the playing field because anyone can access and use the structural information that underlies much professional work. Novices have access to the same tools as experts and professionals. Not only can novices design custom homes, automobile assembly lines, or even legal documents—they can also work with manufacturers of these products, learn what customers want, and develop an extraordinary repertoire of potential designs and ideas.

Designers of workplace learning, too, must think in terms of creating tools for learners to create their own learning programs—from simple self-directed learning designs to more complex, web-enabled knowledge management tools that draw on knowledge repositories. An example, designed for reading with elementary school children, put at teachers' disposal multimedia, interactive lessons emanating from printed children's books that were almost infinitely adaptable by both the teacher and the children. Children could read the story, become virtual reporters interviewing the characters who respond orally, or "google™" various terms to learn more.

Open-ended, influence-able designs are needed that start with where learners are and can be controlled by both the learner and their guide. Electronic courses seldom draw on all available options. They resemble an electronic textbook more than a software program for learning integrated with work. By contrast, one organization envisions a desktop knowledge management system that would enable assembly line workers to access a brief seven-minute learning module or a longer, more interactive learning program on the task. Workers could search a "stockpile" of sample assembly designs along with ratings of their effectiveness. They could access both a tutor and continually updated information on how others rated the tutor's helpfulness. The tutor could import the novice's assembly design to his computer and make suggested changes that the novice would see as notations initialed by the tutor, and which the novice could accept or reject. The novice's proposed assembly design would be added to the in-house repertoire or stockpile of possible designs. What makes tools like this so powerful is immediate, continuous updating and responsiveness to varying ability levels. These tools are fully focused on getting the task done with the requisite learning strategically targeted, modular, and "just enough."

## Tensions for workplace learning practitioners

Lifelong learning in the workplace offers both hope and caution. Hope arises from democratization of knowledge and flexible options for learning. The trend in workplace learning is learner-defined, idiosyncratic learning with the role of the workplace learning professional often moving to virtual or personal coach. Making learning available when and how it is needed requires changes in design and support. Tools can help people tailor learning experiences and collaborate with others to co-create knowledge. Organizations need to create learning–rich environments that emphasize informal learning and open learning designs rather than formal, less flexible learning approaches.

But as lifelong learning moves from vision to reality, tensions arise around solutions that are being put into place. Certification can be a double-edged sword, as noted by Gorard *et al.* (1999), who argue that credentialing privileges learning in some domains over other areas for enrichment. A tension surrounding credentialing is the lack of portability of all skills. How does one translate knowledge gained informally through work and learning experiences into transportable, meaningful "credentials"? Certification carries many benefits, not the least of which is the protection of demonstrated excellence. In an age when people frequently change jobs, by necessity as well as choice, certification helps explain skill sets to new employers. At the same time, it requires a common body of knowledge and mechanisms for certification that are fairly implemented. Given the value placed on knowledge today, and the blurring of national boundaries in knowledge work, questions can also be raised about how societies are rethinking policies that support access to needed resources for lifelong learning for all people.

## Implications for learning in the workplace

Increasingly, human resource and organizational developers, and adult and continuing educators, are finding that their fields have become too diffuse and pervasive to define—and to control. Just as education is no longer the domain of schools or universities, training and development and lifelong learning are less and less the exclusive territory of professional adult educators or trainers. Perhaps they never were. As the authors cited in this chapter note, learning and innovation are being democratized and we will be impacted by this trend as have other professional fields. Lifelong learning as a concept has caught our imagination as never before because people are working longer, and work is changing at a rate that requires that they learn at an equal rate. To make the problem even more dramatic, the learning demands of all jobs are escalating at a significant rate—making the learning needs of every individual in the workplace that much more intense and continuous. Where workplace learning has traditionally focused primarily on new hires, management, and professional/technical workers, it now must provide tools to support learning at all levels of the organization. Little wonder that the emphasis has moved to greater reliance on informal learning strategies such as self-directed learning, mentoring and coaching, electronic support systems, and e-learning and other desk-top learning approaches. Those who hope to facilitate workplace learning have to be sufficiently agile, with a deep portfolio of learning approaches and opportunities to support the learning needs of individuals in this context.

The capacity to collaborate across borders, barriers, and boundaries will become a discriminating feature of a global economy. As it has in the past, it will be one of the most important roles of human resource and organization developers going forward—helping engineers work with non-engineers, helping corporations with different cultures work together, helping individualist Western cultures interact with more collectivist cultures. We will need to focus our efforts on the contexts of workplace learning—both organizationally and societally—and work to enact policies and practices that ensure a learning rich culture.

We will be designers of tools for others' learning rather than developers and deliverers of all of that learning in the future. We need to design and support instructional approaches through which learners co-create knowledge, such as action learning, knowledge communities, and knowledge management tools.

These then are the emerging tasks of those who would facilitate learning in the workplace of the future. They will be multilingual, operating across cultures and languages, and facile in multiple pedagogies. As always in the intensely interpersonal and interactive world of human resource developers, they themselves remain the primary tool—their capacity to learn their life long; to model and coach others in living and working in a multilingual, multicultural, multimedia context—will determine their effectiveness. In *Rising Above the Gathering Storm* (Committee on Prospering in the Global Economy of the 21st Century, 2005):

A letter from the leadership of the National Science Foundation to the President's Council of Advisors on Science and Technology put the case even more bluntly: "Civilization is on the brink of a new industrial order. The big winners in the increasingly fierce global scramble for supremacy will not be those who simply make commodities faster and cheaper than the competition. They will be those who develop talent, techniques and tools so advanced that there is no competition."

(2005: 1–3)

## References

Baldwin, C. and Clark, K. (2005) *Designs and Design Architecture: The missing link between "knowledge" and the "economy,"* Paper presented at the Advancing Knowledge and the Knowledge Economy Conference, National Academies, Washington, DC.

Bassi, L., Cheney, S., and Lewis, E. (1998) "Trends in workplace learning: supply and demand in interesting times," *Training & Development* 52(11): 51–75.

Benner, C. (2002) *Work in the New Economy: Flexible labor markets in the Silicon Valley*, Malden, MA: Blackwell Publishing.

Bruce, L., Aring, M.K., and Brand, B. (1998) "Informal learning: the new frontier of employee and organizational development," *Economic Development Review* 15(4): 12–18.

Campbell, J.L. (2004) *Institutional Change and Globalization*, Princeton, NJ: Princeton University Press.

Cappelli, P. (1999) *The New Deal at Work: Managing the market-driven workforce*, Boston, MA: Harvard Business School Press.

Chang, Richard Y. (2006) "Workplace trends and leadership resolutions for 2007," *Chief Learning Officer* 5(12): 18.

Cahondet, P. (2005) *On Knowing Communities*, Paper presented at the Advancing Knowledge and the Knowledge Economy Conference, National Academies, Washington, DC. Available online at http://advancingknowledge.com/drafts.htm (accessed October 8, 2005).

Committee on Prospering in the Global Economy of the 21st Century (2005) *Rising Above the Gathering Storm: Energizing and employing America for a brighter economic future*, an Agenda for American Science and Technology, the National Academy of Sciences, National Academy of Engineering, Institute of Medicine. National Academy of Sciences. Available online at www.nap.edu/catalog/11463.html (accessed August 24, 2005).

Cross, J. (2007) *Informal Learning: Rediscovering the natural pathways that inspire innovation and performance*, San Francisco, CA: John Wiley & Sons.

Dale, M. and Bell, J. (1999) *Informal Learning in the Workplace*, DfEE Research Report No. 134, London: Department for Education and Employment. Available online at www.dfes.gov.uk/research/data/uploadfiles/RB134.doc (accessed January 3, 2007).

Educational Testing Service (2007) *America's Perfect Storm: Three forces changing our nation's future*, Princeton, NJ: Educational Testing Service.

Faure, E. (Chair), Herrera, F., Kaddoura, A.-R., Lopes, H., Petrovsky, A.V., *et al.* (1972) *Learning to Be*, Paris: UNESCO.

Gandossy, R. P., Tucker, E., and Verma, N. (2006) *Workforce Wake-up Call*, Hoboken, NJ: Hewitt Associates and John Wiley & Sons.

Gorard, S., Fevre. R., and Rees, G. (1999) "The apparent decline of informal learning," *Oxford Review of Education* 25(4): 437–54.

IBM Learning Solutions (2005) *On Demand Learning: Blended learning for today's evolving workforce*. Available online at www.clomedia.com/content/templates/wp_clo_whitepaper.asp?articleid=1128&zoneid=26 (accessed January 2, 2007).

Institute of Management and Administration (2004) "The top 6 trends training managers can expect in '05," *Managing Training & Development* 4(12): 1–14.

Lave, J. and Wenger, E. (1991) *Situated Learning: Legitimate peripheral participation*, Cambridge: Cambridge University Press.

Malcolm, J., Colley, H., and Hodkinson, P. (2003) "The interrelationships between informal and formal learning," *Journal of Workplace Learning* 15(7/8): 313–18.

Marsick, V.J. and Volpe, M. (eds) (1999) *Informal Learning on the Job*, Advances in Developing Human Resources 3, San Francisco, CA: Berrett Koehler Communications.

—— and Watkins, K. (1990) *Informal and Incidental Learning in the Workplace*, London and New York: Routledge.

—— and —— (1999) *Facilitating Learning Organizations: Making learning count*, London: Gower Press.

——, ——, Callahan, M.W., and Volpe, M. (forthcoming, 2009) "Informal and incidental learning in the workplace," in M.C. Smith and T.G. Reio (eds) *The Handbook of Research on Adult Development and Learning*, Mahwah, NJ: Lawrence Erlbaum Associates.

O'Neil, J. and Marsick, V.J. (2007) *Understanding Action Learning*, New York: AMACOM.

Osterman, P. (1999) *Securing Prosperity: The American labor market: How it has changed and what to do about it*, Princeton, NJ: Princeton University Press.

Rand Corporation (2004) "The future at work: trends and implications," Research brief. Available online at www.rand.org/publications/RB/RB5070 (accessed August 21, 2005).

Revans, R.W. (1982) *The Origins and Growth of Action Learning*, Bickly: Chartwell-Bratt/Lund, Sweden: Studenlitteratur.

Rossett, A. (2007) "Leveling the levels," *Training and Development* 61(2): 49–53.

Salopek, J. (2005) "The new brain drain," *Training and Development* 59(6): 23–4.

Scully, E. (2006) "New media as a new medium: work, learning and institutionalization in emerging, project-based occupations," unpublished dissertation proposal, New York: Teachers College, Columbia University.

Society for Human Resource Management (2005) "Workplace Visions®: learning to compete in a knowledge economy," *SHRM Workplace Trends Program*, Issue 3. Available online at www.shrm.org/trends/visions/ (accessed August 21, 2005).

von Hippel, E. (2005) "Democratizing innovation: the evolving phenomenon of user innovation," Paper presented at Advancing Knowledge Conference, The National Academies, Washington, D.C.

Watkins, K. and Marsick, V.J. (1993) *Sculpting the Learning Organization*, San Francisco, CA: Jossey-Bass.

Wenger, E. (1998) *Communities of Practice*, Cambridge: Cambridge University Press.

# 12

# Trade unions
## From workers' education to lifelong learning

*John Holford*

## Introduction

For two centuries, trade unions and workers' movements have been moving forces in adult education and lifelong learning. For most of the twentieth century this was most evident in the major institutions of the field. In Britain, for instance, the Workers' Educational Association (WEA) has long been the largest single provider of adult education courses; for extended periods similar organisations have flourished in Australia, Canada, New Zealand and across Scandinavia (Peers, 1972). Sixty years after Arbeit und Leben ('Work and Life') was established by the Federal German trade unions to support post-war democratic reconstruction, it still provides political education for 300,000 young people and adults each year (Arbeit und Leben, 2007).

Yet trade unions' importance in lifelong learning by no means stops with the stimulus they provided to famous educational providers; neither is it merely historical. Trade unions, and the political parties and pressure groups they have generated, have also contributed to lifelong learning through the direct provision of education and training; through supporting autonomous or semi-autonomous educational bodies; through pressing for public or institutional policies and provision that will (in their view) encourage adult learning, or shape it in desirable ways; and through bargaining with employers to ensure better provision of education and training in the workplace.

This chapter provides an account and discussion of trade union engagement with lifelong learning. The account is historical and developmental, and is grounded principally in the British experience, although some examples from other countries are considered. It is not suggested that the British experience is typical, let alone exemplary; but focusing on a single country, for which there is a reasonable body of research, does permit a more rounded longitudinal account. In addition, at various times British models have been adopted – arguably, even imposed – on other countries, and this may also prove instructive.

## Background

Twentieth century politics were shaped by labour movements. In Europe and North America, the century began with syndicalism and socialism in the ascendant. The October Revolution dominated geopolitics for seven decades. In some countries, such as Germany and Spain, authoritarian opposition to revolutionary socialism was key. In others, such as Britain, socialist revolution took a more muted, social-democratic, form; the changes it brought about were nonetheless fundamental. By mid-century, Britain's Labour Party – very much, at that time, the child of the trade union movement – had established a 'mixed economy' and a 'welfare state'. Trade unions had a central role to play in this: many prominent former trade union leaders were members of Labour governments; even under Conservative governments, trade unions were consulted. The pivotal British pressure group was the Trades Union Congress (TUC), whose deputations were 'well briefed and able to discuss matters on equal terms with government ministers' (Griggs, 2002: 7). As Griggs points out, though lacking the power to make the decisions, 'they often won the argument' (p. 7). Indeed, it was in response to an expression of concern by the TUC that Winston Churchill, as Prime Minister, penned his celebrated defence of adult education:

> There is perhaps no branch of our vast educational system which should more attract ... the aid and encouragement of the state than adult education ... This ranks in my opinion far above science and technical instruction ... The appetite of adults to be shown the foundations and processes of thought will never be denied by a British administration.
>
> (Churchill, 1953)

Many mid-twentieth-century British trade union leaders concerned themselves with education; relatively few had received a substantial formal education. The best educated had generally pursued their own education, often in evening classes, and often in private study. Arthur Creech Jones, for instance, a Cabinet Minister in the 1945–50 Labour government, studied in evening classes after leaving school, eventually finding work in the Civil Service at the age of 16. Imprisoned for three years during the Great War for opposing conscription, he studied alone in gaol (Holford, 1995). Though incarceration was untypical, Creech Jones was one of a stratum of 'working-class autodidacts', studying in the evenings for self-improvement, often attending evening classes. Many were drawn to trade union activity and socialism (Macintyre, 1986). This 'earnest minority', comprising 'trade union and labour activists and a sprinkling of Marxists' (Macintyre, 1986: 39), formed the bedrock of British union leadership from the 1920s until the 1970s – the years of trade union growth and ascendancy.

Such people valued education – serious study – highly, not only as an abstract social necessity but from personal experience as a means to self-improvement. They were personally committed to adult education; many continued to enjoy participation in classes and study-conferences; and many saw provision of classes as a good means of social improvement for working-class adults. While they led the labour movement – and they formed not only the national, but also the local and often the workplace leadership – the value of adult education was taken largely for granted. Thus we find during this period trade unionists in strong support of the work of such organisations as the WEA, the Workers' Educational Trade Union Committee (WETUC), the National Council of Labour Colleges (NCLC), and residential colleges for workers such as Ruskin in Oxford, Newbattle Abbey in Scotland, and Coleg Harlech in Wales.

This enthusiasm for adult learning was not peculiar to twentieth-century trade unions. The very earliest stirrings of working-class organisation in Britain in the late eighteenth and early nineteenth centuries were marked by what Brian Simon called 'extraordinary efforts at self-education among the nascent working class' (1992: ix). The first meetings of the London Corresponding Society in 1792, for instance, did not just call for parliamentary reform; they did so after five nights discussing 'every point of view in which we were capable of presenting the subject to our minds' (quoted in Thompson, 1963: 18). In the broadest sense, self-education became fundamental to working-class organisation, as the very fabric of labour movements over the two succeeding centuries testifies. Trade unions have not just defended their members: their members have assembled in meetings and discussed what they should do, what approaches would work and why. They have become aware of gaps in their knowledge and understanding, and tried to fill them. In the process, they have formed views of who they were, why they were entitled to be treated fairly, what fairness means, and so forth.

All social movements form identities, organisation and strategies; but each does it in its own way. By and large – there were, of course, national variations – labour movements have put education at a premium. 'Instruction is the want of all,' declared the London Corresponding Society in 1794; it sought 'to place instruction within the reach of every citizen' (quoted in Simon, 1974: 180). So, quite soon, labour organisations were not only engaged in *self*-education; they set about demanding, and campaigning for, education for all. At its second annual meeting (1869), the British TUC, for instance, called for 'nothing short of a system of national, unsectarian, and compulsory education' (quoted in Simon, 1974: 362).

## Unions and educational reform

Trade union advocacy of public education has had both quantitative and qualititative aspects: pressure to expand the volume of public education, and to influence what went on within the public educational system. The British TUC, for instance, focused in the 1930s on raising the school-leaving age, and breaking down the 'class barrier which assumes children of working-class parents do not require the fuller education given as a matter of course, to those fortunate enough to be born in families substantially above the poverty line' (quoted in Griggs, 2002: 33). In the 1960s it argued for the abolition of selective secondary schools – and for comprehensive secondary schooling. On the qualitative side, it addressed issues from school medical treatment to the political content of school textbooks between the wars, the nature of work experience in the 1950s, and the provision of school meals in the 1960s (Griggs, 2002).

Of course, the nature of initial education is a fundamental aspect of *lifelong* learning, but trade unions have also pressed for reforms in public post-school education. In the 1960s, for instance, British trade unions pressed for day-release arrangements so that young workers (15–17-year-olds) could broaden their vocational education (Griggs, 2002: 268–70). The TUC supported the formation of the Open University in the 1960s, but was concerned that efforts should be directed mainly toward 'helping those where educational needs were greatest' – that is, the generally working-class people who had themselves left school at the minimum school-leaving age (quoted in Griggs, 2002: 317). Concern for social equity has been a continual theme in trade union educational thought. With the advance of neo-liberal political and economic agendas since the 1980s, this concern has often been combined with a more apparently conservative defence of the status quo; at the same time, the impact of labour and trade union attempts to influence public educational policy has diminished.

## Workers' education and role education

While trade union and labour concern about education has often been expressed through attempts to shape public policy, the self-help dimension has always been strong. As we have seen, this is to be found from the very first days of the labour movement, and played a strong role in shaping the movement's identity. During the early twentieth century trade unions began to construct more formal educational institutions. We find trade unions engaging supportively with the formation of Ruskin College at the turn of the century, and trade unionists were ever-present in the early years of the WEA. At a meeting to set up what became the first WEA branch, for example, over 20 trade unions were represented (Jennings, 1973: 15). These initiatives were deeply invested with the ideologies of the time: trade union members were at the forefront of the disputes with Ruskin College, for instance, which led largely Marxist supporters of 'independent working-class education' to break away and form a separate, overtly socialist, Central Labour College in 1909; this ideological dispute framed the institutions of workers' education in Britain until the 1960s, and its echoes could be heard for another decade or two.

What these bodies shared was a commitment to provide 'workers' education'. This was self-help, but with strongly collective overtones. As early as the 1920s, Margaret Hodgen explained it comparatively. 'As a man and a bread-winner,' she wrote, 'the worker seeks knowledge in order to . . . improve his earning power.' This was the role of vocational training: by enhancing their skills, a few might 'emerge from the constraints of working-class existence' entirely. But workers' education was 'fundamentally different':

> As a unit in a group effort for more complete participation in the common life, the working-man . . . has been frankly sectarian. He has sought information as a member of a social class, a voter or a trade union official . . . [W]orking-men enrolled as students in the [workers' education] movement are committed to some programme of class action, for which special knowledge and a peculiar technique are necessary. In other words, Workers' Education . . . is a discipline for a specific purpose. It concerns itself in teaching the social sciences to men and women who seek to use that knowledge for class, and possibly social, advancement.
>
> (Hodgen, 1925: 4–5)

Such workers' education was in many respects the successor to nineteenth-century self-education: motivated by the desire to strengthen labour's organisational capacity, and by the belief that doing so would bring collective benefits for workers – whether for members of a union, or for an entire social class.

Through the twentieth century, unions developed this agenda. In Britain until the Second World War, they largely 'subcontracted' education to the WETUC and the NCLC, specialist educational bodies that were fiercely opposed to one another. (The chief ostensible reason for this was that the WETUC accepted funding from the government, and was committed to education in pursuit of objective truth; the Marxist labour colleges took acceptance of state funding as evidence that the WEA and WETUC had become agents of the capitalist state, and that *ipso facto* their teaching would be biased.) After the Second World War, unions both developed the capacity and saw the need to develop their own educational operations: in the 1940s and 1950s, the TUC and several individual trade unions developed education departments and training colleges. By the mid-1960s these were strong enough to supplant the NCLC and the WETUC, both of which were absorbed into a new TUC Regional Education Service (Corfield, 1969; Holford, 1993; Millar, 1979).

The TUC's first move was to assert its direct control over the field. As George Woodcock, the TUC's general secretary put it, when the TUC 'moved into a field of activity . . . we must move in with TUC traditions and TUC characteristics' (TUC, 1964: 484). Having established control, the question was what to do with it. The starting point was to consign the ideological disputes that had dominated NCLC–WETUC relations, and the attitudes of many trade unionists educated by them, to history. This was achieved through focusing on the key priority for trade unions at the time – arguably, at any time: the education of workplace union representatives. These people – volunteers elected by their fellow-workers to represent them in the workplace – were responsible for day-to-day bargaining with management on labour relations matters; they were also key to union organisation in the workplace. No one knew for sure exactly how many there were in Britain, but estimates in the 1960s ran between 100,000 and 200,000 (Holford, 1993: 77). As with any large group of volunteers, asked to undertake an often challenging role, there was considerable turnover. The challenge was therefore a considerable one, but, by the late 1960s, the TUC had settled on a clear strategy.

The strategy had five main elements. First, the focus was on 'role education': the education of union workplace representatives (or 'shop stewards' as they were then commonly known) in how to undertake their work in that role. This approach had been developed since the early 1950s, by tutors in trade unions, universities and the WEA, and involved active methods (such as role playing) and the use of 'genuine' material (such as collective workplace agreements), rather than subject-based study. Second, although the programmes were to be controlled by the trade unions, they were to be delivered through collaboration with public educational organisations. After a decade or so of debate and negotiation, this came to mean not only using the facilities of colleges and universities, but also obtaining an annual grant from the government to help pay the fees that the educational institutions charged. Third, the TUC sought, and eventually achieved, legal rights for union representatives to take time off work with pay to attend trade union courses. Fourth, although there was to be a partnership with the state, employers were to be kept as far as possible at arm's length: beyond allowing the shop stewards time off work to undertake the training, the control of what went on in trade union courses was to be a matter for the trade union to decide – in conjunction with the professional educators in the colleges and universities. This was achieved mainly through the establishment of a course development unit at the TUC, staffed by professional educators, which prepared a range of printed learning packages; these not only set out what was to be taught, but also provided model activities and timetables. Fifth, and finally, there was a very assiduous 'courting' of the college and university tutors who were to teach the courses: this included not only staff development events for them, but also the development of a professional ideology. Tutors were to be committed to union aims, rather than merely knowledgeable about labour relations; those who did not measure up were progressively eased out (Holford, 1993).

This structure was introduced during the 1960s and 1970s – the period of trade union growth and hegemony that coincided with extended periods of Labour government. No sooner had it been consolidated, however, than the 1980s ushered in the era of neo-conservative politics and rapidly globalising market capitalism that is with us today. This has radically reduced trade union membership and density, and shifted the balance of those union members who remain from private sector, manufacturing industries to public sector services. For over a decade British trade unions defended the institutional status quo in union education; and, given the adverse circumstances, with some success. But in the early 1990s the government grant, diminishing for some time, was finally lost. Legal rights to time off for union training remained, but in the adverse climate became increasingly difficult to enforce. In the circumstances, the network of colleges and tutors providing trade union courses was substantially eroded – a process reinforced by massive institutional changes in public sector post-compulsory education.

## Union education in the learning age

In the face of the neo-conservative onslaught of the 1980s, British trade unions began to evolve new strategies – though this was an extended and sometimes painful process. Initially labelled the 'new realism', these new approaches stressed services and support for members rather than collective bargaining. This was a distinct shift away from the ethos and approach that had dominated 'role education'. However, it was not only that the stratum of union workplace representatives was now much smaller; more significantly, the labour relations strategies on which union educational curricula had been based were losing credibility. Union education was training shop stewards to fight battles they could no longer hope to win.

Of course, the fundamental sources of union weakness lay not in educational curricula but in politics, economics and the legal framework that shaped workplace industrial relations. From the Second World War until about 1980, 'relationships between employers and employees [in Britain] were characterised by extensive involvement of trade unions'. But collective bargaining, the norm in 1980, had become 'something of a rarity by 1998', according to the (authoritative) Workplace Industrial Relations Surveys (Millward *et al.*, 2000: 227–8). Managers tended to communicate directly with employees, rather than working with unions – despite the fact that, revealingly, 'only union-based channels [of communication], and those indicating a well-established union presence, were positively associated with greater perceptions [on the part of employees] of fair treatment by management' (p. 230).

In these bleak conditions, union educators sought more appropriate and 'realistic' strategies and curricula. One of these was to prove important not only for what union education comprised, but also more generally for union activities and strategies. At the end of the 1980s, the National Union of Public Employees (NUPE), working closely with trade union studies tutors from the WEA, began to develop 'Return to Learn' courses. From the perspective of union strategy, these were very different from the role education approach that had dominated the post-war period. They addressed not the union member *qua* representative, but *qua* union member: in that sense, they constituted a direct service by unions to their members. But in other respects there were strong continuities: confidence-building and personal development had been strong features in WETUC and TUC courses, but were 'brought forward to hold centre stage in the new courses', which emphasised 'the building up of study skills from scratch, using as primary materials students' own personal experiences and moving outwards and onwards from there' (Caldwell and Roberts, 2003: 268).

These new courses became the foundation for a new direction in union education. The formula proved remarkably adaptable:

> Programmes could be tailored to the needs of specific groups of union members; forms of open learning could be developed to take account of learners' needs; the curriculum could be developed and reviewed by students and tutors working co-operatively, and the courses could lead to a variety of outcomes according to individual students' needs.
>
> (p. 269)

It proved remarkably effective at attracting union members who were not 'traditional' union activists, including high proportions of women, part-time workers, the poorly paid and people whose education had ceased at the minimum school-leaving age (p. 269). When NUPE amalgamated with other public sector unions, the developing programme was adopted by the new 'super-union', UNISON. By 2006 the union was offering the following:

Through UNISON the following courses can be delivered with support from an employer:

- Communication at Work: develops practical and relevant skills in written and verbal communication.
- Starting Points: a tailor made opportunity to brush up on literacy, language and numeracy. The course has been developed by UNISON and the WEA in conjunction with the Basic Skills Agency with units mapped against emerging national standards for these skills.
- Using English at Work: this is designed for people whose first language is not English and is structured around the writing, speaking, reading and listening skills required by support employees at work.
- Learning for You: a course for those returning to education. It can provide an effective stepping stone into vocational and professional training.
- Improve your Study Skills: will help brush up academic study skills for those who want to study for a qualification at higher education level.
- Development Review Workshop: introduces employees to the development review process and builds confidence to help them get the most out of it.
- National Tests: Students on all Learning@Work courses have the opportunity to have their literacy and numeracy skills assessed with a view to preparing for and taking tests leading to Adult Certificates in Literacy and Numeracy.

(UNISON, 2006: 16)

In addition, the union had a national agreement with the Open University to provide access to a range of higher education courses.

Three significant features of these programmes deserve mention. First, they provided a new framework for collaboration with the state. Within trade union education, the tradition of suspicion about dealings with government had run deep. Marxist views of the state had extensive influence; the labour colleges may have been wound up in 1963, but the attitudes that underpinned them re-emerged in the debates around public funding in the 1970s and 1980s (Holford, 1993, esp. chs. 5–6). Arguably, training of union representatives was validated by their activity in the workplace. But if the aim of the new programmes was to provide a basis for educational progression by union members, they had to be recognised more widely. In the 1980s and 1990s, this meant securing accreditation from state-endorsed agencies in the further and higher education sector. Second, the development occurred in parallel with the re-emergence of 'lifelong learning' in international policy arenas in the early 1990s (see Field, 2006: 15–16). Of course, it is arguable that these had a common cause; but the result was that British unions found they had a workable vehicle with which to engage with the new policy agenda. The 'New Labour' government, returned to power in 1997, was unwilling to reintroduce the funding for the training of union representatives discontinued in the early 1990s, for example; but it did establish a Union Learning Fund (ULF), which provided support for initiatives that developed learning among union members more generally to support the creation of a 'learning society'. Key aims of the ULF in 2007 included 'build[ing] union capacity to sustain and embed work on learning and skills so that this becomes a core activity for all trade unions', and 'raising demand for learning, especially amongst workers with low skill levels and those from disadvantaged groups' (Unionlearn, 2007a: 3).

Third, the extension of a central thrust of union strategy beyond the education of workplace representatives meant a new role for the latter. Initially this was met informally, with former students advising those considering taking up learning. But these were gradually formalised, initially as Voluntary Educational Advisors (Caldwell and Roberts, 2003: 269). By the late 1990s the TUC had endorsed the appointment of Union Learning Representatives, and under the Employment Act 2002 it secured legal recognition for this new type of union representative. This entitled union learning representatives to 'take reasonable time off' – with pay, if they had taken appropriate education – in relation to:

- analysing learning or training needs
- providing information and advice about learning or training matters
- arranging learning or training
- promoting the value of learning or training
- consulting the employer about carrying on any such activities
- preparation to carry out any of the above
- undergoing relevant training.

(ACAS, 2003: 6–7)

The introduction of workplace union learning representatives was a major shift in British trade union strategy. Previously, the rationale for workplace representatives had always been collective negotiation and bargaining; although the day-to-day business of a 'union rep.' was often representing his or her members individually, it was overwhelmingly in ensuring fair treatment from the employer in the workplace. The starting point for the union *learning* rep., in contrast, was the personal development of the member – although an important dimension of this is ensuring the employer's endorsement of learning provision, and of appropriate time and opportunity for study.

Of course, the approach represented by the UNISON programme, and the role of the learning rep., is susceptible to the critique, as Margaret Hodgen might have put it, that union education now concentrates on knowledge to improve workers' individual 'earning power', rather than for a 'programme of class action'. Such a criticism is valid in part – but only in part. The whole strategy of unions' development of services for their members, in place of bargaining for the provision of such services from employers or governments, certainly represents a shift in the view of the role trade unions should (or can) play. However, there is a clear emphasis in much of the trade union literature that union learning fund projects, for example, should demonstrate 'the clear links between the learning and organising agendas for unions' (Unionlearn, 2007a: 3). And 'return to learn' type courses have complemented, rather than replaced, more 'traditional' programmes for union representatives: 9,594 union representatives, for instance, attended TUC day release courses in 2006/07, with a further 39,518 attending TUC short courses (Unionlearn, 2007b: 20). That this is considerably fewer than attended TUC day-release courses a quarter of a century earlier is testament to the movement's declining bargaining strength, alluded to above, rather than to lack of desire to train union representatives.

## Unions and lifelong learning policy

The direction of British trade union policy on lifelong learning has reflected the drift of trade union strategy generally since the late 1980s: an accommodation to the realities of a reduced role, and specifically a much circumscribed role at the workplace, in the context of globalised and ascendant capitalism. Any hopes – and there were very few – that under a 'New Labour' government unions would achieve the 'insider' status that they had enjoyed under previous

Labour governments proved unfounded. At the same time, while still on the periphery of policy-making, unions have rescued themselves from the 'outer darkness' into which the Conservative governments had cast them; one of the ways they have achieved this is through identifying areas in which they can ensure union concerns are broadly in line with government policy priorities.

One of the policy areas that unions have sought to make their own has been lifelong learning. The foundation on which union policy has been built is that there is a common union and national interest – which, they would argue, employers should also share – in the fundamental aim of increasing skill levels among the British workforce. This is clearly in line with long-standing trade union concerns to strengthen educational attainment, and to extend learning opportunities. While supporting this central thrust, however, trade unions have developed a specific agenda, which seeks to steer national policy in the interests of working people and their families. An example of this can be seen in unions' response to a major recent policy initiative, the Leitch review of skills.

The Leitch review (*Prosperity for All in the Global Economy: World class skills*) is the report of a working group established by the then Chancellor of the Exchequer and the then Secretary of State for Education and Skills in 2004 'to identify the UK's optimal skills mix in 2020 to maximise economic growth, productivity and social justice, and to consider the policy implications of achieving the level of change required' (Leitch Review of Skills, 2006: 143). It was chaired by Lord (Sandy) Leitch, formerly Chief Executive of Zurich Financial Services and chairman of the National Employment Panel, though its 'team' (whose role was not clearly defined in the final report) comprised officials from the two departments. It recommended 'that the UK commit to becoming a world leader in skills by 2020, benchmarked against the upper quartile of the OECD'; this implied 'doubling attainment at most levels' (p. 3). This was to be achieved by moving forward in accordance with 'principles', including:

- *shared responsibility*. Employers, individuals and the Government must increase action and investment . . .;
- *focus on economically valuable skills*. Skill developments must provide real returns . . . Wherever possible, skills should be portable to deliver mobility in the labour market for individuals and employers;
- *demand-led skills*. The skills system must meet the needs of individuals and employers. Vocational skills must be demand-led rather than centrally planned;
- *adapt and respond*. No one can accurately predict future demand for particular skill types. The framework must adapt and respond to future market needs.

(pp. 3–4)

The report is too substantial (147 pages) to be dissected in detail here. What matters, for present purposes, are the main features of trade union response. The TUC welcomed Leitch's 'broad thrust' and, in particular, its 'ambitious targets to virtually eradicate low skills and to increase intermediate and higher skill levels by 2020'. It was also pleased at various other features of the report, such as its recognition of 'the positive role of collective approaches in the workplace, such as learning agreements, workplace learning committees and collective learning funds' (TUC, 2007a: 115), though these were peripheral rather than central to Leitch's approach. However, the response was also critical in various ways. Some of the TUC's criticisms were matters of principle about how the process ought to be managed: it was concerned about 'the emphasis . . . on moving to a largely employer-led skills system' and the 'lost opportunity to develop more of a social partnership model'. It was essential that the 'voice of learners' was 'given equal weight to that of employers' and that employee needs should be 'articulated via trade unions' (p. 118). Its support for Leitch's proposal for a voluntary 'Skills Pledge' by employers was conditional on the government's remaining 'clearly committed to introducing a statutory right to training if the pledge does not lead to a sufficient rate of improvement in investment in training by employers by 2010' (TUC, 2007b: 19).

However, trade union criticisms were not limited to matters of process. The TUC also emphasised the 'important role for the public sector' in delivering skills-related programmes (TUC 2007a: 118). And, more centrally, it has stressed the importance of equity in skills development. In a paper issued in mid-2007, for instance, it focused 'on the divide between the training "haves" and "have-nots" in UK workplaces and in particular [on] the level of discrimination faced by low-skilled employees when it comes to accessing workplace training'. This divide in the labour market was 'morally, socially and economically wrong' and must be 'tackled' if the UK was to move 'to the highskills trajectory necessary for improving social cohesion and productivity' (TUC, 2007c: 1). The paper argued this case in some detail, for a policy and trade union audience, drawing on a range of recent research literature.

The trade union approach to lifelong learning in Britain can thus be characterised as endorsing government commitment to strengthening skills across the labour market. In this respect, for instance, it is at best marginally critical of the government's strong emphasis on work-related skills as forming the heart of lifelong learning. However, it is sharply sceptical that this can be effectively delivered through a market-led approach (even supplemented by government if this is restricted to episodes of 'market-failure'). It stresses the importance of public sector mechanisms of provision, and – perhaps above all – the need for approaches that will achieve social equity. It argues that workplace trade union organisation and bargaining can be valuable in encouraging employers to move the skills agenda forward for their own employees.

This shift – from seeing unions' principal function in terms of collective bargaining in the workplace, to delivering services to their members and encouraging government policies that enable their members to survive and prosper in the labour market – is one that is more strongly embedded in a number of other countries. In large part it reflects a 'realist' engagement with global markets on the part of trade unions. Singapore's National Trades Union Congress has perhaps moved furthest, and more enthusiastically, down this road, but other examples can be found internationally.

## Union education: international trends

The pattern of unions' provision of education and engagement with lifelong learning issues internationally shows some parallels with that in Britain. Surveying union education in the countries of the world, Hopkins (1985) identified five main types of objective in workers' education: individual development for its own sake – an important factor, perhaps, in Return to Learn type courses; the stability and coherence of society – particularly noticeable, at the time he wrote, in the USSR, the People's Republic of China, and their satellite countries, though he also found examples in India and Israel; social change and transformation; efficient workers' organisations; and 'improved socio-economic contributions from the workers and their organisations' (Hopkins, 1985: 26–33). The last referred to the need to train workers to participate effectively in 'health, safety and environment committees and in participatory management schemes' – and also in such workers' ventures as workers' banks, cooperative supermarkets, fishing cooperatives and cooperative housing. In terms of what should be learned, he found five main categories of curricula: 'basic general skills, "role skills" for union and workers' organisation activity; economic, social and political background studies; technical and vocational training; [and] cultural, scientific and general education' (Hopkins, 1985: 43). Such workers' education was delivered through a variety of agencies: by governments, by NGOs, by workers' organisations (especially trade unions), and by a range of 'umbrella organisations' such as UNESCO, the International Labour Organization (ILO), and various international trade union organisations.

At the international union level, education had first emerged as a priority in the 1950s and 1960s. The International Confederation of Free Trade Unions (ICFTU), for example – the largest international union organisation – first set goals for union education in 1952, and over the following decade established a fund to support such work, particularly for 'building the capacities of unions in developing countries' (Bélanger et al., 2007: 5), and was used particularly in order to fund labour colleges and ICFTU regional organisations, supporting national unions, and the educational activities of international trade secretariats (which coordinated the international activities of trade unions in specific industrial sectors). By the early 1990s, the ICFTU's education policy proposed an action programme that encompassed building union capacity, especially in developing countries and countries in transition, 'developing participative methods and regionally adaptable educational material', the global exchange of information through computers, 'integrating international issues into regional and local educational activities', and 'ongoing programme evaluation' (Bélanger et al., 2007: 6).

Summarising the common features of the educational strategies and policies adopted by the main international union bodies, Bélanger et al. identified a number of 'shared values and goals':

- Working people are not commodities to be bought and sold like goods on the global labour market, but are human beings with social, economic and political aspirations for their lives at work, at home and in society.
- Democratic political systems which promote respect for human rights, freedom of expression, cultural, ethnic and religious diversity and gender equality and which guarantee the rights of individuals of all sexual orientations and of all those with physical disabilities are best for building human-centred societies.
- All governmental bodies and employer entities, such as corporations, exist to serve the economic and social needs of people, not the reverse.
- Decent work is a basic human right which must be guaranteed to all.
- Freedom to associate in independent unions and to bargain collectively with employers under legislative protection are basic rights that workers should be able to enjoy without interference.
- Unions should be agents of social change aimed at improving the lives of their members and everybody in society.
- Education, both at the start of life and lifelong, is a basic human right and must be respected, especially as globalization is changing employment patterns and as economies are increasingly based on information handling and knowledge creation.
- Public education should be funded and organized by democratic governments and should not be subject to the privatization imperatives of international trade arrangements.

(2007: 9–10)

Bélanger et al. argue that these values and goals constitute 'the core of a global union culture', which union education promotes in various ways:

149

It can provide workers with the basic training needed to create and maintain economically viable and democratic labour organizations. It can create opportunities for reflection on the complicated issues facing labour organizations today. It can build political awareness as working people struggle to understand why their needs are subordinated to the needs of corporations and undemocratic global governing structures. It can provide working people with opportunities to see how their interests can be better served by collaborating with co-workers rather than relying exclusively on the good will of employers. It can promote gender equality and respect for cultural, linguistic, sexual and physical diversity. It can encourage young people to join and remain in unions as they struggle with precarious employment, frequently changing jobs and a lack of basic benefits such as health care and pension plans. It can help organize workers in informal economies into unions. It can help serve the lifelong learning needs of union members. And it can do much more to help develop the labour movement. Union education is an essential tool in the building of participative lifelong learning for union members, staff and leaders, as they create and strengthen unions.

(2007: 10)

They concluded, moreover, that 'whenever labour organisations come together', they emphasise the importance of education – either of union members or of the general public.

This is an impressive statement of purpose for union education internationally, but it is ambition rather than reality. While examples can be found to support all the claims made, an overall and objective assessment of achievement would be more modest. Education is always asked to deliver too much; and this is no less true of what unions ask of it than of what national governments expect. As with any educational activity, there is continual uncertainty as to whether programmes are delivered efficiently and effectively. In developing countries especially, corruption has sometimes led to misappropriation of funds. With scarce resources, the best focus for efforts and resources is by no means always easy to identify; trade unions are by their very nature highly political bodies, and resources may go where the lobby is loudest, rather than where the need is greatest. Sometimes there is insufficient capacity – expertise – to develop good programmes, or to teach them well.

In recognition of some of these problems, international trade union organisations have set out a range of priorities. These include helping unions to acquire IT equipment and to learn how to use it; developing a database and network to help share information; establishing a network of labour educators; developing a global database of information about education departments, programmes and educators; developing basic educational materials about the international labour movement, and making them available via the internet; and developing internet-based distance education programmes (Bélanger et al., 2007: 21). In order to achieve this, however, the movement needs to locate and deploy substantial additional resources.

## Conclusion

In the programme adopted by its Founding Congress, the ITUC – the international trade union organisation that, in 2006, brought together the ICFTU with the World Confederation of Labour (WCL) – asserted that 'educational programmes should reflect the main lines of action of the ITUC':

This means that union education is not an academic pursuit aimed at the impartial study of a subject such as labour relations or economics . . . Union education is not impartial.

It is aimed resolutely at the strengthening of unions as they struggle for better working and living conditions for all working people. It is education for political and workplace action with its aims set by members or affiliates. It is up to labour educators to support the work of their organizations in pursuing those aims.

(Bélanger *et al.*, 2007: 11)

This is a statement that chimes with the views about British and American workers' education summarised 80 years ago by Hodgen. Trade unions have an interest in encouraging lifelong learning by their members; they have an interest in pressing for learning opportunities to be distributed fairly within society. They know that the business of union organisation, of negotiation and bargaining, and of political lobbying and representation, is complex. Their members need educational support in order to overcome the educational, social and economic gaps between themselves and the agents of global capital. In an era of ascendant global capitalism, they have little choice but to seek accommodation with governments, and with business. Workers' education continues to support unions' organisation, strategy and identity. Their achievements are typically modest, but nonetheless provide essential defence for union members. They are likely to encourage an equity dimension in lifelong learning policy discourse. In educational terms, unions have achieved much in recent years, in profoundly adverse conditions, and have shown themselves able to adapt in the interests of their members.

# References

Advisory, Conciliation and Arbitration Service (ACAS) (2003) 'Time off for trade union duties and activities including guidance on time off for union learning representatives', *Code of Practice* 3, London: The Stationery Office.

Arbeit und Leben (2007) 'Working toward a democratic culture of citizen participation'. Available online at www.arbeitundleben.de/ (accessed 29 October 2007).

Bélanger, M., with Cunniah, D., Cairola, E. *et al.* (2007) *The Role of Trade Unions in Workers' Education: The key to trade union capacity building*, Background paper for the International Workers' Symposium, Geneva, 8–12 October, Geneva: International Labour Office.

Caldwell, P. and Roberts, S.K. (2003) 'From day release to lifelong learning: workplace education and the WEA after 1964', in S.K. Roberts (ed.) *A Ministry of Enthusiasm: Centenary essays on the Workers' Educational Association*, London: Pluto Press, pp. 259–73.

Churchill, W.S. (1953) 'Letter to the Trades Union Congress', in C. Griggs (2002) *The TUC and Education Reform 1926–1970*, London: Frank Cass, p. 205.

Corfield, A.J. (1969) *Epoch in Workers' Education: A history of the Workers' Educational Trade Union Committee*, London: WEA.

Field, J. (2006) *Lifelong Learning and the New Educational Order*, 2nd edn, Stoke on Trent: Trentham Books.

Griggs, C. (2002) *The TUC and Education Reform 1926–1970*, London: Frank Cass.

Hodgen, M.T. (1925) *Workers' Education in England and the United States*, London: Kegan Paul, Trench, Trubner.

Holford, J. (1993) *Union Education in Britain: A TUC activity*, Nottingham: Nottingham University.

—— (1995) 'Britain's forgotten Minister of Adult Education: Arthur Creech Jones and a socialist strategy for development and democracy in Africa', in S. Scott and D. Collett (eds) *Proceedings of the 35th Adult Education Research Conference*, Edmonton: University of Alberta, pp. 171–6.

—— (2003) 'Unions, adult education and post-war citizenship: the WEA and the construction of trade union education', in S.K. Roberts (ed.) *A Ministry of Enthusiasm: Centenary essays on the Workers' Educational Association*, London: Pluto Press, pp. 153–75.

Hopkins, P.G.H. (1985) *Workers' Education: An international perspective*, Milton Keynes: Open University Press.

Jennings, B. (1973) *Albert Mansbridge*, Eighth Mansbridge Memorial Lecture, Leeds: Leeds University Press.

Leitch Review of Skills (2006) *Prosperity for All in the Global Economy: World class skills*, Final Report, London: The Stationery Office, with the permission of HM Treasury on behalf of the Controller of Her Majesty's Stationery Office.

Macintyre, S. (1986) *A Proletarian Science: Marxism in Britain, 1917–1933*, 2nd edn, London: Lawrence & Wishart.

Millar, J.P.M. (1979) *The Labour College Movement*, London: NCLC Publishing Society.

Millward, N., Bryson, A. and Forth, J. (2000) *All Change at Work? British employment relations 1980–1998, as portayed by the Workplace Industrial Relations Survey series*, London: Routledge.

Peers, R. (1972) *Adult Education: A comparative study*, 3rd edn, London: Routledge & Kegan Paul.

Simon, B. (1974) *The Two Nations and the Educational Structure 1780–1870*, London: Lawrence & Wishart.

—— (1992) 'Foreword', in T. Kelly (ed.) *A History of Adult Education in Great Britain*, 3rd edn, Liverpool: Liverpool University Press, pp. ix–x.

Thompson, E.P. (1963) *The Making of the English Working Class*, London: Victor Gollancz.

Trades Union Congress (TUC) (1964) *Annual Report*, London: TUC.

—— (2007a) *General Council Report: The 139th Annual Trades Union Congress 10–13 September, Brighton*, London: TUC.

—— (2007b) *Implementing the Leitch Review of Skills*. Available online at www.tuc.org.uk/skills/tuc=13596-f0.pdf (accessed 12 November 2007).

—— (2007c) *Time to Tackle the Training Divide*. Available online at www.tuc.org.uk/skills/tuc-13698-f0.pdf (accessed 12 November 2007).

Unionlearn (2007a) *Union Learning Fund Prospectus Round 11 2008/2009*, London: Unionlearn. Available online at www.unionlearningfund.org.uk/files/seealsodocs/24308/ULF%20round%2011%20Brochure.pdf (accessed 2 November 2007).

—— (2007b) *TUC Education Annual Report 2007*. Available online at www.unionlearn.org.uk/education/learn-1811-f0.pdf (accessed 3 November 2007).

Unison (2006) *Employers Guide: Partnership workplace learning with Unison*, London: Unison.

# 13

# Lifelong learning and community

*John Field*

Ideas about the relationship between education and community have been widespread since the late nineteenth century. Concepts of community education were developed on a relatively systematic basis in the 1930s, and were taken up with some enthusiasm in the 1960s and 1970s. In some countries, such as Scotland, community education (or community learning) became synonymous with what is usually known elsewhere as adult education. Particularly in adult education, then, ideas about community education remain influential – and controversial – at a time when wider social debate has all but abandoned the notion of community. Some of the most influential social theorists of our time have focused on processes of individualisation and differentiation; today, the concept of community appears ill-suited to what Zygmunt Bauman describes as 'a society of individuals' (2005: 23). Yet for all the trials and tribulations associated with these debates, notions of community represent something important about the way in which we live together and relate to one another, and they have been used in significant ways to challenge some powerful inherited dominant ideas about the purpose and practice of education.

   This chapter provides a critical overview of the various debates about community and lifelong learning. It begins with a discussion of terminology and theory. It then goes on to trace the origins of contemporary debates about community development and lifelong learning to developments in the late 1960s and early 1970s, as part of the radical educational ferments of the same period. The chapter then examines ways in which the debate has shifted ground subsequently. First, it examines the significant linguistic shift from ideas of 'lifelong education', the term that became pervasive in the early 1970s, to 'lifelong learning' as it emerged in the late 1990s. It then looks at changing ideas of community, as a new language emerged of community enterprise and capacity building in the late 1980s, which was then challenged and supplemented – but not replaced – by a discourse of social capital at the start of the new millennium. As so often in this field, these linguistic shifts generated heated debate, and the chapter concludes by taking stock of these lively but so far inconclusive discussions.

## What is community?

What do people mean by the word 'community'? This is where controversy begins, for community is, as Newman put it, an 'imprecise, foggy word' (1979: 197). Thirty years on, it remains, according to Tett, 'a slippery concept that is difficult to define' (2006: 2). It is often used to refer to a particular geographical place, such as a neighbourhood or village; it is used to describe interest groups, such as members of a faith community; it is used to denote a shared identity, whether national, linguistic or other; and it sometimes refers to a common function, such as an occupation or profession.

Community is a broad concept that is used in many different ways, virtually all of them positive. In his concise examination of the word, Raymond Williams notes its origins in Norman French, and suggests that most uses tend to fall into five basic groups, referring to: (1) ordinary people (initially as distinguished from those of rank); (2) a state or organised society; (3) the people of a defined district; (4) the quality of holding something in common; and (5) a sense of common identity and characteristics (1976: 65). According to Williams, the belief that community represented something more immediate than society first emerged in the seventeenth century, becoming much more pervasive in the context of larger and more complex industrial societies. This sense of community meant that the word was easily absorbed into some of the radical movements of the 1960s, which saw community politics or community action as somehow more authentic and direct than more established types of voluntary work or local politics. Williams also commented that, 'unlike all other terms of social organization (state, nation, society, etc.), it seems never to be used unfavourably, and never to be given any positive opposing or distinguishing term' (1976: 66).

Sociologically, the term is often traced back to nineteenth century preoccupations with the impact of industrialisation and urbanisation on existing social arrangements. One important contribution was that of the German social theorist Ferdinand Tönnies, who distinguished between two broad types of human relationships (2001). Tönnies used the German word *Gemeinschaft*, or 'community', to describe systems of immediate face-to-face relationships that were lasting, personal and clearly understood; he believed that this type of social arrangement was being replaced by *Gesellschaft* (which can be translated as 'society' or 'association'), where relationships were more likely to be based on less personal and more formal and – he believed – artificial foundations. The French educationalist and sociologist Émile Durkheim similarly thought that the nature of society was undergoing a profound transformation, distinguishing between the mechanical solidarities of social relations in pre-industrial societies, with their simple and pre-ordained hierarchies based on habitual obedience and shared belief systems, and what he saw as the organic solidarity of modern urban capitalist societies, where people's relationships were based on the goods and services that they performed for one another, often without regard to their formal status and despite a diversity of values and beliefs (Durkheim, 1933).

Durkheim's and Tönnies' sociologies of community present quite different perspectives. Yet both are thoroughly modernist, drawing a clear distinction between past social formations and those of the present. Their ideas of *Gemeinschaft* and mechanical solidarity were applied to earlier societies, while *Gesellschaft* and organic solidarity were applied to the here and now. As Gouldner put it in a prescient review of the predicament facing sociology as a discipline, 'Modern industrial society was being conceptually cut out of its former place in a multiphased series of societies; it was being used as a central point of development' (1971: 119–20).

Much of what followed tended to be similarly ahistorical, presenting a vision of loss and breakdown as the supposedly supportive, secure and reciprocal close relations of the past gave way to the atomised individualism of the modern world. For many late-nineteenth-century adult educators, the story of community lost became a shared intellectual foundation for their educational activities, which presented an opportunity for rediscovering and rebuilding community – or 'fellowship', as it was often expressed – in the new circumstances of urban capitalism (Harrison, 1961: 307).

These themes were particularly marked in writing inspired by Christian religious ideals, which brought young middle-class social critics into the settlement movement as well as helping found the early adult residential colleges (Harrison, 1961; Bowpitt 1998; Knight 2005). Basil Yeaxlee, one of the earliest writers to use the term 'lifelong education', complained that the Great War and industrialisation together had killed off 'the spirit of fellowship', a spirit that he believed was carried into practice by the contemporary adult education movement (1925b: 52). For Yeaxlee, spiritual values represented the only durable basis of social solidarity; adult education only had a lasting impact insofar as it expressed a shared humanity – and indeed a community of interest not only among humans but of all Creation. He believed that, in the adult education movement:

> enduring results have been achieved ultimately because it has done something, whether little or much, to bring the personality of the child, the adolescent or the adult, into a living relationship with reality in other personalities, in the material world, and in the universe. It makes a man consciously a member of a universal spiritual fellowship.
>
> (Yeaxlee, 1925a: 46)

Christian influence has been largely neglected by adult education historians, yet its impact on thinking about community and education was significant, and it remains an important, if now a minority, influence in Europe and North America.

Theories of community continued to exercise social scientists in the decades after the Second World War. Social and economic changes, linked to the development of welfare state systems in much of the industrial West, meant that much attention was again focused on the fate of the working-class community as old neighbourhoods changed and established support systems were supplanted. Again, this was often presented as a story of loss – in particular, a loss of old forms of social solidarity based on locale and on similarities of collective experiences. Many of the studies of this period were based on empirical investigations into particular localities populated largely by manual workers and their families – notably, in the case of Britain, Bethnal Green in east London (Willmott and Young, 1962) and Hunslet in Leeds (Hoggart, 1957).

So far, much of this survey has been historical. And the nineteenth- and twentieth-century origins of the present debate are important; their influence lives on in a number of contemporary concerns about community and learning. However, debate continues over the concept of community, retaining a sharp political edge. Three discussions in particular have implications for people interested in adult learning. First, communitarian ideas enjoyed some popularity at the end of the twentieth century. As developed by writers such as Amitai Etzioni (1993), communitarianism was radically opposed to what its exponents viewed as the extreme individualism of contemporary Western societies. Second, the concept of social capital has recently had a dramatic impact across the social sciences; in some cases it has been used to complement existing thinking on community (as in the work of Robert Putnam (2000)), while others have tended to supplant it, to the extent that some people are extremely cautious about what appears to be a faddish intruder. Third, a number of writers have identified what they see as a profound tendency for people to take a more provisional and conditional approach to their social relationships, including intimate relationships; collective ties are loosening as people become more reflexive about, and sometimes critical of, inherited forms of behaviour and institutions.

Communitarianism attracted relatively little attention among those concerned with adult learning (the exceptions include brief discussions in Bron, 1998; Jansen *et al.*, 1998). Although there is a range of communitarian thinking, its core idea is that the demise of *Gemeinschaft*-type relations has had extremely damaging consequences for our collective well-being, and that what is now needed is to re-create forms of social solidarity that will enforce collective norms, and prevent deviant minorities from disrupting the lives of the majority. This in turn means placing a stronger emphasis on balancing individual rights with social responsibility.

Communitarianism has been widely attacked as backward-looking and patriarchal. Jansen *et al.* criticise communitarians for their focus on traditional forms of bounded solidarity and their neglect of new modes of affiliation (1998: 90). It is indeed hard to see how it can be easily aligned with a diverse and pluralistic society, where it can be difficult to identify widely shared core values. Even in a relatively stable society like Britain, the efforts of Gordon Brown in 2007 to identify and promote the core values of 'Britishness' met with widespread derision. And when strongly shared values do form a rallying point for significant swathes of popular opinion, they can then provide a basis for trying to impose a dominant orthodoxy on the wider public. Michał Bron presciently anticipated the risk of such a 'tyranny of the majority' among militant Catholic groups in Poland (1998: 34).

If some types of communitarianism can be dismissed relatively easily, the desire for collective belonging still holds considerable appeal. Mark Olssen argues for a version of cosmopolitan democracy based on what he describes as 'thin communitarianism', in the sense that 'it has no common bond or goal which is characterized by integration or consensus', but is rather 'an all-encompassing arena without fixed borders or unity, which comprises an assortment of different ways by which life is lived' (2006: 271). For Olssen, thin communitarianism dissolves the tension between social norms and practices on the one hand and individual agency and social difference on the other. He cites a number of thinkers in support of this proposition, including such influential writers as Martha Nussbaum and Michel Foucault.

In a parallel intellectual development, the concept of social capital has been described as matching 'the spirit of an uncertain, questing age' (Schuller *et al.*, 2000: 38). The idea of social capital has enjoyed spectacular popularity in recent years; essentially, the concept draws attention to the resources that people enjoy as a result of their social networks (Field, 2003). Some welcome social capital as bringing a fresh conceptual energy, and a sharp empirical edge, to what they see as very tired debates about community; furthermore, the concept is inherently multi-disciplinary, and appears to resonate with some practitioners and policymakers.

Often inspired by Robert Putnam's massive collection of data relating to the USA, a substantial body of empirical work has broadly shown that people's social networks do indeed affect various aspects of their well-being. As well as a body of evidence on schooling, health, job-seeking, innovation and security from crime, there is also some work suggesting that networks can affect the probability of people participating in adult learning (this work is summarised in Field, 2003: 44–90, and Field, 2005). However, others suggest that using the term 'capital' is misleading, since social networks can neither be owned nor sold; some of these writers acknowledge the value of research presented under the label of social capital, but suggest that much the same could have been achieved if the authors had used the term 'community' to describe the ways in which people cooperate to govern aspects of their own lives (Bowles and Gintis, 2002).

Some have suggested that ideas of social capital are closely related to communitarian thinking. Putnam (2000) certainly appears in some ways close to communitarianism, with his concerns over the decline of familiar bonds such as bowling leagues, and his interest in rebuilding community. Coleman (1991) blends the conservative nostalgia of a Tönnies with a sharp dash of patriarchy, locating social capital primarily in the 'primordial' relations based on childbirth, which he contrasts with 'constructed' forms of social organisation that could only exercise weak types of social control. However, the same clearly cannot be said of Pierre Bourdieu (1984), who used the concept largely as a means of explaining the role of networks among the upper and middle strata as a means of sustaining their social position and upholding the subjugation of subordinate strata.

As well as social capital theories, reflexive modernisation approaches are also highly relevant for ideas about community in contemporary Western societies. In his influential book *Risk Society* (1992), Ulrich Beck outlined a theory of social change that emphasised response to risk – particularly risk produced by human endeavour – as a key organising principle of life in late modernity (or 'second modernity', as Beck put it). Manufactured risk, for Beck, arises out of human agency, and is accelerated by the application of new ideas and new knowledge in a continuing process that Beck, like the British social theorist Anthony Giddens, defines as 'reflexive modernisation'. This process also changes social relationships, which are increasingly individualised; social structures and inequalities, including intimate relations such as love, are based on the accumulation and application of knowledge as well as material wealth.

A number of writers have explored the implications of reflexive modernisation theories for community. For example, Szerszynski suggests that many people are now creating communities based on lifestyle choices, rather than on ascribed characteristics such as class or where you happen to be born. He favours a 'fragile, emergent, pluralised mode of citizenship . . . characterised by a cosmopolitan *awareness* of difference', with social solidarity emerging on the basis of interaction around shared lifestyle interests (1998: 154). Similarly, Jansen *et al.* advocate what they call 'aesthetic communities' based on elective affiliations (1998; see also Baert and Jansen, 1997). Ulrich Beck (2006) has recently advocated a cosmopolitan critical theory as an alternative to the limited state focus of traditional nation-state politics on the one hand, and uncritical celebration of global capitalism on the other, and Giddens has also written of cosmopolitanism in his attempt to theorise dialogic democracy as the basis for active trust and renewed community (1994: 124–32). What is striking about these prescriptions is that they seek to relocate community in a global context, and this marks a clear departure from those theories that really identify community in terms of a very specific locale.

## Community education and adult learning

Debates over community education can be traced back to socially committed Christian movements in the nineteenth century. Education was an important part of the settlement movement, and the movement also influenced several early initiatives in residential adult education. The movement was given further impetus, as well as some theoretical sophistication, as a result of Henry Morris's influence during the interwar years; as chief education officer for Cambridgeshire, Morris persuaded a somewhat conservative county council to pioneer a small number of community colleges, which housed schools alongside other social and educational facilities (Rée, 1973). Morris was particularly interested in protecting and promoting rural community life, but the next wave of community education innovation – and one that is highly relevant for this chapter – was rooted in inner-city developments during the 1960s. Two programmes sponsored by Harold Wilson's Labour government were specifically aimed at tackling deprivation in run-down urban neighbourhoods. Both started with rather limited objectives: the Educational Priority Areas (EPAs) were intended to raise achievement in primary education, while the Community Development Projects (CDPs, sponsored by the Home Office) were intended to engage residents in the process of housing improvement. Both EPAs and CDPs rapidly broadened their remits; the final EPA report warmly endorsed the idea of community schools, which would house adult education and social facilities as well as placing local concerns in the school curriculum (Mark, 1980).

Radical adult educators such as Tom Lovett (a Workers' Educational Association tutor-organiser seconded to work with the Liverpool EPA) and Keith Jackson (an extra-mural lecturer at Liverpool University responsible for community development) allied themselves with the idea of community-based learning as a way of breaking what they saw as a middle-class monopoly on adult education provision. But the radical adult educators were also deeply critical of what they saw as the failure of conventional community education to challenge the power structures and economic inequalities of the society that had bred deprivation.

The radical critique was expressed particularly clearly by Tom Lovett, who in a book published originally in 1975 distinguished between three basic models of community education (Lovett, 1982):

1   Community-based delivery, using outreach approaches and informal methods to bring institutional resources together with resources in the community in order to recruit under-represented groups.
2   Community development approaches, which developed a community dimension to their pedagogy and curriculum in order to provide leaders in the community with skills and knowledge to tackle local problems.
3   Community action-based approaches, which emphasised learning through doing, using Freirian methods and techniques to link educational activities with the wiser struggle to build alternative local institutions.

While Lovett did not see the three models as mutually exclusive, he made it clear that the third was the more radical, since it could help challenge the social and economic foundations of injustice and inequality.

Looking back, Lovett identified the key intellectual influences on Western radicals as being Basil Bernstein, Ivan Illich and Paulo Freire (Lovett, 1988: 145). Bernstein's ideas on language and class were widely debated by educationalists, reinforcing the belief that culture and language constituted barriers to working-class participation and achievement in education. Illich drew attention to the radical potential of informal and deinstitutionalised forms of learning. Freire, the most widely cited author in Western adult education circles, was often quoted to the effect that education was never a politically neutral process, but there was also considerable interest in his ideas about rooting educational activities in everyday life, as well as his emphasis on dialogue as a key process. To these we should possibly add the ideas of the Italian Marxist Antonio Gramsci, who also drew attention to the importance of cultural – and counter-cultural – activity. And we should certainly acknowledge the influence of contemporary social movements, and in particularly the women's movement, with its strong belief that the personal is political.

The radical approach, exemplified by Lovett but also promoted by others such as Marjorie Mayo and Keith Jackson, had considerable influence on community-based adult education in the 1970s and 1980s. Many others shared similar intellectual and political influences, and sought to develop community-based education for adults along broadly Freirian lines. This approach became particularly influential in Scotland (Kirkwood and Kirkwood, 1989), where it was associated with political engagement at the local level.

Of course, not everyone used the language of community in an overtly radical way. For many, community education was virtually a synonym for outreach – which itself was a shorthand for approaches that were aimed at a working-class constituency.

In a report originally written for the Russell enquiry in the early 1970s, Peter Clyne was able to describe adult education as 'a community service', which was concerned equally with 'the individual in the community' as with 'the needs of all adults in all communities'; its purpose was to concern itself with 'people as human beings' (1972: xiii). Clyne's explicitly humanist and universal conception of the community did not prevent him from defining community-based adult education in contrast to the 'typically middle-class and middle-aged design' of conventional adult education programmes (p. xiii). Clyne also defined it in curricular terms as a form of civic education, carried out above all by community associations; 'community education' in this sense, he wrote, was concerned with 'enabling individuals to understand more completely the structure of society, the powers and responsibilities of local and national governments, and capacity of men and women to create public pressure, influence and change' (p. 21).

Others focused more on process issues. Thus Colin Fletcher took issue with those who saw it as concerned with 'deprived groups', preferring to theorise community education as a *process* that was defined by reflection and dialogue, rather than a curriculum or a set of institutions. It involved dedicating educational resources 'to the articulation of needs and common causes' in the community, which required adult educators to 'alternate between the roles of student, teacher and person' (1980: 67).

As well as these essentially humanistic approaches to community education, there was also a more fundamental challenge to the whole idea of community as a philosophical basis for educational work. Lawson (1977) launched a particularly trenchant attack, based on what he presented as confused and sometimes self-contradictory uses of the concept of community, and attacked what he saw as the narrow, sectional and instrumental curriculum being promoted by community educators.

In recent years, community-based learning for adults has continued to be associated with attempts to engage with disadvantaged, non-participant groups. In particular, it has become increasingly important as an aspect of community development and urban regeneration, or neighbourhood renewal as it is sometimes called in Britain. In community development strategies, community-based learning is seen largely as a means to an end, serving other goals as economic regeneration, public health improvements or environmental upgrading. This raises difficult questions of measurement and evaluation in a field of practice that is often diffuse and process-focused. While it is possible to identify evaluation approaches that gather process information (Smart, 1999), this tends both to accentuate existing trends for community learning to be process-focused and to confirm its secondary status. More importantly, it leads to a neglect of longer-term outcome measures that relate to the goals that community educators might reasonably set for their own efforts.

I now turn to a brief discussion of one example of policies that place a value on community-based adult learning. For the Scottish Executive, community education is seen as 'a key contributor to lifelong learning and plays a significant part in combating social exclusion' (1999: 3). Communities Scotland, the Scottish Executive's agency for housing and regeneration, is also charged with promoting community education, which since 2003 has been called 'community learning and development'. It sets out to do so by promoting:

> learning and social development work with individuals and groups in their communities using a range of formal and informal methods. A common defining feature is that pro- grammes and activities are developed in dialogue with communities and participants.
>
> (2004: 33)

159

Process issues are clearly central to this definition. For the Scottish Executive, community learning and development (CLD) should be based on a number of underpinning principles:

- Empowerment – increasing the ability of individuals and groups to influence issues that affect them and their communities;
- Participation – supporting people to take part in decision-making;
- Inclusion, equality of opportunity and anti-discrimination – recognising that some people may need additional support to overcome the barriers they face;
- Self-determination – supporting the right of people to make their own choices;
- Partnership – recognising that many agencies can contribute to CLD to ensure resources are used effectively'.

(Communities Scotland, 2004: 7)

Evaluation approaches are proposed that attend centrally to these process issues, as a way of valuing the underlying principles that guide the development of, and bring coherence to, educational activities of various kinds.

The Scottish government's approach is, though, not solely concerned with process; community learning and development are also seen as means of securing longer-term changes in society. A joint statement by the Scottish Executive with Scottish local authorities described community learning and development as 'central to increasing the supply of "social capital" – a way of working with communities to increase the skills, confidence, networks and resources they need to tackle problems and grasp opportunities' (quoted in Communities Scotland, 2004: 7). This is a relatively loose way of using the concept of social capital, of course, but not unusually so in the policy community.

## Conclusions

The idea of community is a broad and flexible one, and it invariably carries positive associations. The word is therefore used widely, both as adjective and noun, in a variety of contexts and for a plethora of purposes. The same is almost equally true of the concept of social capital, or the idea of lifelong learning. We should therefore exercise care when any two of these concepts are coupled together.

Nevertheless, it would be wrong to try and close the debate over community and lifelong learning. Some are profoundly sceptical of the new language and approaches associated with concepts of lifelong learning and social capital (Crowther and Martin, 2005), and there can be little doubt that the politicised radical adult education approaches of the 1960s and 1970s are in retreat. Yet, as well as foreclosing some possibilities, and hindering some ways of thinking, the new language and approaches also offer new possibilities. Partly inspired by ideas of lifelong learning and partly by theories of communities of practice, for example, some local authorities, employers, trade unions and voluntary bodies have come together with educators to develop ideas about their workplace, neighbourhood, school or town as a 'learning community' (see Duke et al., 2005 for further elaboration).

Ultimately, there are choices to be made. On the one hand, there is a strong risk that policies developed around the two poles of social capital and lifelong learning will simply shift responsibility away from the wider community; as Jane Thompson puts it, the danger is that 'the blame for social exclusion and poverty is placed on apathetic or wilful non-participating individuals rather than on wider structural and societal trends and influences' (2001: 11). Equally, there is considerable potential for developing policies and practices around the two poles of social capital and lifelong learning that can achieve real and sustainable change. Both concepts are broad ones, allowing due attention to be given to learning and engagement in everyday social and cultural life as well as in more formal settings or shaped by economic purposes. What has yet to be made clear is the extent to which they really do allow for innovative developments in policy and practice, or conversely are simply new ways of defining problems that have been discussed in one way or another since the late nineteenth century.

## References

Baert, H. and Jansen, T. (1997) 'Community education in the perspective of social integration and participation', *Lifelong Learning in Europe* 2(4): 223–32.

Bauman, Z. (2005) *Liquid Life*, Cambridge: Polity Press.

Beck, U. (1992) *Risk Society: Towards a new modernity*, London: Sage.

—— (2006) *The Cosmopolitan Vision*, Cambridge: Polity Press.

Bourdieu, P. (1984) *Distinction: A social critique of the judgement of taste*, London: Routledge.

Bowles, S. and Gintis, H. (2002) 'Social capital and community governance', *The* Economic Journal 112: 419–36.

Bowpitt, G. (1998) 'Evangelical Christianity, secular humanism and the genesis of British social work', *British Journal of Social Work* 28(3): 675–93.

Bron, M. (1998) 'Active democratic citizenship: the ESREA network and its field of study', in G. Bisovsky, E. Bourgeois, M. Bron, G. Chivers and S. Larsson (eds) *Adult Learning and Social Participation*, Vienna: Verband Wiener Volksbildung, pp. 29–45.

Clyne, P. (1972) *The Disadvantaged Adult: Educational and social needs of minority groups*, London: Longman.

Coleman, J.S. (1991) 'Prologue: constructed social organisation', in P. Bourdieu and J.S. Coleman (eds) *Social Theory for a Changing Society*, Boulder, CO: Westview Press, pp. 1–14.

Communities Scotland (2004) *Working and Learning Together to Build Stronger Communities: Scottish Executive guidance for community learning and development*, Edinburgh: Scottish Executive.

Crowther, J. and Martin, I. (2005) 'Is there any space left for "really useful knowledge" in the knowledge society?', in A. Bron, E. Kurantowicz, H.S. Olesen and L. West (eds) *'Old' and 'New' Worlds of Adult Learning*, Wrocław: Wydawnictwo Naukowe, pp. 442–51.

Duke, C., Doyle, L. and Wilson, B. (eds) (2005) *Making Knowledge Work: Sustaining learning communities and regions*, Leicester: National Institute of Adult Continuing Education.

Durkheim, É. (1933) *The Division of Labour in Society*, New York: Macmillan.

Etzioni, A. (1993) *The Spirit of Community: Rights, responsibilities and the communitarian agenda*, New York: Crown.

Field, J. (2003) *Social Capital*, London: Routledge.

—— (2005) *Social Capital and Lifelong Learning*, Bristol: Policy Press.

Fletcher, C. (1980) 'The theory of community education and its relation to adult education', in J. Thompson (ed.) *Adult Education For A Change*, London: Hutchinson, pp. 65–82.

Giddens, A. (1994) *Beyond Left and Right: The future of radical politics*, Cambridge: Polity Press.

Gouldner, A. (1971) *The Coming Crisis of Western Sociology*, London: Heinemann.

Harrison, J.F.C. (1961) *Learning and Living 1790–1960: A study in the history of the English adult education movement*, Routledge, London.

Hoggart, R. (1957) *The Uses of Literacy: Aspects of working class life*, London: Chatto and Windus.

Jansen, T., Finger, M. and Wildemeersch, D. (1998) 'Lifelong learning for social responsibility: exploring the significance of aesthetic reflectivity in adult education', in J. Holdford, P. Jarvis and C. Griffin (eds) *International Perspectives on Lifelong Learning*, London: Kogan Page, pp. 81–91.

Kirkwood, G. and Kirkwood, C. (1989) *Living Adult Education: Freire in Scotland*, Milton Keynes: Open University Press.

Knight, L.W. (2005) *Citizen: Jane Addams and the struggle for democracy*, Chicago, IL: University of Chicago Press.

Lawson, K. (1977) 'Community education: a critical assessment', *Adult Education* 50(1): 6–13.

Lovett, T. (1982) *Adult Education, Community Development and the Working Class*, Nottingham: University of Nottingham.

—— (1988) 'Community education and community action', in T. Lovett (ed.) *Radical Approaches to Adult Education: A reader*, London: Routledge, pp. 141–63.

Mark, H. (1980) 'The roots of the community college in England and Wales', in B. Jennings (ed.) *Community Colleges in England and Wales*, Leicester: National Institute of Adult Education, pp. 15–21.

Newman, M. (1979) *The Poor Cousin: A study of adult education*, London: George Allen & Unwin.

Olssen, M. (2006) 'Neoliberalism, globalisation, democracy: challenges for education', in H. Lauder, P. Brown, J.-A. Dillabough and A.H. Halsey (eds) *Education, Globalization & Social Change*, Oxford: Oxford University Press, pp. 261–87.

Putnam, R. (2000) *Bowling Alone: The collapse and revival of American community*, New York: Simon and Schuster.

Rée, H. (1973) *Educator Extraordinary: The life and achievement of Henry Morris*, London: Longman.

Schuller, T., Baron, S. and Field, J. (2000) 'Social capital: A review and critique', in S. Baron, J. Field and T. Schuller (eds) *Social Capital: Critical perspectives*, Oxford: Oxford University Press, pp. 1–38.

Scottish Executive (1999) *Communities: Change through learning – Report of a working group on the future of community education*, Edinburgh: Scottish Executive.

Smart, H. (1999) 'Evaluating community development for health: a survey of evaluation activity across the Lothians', *Health Education Journal* 58(4): 355–64.

Szerszynski, B. (1998) 'Communities of good practice', in I. Christie and L. Nash (eds) *The Good Life*, London: Demos, pp. 148–54.

Tett, L. (2006) *Community Education, Lifelong Learning and Social Inclusion*, Edinburgh: Dunedin.

Thompson, J. (2001) *Rerooting Lifelong Learning: Resourcing neighbourhood renewal*, Leicester: National Institute of Adult Continuing Education.

Tönnies, F. (2001) *Community and Civil Society*, Cambridge: Cambridge University Press.

Williams, R. (1976) *Keywords: A vocabulary of culture and society*, London: Fontana.

Willmott, P. and Young, M. (1962) *Family and Kinship in East London*, Harmondsworth: Penguin.

Yeaxlee, B.A. (1925a) *Spiritual Values in Adult Education: A study of a neglected aspect*, vol. 1, London: Oxford University Press.

—— (1925b) *Spiritual Values in Adult Education: A study of a neglected aspect*, vol. 2, London: Oxford University Press.

# 14

# Learning regions in lifelong learning

*Shirley Walters*

The discussion and development of 'learning regions' in various parts of the world provides fertile ground for understanding how lifelong learning is enmeshed in the socio-economic and political approaches regionally and globally. The language of learning regions or societies is in many instances used synonymously with knowledge-based or information societies. In this chapter, we will explore what a 'learning region' is, what its genesis is and whether it has substance beyond political symbolism. To do this, learning regions and their relationships to lifelong learning are discussed through the prism of a particular case in South Africa. The case has heuristic value as it throws light on how complex and contested lifelong learning and learning regions are. Through the case study, a range of paradoxes is identified, which are at the heart of lifelong learning.

## A learning region and its characteristics

Kuhn (2007), in a volume that brings together analyses of learning societies from most regions of the world, states that the terms 'learning society' or 'knowledge-based society' are concepts that originate in the leading economies of the world and they are tied very closely to economic globalisation. He observes that how the concepts are interpreted is of course shaped profoundly by a nation-state's leading or peripheral position in the global economy. Different analysts, rather than debating whether the learning or knowledge-based society is a desirable aim, are concerned mainly with difficulties to adjust existing societies to this new societal model, and to the challenges of globalisation. As Field says: 'Critical perspectives on the learning society have been relatively subdued . . . In so far as critical perspectives are aired in the public sphere . . . the critique focuses on unpopular consequences and side-effects of the learning society' (2007: 221).

Mehault, writing about France, says that the learning society is a normative concept that is more a political slogan and prospect than a social reality (2007: 68). The concept was developed politically and as part of policy agendas. Social scientists, Kuhn states, have been more inclined to reflect critically on how to make a political decision become a social reality than to question its objectives. The learning society has remained a 'black box'. Mazawi, in reflecting on the

Arab States, says, 'Debates over the "knowledge society" are powerfully enmeshed in geopolitical struggles and local resistance movements' (2007: 337). He highlights the contests between those in the region who support the Western driven version of modernity and those who argue to engage modernity from within Islamic epistemological traditions.

Linquist (2005), who has been facilitating a website for those involved in the development of learning regions, identifies a continuum of interpretations from seeing 'the learning region as an entity that is learning' to it being a 'geographical area in which lifelong learning takes place'. He argues that the learning region as an entity implies a societal change perspective with 'community development and learning as a societal change mechanism'. He sees the 'learning region as a geographical area' – as a reflection of the aggregate of lifelong learning that is taking place.

In his analysis he highlights the overall purpose of the learning region as relating either to a strategy for change or a reflection of the status quo. This he sees as connected to where, or by whom, the concepts originated. He argues that if educators are involved then the majority of attention, resources and efforts are mainly concerned with facilitating, supporting and developing learning service provision. There is concentration on the supply side of learning. This seems to be confirmed in case studies of Bulgaria (Illieva, 2005) and Korea, where the Ministry of Education supported 19 learning cities (Byun and Chae, 2005), although this number has now increased.

As the above examples attest, there is not one understanding of a 'learning region'. For some it is a political slogan tied closely to the political and economic agenda of the United States and the European Union. It has little material reality beyond this. For others who are involved in translating the policy rhetoric into forms of reality, it has a range of other meanings. Within this latter group, the different meanings are embedded within different understandings of economic and social development and the role of learning regions within them (Coffield, 2000; Duke et al., 2005) At the one end a neo-liberal view could encourage an extreme form of competitive individualism within a limited state; at the other end there could be emphasis on social solidarity with an interventionist and developmental state. These in turn refer to various theories of democracy and citizenship.

These differences are also reflected in the different understandings of social capital, which is a key concept in learning regions. For example, some may be highlighting the importance of social capital within a neo-liberal framework. As Mowbray (2004) pointed out, in this scenario people are being urged to volunteer, and to take on more and more community work while the government reduces its public spending in the social sector. There is a new type of social contract in the 'risk society', where individuals are being told to invest in education throughout their lives. If they fall by the wayside it is their fault. Others, who support a participatory democratic view of development, would be urging strengthening of social capital in communities, families and workplaces, for the building of capacity among the citizenry broadly to engage in governance at all levels in the society (Welton, 2006).

Within this political range, among some city planners, the learning city is linked to an ecological sensibility and the goal of the 'sustainable city'. Candy (2003) argues that the ability to move in more sustainable directions is fundamentally linked to the society's ability to learn. She sees learning for the sustainable city as operating at the level of social learning, which is at a higher level than that of the individual. The goal of sustainability is also promoted by the Canadian, Faris (2001), who argues that building sustainable communities is linked to creating learning communities. He states that in learning communities both formal and non-formal lifelong learning of individuals and communities are systematically fostered in order to enhance social, economic, cultural and environmental conditions of their community. He argues for a bottom-up approach, which is 'to build a learning nation community by community'. Both he and Candy link the building of learning communities to more participatory democratic forms of development. Others who are arguing for a bottom-up approach by working through local government structures are Africa and Nicol (2005), who describe 'peer review' mechanisms among ten municipalities in South Africa as powerful instruments for building learning networks to assist members 'to make sense of hard experiences and to strengthen democratic structures'.

For those who regard a learning region as being in the realm of the possible, regardless of the different political orientations, there seem to be certain essential characteristics of a learning region. One of these is to have a new understanding of the centrality for economic and social development of all forms of learning – informal, non-formal and formal – for people of all ages and in all sectors and spheres of family, community and working life. A second is to prioritise excellent education and training systems at all levels. A third is to provide frequently updated, easily accessible information and counselling services to enable citizens to maximise their learning opportunities. A fourth is to have world-class systems for collection, analysis, management and dissemination of information in order to monitor progress towards being a learning region. A fifth is the creation of social capital through partnerships and networks. This is summarised as follows:

- *Education:* World-class education and training systems at all levels, with high participation rates.
- *Partnerships and networking:* High levels of collaboration, networking and clustering within and across economic and knowledge sectors, especially around areas of innovation.
- *Information:* World-class systems for the collection, analysis, management and dissemination of information.
- *Out of the silos:* A constant challenging of traditional knowledge categories to suit rapidly changing social and economic realities.
- *Accessibility:* Providing frequently updated, easily accessible information and counselling services to enable citizens to maximise their learning opportunities.
- *Lifelong learning valued:* High value placed on formal, non-formal and informal learning throughout life; that value is expressed in tangible improvements in the learner's employment and community situations.
- *Social cohesion:* Learning supports high levels of social cohesion (across social class, ethnicity, gender, ability, geography and age) within a society of limited social polarities.

In brief, there is an understanding, which could be that a learning region is a geographical area, which could be small or big, for example a city, village or province, which links lifelong learning with economic development to compete globally. It is a response to economic globalisation, where informal, non-formal and formal learning are recognised as important, for people of all ages, to assist the processes of innovation that can lead to economic distinctiveness. There is an assumption that countries will not be able to move to competitive knowledge economies if there is not sufficient social cohesion. The concept of a 'learning region' can focus attention on the interconnectedness and interdependence of the local and the global. While it focuses attention on a local region, it can also encourage understanding of the world as a single space.

The concept, 'learning society', is summarised by Field as, 'best seen as an umbrella concept, valuable for its heuristic potential as well as questionable for its normative, even utopian content' (2007: 225).

In the case study that follows, the concept, while recognised as utopian, is seen as having the potential to try to shift social reality in a context of widespread poverty and social polarisation. The case is used as a prism to throw light on how complex and contested lifelong learning and learning regions are (Walters, 2005).

## The case of the Learning Cape

The Western Cape is the second wealthiest of the nine provinces in South Africa. It has a population of about 4.5 million. On the one hand, certain parts of the economy are fairly buoyant, such as tourism, services for film, media and IT, and the fruit and wine industry. On the other hand, 65 per cent of people earn below US$200 per month, there is 24 per cent unemployment, 30 per cent of adults are 'illiterate', 75 per cent of pre-schoolers do not have access to early childhood development opportunities, and the number of tuberculosis- and HIV/Aids-infected people is increasing rapidly. The disparities between rich and poor are among the most extreme in the world. In terms of party politics the Western Cape is one of two provinces in the country that do not reflect a clear majority for the African National Congress (ANC), the party in power nationally. Although this makes for vibrant party politics, the ANC is itself a 'broad church' in which tendencies from liberal, to social democratic, to socialist coexist.

In 2001 the Provincial Government, after lengthy consultative processes, adopted an economic development White Paper (PAWC, 2001) that argued for an intimate relationship between economic development and learning within a learning region framework, coining the term 'Learning Cape', as one of four key pillars for economic and social development (Walters, 2005). As a way of testing whether the Learning Cape had anything other than symbolic value and following recommendations in a paper commissioned by the Department of Economic Development (DLL, 2001), a group of activists from civil society, trade unions, government and higher education set up an annual month-long Learning Cape Festival, which profiled lifelong learning across sectors and sites (Walters and Etkind, 2004). The Department also commissioned a research and development project to develop indicators for the Learning Cape. It was in the process of undertaking the latter project that the ambitious and complex nature of the undertaking became clearer.

### Indicators of success for the Learning Cape?

The research team[1] undertook a limited, four-month project. We saw the indicators as primarily a tool for development to 'help make things happen', rather than as a measurement instrument alone. The task was to develop learning indicators, not indicators of education and training. This expressed the broad lifelong learning focus of the exercise, away from an emphasis on formal education and towards the informal and non-formal. To capture the centrality of the relationship of learning to economic and social development, we drew on Bélanger's (1994) work, which circumscribed three broad areas that are interlinked and represent the life cycle and the learning contexts:

- *Initial Learning*, including non-formal learning of children from birth, and schooling at general and further educational levels.
- *Adult Learning*, including adult basic education and training (ABET) and higher and continuing education throughout adult life until death.

- *Diffuse Learning Environments*, which are enhanced through the educational quality of libraries, the media, cultural activities, learning cultures in families, voluntary associations, and so on.

The approach was to start with the characteristics, as described earlier. We accepted that, in order to have learning regions, there is need of 'an excellent education and training system', without subscribing to the view that there is a linear process whereby the existence of an excellent formal system must precede any attempt to develop a broader learning culture. There is ample evidence that an excellent formal system is not possible without facilitative learning cultures in families, in workplaces and in communities. This led us to identify the formal education system as part of the bedrock of a learning region, and a set of bedrock indicators for which different parts of the formal education system are responsible. These acted as a backdrop to the more specific Learning Cape indicators.

We also recognised that the development of learning indicators was not a politically neutral process and would inevitably reflect different political positions and understandings of a learning region. As Duke (2004) points out, in the international literature on learning neighbourhoods, communities, cities and regions, there are important differences of purpose and priority, as well as different ways of going about policy interventions. He identifies the commonest tensions as between economic and social dimensions and between the individual and the collective. Some stress the importance of social indicators, such as those of health and social welfare, while others will highlight specifically economic indicators. In most cases the intention is to create a sufficiently upward spiral to enable economic and social development.

Background research highlighted the fact that indicator construction is a social process. It requires consultation and is therefore slow. The process was seen as being able to be used to win supporters for the Learning Cape initiative and to spread the discussion within the province on how to promote a learning region and learning communities.

We developed a matrix to draw together chronological and locational aspects of learning, which included formal, informal and non-formal learning within civil society, including the family, formal education and training, workplaces, the media, ICT and communities. Since every sector potentially has its own form of indicators and measures to evaluate progress, we operated on the assumption that what makes the Learning Cape indicators unique is the combination of indicators across the sectors, and how they relate to the characteristics of a learning province. Our methodology deliberately left open the possibility for other parts of the provincial government, other spheres of government, or organisations of civil society to sponsor 'data baskets'.

Using the three organising categories of initial, adult and diffuse, a cluster of indicators was identified from the initial and adult categories that form the foundation of a learning region. As the bedrock of learning, a positive assessment of these indicators is essential to the development of lifelong learning in the region. These indicators are mainly but not solely the responsibility of the Education Departments. An illustrative example of these is the proportion of children of 0–4 years attending Early Childhood Development; the number of computers per learner in public schools; or improvement in throughput rates in Further Education and Training colleges. It was assumed that sources of data for the bedrock indicators are mostly available through statistics within the Department of Education.

The bigger challenge was to imagine the indicators that would be more specific to the Learning Cape and less reflective of mainstream education. In order to decide on these indicators, the 'essential characteristics of a learning region' were used, with the three lifelong learning categories: 34 indicators were developed and reflected against the characteristics.

Attempting to decide on Learning Cape indicators opens a host of difficult issues. One of the challenges is to work with people coming out of different traditions and professional fields, with different and competing understandings. For example, working with city planners who may emphasise 'social learning for sustainability' (Candy, 2003), or educationists who may emphasise individual attainment within a formal schooling context, is part of the challenge. In the process of mediating the indicators, it is not necessarily clear what are professional or political differences. To illustrate this I use a brief example of children under the age of 5.

The proposed indicators were:

- proportion of children 0–4 attending an early childhood facility;
- proportion of children recognised as vulnerable in terms of their weight, cognitive and physical development, HIV/Aids status or poverty level.

Given the scenario that less than 22 per cent of the under-5 population currently attend an early childhood facility, that 42 per cent of the households in the Western Cape have an annual income below US$3,000, and that there is an important relationship between nutrition and ability to learn, these seemed to be potentially useful indicators. The researchers argued that there was in all likelihood a relationship between improving socio-economic conditions and improving educational opportunities.

The initial response from one economist was that 'five-year-old children had nothing to do with the economy'. Another response was from the marginal early childhood sector, which was thrilled to have the connection between early childhood facilities and the socio-economic conditions recognised. Supporters of lifelong learning continually stressed the importance of early learning experiences in terms of developing lifelong learners for socio-economic development more broadly. It was a working mother who most clearly pointed out the real benefit, in her view, of good early childhood education. It was to free her up to rejoin the workforce. The economists were persuaded on hearing this. The indicator was retained for the time being.

Another major concern related to the processes of development of the indicators. There had been an initial intention to produce the preliminary indicators through participatory processes, but this was short-circuited because of unfolding economic policy developments. In the midst of the process, there was pressure to make the indicators more obviously connected to the emerging micro-economic development strategy and to relate to more conventional, internationally comparable, economic and human development data. The researchers began also to see more clearly the vastness of the project, which needed to establish legitimacy for new indicators for which there were no ready data. The leadership in the Department of Economic Development, quite reasonably, did not see their role as leading innovative thinking about the learning region and the role of lifelong learning in it. This begs the question, where should a cross-cutting project like this be housed? The indicators project stalled and it is not clear if the work done will ever see the light of day.

## Discussion

The issues that were raised in this project, beyond the specific indicators themselves and their use, are of direct relevance for many lifelong learning projects or programmes.[2]

## Social purposes

The literature on lifelong learning reflects very different understandings of its social purposes. It is a contested term (Crowther, 2004). The conception of a learning region, which has lifelong learning tied to socio-economic development strategies, is equally contested. The social purposes imagined for the learning region will certainly shape the indicators. However, in most contexts where the learning region will want to include divergent views, there are competing development strategies, or at least competing emphases. Field poses the issue clearly when he asks, 'if we place sustainability and justice at the heart of our approach' what policies might be adopted (2006: 3)? The starting point then for understanding the relationship between lifelong learning and society is the development framework, which is implied.

In the South African case, there is a continuum of development discourses that jostle for position from socialist, to social democratic, to neo-liberal, which are mobilised by different constituencies within government, civil society, business and labour. There is an ongoing contest for hegemony of one development approach over another. There is no reason to believe that these same political contestations would not also be present in processes towards building a learning region and within understandings of lifelong learning.

## Ownership

Linked to the above, who initiates the development of the learning region and for what purpose is critical. For some, the primary purpose of a learning region may mainly be a marketing opportunity to profile the region; or it may be to widen access to learning opportunities for a broader range of citizens; or it may be a deliberate intervention to bring about changes in the socio-political and economic relationships within a region; or it may be purely symbolic. The question of ownership is equally pertinent for lifelong learning generally.

In some situations the Department of Education is the key agency. The limits may be that the project is seen narrowly in terms of conventional educational concerns. It might also be that the learning region is seen as the aggregate of lifelong learning opportunities as reflected by Linquist (2005). If the lead agency is an Economics Department, there may be other constraints, which could reflect a very narrow economistic orientation and an instrumentalist view of lifelong learning. If it were driven by social welfare, perhaps the economists and educators would not see it as 'their' concern. This raises the question, where in government should the learning region project be located? Who should drive lifelong learning?

The 'learning region', as with lifelong learning itself, is trying to break out of silos, to promote 'joined up' ways of working. Therefore, the question of who drives it, or how, is pertinent. Is the answer, where there is strongest political will and influence? If the vision of the learning region is to be a lever for change then more than political buy-in is required. It needs translation into budgets and programmes that challenge government departments, at local, provincial and national levels, to move 'out of their silos' and engage in the 'border skirmishes' that may follow. As different tiers of government also have their own relationships to the state and the economy with their own rules, legislative or regulatory changes may be required.

## The lifelong learning framework

In reading about learning regions, which have lifelong learning as a centrepiece, there are few who set out what framework of lifelong learning they are using. Given that lifelong learning is so contested, this is surprising. Because lifelong learning so often is translated to mean adult learning, or formal education and training, we deliberately chose a framework that is holistic.

Bélanger's framework challenges the conventional boundaries between formal and informal learning and includes learning that is lifelong, lifewide and life deep. However, its all-inclusive nature also made it difficult to operationalise in the indicators project. It is a framework that was not well known among the key constituencies, was difficult for those not familiar with lifelong learning to understand, and empirical data was not readily available within the categories. Because conceptually it did cut across sectoral boundaries, it made political and bureaucratic ownership of the project difficult. Its power conceptually made it difficult to use organisationally.

The question is, what framework could be used for lifelong learning within a learning region, which does not reinforce the formal, narrow notions of education and training? What conceptions of lifelong learning are able to be mobilised, which can be integrated, both in terms of policy and practice, into all aspects of economic and social life, and which can be monitored in some way?

## *Indicators*

The unique aspect of learning communities or regions is the new relationships that they are forging. In the case study the indicators specifically tried to target the areas relating to relationships, such as partnerships, networks or inter-sectoral functioning. However, the indicators were quite inward-looking. They focused on the province. They did not especially look for connections with other provinces, or nationally, or with the African region, or globally. This highlights a key paradox within lifelong learning and the learning region.

A learning region requires to be both inward- and outward-looking. If it is to materialise it needs strong social capital to be built both at home locally and with others globally. It needs to develop sufficient social cohesion among communities, while at the same time it must be forging new relationships and connections. It needs to be oriented both locally and globally. However, in some situations, where the notion of the learning region is a defensive one, where the 'learning region' idea is being used to help an embattled, depressed community to have a new sense of themselves, the emphasis on social cohesion can have conservative outcomes (Field, 2006). It is similar in institutions or learning communities that focus their attention on the micro teaching and learning contexts and neglect the importance of the new connections, partnerships and interdisciplinary possibilities with social movements, workplaces or other communities both at home and abroad.

Forging new partnerships, working across different sectors and breaking 'out of silos' are inevitably political acts. They transgress various boundaries. The challenge for lifelong learning is that it too challenges boundaries and trespasses on others' turf, as it strives for a holistic, integrated view of human development.

## Concluding remarks

Discussions of lifelong learning within a learning region force the conversation to the relationships between lifelong learning and socio-economic development. This is highly political. Identifying indicators for a learning region makes the connections between teaching and learning issues at the micro level, to organisational issues at the meso level, to the developmental issues at the macro level. For example, an indicator that is 'whether people can build their own house' will signal the value of people being multi-skilled to undertake a project for the collective social good, as opposed to another one that highlights the number of individuals who attain particular qualifications.

The building of a learning region, which has a transformational agenda, is clearly complex, will be contested and requires very long-term time horizons. Political leadership often comes and goes within five years or less. The question then is, who holds the vision and pursues the transformational agenda that is required for it to come about? What are the roles of civil society, business, labour and government? Over an extended time there will always be contests for the hegemony of particular views of the learning region, and within it lifelong learning. Building a learning region is no doubt in the end a political project.

Those involved in conceptualising and building the learning region are implicated in some way at both the intellectual and the political levels. They are inevitably advocates for some 'indicators' rather than others, for some conceptual frameworks rather than others and, therefore, for particular understandings of the 'learning region'. However, the nature of the project is to open up possibilities and spaces for innovative ways of thinking and acting, to allow new connections to be made and to challenge 'silo' thinking. This, as Field (2006) suggests, requires particular capacities. If political views are held dogmatically they will work against finding new ways to think and act. The actors need themselves to be accomplished lifelong learners and to have the capabilities to be 'boundary spanners'.

A learning region, like that in South Africa, is a geographical space that includes great polarities of economic, social and human need, with unequal and uneven forms of development. To translate learning region policy from symbolism to reality, where the degrees of polarity are to be lessened and where social conditions are dramatically improved, serious and sustained political will is required at every level of government, and also within civil society and among businesses. It is a very ambitious project, which is no doubt utopian but which can be a spur for learning activists to grapple with changing realities through organisation, pedagogy and politics.

## Notes

1    The project, commissioned by the Department of Economic Development (DED) of the Provincial Administration of the Western Cape (PAWC), was undertaken by Zenobia Africa, Martin Nicol (Organisation Development Africa, ODA), Kathy Watters, Roger Etkind and Shirley Walters (Division for Lifelong Learning (DLL), University of Western Cape).

2    I wish to acknowledge useful ideas, which colleagues raised at a seminar at UWC on 'Indicators for the Learning Cape' during March 2006, when Professor Tom Schuller of the Centre for Research and Innovation (CERI) at the OECD visited Cape Town.

## References

Africa, Z. and Nicol, M. (2005) *The Power of Peer Reviews in Building a Learning Network for Local Government in South Africa*, Cape Town: Organisation Development Africa (ODA).

Bélanger, P. (1994) 'Lifelong learning: the dialectics of lifelong education', *International Review of Education* 41: 353–81.

Byun, J. and Chae, J. (2005) 'An evaluation of the lifelong learning cities in Korea', in J. Allan, L. Doyle, J. Field, P. Gray, S. Mills, *et al.* (eds) *Making Knowledge Work: Conference proceedings*, Stirling: University of Stirling, pp. 29–34.

Candy, J. (2003) 'Planning learning cities: addressing globalisation locally'. Available online at www.isocarp.net/data/case_studies/251.pdf (accessed 25 March 2008).

Coffield, F. (ed.) (2000) *Differing Visions of a Learning Society: Research findings*, vol. 2, Bristol: Policy Press.

Crowther, J. (2004) 'In and against lifelong learning: flexibility and the corrosion of character', *International Journal of Lifelong Education* 23(2): 123–36.

Division for Lifelong Learning (DLL) (2001) 'Developing the "Learning Cape"', Paper commissioned by the Department of Economic Affairs, Agriculture and Tourism, Provincial Administration of the Western Cape, prepared by the Division for Lifelong Learning, University of Western Cape, June.

Duke, C. (2004) *Learning Communities: Signposts from international experience*, Leicester: NIACE.

——, M. Osborne and B. Wilson (2005) *Rebalancing the Social and Economic: Learning, partnerships and place*, Leicester: NIACE.

Faris, R. (2001) 'The way forward: building a learning nation community by community', Working Paper, Vancouver, Canada.

Field, J. (2006) 'Social networks, innovation and learning: can policies of social capital promote both economic dynamism and social justice?', Pascal Hot Topic. Available online at www.obs-pascal.com/hottopic.php (accessed 28 October 2007).

—— (2007) 'Lifelong learning and the learning region: trends and prospects in Europe', in M. Kuhn (ed.) *New Society Models for a New Millennium: The learning society in Europe and beyond*, New York: Peter Lang, pp. 47–66.

Illieva, K. (2005) 'Lifelong learning: institutionalisation and regulating mechanisms. Bulgarian case lost in translation', in J. Allan, L. Doyle, J. Field, P. Gray, S. Mills, *et al.* (eds) *Making Knowledge Work: Conference proceedings*, Stirling: University of Stirling, pp. 185–90.

Kuhn, M. (ed.) (2007) *New Society Models for a New Millennium: The learning society in Europe and beyond*, New York: Peter Lang.

Lindquist, K. (2005) 'Lifelong learning as a mechanism for change', in J. Allan, L. Doyle, J. Field, P. Gray, S. Mills, *et al.* (eds) *Making Knowledge Work: Conference proceedings*, Stirling: University of Stirling, pp. 249–56.

Mazawi, A. (2007) 'Globalisation, development and policies of knowledge and learning in the Arab States', in M. Kuhn (ed.) *New Society Models for a New Millennium: The learning society in Europe and beyond*, New York: Peter Lang, pp. 335–83.

Mehault, P. (2007) 'Knowledge economy, learning society and lifelong learning: a review of the French literature', in M. Kuhn (ed.) *New Society Models for a New Millennium: The learning society in Europe and beyond*, New York: Peter Lang, pp. 67–91.

Mowbray, M. (2004) 'Beyond community capacity building: the effect of government on social capital', Pascal Hot Topic. Available online at www.obs-pascal.com/resources/mowbray2004.

Provincial Administration of the Western Cape (PAWC) (2001) *Preparing the Western Cape for the Knowledge Economy of the 21st Century*, White Paper, Cape Town: PAWC.

Walters, S. (2005) 'South Africa's Learning Cape aspirations: the idea of a learning region and the use of indicators in a middle income country', in C. Duke, M. Osborne and B. Wilson (eds) *Rebalancing the Social and Economic: Learning, partnerships and place*, Leicester: NIACE.

—— and Etkind, R. (2004) 'Developing a learning region: what can learning festivals contribute?', Paper presented at the AERC Conference, Victoria, Canada.

Welton, M. (2006) *Designing the Just Learning Society: A critical inquiry*, Leicester: NIACE.

# 15

# Lifelong learning through heritage and art

## *Henrik Zipsane*

John Dewey made an important point about the specific role of history in connection with the formation of perspective in human life:

> Geography and history are the two great school resources for bringing about the enlargement of the significance of a direct personal experience. The active occupations . . . reach out in space and time with respect to both nature and man. Unless they are taught for external reasons or as mere modes of skill their chief educational value is that they provide the most direct and interesting roads out into the larger world of meanings stated in history and geography. While history makes human implications explicit and geography natural connections, these subjects are two phases of the same living whole, since the life of men in association goes on in nature, not as an accidental setting, but as the material and medium of development.
>
> (1916: 217–18)

Dewey seems to have regarded history and geography with great passion as pedagogical tools for time and space perspectives respectively. He even insisted on the interdependency between the two and he was continuously interested in the relation between the individual or personal time and space recognition and the historical and geographical perspective. Until the 1970s the aim of history lessons in the compulsory system of education in many Western countries was defined within the framework of Dewey's logic. The (national) identity was produced and reproduced through the method of postulating a relation between (national) history and personal life development. During the last three decades of the twentieth century the political and economic agenda of globalization had less need for national history and heritage and art organizations and institutions searched for other challenges.

Following the latest developments in Europe after 2000 with a focus on third world immigration and European integration, we see in some young nation states and even in some older ones a revival of nationalism and the use of history as a tool in this respect. Countries such as Denmark, the Netherlands and the UK have been, since the year 2000, examples of countries that revived the close relation between a nation state history curriculum for compulsory education and production of pedagogical programmes in public museums, archives and art collections. The revival of the usefulness of Dewey's logic of the relation between the history of society and personal history in pedagogy does, however, underline the enormous strength in the learning possibilities from both material and non-material heritage.

In this chapter I will try to give an impression of these possibilities from three angles. First, we will concentrate on the learning possibilities that have developed on the basis of the organizational traditions and the nature of the collections in heritage and art institutions, such as archives, museums and galleries. Second, we will focus on the work done by researchers in order to understand the effect of using heritage in learning processes. Third, I shall try to place heritage learning in the context of target groups and thereby in the wider perspective of lifelong and lifewide learning (Ekholm and Härd, 2000). In order to understand the learning implications I suggest that, instead of writing about visitors, users or even participants, we shall here regard them all as learners.

## Disciplines and organizational traditions in heritage learning

Heritage learning can be defined as a specific part of cultural learning that is specified by the use of a time perspective in pedagogical practice. This may include the use of a historical perspective but it doesn't have to since the present time perspective is often apparent. Even the difficult border between the present time and timelessness occurs: but a time perspective always will be there some way or another.

Heritage learning is used as a term for the sum of learning activities from four different disciplines and traditions: museum pedagogy, archival pedagogy, heritage site pedagogy and art pedagogy. If we see the four learning activities as heritage learning disciplines, we focus on the pedagogical practice and possibilities related directly to the use of museum objects, archival records, heritage sites and art. When we see the four pedagogical practices as traditions we emphasize the organizational background for the pedagogical development. For most of the twentieth century, museums, archives, galleries and the organizations working with heritage sites developed different ways of pedagogical practice.

In real life it may be very difficult or impossible to keep the perspectives of discipline and tradition apart from each other and it may even be difficult to separate the different disciplines from each other as many archives also hold museum or art collections. There is, however, an important point that becomes very clear when we see these four different disciplines and traditions in heritage learning: archives, museums and galleries do as a rule find their roots in different sectors of society and have performed different basic public tasks. Consequently, different cultures have developed in the organizations and they have also developed different pedagogical practices. At the start of the twenty-first century, we still see fundamental differences between archives, museums and galleries in their approach to heritage learning in many countries, but some of the differences can be traced to the different status of pedagogical work in the organizations.

By focusing on the pedagogical method we can from an abstract perspective describe the four disciplines and traditions in the following way.

### *Archival pedagogy*

Archival pedagogy has its starting point in the archival material that will often be unique written material that has survived through time and has been collected by the archival institution. The uniqueness and the authenticity of the material are essential for the special possibilities of archival pedagogy. This is the real authentic document, which by definition reflects the time and situation in which it was written! In pedagogical practice it therefore becomes crucial to recognize that the past is talking to us!

When the learning situation is working most effectively, the learners sense and are brought to realize that, beyond the archival material in focus at the moment, there once was a real person in a social setting, which might introduce them not only to this historical environment but also to a diverse collection of other archival material in the storeroom. This feeling incites curiosity and stimulates the experience of the possibility for further digging and research and thereby even the possibility of the true experience and joy of being a discoverer or a detective. And as the archival institutions seek to make the collections accessible in research rooms, many pedagogical activities have been developed with that traditional experience as the starting point. We may conclude from the practice of archival pedagogy that authenticity, uniqueness and potential discoveries are main factors in the learning process.

## Museum pedagogy

Museum pedagogy initially appears to make a less definable impression. It takes its starting point as the different collections in the museum, but also in the illusion of authenticity that the museum curators have endeavoured to give these collections. Since the collections are almost always removed from their original or pre-museum context, it is essential for the museums to seek to create possibilities for experiencing a sense of authenticity.

The collections are primarily accessible through professional presentations. Traditionally this takes the form of exhibitions and the pedagogical programmes that will have been developed together with the exhibition. Therefore the pedagogical programme will also present an interpretation – more or less obvious – and the heritage presentation will be arranged in order to give the learner an experience with a predefined purpose. The visitors' or participants', that is, the learners', ability to adapt to the impressions and feel sympathy with the different experiences in the presentation is central to the learning experience. It may very well have been like this! Or, if it is a presentation of the present time, the basic impression of the learners should be: It probably is like this! That is true for both indoor and open air museums.

On the basis of experience from the practice of museum pedagogy we may conclude that the convincible illusions of authenticity through the presentation of the collections and the use of the learners' ability to feel sympathy are the main factors in the learning process.

## Heritage site pedagogy

Heritage site pedagogy has its starting point in the landscape with archaeological excavation sites still existing as houses or other human constructions. As with archival pedagogy, the authenticity of the material is central, but now we have the authentic object placed in the original surroundings. Heritage site pedagogy is probably the oldest discipline of all heritage pedagogies: even in the oldest times the heritage site was used as a place for storytelling. Also, in our time, the visual experience of the heritage site will often be accompanied by a guide or information text.

The strong feeling of authenticity at the heritage site is central to this pedagogy. It happened here! The experience of the authentic three-dimensional rudiments of the past creates an atmosphere of standing in the middle of the 'history'. The learners thereby get help to imagine the past. By combining the visual impression and maybe even sounds, smells and the possibility to 'touch the past', the learners through the use of all senses create images. From the practice of heritage site pedagogy we can conclude that the authentic object placed in the original surroundings is the sole important factor in the learning process.

## Art pedagogy

Art pedagogy may be said to have two equally important starting points. It is not least because of this equality that art pedagogy stands out as very different from the other disciplines and traditions of heritage pedagogy. On the one hand, art pedagogy deals with the images and other creations of art that surround us. On the other hand, it includes such pictures, films or other creations that to some extent claim to be documentary.

The field between the two aspects is often an interesting field of tension, which is exploited in this form of pedagogy. The border between fact and fiction seems to disappear.

In another way, art pedagogy also has two other equally important starting points, since it often includes both the pedagogical possibilities of the experience of other people's works of art and the learners' own creative work. We may conclude from the practice of art pedagogy that the conscious use of the borderland between fact and fiction and the meeting between the interpretation of other people's work and the learners' own creativity are the main factors in the learning process.

This perspective on the disciplines and traditions within heritage learning has so far proved to be quite operational in analytical practice. Even in recent times, when many initiatives have been taken to strengthen collaboration between the old institutions behind these pedagogical traditions, we can often see the characteristics of the basic disciplines.

## The outcomes or effects of heritage learning

When John Dewey placed history in an educational context almost a hundred years ago it was natural to expect that a historical perspective was the essential learning outcome. By transferring the focus from the traditional term 'history' to the postmodern use of the term 'heritage', the expectations of the outcomes have also changed.

The study of the learning process as such has been at the centre of learning research for three decades or more (Kolb, 1984; Jarvis, 1987, 2006). Different heritage and art organizations have chosen to follow one or another school (Gibbs *et al.*, 2007). In recent years the branch of heritage and art organizations has focused more on the learning outcome. The UK may serve as the most coherent example. The Department of Museum Studies at Leicester University has, for the Museums, Libraries and Archives Council (MLAC), developed a fivefold description of what they call the GLO – generic learning outcome – from heritage learning activities (MLAC, 2005). The description is interesting and represents professional heritage thinking as it is presented at the beginning at the twenty-first century and, at the same time, some of the challenges in thinking we have before us:

### Making links and relationships between things

*Communication skills – Physical skills*

| *Knowledge and understanding* | *Skills* |
| --- | --- |
| Knowing what or about something | Knowing how to do something |
| Learning facts or information | Being able to do new things |

Making sense of something
Deepening understanding
How museums, libraries and archives
   operate

Intellectual skills
Information management skills
Social skills

*Attitudes and values*

Feelings
Perceptions
Opinions about ourselves, e.g. self
   esteem
Opinions or attitudes towards other
   people
Increased capacity for tolerance
Empathy
Increased motivation
Attitudes towards an organization

*Enjoyment, inspiration, creativity*

Having fun
Being surprised
Innovative thoughts
Creativity
Exploration, experimentation and
   making
Being inspired

*Positive and negative attitudes about an experience*

Activity, behaviour, progression
What people do
What people intend to do
What people have done
Reported or observed actions
A change in the way that people manage their lives

It is interesting and central to this form of understanding of learning in heritage organizations that the classic description of learning outcomes in knowledge, skills and attitudes seems not to be enough. The classical learning process, defined as the processes through which an experience is transformed into knowledge, skills and attitudes, seems only to cover some of the outcome from heritage learning (Jarvis, 1987). From a traditional perspective one might claim that the outcomes here labelled 'enjoyment, inspiration, creativity' form an integrated part of attitudes and values. In the same way the outcome labelled 'activity, behaviour, progression' can be seen as just one special aspect of skills. But there is an interesting point that comes to light when we see enjoyment and changed behaviour as independent learning outcomes.

The outcomes in the forms of enjoyment and changed behaviour are given attention first of all because these outcomes exist and have done so for as long as we have had real, engaging heritage pedagogical programmes. Many people who have been engaged in heritage or art learning 'know' this, but these special outcomes are probably also given special attention because this approach to heritage learning outcomes becomes more special than if they are seen as part of classical thinking about attitudes and skills.

The most interesting effect of this structuring of the outcomes of heritage learning is that formal, non-formal and informal settings can all be included. This makes it relatively easy to use the structure and terminology in a very broad spectrum of (learning) activities in heritage and art organizations. The possibility to describe and analyse the learning situations of users of both heritage and art as leisure and as self-directed studies and in formalized educational programmes within the same conceptual framework will probably be of outstanding value to the branch in the coming years.

## Heritage learning and its place in lifelong and lifewide learning

The major challenge for heritage and art organizations is now to get the newly defined outcomes of heritage learning to correspond with the competences demanded by society. Within the conceptual framework of lifelong and lifewide learning, the international arena provides some indications about what is in demand now and will be in the near future – at least in Western society. There is a clear relation in the thinking behind the concepts of key competences from the European Union (EU), the Organization for Economic Cooperation and Development (OECD) and UNESCO (Eurydice, 2000; OECD 2001, 2005; EU 2001, 2004, 2005). The focus on key competences is now also clear on an interregional and national level.

As a well-developed example of this thinking we may look more closely at the EU. The European Commission has identified eight key competences that shall be promoted and stimulated both in compulsory basic education and throughout adult education:

- communication in the mother tongue;
- communication in another language;
- basic competences in maths, science and technology;
- digital competence;
- learning to learn;
- interpersonal and civic competences;
- entrepreneurship;
- cultural expression.

The reasoning behind this can be described as a concern for employability and social cohesion (Negt, 2000; Ehlers, 2007; Zipsane, 2007b, d). The challenge for the heritage and art organizations in Europe is now to see how the learning outcomes match these competences.

Two different perspectives exist here that are very important and that indicate some advantages for museums, archives and galleries. The first perspective is about learning outcomes from experience in heritage and art organizations and this matches competences demanded for the average learner possibly better than the learning outcomes that come from some other providers. It might be claimed that this or that is learned more effectively – or may actually only be learned – through heritage learning, and this may be the case with respect to interpersonal and civic competences as well as to some forms of cultural expression (Hargreaves, 1983, 1989; KEA European Affairs, 2006). The second perspective is just as important. It seems to have been proven again and again that the environment of heritage and art organizations offers learning experiences for people who may have difficulties in other settings. This experience is most obvious when we refer to the formal educational system. Something really happens for many people when they move from the classroom to the museum (Wood, 1988; Selmer-Olsen, 1993)! And what seems to be true for children seems also to be the case for adults (Brookfield, 1986; Padro, 2004; Westergren, 2005).

Heritage and art organizations may be very interesting as providers of learning outcomes that match the demanded key competences. The way the EU explains the knowledge, skills and attitudes perspective on the key competences may serve almost as a delivery list for the heritage sector. An example may be the competence of learning to learn:

LEARNING TO LEARN – essential knowledge, skills and attitudes related to the competence. Where learning is directed towards particular work or career goals, an individual should have **knowledge** of the competences, knowledge, skills and qualifications required. In all cases, learning to learn requires an individual to know and understand their preferred learning strategies, the strengths and weaknesses of their skills and qualifications, and to be able to search the education and training opportunities and guidance/support available to them.

Learning to learn **skills** require firstly the acquisition of the fundamental basic skills such as literacy, numeracy and ICT that are necessary for further learning. Building on this, an individual should be able to access, gain, process and assimilate new knowledge and skills. *This requires effective management of one's learning, career and work patterns, and in particular the ability to persevere with learning, to concentrate for extended periods and to reflect critically on the purposes and aims of learning. Individuals should be able to dedicate time to learning autonomously and with self-discipline, but also to work collaboratively as part of the learning process, draw the benefits from a heterogeneous group, and to share what they have learnt.* They should be able to evaluate their own work, and to seek advice, information and support when appropriate.

A positive **attitude** *includes the motivation and confidence to pursue and succeed at learning throughout one's life. A problem-solving attitude supports both learning and an individual's ability to handle obstacles and change.* The desire to apply prior learning and life experiences and the curiosity to look for opportunities to learn and apply learning in a variety of life-wide contexts are essential elements of a positive attitude.

(EU, 2005: 16; my bold; italics in original)

The script in italics will, I believe, be recognized by many of my colleagues in the heritage and art sector as areas close to the learning outcomes designed for our guests, users and other learners, although the learning style and environment may differ. This is just an example among many, many others. The heritage and art organizations do indeed form an integral part of lifelong and lifewide learning provision. The time and space perspective, as John Dewey saw it, is still active in heritage and art learning, but the developed disciplines, the outcomes and the production of competences in the twenty-first century go far beyond that.

## Bibliography

Alexander, T. and Clyne, P. (1995) *Riches Beyond Price: Making the most of family learning*, National Institute of Adult Continuing Education Policy Discussion Paper, Leicester: NIACE.

American Association of Museums (AAM) (1992) *Excellence and Equity: Education and the public dimension of museums*, Washington, DC: AAM.

Anderson, D. (1999) *A Common Wealth: Museums in the learning age*, Report to the Department for Culture, Media and Sport, London: DCMS.

—— (2000) 'A conceptual framework', in A. Chadwick and A. Stannett (eds) *Museums and the Education of Adults*, Leicester: NIACE.

Aronsson, P. (2004) *Historiebruk: att använda de förflutna*, Lund: Studentlitteratur.

Association of Art Museum Directors (AAMD) (1992) *Different Voices: A social, cultural and historical framework for change in the American art museum*, New York: AAMD.

Ball, C. (1994) *Start Right: The importance of early learning*, London: Royal Society of Arts.

Best, D. (1992) *The Rationality of Feeling: Understanding the arts in education*, London: Falmer Press.

Bicknell, S. and Farmelo, G. (1993) *Museum Visitor Studies in the 90s*, London: Science Museum.

Brookfield, S. (1986) *Understanding and Facilitating Adult Learning*, San Francisco, CA: Jossey-Bass.

Bruner, J., Jolly, A. and Sylva, K. (1976) *Play: Its role in development and evolution*, Harmondsworth: Penguin Books.

179

Chadwick, A. and Stannett, A. (eds) (1995) *Museums and the Education of Adults*, Leicester: NIACE.

Clarke, A., Dodd, J., Hooper-Greenhill, E., O'Riain, H., Selfridge, L. and Swift, F. (2002) *The Department for Education and Skills – Museums and Galleries Education Programme: A guide to good practice*, Leicester: University of Leicester, Research Centre for Museums and Galleries (RCMG).

Classen, C. (1993) *Worlds of Sense: Exploring the senses in history and across cultures*, London: Routledge.

Colardyn, D. and Björnavold, J. (2004) 'Validation of formal, non-formal and informal learning: policy and practices in EU member states', *European Journal of Education* 39(1).

Department for Education and Employment (1997) *Connecting the Learning Society*, London: DfEE.

Department of National Heritage (1996) *Treasures in Trust: A review of museum policy*, London: DNH.

Desai, P. and Thomas, A. (1998) *Cultural Diversity: Attitudes of ethnic minority populations towards museums and galleries*, London: Museums and Galleries Commission.

Dewey, J. (1916) *Democracy and Education*, New York: Free Press.

Dodd, J. and Sandell, R. (1998) *Building Bridges: Guidance for museums and galleries on developing new audiences*, London: Museums and Galleries Commission.

Donaldson, M. (1987) *Children's Minds*, London: Fontana.

Duke, C., Osborne, M. and Wilson, B. (eds) *Rebalancing the Social and Economic: Learning, partnership and place*, Leicester: NIACE.

Edwards, B.D. (2006) 'New key competences: the European Certificate in Basic Skills', *Lifelong Learning in Europe* No. 2, Helsinki: Helsingki Universitet.

Ehlers, S. (2006) 'Four Danish strategies towards adult learning', in S. Ehlers (ed.) *Milestones Towards Lifelong Learning Systems*, Copenhagen: Danmarks Pädagogiske Universitet.

—— (2007) 'En kulturarvspædagogik må rumme mere end det nationale', in M. Eivergård and H. Zipsane (eds) *Friluftsmuseer, kulturarv och lärande*, Östersund: Jamtli förlag.

Ekholm, M. and Härd, S. (2000) *Lifelong Learning and Lifewide Learning*, Stockholm: Liber Distribution Publikationstjänst.

Elsdon, K. with Reynolds, J. and Stewart, S. (1995) *Voluntary Organisations: Citizenship, learning and change*, Leicester: NIACE.

European Task Force on Culture and Development (1997) *In from the Margins: A contribution to the debate on culture and development in Europe*, Strasbourg: Council of Europe.

European Union (EU) (2001) *Making a European Area for Lifelong Learning a Reality*, COM (2001) 678 final, Brussels: Commission of the European Communities, 21 November.

—— (2004) *Implementation of Education and Training 2010: Work programme – Key competences for lifelong learning – A European reference framework*, Brussels: Commission of the European Communities, November.

—— (2005) *Proposal for a Recommendation of the European Parliament and of the Council on Key Competences for Lifelong Learning: A European reference framework*, COM (2005) 548 final – 2005/0221 (COD), Brussels: Commission of the European Communities, 10 November.

Eurydice (2000) *Key Competencies: A developing concept in general compulsory education*, Survey 5 (October), Paris: Eurydice.

Falk, J. and Dierking, L. (1995) *Public Institutions for Personal Learning: Establishing a research agenda*, Washington, DC: American Association of Museums.

—— and —— (1997) 'School field trips: assessing their long-term impact', *Curato* 40(3) (September).

Falk, J. (1998) 'Investigating the long-term impact of a museum on its community: the California Science Center L.A.S.E.R. Project', *Insights* 1(1) (Spring).

Field, J. (2005) 'Social networks, innovation and learning: can policies for social capital promote both dynamism and justice?', in C. Duke, M. Osborne and B. Wilson (eds) *Rebalancing the Social and Economic: Learning, partnership and place*, Leicester: NIACE.

—— (2006) Lifelong Learning and the New Educational Order, 2nd edn, London: Trentham Books.

Fraser, J. and Wardlaw, V. (1998) *Museum Education in Scotland: A survey of current practice, 1998 update*, Edinburgh: Scottish Museums Council.

Gibbs, K., Sani, M. and Thompson, J. (eds) (2007) *Lifelong Learning in Museums: A European handbook*, Ferrara: SATE srl.

Goleman, D. (1996) *Emotional Intelligence*, London: Bloomsbury.

Greany, T. (ed.) (1998) *Attitudes to Learning '98: MORI state of the nation survey: summary report*, London: Campaign for Learning.

Group for Education in Museums (GEM) (1995) *Developing Museum Exhibitions for Lifelong Learning*, London: The Stationery Office.

Hargreaves, D. (1983) 'Dr. Brunel and Mr. Denning: reflections on aesthetic knowing', in M. Ross (ed.) *The Arts: A way of knowing*, London: Pergamon Press.

—— (1989) 'Developmental psychology and the arts', in D. Hargreaves (ed.) *Children and the Arts*, Buckingham: Open University Press.

—— (ed.) *Children and the Arts*, Buckingham: Open University Press.

Harland, J., Kinder, K. and Hayness, J. (1998) *The Effects and Effectiveness of Arts Education in Schools: Interim Report I*, Slough: National Foundation for Educational Research.

Hein, G. (1998) *Learning in the Museum*, London: Routledge.

—— and Alexander, M. (1998) *Museums: Places of learning*, Washington DC: American Association of Museums.

Hooper-Greenhill, E. (1994) *Museums and Their Visitors*, London: Routledge.

—— (ed.) (1996) *Improving Museum Learning*, Nottingham: East Midlands Museums Service.

Illeris, H. (2006) 'Museums and galleries as performative sites for lifelong learning: constructions, deconstructions and reconstructions of audience positions in museum and gallery education', *Museum and Society* 4(1): 15–26.

Jarvis, P. (1987) *Adult Learning in the Social Context*, London: Croom Helm.

—— (2006) *Towards a Comprehensive Theory of Human Learning*, Lifelong Learning and the Learning Society, vol. 1, London and New York: Routledge.

——, Holford, J. and Griffin, C. (2005) *The Theory and Practice of Learning*, 2nd edn, London: Routledge.

KEA European Affairs (2006) 'The contribution of the creative and cultural sector to European growth and cohesion', KEA, Brussels. Available online at http://ec.europa.eu/culture/eac/index_en.html (accessed 13 November 2006).

Knoll, J.H. (2004) 'International adult education as education policy: lifelong learning and Europeanization', *Adult Education and Development* 62.

Kolb, D.A. (1984) *Experiential Learning: Experience as the source of learning and development*, Upper Saddle River, NJ: Prentice Hall.

Märja, T. (2005) 'Learner-centred lifelong learning policies', *LLinE – Lifelong Learning in Europe* 1, Helsinki.

Museums & Galleries Commission (1996) *Guidelines on Museum Education*, London: MGC.

Museums & Galleries Commission (1998) *European Museums Beyond the Millennium*, London: MGC.

Museums Association (1996) *The National Strategy for Museums: The Museums Association's recommendations for government action*, London: MA.

Museums, Libraries and Archives Council (MLA) (2005) 'GLO: generic learning outcomes', from homepage *Inspiring Learning for All: What are the generic learning outcomes?* Available online at www.inspiringlearningforall.gov.uk/measuring_learning/learningoutcomes/why_do_we_need_glos/_217/default.aspx (accessed 18 October 2005).

—— (ed.) (2006) *Museum Learning Survey: Final Report*, London: MLA.

Negt, O. (2000) Learning throughout life: the contribution of adult education to the establishment of European identity, *Adult Education and Development* 54.

Organisation for Economic Co-operation and Development (OECD) (2001) *Knowledge and Skills for Life: First results from PISA 2000*, Paris: OECD.

—— (2005) *From Education to Work: A different transition for young adults with low levels of education*, Paris: OECD.

Ottersten, E.K. (2004) 'Lifelong learning and challenges posed to European labour markets', *European Journal of Education* 39(2).

Padro, C. (2004) *Mapping Learning Theories in Museums*, Collect and Share Report, Barcelona: Departamento de Dibuix – Unitat d'Educació Artistica.

Rasmussen, P. (2006) 'Globalisation and lifelong learning', in Sören Ehlers (ed.) *Milestones Towards Lifelong Learning Systems*, Copenhagen: Danmarks Pädagogiske Universitet.

Rayner, A. (1998) *Access in Mind: Towards the inclusive museum*, Edinburgh: The Intellectual Access Trust.

Reding, V. (2001) 'Lifelong learning in Europe', *Adult Education and Development* 58.

Ross, M. (ed.) *The Arts: A way of knowing*, London: Pergamon Press.

Sandell, R. (2003) 'Social inclusion, the museum and the dynamics of sectoral change', in *Museum and Society* 1, Leicester University.

Sargant, N. (1991) Learning and Leisure: A study of adult participation in learning and its policy implications, Leicester: NIACE.

——, Field, J. and Francis, H. (1997) *The Learning Divide: A study of participation in adult learning in the United Kingdom*, Leicester: NIACE.

Saunders, D. and Wyn-Lewis, E. (2003) 'Exploring the links between informal learning and social action campaigns: a public broadcasting case study', *Journal of Widening Participation and Lifelong Learning* 5(1), Staffordshire University.

Scheffler, I. (1991) *In Praise of the Cognitive Emotions*, New York: Routledge.

Selmer-Olsen, I. (1993) 'Barn, kultur, kulturformidling og barns kultur', in I. Selmer Olsen, *Kulturens fortellinger*, Oslo: Ad Notam Gyldendal.

Weil, S. and McGill, I. (eds) (1989) *Making Sense of Experiential Learning: Diversity in theory and practice*, Milton Keynes: Society for Research into Higher Education/Open University Press.

Westergren, E. (2005) 'Holy cow – this is great! Historic environment education. How did it all start?, in E. Westergren (ed.) *Holy Cow – This is Great! Report from a symposium on historic environments, education and time travels in Vimmerby, Sweden, November 2004*, Kalmar: Kalmar Läns Museum.

—— (ed.) (2005) *Holy Cow – This is Great! Report from a symposium on historic environments education and time travels in Vimmerby, Sweden, November 2004*, Kalmar: Kalmar Läns Museum.

Wood, D. (1988) *How Children Think and Learn: The social context of cognitive development*, Oxford: Blackwell.

Zipsane, H. (2005a) 'The Open Air Museum and its new role as a museum of many cultures', in *Papers from the 21st Conference of the European Association of Open Air Museums August 2003 in Scotland*, Glasgow: Bryson Print.

—— (2005b) 'Refugees at the Open Air Museum: the museum as a place for informal lifelong learning. A case study', in *Making Knowledge Work: International Conference – Conference Proceedings*, Pascal Observatory, Stirling: University of Stirling

—— (2007a) 'Lifelong learning in open air museums – a fascinating part to play in Europe', in *Papers from 22nd Conference of the European Association of Open Air Museums, August 2005 in Finland*, Turku: Turku Provincial Museum.

—— (2007b) 'Heritage learning: not so much a question about the past as about the present, here and now!', in H. Hinzen (ed.) *Journal for Adult Education and Development* 68.

—— (2007c) 'Cultural learning as key word in transition from social client to learner', in *The Times They are A-changing: Researching transitions in lifelong learning – Conference Proceedings'*, CRLL, Stirling: University of Stirling

—— (2007d) 'Cultural heritage, lifelong learning and social economy of senior citizens', in *ICOM/CECA 2007: Museums and Universal Heritage – Heritage Learning Matters – Conference Proceedings*, Wien: Österreichisch Galerie Belvedere (in print).

# 16

# Libraries and lifelong learning

*Susan Imel and Kim Duckett*

By their very nature, libraries are inextricably linked to lifelong learning. Accordingly:

> [libraries] do not approach the issue of lifelong learning support as though it were entirely revolutionary and . . . [they] have a strong tradition of support on which they can build, from the public library offering myriad opportunities for informal learning to the university library supporting leading-edge research.
>
> (Brophy and MacDougall, 2000: 12)

A number of factors are affecting how libraries serve lifelong learners. Chief among these are changes in technology that create multiple ways of information access and dissemination. These changes mean that individuals can actually build libraries on their personal computers and disseminate information on their own (Longee, 2006). "Historically, most libraries have offered very little in the way of support to learners who were not willing to present themselves physically in the library" (Brophy and MacDougall, 2000: 12), but the change in control and access of information has caused libraries to re-examine their services and their role in serving lifelong learners.

Despite the fact that libraries and lifelong learning share many similar goals, librarians and adult educators often seem to operate on parallel tracks with little or no crossover between the fields. It was only in 1997, for example, that one of the International UNESCO Conferences on Adult Education—CONFINTEA V—provided space on the agenda for a workshop that focused on adult education documentation and information (Adams *et al.*, 2002). The CONFINTEA V Mid-Term Review Conference held in 2003 continued the work of emphasizing the role of libraries in lifelong learning by declaring that "libraries are important agents in our new learning societies. Their roles are both educative and educational" (Thinesse-Demel, 2005: 2).

The goal of this chapter is to weave together information from the fields of adult education and library science and provide a snapshot of the current status of lifelong learning in libraries. Although the term "lifelong learning" applies to learning across the lifespan, in this chapter the emphasis is on the adult years. The chapter discusses three major themes. The first two concern the role of public and academic libraries in lifelong learning. The third focuses on information literacy and its role in lifelong learning.

## Public libraries and lifelong learning

Public libraries throughout the world seek to support adult learners by offering access to information and specialized personal assistance in finding and using that information, and by hosting meetings and discussions (Adams *et al.*, 2002). According to the International Federation of Library Associations (IFLA), "public libraries can . . . play a role of fundamental importance in the development of future systems of lifelong learning" by connecting local learners "with global resources of information and knowledge" (2004: 3). As a result of its efforts to collect information about activities related to lifelong learning in the 267,219 public libraries worldwide, IFLA found a number of examples but also concluded that in many countries only a few libraries are actively engaged as partners in the learning process. In Europe, the European Commission's research program for a User-Friendly Information Society launched Public Libraries Mobilising Advanced Networks or PULMAN. Public libraries from 26 countries were included in this effort, which was designed to increase support for adult learners (www.pulmanweb.org). Evidence of the importance of the public library's role in lifelong learning in the United States is found in the results of a survey that revealed that the public library is used most frequently for educational purposes. Furthermore, 91 percent of the survey respondents reported that they believe the library will exist in the future despite the emergence of the internet as an information source (American Library Association, 2002). Clearly, public libraries play a major role in supporting and providing lifelong learning. Following an overview of the history of public libraries in adult education, the balance of this section of the chapter examines how public libraries support adult learners.

## Historical and recent links to adult education and adult learning

The first examples of public library programming for adults began appearing in Great Britain and the United States in the late 1800s (Lear, 2002). In tracing the origins of the "non-book activities in public libraries," Davies (1974: 1) found that, in the late nineteenth century, links developed between public libraries and cultural societies such as lyceums and mechanics institutes. Although some cultural societies developed their own libraries, many public libraries promoted books and reading in conjunction with the activities sponsored by the societies (Adams *et al.*, 2002; Davies, 1974). Lines between the societies and the libraries began to blur, with libraries initiating more functions that were similar to those of the cultural societies. In Great Britain the Libraries Amendment Act of 1884 permitted public libraries to apply for funds to support classes in areas such as painting, drawing, and architectural design. Funds from the act could to be used for payment of instructors, purchase or lease of sites, and equipment and supplies. As a result, Davies notes that "British libraries were . . . on their way to becoming atheneums, mechanics' institutions and lyceums" (1974: 78). During this same period, public libraries in the United States also began the shift into becoming centers of community culture and began offering classes and exhibits to supplement reading (Davies, 1974; Lear, 2002).

During the twentieth century, library activities related to lifelong learning experienced a number of phases. In the United States, librarians and adult educators worked closely together, beginning in the 1920s and continuing through the mid-1950s. This collaborative work was encouraged by funding from the Carnegie Foundation and then later by the Ford Foundation's Fund for Adult Education and involved the American Association for Adult Education and the American Library Association (Monroe, 1963). During this period in Great Britain, librarians turned from their previously active roles as promoters of adult education to become more passive in their interactions with adult clients. Bacon attributes this change in attitude to the growth of professionalism in the field resulting in concepts about what was appropriate for libraries to do, and that did not include "uplifting the cultural level of the masses" (1980: 53).

On a global level resource centers began to emerge as an alternate form of libraries in the latter part of the twentieth century. In Africa, for example, where Anglo-American ideas of library service had dominated, resource centers that reflected the values and cultures of local communities were developed. In addition to providing information, these resource centers took on the role of referral centers and provided advice and guidance (Rosenberg, 1993, 1994). In Brazil, resource centers grew out of urban social movements, beginning as ways to document the movement's history, but evolving into collecting, preserving, and disseminating documents produced by or about popular movements (Cardoso, 1993).

One final significant development on the eve of the twenty-first century was the development of the Adult Learning Documentation and Information Network (ALADIN). ALADIN, which is coordinated by the UNESCO Institute of Lifelong Learning, emerged as a result of the CONFINTEA V workshop, "Global Community of Adult Learning through Information and Documentation: Developing a Network of Networks" (Giere and Imel, 2000). ALADIN has developed a global network of approximately 100 libraries, resource and documentation centers, and other organizations that support adult learners and learning. ALADIN network members come from 40 countries representing all regions of the world. ALADIN seeks to promote the sharing of information and resources and it also supports training for resource center staff in developing countries. For more information on ALADIN, see www.unesco.org/education/aladin/.

## Public libraries as partners in lifelong learning

Currently, public libraries support lifelong learning as a natural extension of their missions. In Europe, libraries are considered to be partners in lifelong learning initiatives that are promoted by governmental units (Häggström, 2005). The European Commission's Commission on Lifelong Learning, for example, suggests that libraries should serve as access points for internet telecommunications services and recognizes that libraries can partner with educational institutions to serve as local learning centers. Although the EC tends to view libraries more as service providers than as "active partners offering access to global resources, professional guidance and training in a local setting," they do acknowledge a role for public libraries in lifelong learning (Häggström, 2005: 4).

Support of adult learners by public libraries can be divided into two distinct categories. Educational and cultural programs comprise the first category. The programs, which are sometimes developed in collaboration with other community groups, may include lectures, short courses, book talks and discussions, exhibits and displays, and other activities. Since most public library mission statements include some reference to continuing education or lifelong learning, this type of programming is a natural part of a library's purpose (Robertson, 2005). The impulse behind these programs may be as simple as providing a community service but frequently involves more complex reasons, such as the need to attract both new patrons and former library clients who may have been lured away by other attractions (Lear, 2002). The public library as an educational and cultural center is rooted in its history, in which adult programming grew out of ties to cultural societies (Davies, 1974; Lear, 2002; Robertson, 2005).

Public libraries also provide support for lifelong learning by assisting those adults who are independent, self-directed learners. Although less visible than educational and cultural programs, this category of support is no less important. Sometimes classified as informal learners, these are adults who come to the library seeking information for a variety of reasons related to their learning needs. Sense-making methodology as developed by Brenda Dervin (http://communication.sbs.ohio-state.edu/sense-making/) has been used to frame how some libraries and librarians seek to help adult learners. Carr (1999/1988), using Dervin's research on information seeking and use, says that the information needs of adults are personalized and that they may be seeking information because what used to make sense no longer does. They are experiencing an information gap and are searching for information to fill that gap and then to use it in a way that addresses the situation or problem (Dervin, 2002, cited in Worchester and Westbrook, 2004). According to sense-making methodology, to be effective, librarians need to help these adults construct a response that makes sense in terms of their own experiences and prior knowledge. Carr (1999/1988) sees this as a multiple-step, collaborative process, in which the librarian assists by asking the learner to articulate the information needed in a way that contextualizes it (why they need the information, for what purpose); works with the learner to find and bring order to the resources that address the need; and then helps them in constructing new meaning. As outlined by Carr, assisting independent adult learners is a complex process for which libraries and librarians may not be prepared.

A research study (McNicol and Dalton, 2003) conducted in Great Britain sheds light on how libraries do support informal adult learners. Six stages of informal learning that occur in a library context were identified as follows: engagement, planning, exploration, reflection, generalization and implementation, and evaluation. Using the stages as a filter, the practices of selected public libraries in Great Britain were examined using library documents and interviews. The researchers found that libraries focused most of their efforts in the first three areas of engagement, planning, and exploration because these areas involve processes that are external to the learner. Reflection, generalization, and implementation and evaluation, on the other hand, are processes that are internal, making it more difficult to evaluate the role libraries play in those areas. The study concluded that support for learners could be improved by hiring additional staff and by forming partnerships with other providers when it is not feasible for the library to play a major role in learning.

One recent effort that demonstrates how libraries are effectively supporting lifelong learning is found in the redesign of libraries and learning centers in the London Borough of Tower Hamlets (Wills, 2003). The principles behind the redesign efforts involved extensive needs assessment through consultation with community residents and collaboration between libraries and educational providers. As a result of extensive research to find out what needed to be done to encourage community residents to use libraries and learning centers, the existing library and learning center facilities were combined, relocated, redesigned, and renamed as "Idea Stores." To compete with other options adults have for their discretionary time, the Idea Stores were located near shopping areas and designed by a company that specializes in brand development, and graphic, interior, and architectural design. Service was also redesigned so that, instead of sitting behind a desk, all staff members are expected to circulate on the floor and all are responsible for providing information. Staff members are hired on their customer service qualities rather than on their knowledge of library services. The buildings themselves incorporate the model of service and the set of values on which the Idea Stores are based, with seamless support for adult learning throughout.

The Idea Stores have given community members a place to come and congregate, have coffee, read the paper, take a course, and access the internet. In the first facility opened, visits were up threefold over the two library facilities it replaced and enrollments in learning center courses doubled in comparison to the learning center facility it replaced. Because many of the customers tend to be wary of education, the Idea Stores provide short, "taster" courses. One user reported that, after doing a taster course in computing, he plans to do an entire course because "I think I've got the bug," and went on to say "I didn't used to use the old library but I'm definitely coming back here" (Wills 2003: 120). (For further information see www. ideastore.co.uk/.)

Throughout the world public libraries are engaged in a myriad of activities that support lifelong learning. The most visible are educational and cultural programs, many of which can be found simply by accessing public library websites. No less important, however, is the work that librarians do with independent, self-directed adult learners to help them with their learning projects.

## Academic libraries and lifelong learning

Academic libraries support the teaching and research taking place at higher education institutions such as community colleges, colleges, universities, and professional schools. The missions of such libraries include efforts to support the instructional, learning, and research activities of an academic community by purchasing and curating collections of information resources, helping users find information, and teaching research skills. Additionally, academic libraries often serve the information needs of the broader community outside the institution, especially if the institution is publicly funded.

The latter half of the twentieth century spawned many changes in higher education, with the increased use of technologies on campuses and the development and adoption of new educational delivery methods (i.e. distance education, technology-enhanced instruction, etc.). Academic libraries were a part of these transformations as well. Librarians began to leverage technologies to make information collections more discoverable and usable and developed services to support students at a distance, many of whom are adult learners. Now, at the beginning of the twentieth-first century, institutions of higher education are more diverse than ever, including some colleges and universities serving completely distance education communities. Sometimes there may even be little or no physical "campus." The development of information technologies such as the internet and the growth in availability of information on the World Wide Web have enabled libraries to build online collections of information resources for their user communities, thereby decreasing the need to visit a physical library. These changes have fostered a shift in perception of the academic library, which has typically been understood as a physical place where information resources are stored and learners go to find information. The growing access to the web, however, has challenged the perceived importance of the library, both as a physical space and as a virtual collection. As a result, academic libraries throughout the world give great attention to the development of their virtual spaces—websites, search tools such as the library catalog, and the development of online services for library users to receive research assistance.

As centers of information and learning—both physical spaces and increasingly as virtual collections of resources and services—academic libraries and librarians play an important role in fostering lifelong learning, both for campus community members of all ages and for individuals in the broader community who turn to the academic library for research assistance and cultural programming.

187

## Support for Distance Education

In response to the increase in distance education in the latter half of the twentieth century, academic libraries throughout the world began to develop library services to support learners at a distance (Slade, 2005). Library associations in the United States, Canada, and India have created standards related to library services for distance learners that are used widely in their respective countries (Association of College and Research Libraries, 2004; Canadian Library Association, 2000; Indian Library Association, 2001). The UK-based Society of College, National and University Libraries (SCONUL, 2001) has also created a briefing paper related to the topic. Additionally, Needham and Johnson (2007) have proposed a set of ethical guidelines for providing library support to distance learners, so that these students are assured an equivalent level of access to library resources and services and treated with respect.

According to Slade and Kascus (2000: xx–xxii), there are four main service models for academic library support of distance learners. These models include:

- Onsite collections and library resources at remote centers such as extended campuses and regional and local study centers.
- Interlibrary cooperation, resource sharing, and student use of unaffiliated libraries—particularly public libraries.
- Delivery of library materials to the student from a main campus of the parent institution to the student's home, office, or another central pickup location.
- Use of information and communication technologies (ICT) to enable learners to access online resources from remote locations.

Many academic libraries now have websites dedicated to informing distance education students about using the library's resources from off-campus and about special services tailored to their educational needs. One or more librarians may be assigned the role of "distance education librarian" and oversee the services available for distance learners.

It is common for academic libraries to provide services that allow distance learners to request home delivery for books and other print materials in the library's collection. Through web-based delivery services, journal articles may also be electronically sent to off-campus users. Additionally, an emphasis on the provision of online information resources is currently found throughout academic libraries, which enables all affiliated library users to find information without necessarily coming to the library. The costs of such conveniences are not cheap, however. Budgets for the acquisition and management of online journals, books, and reference materials frequently exceed budgets for print materials. To offset the impact of the high costs associated with online resources—especially online journals—academic libraries around the world frequently depend on consortium participation to leverage purchases and negotiation with publishers (Subramanian, 2002).

Academic librarians have developed services to provide one-on-one assistance for distance learners via email, phone, and synchronous online communication systems. In a number of countries, most notably in the United Kingdom, Australia, Canada, and the United States, librarians are also designing and delivering information literacy instruction for groups of distance learners using web-based synchronous tools as well as online guides and tutorials that learners can access at their convenience (Slade and Kascus, 2000).

## Support for adult learners

Adult learners who take higher education courses are often challenged by a shortage of time arising from work and family responsibilities. The increase in online information available through the library enables these students to access needed information from home or the office at any time of the day. There are a number of potential challenges for adult learners using these systems, however. For many adults returning to higher education, it has been years since they used a library for academic purposes and the functioning of the library has radically changed to an online environment. They may feel intimidated by using the library's website, online catalog, and other subscription-based resources such as e-journals and article databases (i.e. indexes of disciplinary literature). Adult learners might also vary widely in their computer skills as well as familiarity with academic writing and research. As a result, they may need both technical and instructional support (Ezzo and Perez, 2000).

The online world of information can be frustrating and overwhelming for some users. Although libraries, publishers, and online resources vendors are constantly redesigning their search tools to be more user-friendly and interoperable, the web of resources available and the lack of easy connections between them can be challenging for some users. Adult learners will benefit from library staff members who are sensitive to the varying computer competencies of adult learners and are skilled in troubleshooting technical problems at a distance.

Additionally, the sheer amount of information available can lead to "information overload" (Ezzo and Perez, 2000). Adult students may need assistance in selecting appropriate resources and in evaluating information to help them research effectively and efficiently. As a result, it is important that academic libraries develop information literacy instruction aimed towards these students. The use of point-of-need online instruction, web-based tutorials, and easy ways to contact a librarian for help in person or via phone, email, and synchronous online communication tools provide important instructional support for adult students.

## Information literacy: skills for lifelong learning

One of the primary ways academic and public libraries throughout the world support lifelong learning is through the promotion of information literacy for all individuals, regardless of age or education level (Rader, 2001). Information literacy is frequently characterized as a set of abilities enabling an individual to "recognize when information is needed and have the ability to locate, evaluate, and use effectively the needed information" (Association of College and Research Libraries, 2000: 2). This literacy is viewed as encompassing both information skills and information technology skills, which together enable individuals to find and use information as part of their daily lives and to be informed citizens (SCONUL, 1999; Association of College and Research Libraries, 2000). The terms "information competency" and "information fluency" are also used to characterize this kind of knowledge and skills. In relation to libraries, the terms "bibliographic instruction," "library instruction," and "user instruction" may be used to describe the work of librarians to help students and members of the community develop information literacy. Increasingly in higher education, visual literacy—a set of skills surrounding the interpretation and evaluation of images—is being viewed as a corollary to information literacy in recognition of the importance of visual media in contemporary cultures throughout the world (Jones-Kavalier and Flannigan, 2006).

In 2005, The United Nations Educational, Scientific and Cultural Organisation (UNESCO), IFLA, and The National Forum on Information Literacy (NFIL), organized the High-Level

Colloquium on Information Literacy and Lifelong Learning. The colloquium's report from the meeting (Garner, 2006) encourages international, national, and regional organizations to advocate for "Information Literacy for All" in addition to "Information for All." The members of the colloquium declared that:

> Information literacy lies at the core of lifelong learning. It empowers people in all walks of life to seek, evaluate, use and create information effectively to achieve their personal, social, occupational and educational goals. It is a basic human right in a digital world and promotes the social inclusion of all nations.
>
> (Garner 2006: 3)

Similarly, in its *Information Literacy Competency Standards for Higher Education*, the Association of College and Research Libraries (2000), a division of the American Libraries Association, stated a connection between lifelong learning and information literacy that is reiterated frequently in the literature surrounding the concept:

> Information literacy forms the basis for lifelong learning. It is common to all disciplines, to all learning environments, and to all levels of education. It enables learners to master content and extend their investigations, become more self-directed, and assume greater control over their own learning.

Although librarians have been working to promote research and library skills for decades, information literacy became an issue of increasing importance in the 1980s with the increase in information technologies. Global awareness and concern about information literacy further increased during the 1990s and continues today (Rader, 2001). Library and information professional associations as well as individual higher education institutions throughout the world have written competency standards and guidelines that are used to define information literacy and the skills it encompasses. These standards are used by many libraries as well as other academic units to shape the development and assessment of information literacy initiatives. Among the well-known competency standards are those created by SCONUL in Europe (1999), the Association of College and Research Libraries in the United States (2000), the Council of Australian University Librarians (2001), and the Australian and New Zealand Institute for Information Literacy (2004).

The competencies outlined by these organizations follow similar patterns and, although using different language, describe that the information literate student:

- recognizes that he or she needs information and constructs strategies for locating it;
- identifies various information resources and searches effectively and efficiently for information;
- critically compares and evaluates information and its sources and incorporates the information into his or her knowledge base;
- effectively organizes, synthesizes, and applies information to accomplish a specific purpose;
- expands, re-frames, or create new knowledge by incorporating new information into prior knowledge.

Additionally, information literacy competencies may include concepts related to understanding the economic, cultural, and legal issues surrounding information in society—including respect for copyright and intellectual property and awareness of plagiarism (Association of

College and Research Libraries, 2000; Council of Australian University Librarians, 2001). The Council of Australian University Librarians' information literacy standard seven also specifically delineates that "the information literate person recognizes that lifelong learning and participative citizenship requires information literacy" (2001: 19).

Information literacy initiatives by academic libraries often include campus advocacy for incorporating information literacy into the curriculum, research skills workshops, credit courses, and the development of web-based tutorials and guides. The audiences for such instruction include undergraduate, graduate, and continuing education students, as well as faculty and staff. Academic librarians may also collaborate with public libraries to provide information literacy outreach to community members not affiliated with a higher education institution. In response to the growth in distance education, librarians are using instructional technologies to reach people at a distance and traveling to off-campus sites to visit student groups. The instruction may range from skills in using online research tools such as library catalogs and article databases to the evaluation of information. Increasingly, librarians are also asked by instructors to teach students about plagiarism and ethical uses of information.

Public libraries also engage in activities to promote information literacy. Like their counterparts in academic libraries, public librarians assist their clients in using online research tools such as the library catalogs and information databases. Although library patrons have access to information through their home computers and may work independently in the library, librarians frequently provide the personalized service that they may need to locate and identify the most appropriate information (American Library Association, 2002; Wilson, 2000).

## Conclusion

Public and academic libraries support lifelong learning in multiple ways. Academic libraries by their very nature engage in activities designed to support learners enrolled at their institutions. They actively promote information literacy, provide services to distance learners, and so forth. In public libraries, efforts related to lifelong learning may be less visible but, nevertheless, they are an integral part of the services provided.

## References

Adams, S., Krolak, L., Kupidura, E., and Pahernik, Z.P. (2002) "Libraries and resource centres: celebrating adult learners every week of the year," *Convergence* 35(2–3): 27–39.

American Library Association (2002) *ALA Library Fact Sheet Number 6*, ALA, Chicago. Available online at www.ala.org/ala/alalibrary/libraryfactsheet/ALA_print_layout_1_201599_201599.cfm (accessed April 2, 2007).

Association of College and Research Libraries (2000) *Information Literacy Competency Standards for Higher Education*, Chicago, IL: ACRL. Available online at www.ala.org/ala/acrl/acrlstandards/ informationliteracycompetency.htm (accessed April 22, 2007).

—— (2004) *Guidelines for Distance Learning Library Services*, Chicago, IL: ACRL. Available online at www.ala.org/ala/acrl/acrlstandards/guidelinesdistancelearning.htm (accessed April 22, 2007).

Australian and New Zealand Institute for Information Literacy (2004) *Australian and New Zealand Information Literacy Framework: Principles, standards, and practices*, Adelaide: ANZIIL. Available online at www.anziil.org/resources/Info%20lit%202nd%20edition.pdf (accessed April 22, 2007).

Bacon, A. (1980) "The role of the public library in a continuing education service," in The Library Association (eds) *Adult Education and Public Libraries in the 1980s: A Symposium*, London: The Library Association, pp. 41–68.

Brophy, P. and MacDougall, A. (2000) "Lifelong learning and libraries," *New Review of Libraries and Lifelong Learning* 1: 3–17.

Canadian Library Association (2000) *Guidelines for Library Support of Distance and Distributed Learning in Canada*, Ottawa: CLA. Available online at www.cla.ca/about/distance.htm (accessed April 22, 2007).

Cardoso, A.M. (1993) "Popular documentation and communication centres in Brazil," *Information Development* 9(4): 215–20.

Carr, D.W. (1999/1988) "The situation of the adult learner in the library," reprinted from a 1988 presentation, in P.O. Libutti (ed.) *Librarians as Learners, Librarians as Teachers*, Chicago, IL: Association of College and Research Libraries, American Library Association, pp. 18–35.

Council of Australian University Librarians (2001) *Information Literacy Standards*, Canberra: CAUL. Available online at www.caul.edu.au/caul-doc/InfoLitStandards2001.doc (accessed April 22, 2007).

Davies, D.W. (1974) *Public Libraries as Culture and Social Centers: The origin of the concept*, Metuchen, NJ: Scarecrow Press.

Ezzo, A. and Perez, J. (2000) "The information explosion: continuing implications for reference services to adult learners in academia," *Reference Librarian* 69/70: 5–17.

Garner, S. (ed.) (2006) *High-Level Colloquium on Information Literacy and Lifelong Learning: Report of a meeting held at the Bibliotheca Alexandria, Alexandria, Egypt, November 6–9, 2005*. Available online at www.ifla.org/III/wsis/High-Level-Colloquium.pdf (accessed April 22, 2007).

Giere, U. and Imel, S. (2000) *From Idea to Virtual Reality: ALADIN—Adult Learning and Documentation and Information Network*, Report of a CONFINTEA workshop and its follow-up, Hamburg: UNESCO Institute for Education. Available online at http://eric.ed.gov/ (accessed April 22, 2007).

Häggström, B.M. (2005) "Libraries as sources of knowledge and spaces for learning," in J. Thinesse-Demel (ed.) *Museums, Libraries and Cultural Heritage: Democratising culture, creating knowledge and building bridges*, Report on the workshop held at the CONFINTEA V Mid-Term Review Conference, Bangkok, Thailand, September 2003, Hamburg: UNESCO Institute for Education, pp. 4–8.

Indian Library Association (2001) *Guidelines for Library Services to Distance Learners*, Approved by the Council of Indian Library Association on July 28, 2001. Available online at http://uviclib.uvic.ca/dls/LSDL_Guidelines.pdf (accessed April 22, 2007).

International Federation of Library Associations (IFLA) (2004) *The Role of Libraries in Lifelong Learning*, Final report of the IFLA project under the Section for Public Libraries. Available online at www.ifla.org/VII/s8/proj/Lifelong-LearningReport.pdf (accessed April 22, 2007).

Jones-Kavalier B. and Flannigan, S. (2006) "Connecting the digital dots: literacy in the 21st century," *Educause Quarterly* 2: 8–10.

Lear, B.W. (2002) *Adult Programs in the Library*, Chicago, IL: American Library Association.

Longee, W.P. (2006) "Scholarly communication and libraries unbound: the opportunity of commons," in C. Hess and E. Ostrom (eds) *Understanding Knowledge as a Commons*, Cambridge, MA: MIT Press, pp. 311–32.

McNicol, S. and Dalton, P.(2003) "Broadening perspectives on the learning process in public libraries," *New Review of Libraries and Lifelong Learning* 4(1): 27–43.

Monroe, M.(1963) *Library Adult Education: The biography of an idea*, New York: Scarecrow Press.

Needham, G. and Johnson, K. (2007) "Ethical issues in providing library services to distance learners," *Open Learning* 22(2): 117–28.

Rader, H. (2001) *Information Literacy: An emerging global priority*, A White Paper prepared for UNESCO, the US National Commission on Libraries and Information Science, and the National Forum on Information Literacy, for use at the Information Literacy Meeting of Experts, Prague, Czech Republic. Available online at www.nclis.gov/libinter/infolitconf&meet/papers/rader-fullpaper.pdf (accessed April 22, 2007).

Robertson, D.A. (2005) *Cultural Programming for Libraries: Linking libraries, communities, and culture*, Chicago, IL: American Library Association.

Rosenberg, D. (1993) "Rural community resource centres: a sustainable option for Africa?," *Information Development* 9(1/2): 29–35.

—— (1994) "Can libraries in Africa ever be sustainable?," *Information Development* 10(4): 247–51.

Society of College, National and University Libraries (SCONUL) (1999) *Information Skills in Higher Education: A SCONUL position paper*, London: SCONUL, Advisory Committee on Information Literacy. Available online at www.sconul.ac.uk/groups/information_literacy/papers/seven_pillars. html (accessed April 22, 2007).

—— (2001) *Access for Distance Learners: Report of the SCONUL Task Force*, London: SCONUL. Available online at www.sconul.ac.uk/publications/pubs/index.html (accessed April 22, 2007).

Slade, A. (2005) *Library Services for Distance Learning: The fourth bibliography*. Available online at http://uviclib.uvic.ca/dls/bibliography4.html (accessed April 22, 2007).

—— and Kascus, M. (2000) *Library Services for Distance and Open Learning: The third annotated bibliography*, Englewood, CO: Libraries Unlimited.

Subramanian, J. (2002) "The growing and changing role of consortia in providing direct and indirect support for distance higher education," *Reference Librarian* 77: 39–62.

Thinesse-Demel, J. (2005) "Introduction," in J. Thinesse-Demel (ed.) *Museums, Libraries and Cultural Heritage: Democratising culture, creating knowledge and building bridges*, Report on the workshop held at the CONFINTEA V Mid-Term Review Conference, Bangkok, Thailand, September 2003, Hamburg: UNESCO Institute for Education, pp. 1–3.

Wills, H. (2003) "An innovative approach to reaching the non-learning public: the new Idea Stores in London," *New Review of Libraries and Lifelong Learning* 4: 107–20.

Wilson, M. (2000) "Understanding the needs of tomorrow's library user: rethinking library services for the new age," *APLIS* 13(2): 81–7.

Worcester, L. and Westbrook, L. (2004) "Ways of knowing: community information needs analysis," *Texas Library Journal* 80(3): 102–7.

# 17

# Tourism development in the Asia-Pacific region

## Opportunities for lifelong learning

*Jean-Louis Vignuda[1]*

While tourism has been practised in some form or another over many centuries, the phenomenon of tourism as an industry is a comparatively recent one. It is generally considered to have had its origins in Britain during the mid-1800s (Weaver and Opperman, 2000). And since then, the industry has shown continuous expansion, despite regional and temporal setbacks. Nowadays, tourism is often referred to as the world's largest growth industry, with an ever-increasing number of people travelling from, to and within more countries and the regions of the world. Leading industry in the service sector at the global level, tourism has become a major provider of jobs and a significant generator of foreign exchange at the national level.

Over the period 1995–2005, international tourist arrivals grew at an average annual rate of 4.1 per cent, exceeding the 800 million mark of arrivals in 2005, an all-time record, compared to 540 million as reported in 1995. This outstanding performance can be attributed to several factors, including, among others, the improvement of transportation and the introduction of low-cost airline services, easier access from traditional source markets and the emergence of new markets, such as China and India, rising levels of disposable income, and the diversification of the industry with new market niches such as, among others, cultural tourism, ecotourism and adventure tourism.

## International tourism development

### International tourist arrivals

Table 17.1, which presents international tourist arrivals by regions for two selected years, shows that, during the period 1995–2005, Asia and the Pacific region outperformed the rest of the world in tourism growth, with arrivals averaging an increase of 6.5 per cent annually, raising the global share from 15.3 per cent in 1995 to 19.2 per cent in 2005.

By contrast the two more mature regions – Europe and the Americas – have seen their respective global shares decrease from 58.3 per cent in 1995 to 54.8 per cent in 2005 for Europe and from 20.2 per cent to 16.6 per cent for the Americas over the same period. With such increases in numbers of international visitors, there is no doubt that in many destinations

*Table 17.1* International tourist arrivals by regions, 1995–2005

| Destinations | Arrivals (millions) | | Percentage of market share | | Average annual growth rate |
| --- | --- | --- | --- | --- | --- |
| | 1995 | 2005 | 1995 | 2005 | 1995–2005 |
| Africa | 20.3 | 36.7 | 3.7 | 4.6 | 6.1 |
| Americas | 109.0 | 133.5 | 20.2 | 16.6 | 2.1 |
| Asia–Pacific | 82.4 | 155.4 | 15.3 | 19.2 | 6.5 |
| Europe | 315.0 | 441.5 | 58.3 | 54.8 | 3.4 |
| Middle East | 13.3 | 39.1 | 2.5 | 4.8 | 11.4 |
| **World** | **540.0** | **806.0** | **100.0** | **100.0** | **4.1** |

Source: UNWTO (2004, 2005, 2006).

expenditures incurred by tourists on accommodation, food and drink, and other tourist-related services are important resources for the economy of the concerned countries. The United Nations World Tourism Organization estimated that in 2005 some 70 countries earned more than $US 1 billion from international tourism activities (UNWTO, 2006).

## International tourism receipts

Table 17.2 presents the international tourism receipts by regions of the world. Globally, in 2005, international tourists spent some $US 680 billion, a net increase of $US 269.2 billion in absolute terms since 1995. This is equivalent to an average increase of 5.2 per cent over the period. The Asia-Pacific region posted significant increases in international tourism receipts with an average annual growth rate of 5.4 per cent, in line with its growth performance in terms of arrivals over the previous ten years. This is slightly higher than the world rate of 5.2 per cent, outclassing the mature regions of Europe and the Americas in terms of tourism receipts. As a result, the global share of the Asia-Pacific region increased from 19.9 per cent in 1995 to 20.4 per cent in 2005, while shares of the Americas and Europe decreased over the same period.

*Table 17.2* International tourism receipts by regions, 1995–2005

| Destinations | Receipts (billion USD) | | Percentage of market share | | Average annual growth rate |
| --- | --- | --- | --- | --- | --- |
| | 1995 | 2005 | 1995 | 2005 | 1995–2005 |
| Africa | 8.5 | 21.5 | 2.1 | 3.2 | 9.7 |
| Americas | 98.4 | 144.6 | 24.0 | 21.2 | 3.9 |
| Asia–Pacific | 81.9 | 138.6 | 19.9 | 20.4 | 5.4 |
| Europe | 212.2 | 348.2 | 51.6 | 51.2 | 5.1 |
| Middle-East | 9.8 | 27.6 | 2.4 | 4.0 | 10.9 |
| **World** | **410.8** | **680.0** | **100.0** | **100.0** | **5.2** |

Source: UNWTO (2004, 2005, 2006).

## The economic dimension of tourism

The economic impact of the tourism industry can be seen in terms of revenue, especially its contribution to a country's gross domestic product (GDP). Table 17.3 illustrates the contribution that tourism made to the GDP in a selected number of developing countries of the Asia-Pacific region in 2006 as well as to their total exports.

The highest contributions to GDP are those from island states (the Maldives, Fiji, Tonga, and Vanuatu), where the tourism sector is predominant as few other economic alternatives exist. Indeed, many of these small Pacific island economies are highly dependent on tourism as evidenced by their significant share of tourism in their total export earning, to an extent comparable with the dependence on single developing primary commodities. For instance, tourism together with sugar are Fiji's two economic mainstays. In 2006, tourism alone contributed 43.5 per cent of total export earnings of Fiji and one third of its GDP. Similarly, in the Maldives tourism is the top export sector, well before the fisheries industry, capturing a 65.9 per cent share of total foreign exchange earnings and contributing two thirds of its GDP. Other small islands are dependent on tourism for about, or more than, half of their exports, such as Tonga (47.2 per cent) and Vanuatu (73.7 per cent).

*Table 17.3* Contribution of tourism (direct and indirect) to GDP and total exports in the Asia-Pacific region, 2006

| Countries | To GDP (per cent) | To total exports (per cent) |
|---|---|---|
| *Northeast Asia* | **10.3** | **8.2** |
| China | 13.7 | 7.4 |
| Republic of Korea | 6.8 | 6.8 |
| *Southeast Asia* | **7.0** | **8.4** |
| Cambodia | 19.6 | 22.3 |
| Indonesia | 8.7 | 11.5 |
| Lao PDR | 9.3 | 21.4 |
| Papua New Guinea | 9.2 | 7.5 |
| Philippines | 9.1 | 8.3 |
| Singapore | 10.3 | 4.2 |
| Thailand | 14.3 | 12.6 |
| Vietnam | 10.9 | 9.4 |
| *South Asia* | **5.5** | **5.4** |
| India | 5.3 | 4.7 |
| Iran (Islamic Rep. of) | 9.8 | 12.1 |
| Maldives | 66.6 | 65.9 |
| Nepal | 8.2 | 22.6 |
| Sri Lanka | 9.6 | 14.9 |
| *Oceania* | **13.1** | **22.4** |
| Fiji | 33.1 | 43.5 |
| Tonga | 17.5 | 47.2 |
| Vanuatu | 47.0 | 73.7 |

Source: World Travel and Tourism Council (WTTC, 2006).

Note: The data used in the table refer to the *Travel and Tourism Economy* (direct and indirect impact) as these provide a more comprehensive account of the tourism sector.

Tourism in China also provides a substantial contribution to its GDP, amounting to 13.7 per cent in 2006, reflecting the remarkable growth of its tourism industry. Taking full advantage of the potential of their natural and cultural tourism resources, countries from the Greater Mekong sub-region are now reaping the benefits of the development of their tourism industry. In 2006, tourism in Cambodia and the Lao People's Democratic Republic respectively accounted for 22.3 and 21.4 per cent of their total exports and respectively contributed 19.6 and 9.3 per cent to their GDP.

In the other countries, the contribution of tourism to GDP and to total exports averaged between 7 and 10 per cent, mainly because their economies are much more diversified. However, in the light of the expected continuous growth of the tourism industry in the foreseeable future, it can be assumed that the part tourism plays in the Asia-Pacific region's economy will become more significant across the board.

## *The social dimension of tourism*

While there are various definitions of social development depending on the context in which the analysis is made, all of them tend to converge, in essence, around the concept of improving the well-being of a country's citizens, by promoting higher standards of living, employment and economic conditions through social policy and economic and political initiatives (ITU, 2006). Therefore, in the absence of better indicators to measure the impact of tourism on the social development of a region, the importance of the tourism workforce has been chosen to assess such an impact.

The tourism industry significantly contributes to the creation of employment, both directly and indirectly. Table 17.4 compares the number of employees in the tourism sector in the Asia-Pacific region by country and their share in total employment in 2006.

The tourism industry in the whole Asia-Pacific region was able in 2006 to provide jobs to about 140 million, representing an average of 8.9 percent of total employment. Looking at the sub-regional level, tourism employment in Northeast Asia was estimated at 86 million jobs or 10.1 percent of total employment, representing 1 in every 9.9 jobs. This is mainly attributed to the remarkable development of the tourism sector in China, where one Chinese out of ten works in a tourism-related industry. In Oceania, where the tourism industry is one of the main economic sectors, the workforce in the tourism sector accounted for 14.5 percent of total employment or 1 in every 6.9 jobs. The importance of tourism becomes more acute when we analyze the structure of the workforce in selected Pacific island economies. For instance, in 2006 one Fijian out of three was employed in the tourism sector, while in Vanuatu the ratio was one to 2.4 jobs. In the Maldives one in every 1.7 jobs was created by tourism, representing 57.6 percent of the total employment.

A comparison of tourism-dependent countries in the other sub-regions, namely Southeast Asia and South Asia, highlights that employment in the tourism sector, as a share of the total employment in 2006, varied between 5.4 percent in India to more than 10 percent in both the Philippines and Thailand.

## Cultural tourism in the Asia-Pacific region

A notable feature of the tourism industry is its focus on market segmentation as a way to provide better services to specific groups of tourists depending on their social, cultural, and economic characteristics. New market segments are continually being sought by the industry as older segments mature and evolve. Cultural tourism emerged as a product in the late 1970s and rapidly became a specialized niche tourist activity that initially was thought to attract a small number of better educated and more affluent tourists whose primary interest was to enjoy a cultural experience rather than the standard sand, sun, and sea holiday. However, since the early 1990s cultural tourism continues to evolve and has gradually become a high-profile mainstream tourism activity. Indeed, all travel involves cultural elements, such as visits to landmarks, historic sites and museums.

The long and diverse history of the Asia–Pacific region and its rich cultural heritage have long been major attractions for tourists from across the world. The Asia–Pacific region is home to some 168 cultural World Heritage sites, many of which are very popular tourist destinations attracting millions of visitors every year. For example, according to the Cambodia Tourism Ministry, during the first six months of 2007, there were 615,448 visitor arrivals to Angkor Wat, one of the most famous World Heritage sites in the region, a 55.67 percent increase from the 395,360 arrivals reported in the same period the previous year.

*Table 17.4* Contribution of tourism (direct and indirect) to employment in the Asia–Pacific region, 2006

| Countries | To employment | | Ratio of tourism employment to total employment |
|---|---|---|---|
| | *(thousand jobs)* | *(per cent)* | |
| *Northeast Asia* | **85,577** | **10.1** | **1:9.9** |
| China | 77,600 | 10.2 | 1:9.8 |
| Republic of Korea | 1,731 | 7.4 | 1:13.4 |
| *Southeast Asia* | **21,743** | **8.6** | **1:11.7** |
| Cambodia | 1,072 | 15.4 | 1:6.5 |
| Indonesia | 7,332 | 7.2 | 1:13.8 |
| Lao PDR | 203 | 7.3 | 1:13.7 |
| Papua New Guinea | 194 | 7.5 | 1:13.3 |
| Philippines | 3,336 | 10.8 | 1:9.2 |
| Singapore | 191 | 8.3 | 1:12.0 |
| Thailand | 3,820 | 10.7 | 1:9.4 |
| Vietnam | 3,364 | 8.7 | 1:11.5 |
| *South Asia* | **30,891** | **5.2** | **1:19.4** |
| India | 24,349 | 5.4 | 1:18.4 |
| Iran (Islamic Rep. of) | 1,712 | 8.7 | 1:11.4 |
| Maldives | 69 | 57.6 | 1:1.7 |
| Nepal | 726 | 6.4 | 1:15.5 |
| Sri Lanka | 662 | 7.9 | 1:12.7 |
| *Oceania* | **1,911** | **14.5** | **1:6.9** |
| Fiji | 196 | 31.0 | 1:3.2 |
| Tonga | 5 | 15.2 | 1:6.6 |
| Vanuatu | 26 | 42.4 | 1:2.4 |

Source: WTTC (2006).

## Human resources development

Such a continuing growth in tourist arrivals is exerting an ever increasing demand on trained manpower in the hospitality and travel sectors. The challenges for countries are thus to provide a balanced blend of academic education and professional training via formal courses and accredited programmes delivered through educational and training institutions. Indeed, international tourists expect international standards of service.

In this context, efforts are made by several universities and colleges in the region to offer programmes on the tourism business and hotel management at under- and postgraduate levels, with a view to equipping students with professional knowledge and technical competence in preparation for their leadership responsibilities in the tourism industry. Also very valuable is education provided beyond the formal setting of universities and colleges, for example certificates and diplomas delivered by professional institutions in areas such as front desk management, housekeeping, cookery, bakery and confectionery.

With the emergence of cultural tourism, the industry in addition requires a set of skilled personnel who are particularly trained in the cultural value of tourist destinations and are able to convey informative messages to the visitors on cultural tourism sites. Who are these personnel? They comprise all persons who come in direct contact with the visitors, from the time they arrive at the host destination until their departure. They include primarily taxi drivers, local tour guides, and tour escorts.

Among them, local tour guides play an important role as they have the potential to help visitors to enjoy their tourism experience and carry home images of the host destination. The responsibility of these local tour guides is to bring to life the historical sites and tell the story attached to it. However, the quality of the message conveyed and the effectiveness of the experience mainly depend on the type of knowledge that the guide has about the cultural site and its interpretation.

The first people that visitors meet on arrival at a tourism destination are often taxi drivers. They also have in their own way the potential to create a lasting impression on tourists in providing information on the cultural value of the host destination. Indeed, they may provide useful information on the various cultural landmarks that they pass by on their way to the hotel or other destinations. It is therefore important that such information be of a quality that in turn may add interest to the whole tourism experience.

Unlike the local tour guides who operate at destinations, a tour escort accompanies a tour group for the entire duration of their visit. The escort's primary role is to ensure the smooth conduct of the tour and thereby contribute to the visitors' experience through setting up customized tours, which may well include visits to attractions at a cultural destination. While local tour guides will take over the group at the cultural destination, escorts may prepare the visitors by providing preliminary information on the cultural sites to be visited. In contrast to local tour guides, the basic employment requirements of tour escorts are not their cultural or heritage backgrounds. It is therefore important that they are provided with specific training to equip them with real knowledge of the cultural places that could be included in their prospective tours.

## Tourism education in the region

In response to the demand of the tourism industry in terms of trained manpower, government education and training institutes, as well as private ones, offer a number of programmes particularly aimed at these above-mentioned areas in addition to formal academic programmes. In the following paragraphs are some examples of initiatives taken by both public and private educational and training institutes in the Asia-Pacific region in this regard.

The Institute for Tourism Studies (IFT), established in 1995, is a public institution of higher education in Macao (China) offering tourism and hospitality management degree programmes, as well as professional training. The *Prospectus* further emphasizes that IFT programme are designed and delivered with a clear focus on the demands and challenges unique to tourism and hospitality. The Institute also offers practical training and on-the-job work opportunities through its internship and practicum programmes. Since the addition of 'the Historic Centre of Macao' to the World Heritage list in 2005, IFT has introduced two new Bachelor Degree Programmes – Heritage Management and Tourism Event Management – since the academic year 2005–6.

One of the interesting initiatives of IFT is the Professional and Continuing Education School (PACES), which enables the Institute to be linked with the industry and the local community. Within this programme, the Institute provides professional and continuing education at all levels, particularly to mature individuals for self-development and career advancement. IFT proposes customized training programmes to public and private entities to upgrade their employees' professional skills and knowledge. PACES training programmes are conducted in areas such as tourism and events, hospitality and catering, languages, customer service and management. They are made available to the general public, secondary schools, and local industry partners.

In India, the central government and the state governments have collaborated to provide resources in order to train people in the hospitality sector, through the establishment of institutes of hotel management throughout the country. These institutes conduct several types of courses in hotel management, craftsmanship, and food and beverage services. These include three-year diploma courses, postgraduate diploma courses, six-month courses and certificate courses. In addition to the central government's support for training tourism industry personnel, there are other training courses and programmes carried out by various agencies, including universities, state governments and private organizations. These agencies offer training courses and short courses lasting between three months and one year in areas such as cooking, bakery, confectionery, housekeeping and other services.

## Support from international organizations for tourism education

Issues related to human resources development in the tourism sector go beyond the number of people employed. They relate to the quality of manpower, their conditions of work, their training and educational opportunities, the role of the private sector, and the role of governments in giving attention to and finding solutions to problems and constraints. While individual countries are taking necessary steps to develop their human resources capacity, achievements in some countries remain uneven due to a number of factors. For example, some countries suffer from a lack of adequate training and education facilities necessary to meet the growing demand for skilled and trained personnel in the industry. There might also be shortages of skilled trainers, instructors and teaching staff to meet industry needs. The curriculum and skill standards may also need to be upgraded. Some other countries may lack the resources available to expand or improve their existing capability to develop the required human resources for the tourism industry. Closer cooperation among countries is one way to overcome some of these constraints and shortcomings effectively. Indeed, countries could usefully share their strengths and expertise with those lacking them. To this end, strengthening institutional links among tourism training institutes can form a basis for exchanges of experience and information.

## Network of Asia-Pacific Education and Training Institutes in Tourism (APETIT)[2]

It was against that background that the Network of Asia-Pacific Education and Training Institutes in Tourism (APETIT) was established by UNESCAP[3] in 1997, as networking was then considered the most practical mechanism for regional cooperation and collaboration. APETIT has since been functioning as an effective mechanism for promoting cooperation and training. The Network started with 24 members and by July 2007 it had grown to 248 education and training institutes, and national tourism organizations in 44 countries and areas. APETIT is administered by an Executive Committee and a General Council with the UNESCAP secretariat acting as regional coordinator.

The main purposes of the Network are threefold, namely to strengthen the institutional capabilities of various countries' tourism training, education, and research institutes; to encourage cooperation among them; and to overcome the quantitative and qualitative shortages of human resources in the tourism industry. Since its inception, the APETIT has facilitated the implementation of specific operational activities that benefited a number of APETIT members. These included the exchange of experience among tourism education and training institutes and national tourism organizations in the region; the conduct of seminars and training programmes with experts drawn from member institutes acting as resource persons; the provision of advisory services on human resources development; the organization of students' and faculty members' exchange programmes; the organization of study tours; and the conduct of joint research activities in the area of human resources development.

The following specific examples of cooperative activities demonstrate the commitment of APETIT membership to meeting the challenges faced by the tourism industry in the region and to cooperating in raising the training standards of tourism education programmes. Several training programmes in the areas of restaurant and front office operations were conducted in Vietnam with the support of Thai experts. Groups of students from Vietnam participated in a programme on cultural heritage organized by Thailand. Vietnam conducted two three-month courses on public management in tourism, the first one for officials from the Laos National Administration of Tourism and the second one for middle-level managers from the Ministry of Tourism of Cambodia. Macao (China) offers, on a continuous basis, courses to APETIT members in the fields of heritage tourism, train-the-trainers on tourism and hospitality. With the cooperation of APETIT member institutes and organizations in Hong Kong (China), India, Macao (China), the Philippines and Thailand, which made available their experts to act as resource persons, several capacity-building seminars and national training workshops on sustainable tourism development, including human resources development, were organized in various countries of the region such as the Lao People's Democratic Republic, Vietnam, Cambodia, Mongolia, Kyrgyzstan, Azerbaijan and Bangladesh.

With the aim of fully operationalizing the Network, new initiatives have been added to its programmes of activities. In 2005, a *Directory of Student and Staff Exchanges* was published, providing a range of very useful information on APETIT member institutes interested in entering into students' and faculty members' exchanges within the framework of the Network. Simultaneously, a *Directory of APETIT Expertise* was compiled and published. The *Directory* provides basic information on potential experts from APETIT member institutes who can be called upon to render advisory and/or expertise services to other APETIT members. The Network has recently launched an initiative aimed at promoting and intensifying student exchange within APETIT. This initiative, the *APETIT Marco Polo Programme*, is based on the European Union 'Erasmus Programme', allowing tourism and hospitality students to study at various institutions in the Asia-Pacific region and accumulate credits for graduation. Following the principles of the 'Erasmus programme', the initiative seeks to enhance quality and develop a pan-Asian and Pacific cultural spirit. The advantages of the proposed scheme would thus encompass student mobility, learning experience in diverse environments and a cross-cultural experience.

The latest initiative of the Network is a proposal to open an APETIT knowledge portal that would encourage APETIT member institutions to make available Open Education Resources (OER) in the form of digitally based, as well as other course material, lectures and links to other sources to APETIT member institutions. The knowledge portal would be divided into several sections including (1) course outlines and objectives; (2) course material in a form of PowerPoint; (3) video material; (4) lectures that have been videotaped; and (5) links to sites where network members can access further information. The proposed portal would enable APETIT member institutions to gain access to the experience of more established institutions in developing their programmes. It was also felt that the knowledge portal could serve as a focus point for cooperative ventures in developing digitally based distance education materials. The modalities of this initiative are being elaborated.

## UNESCO Cultural Heritage Specialist Guide Training and Certification Programme

In order to improve the sustainability at World Heritage sites, UNESCO-ICCROM[4] Asian Academy of Heritage Management (AAHM) initiated in 2005 a regional programme to improve training for heritage guides, particularly those working directly at the sites. The UNESCO Cultural Heritage Specialist Guide Training and Certification Programme responds to the need to provide specialized and enhanced training for professional guides in the Asia-Pacific region. This guide training programme is jointly implemented by the IFT in Macao (China) and UNESCO. The programme has several objectives. First, it offers advance training for guides that will complement existing national training and certification programmes. It also helps improve the interpretation of the sites, thereby enhancing the experience of visitors and increasing stays. The programme also aims at promoting positive interaction and benefits for local communities, contributing to the sustainability of the sites, and improving the career prospects and incomes of the guides. Finally, it is expected that, with the implementation of the programme, the capacity of National Tourism Organizations (NTOs) and partner training institutions would be strengthened.

The programme entails the production of customized training materials and train-the-trainers courses at national level, and conducts train-the-trainers sub-regional workshops and national-level training workshops, including certification of guides. The beneficiaries of the programme include: (1) guides working at UNESCO World Heritage Sites; (2) visitors to UNESCO World Heritage sites; (3) World Heritage sites and management authorities; (4) local communities, including local tourism businesses; and (5) National Tourism Organizations and training institutions.

The programme has been adopted under the Asian Development Bank (ADB) South Asia Sub-regional Economic Cooperation (SASEC) Tourism Development Plan and the ADB Greater Mekong sub-region (GMS) Tourism Strategy. The first phase of the programme has been completed under ADB sponsorship in South Asia and the GMS through the organization of two sub-regional workshops in Paro, Bhutan (6–11 May 2006) and Luang Prabang,

Lao People's Democratic Republic (6–14 October 2006). Workshop participants included trainers from Bhutan, India, Nepal and Sri Lanka along with Cambodia, China (Yunnan), Lao People's Democratic Republic, Myanmar and Thailand.

## UNESCAP Project on Human Resources Development in Tourism in the Greater Mekong sub-region

The six countries of the GMS[5] have recognized the value of their cultural heritage sites and the importance of managing these sites properly in order to further improve and develop their tourism sectors. However, there are indications that, in most of the GMS countries, agencies or institutions responsible for managing these sites suffer from weak human resources and lack of high standards in the management of cultural tourism sites. It was therefore generally felt that it would be useful and highly beneficial to develop a standardized training package for trainers in cultural tourism sites management.

In response to this need, UNESCAP launched a technical project in 2006, designed to strengthen the teaching capacity of the six GMS countries in cultural tourism sites management. The underlying aim is to assist countries in raising the standards of their education and training institutions offering tourism and hospitality management courses through the provision of a training manual for trainers and the conduct of national training workshops.

The topics covered in the training manual for trainers are divided into eight modules. The first six modules are designed to help develop trainers' knowledge and understanding of cultural tourism: cultural heritage; management issues related to cultural tourism sites; facilities management; visitor management; community participation; and integrated management on cultural tourism sites. In addition to the core knowledge, this module provides examples of various teaching methods, such as worksheets, workshops and group discussions, that can be adopted by the trainers in their own training programmes. Modules 7 and 8 are designed to help develop the teaching capacity of the trainers. They provide guidelines on how a trainer can plan and run an effective training programme for cultural tourism sites management and how the trainer can enhance her or his knowledge of the subject through a self-learning programme.

The project entered its second phase with the organization of national training workshops to be conducted at a cultural tourism site of the selected country, in order to enable the organization of field visits to support the theoretical part of the training. National training workshops have accordingly been conducted in Hoi An, Vietnam (23–28 July 2007) and Bangkok, Thailand (30 July–4 August 2007). Participants at both workshops were professors and lecturers on tourism destination management from leading universities and colleges of the two countries. Similar training workshops were planned in the later part of 2007 in Wat Phou, the Lao People's Democratic Republic and in Siem Reap, Cambodia.

## Conclusion

Tourism has become one of the most important economic activities in the world today and the tourism sector in the Asia-Pacific region has shown over the past few years impressive performance in terms of increases in international tourist arrivals and growth in volume of international tourism receipts. As a result, tourism directly generates services, products, foreign exchange earnings, employment and investment. However, the rapid growth of tourism can lead to challenges for governments in policy-making, planning and managing tourism development in a sustainable and responsible manner and in ensuring adequate resources development.

Universities and education institutes have designed a complete range of specialized graduate and postgraduate programmes on tourism and hospitality management to prepare younger managers to take up key positions in a growing tourism industry. However, jobs in the tourism sector now carry more emphasis on developing social and language skills in a cross-cultural environment. Indeed, hotels and tourism enterprises, including travel and tour operators, are recruiting young people with little technical training but with well-developed social and language skills. With larger numbers of staff being recruited directly from high schools, it is essential to further improve in-service training. Indeed, work-based training will facilitate programmes organized jointly by the tourism industry and training institutions.

The Asia-Pacific region also has a rich cultural heritage, and special attention needs to be taken to preserve its uniqueness when developing human resources for the tourism sector. Personnel should therefore be trained to identify themselves with their own cultures as well as to learn to appreciate and respect the cultures of visitors.

There is thus strong evidence that tourism could form the basis for lifelong learning and this form of education should be further developed not only for responding to the demand of the industry as a whole, but also to ensure that cultural heritage is treasured and preserved.

## Notes

1   The views expressed herein are those of the author and do not necessarily reflect the views of the United Nations.
2   For details of APETIT consult www.apetit-network.org.
3   The United Nations Economic and Social Commission for Asia and the Pacific (UNESCAP) is one and the largest of the five regional commissions of the United Nations. It currently comprises 62 member governments representing more than 50 per cent of the global population. The primary function of UNESCAP is to promote economic and social development through regional and sub-regional cooperation.
4   ICCROM, the International Centre for the Study of the Preservation and Restoration of Cultural Property, is an intergovernmental body founded in 1956, which provides expert advice on how to conserve World Heritage sites, as well as training in restoration techniques.
5   Cambodia, the People's Republic of China (Guangxi and Yunnan), the Lao People's Democratic Republic, Myanmar, Thailand and Vietnam.

## References

International Telecommunications Union (ITU) (2006) *World Telecommunication/ICT Development Report*, Geneva: ITU.

Institute For Tourism Studies (ITS) (2007) *Prospectus 2007–2009,* Macao, China: ITS.

*Travel Trade Report* (2007) 'Cambodia's arrivals in big leap', 30(30) (August): 22–8, Bangkok, Thailand: TTR.

UNWTO (2004) *Tourism Market Trends Asia*, Paris: World Tourism Organization.

—— (2005) *Tourism Market Trends Asia*, Paris: World Tourism Organization.

—— (2006) *Tourism Highlights*, Paris: World Tourism Organization.

Weaver, D. and Opperman, M. (2000) *Tourism Management,* Milton Park, QLD: John Wiley and Australia.

World Travel and Tourism Council (WTTC) (2006) *Tourism Satellite Accounts: Regional reports*. Available online at www.wttc.org/frameset2.htm (accessed 25 November 2007).

# Part 4
## Modes of learning

# 18

# A critique of self-directed learning in the modern context

*Richard Taylor*

## Introduction: self-directed learning, individualism and democracy

At first sight the concept of self-directed learning would appear to be an uncomplicated good. Putting the learner centre stage, ensuring that his or her needs and interests are given the highest priority, and thereby ensuring that educational provision and the necessary structures are 'relevant' and 'fit for purpose' (to use two of the more tired pieces of jargon of the day) – all these are part of the mainstream political agenda.

Underlying these contemporary emphases is the longstanding but now especial dominance of individualism in political culture. 'Possessive individualism' has long been recognised as one of primary ideological features of liberal capitalism: and, in the British context, particularly of the Liberal Party and the social democratic wing of Labour. The rise of populist conservatism in the 1980s and its profound influence upon society and politics gave a new prominence to individualist rhetoric.

New Labour from the 1990s significantly developed and extended this ideology within the Third Way politics espoused by Tony Blair. Although this became increasingly beset by a whole series of problems – some in the domestic sphere but more importantly those in foreign affairs, in particular of course the war in Iraq and its aftermath – New Labour's ideology remains at its core one of 'marketised welfarism', as I have argued at length elsewhere (Taylor, 2006).

Education policy in general reflected these trends, and arguably in the post-compulsory sector the changes in emphasis were even more marked than elsewhere. There are two overwhelming and obvious changes in this sector as far as lifelong learning is concerned: one is the rapid expansion, particularly, of higher education; and the second, linked to it, is the recognition that education and training are the most important priorities for modern liberal capitalist societies if they are to remain both economically competitive in a globalised world, and cohesive and dynamic in their social and political cultures. (Interestingly, Will Hutton's 2007 book on China argues that it is precisely because the latter element is missing in monolithic Communist structures that China is unlikely to assume in the long term the dominant world role predicted by many on the basis of its phenomenal rates of economic growth.)

These themes of change impact directly upon the ways in which self-directed learning is conceptualised and practised. In the early years of the Labour Government, for example, David Blunkett articulated the concern for cultural and social educational perspectives with some passion: his introduction to *The Learning Age*, the Government's 1998 policy paper, includes an oft-quoted passage lauding democratic and, by implication, self-directed learning:

> The Learning Age will be built upon a renewed commitment to self-improvement and on a recognition of the enormous contribution learning makes to our society. Learning helps shape the values that we pass on to each succeeding generation. Learning supports active citizenship and democracy, giving men and women the capacity to provide leadership in their communities.
>
> (DfEE, 1998)

But this enthusiasm was relatively short-lived (and, as some critics have observed, even in *The Learning Age*, the radicalism of Blunkett's 'Foreword' is not carried through into the body of the text itself). As will be argued below, New Labour's policy has been dominated, as has happened in most comparable societies, by human capital, economic competitiveness arguments (Taylor, 2006).

There are two other aspects of the changes that are directly relevant to the theme of self-directed learning. The coming of a *mass* system has resulted, among other things, in an increased degree of student choice, partly because of modularity, and partly because of a whole series of other developments, including open and distance learning opportunities and the growth of flexible modes of study, through part-time degree provision, for example.

The second characteristic is at a different level altogether: traditional subject disciplinary assumptions and the epistemological perspectives that underpinned them have come under persistent attack. Both postmodernists and the advocates of a more 'relevant' vocational higher education have struck at the very roots of traditional approaches to the academy (see Jessop, 1991; Scott, 1995; Smith and Webster, 1997; Taylor *et al.*, 2002; Usher and Edwards, 1994). More or less by default, this has also empowered learners, as the previously established disciplinary canons increasingly came into question. Not that this should be exaggerated: for example, at least two of the key parts of the bureaucratic system of higher education – the QAA (Quality Assurance Agency) and the RAE (Research Assessment Exercise) – are based four-square on traditional disciplinary boundaries and the accompanying assumptions.

There is therefore abundant evidence that the centrality of self-directed learning has increased significantly. And, as individualist assumptions are widely held, as noted, to characterise a proper democracy, is there any reason to question self-directed learning as an uncomplicated good? I believe there is. In my view, there is a marked dichotomy between the deep-seated democratic tradition of self-directed learning and learner empowerment, and the contemporary, New Labour orientation.

## The democratic tradition of self-directed learning

In a 1968 lecture, E.P. Thompson referred to the symbiotic relationship, in adult education, between the worlds of life experience and work, and the abstract theorisation and historical knowledge of the academy:

> All education which is worth the name involves a relationship of mutuality, a dialectic: and no worthwhile educationalist conceives of his material as a class of inert recipients

of instruction. But, in liberal adult education, no tutor is likely to last out a session – and no class is likely to stay the course with him – if he is under the misapprehension that the role of the class is passive. What is different about the adult student is the experience which he brings to the relationship. This experience modifies, sometimes subtly and sometimes more radically, the entire education process . . . To strike the balance between intellectual rigour and respect for experience is always difficult. But the balance today [1968] is seriously awry . . . [I wish to redress it a little] by reminding us that universities engage in adult education not only to teach but also to learn.

(Thompson, 1968)

Although specific to *adult* education, and somewhat dated, this notion of symbiosis, of the interaction between life and experience on the one hand, and the abstract and detailed knowledge of the academy on the other, remains central to good educational practice. But, and this is the crucial point in this context, self-directed learning is held to be about much more than this. First of all it is a collective, group learning experience as well as an individual one. Education and learning are about more than individual personal development, let alone education construed as primarily a means of self-advancement materially. Second, it is concerned in the broad sense with social purpose, with organic growth, through education and learning, of participative democracy; and it is concerned too with equality, with enabling the working class and other disadvantaged groups to have access to knowledge and education, partly for personal development and fulfilment (the 'sheer joy of learning') and partly to create and nurture a dynamic civil society. Third, it is based upon a concept of education and learning as a mutual, shared experience, valuing the life experience and collective voice of the group as much as that of the abstract knowledge of the academy and the tutor.

The social purpose, though, had an explicitly political dimension too. This tradition of self-directed learning saw the partnership between the academy and the learners as facilitating progressive, democratic social change, often through social movements. Obvious examples are the labour movement, through partnership in educational provision with trade unions, and 'New Opportunities', access and women's studies programmes linked to the women's movement. 'Knowledge is power' has been a firm conviction of the Left, in all its forms: from William Lovett of the Chartists, to the Italian Communist Gramsci, to Shirley Williams and the Social Democratic Party (SDP).

The democratic tradition has thus held to a no doubt rather romantic belief that a mix of education and learning, social purpose, individual enlightenment, and progressive political commitment can produce a centrally important element in a democratic political culture.

Of course there are problems with this conceptualisation, and it has been strongly contested. Before moving on to consider New Labour's very different orientation, we should note some of the main elements of this critique. Essentially, these fell under two heads: the complexity and fractured nature of the political commitments, and the contested nature of the 'liberal tradition'. There is of course a whole literature on the British Left. Here, the key points are that lifelong learning has been centred on Left Labourism (or democratic socialism, as its advocates prefer), with strong, vociferous but minority currents on the Marxist Left – including both orthodox Communists and more libertarian socialists (for example, E.P. Thompson and Raymond Williams). Within the mainstream Labourist tradition, commitment to learner empowerment was at best patchy. The shifting orthodoxy of Labourism was very evident, particularly in the Cold War years from the 1940s onwards (Fieldhouse, 1985, 1996). The learner-centred approach was often blocked at one level or another because of a conservative insistence on both established bureaucratic practice and ideological orthodoxy.

Although this democratic tradition has thus been somewhat intermittent, it has always been there: and, outside this Labourist framework, radical adult education has flourished, at particular times and in response to particular social and political circumstances (Harrison, 1961; Johnston, 1997; Lovett, 1983; Mayo and Thompson, 1995; Taylor *et al.*, 2002; Thompson, 1963, 1983; Ward and Taylor, 1986).

The second issue – the contested liberal tradition – is relevant because self-directed learning, and the whole democratic educational tradition, has taken place very largely within this overriding framework. However, the liberal tradition has been often far from democratic and learner-centred – or, for that matter, 'radical'. Some, such as Robin Usher, have seen the liberal tradition as conservative, elitist and permeated by a series of unwarrantable progressive, modernist assumptions (Usher, 1997). Feminist critics, such as Jane Thompson, have seen the liberal tradition as patriarchal and exclusive; and vocationally orientated critics have seen the liberal tradition as anachronistic and a brake upon a more vocational, professional approach (Jessop, 1991; Thompson, 1983).

Whatever the validity or otherwise of these criticisms, it is beyond doubt that the liberal tradition derives from the wider ideological perspective of liberalism; and this in turn is centred on individualism and, in particular, the importance of freedom for the individual in the economic and social spheres, and in civil society generally (Coffield and Williamson, 1997; Fieldhouse, 1996; Ryan, 1999; Taylor 1996; Taylor *et al.*, 1985). Thus, educationally, the individual is at the centre of the system – and his or her personal development is the key criterion. Clearly, there is a tension here with the collective, social purpose approach. In addition, there are assumptions about linearity of knowledge, the sanctity of traditional disciplinary boundaries and an unquestioning acceptance of the 'bourgeois canon' in terms of curriculum – and there is certainly a conservative dimension, to put it mildly, to the liberal tradition. All this is mirrored to a large extent in the traditional mainstream epistemology and culture of the academy (Barnett, 2000; Scott, 1995).

Finally, there is the obvious empirical point that the large majority of those attending liberal adult education provision is now, and always has been, middle class, white and relatively well educated (and often late middle aged or elderly). Of course, the same applies – with the exception of the generational point – to an even greater extent to mainstream higher education.

Undoubtedly, therefore, the liberal tradition is both pluralistic and contested. But, in its radical, democratic, social purpose dimension, there is a particular perception of self-directed learning that is centrally concerned with progressive educational and social change. This stands in sharp contrast to New Labour perspectives and practice.

## New Labour and self-directed learning

New Labour ideology derives in part from the bruising experiences of Labour's years in opposition under the Thatcher and later Major governments, and the repeated electoral disappointments from 1979 to the mid-1990s; and partly from a series of revisionist social democratic arguments. The former is self-explanatory – though the consequent policy positions adopted by Tony Blair as a result have been arguably deeply misguided, even by straightforward electoral criteria, let alone any *socialist* ones. It is the latter, ideological, stance that is relevant here for the purpose of 'placing' self-directed learning in the overall educational policy framework.

There is clearly a Christian element to Tony Blair's personal ideological perspective, though it is doubtful whether this has applied to New Labour more generally: we do, for good or ill, live in a largely secular society. (As Alastair Campbell put it, 'We don't do God.') It is important though to differentiate this from the Labour Party's historically significant Christian socialism – such a key element in the Party's early years. Blair's Christianity clearly has much more in common with personal moral and spiritual aspects of Christian belief than with the strongly social and radical perspectives of Christian socialism.

More important than any form of Christian inspiration, however, has been the political legacy of the social democratic ideology of the SDP – and the personal influence of Roy Jenkins. This in turn is based, I would argue, on the more intellectually weighty revisionism of the 'Fabians' of the 1950s and early 1960s: in particular, Anthony Crosland, whose *The Future of Socialism* (1956) remains a powerful critique of Marxist-inspired socialist theory. Crosland argued that, because of the marked changes in the structure of modern capitalism, issues of social class based upon 'ownership and control of the means of production' had become literally an irrelevance: there was, by the mid-twentieth century, a clear separation between ownership and control, and as a consequence the rise of a powerful professional elite based much more than in the past upon a meritocratic social structure (Perkin, 1989). The social democratic agenda, therefore, was concerned with a mixed economy capitalism ('welfare capitalism') characterised socially by a meritocratic emphasis upon equality of opportunity.

It is not relevant here to debate whether or not this analysis and the prescription that followed from it was correct. But it is worth noting that the continued growth predicted by the neo-Keynesian social democrats of the period was short-lived (see the economic crisis precipitated by the oil shortages and price rises from 1973), and that subsequently neo-liberal free market economics as advocated by Margaret Thatcher and Ronald Reagan – and continued in most ways by their successors, including Tony Blair – became dominant.

However, the main point here is that New Labour's ideology, stripped of the hype and the 'spin', is an updated version of Crosland's social democracy, and Giddens' (1998) *Third Way,* which is little more than a superficial, even more revisionist version of the same thesis. In this context, socialism as a whole has of course changed irrevocably since Crosland's time. In particular, the collapse of the Soviet Union and Marxism-Leninism as a world ideology has had reverberations that are very much with us still. Less dramatically, but important nonetheless, social democracy and related socialist politics in the West have also retreated and become subject to persistent revisionism.

How has all this impacted upon the specific theme of self-directed learning? There are, I would argue, three aspects in particular in which New Labour thinking has a particular purchase on this theme. There is, first, a real as well as rhetorical commitment to learners as stakeholders: and specifically to learners as individual customers in the market place, paying for and thus purchasing the educational goods to suit their perceived needs. However, within this there is a strong emphasis, which has steadily become virtually an *exclusive* emphasis as the New Labour era has unfolded, upon skills enhancement – an extension of the ideological instrumentalism of Margaret Thatcher and her belief that education was worthwhile in the end only if it enhanced economic competitiveness. (Needless to say, there is no talk in New Labour of education for socialist, or even social, purposes – of empowering people through education and learning to appreciate an alternative analysis to the dominant 'common sense' of capital.)

Learning has thus become commodified. All the talk in New Labour in 2006–7, for example, of the 'personalisation' of learning should be seen in this context. There is much rhetoric about personalisation in the 2006 White Paper *Further Education: Raising skills, improving life chances,* but, despite its stress on seeking and responding to the views of the learners, it is in reality a part of the privatisation and marketisation of social policy in general.

The third element is the individualism that underpins New Labour's ideology, in contrast to Labour's more collectivist community tradition. (Insofar as 'community' features in New Labour policy – and it does quite frequently – almost always community is equated with *business* community: a good example of an Orwellian use of language.) Thus it is the *individual*, and his or her responsibility for their own destiny, that is New Labour's reference point: rather than the group, particularly the *social class* that has featured so strongly in all varieties of socialist perspectives in the past. This orientation can be seen clearly in policy programmes: for example, the Higher Education Funding Council for England's Widening Participation strategy focuses very strongly on the *individual's* accessibility and progression. (See successive HEFCE policy papers on Widening Participation from 1998 onwards.) Putting these elements together produces a version of self-directed learning sharply different from that of the democratic tradition: in New Labour's framework, self-directed learning is in part inspired by liberal humanism, but very largely by a consumerist, individualistic conception of the learner, operating within a perspective of a neo-liberal market place, and assumed to be motivated by an uncritically accepted market ideology.

## Conclusion

From any progressive educational point of view, and especially from a socialist perspective, this paints a pessimistic picture. Should we, therefore, dismiss self-directed learning as a concept and practice that has been captured by the New Labour Right, and must thus be opposed? Most emphatically not. No social processes are monolithic. These are still very much contested issues. Merely because the Right has tried to hijack and falsely reinterpret radical educational ideas does not lead to their being lost. Contested ideological perspectives are by definition sites of conflict, and there are, as always, contradictory tendencies at work, both in this specific debate and in Labour social policy politics more generally. The role of the progressive educator is to encourage and support the democratic and empowering articulation of self-directed learning and to oppose the more reactionary and negative perspectives. This is one important part of a much wider intellectual and political debate in Labour politics in what promises to be both an interesting and volatile political decade.

## References

Barnett, R. (2000) *Realising the University in an Age of Super-complexity*, Buckingham: SRHE and Open University Press.

Coffield, F. and Williamson, B. (1997) *Repositioning Higher Education*, Buckingham: Open University Press.

Crosland, A. (1956) *The Future of Socialism*, London: Cape.

Department for Education and Employment (DfEE) (1998) *The Learning Age*, London: HMSO.

Fieldhouse, R. (1985) *Adult Education and the Cold War*, Leeds Series in Adult Education, Leeds: University of Leeds.

—— (ed.) (1996) *A History of Modern British Adult Education*, Leicester: NIACE.

Giddens, A. (1998) *The Third Way*, Cambridge: Polity Press.

Harrison, J.F.C. (1961) *Learning and Living*, London: Routledge and Kegan Paul.

Hutton, W. (2007) *The Writing On The Wall: Why we must embrace China as a partner or face it as an enemy*, London/New York: Little, Brown.

Jessop, G. (1991) *Outcomes: NVQs and the emerging model of education and training*, Brighton: Falmer Press.

Johnston, R. (1997) 'Adult learning for citizenship', in R. Usher, I. Bryant and R. Johnston (eds) *Adult Education and the Postmodern Challenge: Learning beyond the limits*, London: Routledge, pp. 40–9.

Lovett, T. (1983) *Adult Education, Community Development and the Working Class*, London: Croom Helm.

Mayo, M. and Thompson, J. (1995) *Adult Learning, Critical Intelligence and Social Change*, Leicester: NIACE.

Perkin, H. (1989) *The Rise of Professional Society: England since 1880*, London: Routledge.

Ryan, A. (1999) *Liberal Anxieties and Liberal Education*, London: Profile Books.

Scott, P. (1995) *The Meanings of Mass Higher Education*, Buckingham: SRHE/Open University Press.

Smith, A. and Webster, F. (eds) (1997) *The Post Modern University? Contested visions of higher education in society*, Buckingham: SRHE/Open University Press.

Taylor, R. (1996) *Preserving the Liberal Tradition in 'New Times'*, in J. Wallis (ed.) *Liberal Adult Education: The end of an era?*, Nottingham: Nottingham University Press.

Taylor, R. (2006) 'Lifelong learning and the Labour Government, 1997–2004', in G. Walford (ed.) *Education and the Labour Government: An evaluation of two terms*, London: Routledge, pp. 99–116.

——, Rockhill, K. and Fieldhouse, R. (1985) *University Adult Education in England and the USA: A reappraisal of the liberal tradition*, London: Croom Helm.

——, Barr, J. and Steele, T. (2002) *For a Radical Higher Education: After postmodernism*, Buckingham: SRHE/Open University Press.

Thompson E.P. (1963) *The Making of the English Working Class*, Harmondsworth: Penguin Books.

—— (1968) *Education and Experience*, Fifth Albert Mansbridge Memorial Lecture, Leeds: University of Leeds.

Thompson, J. (1983) *Learning Liberation: Women's response to men's education*, London: Croom Helm.

Usher, R. and Edwards, R. (1994) *Postmodernism and Education*, London: Routledge.

——, Bryant, I. and Johnston, R. (1997) *Adult Education and the Postmodern Challenge*, London: Routledge.

Ward, K. and Taylor, R. (eds) (1986) *Adult Education and the Working Class: Education for the missing millions*, London: Croom Helm.

213

# 19

# On being taught

*Stephen Brookfield*

Discourses on lifelong learning may seem to be dismissive of learning from teaching; indeed, within adult and continuing education generally, learning is given much greater attention than teaching (English, 2005; Wilson and Hayes, 2000). In this chapter I intend to challenge the unproblematized hegemony of a discourse of learning and to argue that learning from teaching needs to be considered as seriously as learner-driven modalities such as self-directed, self-regulated, and self-paced learning. Three rationales for learning from teaching are explored—empirical, experiential, and critical. Empirically, research on self-directed learning does not support the contention that teachers are somehow absent. As we shall see, the opposite is true; learners who plan, conduct, and evaluate learning projects frequently decide to place themselves under the episodic direction of a teacher. Experientially, a whole corpus of research on forms of adult learning points to the importance of teachers as intentional engineers of dissonance (Sinnott, 2007). This is particularly the case where transformative learning—probably the most heavily researched form of contemporary adult learning—is concerned (Mezirow, 2000). Critically, a strong case can be made that learning to challenge dominant ideology, and learning to recognize how repressive tolerance successfully moves the goalposts of resistance so that people are fooled into thinking progress has been made, can best happen when a critical animateur forces people to become aware of these realities.

## The empirical rationale for learning from teaching

In the 1960s and 1970s the Canadian researcher, Allen Tough, initiated a stream of research into learning conducted outside formal educational institutions (Tough, 1979). Tough's own research, and that of his research teams, explored how adults taught themselves across the gamut of possible learning projects—from learning to organize political resistance to learning how to rewire a basement or play golf. Tough's rubric for this began as self-teaching, broadened into major learning projects, and then focused on intentional change. The umbrella term of self-directed learning finally gained widespread acceptance and came to form the focus of numerous dissertation projects and led to a series of annual conferences devoted solely to research reporting on its presence (the 2006 International Self-Directed Learning Symposium in Cocoa Beach, Florida was the twentieth consecutive North American conference).

Tough's terminological shift represented more than a semantic change; instead, it signaled an increasing recognition of the importance of teachers in self-directed learning projects. Instead of being conducted in some sort of splendid isolation, self-directed learning involved adults regularly deciding to place themselves in the role of dependent and directed learner who benefited from the teaching of an expert they had selected. My own dissertation research (Brookfield, 1980) was a very small contributor to this shift. To my surprise, my study of how rural working-class adults with no formal qualifications had developed local and regional reputations in different areas of expertise found that such learners overwhelmingly saw their learning as located in broader learning networks. And within these networks the adults I studied frequently identified particular individuals as their teachers—people who showed them particular skills, taught them new ways of thinking, and helped them assess how well their own learning was progressing.

In the subsequent three decades the voluminous body of work on self-directed learning has only served to confirm this finding. No longer are self-direction and teaching placed at opposite ends of a continuum as used to be the case when Knowles (1970) and others contrasted andragogy (said to be a quintessentially adult way of organizing one's own learning) with pedagogy (said to be suitable for children and adolescents who lacked sufficient life experience to organize their own learning). Instead, as recent handbooks on self-directed learning make plain (Costa and Kallick, 2003; Gibbons, 2002) teachers are now seen as having a major responsibility for nurturing self-directed learning capabilities in their students. So, from being regarded as irrelevant to self-directed learning, teachers are now viewed as process experts charged with inculcating and assessing students' powers of self-direction. Tools such as the Self-Directed Learning Readiness Scale are now accepted as part of the adult teacher's armory.

One consequence of the expansion of tools and techniques for teaching self-directedness has been the development of a critical perspective on the instrumentalization of self-direction. Prominent in this regard is the Canadian educator Michael Collins (1998), who argues that the early free spirit of self-direction has been turned (through the technology of learning contracts and readiness scales) into a masked form of repressive surveillance—one more example of the infinite flexibility of hegemony, of the workings of a coldly efficient form of repressive tolerance. What began as a cultural challenge, a counter hegemonic effort, is seen as taking a technocratic, accommodative turn in which individual needs are sublimated to institutional interests.

Following Foucault's (1980) analysis of disciplinary power, it is certainly highly plausible to see the technology of self-directed learning—particularly the widespread acceptance and advocacy of learning contracts—as a highly developed form of surveillance. By ensuring that students interiorize what Foucault calls the 'normalizing gaze' (teacher developed norms concerning what's acceptable), learning contracts transfer the responsibility for overseeing learning from the teacher to the learner. Using Foucault's principle of reversal (seeing something as the exact opposite of what it really is) learning contracts can be reframed and understood as a sophisticated means by which the content and methodology of learning can be monitored without the teacher needing to be physically present. Self-directed learning thus becomes self-discipline. Notwithstanding this critique, it is clearly false to assume that the concept and practice of self-directed learning somehow renders learning from teaching irrelevant. Instead, it needs to be understood in its totality as something a teacher moves in and out of according to the learner's recognition of his or her need for external direction and assistance.

## The experiential rationale for learning from teaching

An important strand of theorizing within adult learning is grounded in the developmental tasks of adulthood (Merriam *et al.*, 2006). This theorizing explores how entering the world of work, assuming political responsibilities, and developing intimate relationships entails a form of cognitive development often called post-formal reasoning (Hoare, 2006; Taylor *et al.*, 2000; Tennant and Pogson, 2002). Although conventional wisdom holds that "experience" is the teacher as people become adult, these texts argue that analyzing—and learning from—experience often needs assistance from a teacher. They argue that the simple equation of chronology and richness of experience—the idea that because adults have lived longer than children they have had better, or more diverse, experiences—is empirically shaky. It is quite possible for adults to live their years within a narrow social, cultural, and political setting in which values, assumptions, and perspectives learned in childhood are continually reinforced. Even at the height of a supposedly postmodern era, when sensibilities are fractured and contradictions rule, there are many adults who live a unitary existence in which the same emotions and perceptions recur in a self-confirming loop. When contradictory events happen that might challenge these emotions or perceptions they are either dismissed as deviant aberrations or rationalized in such a way that they justify existing beliefs. The old saw that 40 years' experience is often one year repeated 40 times is undeniable.

So there is no necessary empirical basis for assuming that a learner's experience always constitutes a rich resource for learning that inevitably teaches them about contextuality, broadens their perspectives, or helps them realize the limits to their assumptions. In fact, developmental literature indicates that the converse is sometimes the case. Adults' past experiences can be distorted, self-fulfilling, unexamined, and constraining. Simply having experiences does not mean that these are reflected on, understood, or analyzed critically. Neither are experiences inherently enriching. Experience can be construed in a way that confirms habits of bigotry, stereotyping, and disregard for significant but inconvenient information. It can also be narrowing and constraining, causing us to evolve and transmit ideologies that skew irrevocably how we interpret the world. It is overly simplistic to assume that, merely by sticking around on the planet long enough to reach adult age, this necessarily and sufficiently confers a corresponding capacity to learn from experience. Here I am defining learning from experience similarly to Sinnott (2007) as the capacity to unearth the assumptions that have framed one's thought and action and then to subject these assumptions to research and critical inquiry by reviewing them through different lenses. Some of us are never able to learn from experience; others do it only intermittently. We all know people who repeat the same mistakes each time a similar situation arises, and we all know people who make disastrously wrong readings of the meaning of the crises through which they pass.

There is also an epistemological confusion surrounding the way in which discussions of learning from experience treat experience as an objective artifact. Experience is often viewed as a fixed category—something that is bestowed upon us, or something that happens to us, from which we draw appropriate lessons. But experiences don't happen to us, events happen to us. Experiences are constructed *by* us as much as they happen *to* us: the interpretive frames we employ to assign meaning to events shape fundamentally how we experience them. It is a mistake to think that we have experiences in the sense that our own being stands alone while the river of experience flows around us. This separates the knower from the known in a misleading way. It is more accurate to say that the knower creates and continually recreates the known. So a consequence of viewing experience naively is that we end up as educators regarding the celebration of our learners' experiences as the legitimate start and finish of adult education. We get them to tell their stories, to write their narratives, and to share their experiences (usually in a circle of voices) in the belief that this represents the ultimate form of democratic, empathic, adult education. But idealizing or romanticizing experience through an uncritical sharing is not, in and of itself, educational. For the celebration of experience to become educational it has to be allied to critical analysis. We have to ask how that experience might be understood from different perspectives, what aspects of the experience need questioning and further inquiry, and what parts of the experience have been misapprehended, ignored, or omitted in recollection.

This is where the teacher's role in helping adults learn from experience becomes crucial. Sometimes the focus is on the teacher as designer of role plays, games, and simulations that will help participants learn team-building, develop emotional intelligence, experiment with different learning styles, and so on (Beard and Wilson, 2006). At other times, particularly in transformative learning (Cranton, 2006; O'Sullivan, 2006), the teacher assumes a more provocative, potentially explosive, role. Work on transformative learning grants to the teacher the role of dissonance-engineer. The teacher's responsibility becomes to create situations in which students are required to confront contradictions in their position, to respond to unexpected information, and to resolve discrepancies between how they feel the world should work and how it actually operates. This pedagogic function is grounded in empirical work in the area that stresses the importance of disorienting dilemmas as triggers to transformation. Since adults will not usually seek out traumatic events of their own volition, creating these becomes an important teacher behavior. Work on mentoring adult learners (Daloz, 1999; Herman and Mandell, 2004) has stressed how teachers need to research their students' backgrounds, expectations, and perceptions as a prelude to determining how much dissonance learners can tolerate as a spur to difficult learning before deciding they are being asked to engage in learning that is too personally challenging.

Determining the balance between support and challenge is difficult enough with a single student let alone a group of diverse individuals. One of the areas where this balance is hardest to strike is in anti-racist education, where teachers work to create exercises that bring learners' own complicity in racism to their attention. Other areas in which teachers are seen as necessary prompters of learning from experience are those clustered around the concept of reflective practice (Brookfield, 1995; Jarvis, 1999), psychotherapeutic and psychoanalytic learning (Charles, 2004), multicultural and identity struggles (Moya, 2002), and learning in social movements (Holst, 2002).

## The critical rationale for learning from teaching

This section explores a critical theory perspective on learning from teaching. Central to such a perspective is the idea that dominant ideology is such a permeating and all-pervasive force that, on their own, students are unlikely to seek to challenge it, preferring instead to view ideas and practices they have internalized as common sense, obvious explanations of what they see around them. Critical theory holds that ideological obfuscation is so successful that the only way people will learn to perceive its existence is if something—often a teacher—brings this to their attention. Indeed, Gramsci's (1971) concept of organic intellectuals—teachers, leaders, and persuaders drawn from the ranks of a class or movement who then direct its activities—has been influential on some adult educators who have seen it as a useful way of delimiting what is particular to the field (Coben, 1998; Mayo, 1998).

In Gramsci's view a necessary trigger to workers coming to realize their true situation of oppression and deciding to change this through political action is a group of organic intellectuals. The existence of this group is crucial to the awakening of revolutionary fervor. Organic intellectuals have the responsibility to help people understand the existence of ruling-class hegemony and the need to replace this with proletarian hegemony. In order to do this, these intellectuals need a capacity for empathic identification with how it feels to be oppressed. They must inhabit the life-world of the masses, feeling the elementary passions of the people and helping them develop a collective identity as a class for themselves.

Well-meaning middle-class radicals cannot become organic intellectuals. Despite Freire's injunctions concerning the need for middle-class adult educators to commit class suicide so they can work in an authentic way with the peasantry and other oppressed groups (Freire, 1970), this transition is highly problematic. And what of attempts to commit racial, rather than class, suicide? How can White adult educators ever experience the systemic racism visited daily on non-Whites? As Holst (2002) points out, discussions of organic intellectuals that focus on Martin Luther King tend to ignore the way the civil rights movement produced organic intellectuals from the Black share-croppers and working class throughout the South. Gramsci argues that a condition of being an organic intellectual is the educator being a member of the racial or class group concerned, and not a sympathetic fellow traveler, however well intentioned. Myles Horton understood this when he insisted that the literacy teachers in the campaign to help St John's islanders learn to read and write (so they could register to vote) should all be African American (Horton, 1990). No matter how sincere a White teacher might be, he or she lacked the racial membership to feel 'the elementary passions of the people', which was a precondition of being trusted by the people.

The idea that learning critically can happen from teachers is inherent in critical theory's formulations, in particular the idea that teachers have moved beyond false consciousness and can help learners see how they are trapped in dominant ideology. From Marx's eleventh thesis on Feuerbach onwards, it is clear that the theory is full of activist intent in which people are directed toward revolutionary change. Indeed, as Horkheimer (1995) argued in his essay defining critical theory (first published in 1936), the theory can be considered successful only if it is used by its adherents—including teachers—to produce revolutionary change. Theorizing exists, and theorists teach theorizing, so that people can understand the dynamics of political, economic, racial, and cultural oppression. With that understanding they can then begin to challenge these dynamics and learn to create new social forms, particularly new conditions of labor, that allow them to express their creativity. So learning to correctly perceive one's own interests is seen as being partly dependent on teaching and teaching informed by critical theory is, by implication, to teach with a specific social and political intent. Critical theorists intend that their analyses and concepts will help people create social and economic forms distinguished by a greater degree of democratic socialism.

Although there are noticeable differences in the ways different theorists pursue teaching critically, one theme—the inevitably directive nature of education (and, hence, the connection of learning to teaching)—remains fairly constant in the tradition. Critical teaching begins with developing students' powers of critical thinking so that they can critique the interlocking systems of oppression embedded in contemporary society. Informed by a critical theory perspective, students learn to see that capitalism, bureaucratic rationality, disciplinary power, automaton conformity, one-dimensional thought, and repressive tolerance all combine to exert a powerful ideological sway aimed to ensure the current system stays intact. Critical thinking in this vein is the educational implementation of ideology critique; the deliberate attempt to penetrate the ideological obfuscation that ensures that massive social inequality is accepted by the majority as the natural state of affairs.

This form of critical thinking is, however, only the beginning of critical theory's educational project. The point of getting people to think critically is to enable them to create true democracy—what critical theorists regard as the cornerstone of socialism—at both the micro and macro levels. If adults think critically in this view they will be demanding worker cooperatives, the abolition of private education, the imposition of income caps, universal access to health care based on need not wealth, and public ownership of corporations and utilities. Critical thinking framed by critical theory is not just a cognitive process. It is inevitably bound up with realizing and emphasizing common interests, rejecting the privatized, competitive ethic of capitalism, and preventing the emergence of inherited privilege.

Although critical theorists share a common recognition of the politically directive nature of education, they do not advance any kind of methodological orthodoxy to describe how such education should take place. However, four contrasting methodological clusters or emphases are discernible in critical theory. One of these is the importance of teaching a structuralized worldview. A structuralized worldview always analyses private experiences and personal dilemmas as structurally produced. At root, this idea is grounded in Marx's theory of consciousness with its argument that what seem like instinctive ways of understanding the world actually reflect the material base of society. This idea recurs throughout critical theory in concepts such as the colonization of the life-world, one-dimensional thought, and disciplinary power.

A second pedagogical emphasis in critical theory explores the need for abstract, conceptual reasoning—reasoning that can be applied to considering broad questions such as how to organize society fairly or what it means to treat each other ethically. Critical theorists, particularly Marcuse (1964) and Habermas (1984), argue that critical thought is impossible if adults have learned only to focus on particulars, on the immediate features of their lives. For example, people need some basis for comparing the claims of various groups that they should be treated differently because of their history, race, culture, religion, and so on. As long as we live in association with others there have to be restrictions placed on the liberty of those who behave in ways likely to injure others. How we decide what these limits should be is based on some broad concepts of fairness or social well-being. Your right to smoke a cancer-inducing cigarette cannot be exercised regardless in a small room containing asthma, lung cancer, or emphysema sufferers. So if living socially requires the development of rules of conduct that have a level of generality beyond that of individual whims then we need to be comfortable thinking in broad abstract terms. Deciding which rules should be followed, and how these might be established in ways that ensure their general acceptance, are matters that require a level of thought beyond that of saying "this is what I want because it works for me in my life." Freedom, fairness, equity, liberation, the ethical use of power—all these "big" ideas are central to the critical tradition and all contain a level of universality entailing the exercise of abstract, conceptual thought.

A third element stressed in some variants of critical theory is the need for adults to learn how to separate themselves from the demands and patterns of everyday life so that they can view society in a newly critical way. Both Gramsci (1971) and Marcuse (1964) argue that a temporary detachment from social life is a necessary spur to critical thought, with Marcuse conducting a sustained analysis of how separation, privacy, and isolation help people to escape one-dimensional thought. This strand of critical theory connects directly to adult educators' concern mentioned earlier with self-directed learning and the practices that foster this. This element in critical theory receives less contemporary attention probably because privacy is now, as Marcuse admits, a resource available chiefly to the rich. Also, Marcuse's emphasis on how a powerfully estranging, private engagement with a work of art leads to the development of rebellious subjectivity smacks to some of elitism. It also raises the specter of unrestrained individualism, an element of dominant ideology that prompts deep skepticism among many of a critical cast.

Cohort groups and other forms of social learning are the setting for a fourth pedagogic emphasis in critical theory, that of dialogic discussion. Fromm (1956) and Habermas (1984) are the two theorists discussed who emphasize this approach most strongly with both of them viewing a widespread facility with dialogic methods as the guarantee of democracy. Fromm's emphasis on the dance of dialogue in which speakers lose their ego in a selfless attempt to understand the positions advanced by others is very much a forerunner to Habermas's ideal speech situation. Both theorists believe that decisions arrived at through fully participatory, inclusive conversation are the cornerstone of democracy, and both believe education can play a role in teaching adults the dispositions necessary to conduct such conversations.

It is important to stress that learning dialogic practices often depends on a teacher's intervention. I have argued elsewhere (Brookfield and Preskill, 2005) that most discussions are not distinguished by automatic goodwill on the part of all participants. After all, most people do not have the chance to practice the kinds of democratic dispositions good discussions require. Ideal speech situations are virtually extinct for many of us. We must not assume that adult education classrooms are safe havens or power-free zones. Neither learners nor teachers leave their racial, class, or gender identities at the classroom door, nor do they forget their previous participation in discussions with all the humiliations and manipulations these often entailed. For an adult education group to look anything remotely like the ego-less dance celebrated by Fromm, or the ideal speech situation described by Habermas, its participants will need to evolve, and adhere to, rules of discourse that exemplify these features. Since the exercise of these rules cannot be left to chance, the group will have to find some way to monitor observance of these.

Because groups are often unwilling to acknowledge and confront the hierarchies and power dynamics they import into the classroom, teachers can help illuminate these. Discussion leaders can consistently draw attention to the need for inclusive models of conversation such as the circle of voices, circular response, snowballing, or newsprint dialog (Brookfield and Preskill, 2005). They can intervene in conversations to stop the most privileged and vociferous from dominating, by declaring a ground rule that the next couple of minutes of conversation are reserved for those who up to now have not had a chance to contribute. They can also democratize the conversation by advocating something like the three-person rule. This rule holds that, once someone has made a comment, they are not allowed to contribute again until at least three other people have spoken. The only exception to this is if someone else in the group directly asks a speaker to say more about their original comment. Teachers can also distribute to the group the results of anonymous student classroom evaluations if these reveal that some people feel shut down and unheard. And they can acknowledge constantly the fact of their own power and how this is being exercised to create conversational structures that equalize participation and prevent the emergence of an unofficial pecking order of contributions.

Australian Michael Newman (2006) draws on the critical tradition to position adult teachers as activists unable to avoid taking a stand and fated to declare allegiances. He grounds his conception of adult education in a familiar lexicon, that of helping adults think critically. However, his definition of critical thinking is distinctly unfamiliar to many adult educators. For him it is irrevocably linked to the exposure and overthrow of oppression, ruling class hegemony, and capitalism. Newman argues that critical thought involves a clear-sighted and explicitly judgmental pointing of the finger of blame. Along with the act of laying blame comes the commitment to choose sides in a struggle and live with the implications of one's choice.

Building on Newman's analysis, Grenadian-born adult educator Ian Baptiste (2000) argues for an ethically grounded pedagogy of coercion in which adult educators help learners identify their true enemies. To Baptiste, adult educators often function as persuaders and organizers but choose not to acknowledge this. He argues that they already use forms of justifiable coercion but are queasy about admitting to that reality. In Baptiste's view it is naive, and empirically inaccurate, for adult educators to insist that their job is not to take sides, not to force an agenda on learners. Like it or not (and Baptiste believes most of us do not like to acknowledge this) adult educators cannot help but be directive in their actions, despite avowals of neutrality or non-interference.

## Conclusion

Learning from teaching happens in formal, informal, and non-formal adult educational contexts. The three rationales for teaching explored in this chapter argue that, despite the shift in discourses in the field from teaching to learning, teaching retains a central role as the instigator of significant learning. Self-directed learning in the total absence of teachers is relatively rare, experiential learning without teacher analysis risks chasing its own tail in an uncritical celebration, and learning to challenge dominant ideology will often only happen when adults are encouraged by teachers to recognize their own cultural complicity.

## References

Baptiste, I. (2000) "Beyond reason and personal integrity: toward a pedagogy of coercive restraint," *Canadian Journal for the Study of Adult Education* 14(1): 27–50.

Beard, C. and Wilson, J. (2006) *Experiential Learning: A handbook of best practices for educators and trainers*, London: Kogan Page.

Brookfield, S.D. (1980) "Independent adult learning," unpublished doctoral dissertation, Leicester: University of Leicester.

—— (1995) *Becoming a Critically Reflective Teacher*, San Francisco, CA: Jossey-Bass.

—— and Preskill, S. (2005) *Discussion as a Way of Teaching*, San Francisco, CA: Jossey-Bass.

Charles, M. (2004) *Learning From Experience: A clinician's guide*, Mahwah, NJ: Analytic Press.

Coben, D. (1998) *Radical Heroes: Gramsci, Freire and the politics of adult education*, New York: Garland.

Collins, M. (1998) *Critical Crosscurrents in Education*, Malabar, FL: Krieger.

Costa, A.L. and Kallick, B. (2003) *Assessment Strategies for Self-directed Learning*, Thousand Oaks, CA: Corwin Press.

Cranton, P. (2006) *Understanding and Promoting Transformative Learning: A guide for educators of adults*, San Francisco, CA: Jossey-Bass.

Daloz, L.A. (1999) *Mentoring: Guiding the journey of adult learners*, San Francisco, CA: Jossey-Bass.

English, L. (ed.) (2005) *International Encyclopedia of Adult Education*, New York: Palgrave/Macmillan.

Foucault, M. (1980) *Power/Knowledge: Selected interviews and other writings, 1972–1977*, New York: Pantheon Books.

Freire, P. (1970) *Pedagogy of the Oppressed*, New York: Continuum.

Fromm, E. (1956) *The Sane Society*, London: Routledge and Kegan Paul.

Gibbons, M. (2002) *The Self-directed Learning Handbook: Challenging adolescent students to excel*, San Francisco, CA: Jossey-Bass.

Gramsci, A. (1971) *Selections from the Prison Notebooks* (ed. Q. Hoare and G.N. Smith), London: Lawrence and Wishart.

Habermas, J. (1984) *The Theory of Communicative Action, vol. 1: Reason and the rationalization of society*, Boston, MA: Beacon Press.

Herman, L. and Mandell, A. (2004) *From Teaching to Mentoring in Adult Education: Principles and practice, dialogue and life in adult education*, New York: Routledge.

Hoare, C. (ed.) (2006) *Handbook of Adult Development and Learning*, New York: Oxford University Press.

Holst, J.D. (2002) *Social Movements, Civil Society and Radical Adult Education*, Westport, CT: Bergin and Garvey.

Horkheimer, M. (1995) *Critical Theory: Selected essays*, New York: Continuum.

Horton, M. (1990) *The Long Haul: An autobiography*, New York: Doubleday.

Jarvis, P. (1999) *The Practitioner-Researcher: Developing theory from practice*, San Francisco, CA: Jossey-Bass.

Knowles, M.S. (1970) *The Modern Practice of Adult Education: From pedagogy to andragogy*, Chicago, IL: Follett.

Marcuse, H. (1964) *One Dimensional Man*, Boston, MA: Beacon.

Mayo, P. (1998) *Gramsci, Freire and Adult Education: Possibilities for transformative action*, New York: ZED Books.

Merriam, S.B., Caffarrella, R., and Baumgartner, L.M. (2006) *Learning in Adulthood: A comprehensive guide*, San Francisco, CA: Jossey-Bass.

Mezirow, J. (ed.) (2000) *Learning as Transformation: Critical perspectives on a theory in progress*, San Francisco, CA: Jossey-Bass.

Moya, P.M.L. (2002) *Learning from Experience: Minority identities, multicultural struggles*, Berkeley, CA: University of California Press.

Newman, M. (2006) Teaching Defiance: Stories and strategies for activist educators, San Francisco, CA: Jossey-Bass.

O' Sullivan, E. (2006) *Transformative Learning: Educational vision for the twenty first century*, New York: ZED Books.

Sinnott, J.D. (2007) *The Development of Logic in Adulthood: Postformal thought and its applications*, New York: Springer.

Taylor, K., Marienau, C., and Fiddler, M. (eds) (2000) *Developing Adult Learners: Strategies for teachers and trainers*, San Francisco, CA: Jossey-Bass.

Tennant, M. and Pogson, P. (2002) *Learning and Change in the Adult Years: A developmental perspective*, San Francisco, CA: Jossey-Bass.

Tough, A.M. (1979) *The Adult's Learning Projects: A fresh approach to theory and practice in adult learning*, New York: Pfeiffer.

Wilson, A.L. and Hayes, E.R. (eds) (2000) *Handbook of Adult and Continuing Education*, San Francisco, CA: Jossey-Bass.

# 20

# The contribution of open and distance education to lifelong learning

*Otto Peters*

In order to deal with this subject in productive ways, distinct features of 'lifelong learning' and 'distance education' are characterized. A comparison of the two concepts shows inherent and evident similarities and parallelisms, which suggest possible theoretical and practical contributions of distance education to the further development of lifelong learning. These notable correspondences mark distance education as the most significant contribution to lifelong learning.

## Lifelong learning

As there is widespread misunderstanding and even ignorance of the real meaning of lifelong learning, it is necessary to delineate this concept first. Most educators support this concept, but too often simply because of its underlying idea that learning is not restricted to childhood and adolescence, but must be continued throughout the entire lifetime, from 'the cradle to the grave', as the saying has it. This understanding of the term is, of course, true, but there is much more to it. The concept involves no less than the vision, creation and establishment of a comprehensive new learning culture with far-reaching consequences for our economic, technological, social and cultural life. For instance, one possible effect of the fast-growing interest and involvement in lifelong learning could be the creation of 'the largest and fastest growing market segment, while the market for traditional educational services . . . and traditional institutions . . . will decline' (Finke, 2000: viii).

### General meaning

The concept of lifelong learning was widely discussed in the early 1970s, inspired and initiated by the lifelong learning policies of UNESCO, the European Commission, the Council of Europe, the Organization of Economic Cooperation and Development (OECD) and the Club of Rome. The discussion intensified in the 1990s and culminated in 1996, when this concept assumed not only educational and economic, but also remarkable political importance: in 1996 the Education Ministers of OECD countries met at a conference to discuss the issue of *Making*

*Lifelong Learning a Reality for All*. In the same year UNESCO published a report about the results of the International Commission on Education in the Twenty-First Century dealing with *Learning Throughout Life*. The European Union even designated 1996 as the Year of Lifelong Learning, and in the same year the German Federal Ministry for Education, Science, Research and Technology published three brochures dealing with lifelong learning, one with the title: *Lifelong Learning: Guidelines for a modern policy of education*. All these efforts received unusual national and international publicity. Reading these documents makes us aware of the great urgency of this unprecedented challenge.

Why did this radical new pedagogical concept emerge?

Suzy Halimi (2005: 11) answers this question by pointing to the necessity of adapting to the changes caused by scientific and technological advances, spectacular developments of information and communication technologies and the emergence of new ways of creating knowledge. She refers also to the 'race in which states know full well they need to equip themselves with the best skilled and qualified human resources possible', to 'the necessity of re-skilling and reorientation in order to find work', and to 'the necessity of opening doors of higher education to people who have so far been underrepresented there – women, ethnic and cultural minorities, the disabled, young and not so young people from underprivileged social backgrounds'.

Günther Dohmen (1996: 1, 5) judges the necessity of immediate change even more severely. He characterizes the precarious situation by spelling disaster to mankind and shows deep concern over powerful societal trends that are likely to destroy the fundamental preconditions of human life on this globe. According to him people are also confronted with radical changes and far reaching transformations: ecological destruction, growing structural unemployment, a high and still growing proportion of old people, lowering of the standard of living, the debt crisis of public budgets, the increasing numbers of immigrants, economical egoism, growing corruption, violence and crime, and the penetration of Mafia structures into industry, sports, media and politics.

Today even more dangers must be added to his catalogue of serious developments: the economic consequences of globalization, aggravated conflict between industrialized and developing countries, increased cultural, religious and ethnic antagonisms, terrorism, war and nuclear armament. In order to be prepared and able to meet these challenges, the advocates of lifelong learning insist that an entirely new educational system must be established. Even more, they believe that our traditional educational institutions are neither equipped nor ready to react to the ongoing transformation and to its dangerous consequences.

As practically everyone is already affected by these consequences today and will be much more so in the future, it is only natural that far-sighted educational planners and politicians devise plans for facing and overcoming them. They recommend lifelong learning *for all* as an alternative educational approach. It is to equip people for solving the unusual problems they will have to face in this time of transformation and radical change. Dohmen interpreted lifelong learning for all as the 'vital question for the survival of mankind'. According to him 'the simple alternatives are lifelong learning or destruction' (1996: 18–19).

## General features of the concept

Unfortunately, for most people the contours of the new concept are blurred, as 'lifelong learning' has become a popular slogan that is often used by educationists in order to reinterpret their own teaching approach in terms of lifelong learning. In these cases the slogan serves as a 'modern cloak' in which traditional forms of education are 'clothed' (Osborne, 2003: 16). Osborne himself co-edited a book dealing exclusively with university continuing education under the title *Lifelong*

*Learning in a Changing Continent*. Finke (2000) also used this term in a similar way, although dealing almost exclusively with net-based learning. Furthermore it can be argued that lifelong learning should not be mixed up with continuing education – be it general, vocational or professional, nor with traditional adult education, recurrent education, and especially not with the mere expansion of available education and training opportunities.

Because of widespread misapprehensions it is important to conceive lifelong learning in a much broader context. It is a comprehensive form of learning with unusual new goals, approaches, methods and media. It is varied and full of radical new aspects. According to Hasan (1996: 35):

- it 'focuses on the standards of knowledge and skills needed by all, regardless of age';
- it 'emphasizes the need to prepare and motivate all children at an early age for learning over a lifetime';
- it directs efforts to ensure 'that all adults, employed or unemployed, who need to retrain or upgrade their skills, are provided with opportunities to do so'.

This concept is still under discussion in many countries. Present contributions are based on a consensus about a 'core of common elements' reached ten years ago (Hasan, 1996: 35). There is:

- a common desire for universal access to learning opportunities, regardless of age, gender or employment status;
- the recognition of the importance of non-formal learning in diverse settings;
- the recognition of a diversity of new means and methods of teaching;
- the emphasis on self-managed independent learning;
- the critique of conventional institutionalized education.

This vision of lifelong learning has imposed new imperatives for learning and training and has assumed extraordinary importance to educational policy makers in most industrialized countries, as well as in developing countries (Daniel, 2005: ix).

## Special pedagogical features

### New general goals

Lifelong learning is considered 'a natural basic function of human life' (Dohmen, 1996: 1, 5). It focuses on new competences for understanding our world and for dealing with life's pressing tasks. It mobilizes all competences and the creative problem-solving potential that has up to now been left unexploited. In order to achieve this, learning is individualized in the sense that individual demand is taken care of and personal development is fostered. Furthermore, social cohesion is maintained, community life is cultivated and innovative productivity and economic growth are promoted (see Hasan, 1996: 35).

### New methods of learning

Lifelong learning describes possible alternatives to the methods of conventional education in schools and universities. The *Memorandum on Lifelong Learning* (CEC, 2000: 10–19) conveys key messages in order to develop and establish them:

- new basic skills for all;
- innovation in teaching and learning;
- valuing learning;
- rethinking guidance and counselling;
- bringing learning closer to home.

Furthermore, learners are to be addressed in their everyday life and work situations as, for instance, when they have to deal with problems, such as tensions between those with power and the powerless, and between males and females, social and ethnic unrest, political and religious opposition, unemployment, conflicting interests and violence.

With regard to the actual teaching–learning a diversity of methods is to be used, some of which are unorthodox. They are to be developed in contrast to the still dominating traditional practice of expository teaching and receptive learning. Dohmen (1996: 29–35) distinguishes between:

- *Nonformal learning*, which takes place at home, at work and in the community. It is organized, but does not lead to any certificate, diploma or degree.
- *Informal learning*, which takes place in a spontaneous and not regulated way. Its aim is to solve the problems of everyday life.
- *Autonomous and self-regulated learning*, which is highly individualized and usually inspired and supported by tutors and advisers.
- *Innovative learning*, which is based on digitized information and applied in order to study new developments and to solve new problems in new ways.

Generally speaking, learning means 'constructive assimilation and transformation of information and experience into knowledge, insights and competence' (BLK, 2004: 5). The 'focus is on individual learning needs and competencies to perform complex real-life situations' (Finke, 2000: viii). Protagonists of lifelong learning often refer to the report of the Delors Commission. This commission felt that 'education throughout life is based upon four pillars: learning to know, learning to do, learning to live together and learning to be' (Delors, 1996: 86–97). This metaphor signifies aptly the methodical complexity required in the new system of lifelong learning so often neglected in traditional teaching and learning.

# Distance education

## The traditional concept

The precise meaning of distance education is also not really known by most people, and not even by most educationists. The notion of 'correspondence education' as performed by commercial correspondence schools still lingers in the public memory. This means that people are only aware of a form of distance education in which teachers and students are separated by geographical distances and in which the gap between teacher and taught is usually bridged by means of posted printed course material and by the exchange of letters. This concept of distance education, although still practised globally, is more than 150 years old and hence pedagogically and technologically outdated.

## The open learning movement

It is important to realize the conceptual development of distance education after the Second World War. In the 1950s and 1960s a remarkable movement advocated 'open learning' in England (Paine, 1988). In the 1970s there was great interest in 'non-traditional studies' (Gould and Cross, 1977) and in *Adults as Learners* (Cross, 1981) in the USA. Educational reform was in vogue in those years. It became fashionable to provide access to universities for a new clientele with the help of new media. Several versions of a 'University Without Walls' were created in the USA, of which the Empire State College is still the most notable achievement. The supporters of open learning not only envisaged the application of new technical (mass) media, but also the development of innovative teaching methods, the creation of a new learning behaviour and the achievement of political, economic and social goals as well. According to Norman MacKenzie *et al.* (1975: 16–17, 22), the message of this movement was that:

- the acquisition of knowledge, skills and attitudes was to be open to all – nobody should be excluded;
- traditional educational barriers were to be removed, e.g. financial difficulties, gender-specific educational practices, unfavourable sociocultural milieus or membership of minority groups;
- learning was not bound to defined life cycles or to specific locations and times – it must be possible to learn at any time and everywhere;
- teaching programmes were not to be completely developed and determined beforehand in an empirical-scientific manner, but should be 'open' for unforeseen developments in the build-up of individual ability to act;
- the course of learning was not to be stipulated rigidly and independently of the students, but start from and be shaped by their individual value perspectives, interests and experiences;
- students were not to be objects but subjects of the teaching process; for this reason, learning and teaching institutions were to be created in which students could organize their learning themselves;
- learning itself was not to be initiated and steered by means of ritualized presentation and reception processes, but by discussion and active management of the student.

We can see that the underlying principles of this movement are still valid and have acquired particular significance in the present lifelong learning campaign: the principles of egalitarianism, of equality of educational opportunity, of lifelong and ubiquitous learning, of flexible curricula, of learner orientation, of autonomous learning, and of learning through communication and interaction. These principles inspired the advocates and founders of 'open' learning systems, especially of 'open universities'.

## Open universities

The impact of the open learning movement induced politicians and educational experts to establish forms of teaching and learning that were mainly based on correspondence education combined with the technical (mass) media that were available at the time.

The founders of the National Extension College in Cambridge, an influential distance teaching institution, and later on of the Open University in Milton Keynes, devoted themselves to realizing such goals in a pioneering way. The Open University, a single-mode distance teaching institution, became famous for its open entrance policy, its focus on teaching adults, and for its extraordinary success in producing more graduates than all other universities of the country put together. Its great example initiated a spectacular and unforeseen development of distance and open education all over the world. The reason for this success was the innovative approach to open learning.

The learning system of open universities consists of the following eight elements:

- careful creation of high-quality learning material pre-prepared by multi-skilled academic teams;
- multimedia approach: printed matter, radio, television, satellite communication, audio and video tapes;
- optional or obligatory face-to-face meetings in study centres;
- the students are obliged to plan, organize and evaluate their own learning;
- dedicated personal academic support from specialized tutors, mentors, counsellors;
- learning by communicating and collaborating on the internet: the net provides 'a communicative glue that increases the synergy between those other media' (Daniel, 1998b: 29), the necessity of enabling the students to become autonomous;
- an absolutely reliable professional logistical system;
- academic research as a necessary foundation of the teaching.

Through the interplay of these eight elements it is possible to reach large numbers of students who are unable to take part in education in the traditional way because of circumstances. And yet open learning institutions focus on individual learning. Students are flexible with regard to their place and time of learning. They may study at home, at the workplace, on a train or in a plane. They may study alone, with real or virtual partners, or face-to-face in study centres. Obviously students have adjusted to this new form of alternative education and like studying in this way. In the UK the 2005 and 2006 National Student Surveys show that the Open University is *more popular* with its students than any other publicly funded university in the country (Curtis, 2005). As large numbers of students can be accepted, open universities profit from economies of scale. Furthermore, they are able to appoint well-known and reputable professors and develop the most reliable technical-administrative system available.

The development of open learning culminated in the proliferation of more than 50 open universities in many industrialized and developing countries (Peters, 2008). A significant number of them are 'mega-universities' (Daniel, 1996) catering for more than one hundred thousand, often several hundred thousand, and in some cases even more than a million students each. These mega-universities 'provide a powerful response to the crisis of access and costs' (Daniel, 1999: 8). The emergence of such an entirely new type of university signifies a unique development in the history of education that will assume even greater importance in the future. Terry Evans and Daryl Nation (1996: 1–6; 2003: 777–92) described the global lines and local connections of 'opening education' and predicted how it will change university teaching (2000: 160–75).

## Online distance education

The rapid development of digital technologies, especially within the last ten years, changed the concept of multimedia distance education in a way that, in its radicalization, was never experienced before. The growing use of 'knowledge media' and the 'knowledge web' (Eisenstadt and Vincent, 1998) caused the emergence of 'online distance education', a new distinct format. It increases the unique possibilities of distance education (e.g. distributed learning, self-learning, mediated learning, student–teacher dialogue) by enlarging, extending, intensifying and perfecting them. At the same time it includes new pedagogical approaches such as, for example, data mining, critical selection of information, knowledge construction, learning with multiple digital media, simulations and hypertexts, as well as learning by communication and collaboration. All these new elements make distance education even more effective (see Bates, 2005: 139–40; Thorpe, 2005: 24).

Online distance education in open universities differs from online learning offered by campus universities as it is based on and profits from the pedagogy and practice of distance education: ingenious course development, high-quality learning material (teaching texts for self-learning), painstaking student support, tutoring or mentoring, specific evaluation methods, additional face-to-face meetings, and long experience in teaching working adults. Hence online distance education has a different, very specific and peculiar pedagogical profile.

## Main conceptual features

The rise of distance education has been caused by several factors: distance education not only uses, but is based entirely on, technical media. It developed 'distributed learning' 150 years before this term became fashionable among advocates of online learning. Students may live widely spread over regions, nations or even continents. All of them can be reached at one time. Study material can be mass-produced and delivered by mass media to great numbers of students. This means that distance education provides access to education to a larger segment of the population. It reaches the previously unreachable, especially new groups of students who had previously been prevented from enrolment. And it forges closer links with companies. Because it shows an inherent tendency towards large-scale operations, it can be beneficial with regard to cost-effectiveness (Daniel, 1999: 39; Moore and Thompson, 1990: 34). Distance education paves the way from elitist education to mass education. It has developed a special pedagogy for distant students, and accumulated rich and detailed experience with the systematic use of multimedia and new information and communication technologies in higher education. It emphasizes additional face-to-face communication in study centres.

These features mark a significant departure from all formats of traditional education. Beaudoin (2006: 6) criticizes traditional universities by arguing that they cannot adopt technology-driven opportunities for new formats of open learning as 'they remain handicapped by a persistent preoccupation with the accoutrements of academia, and what they perceive to be most important and prestigious: stressing faculty scholarship, research and grants, and the preservation of existing infrastructure'. Distance education, however, not only opens the doors for new students, but is already meeting many requirements and challenges of the educational paradigm shift, which most educational systems will have to face in the near future. This may be another reason for its unparalleled evolution, especially during the last decades. There is now a 'growing allure of, and increased demand for distance education options' (Beaudoin, 2006: 3). Distance education 'continues its advance from the margins to the epicentre of the knowledge and information age' (p. 19).

## Similarities and parallelisms

### A comparison

Lifelong learning and distance education *differ* in many significant ways. Distance education emerged slowly in the middle of the nineteenth century unexpectedly and was not at all

229

welcomed by educational experts, professors and even the public. It developed in an atmosphere of hostility, contempt and even ridicule. Lifelong learning, however, has been strongly advocated during the last decades only, is still praised to the heavens and is promoted by national governments, the European Union and reputable educational planners. The two concepts of education were created in entirely different periods of time, by different initiators and advocated by different protagonists: distance education as an expression of industrialization and the modern age by individual entrepreneurs and progressive universities, and lifelong learning as a manifestation of post-industrialism in a postmodern knowledge-society created by leading European government officials and professional educational planners.

Distance education developed unnoticed and bottom up, whereas lifelong learning seems to be generally accepted and is in the process of being realized top down with great zeal and emphasis as part of a great international campaign. However, distance education is a reality that has stood the test of time and lifelong learning is still a great vision, an innovative reform programme, an ambitious project.

In sharp contrast to these structural differences it is easy to identify conspicuous similarities and parallelisms. A great number of them are absolutely obvious. Both formats:

- respond to significant new general societal trends, issues and challenges, and anticipate and realize change;
- are urgency measures as they have to cope with acute and dangerous technological and societal transformations;
- have a tremendous innovative impact;
- strike forcibly against traditional educational patterns;
- transcend conventional academic institutional structures;
- transgress boundaries of locations, regions and states;
- establish new pedagogical approaches, and employ new methods, media, unorthodox ways of learning and learning places;
- integrate advanced interactive telecommunications and information techniques into their learning and teaching programmes;
- envisage and support collaborative learning as a means of creating knowledge;
- emphasize the capacity for self-learning;
- are committed to tutoring and mentoring;
- are dedicated to human self-development;
- link learning and work;
- concentrate on the universalization of education by extending access on a great scale;
- are able to meet the needs of persons of all age groups;
- practise a continuum of learning throughout life;
- are similar in the ways they manage time, space and human resources;
- perform a special humanistic mission as they endeavour to achieve the social advancement of disadvantaged groups, of persons previously underrepresented in education;
- are keys to a better quality of life;
- require unorthodox organizational set ups;
- develop entirely new ways of structuring and financing education;
- express reservations about traditional education.

These similarities suggest that distance education and lifelong learning correspond to each other with regard to significant trends, issues and challenges.

## *An elaboration of selected similarities and parallelisms*

### Urgency measures

Dohmen described the present societal emergency situation by maintaining that there are only the simple alternatives 'lifelong learning or destruction' (1996: 19). For about 150 years the emergency situation for millions of persons could be described by a similar simple alternative: distance education or no education at all, no training at all, being barred from access to higher education, having reduced chances for promotion in the labour market and being excluded from the possibilities of upward mobility. Restrictions of this kind are certainly of vital significance for these persons as they reduce the possible basis of their livelihood.

In the nineteenth century industrialization brought about new demands for education and training that could not be met by traditional educational institutions, as these were geared to adolescents and face-to-face instruction and were not prepared and were practically unable to teach adults who had to work. These persons often lived quite far away from educational institutions, many of them abroad in English or French colonies, or they were hospitalized, home-bound or in prison. In such emergency situations distance education was often the only way out. This held true during the period of industrialization and still holds true in our post-industrial knowledge and learning society. This is due to the rise and growing importance of online distance education offered by open, virtual and corporate universities. In most countries in the world distance students are gaining and renewing the skills needed for sustained participation in the knowledge and learning society.

Distance education as an urgency measure became especially important in developing and threshold countries, where it is used and intensified for fostering the economic and cultural development of these countries for millions of persons (Dikshit *et al.*, 2002).

There is still another and more general aspect of urgency. Distance education can also be interpreted as a means of coping with acute societal problems, as it has helped to adapt the workforce to technical innovation and change. The late Charles A. Wedemeyer, still the leading expert and great visionary of distance education, wrote the following lines in 1981 to describe the role of distance education:

> The new urgency respecting learning to cope with societal behavioral problems (health, energy, crime, human rights, resources, peaceful co-existence, population, pollution etc.), signals the need for educational approaches that recognize and acknowledge the significance of non-traditional learning throughout life.
>
> (1981: 206)

These lines could also be part of one of the recent official memoranda on lifelong learning. The similarity of attitude, outlook and approach is impressive. In a way, Wedemeyer was a forerunner of the lifelong learning movement.

### Innovative impact

Distance education and lifelong learning collide with traditional concepts and practices of education in a similar way because of their strong innovative ideas and approaches.

The development and promotion of distance education in the nineteenth century was already a revolution. It brought about the abrupt change from oral face-to-face learning to mediated

231

and distributed learning, which created an entirely new structure of learning times and locations and required new specific learning behaviours. The second revolution took place when distance education was delivered by combined technical (mass) media at open universities. At present we are experiencing the third revolution of distance education, which is caused by computers and the internet.

There is still another important aspect of educational innovation: distance education caters mainly for adults of any age group who may learn at home, at work or in local study centres or even when travelling. It promotes learning in the lifespan, advocates a new understanding of learning and enables students to become self-regulated autonomous learners. This is one of the reasons why distance students will make good lifelong learners.

Distance education has a long tradition in being innovative in many ways and can integrate its respective achievements into the system of lifelong learning – much more so than campus-based education.

## New pedagogical approaches

The CEC *Memorandum on Lifelong Learning* deplores that 'most of what our education and training systems offer is still organized and taught as if the traditional ways of planning and organizing one's life had not changed for at least half of the century and demands adaptations' (CEC, 2000: 14). Distance education adapted early to the specific life conditions of the learners. It is not just a variation or replica of traditional face-to-face education, but breaks institutional boundaries, reorganizes teaching and learning processes thoroughly by the application of principles of industrialization, and establishes entirely new systems of education beyond classical educational institutions. Distance education, and especially digitized distance education, supports 'seamless, ubiquitous access to lifelong learning' (Koper *et al.*, 2005: 71). They both use technical media for the production and distribution of teaching material and the computer for providing virtual spaces for instruction, documentation, information, communication, collaboration and simulation for the learner. This new approach to learning changes the teaching behaviour of teachers and the learning behaviour of learners drastically. Teachers become designers of specific teaching materials, mentors, guides, moderators, advisers and managers of extensive learning systems. Students take over responsibility for their own learning, manage their own learning and develop formats of independent learning.

It is especially the extraordinary pedagogical flexibility that could greatly contribute to lifelong learning.

## Emphasis on self-learning

As experts of lifelong learning deplore that we 'still know and share too little . . . about how to generate productive self-directed learning' (CEC, 2000: 14), it might be sufficient to point to the fact that, to a degree, all distance learners are self-learners per se as they at least have to fix the times, location and duration of their learning. There are also models of teaching at a distance in which learners also determine the goals, methods and media of their self-learning (e.g. contract learning). Autonomous, self-regulated learning has been a guiding principle of several theories of distance education (Holmberg, 2005: 112–7; Jarvis, 1993: 171; Keegan, 1994: 51–72; Moore, 1993: 31–2; Moore and Kearsley, 2005: 227–8; Peters, 2004: 203–14; Wedemeyer, 1981: 50–3).

## The universalization of education

The great asset of the concepts of lifelong learning and distance education is the improvement of access to education for many of those persons who cannot afford to attend classes in traditional educational institutions. Distance education reaches out to persons who for quite a number of reasons cannot attend schools or institutions of continuing education, because of, for example, vocational, professional, military or family obligations, handicaps, low social standing or neglect. These persons can enrol in correspondence schools in order to upgrade their vocational knowledge and skills, or enrol in open high schools to improve their education, or they can take courses at open universities, virtual universities or corporate universities. The number of learners can be increased by means not available in traditional institutions of learning.

In this way the maxim of lifelong learning – learning for all regardless of age, location and social status – has been put into practice already to a remarkable extent.

## Humanistic mission

'Learning, whether traditional or non-traditional, should lead to humanistic ends' (Wedemeyer, 1981: 207). This statement certainly holds true for any learning. Distance education and lifelong learning, however, show a particularly strong and distinct tendency to achieve the social advancement of disadvantaged groups as well, especially of persons previously underrepresented in education. For about 150 years, distance education helped to enable ambitious and gifted persons to upgrade their knowledge and to earn certificates, diplomas and academic grades *outside* traditional educational systems. In the industrialized economy this quite often meant better jobs, better salaries, advancement in the operational hierarchies and improvements in standard of living and social status. This contribution is by no means a peripheral matter. Many of the more than 50 open universities in all parts of the world established themselves as major providers of continuing and higher education in their respective countries.

There is another significant parallel: according to the *Memorandum on Lifelong Learning* (CEC, 2000: 4), learning should be reinterpreted in order to be ready to 'offer equal opportunities for access to quality learning throughout life to all people' regardless of gender, age and social status. And education and training provision should be based 'first on the needs and demands of individuals' (p. 4). This objective reminds us of the 'legacy of distance education' (Daniel, 1998a: 3), which refers to the fact that distance education has a long tradition of taking care of the underprivileged, disadvantaged, neglected, ill and handicapped. In these cases in particular, learning leads to humanistic ends in distance education as well, including in the sense that it fosters their quest for understanding complex societies and for a better life.

## Reservations about traditional education

The early influential and invigorating supporter of the idea of lifelong learning, Edgar Faure, and his team started criticizing contemporary forms of education by pointing to inadequacies and the irrelevance of elements of traditional curricula and by considering alternative models of education (Faure, 1972). In the same way, most proponents of online learning disapprove of traditional forms of teaching and learning by recommending new and unorthodox pedagogical models. Their most important criticism is that educational institutions take care of sections of the clientele only, whereas other sections remain under-served.

In a similar way, theorists and practitioners of distance education develop their systems as they see that conventional educational institutions are not used and even not able to fulfil

233

necessary tasks for individual and social survival in a post-industrial knowledge society. Wedemeyer (1981: xix) wrote, 'The traditional ways of learning do not satisfy urgent needs rapidly and equitably enough.' And H.P. Dikshit, the Vice-Chancellor of the Indira Gandhi National Open University in New Delhi, considers 'access and equity' to be the most important challenges for distance education (Dikshit *et al.*, 2002: 24). According to him 'higher education witnessed tremendous innovative developments'. These, however, have raised doubts about the viability, or even desirability of the *wholesome* conventional face-to-face education in classroom environment. For him distance education is one of the alternatives that 'can cater for more flexible educational delivery, encourage self-learning, and are more cost-effective than the conventional education' (p. 24).

## Possible contributions

Because of the significant similarities and parallelisms referred to above, distance education can be considered a form of education that is *most suitable* for integration in comprehensive systems of lifelong learning. It provides a wealth of opportunities and challenges for this purpose. This can be explained with regard to its philosophy, its traditions, its transgression of the boundaries of place and time, its keeping up with technological progress, its unparalleled use of technical media, its expanded and intensified experiences in online learning, its extraordinary flexibility, responsiveness and accessibility, its singular pedagogical achievements outside traditional educational institutions and its unique learning experiences with adults working for a living.

### Pedagogical practices

In the face of the activities in distance teaching institutions all over the world – commercial, state-run or corporate – and especially of the unimaginable impact of more than 50 open universities in highly industrialized and developing countries, one cannot but recommend the practices developed there. Lifelong learning can profit a great deal from their specific *pedagogical* achievements.

The following *practices* in particular can be taken over, adapted and developed further: mediated education, distributed education, ubiquitous learning, online learning, autonomous learning, the combination of mass and individualized education, the integration of work and learning, the marked change of the roles of teachers, techniques of online communication and collaboration, the course team idea, pre-prepared high-quality learning material, techniques of modularization of contents, face-to-face sessions and individual counselling in study centres, experiences in tutoring and mentoring, intensified and efficient support of students *and* teachers, computer-based and tutor-based examinations, various forms of cooperation with corporate personnel departments or human resources departments, and, finally, distinct techniques of administering large, and even extremely large, numbers of students at a time.

### Pedagogical concepts

Supporters and developers of lifelong learning could also profit from becoming familiar with some of the assumptions, beliefs, visions and ideologies inherent in the tradition of distance education. Most of them will only be partly realized, or never fully realized, but it is certainly a distinct advantage when proponents and practitioners of lifelong learning have internalized them and have become able to act respectively.

Among others, the following theoretical *assumptions* may also become important for lifelong learning:

- Communication and collaboration must be emphasized.
- Guidance and support must be reinterpreted and decisively enhanced.
- A constructivist interpretation of learning is conducive to developing and enhancing online learning.
- It is necessary to enable students to become autonomous learners.
- Students can be guided and enabled to assess and evaluate their learning themselves.
- Teachers and students must become aware of the essential difference between traditional and computer generated knowledge – and they must become skilful in applying these two forms of knowledge.

### Education policy concepts

The following ideas and visions have become prevalent in distance education. They show a strong affinity to lifelong learning:

- The quest for *equality of educational opportunity* and *equity*, so important in open universities, e.g. in China, Korea, India and Venezuela.
- The declared belief in the goal of *education for all* which is the official motto of open universities, e.g. in Hong Kong and New Delhi.
- The accentuation of egalitarian tendencies in education, which means advocating new forms of mass education and of mass higher education.
- The strong conviction that learning can be *brought closer to home and job* in several ways.
- The goal of developing strategies of dealing with *diverse age groups of adults* in different learning contexts.
- The realization of the legacy of distance education, which is a specific *humanistic approach* in teaching.
- The vision and justification of the *autonomous, self-regulated learner*, which has always been a goal of distance education theorists for pedagogical and personality building reasons.

## Conclusion

Compared to all traditional formats of teaching and learning, distance education lends itself most easily and effectively to fulfilling new tasks in lifelong learning. It could even be maintained that it has already performed significant functions of lifelong learning in its long history. In a way it can even be considered a forerunner of lifelong learning. 'The practice of lifelong learning has been facilitated by the demonstrable fact of thousands (and now millions worldwide) of adults studying beyond school age using a range of media, and pursuing both occupational and leisure goals' (Daniel, 1996, quoted in Thorpe, 2005: 23). These significant experiences suggest that distance and open education will play a supremely important role in establishing, supporting and enhancing lifelong learning. Distance education will be 'a powerful tool for supporting lifelong learning' (Daniel, 2005: ix).

# References

Bates, T. (2005) 'Charting the evolution of lifelong learning and distance higher education: the role of research', in C. McIntosh (ed.) *Perspectives on Distance Education: Lifelong learning and distance higher education*, Vancouver and Paris: Commonwealth of Learning and UNESCO, pp. 133–49.

Beaudoin, M.F. (2006) 'The impact of distance education on the academy in the digital age', in M.F. Beaudoin (ed.) *Higher Education in the Digital Age,* New York: Nova Science Publishers, pp. 1–20.

Bund-Länder-Kommission für Bildungsplanung (BLK) (2004) *Strategie für lebenslanges Lernen in der Bundesrepublik Deutschland*, Bonn: BLK.

Commission of the European Communities (CEC) (2000) *A Memorandum on Lifelong Learning*, Brussels: CEC.

Cross, K.P. (1981) *Adults as Learners*, San Francisco, CA: Jossey-Bass.

Curtis, P. (2005) 'Popular crusade: at last staff see themselves as students see them', *Education Guardian*, September 27. Available online at http://education.guardian.co.uk/higher/comment/story/0,,1578671,00.html (accessed 20 October 2007).

Daniel, Sir John (1998a) 'Knowledge media for mega-universities: scaling up new technology at the UK Open University', Keynote speech at the 1998 Shanghai International Open and Distance Education Symposion, in *Proceedings of the Shanghai Television University: Symposion: Abstracts*, Shanghai: Television University, p. 3.

—— (1998b) 'Can you get my hard nose in focus? Universities, mass education and appropriate technology', in M. Eisenstadt and T. Vincent (eds) *The Knowledge Web: Learning and collaborating on the net*, London: Kogan Page.

—— (1999) *MegaUniversities and Knowledge Media*, London: Kogan Page.

—— (2005) 'Preface', in C. McIntosh (ed.) *Lifelong Learning and Distance Higher Education*, Paris: Commonwealth of Learning/UNESCO, pp. ix–x.

Delors, J. (Chair) (1996) *Learning: The treasure within*, Paris: UNESCO.

Dikshit, H.P., Garg, S., Panda, S. and Vijayshri (2002) *Access and Equity: Challenges for open and distance education*, New Delhi: Kogan Page Private.

Dohmen, G. (1996) *Das lebenslange Lernen: Leitlinien einer modernen Bildungspolitik*, Bonn: Ministerium für Bildung, Wissenschaft, Forschung und Technologie.

Eisenstadt, M. and Vincent, T. (eds) (1998) *The Knowledge Web: Learning and collaborating on the net*, London: Kogan Page.

Evans, T. and Nation, D. (eds) (1996) *Opening education: Policies and practices from open and distance education*, London: Routledge.

—— and —— (2000) 'Understanding changes to university teaching', in T. Evans and D. Nation (eds) *Changing University Teaching*, London: Kogan Page, pp. 160–75.

—— and —— (2003) 'Globalization and the reinvention of distance education', in M.G. Moore and W.G. Anderson (eds) *Handbook of Distance Education,* Mahwah, NJ: Lawrence Erlbaum, pp. 777–92.

Faure, E. (Chair) (1972) *Learning to Be: The world of education today and tomorrow*, Paris: UNESCO.

Finke, W.F. (2000) *Lifelong Learning in the Information Age*, Bueren: Fachbibliothek Verlag.

Gould, S.B. and Cross, K.P. (eds) (1977) *Explorations in Non-traditional Study*, San Francisco, CA: Jossey-Bass.

Halimi, S. (2005) 'Lifelong learning for equity and social cohesion: a new challenge for higher education', in C. McIntosh (ed.) *Lifelong Learning and Distance Higher Education*, Paris: Commonwealth of Learning/UNESCO, pp. 11–22.

Hasan, A. (1996) 'Lifelong learning', in Albert C. Tuijnman (ed.) *International Encyclopedia of Adult Education and Training*, 2nd edn, Tarrytown, New York: Pergamon, pp. 33–41.

Holmberg, B. (2005) *The Evolution, Principles and Practices of Distance Education*, Olderburg: Bibliotheks- und Informationssystem der Universität Oldenburg.

Jarvis, P. (1993) 'The education of adults and distance education in late modernity', in D. Keegan (ed.) *Theoretical Principles of Distance Education*, London: Routledge, pp. 165–74.

Keegan, D. (1994) *Foundations of Distance Education*, London: Routledge.

Koper, R., Giesbers, B., van Rosmalen, P., van Bruggen, J., Tattersall, C., Vogten, H. and Brouns, F. (2005) 'A design model for lifelong learning networks', *Interactive Learning Environments* 13(1–2). Available online at http://dspace.learningnetworks.org/handle/1820/32 (accessed 20 October 2007).

McIntosh, C. (2005) 'Introduction', in C. McIntosh (ed.) *Lifelong Learning and Distance Education*, Vancouver and Paris: Commonwealth of Learning and UNESCO.

MacKenzie, N., Postgate, R. and Scupham, J. (1975) *Open Learning Systems and Problems in Post-secondary Education*, Paris: UNESCO.

Moore, M.G. (1993) 'Theory of transactional distance', in D. Keegan (ed.) *Theoretical Principles of Distance Education*, London: Routledge, pp. 22–38.

—— and Kearsley, G. (2005) *Distance Education: A systems view*, Belmont, CA: Thomson Wadsworth.

—— and Thompson, M. (1990) *The Effects of Distance Education: A summary of the literature*, University Park, PA: American Center for Distance Education.

Osborne, M. and Thomas, E. (2003) *Lifelong Learning in a Changing Continent: Continuing education in the universities of Europe*, Leicester: NIACE.

Paine, N. (ed.) (1988) *Open Learning in Transition*, Cambridge: National Extension College Trust.

Peters, O. (2004) 'Visions of autonomous learning', in O. Peters (ed.) *Distance Education in Transition,* 4th edn, Olderburg: Bibliotheks- und Informationssystem der Universität Oldenburg, pp. 215–34.

—— (2008) 'Open universities', in T. Evans, M. Haughty and D. Murphy (eds) *The World Handbook of Distance Education*, Chennai: Elsevier.

Thorpe, M. (2005) 'The impact of ICT on lifelong learning', in C. McIntosh (ed.) *Lifelong Learning and Distance Education*, Vancouver and Paris: Commonwealth of Learning and UNESCO, pp. 23–32.

Wedemeyer, C.A. (1981) *Learning at the Backdoor*, Madison, WI: The University of Wisconsin Press.

# 21

# The development and transformation of e-learning

## An international review[1]

*Weiyuan Zhang*

In the last ten years, e-learning has become one of the most popular and widely used learning modes in open, distance and conventional institutions. E-learning is now regarded as an effective method to support the establishment of a lifelong learning society. Zhang and Huang (2002) stated four distinct advantages of e-learning: flexibility, interactivity, resource-sharing and openness. First, e-learning offers a tremendously flexible learning opportunity without the limitations of time or location. Students can learn at any time and anywhere based on their own pace and their preferred learning methods. Second, the internet has powerful functions for interaction and communication. Learners can interact with instructors and other learners using asynchronous and synchronous communications. Third, quality education resources can be linked through online databases and shared by all learners and instructors, both locally and internationally. Fourth, e-learning is fully open to people independent of gender, age, ethics, beliefs, religion and the like. However, e-learning is also a most controversial issue in both philosophy and practice. The purpose of this chapter is to review the development and changes of e-learning from an international perspective. It offers an analysis of both the theory and the practice of e-learning.

## The development of e-learning

In the early 1990s, a few universities in Western countries realized the great potential of e-learning and started to develop online courses. During that period, HTML or other web programming languages were used to develop online courses, which required professional web programmers with expensive technological resources. Therefore, only universities with advanced technological support and sufficient resources were able to develop a limited number of online courses.

In the mid-1990s, with the rapid development of web technology and the increasing need for flexible learning, some educational and business organizations took the market opportunities to develop e-learning platforms, such as WebCT, Blackboard and First Class, among others. These tools integrated functions of course design, communication and interaction, administration and management. With these kinds of e-platforms, instructors could develop their own courses easily without the need for web programming skills. As a result, these platforms have greatly promoted e-learning development worldwide since the late 1990s.

## Three schools of thought in e-learning

With the increasing demand for e-learning in educational institutions, educational researchers have been exploring the philosophy and practices of the format since the late 1990s. Zhang and Wang (2004) reviewed the literature and identified three schools of thought in e-learning, which explore e-learning from a technological aspect, from a pedagogical aspect, and from technological and pedagogical aspects.

### E-learning from a technological aspect

The first school examines e-learning from a technological aspect, such as studied by Khan (1997), Ross (1998) and Firdyiwek (1999). Table 21.1 summarizes the details.

*Table 21.1* E-learning from a technological aspect

---

*Components of e-learning*

---

*Hardware technology – based on functions of web hardware*
- Content development (learning and instructional theories, instructional design, curriculum development)
- Multimedia component (text and graphics, audio streaming, video streaming, graphical user interfaces, compression technology)
- Internet tools (communication tools, remote access tools, internet navigation tools, search and other tools)
- Computers and storage devices (computer platforms, servers, hard drives, CD ROMs, etc.)
- Connection and service providers (modems, dial-in services, gateway service providers, internet service providers, etc.)
- Authoring programs (programming languages, authoring tools, HTML converters and editors, etc.)
- Servers (HTTP servers, common gateway interfaces)
- Browsers and other applications (text-based browsers, graphical browsers, links, plug-ins)

(Khan, 1997)

*Software technology – based on functions of e-learning platforms*
- Student tools (glossaries, indexes, book marking, searching, related links pages, notebooks, online help)
- Collaboration tools (asynchronous communication, synchronous communication, class lists)
- Administration and security (log-in/log-out, counters, multi-browser use)
- Testing and record-keeping (online grade books, quick quizzes, essay submission forms)
- Functionality (site maps, tracking, better use of multimedia technology)
- User interface (consistency of layout, intuitive interface, user feedback, measures for individualized instruction, reasonable load time, appropriate use of media, new windows for external browsing)
- Non-technical features (student handbooks, orientation days, student surveys, computers-as-tools, assessing learning styles)

(Ross, 1998)

- Administration (set-up and maintenance, enrolment and registration, access control, use tracking)
- Instruction (look-and-feel, instructional tools, assessment tools, course management)
- Student use (authoring, self assessment)

(Firdyiwek, 1999)

---

239

*Table 21.2* E-learning from a pedagogical aspect

| Basis | Components of e-learning |
| --- | --- |

*Distance education principles*

- Pedagogical philosophy: constructivist
- Learning theory: cognitive
- Goal orientation: general
- Task orientation: general
- Source of motivation: intrinsic
- Teacher role: facilitative
- Metacognitive support: integrated
- Collaborative learning strategies: integral
- Cultural sensitivity: respectful
- Structural flexibility: open

(Reeves and Reeves, 1997)

- Structure discussions: breaking large numbers of students into small groups, providing specific tasks, setting timelines for discussion
- Collaborative activities: group work, peer commenting
- Online assessment: assignment submission, self-tests
- Interactive course materials: choice of learning routes and methods, video, audio and text materials, interaction with content
- An online pedagogy: importance of interactivity in the learning process, changing role of the teacher from sage to guide, need for knowledge management skills and for team working abilities, move towards resource-based rather than packaged learning

(Mason, 1998)

*Transnational distance theory*

- Communication variable: academic interaction, collaborative interaction, interpersonal interaction
- Learning variable: learner autonomy, learner collaboration
- Teaching variable: content expandability, content adaptability, visual layout

(Jung, 2001)

## E-learning from a pedagogical aspect

The second school explored e-learning from a pedagogical aspect and explored principles in an e-learning environment. The examples of this group are shown in Table 21.2.

## E-learning from technological and pedagogical aspects

The third school examined e-learning from technological *and* pedagogical aspects. An example is shown in Table 21.3.

In the third group, some educationists adapted interaction theories in distance education, such as learner–content interaction, learner–instructor interaction, learner–learner interaction (Moore, 1989) and learning-interface theory (Hillman *et al.*, 1994), to explore e-learning. A comprehensive model of e-learning based on interaction theories, which is from a pedagogical aspect supplemented by technological utilization, was developed by Anderson in 2004 (see Figure 21.1). This model illustrates two basic e-learning modes based on interaction among learners,

*Table 21.3* E-learning from technological and pedagogical aspects

---

*Components of e-learning*

---

*Technology and pedagogy – based on principles of using ICT in teaching and pedagogy*

- Descriptive dimension: site identification (name, URL, author, etc.), site evolution (creation date, last updating, sections under development), language or languages used in the site, target population, size, subject matter

- Pedagogical dimension: instructional configuration (web-only or links to external resources), instructional model (inquiry-oriented, open-ended), instructional means (hypermedia, virtual 3-D), instructional type (browsing, answering questions, interacting with experts or peers), cognitive process elicited (plain information retrieval, problem solving, invention), locus of control over the learning process, feedback (automatic evaluation answers, human expert response), help functions offered in the site, learning resources (embedded in the site or external), evaluation

- Knowledge dimension: representational structure (linear, branching, or web structure), representational means (text, still image, interactive image, sound), type of knowledge (declarative, procedural, dynamic), navigation tools (time lines, search facilities, location maps)

- Communication dimension: types of tele-learning (tele-information handling, tele-interaction, tele-manipulation), types of communication (synchronous and asynchronous), link structure of the site (links within the site, to other sites, non-web tools, humans), communication means (email, discussion group, chat, videoconference)

(Mioduser *et al.*, 2000)

---

teachers, content and interface. The first mode on the left illustrates paced and collaborative e-learning, while the second mode on the right describes dependent e-learning.

Zhang and Wang (2004) stated that these different approaches for exploring e-learning reflected a continuous development of its conception and practice. In its early stages, e-learning was still new to most educators. Scholars in educational technologies tried to introduce and emphasize the hardware and software needed for e-learning. After becoming familiar with the technologies and gaining first-hand experience in e-learning, educational scholars became more concerned about the pedagogical applications. After all, technologies facilitate the learning process but cannot replace the pedagogy for effective learning. The third school of educators tried to adapt theories of distance education into e-learning, which combined the technological aspects with pedagogy for more effective e-learning.

## Functions and features of e-learning platforms

E-learning courses are delivered and managed by e-platform support. Many e-platforms were developed by educational institutions and business enterprises in the USA, UK, Singapore, mainland China, Hong Kong and India. Zhang and Wang (2004, 2005) examined 17 e-learning platforms that have been widely used by open and conventional universities around the world. These 17 e-learning tools were WebCT, BlackBoard, FirstClass, FlexEducation, ANGEL, Anlon, Avilar WebMentor, BluePower, CentraOne, Click2learn Aspen, Dianda-online, eCollege, IVLE, Learning Space, The Learning Manager, TopClass and Virtual Campus. The functions of e-learning tools based on these platforms are classified and summarized in Table 21.4.

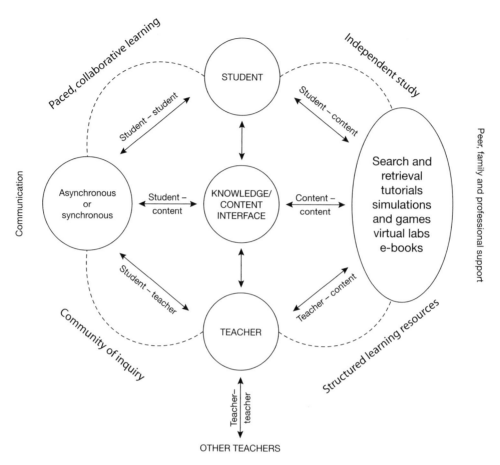

*Figure 21.1* A model of online learning showing types of interaction.

Source: Anderson (2004: 49).

Table 21.4 shows that the functions of e-learning platforms can be classified into three types: course design, communication and collaboration, and administration and management. This reflects three main factors in teaching: course, delivery and management. Within these three types of functions, there are 17 sub-functions. Zhang and Wang's studies (2004, 2005) found that Web-CT and BlackBoard incorporated all 17 functions, while all other e-platforms had only some of them.

Zhang and Wang (2004) further reviewed over 100 online courses using the e-platforms mentioned above, and identified the 32 common features of e-learning courses indicated in Table 21.5.

Table 21.5 reveals the 32 features subdivided into five types: course, communication and collaboration, administration and management, technical support, and assignment and assessment.

Understanding the functions and features of e-learning platforms is helpful for educationists in order to develop and use the most suitable ones depending on the specific context.

*Table 21.4* Common functions of e-learning platforms

| Course design functions | Communication and collaboration functions | Management and administrative functions | |
|---|---|---|---|
| | | Course management functions | Administrative functions |
| Instructional design tools | Asynchronous communication: discussion forums | Module management | Secure login |
| Course layout template | Asynchronous communication: internal email | Quiz management | Technical support |
| Search tool for course website | Synchronous communication: text-based chat | Grade management | |
| Student homepage | Synchronous communication: audio/video conferencing | Student tracking | |
| | File sharing | | |
| | Workgroup | | |
| | Whiteboard | | |

Source: Zhang and Wang (2004; 2005).

*Table 21.5* Common features of online courses

| Course | Communication and collaboration | Administration and management | Technical support | Assignment and assessment |
|---|---|---|---|---|
| Syllabus | Email | Course unit management | FAQs | Receiving assignments online |
| Online course materials | Discussion forums | Announcements | Online technical support | Submitting assignments online |
| Video lectures on demand | Teachers' feedback | Grading management | Online teacher support | Online self-assessment |
| IP courseware | Whiteboards | Statistics of online activities | Software maintenance | Online exams |
| Links to supplementary materials | Workgroups | Online registration | Hardware maintenance | Automatic grading |
| Course website search engines | File sharing | Secure logins | Technical training | Timetables for assignments and exams |
| Course notes | Student homepage | | | |

Source: Adapted from Zhang and Wang (2004).

## Analysis of success and failure of e-learning practices

In the late 1990s, e-learning was the most fashionable teaching and learning mode that higher education institutions strove to pursue. However, after several years of effort, e-learning has become the most controversial learning mode because of its failure in some newly established e-learning institutions/consortiums in the early 2000s. Examples of failed e-learning institutions are shown in Table 21.6 (Zhang, 2005).

Table 21.6 shows that e-learning in some educational institutions faced serious challenges in the early 2000s. However, at the same time, e-learning in other universities has been successful, as shown in Table 21.7.

It is valuable to explore why e-learning failed in some educational institutions in such a short period while it is still successful in others. Zhang (2005) proposed the main reason for failure: the institutions that failed in running e-learning were newly established and lacked expertise and experience in distance education. They wrongly regarded e-learning as simply putting existing face-to-face course materials on the web supplemented by limited online discussion. Through web technology, they could make great profits by enrolling massive numbers of local and international students. However, they did not realize or understand that e-learning, as a distance education mode that is distinctly different from face-to-face learning, needs to follow the pedagogical principles of distance teaching and learning, including all aspects of administration and management, instructional design, course development, learning support, technical support, quality assurance and so on. According to experiences from successful open education institutions, the most expensive cost in distance education is course development and student support, rather than technology. Effective e-learning needs professional experts in distance education and a great deal of investment. Cost-effectiveness – let alone profit – can only be achieved when a large number of students share *quality* e-learning courses.

The explanation above could be supported by the successful e-learning institutions listed in Table 21.7, which have either had experience in open and distance learning or have experts in open and distance learning involved in e-learning. These institutions have *evolved* from distance learning to e-learning, rather than dramatically changing from face-to-face learning to e-learning without expertise and experience.

## Transformation from e-learning to blended/integrated learning

Because of the failure of some newly established institutions using purely e-learning, educational scholars attempted to explore how and why the successful e-learning institutions *were* successful. It was found that the majority of successful institutions use e-learning in their courses as an *adjunct* to conventional modes. According to the results of a survey on e-learning in Commonwealth Universities (International Strategic Information Service, 2002), e-learning in the majority of universities was integrated with face-to-face learning and printed materials. In that study, the term 'e-learning' was defined as 'us[ing] Internet to enhance teaching and learning'. Another large-scale survey on e-learning in Asian open universities (Zhang, 2004) revealed that very few purely online courses were provided in 11 leading e-learning institutions in Asia. Zhang's study defined 'e-learning' as 'us[ing] computer and Internet to provide teaching information and educational resources, and to enhance communication and interaction of teaching and learning' (p. 5).

In this situation the definition of e-learning and its relationship with other learning modes needs to be reconsidered and re-examined. The earlier concept was that e-learning and other

*Table 21.6* Examples of failing e-learning institutions and consortiums

| Founding institution/ consortium | Name of e-learning institution | Purpose | Process and result | |
|---|---|---|---|---|
| Columbia University | Fathcom.com | Deliver existing programmes/ courses within the university through the web for profit-making purposes | Founded in 2000 and closed in 2002 because of lack of students | Lost US$25 million |
| Temple University | Virtual Temple | Deliver existing programmes/ courses within the university through the web for profit-making purposes | Founded in November 1999 and closed in July 2001 because of lack of students | Lost over US$10 million |
| New York University | NYUonline | Deliver existing programmes/ courses within the university through the web for profit-making purposes | Founded in 1998 and closed in December 2001 because of lack of students | Lost over US$10 million |
| University of California, California State University and California Community Colleges | California Virtual University | Deliver existing programmes/ courses within the university through the web for profit-making purposes | Founded in 1997 and closed in December 1999 because of lack of students | Lost over US$10 million |
| 19 Western States, Gates Foundation, IBM and State Consortium | Western Governor's University (WGU) | Deliver existing programmes/ courses from educational institutions throughout USA via web for the purpose of profit-making | Founded by 19 Governors in 1997 and planned to be a top online university, but lack of students since 2001 caused WGU to change its direction and only provide a teacher training project | No data |
| Higher Education Funding Council (UK) | UKeU | Deliver existing programmes/ courses from well-known universities in the UK through the web and make profits | Founded in May 2001 and closed in February 2004 because of lack of students | Lost over £62 million |

Sources: Hafner (2002); Liu (2005); Cheng (2005).

*Table 21.7* Examples of successful e-learning institutions

| Country/Region | Institution (examples) |
| --- | --- |
| UK | The Open University |
| USA | University of Phoenix |
| Canada | Athabasca University |
| Germany | FernUniversität |
| Australia | University of Southern Queensland |
| China | China Central Radio & Television University; Online Education Colleges affiliated to 67 universities |
| Hong Kong | The Open University of Hong Kong |
| India | Indira Gandhi National Open University |
| Thailand | Sukhothai Thammathirat Open University |
| Malaysia | Open University of Malaysia |
| South Africa | University of South Africa |
| Israel | Open University of Israel |
| Pakistan | Pakistan Virtual University |
| Korea | Korea National Open University |
| Finland | Finnish Virtual University |
| Turkey | Anadolu University |

Source: Adapted from Bacsich (2004).

learning modes were mutually exclusive. However, after a decade's practice of e-learning, it was realized that the e-learning mode should be combined with other learning modes. Therefore, the term 'blended e-learning' appeared, which was developed from the earlier term 'blended learning'.

There are so many explanations of the term 'blended learning'. Graham (2006) identified and summarized three types of different opinions as follows:

- Blended learning = combining instructional modalities (or delivery media).
- Blended learning = combining instructional methods.
- Blended learning = combining online and face-to-face instruction.

Graham (2006) pointed out the shortcomings of the first two positions, because any learning system involves multiple instructional methods and multiple delivery media. So, defining blended learning in either of these two ways did not get at the essence of what blended learning was and why the concept was exciting to so many people. The third position more accurately reflects the historical emergence of blended learning systems and is the foundation of the author's working definition.

With the acceptance of blended e-learning, which replaced e-learning, the term blended e-learning was questioned. The word 'blend' means 'mixed', which seems to combine learning modes casually without the need for an instructional design. Therefore, the term 'blend' might not be proper in this situation because it doesn't mean to 'mix' different learning modes. What is meant here is to integrate e-learning with other learning modes, which could provide the best combinations in order to use the advantages of each learning mode. Therefore, 'integrated e-learning' might be a better term because it reflects what is really being talked about.

246

## Conclusion

E-learning has become one of the main learning modes used in establishing a lifelong learning society, although the debates on how to use e-learning effectively continue. This chapter examined the global development and three schools of thought in e-learning. The functions of e-learning were clarified and analysed. The experiences and lessons of e-learning were examined from an international perspective. It was suggested that the term 'integrated e-learning' could reflect the meaning of the best combination of e-learning and other learning modes as well as marginalizing the disadvantages of each mode.

## Note

1    I would like to thank Dr Rex G. Sharman, HKU SPACE, for his constructive comments and editorial suggestions.

## References

Anderson, T. (2004) 'Toward a theory for online learning', in T. Anderson and F. Elloumi (eds) *Theory and Practice of Online Learning*, Athabasca, Alberta: Athabasca University, pp. 33–60.

Bacsich, P. (2004) 'Introduction to virtual universities and e-universities', in P. Bacsich and S. Frank Cristow (eds) *The E-University Compendium: Cases, issues, and themes in higher education distance e-learning*, York: The Higher Education Academy. Available online at www.heacademy.ac.uk/learningandteaching/eUniCompendium_front.doc (accessed 13 October 2006).

Cheng, X. (2005) 'Lessons from distance education in USA', *China Distance Education* 4: 72–5 (in Chinese).

Firdyiwek, Y. (1999) 'Web-based courseware tools: where is the pedagogy?', *Educational Technology* 39(1): 29–34.

Graham, C.R. (2006) 'Blended learning systems: definition, current trends, and future directions', in C.J. Graham and C.R. Graham (eds) *Handbook of Blended Learning: Global perspectives, local design*, San Francisco, CA: Pfeiffer Publishing, pp. 3–21.

Hafner, K. (2002) 'Lessons learned at dot-com U', *The New York Times*, May 27.

Hillman, C.G., Wills, D.J. and Gunawardena, C.N. (1994) 'Learner–interface interaction in distance education: an extension of contemporary models and strategies for practitioners', *The American Journal of Distance Education* 8(2): 30–42.

International Strategic Information Service (2002) *Online Learning in Commonwealth Universities: Selected data from the 2002 Observatory Survey – Part 1*, London: The Observatory on Borderless Higher Education.

Jung, I. (2001) 'Building a theoretical framework of web-based instruction in the context of distance education', *British Journal of Educational Technology* 32(5): 525–34.

Khan, B.H. (1997) 'Web-based instruction (WBI): what is it and why is it?', in B.H. Khan (ed.) *Web-based Instruction*, Englewood Cliffs, NJ: Educational Technology Publications, pp. 5–18.

Liu, D. (2005) 'Disappeared quicker than dot-com', *China Distance Education* 2: 23–5 (in Chinese).

Mason, R. (1998) 'Models of online courses', *ALN Magazine* 2, The Sloan Consortium (SloanC), p. 2.

Mioduser, D., Nachmias, R., Lahav, O. and Oren, A. (2000) 'Web-based learning environment: current pedagogical and technological state', *Journal of Research on Computing in Education* 33(1) (Fall): 55–77.

Moore, M.G. (1989) 'Editorial: three types of interaction', *The American Journal of Distance Education* 3(2): 1–6.

Reeves, T.C. and Reeves, P.M. (1997) 'Effective dimensions of interactive learning on the world wide web', in B.H. Khan (ed.) *Web-based Instruction*, Englewood Cliffs, NJ: Educational Technology Publications, pp. 59–66.

Ross, J.L. (1998) 'Online but off course: a wish list for distance educators', *International Electronic Journal for Leadership in Learning* 2(3). Available online at www.acs.ucalgary.ca/~icjll/volume2/Ross2_3.html (accessed 13 October 2006).

Zhang, Weiyuan (2004) 'Comparison of e-learning in open universities in Asia', *Journal of Distance Education* (Taiwan) 16: 1–19 (in Chinese).

—— (2005) 'An analysis of the reasons why some e-learning institutions failed', *China Distance Education* 11: 32–5 (in Chinese).

—— and Huang, C. (2002) 'Development of online learning: cases of Hong Kong and Taiwan', in W. Zhang (ed.) *Current State and Trends in Open and Distance Education*, Beijing: China Central Radio and Television University Press, pp. 82–95 (in Chinese).

—— and Wang, L. (2004) 'Global collaboration in the development of an online learning environment scale', *Staff and Educational Development International* 8(1): 47–64.

—— and —— (2005) 'Learning management system (LMS) for web-based distance education: an international review', in Y.L. Visser, L. Visser, M. Simonson and R. Amirault (eds) *Trends and Issues in Distance Education: International perspectives*, Greenwich: Information Age Publishing, pp. 245–59.

# 22

# The World Wide Web and lifelong learning

*Santosh Panda*

The World Wide Web (WWW, or the web) is the most significant aspect of the internet (or Net) and provides lifelong learners with access to enormous resources, sometimes filtered and arranged by many search engines and web-access preferences. Besides e-commerce, e-governance, e-health and e-dating, among others, the Net is considered as the perpetuator of lifelong learning (Harasim *et al.*, 1995; Walker, 1998). Technology-enabled interactive e-learning is positioned to result in continuous lifelong learning anywhere, anytime (Halal and Liebowitz, 1994). These developments provide for unlimited learning opportunities and increasing participation in adult education. A learning age (DfEE, 1998) and a technological vision of a learning society are part of the rhetoric promised by innumerable developments across the globe. What promises, then, do we have for the WWW in the context of lifelong learning in the information society? This chapter examines these aspects and reflects on the possibilities we might consider.

## Society and the Net

The Net today provides for virtually everything – from information to collaboration, from e-marketing to community service, from cybersex to blogging. The past decade has provided opportunities for the convergence of technologies – broadcasting, telecommunication and computing – leading to increasing networking and presence in consumers' lives. The web as an ICT resource is progressively supported by emerging platforms created by the convergence of technological artefacts, such as digital broadcasting, mobile phones and the latest generation of personal computers. All this is happening under the banner of what is called an 'information society'.

The proliferation and increasing commercial use of the Net in the 1990s focused the attention of governments and policy makers on the emergence of the information society. Governments would provide significant budgetary provisions for making computers and the Net accessible to as many as possible, thereby bridging the new monster in the discrimination bandwagon – the digital divide. The post-industrial society – the information society – necessitated the adoption of information and communication technology (ICT), particularly the Net, in all spheres of human life. There are significant economic, technological, sociological and historical explanations for the proliferation and consolidation of information technology in an information society. There have also been contrasting views on the adoption of ICT. For instance, Castells (1998) argues that the development of global communication networks drives contemporary economic changes, while Giddens (1999) underlines that globalisation is driven by the adoption of ICT within broader socio-economic changes. 'The information society,' writes Feather, 'is an essentially social phenomenon: it is about how people live and work both individually and with each other. Therein lies its importance and its unending fascination' (2003: 16). Black, on the other hand, argues that 'the information society proposition is in reality a mirage: a vision built on the shifting sands of the disquietening social change that has characterised recent decades' (2003: 20). He criticises the widely held notion of reducing information into bits of disaggregated data, and treating information as an item rather than a process, as a thing rather than an action.

The Net, though, facilitates the retrieval and processing of information – information as a process and not as a thing; this should also facilitate self-reflection and critical thinking in adult learners. In a recent work, Selwyn *et al.* (2006: 9) critically discuss the concept and application of 'le@rning society' for 'practical achievement of the learning society vision through technological means'. Instant availability of information should not delimit the culture of communities or the capacity for imagination; and, as Beeson (2003) argues, 'submersion in a global information culture' must be resisted. Therefore, 'technology needs to be geared towards culturally induced reforms in all spheres of life which further sustain cultural and individual identity and develop critical reflection on what could be set right for progress and development' (Panda, 2007: 446).

Castells (1996), in an earlier work, had interpreted these developments within the framework of what he coined a 'network society', based on the stark realities of global economics, and in which the technological developments drive the networking of the basic structure of such a society. Networks govern functions and processes, and also contribute to the modification of 'the operation and outcomes in the processes of production, experience, power and culture' (Castells, 1996: 469). Among the results of the Net and the network society are: the rise of new technical, professional and scientific groups; the networking of labour and enterprises; and the global economy. These new social and economic activities are characterised by the changing nature of: work and occupations; the creation and retrieval of knowledge; and economic and social exchanges. The Net has facilitated flexible working (in place of Monday to Friday, nine to five), changing patterns of employment, and especially the service sector. It is therefore not surprising that almost all kinds of work, including agriculture, today require, in one way or the other, the use of IT. With significant transition from an industrial society to post-industrial/knowledge-based learning society, public authorities and local community leaders have realised that all citizens should acquire high-quality general and vocational education, in order to be able to engage in productive work and further education and training throughout the entire lifespan within a scenario of the contexualisation of learning in social practice, and the convergence of traditional learning with the knowledge explosion in the learning society. It is pertinent therefore to analyse the changing interpretation of the context of lifelong learning, and in what way the web/Net could address this.

## Lifelong learning in context

Learning in the context of lifelong learning (Edwards, 1997) and the use of ICT can happen at one's pace and place – workplaces, marketplaces, social environments, homes and the like.

The power of the web provides ample scope to learn at a distance, and gives significance to continuing lifelong learning. Learning happens in a context, and it is important to appreciate this 'context' within which learning takes place. This, in a way, is the analysis of context–practice–learning.

Besides the influence of workplaces, homes, communities and social environments, the Net also facilitates distributed, structured and self-structured learning (Lea and Nicoll, 2002). Descriptive, explanatory and complex contexts of learning have been provided by Edwards (2006), who underlines 'context to be extended into the dimension of relationship between individuals and variously defined others, mediated through a range of social, organisational and technological artefacts'. The earlier interpretation of 'context' as a bounded container for learning – for instance, school, college, classroom and textbooks, which bound formal learning together away from everyday practice – needs further expansion to include views on the situatedness of learning (Lave and Wenger, 1991; Lave, 1996), wherein decontexualised knowledge within socially situated practices (or, in other words, contexualisation of formal learning in social practice) assumes considerable significance. Learning is a change in understanding in practice in social contexts, and therefore all social practices are learning contexts. The focus is on 'contexualisation', that is, 'a set of practices through which a context emerges' rather than on 'context' as a 'bounded, pre-existing container for practice' (Edwards, 2006). Practice could be interactive, intersubjective and intertextual or discursive; hence the need for interpreting poly-contexualisation of practice and/or learning, rather than distinguishing between formal, informal and non-formal adult learning. Does the web address this?

## The promise of the WWW in lifelong learning

Ahead of all other media, the web provides wider scope for information storage, retrieval, exchange, collaboration and networking. The web comprises interlinked hypertext resources that are accessed through the Net. These resources may include any or all of these: texts, images, audios, videos and multimedia, hyperlinked to each other. A variety of facilitating mechanisms such as IP (Internet Protocol) addresses, URLs (Uniform Resource Locators), HTML (HyperText Markup Language), HTTP (HyperText Transfer Protocol), hyperlinks, caching and search engines, among others, help adult learners access and handle the web with ease.

Created in 1989 by Sir Tim Berners-Lee and Robert Caillaiau, the web took off in 1992 by using web standards such as 'markup languages'. Based on Berners-Lee's book *ENQUIRE* (*Enquire Within Upon Everything*), written in 1980, the detail of the WWW was developed by him in 1990 in collaboration with Robert Caillaiau. Starting from NexTcube as the first web server and the WWW as the first web browser, these have diversified into innumerable options for adult learners in respect of interest, capacity, area of study and specialisation. The WWW scored over the Gopher protocol when the former was declared as an open source and therefore free to all users; this was further strengthened when the Mosaic web browser, which supported the mix of graphics with text-based web pages, was introduced in 1993. The other developments, such as Uniform Resource Identifiers (URIs: the global system of internet referencing), HyperText Transfer Protocol (HTTP: specification of the communication between web browser and web server) and Sun Microsystem's JavaScript (which facilitated the user interfaces of web pages) added to the strengths of the web. Web publishing free of cost and by creating one's own blog facilitates adult learners to create and share their views and documents with others. There are now new means of communication such as Skype; new places to communicate such as MySpace for social networking; and new platforms for communication such as YouTube for sharing video files. With 11.5 billion web pages in 2005 (Gulli and Signorini, 2005), today this has increased to above 24 billion – from nearly 16 billion in August 2007 to about 24 billion in October 2007. This clearly shows the pace of change for the future.

The development of 'Semantic Web' (SW) by Berners-Lee in the recent past heralded a new era in the use of the web. SW extends the use of the web (used generally through natural languages by the user) to software agents that can locate, furnish and integrate information at ease. The web was visualised as a medium for the exchange of data, information and knowledge; and the SW extends this towards describing concepts, terms and relationships in a knowledge domain by using new elements such as working groups; Resource Description Framework (RDF: common standard for websites); data interchange formats such as RDF/XML, N3 and N-Triples; RDF Schema (RDFS); and Web Ontology Language (OWL). Extending the earlier format of the web for only human beings interacting with human beings for the exchange of information, the SW facilitates computers and the Net to do this instead. The web is now capable of analysing all kinds of data – contents, links, exchanges – on the web itself without the help of human beings. It also facilitates real-time publishing – semantic publishing – and instant sharing on the web. While HTML links documents anywhere in the globe, the SW, by using RDF, links anything – documents, human beings, events, etc. However, like the Google Earth search, criticism of SW also concerns privacy and censorship.

Adult/lifelong learners today are further assisted by new social software systems for greater informal learning. These provide access beyond the classroom to communities of practitioners and experts within one's context and across the globe. Lifelong learners can carry out activities within digital social networks (Shirky, 2003; Klamma et al., 2006) with the help of social software, that is, socially based tools and systems. The development of the second generation Net and Web 2.0 goes beyond the traditional publishing and distribution of learning resources to contribute to the creation of communities in digital social networks with freedom for self-direction and self-management (Klamma et al., 2007). Web 2.0 has created projects such as Wikipedia, which goes beyond publishing to 'participation', from personal websites to 'blogging' (Blood, 2004), from content management to 'wikis', from directories to 'tagging', and from stickiness to 'syndication' (O'Reilly, 2005). Lifelong learning presupposes much of learning beyond the conventional institutional boundaries; and the new web supports lifelong learning driven by and for the learners. Blogging, for instance, facilitates the creation of lifelong learners' own content and links to others, thereby allowing them to add material and comment – collaborative and critical knowledge generation in the communities of practice (Wenger, 1998).

Brown et al. (1989) argued that, in 'situated cognition' (and situated learning), context plays an important role in learning since it forms an integral part of the knowledge base that guides that learning. In Collins et al.'s (1987) context for a 'cognitive apprenticeship' approach to learning, instead of predetermined instructional sequences, learning takes place through solving real-world problems. In the design of learning environments and the web of constructivism, Jonassen (1994) underlines three common elements: context, collaboration and construction. Herein, construction involves both internal and social negotiations—the latter being mediated by articulation and reflection. Here, situated learning defines the context. In another work, Panda and Juwah (2006) identified three types of contexts: culture, community of practice and online learning community; these are consistent with Brown et al.'s (1989) idea that knowledge is contextually situated and is influenced by activity, context and culture. Similarly, Herrington and Oliver (1995) have argued that learning and development in instructional design for situated learning in a multimedia environment will be more meaningful if they are embedded in the social and physical contexts of their use. Quoting Brown and Duguid (2000), in contexts of lifelong learning through the web/Net, Panda and Juwah (2006) remarked that:

> They further suggest that any educational provision must have access to an authentic learning community, authentic resources for creation of knowledge and accreditation of the process and product . . . the Internet can support the existing professional community of practice as online learning community. The existence of the local community of practice and its working on collaborative reflective projects shall ensure credibility, authentication and accreditation.
>
> (p. 214)

The web and the Net are capable of meeting the new interpretations of learning in practice – beyond the conceptualisation of the context as container with boundaries – through communities of practice (Lave and Wenger, 1991), actor-networks (Nespor, 1994), activity systems (Engestrom *et al.*, 1999) and distributed learning (Lea and Nicoll, 2002). In web-supported/web-based learning, it is not only possible but rather desirable to create online contexts by contexualising practices, creating virtual surrogates of work environments, and converging online learning communities and offline communities of practice (Panda and Juwah, 2006) – rather than creating predetermined contexts as bounded containers for practice.

The Net/web facilitates both individuals and learning organisations through formal (largely teacher-controlled) and non-formal (largely learner-controlled) learning mechanisms. As long as institutions vie for assessment and accreditation, there will be limited learner control over the curriculum and its delivery, meaning that the curriculum will still have its drawn boundary. The opportunities the web provides need to gel well with greater learner control, less institutionalisation, and less tutor dominance over (including asynchronous) communication.

Today, the web provides ample opportunities to (adult) learners to access, in one's area of interest, a wealth of resources that could range from beginner level to the level of mastery, and to engage in a variety of virtual contexts. For instance, partnering for discussion on an informal and wider scale anywhere in the globe, as Illich (1971) argued in his *Deschooling Society*, is possible through networked computers with ever increasing intellectual resources on the web. This transforms the very nature of learning – moving from teacher-dominated to student-centred activity, and the formal curriculum being replaced by a postmodern curriculum (Pickering, 1995), characterising a change in the culture of textual education to a more multimedia-based interactive hypertext.

Also, the promotion of online learning in regional languages has been possible through such initiatives as, for instance, the Digital College in Wales (Selwyn *et al.*, 2001), the University of the Third Age in China, promoted by the China Association of Universities for the Aged (Caiwei, 2000), Tamil Virtual University in India, and many others. The Digital College offered 'non-participating groups' the opportunity to learn new skills in vocational and non-vocational areas with the provision of continued support (Digital College, 1998).

Technology propagators and researchers have argued for the facilitation of critical thinking (Anderson, 2003), reflection, and social and collaborative experiences (Hammond and Trapp, 1992; McLoughlin and Oliver, 1998; Juwah, 2006), though the new ICT-based learning could be labelled as a pseudo-new form of adult learning (Kenway *et al.*, 1994). Nevertheless, many big industrial houses are encouraging their employees to continuously upgrade their knowledge and skills through such provisions as IBM's 'Global Citizen's Portfolio'. As the chief of IBM puts it: 'expertise is not static. To be competitive, any individual – like any company, community or country – has to adapt continuously, learning new fields and new skills' (quoted in Monies, 2007).

## Limitations

Given the above discourse, it is pertinent to underline that the use of the web in the larger context of ICT and lifelong learning requires a range of considerations to facilitate the individual and the groups within their contexts. The limitations of such considerations, as outlined below (Gray, 1999; Mayes, 2000; Selwyn *et al.*, 2001; Aviram and Eshet-Alkalai, 2006; Panda, 2007) require further examination.

- The average lifelong learner needs sufficient prior knowledge, practice and experiences in using structural knowledge to make use of the navigational tool of hypertext.
- Referring to two pedagogies involved in ICT – IT as linear and C as conversations – Mayes argues that, 'in the context of lifelong learning policy the real problem is that 'IT' is cost-effective and the 'C' not. Unfortunately, in terms of pedagogic effectiveness the second is better than the first' (2000: 3).
- The free availability of required learning resources as an open source on the web is a myth. Copyright and intellectual property rights are issues that need to be addressed for effective web-based lifelong learning.
- The required bandwidth to flexibly access multimedia resources is yet to come. Learner exasperation, alienation and lurking may be due to the technology rather than to learners' intellectual skills.
- The digital divide is not only about access (to computer, Net and broadband), but more about the still elitist ability to access and handle the web to one's advantage.
- There is also gender, language, skill, culture and class imbalance in the use of technology. While technology is intended to provide access and ensure equality, this may itself become a hindrance to it, thus exacerbating existing societal discriminations and inequalities.
- In educational discourse, learning engagement involves personal relationships, belongingness and non-verbal communication. The web/Net has not been able to address these essentials to date. Selwyn *et al.*'s (2001) comment in the context of Wales may be equally applicable to other societies:

> merely dealing with the 'technology' side of the 'technology-based lifelong learning' equation may be to avoid tackling the fundamental problems of why people do not participate in education – many of which are not related to technology any way . . . instead of repackaging and delivering existing traditional materials via the Internet, lifelong learning providers should consider how the Internet can add value to the learning process via its more innovative features. Moreover, of utmost import-ance to providers . . . is how non-participants can be encountered and attracted to engage with learning of any kind (whether 'off-line' or 'online') if the 'e-learning' society is not to merely replicate the patterns of inequality it set out to replace.
>
> (p. 217)

While proposing the need for five required literacies in the context of digital literacy – photo-visual literacy, reproduction literacy, branching literacy, information literacy and socio-emotional literacy – and the clash between civilisations (like the established culture of Western societies and the post-modern culture), Aviram and Eshet-Alkalai remarked:

> it is likely that photo-visual skill, branching skill and reproduction skill will be powerfully enhanced, while the ability for criticism, or indeed, rational thinking of

any kind, may deteriorate. Some might take it to be a desired scenario, but if it is, it calls for a conscious decision, rather than being dragged towards it blindly.

(Aviram and Eshet-Alkalai, 2006)

• Writes Panda (2007):

Besides the possibility of creation of pseudo communities, there is criticality in the cultural construction of the cyberspace. Critical voices have been raised such that the Net, in the name of recreating such a society, may in fact undermine the notion of civil society and multiplicity in unity (Jones, 1997). Questions have been raised about unacceptable language, ethical issues, wastage of time and resources, and additional technological skills to use the Net. Sometimes, due to lack of provision to mention gender/race/caste/religion in Net-based communication, there is in fact disrespect to these realities in interaction in the cyber society.

(p. 458)

• In the use of ICT, social activists have raised critical questions in respect of surveillance, pornography, cybersex, cybercrime, etc. in civil society (Panda, 2007). In the case of social software, there are still unresolved social-technical gaps concerning, for instance, trust, security and privacy (Olson and Olson, 2000). Further, as Klamma *et al.* remark, 'Put together the underlying research question here is: How to quantify and qualify learner experiences in deploying social software?' (2007: 80).

• Most of web-based learning, through either the use of established platforms or only open source software, is based on the design consideration of treating the online learning context as bounded, given and created to work on. Online learning as constructivist and contexualising the practices as they emerge needs serious introspection and research.

Therefore, effective, successful and sustainable web-based lifelong learning requires not merely access to the web, but more importantly to the creation of a networked system available anywhere and anytime, and guarded against the maladies it perpetuates. While this all-pervading network in many societies is yet to appear, the question in respect of overdependence on this networked information society is a major part of the current debate on technology itself. The sceptics will still argue if technology is all about the interests of manufacturers, suppliers/vendors and service providers, rather than about facilitating seamless lifelong learning!

## Conclusion

As discussed in this chapter, tremendous developments in web technology and interest in webology have brought significant changes in the way lifelong learners engage in individual and collaborative learning. Web 2.0/Internet 2.0 promises much more to come. The notion and practice of contextualisation in lifelong learning is reinforced by some collaborative web resources and constructivist learning designs.

There is considerable interest in the diffusion of the Net in augmenting the information society (Press *et al.*, 2002); diffusion has been argued to be the most innovative strategy for expansion and use of the Net/web; and frameworks of analyses have been suggested for nation states to self-check if they are progressing along the right path and with earnest. Governments have been heavily investing in the creation of Net infrastructure and broadband and providing access to as many communities as possible based on the diffusion framework: pervasiveness, geographical dispersion, organisational infrastructure, connectivity infrastructure, sectoral absorption and sophistication of use. The basic issue at the grassroots level is digital access and/or the digital divide. A recent survey (Horrigan and Smith, 2007) in the United States shows that, in 2007, 47 per cent of Americans had a broadband connection at home – the situation is not so good in others, especially in developing countries. This is important since one of the major issues for today and tomorrow is accessibility to broadband. This will also affect rural networking and the establishment of community kiosks, rural development, development communication, e-marketing, e-governance, e-health/e-medicine and other such developments.

As was analysed in an earlier section, context is very important to lifelong learning, and the possibilities of the web for contextualisation in practice online are immense. The variety of social software and open source software and platforms could also strengthen this. Just as there is debate between context and contextualisation to put technology-enabled lifelong learning in place, so also is there debate concerning the diffusion of the Net and the social shaping of technology. Technology by itself is not socially and ethically neutral. It is important what individual choices are made towards the contextualisation of social activities in informal life settings. Therefore, diffusion, or in other words access to technology and broadband, is not as much an issue in lifelong learning as the context of the actual (individual and collaborative) use of technology for transforming social practices and for collective social action in a civil society.

## References

Anderson, T. (2003) 'Towards a theory of online learning', in T. Anderson and F. Elloumi (eds) *Theory and Practice of Online Learning*, Athabasca, Alberta: Athabasca University, pp. 33–60.

Aviram, A. and Eshet-Alkalai, Y. (2006) 'Towards a theory of digital literacy: three scenarios for the next steps', *European Journal of Open, Distance and E-Learning* 1.

Beeson, I. (2003) 'Imaginative communities: turning information technology to expressive use in community groups', in S. Hornby and Z. Clarke (eds) *Challenge and Change in the Information Society*, London: Facet Publishing, pp. 104–24.

Black, A. (2003) 'The information society: a secular view', in S. Hornby and Z. Clarke (eds) *Challenge and Change in the Information Society*, London: Facet Publishing, pp. 18–41.

Blood, R. (2004) 'How blogging software reshapes the online community', *Communications of the ACM* 47(12): 53–5.

Brown, J.S., Collins, A. and Duguid, P. (1989) 'Situated cognition and the culture of learning', *Educational Researcher* 18: 32–42.

Caiwei, X. (2000) 'China: lifelong learning and the use of new technology', *TechKnowLogia*, September/October.

Castells, M. (1996) *The Information Age: Economy, society and culture, vol. 1: The rise of the networked society*, Oxford: Blackwell.

—— (1998) *End of the Millennium*, Oxford: Blackwell.

Collins, A., Brown, J.S. and Newman, S.E. (1987) 'Cognitive apprenticeship: teaching the craft of reading, writing, and mathematics', in L. Resnick (ed.) *Learning, Knowing, and Instruction*, Hillsdale, NJ: Lawrence Erlbaum, pp. 453–94.

Department for Education and Employment (DfEE) (1998) *The Learning Age: A renaissance for a new Britain*, London: Stationery Office.

Digital College (1998) *The University for Industry and Wales: A partnership challenge*, Cardiff: Coleg Digidol.

Edwards, R. (1997) *Changing Places? Flexibility, lifelong learning and a learning society*, London: Routledge.

—— (2006) 'Beyond the moorland? Contexualising lifelong learning', *Studies in the Education of Adults* 38(1): 25–36.

Engestrom, Y., Miettinen, R. and Funamaki, R.-L. (eds) (1999) *Perspectives on Activity Theory*, Cambridge: Cambridge University Press.

Feather, J. (2003) 'Theoretical perspectives on the information society', in S. Hornby and Z. Clarke (eds) *Challenge and Change in the Information Society*, London: Facet Publishing, pp. 3–17.

Giddens, A. (1999) *Runaway World: How globalisation is re-shaping our lives*, Cambridge: Profile Books.

Gray, D.E. (1999) 'The Internet in lifelong learning: liberation or alienation?', *International Journal of Lifelong Education* 18(2): 119–26.

Gulli, A. and Signorini, A. (2005) 'The indexable web is more than 11.5 billion pages'. Available online at www.cs.uiowa.edu/~asignori/web-size/ (accessed 2 November 2007).

Halal, W.E. and Liebowitz, J. (1994) 'Telelearning: the multimedia revolution in education', *The Futurist* 21 (November/December).

Hammond, N. and Trapp, A. (1992) 'CAL as a trojan horse for educational change: the case of psychology', *Computers & Education* 19(1/2): 87–95.

Harasim, L., Hiltz, S.R., Teles, L. and Turoff, M. (1995) *Learning Networks: A field guide to learning and teaching online*, Cambridge, MA: MIT Press.

Herrington, J. and Oliver, R. (1995) 'Critical characteristics of situated learning: implications for the instructional design of multimedia', in *Proceedings ASCILITE '95*, Melbourne, VIC: University of Melbourne.

Horrigan, J.B. and Smith, A. (2007) *Home Broadband Adoption 2007 Report*, Pew Internet and American Life. Available online at www.pewinternet.org/pdfs/PIPBroadband%202007.pdf (accessed 2 November 2007).

Illich, E. (1971) *Deschooling Society*, Harmondsworth: Penguin.

Jonassen, D. (1994) 'Thinking technology: towards a constructivist design model', *Educational Technology* 34(4): 34–7.

Jones, S. (ed.) (1997) *Virtual Culture: Identity and community in cyber society*, London: Sage Publications.

Juwah, C. (2006) *Interactions in Online Education: Implications for theory and practice*, London and New York: Routledge.

Kenway, J., Bigum, C., Fitzclarence, L., Collier, J. and Tregenza, K. (1994) 'The new education in new times', *Journal of Education Policy* 9(4): 317–33.

Klamma, R., Spaniol, M., Cao, Y. and Jarke, M. (2006) 'Pattern-based cross media social network analysis for technology enhanced learning in Europe', *Lecture Notes in Computer Science* 4227: 242–56.

——, Chatti, M.A., Duval, E., Hummel, H., Hvannberg, E.T., Kravcik, M., Law, E., Naeve, A. and Scott, P. (2007) 'Social software for life-long learning', *Educational Technology & Society* 10(3): 72–83.

Lave, J. (1996) 'The practice of learning', in S. Chaiklin and J. Lave (eds) *Understanding Practice: Perspectives on activity and context*, Cambridge: Cambridge University Press, pp. 3–33.

—— and Wenger, E. (1991) *Situated Learning*, Cambridge: Cambridge University Press.

Lea, M. and Nicoll, K. (eds) (2002) *Distributed Learning*, London: Routledge.

McLoughlin, C. and Oliver, R. (1998) 'Maximising the language and learning link in computer learning environments', *British Journal of Educational Technology* 29(2): 125–36.

Mayes, T. (2000) 'Pedagogy, lifelong learning and ICT', in Scottish Forum on Lifelong Learning (eds) *Role of ICT in Supporting Lifelong Learning*, Sterling: Centre for Research in Lifelong Learning, University of Sterling.

Monies, P. (2007) 'IBM funds lifelong learning plan', *Knight Ridder Tribune Business News*, August 15.

Nespor, J. (1994) *Knowledge in Motion*, London: Palmer.

Olson, G.M. and Olson, J.S. (2000) 'Distance matters', *Human–Computer Interaction* 15: 139–78.

O'Reilly, T. (2005) 'What is Web 2.0: design patterns and business models for the next generation of software'. Available online at www.oreillynet.com/pub/a/oreilly/fim/news/2005/09/30/ what-is-web-20.html (accessed 2 November 2007).

Panda, S. (2007) 'Globalisation, culture and information communication technology in India', in K. Choudhry (ed.) *Globalisation, Governance Reforms and Development in India*, New Delhi: Sage Publications, pp. 443–61.

—— and Juwah, C. (2006) 'Professional development of online facilitators in enhancing interactions and engagement: a framework', in C. Juwah (ed.) *Interactions in Online Education: Implications for theory and practice*, London and New York: Routledge, pp. 203–23.

Pickering, J. (1995) 'Teaching on the Internet is learning', *Active Learning* 2. Available online at www.cti.uk/pulel/aclea/issue2/pickering (accessed 2 November 2007).

Press, L., Foster, W., Wolcott, P. and McHenry, W. (2002) 'The Internet in India and China', *First Monday* 7(10): 1–34.

Selwyn, N., William, S. and Gorard, S. (2001) '"E-stablishing a learning society": the use of the Internet to attract adults to lifelong learning in Wales', *Innovations in Education and Teaching International* 38(3): 205–19.

Selwyn, N., Gorard, S. and Furlong, J. (2006) *Adult Learning in the Digital Age: Information technology and the learning society*, London: Routledge.

Shirky, C. (2003) 'Social software: a new generation of tools', *Esther Dyson's Monthly Report* 10.

Walker, D. (1998) *Education in the Digital Age*, London: Bowerdean.

Wenger, E. (1998) *Communities of Practice*, Cambridge: Cambridge University Press.

# Part 5
## Policies

# 23

# Policy and lifelong learning

*Colin Griffin*

It has long been accepted that lifelong education or learning is as much an object of policy as it is a description of educational provision throughout a person's lifetime. The reasons for this have been well explored by now, and thousands of policy documents and statements emanating from international, national and other sources have been scrutinised and analysed. In particular, lifelong education as a worldwide strategy of economic, social and cultural policy has been aimed at individual employability, social integration and inclusion. In fact, some fairly exaggerated claims have sometimes been made for the role of education as such in these critically important policy fields. Also, the sheer instrumentality of much lifelong education policy has been opposed, especially by those theorists and practitioners who continue to represent more humanistic traditions of liberal adult education (Jarvis and Parker, 2005). To some extent, since all policy fashions come and go, the wheel of adult learning and lifelong education continues to turn, and despite the mountain of policy documents that has built up over several decades now, little is finally settled.

This chapter presents a discussion of some of the factors that operate nowadays in the field of policy and lifelong learning, and offers some theoretical analyses of this unfinished business, together with the view that the search for definitive solutions in both policy and education is as elusive now as it has ever been.

In the relatively short time since ideas such as lifelong learning and education have come to the fore, however, the whole concept of policy, in whatever context, has changed almost beyond recognition. It is certainly the case that the traditional categories of policy analysis are no longer as useful as they once were: it is not only the nature of analysis that has changed, but that of policy itself. In particular, the distinctions and differentiations of lifelong education, lifelong learning and adult education, about which so much was written, seem less relevant now than was sometimes believed in the past. And this is probably true for all the other related concepts, such as continuing or recurrent education, which fell by the wayside long ago. Some analytic categories remain valid, of course, especially when we think about education and learning in policy terms, the distinction between which is still crucial but still often obscured in the public mind.

This chapter begins with an outline of some aspects of the new context of policy that have emerged since the idea of lifelong learning became as prominent as it is today. The evolution of the idea among a family of related concepts such as permanent, recurrent and continuing education will be briefly described, followed by a discussion of this in relation to the new policy context. There will be a consideration of related problems in the nature of policy analysis itself that arise from the discussion. Finally, a current policy document will be analysed in similar terms and some conclusions suggested.

In general, it is argued that the distinctions that were once thought significant between adult education, lifelong education and lifelong learning are primarily a function of policy discourses. In terms of theory and practice, there are few significant differences between them. For example, education can be an object of policy in ways that learning cannot, but good practice is a concept applicable to both. Similarly, adult education seems age specific whereas lifelong education clearly is not, but again, what theoretical or practical implications follow from this that are *directly* comparative? There are theories of good practice in education and learning and these are distinct from other contingent features of the situation such as age or any other social and individual factors.

Perhaps in the most general theoretical terms we have an instance of that process of de-differentiation associated with postmodern perspectives on social change, and this certainly seems true of the concept of the state as differentiated from other sources of power and legitimacy. This was traditionally the fundamental assumption upon which the possibility of policy itself was based.

## The changing context of policy

Traditional policy analysis, in whatever context, presumed the political nature of policy and the power of the state. The situation today, however, means that the power of the state needs to be re-contexted along many dimensions. A few of these will now be introduced before a consideration of their significance for policy in the context of lifelong learning and education. Such developments are often attributed to the globalisation of capital and media communications. But globalisation is an extremely generalised concept, and there are many forces of social, economic and cultural resistance operating. As far as national policies of the state are concerned, there are intervening factors interposed between globalisation on the one hand and policy implementation on the other.

Nevertheless, it is possible to offer some examples of the changing context of policy in which lifelong learning is now conceptualised:

1   One fairly obvious element of the changing policy context is the increasing absence of clear distinctions between the *public* and the *private* realm when it comes to finance. In other words, policy has ceased to be unambiguously 'public' in the face of corporate financial investment alongside public expenditure from public revenues, and it is often now located in the interface between government authority and market forces.

2   The process of globalisation also implies subordination of policy to *global* forces that are not simply those of corporate capital but that reflect strategic social, political and cultural interests located in global contexts of power.

3   Increasingly, these global contexts reflect concepts of universal *human rights*, and policy is increasingly constructed within the limits of such concepts, perhaps the most obvious example of this being in the case of immigration and population movements worldwide, but the policy constraints of human rights also apply in such contexts as employment, the justice system and so on.

4  The ways in which policy is formulated, implemented and, especially, *communicated* is now strongly determined by developments in information technology. According to this, the scope for surveillance and control has become virtually limitless, with all this implies for the power of governments to secure compliance.

5  At the same time, information and communications technology presents hitherto unimaginable possibilities for the identification and formation of *civil society* and therefore for sources of resistance or opposition to public policy that may prove difficult to repress. Although the democratic potential of new communications technology can be exaggerated, since to some extent it merely reproduces existing relations of production, there seems no doubt that it constitutes a new and significant element in the policy context. Developments such as social enterprise and ethical business also originate in civil society rather than in the public policy sphere. Increasingly, policy is also located in the interface between government authority and social movements of civil society.

6  The onset of *research-driven policy* also reflects the possibilities inherent in the new technologies of information and communication. The claim that policy somehow reflects the 'facts' of society, rather than simply ideological views of it, is more likely than ever before to feature now. By the same token, of course, most social research is policy-driven too: possibly there is an element of self-fulfilling prophecy in this relation, but in any case research is increasingly seen as a validating condition of policy.

7  Another policy context must be the trend to smaller political units in the form of *regionalisation* and *local autonomies*. In an age of globalisation, national identities have never loomed larger, making it possible for different and even opposed policies to exist in close proximity. Devolved government, particularly with regard to particular social policies, co-exists with the worldwide movement towards regionalisation based upon specific economic conditions.

8  Again, at the same time, such shared economic and other conditions have contributed to the increasing significance of international organisations and *international legislation*, either regional or more global. This is perhaps the most evident of the changing policy contexts of autonomous states, and remains politically controversial but influential, especially in an area such as human rights.

9  For example, one of the most important considerations driving international organisation today is that of *environmental* concerns surrounding climate change and global warming. Most policy nowadays must take into account such ecological dimensions as much as human rights legislation.

Whether or not globalisation entails a loss of policy autonomy on the part of individual states, the above are examples of the changing context in which policy is formulated and implemented. Clearly the examples given do not form some kind of seamless web, and may represent, in some cases, contradictory trends. For present purposes, however, the point is that these developments have been of increasing salience during the evolution of ideas such as lifelong learning and lifelong education.

## Evolution of lifelong learning as policy

The concept of lifelong learning had evolved, of course, long before the onset of the new policy context outlined above. The idea that learning is a lifelong process, rather than an early schooling experience, is quite an old one and is well documented (Jarvis and Griffin, 2003).

However, before the concept achieved its present pre-eminence, it had to evolve through a series of related ideas, each of which reflected an earlier policy context, although with some discernible continuities. Broadly speaking, this involved such concepts as liberal adult education, permanent education, continuing education, recurrent education, lifelong education and the learning society. These will be briefly reviewed before a consideration of some of the issues they raise for thinking about them in terms of policy analysis.

## Liberal adult education

Liberal adult education in the UK is an age-specific category of provision (distinguished from child education) for individual leisure, academic or recreational learning on a humanistic basis of personal development: learning for learning's sake, as it was sometimes put. In policy terms its position was, and is, ambiguous. It was never fully incorporated into national policy, and governments were in general resistant to funding on this basis. It retained many of the characteristics of a social movement. There were, however, what might be described as intimations of incorporation when adult education ceased to be an umbrella term and became associated with specific social purposes of political significance, such as literacy or community development. Provision was on a local government basis, together with that of voluntary bodies, universities and other relevant organisations connected perhaps with special areas of interest. It remained associated with social movements in civil society, therefore, rather than with bureaucratic provision. It does, however, raise the issue of where exactly the distinction lies between vocational and non-vocational learning, or indeed whether such a distinction is possible, and this remains important in tracing the evolution of lifelong learning in policy terms. The problem with liberal adult education for policy is that the category of 'adult' is far too generic for practical purposes, and also, being a voluntary activity, it is difficult to turn into conventional policy frameworks. Only when 'adult' is conceptualised as 'worker' or 'citizen' is adult education fully incorporated into policy, and this is what, in effect, subsequently happened under the headings of lifelong education or learning. It also illustrates the point made above, which was that such distinctions and definitions as these exist perhaps more as a function of policy discourse than of teaching and learning practice: the lasting legacy of adult education was a body of professional theory and practice sometimes called andragogy (Knowles, 1970) and even this has been criticised for the rigid distinction of the age category that it reflects.

## Permanent education

Permanent education was an early if short-lived formulation of lifelong learning principles, and was associated in the early 1970s with the Council of Europe. It advocated the availability of learning opportunities throughout an individual's lifetime, and focused on provision for this on much more conventional policy lines. It was a much more comprehensive and integrated view of education, which represented an early rejection of such distinctions that were reflected in the liberal adult education model outlined above. In particular, it sought an integration of compulsory and voluntary education, of liberal and vocational education, of the recreational and the academic, of the instrumental and the expressive and so on. But above all, it was a political and critical vision of education, rather than the conventional liberal one: 'together with social work and community development, permanent education will include social action i.e. it must be an active force in social change' (Council of Europe, 1970: 469). Above all, this is a *critical* vision of the role of education as policy: 'With respect to culture the contents of this permanent education must aim at the development of a critical attitude towards technology, in its industrial, social and educational use' (p. 469). The policy significance of this idea of permanent education therefore lies in its critical perspective. And for the purposes of this chapter, it is precisely the loss of this critical perspective in current formulations of lifelong learning that is most interesting.

## Continuing education

Continuing education as formulated in the UK during the 1980s constituted a swing away from the radicalism of the concept of permanent education and marks the first genuine instance of incorporation of these ideas into national policy (ACACE, 1982). The chances of a critical vision of permanent education being incorporated were non-existent from the beginning. However, continuing education came to be of some significance in relation to the focus on education for workforce formation and employability, which has since played a most prominent part in any lifelong learning vision that has found some degree of incorporation into national policies. In short, continuing education symbolised the rejection of a critical or political function for lifelong learning and was easily assimilated into social and economic policy, and perhaps into economic policy to the exclusion of all else. For present purposes, this raises the issue of whether concepts of lifelong learning are more likely to take a socially and politically more radical form than those emanating from national policy sources. One does not have to look far to find reasons for the policy significance of continuing education. The reports of the Advisory Council for Adult and Continuing Education (ACACE), together with similar policy documents from the Open University, simply assimilated adult education into the needs of the economy for the foreseeable future: 'The increasingly rapid application of recently developed technologies: bringing higher productivity and the need for a more skilled and adaptable labour force' (ACACE, 1982: 181). In the 1980s, continuing education represented a strategy for dealing with economic change. It does not simply deny the distinction between liberal and vocational adult education but consigned the former to a policy limbo from which it has never returned. Significantly, the ACACE (1981) report on liberal adult education, which it called 'adult general education', and which was considerably shorted, was entitled *Protecting the Future for Adult Education*, a defensive posture that has subsequently been more than justified. So the policy origins of today's concept of lifelong learning do not lie in its original formulations as adult or permanent education but in continuing education, although considerably broadened out from its original economic function as employment training. As with the highly contrasted concept of permanent education, that of continuing education has fallen out of sight: appropriately it lingered on as continuing professional education (CPE), which in turn became continuing professional development (CPD). All of which reinforces a view that all of these concepts are a function of policy rather than of theory and practice. There was, however, an earlier version of lifelong learning, again emanating from an international source and with a more radical potential, which, as in the case of permanent education, had little hope of being incorporated into policy.

## Recurrent education

Recurrent education was a concept emanating from the Organization of Economic Cooperation and Development (OECD) during the 1970s as a strategy for lifelong learning that stressed the alternative and recurring sequence of education and other sources of an individual's learning throughout life. In its earlier formulation, this learning was thought of in quite broad and general terms: 'It proposes a frame within which lifelong learning will be organised, this being the alternation and effective interaction between education, as a structured learning situation, and other social activities during which incidental learning occurs' (OECD, 1973: 236). There are features of this definition that constitute recurrent education as an object of policy, although interestingly enough it was usually described as a *strategic* vision rather than a more conventional policy formulation. It also introduces a key feature of early formulations of lifelong learning, namely that of the identification of informal, non-formal or 'incidental' learning alongside formal educational structures. The distinction between policies and strategies is important and will be discussed later. What is important, however, is that learning of an incidental kind is difficult to express in policy terms, rather than strategic ones. In fact, the concept of lifelong education, discussed below, takes no account of learning other than that which may (or may not) occur in other than formal educational settings. In this sense, recurrent education, like permanent education, was a more radical vision of lifelong learning than either continuing education or the concept that has since prevailed in policy terms. This is one reason for the short life of recurrent education as a strategy of lifelong learning. But there was another more radical aspect of it, which was that of an associated strategy of paid educational leave (PEL) as a right. In the UK this was a strand of recurrent education that became particularly prominent (Houghton and Richardson, 1974). Since there was little likelihood that either the state or employers would fund learning not directly relevant to employment, there was virtually no possibility of recurrent education being adopted as national policy. The government was, however, very interested in the formation of a more highly skilled and competitive workforce.

### *Lifelong education*

Lifelong education as a concept had the advantage, from a policy point of view, that its focus was neither upon unquantifiable 'incidental' learning nor upon unaffordable strategies of PEL. The associated idea of the *learning society* was also to find some favour, at least as a rhetorical flourish of policy formation. As an idea, lifelong education goes back a long way (Yeaxlee, 1929), but it was not until the second half of the twentieth century that it began to feature in education policy discourse. There were two main reasons for this: criticism of the effectiveness of the current formal education systems, from various points of view, and also a growing perception that the coming world economic order required a much stronger focus on the need for a highly skilled and competitive workforce. In 1970, therefore, lifelong education was adopted as a desirable policy objective. As an alternative to traditional education, lifelong education encompassed elements of both vocational and adult liberal education, but went further than either of these in its integrative potential and humanistic basis:

> Each period of a person's life in fact represents at the same time a unique and valuable experience and a preparation for future stages . . . each phase of a person's existence should be lived to the full and should constitute experiences, pleasures and satisfactions in the long process by which he or she gradually comes to know himself or herself through a series of revelations.
>
> (Lengrad, 1989: 7)

This is clearly quite a utopian vision of lifelong education, incorporating as it does both the instrumental/vocational as well as the intensely personal possibilities for education. A good deal of the policy discourse since this early formulation has constituted a reflection upon the possibilities of translating such ideas into forms of provision. But behind such reflections has always loomed the possibilities constituted by policy and strategy, and these have generally proved a highly limiting factor. The same kind of analysis can be applied in the case of the concept of the learning society, which again is hardly new (Hutchins, 1968). This simply stood for the idea that whole societies, as well as individuals, could be thought of as learners and learning resources, and it is particularly strongly formulated in relation to the possibilities opened up by rapidly developing technologies of information and communication. It also appears as a more integrated, and therefore possibly more democratic and equitable, society in which the barriers between individuals are diminished through access to information on an unprecedented scale. Above all, the learning society is a response to the new knowledge-based rather than production-based economy, so that learning itself, rather than conventional conceptions of work, functions as the source of political, social, economic and cultural solidarity.

Current conceptions of lifelong learning contain many of the elements of the ideas out of which it evolved and which have been outlined above. There are many common threads, the most important of which is, of course, the view that education or learning in some other, wider contexts such as experience or life itself, should be available to all, or that as many as possible should have access to learning opportunities. There are also tensions between ideas of education, learning and training, or human and social capital, or the construction of visions, strategies and policies in relation to social justice and so on. The question whether education reproduces or transforms social relations, which was associated with the 1960s' disillusion with schooling, may still be one that can be asked of lifelong learning itself. There seem sometimes to be differences between international organisations' views on lifelong learning and the more parochial concerns for it on the part of national governments. But, above all, every one of these evolutionary ideas is rooted in the policy discourses of their time, that is, the last 40 or 50 years.

We need to ask whether present-day conceptions of lifelong learning can be located in what was described earlier as the new policy context. But before that there needs to be a more reflexive account of the process of policy analysis itself. In its most radical form, we might ask whether the market forces of the globalised corporate capital economy have now reduced both policy and its analysis to a spurious academic exercise.

## Analysing policy

The academic analysis of policy involves many methodological possibilities, as well as some more basic differentiations and conceptual distinctions. Two will be briefly indicated here, to make possible an analysis of current policy trends as well as the evolutionary background of lifelong learning itself. These are the distinction between education and learning, and that between policy and strategy, both of which have been deployed in the context of lifelong learning and social welfare reform (Griffin, 2002).

What have been described as the evolutionary concepts of lifelong learning have been, in fact, expressed as *educational* policies, in forms such as permanent, recurrent, continuing and so forth. Quite often, lifelong learning itself has been expressed as lifelong education. The distinction between learning and education, in all of this, has never been convincingly established, and indeed the terms education and learning have been used indiscriminately, which is one reason why lifelong learning has been considered to be a rather vague idea. If it *is* a vague idea, there is little chance of its being incorporated into policy, which, as suggested above, demands for its formulation and implementation some quite measurable and quantifiable outcomes for purposes of evaluation.

With the benefit of hindsight, it is not difficult to predict which of the concepts or 'visions' of lifelong learning described above would be likely to be adopted as policy or strategy; in other words, which kinds of lifelong learning would be translated into funded structures of provision. For this to happen, policies need to have a tight focus with the possibility of demonstrable and hopefully quantifiable outcomes. They also needed some kind of 'social purpose' ideology. The evolution of lifelong learning demonstrates these features fairly clearly. For example, the category of 'adult' is too indeterminate and needed to be expressed in categorical terms to do with employment, citizenship or minority community. Personal fulfilment, or growth and development, although universally acclaimed for their individual and social value, were nevertheless rather subjective and vague. Something such as PEL on a recurring and open-ended basis was simply too expensive. Where benefits are clearly measurable and beneficial to society as much as to individuals, such as was the case with literacy education, or perhaps community development, then the chances of such projects being an object of policy were much higher. Even then, the inevitability of some kind of 'political' dimension to community development might prove an obstacle. All of the evolutionary concepts of lifelong learning contain varying degrees of individual as well as social, economic and cultural benefit, but many remain simply utopian visions.

In analysing lifelong learning as a concept, therefore, it is important to distinguish many diverse features, such as those of vision, policy and strategy, and to distinguish between them. It is possible to analyse lifelong learning as a function of welfare reform (Griffin, 2002) or the learning society in terms of human and social capital (Schuller and Field, 2002), but behind these kinds of analyses lies the fundamental distinction between learning and education, and the distinction of lifelong learning as either vision, policy or strategy, and this section will close with a brief consideration of such analytic distinctions.

Many of the evolutionary ideas of lifelong learning, such as recurrent education, were described at the time as 'strategies' for its achievement. Sometimes the discourse is of policies, and often they are simply confused. But it is important to separate them out. Some of the concepts described above have been translated into policy, many have not. But some, as has been suggested, were never really available for policy formation or implementation. Education as an object of policy entails the same kind of things as every other object of policy, namely, identifiable systems and structures of mandated provision, with all this implies for funding, staffing and so on. In policy terms education is therefore a system of provision and as such has the capacity to achieve many objectives such as access and the redistribution of opportunity, some of which have, in fact, been achieved. But it is important to distinguish education from the kind of learning we associate with the learning society or lifelong learning itself:

> learning is something we *attribute* to people without being able to *mandate* it or secure it in the way that social policy must presume, to some degree at least: learning eludes social policy because it cannot, like educational provision, be directly controlled.
>
> (Griffin, 2002: 126–7)

Individual learning can only be an object of strategy, and not directly of policy. A strategy is an instrumental means to a policy end, and the evolutionary concepts of lifelong learning frequently contain references to this way of thinking about it, so that, for example, adult education itself may be thought of as a particular strategy to achieve the end of lifelong learning or a learning society. In short, the term strategy describes precisely what has happened in practice: 'At the level of government strategy, people may be variously persuaded, cajoled, bribed, threatened or shamed into becoming active individual learners: their learning cannot be mandated' (p. 127).

The above analytic distinctions of education and learning, and policy and strategy, need finally to be located in the new policy context, and the concluding section of this chapter will examine a more recent relevant document in the light of all the foregoing analysis.

## Concluding case study

Both the new policy context (or at least elements of it) and the evolutionary history of lifelong learning can be traced in a recent short paper from the European Commission called *Adult Learning: It is never too late to learn* (EC, 2006). This is a progress report on the role of lifelong learning in implementing policies for competitiveness, employability, social inclusion, active citizenship and personal development. It is particularly concerned with the role of adult learning, defined as all forms of learning after initial education and training. Education and training are seen as 'critical factors' among the strategies for economic growth, competitiveness and inclusion. Implementation of such strategies, however, has proved weak, and the paper argues that the contribution of adult learning towards the achievement of policy goals is essential. The challenge is that:

> Adult learning has not always gained the recognition it deserves in terms of visibility, policy prioritisation and resources, notwithstanding the political emphasis placed on lifelong learning in recent years. This dichotomy between political discourse and reality is even more striking when set against the background of the major challenges confronting the Union.
>
> (EC, 2006: 3)

There follows some account of these challenges of competitiveness and social inclusion. Competitiveness is a function of highly skilled and competent workforces, and insufficient workers are skilled and possess key competences such as those needed for the new information and communication technologies that now constitute the basis of production. The demographic changes brought about by an aging population in Europe are also a factor in this equation, and the skills and competences of migrants represent another major source of competitive strength if, through adult learning, they can be developed and utilised. Social inclusion represents a serious challenge to member states, and there remain many obstacles in the way of their becoming active citizens. An argument is made for diversity of provision, especially in the new policy context: 'Political decisions are made at central, regional or local level, and sometimes at different levels concurrently, with many countries showing high degrees of decentralisation' (EC, 2006: 5).

The paper concludes with five key messages for adult learning stakeholders:

- lifting the barriers to participation;
- ensuring the quality of adult learning;
- recognition and validation of learning outcomes;
- investing in the aging population and migrants;
- indicators and benchmarks.

There is little in the document that cannot be traced back somewhere to the ideas and concepts out of which lifelong learning evolved and which have been outlined in this chapter: from the broad definition of learning to the need for quantifiable outcomes; from skills training to personal development; from access and provision to active citizenship.

From a policy analysis perspective it is clear that the objects of policy are in fact competitiveness and inclusion: lifelong learning is in itself a strategy to achieve these policy objectives, and adult learning is an element of that strategy.

What is also apparent are distinct features of the new policy context that was outlined at the beginning of this chapter, such as globalisation, regionalisation, immigration and population movements, citizenship, information technology, the functions of research and so on. There are some new policy contexts that do not, however, feature prominently: international law and human rights, and environmental concerns perhaps. And it may be significant that the 'stakeholders' in the lifelong learning project tend to be the traditional ones led by states or 'public authorities'. There is little or no concession to the fact that the differences between public and private funding are breaking down in education as elsewhere. To pursue this point in policy analysis terms might lead to an investigation of the political source of such policy documents as these, concerned as they are mostly with states and with public and political authority. But perhaps this is just another indication of the degree to which adult learning has been incorporated into public policy.

## References

Advisory Council for Adult and Continuing Education (ACACE) (1981) *Protecting the Future for Adult Education*, Leicester: ACACE.

—— (1982) *Continuing Education: From policies to practice*, Leicester: ACACE.

Council of Europe (1970) *A Pluralistic Model of Permanent Education* (Strasbourg: Council of Europe), in P. Jarvis and C. Griffin (eds) (2003) *Adult and Continuing Education*, vol. 1, London: Routledge, p. 223.

European Commission (EC) (2006) *Adult Learning: It is never too late to learn*, COM (2006) 614 final, Brussels: EC.

Griffin, C. (2002) 'Lifelong learning and welfare reform', in R. Edwards, N. Miller, N. Small and A. Tait (eds) *Supporting Lifelong Learning, vol. 3: Making policy work*, London: RoutledgeFalmer, pp. 123–49.

Houghton, V. and Richardson, K. (eds) (1974) *Recurrent Education: A plea for lifelong learning*, London: Ward Lock Educational.

Hutchins, R.M. (1968) *The Learning Society*, London: Pall Mall.

Jarvis, P. and Griffin, C. (eds) (2003) *Adult and Continuing Education: Major themes in education*, 5 vols, London: Routledge.

—— and Parker, S. (eds) (2005) *Human Learning: An holistic approach*, London: Routledge.

Knowles, M. (1970) *The Modern Practice of Adult Education: Andragogy vs pedagogy*, New York: Association Press.

Lengrad, P. (1989) 'Lifelong education: growth of the concept', in C. Titmus (ed.) *Lifelong Education for Adults*, Oxford: Oxford University Press.

Organization for Economic Cooperation and Development (OECD) (1973) *Recurrent Education: A strategy for lifelong learning* (Paris: OECD), in P. Jarvis and C. Griffin (eds) (2003) *Adult and Continuing Education*, vol. 1, p. 236.

Schuller, T. and Field, J. (2002) 'Social capital, human capital and the learning society', in R. Edwards, N. Miller, N. Small and A. Tait (eds) *Supporting Lifelong Learning, vol. 3: Making policy work*, London: RoutledgeFalmer, pp. 76–87.

Yeaxlee, B. (1929) *Lifelong Education*, London: Cassells.

# 24

# The European Union and lifelong learning policy

*Peter Jarvis*

The European Community has gradually grown from the initial six countries that embarked upon this rather idealistic enterprise to the 27 that now comprise the European Union (EU), and future growth is still being considered. In the first instance, the countries from Western Europe that started this process were advanced, wealthy capitalist societies having a great deal of their history in common, but as the EU increased in size it took into membership countries from the former Eastern Bloc that had a very different political history and were less economically advanced than those in Western Europe, so it is not surprising that lifelong learning has had at least a dual role in the European Commission (EC)'s policy since it first pronounced on the subject – both political and economic.

The EU did not pronounce a policy on lifelong learning until 1995 (EC, 1995), but by this time issues of lifelong learning were becoming quite significant within education generally as concepts such as the information society and the knowledge economy had begun to emerge. Most of these ideas were related to the emerging knowledge economy and the competitive place of nations was related to global capitalism. But Europe had a second mission, uniting the Member States of this diverse continent into a coherent whole and so from the outset there were two major aims to the European policy: economic competitiveness and citizenship in a new European union. Combining these in both policy and practice has been a very complex process and this chapter seeks only to illustrate some of the major issues that the Commission faced in developing its policy.

Once the EU had adopted the idea of lifelong learning it actively promoted it. For instance, 1996 was declared the European Year of Lifelong Learning and as the policy document *Making a European Area of Lifelong Learning a Reality* shows:

> The theme of lifelong learning runs through all these initiatives, each time addressed from a specific angle. Following the request from the Lisbon European Council, the Education Council adopted a *Report on the Concrete Future Objectives of Education and Training Systems*. The Commission then adopted in September 2001 a report containing a draft detailed work programme on the Follow-up of the Objectives report, which will form the basis of a joint report to be presented, on the invitation of the Stockholm Council, to the Spring European Council in 2002. The *European Employment Strategy* features a horizontal

objective on lifelong learning and specific guidelines that focus on the employment- and labour market-related aspects of lifelong learning. The *European Social Agenda* aims to reduce inequalities and promote social cohesion, including through lifelong learning. The *Skills and Mobility Action Plan* will aim to ensure that European labour markets are open and accessible to all by 2005. The *eLearning Initiative* part of the *eLearning Action Plan* seeks to promote a digital culture and wider use of information and communication technologies (ICT) in education and training. Finally, the *White Paper on Youth* provides the Community with a framework for cooperation in the field of youth policy, focusing on participation of young people, the education, employment and social inclusion.

(EC, 2001a: 8; underlining in original)

Consequently, the 2001a document really brought all of this together and in it there were four aims specified for lifelong learning: personal fulfilment, active citizenship, social inclusion and employability/adaptability (p. 9). Despite the fact that employability is the last mentioned of these four, it has been the predominant one in all the documents published since 1995, but this is probably because of the consultation that the Commission undertook in 2000, when it was widely criticised for its too strong vocational stance and for not emphasising a broader spectrum of lifelong learning aims. Because of the nature of the EU, active citizenship also plays a major role in lifelong learning and, in a sense, social inclusion combines these two since it is about economic and social inclusion in Europe. Personal fulfilment actually receives very little space in these documents and lifelong learning and senior citizens find no place before the document, *Adult Learning: It is never too late to learn* (EC, 2006).

At the same time, the EU has never really flushed out an acceptable definition for lifelong learning that could also embody its practice. For instance, it has traditionally defined it as 'all learning activity undertaken throughout life, with the aim of improving knowledge, skills and competences within a personal, civic, social and/or welfare employment-related perspective'(EC, 2001a: 9), which was an extension of the definition used only one year previously in the *Memorandum on Lifelong Learning* (EC, 2000). However, there are a number of conceptual failings with this definition that need not concern us here, since the major problem with the Commission is that it still separated both 'education and training' and 'higher education' from 'lifelong learning' – producing policy statements about all three at the same time. Actually, the definition would have been more accurate had it referred only to adult learning, as had the Commission's 2006 pronouncement (EC, 2006).

This chapter falls into three main parts: the first looks at employability in a global world; the second examines the EU's developing citizenship policy; and the third looks briefly at some of its programmes.

## Globalisation, employability and lifelong learning

While adult education has been a significant sector of the educational institution for many years, it was only in the last 30 years of the twentieth century that the ideas of lifelong learning came to the fore, so it is not surprising that the European Union's policy statements did not really begin until 1995. Nevertheless, from the very first statement, the emphasis on employability has been dominant and this reflects the changed social conditions since the idea of a European Common Market was first mooted.

Since the Second World War there have been political and economic changes that enabled global capitalism to come to the fore, such as:

- the oil crisis in the 1970s, which dented the confidence of the West;
- the demise of the Bretton Woods Agreement, which eventually enabled both free trade and the flow of financial capital to develop throughout the world;
- the development of sophisticated information technology through the star wars programme, through which the information technology revolution took off, with one development leading to another, as Castells (1996: 51ff.) demonstrates. He makes the point that 'to some extent, the availability of new technologies constituted as a system in the 1970s was a fundamental basis for the process of socio-economic restructuring in the 1980s' (p. 52);
- the economic competition from Japan, which challenged the West;
- the use of scientific knowledge in the production of commodities in the global market;
- the fall of the Berlin Wall – the democratisation of the Eastern Bloc – for, from the time it occurred, there has literally been 'no alternative' (Bauman, 1992) to global capitalism, so the process has been reinforced.

It was in the 1970s that theorists, recognising these processes, first began to suggest that there is actually a world economy (Wallerstein, 1974, among others) based on the capitalist system of exchange. Wallerstein's approach was questioned in part by Robertson (1995), who developed the theory of 'glocalisation' in which he correctly isolates the distinctiveness of individual cultures, as we have pointed out above. Castells (1996) has also argued that the state still has a place to play in a not completely free, but extremely competitive, global market. Nevertheless, corporations had begun to relocate manufacturing and to transfer capital around the world from about the early 1970s, seeking the cheapest places for, and the most efficient means of, manufacture, and the best markets in which to sell their products, so that an international division of labour has been created and a competitive international market generated. Additionally, the corporations have been able to locate themselves in countries where they have to pay fewer taxes, so that they underplay their responsibility to the world (see Cohen (2002) for a recent example), although some of them seek to persuade the world that they are exercising social responsibility by establishing charitable foundations or contributing some financial and intellectual assistance to underprivileged peoples, or to other needy causes. Beck actually suggests that globalisation is 'the *processes* through which sovereign national states are criss-crossed and undermined by transnational actors with varying prospects of power, orientations, identities and networks' (2000: 11; italics in original).

With the advent of global capitalism, the competing corporations need an educated workforce, continuing education so that the workforce can keep abreast of changing scientific knowledge. They also need an understanding of how workers actually learn in the workplace, so a major aim of lifelong learning has become employability. The corporations have to compete in the global market to produce an economic profit, so they need new knowledge in order to produce new commodities that can be produced cheaply and efficiently. An indication of the success of the capitalist enterprise is the 'slimness' of the organisation – hence there are often job redundancies in successful capitalist innovations and corporation mergers. There is a number of outcomes of this: on the one hand, new knowledge, new commodities, new production methods and more efficient organisational processes; on the other hand, cheap resources acquired from wherever in the world they are available, job redundancies, the creation of a reserve army of labour, lower wages and attacks on all forms of costly welfare on the grounds of efficiency and on trade union movements. However, while this latter group of outcomes was well recognised by the EC (2001a), it is still often presented by business and government in terms of positive terms, such as personal fulfilment, the good of the national economy and so on – all sectors of society have become experts in the presentation of their perspectives. The upshot of this is that, for those who own or control the process, there is increased wealth; for those who contribute to the process (knowledge workers and managers), there is a reasonable although relatively decreasing salary; and, for the poor who either supply the resources (often in third world countries) and the labour and for the unemployed, there are decreasing returns or welfare provision.

That this system needs an educated workforce is undeniable: it is at the heart of its success and so lifelong learning – that is 'work-life learning' – has assumed a dominant place in the global world of adult education and many educators of adults have responded to the demands of the core since it has become mainstream further and higher education. That the system also exacerbates the poverty of the third world and in places fails to recognise their human rights, helping to create 'the third world in the first', is also undeniable (e.g. Korten, 1995; Pilger, 2003). However, the system also produces a very high economic standard of living for many of those who live in the developed West, and those elsewhere in the world who exercise power within the framework or the needs of global capitalism, so that the beneficiaries of the system can experience the good things that it offers and be satisfied.

Universities, therefore, play an important role within this new situation: they can provide much of the new knowledge as a result of sponsored research and they can also provide an educated workforce – one that is being continually updated through lifelong learning. It must be pointed out that lifelong learning is actually a combination of learning throughout the lifespan and recurrent education, in which social institutions provide opportunities for individuals to further their learning in topics relevant to their lives, which are most frequently work-based. Universities have, therefore, adapted rapidly in many parts of the world to provide the lifelong learning that the global capitalist system urgently needs. Where, or if, universities and further education fail to respond to these demands, then the simple response is that the corporations start their own universities so that we get Motorola University, Disney University and so on (Meister, 1998; Jarvis, 2001).

Now the important fact about this analysis is that the global core – the economic and technological institutions supported by the political and military might of the USA (see Jarvis, 2007) – cannot make binding policies or laws except in relation to its own organisation. Also, the international agencies can enunciate policies, such as the EU's policies on lifelong learning, but it is only at state level that law can be enacted, so that we find states both producing educational laws and also initiating policies within their own territories. Since the global core is the most powerful layer, it is hardly surprising that both the international and the national agencies include the demands of the core within both their policies and their laws and it is within these that universities function. It is significant, however, that the poverty outcomes of the system are downplayed and the reasons for this vary from the more radical analyses such as Pilger's (2003), which suggests that government is also playing to the same tune as the capitalist system for its own ends, or to the more moderate analyses that suggest that governments may be trying to cushion the harsh effects of the capitalist system (Habermas, 2006: 81) through various policies and laws. A similar argument might be made for organisations such as UNESCO, but certainly not the World Bank or the International Monetary Fund. Whatever the interpretation given to government actions, it is clear that lifelong learning, policy and practice, fits into this framework and that it tends to be work-life learning rather than lifespan learning. The fact that such aims as producing active citizens as a result of lifelong learning are included in most policy statements tends to favour the Habermasian interpretation that either national governments are trying to keep up with the global power of the core or they are trying to protect their citizens from the harsh realities of global capitalism (Habermas, 2006), although it might be pointed out that, in a democratic society, if the government did not appear to be trying to alleviate hardship, however it is produced, then the electorate would soon remove it. At the same time, it has to be acknowledged that different states respond to this situation differently, reflecting their governments' own ideological commitment – with socialist governments providing a greater cushioning effect than right–wing governments.

If the EU is to keep abreast of the productive capacity of many countries in the global capitalist market, then it needs this highly educated and technological workforce. Leaving this to school education was not an option since the world was, and is, changing so rapidly. The workforce had to be educated and re-educated so that, since the Second World War, the idea of adult education has moved from a periphery leisure time interest to part of mainstream education in the change of name from adult education to the education of adults. It has then assumed three other names: continuing professional development, continuing education and recurrent education. Implicit in all of these is the idea of lifelong education, although the term was not used a great deal, except by UNESCO, which adopted it as early as 1972.

However, in the 1990s another change was to occur: education became a problematic term and so learning took its place and lifelong learning emerged as the key concept. There is a number of significant aspects in this change of title but one, above all, is that it made individual members of the workforce responsible for their own learning if they were to continue to be employable. Hence, lifelong learning and employability became central themes in EU policy in the 1990s.

## Active citizenship and lifelong learning

As the EU emerges, it is confronted with a major problem of European citizenship, so that it is not surprising that the other major aim of lifelong learning has been citizenship, but there are considerable problems in trying to introduce a new form of active citizenship in this globalising world. Globalisation has brought about the law of the global market, whereas the laws of the states are still apparently controlled by the democratic (or not so democratic) governments, although the extent to which the national governments are sovereign is much more questionable (see Korten, 1995; Monbiot, 2000). Certainly the laws of the market have simply bypassed the laws of the states and the corporations are now able to exert tremendous pressure on national and local governments in order to pursue their own policies. These processes have made the nation states far less powerful than ever before in their history, so that politicians now call for partnerships between the public and private sectors. Significantly, the Europeanisation process has had the same effect as Member States of the Union cede some of their power to Brussels, which might enable the EU to resist some of the laws of the market. Overall, however, it appears that politicians are only willing to do this and to cooperate with these powerful institutions of the global market because they are realists and recognise where the power lies – it is at least shared, if not lost! But, as Bauman noted:

> Once the state recognizes the priority and superiority of the laws of the market over the laws of the *polis*, the citizen is transmuted into the consumer, and a consumer demands more and more protection while accepting less and less the need to participate in the running of the state.
>
> (1999: 156; italics in original)

In other words, the consumer becomes a less active citizen and the political dimension of citizenship becomes little more than the election of those who will manage the state and they, the citizens, will then receive whatever goods and services the state still provides. There is a danger in this since, as Habermas reminds us, 'the public sphere is a warning system with sensors that, though unspecialized, are sensitive throughout society' (1995: 359). This warning has been picked up in the EC White Paper on European Governance (2001b: 14), when discussing the significance of civil society. When the sensors are not operating, then those who have power can do what they like, within certain limits – and this is precisely what the corporations are tending to do.

However, it might be claimed that the tragic events of 11 September 2001 have actually called into question the socio-economic power of the large corporations, because they do not have the control of legitimate force, so that politicians conceivably have the opportunity to act independently of the corporations. But, as we have suggested already, if the states are part of the superstructure, then those who control the substructures will continue to exercise control over the politicians and get them to defend the corporations' interests, even if it requires using force, and this is what American policy seems to indicate that it will do.

One of the most seminal works of citizenship has been T.H. Marshall's *Citizenship and Social Class* (1950), in which he suggested that citizenship has three dimensions: civil, political and social. Civil citizenship is about human freedoms and rights; political citizenship about the right to participate in political processes; and social citizenship about the right to live, and to be supported if necessary, in a civilised lifestyle according to the standards of the society in which individuals live. This discussion of the rights of citizens makes no reference to the fact that these rights are granted and enforced by nation states, whose power in the world is declining. This is clearly one of the major problems with which we are confronted when seeking to understand citizenship in a global society. Once the state's sovereignty has declined then the significance of the public, that is, the political, sphere has to be reassessed, but so too do the civil and social dimensions that comprise the private one – traditionally viewed as being free from the apparatus of state.

Marshall's three-dimensional formulation, however, has not gone uncriticised (see Heater, 1999: 19–24), but the three dimensions have served as one basis for our understanding of citizenship and, to some extent they still do, even though citizenship itself is being redefined. While Marshall regarded the civil and political dimensions emerging in the eighteenth century, he thought that it was the universal provision of education in the UK in 1870 that signalled the beginnings of the social dimension of citizenship. Moreover, the importance that he placed on education is echoed in the EC paper *Education and Active Citizenship* (1998: 6), among others, but the relationship between having knowledge and doing something about it is very tenuous, to say the least.

Citizenship was originally about being a member of the *polis*, and Barbalet (1988: 1) says it 'defines who are, and who are not, members of a common society' in which members had certain rights. In the light of globalisation and Europeanisation we can see that we no longer live in a common society and we might ask whether the society in which we do live is local, regional, national or global? Held *et al.* suggest, therefore, that 'Political space in respect of effective government and the accountability of political power is no longer coterminous with a delimited national territory' (1999: 499).

Delanty also suggests that we need to think of citizenship as cosmopolitan (2000: 51–67). Certainly, the EU has espoused the idea of European citizenship, and then its members can be regarded as having a form of dual citizenship: that of the nation of birth and that of Europe. Yet there will still be denizens in Europe since many have migrated to the Union in search of freedom or work or have been moved to it by their employers, and this distinction is not drawn in the EU documents on lifelong learning. Additionally, European citizens may also still be regarded as denizens in the countries in which they live and work if they have migrated within Europe in search of employment or for other reasons. Nevertheless, the Commission recognises that the 'concept of citizenship is ... becoming more fluid and dynamic' (EC, 1998: 5). Consequently, these publications do not pursue issues of territory or rights, but concentrate on practices. European citizenship is assumed and active citizenship is an aim. Nevertheless, within the practice of subsidiarity that exists in Europe, that is, with Europe as a pyramid of structures, interest, activity and decision-making within the Union should start at the lowest possible level. In this approach the EU is at the apex of the pyramid with the nation states immediately below, but with many other levels below these. Citizens can play their citizenship roles at any of the levels and in any of the communities that concern them. Held *et al.* (1999: 449), likewise, suggest that we live in an interconnected world with effective power being shared, so that individuals need to develop a sense of multiple citizenships: 'a sense of belonging to overlapping (local and global) communities of interest and affection' – one of these might be the nation state, but as we have already suggested citizens have become more passive and there does seem to be a decline in social capital in Europe similar to that recorded by Putnam (2000) in the USA. However, Held *et al.* (1999) do not elaborate greatly on being a member of communities of conflicting interests, when life-politics becomes a significant factor for individuals (Giddens, 1991).

Nevertheless, from the outset of the EU's concern for lifelong education, citizenship has always been seen as a major policy initiative. The agenda was set by the following:

> The future of European culture depends on its capacity to equip young people to question constantly and seek new answers without prejudicing human values. This is the very foundation of citizenship and is essential if European society is to be open, multicultural and democratic.
>
> (EC, 1995: 10)

Later, there is also reference to 'the principle of equal rights' (p. 23). Within two years, however, the Commission had coupled lifelong learning to citizenship much more explicitly, while still emphasising the need to promote policies to restore the employment situation:

> This educational area (Europe) will facilitate an **enhancement of citizenship** through the sharing of common values, and the development of a sense of belonging to a common social and cultural area. It must encourage a broader-based understanding of citizenship, founded on active solidarity and on mutual understanding of the cultural diversities that constitute Europe's originality and richness.
>
> (EC, 1997: 4; bold in original)

By 1997, the European educational area will have three dimensions:

> The citizens of Europe will be able to develop their fund of **knowledge**, and this area will facilitate the **enhancement of citizenship** and **the development of employ-ability through the acquisition of competencies** made necessary through the changes in work and its organisation.
>
> (EC, 1997: 2; bold in original)

Two things are clear here: that the emphasis is still on education for citizenship, so that the framework of responsibility is organisational and little or no mention is made of the citizens' own responsibility; and that the concern is still with citizenship per se rather than with active citizenship, an emphasis that was to change the following year:

> In 1998, however, the Commission acknowledged that citizenship could not be taught, since it had cognitive, affective and practical dimensions – it could be learned, however, and learning for active citizenship became an aim of lifelong learning. Here, the teaching of citizenship is not enough – it is the learning of citizenship which is essential . . . Learning for active citizenship includes access to the skills and competencies that young people will need for effective economic participation under conditions of technological modernisation, economic globalisation, and, very concretely, transnational European labour markets.
>
> (EC, 1998: 6)

In *Making a European Area of Lifelong Learning a Reality*, it was more specifically recognised that the Europe of Knowledge threatens to bring about 'greater inequalities and social exclusion' (EC, 2001a: 6), so it is claimed that lifelong learning:

> is much more than economics. It also promotes the goals and ambitions of the European countries to become more inclusive, tolerant and democratic. And it promises a Europe in which citizens have the opportunity and ability to realise their ambitions and to participate in building a better society.
>
> (p. 7)

Significantly, the emphasis on the relationship between active citizenship and employability is explicitly downplayed (p. 9); now the aims of lifelong learning have become personal fulfilment, active citizenship, social inclusion and employability/ adaptability. At the same time, building a 'better society' has become an aim of citizenship and, unless the good society is only materialistic, and the EC documents do not really read this way, then space is implicitly being made for political action in the public sphere. However, EC documents are at pains to point out that, in the Europe of Knowledge, active citizens must be aware of the issues and engage in critical debate. Lifelong learning should empower citizens both to meet the challenges of the knowledge-based society and also to respond to the demands and ambitions of the EU and its Member States (p. 8).

Learning for active citizenship is not an optional extra but it is an integral part of living and acting within the EU, demanding autonomy and critical reflection rather than having a fixed list of norms and values. But people have to be encouraged to be citizens, even though they are the authors of their own biographies: 'In this context, the practice of citizenship becomes more like a method of social inclusion, in the course of which people together create the experience of becoming architects and actors of their own lives' (EC, 1998: 5).

Citizenship is now a responsibility rather than a right, but is still to be found in Marshall's social dimension. But there is still a fundamental conceptual difference between citizenship and active citizenship.

## Putting policy into practice

In a wide variety of programmes about lifelong learning, the EU has tried to put its policies into practice – both in economic and in citizenship terms. Space forbids a full discussion of these programmes, but we will highlight a few to illustrate what is happening.

Recognising the diversity of Europe, language learning plays an important part and so there is an extensive language programme, the objectives of which are:

- To contribute through lifelong learning to the development of the Community as an advanced knowledge society, with sustainable economic development, more and better jobs and social cohesion.
- To foster interaction, cooperation and mobility between education and training systems within the Community, so that they become a world quality reference.

(EC, 2007: 4)

A wide variety of 30 programmes are sponsored that include many of the major languages of Europe, including those such as Bulgarian – a new nation at the periphery of the EU.

In precisely the same way, there is an extensive research programme – the Framework programme – whereby universities and other institutions across Europe form Europe-wide teams to research major projects. The Erasmus programme has encouraged joint study at university level and is sponsoring a group of universities to offer a degree-level programme in which students follow the same modules and study together. A different university will host each part of the programme so that the students move between universities. The Grundtvig adult education programme is a joint research and development programme whereby funds are only granted to teams of universities and other adult education institutions from different countries working together. Other programmes could be discussed but space forbids it.

## Conclusion

In all of these programmes the EU has embarked upon a policy initiative that has encouraged each of the Member States to initiate its own national programmes reflecting these wider policies, although the Commission can only encourage, since the principle of subsidiarity means that Brussels cannot overrule national policy, only influence it. At the same time, the Commission has devoted considerable funding to initiate Europe-wide programmes, such as those noted above. Perhaps the relationship between the Commission and the Member States is best summed up in the recent report *Adult Learning: It is never too late to learn* (EC, 2006) when it states:

The Commission therefore proposes that there should be dialogue with the Member States and relevant stakeholders to explore:

- Ways of making the best use of financial mechanisms available at the European level (such as Structural Funds and the Lifelong Learning Programme);
- How to take proper account of adult learning needs in the National Reform Programmes under the Lisbon strategy;
- How best to involve stakeholders to ensure that the messages of this Communication are acted on in the diverse circumstances prevailing in the different Member States;
- How to encourage exchanges of good practices through peer learning activities in the Framework of the 'Education and Training 2010' programme, including on the basis of the results of existing EU programmes;
- Best approaches to improve statistical monitoring.

Based on this reflection the Commission proposes to develop an action plan in 2007 to ensure effective follow-up to the messages set out in this Communication.

(EC, 2006: 10)

# References

Barbalet, J. (1988) *Citizenship*, Milton Keynes: Open University Press.
Bauman, Z. (1992) *Intimations of Post-Modernity*, London: Routledge.
—— (1999) *In Search of Politics*, Cambridge: Polity.
Beck, U. (2000) *What is Globalization?*, Cambridge: Polity.
Castells, M. (1996) *The Rise of the Network Society*, vol. 1 of *The Information Age: Economy, society and culture*, Oxford: Blackwell.
Cohen, N. (2002) 'One way to get very rich', *The Observer* (London), 24 February, p. 31.
Delanty, G. (2000) *Citizenship in a Global Age*, Buckingham: Open University Press.
European Commission (EC) (1995) *White Paper on Teaching and Learning: Towards a learning society*, Brussels: European Commission.
—— (1997) *Towards A Europe of Knowledge*, COM (1997) 563 final, Brussels: European Commission.
—— (1998) *Education and Active Citizenship*, Brussels: European Commission.
—— (2000) *A Memorandum on Lifelong Learning*, SEC (2000) 1832, Brussels: European Commission.
—— (2001a) *Making a European Area of Lifelong Learning a Reality*, COM (2001) 678 final, Brussels: European Commission.
—— (2001b) *European Governance: A White Paper*, COM (2001) 428 final, Brussels: European Commission.
—— (2006) *Adult Learning: It is never too late to learn*, COM (2006) 614 final, Brussels: European Commission.
—— (2007) *Languages for Europe*, Luxembourg: Office of Official Publications of the European Communities.
Giddens, A. (1991) *Modernity and Self-identity*, Cambridge: Polity.
Habermas, J. (1995) *Between Facts and Norms* (trans. W. Rehg), Cambridge: Polity.
—— (2006) *Time of Transitions* (ed. and trans. C. Cronin and M. Pensky), Cambridge: Polity Press.
Heater, D. (1999) *What is Citizenship?*, Cambridge: Polity.
Held, D., McGrew, A., Goldblatt, D. and Perraton, J. (1999) *Global Transformations*, Cambridge: Polity.
Jarvis, P. (2001) *Universities and Corporate Universities*, London: Kogan Page.
—— (2007) *Globalisation, Lifelong Learning and the Learning Society: Sociological perspectives*, London: Routledge.
Korten, D. (1995) *When Corporations Rule the World*, London: Earthscan.
Marshall, T.H. (1950) *Citizenship and Social Class and Other Essays*, Cambridge: Cambridge University Press.
Meister, J. (1998) *Corporate Universities*, revised edn, New York: McGraw Hill.
Monbiot, G. (2000) *Captive State*, London: Macmillan.
Pilger, J. (2003) *The New Rulers of the World*, London: Verso (updated).
Putnam, R. (2000) *Bowling Alone*, New York: Simon and Schuster.
Robertson, R. (1995) 'Glocalisation', in M. Featherstone, S. Lash and R. Robertson (eds) *Global Modernities*, London: Sage.
Wallerstein, I. (1974) *The Modern World System*, New York: Academic Press.

# 25

# The World Bank's view of lifelong learning
## Handmaiden of the market

*William M. Rivera*

In *Lifelong Learning in the Global Knowledge Economy* an impressive list of World Bank specialists involved in its writing conclude that countries need to create "high-performance, lifelong learning systems" (2003: 57), and will consequently require significant changes in the governance and financing of education and training. While changes in education systems may be needed, the use of the phrase "lifelong learning *systems*" deserves examination, especially regarding the various purposes of education, with work orientation being only one.

The ideal of lifelong *learning* is to foster change in the attitude of individuals and groups away from "education for grades and certificates" toward a proactive and learning approach to solving problems, thereby increasing one's ability to think and act. The ideal of lifelong *education* is to provide lifelong "educational" access at all levels and for all needs. Certainly, neither ideal will be socially and economically effective without job and career opportunities, preferably meaningful ones.

Issues that deserve conceptual and programmatic discussion are (1) the fact that the World Bank has spent billions on primary and secondary education, ignoring the potential for adult and continuing (especially continuing professional) education for those adults in or just preparing to enter the work world; (2) the importance of "facilitator teaching" methods, which are talked about but seldom instituted; and (3) the lack of coordination within the World Bank regarding various issues of education, both conceptual and strategic:

> "Lifelong learning" is an attitude. It provides an opportunity to adopt an ideal, not an ideology. Lifelong learning relates as strongly to citizenship education as to utilitarian education geared to market-oriented, market-driven development.
>
> The Bank has developed numerous documents dealing with lifelong learning, including documents on education policy, regional strategies, cross-sectoral strategies, and project papers—with the latter highlighted for Hungary, Romania, and Chile.
>
> (World Bank, 2003: 109)

The "implications of lifelong learning for traditional education have yet to be explored," according to *Lifelong Learning in the Global Knowledge Economy* (World Bank, 2003: 108). However, this has not prevented the World Bank from suggesting the advancement of lifelong learning "systems." The implication for the concept of "lifelong learning" is reductive, referring primarily to work-oriented, market-oriented education.

The essence of what's needed to promote adult opportunities for basic, continuing, and post-secondary education is practical programs provided by specialized facilitators. The ideal of lifelong learning will be fostered in rural areas, for example as the poor gain access to and obtain education for work and advancement in line with the Bank's objectives of socio-economic development along with poverty alleviation. However, lifelong learning is a broader concept than for-work education, and includes other goals such as citizenship and societal concerns (Martin, 2003).

## Definitions and the evolution of lifelong learning

One of the various intellectual products that the World Bank now "sells" (Goldman, 2005: 133) is lifelong learning. Like other products sponsored by the Bank, lifelong learning has become a stated component in its programs and relevant to the types of loans it makes. Specifically, lifelong learning is advocated as a component of what education means for poverty alleviation (World Bank, 2003).

The World Bank's 2005 *Education Sector Strategy Update* (ESSU) states its vision of societies and economies as "increasingly dynamic, knowledge-driven, and cohesive . . . all children complete school, learn well, and adopt healthy behaviors and positive values . . . more adults obtain skills—and gainful employment" (2005: 5). The list goes on, enumerating a host of ideals for realizing their stated vision to "maximize the impact of education on economic growth and poverty reduction." To realize its strategy, the Bank proposes in the ESSU to maximize the impact of education on economic growth and poverty reduction (the latter in line with MDG #1—one of the eight UN-sponsored Millennium Development Goals to reduce poverty and hunger).

Lifelong learning is mentioned over 30 times in the ESSU text. Often it is used without precise meaning. More often it is associated with tertiary education or follows it, as though it were another or "fourth" level of education.

At different points in the ESSU, lifelong learning is referred to variously as a "system" (World Bank, 2005: 59, 107, 123, 166), a "strategy" (p. 80), a "perspective" (p. 126), and a "model" (p. 59). In short, it is used indiscriminately throughout the document.

The ESSU rightly states, "The macroeconomic and labor market context is crucial for mapping out a country's education strategy" (p. 32). It recognizes in this instance the importance of individual situations. But then it speaks of lifelong learning as a "model." The variety of meaning associated with the term "lifelong learning" in this document, written by a committee of specialists, falls into an old error, of bureaucratically adopting one answer to situations that demand more than one "model." The Bank fell into a similar embarrassing error when it adopted the training and visit (T&V) management system as its one-system approach to agricultural extension, which Anderson *et al.* (2006) have documented as the "rise and fall" of the Bank's T&V system.

The ESSU document highlights an anomaly in the Bank's general emphasis on skills and work-oriented education for economic development when it states, "The challenge of integrating education into labor market strategies implies the need to: identify and develop those skills that are most demanded in the global economy, while learning how to learn—rather than occupation-specific skills" (World Bank, 2005: 32). Why would "learning how to learn" be contrasted with learning "occupation-specific skills?" It is this lack of precise term definition that weakens the document and does not add to our understanding. It makes one wonder as to the writers' clarity about what "learning how to learn" means and further puts into question their use of the term "lifelong learning."

Indeed, the ESSU document states, "Lifelong learning 'systems' recognize the need for learning throughout the lifecycle, based on learning needs rather than age, and aim to replace information-based, teacher-directed methods with learning that develops the ability to create, apply, analyze, and synthesize knowledge" (p. 59). *How* does lifelong learning "recognize the need" and accomplish the aim of replacing "information-based, teacher-directed methods with . . . etc."? In the education arena, teachers—whether face-to-face or in distance education programs—will always be responsible for students/participants and their learning whether or not their students/participants are self-directed or "lifelong" learners.

None of the above comments is intended either to undermine the Bank's adoption of these diverse education terms or to suggest that the Bank should not work to promote such attitudes as "learning to learn" and "lifelong learning." Certainly the Bank is in line with other international organizations in promoting these concepts. For example, as noted in *Lifelong Learning in the Global Knowledge Economy*:

> The theme of lifelong learning has been embraced by the OECD, the European Union, the World Bank, and other international organizations. In 1999 World Bank President James Wolfensohn referred explicitly to lifelong learning as a component of what education means for poverty alleviation (World Bank, 1999).
>
> (World Bank, 2003)

"The World Bank has developed," according to that same publication (2003) "strategies for traditional education, but its [the Bank's] involvement is still at an early stage and has not yet fully explored the implications of lifelong learning." To illustrate the Bank's commitment to lifelong learning, however, the publication then cites a number of World Bank documents (18 in all) underlining lifelong learning as a priority, in the organization's education sector policy, regional strategies, cross-sectoral strategies, and a number of projects already labeled "lifelong learning systems."

The World Bank has implemented a number of projects with lifelong learning components (World Bank, 2003: 109), already mentioned, examples being Romania, Chile, and Hungary. In Jordan an e-learning strategy is being developed "for the knowledge economy." *Lifelong Learning in the Global Knowledge Economy* notes, however, that most of the strategies being developed have looked at individual elements of "the lifelong learning system" rather than "seeing the overall framework and connections between these elements" (World Bank, 2003: 108). Presumably the "overall framework" is being developed in countries such as Chile, Mexico, and China, where so-called "lifelong learning systems" are said to be already in place, most of which are simply training projects.

The idea of a lifelong learning "system" begs the question as to what would constitute "a system" in a concept as broad and free-ranging as "lifelong learning"? I suspect that what is meant by Field (2000) and others thinking along these lines is a lifelong *"education* system," in which educational opportunity—rather than "learning"—is made possible from "early childhood to retirement" by a variety of educational institutions and programs.

The Organization of Economic Cooperation and Development (OECD) concept of "recurrent" education is also worth mentioning. This concept would design education around the needs of workers who become "obsolete" at their jobs, or who lose their jobs for whatever reason, and require recurrent education to prepare them for the existing new work arena. This was the first attempt, to my knowledge, to create a *lifelong adult education system geared to the work arena*. The most current concept of the "knowledge society" is linked once again to work and career, with "knowledge workers" at the top of the hierarchy of workers in the "knowledge economy." The concept of the "knowledge economy" underscores the importance of advanced knowledge as a major contributor to economic development. These concepts of lifelong learning, lifelong education, recurrent education, and the knowledge society have different meanings and emphases. The terms "education" and "learning" need to be clarified and de-linked.

Education refers to what goes on in and by institutions and programs—formal, distance, in-service, and non-formal institutions that provide educational information and training. Learning refers to individual and group acquisition of knowledge and skills, whether provided by educational institutions or gained from family and peers or through experience and the incidental access to knowledge. The unsystematic use of these two terms—education and learning—is one of the reasons much of the writing in this domain appears confusing. The lack of clear definition of terms presents a problem not only of nomenclature but of meaning.

In 1976, at the UNESCO international conference on lifelong education, the difference between "education" and "learning" was a point of significant debate, with most Europeans arguing that lifelong *education* was institutionally tangible but that the notion of lifelong *learning* was formless and could not be measured. But representatives from the United States, the United Kingdom, and Australia supported the concept of lifelong learning as it stressed the importance of the individual's capacity and responsibility for learning and, in contrast to the European position, was more open-ended and comprehensive. This was the beginning of adherence to both terms, the one championing the role of institutions in promoting "permanent" or lifelong education and the other espousing the role of the individual in acquiring knowledge and skills. However, the distinction between the two terms is too often blurred and, worse, undifferentiated.

Indeed, in the United States, following passage of the Lifelong Learning Act of 1976, sponsored by then Senator Walter Mondale, US Congressmen were said to have posed indicative questions as to which "education" institutions should be funded to provide lifelong learning. What needed to be clarified then as now is that "lifelong learning" stands as an ideal of the individual attitude toward learning and is not necessarily allied to any specific institutional base or system.

The confusion increases with Bank statements, such as: "Lifelong learning is crucial to preparing workers to compete in the global economy" (2003: xvii). It is not lifelong learning that is crucial but *access to education throughout the working life*. However, some specialists argue that lifelong learning is "an explosive policy issue" and that it has become "a way of thinking about and structuring our society's approach to education" (Field, 2000: 17).

It is not the concept of lifelong learning per se that makes for "an explosive issue"; it is the lack of rethinking and recasting of the already existing formal, in-service, and non-formal education systems and the need to weave these into a whole and to direct them to socio-economic goals related to innovation and development; what I conceptualize as the "Workforce Education System" (Rivera, 2006). Lifelong learning *is* an "explosive issue" for the World Bank, but for other reasons. If it were truer to its banking nature, it seems to me the Bank would recognize adult and lifelong education as central to the business of its immediate work-oriented development purpose.

Lifelong learning is an attitude toward education and learning. It has rightly been called "pedagogy of the self" (Hinchliffe, 2006). Indeed, it harks back to the concept of self-directed learning. There is a distinction between the educational improvement brought about through in-service (job-oriented) training and the learning pursued and acquired by individuals on their own; those engaged in what he termed "vocationally-oriented self-directed learning" (Clardy,

1992). The concept of self-directed learning, like lifelong learning, underscores that learning depends on the individual's attitudes and behaviors toward learning, not on the educational programs of an institution, although those attitudes and behaviors also influence learning within institutions.

Self-directed learning (Tough, 1971) is another powerful concept. It has been described as "a process in which individuals take the initiative, with or without the help of others, to diagnose their learning needs, formulate learning goals, identify resources for learning, select and implement learning strategies, and evaluate learning outcomes" (Knowles, 1975). Mocker and Spear (1982) sought to describe a matrix that would contain formal, non-formal, and self-directed learning. The problem in their case is that of comparing incomparables, for while individuals may learn in formal and non-formal educational arenas, self-directed learning is a different, non-institutional concept. Indeed, adults are continually involved in self-directed learning. Tough (1971) estimated that some 90 percent of adults conduct at least one self-directed learning project per annum, and that these projects most often are carried out outside an educational institution. Cross (1981) calculated that 70 percent of adult learning is self-directed learning.

The concept of lifelong learning is closely associated with the early development of adult education. Adult education practitioners promoted "lifelong learning" concepts as early as the 1920s by thinkers such as Yeaxlee and Lindeman. Concepts and principles related to lifelong learning were quickly integrated into teaching and learning methodologies advanced by adult educators such as Malcolm Knowles, in *The Modern Practice of Adult Education* (1974), and were recognized as being as applicable to pedagogy as they were to "andragogy," as implied in *The Theory and Practice of Learning* (Jarvis *et al.*, 2003).

The relatively recent notions of "knowledge society" and "knowledge economy" represent an effort to re-conceive the values and implications of lifelong learning and lifelong education. The concept of the Knowledge Society was first used, to my knowledge, by Torsten Husèn in his 1974 collection of essays. His contention was that the school no longer served as the influential force that it had once been. To underscore the importance of advanced knowledge acquisition and development to the advance of knowledge societies, another concept—"the knowledge economy"—has been posited. It simply underlines the importance of advanced knowledge as a major contributor to economic development. Peter Drucker, in his famous Harvard University article on "Knowledge work and the knowledge society" (1994), argued for the significance of the "knowledge society" concept and the importance of "knowledge workers," whom he considered "the leading class" in knowledge societies:

> Knowledge workers, although only a large minority of the work force . . . already give the emerging knowledge society its character, its leadership, its central challenges and its social profile. Knowledge workers may not be the *ruling* class of the knowledge society, but they are its *leading* class. In their characteristics, their social positions, their values and their expectations, they differ fundamentally from any group in history that has ever occupied the leading, let along [sic] the dominant position.
>
> (Drucker, 1994; italics in original)

Drucker's argument may be correct, but it is well to remember the warning made in the preamble of UNESCO's *Learning to Be*:

> The great changes of our time are imperiling the unity and the future of the species, and man's own identity as well. What is to be feared is not only the painful prospect of grievous

inequalities, privations and suffering, but also that we may be heading for a veritable dichotomy within the human race, which risks being split into superior and inferior groups, into masters and slaves, supermen and submen.

(Faure, 1972: xxi)

It was not long after Drucker's statement that the concept of the knowledge society was connected to economic development and formed into the concept of the "knowledge economy." The knowledge economy, or knowledge-based economy, concept gained prominence in New Zealand in the mid-1990s as a way of referring to the manner in which various high-technology businesses, especially computer software, telecommunications, and virtual services, as well as educational and research institutions, could contribute to a country's economy.

These relatively new concepts regarding knowledge emerged along with a transformation of knowledge itself, sparked by multiple factors outlined at the International Conference on "Advancing Knowledge and the Knowledge Economy" held in Washington, DC in 2005. This conference brought together specialists to examine how processes for creating and organizing knowledge interact with information technology, business strategy, and changing social and economic conditions. The conference participants cited multiple factors as contributing to the transformation of knowledge:

1    globalization of communications and commerce;
2    commoditization of ICTs (and partial commoditization of codified knowledge;
3    the increasing role of scientific research and innovation;
4    advanced, integrative information infrastructure;
5    modularization, vertical disaggregation, and outsourcing; and
6    expanded value chains and clusters with new categories of actors.

(http://advancingknowledge.com)

The Knowledge Society concept presumes increasing specialization of skills and knowledge that will contribute to society's betterment and advancement of its economy. The concept of "the knowledge economy" links more specifically to the idea that, while "money makes the world go round," knowledge makes it advance.

## The Bank's primary interest

Presumably the Bank's support for lifelong learning and related concepts such as the "knowledge society" and the "knowledge economy" is to promote a more skilled and educated world. This fits with its interest in the development of human career and work advancement, "human resource development," or what economists refer to as "human capital" (Becker, 1975). In turn, the Bank's orientation toward human resource development[1] parallels that of other international organizations, as mentioned earlier. While cognizant of other educational aims, the orientation of international organizations toward work-oriented programs and their utility for entering the human capital market with the ultimate purpose of developing market economies cannot be denied.

While it is understandable that a bank would emphasize a purely socio-economic rationale for lifelong education, one is justified in expecting the World Bank to have longer time horizons, which would include civic education in support of democratic governance, environmental education to meet the challenges of resource degradation, and other societal aims. The editors of the *International Journal of Lifelong Education*, Peter Jarvis and John Holford, claim that "Education is inextricably bound up with collective and democratic action" (Jarvis and Holford, 2006: 445). In supporting this claim they highlight three cases cited in an article by Holford (2006), namely:

> Arthur Creech Jones' advocacy of community education in the post-war British Colonial Office; the Workers Educational Association's efforts to educate workers for "democratic leadership" in Britain; and the European Union's recent attempt to incorporate an active citizenship dimension into its prescriptions for lifelong learning.

The World Bank, whose status is rendered distinct from other UN organizations because of its voting procedures and its profit-making agenda, has consistently advanced programs related to work-oriented knowledge and skills, as have other specialized agencies of the UN. UNESCO, for example, in the 1960s and 1970s, promoted "functional" literacy, that is, not just literacy but literacy related to work. Also, it would be remiss not to mention UNESCO's leadership in the publication and promotion of the lifelong learning concept in its seminal work, *Learning to Be: The world of education today and tomorrow* (1972), which stresses among other things what I hope is implied in this chapter—the argument for "the right to education."

At the same time, during the late 1960s, when UNESCO was promoting the now dominant concepts of lifelong education and lifelong learning, the OECD supported the concept of "recurrent education," education intended to be made available for workers who jobs might be lost or upgraded over time, advancing the idea that these workers would need to be retrained and perhaps reskilled to re-enter the advanced needs of the job market.

The World Bank's support for lifelong learning, the knowledge society, and related concepts involving education and learning makes perfect sense because this position relates to the organization's main concerns, specifically the world of work and economic development. However, there remains a glitch often overlooked in the rhetoric extolling the virtues and value of work-oriented, knowledge-oriented societies. That glitch is a country's actual employment situation. While the issue of employment demand and employee training is frequently mentioned in Bank texts on education, such as *Lifelong Learning in the Global Knowledge Economy* and the ESSU, the critical factor in the state's involvement in the economic and employment policies underlying global, national, and local economies is seldom spelled out.

Employment policy and actual employment situations are keys to the practical discussion of lifelong learning and complementary concepts. The promotion of these useful learning and knowledge concepts pales in practice if employment and employment opportunity are non-existent. The knowledge economy is advanced by lifelong learning attitudes in knowledge societies when those societies provide the basis for knowledge use, through employment. Even so, when education and job opportunities exist and are satisfying, what ultimately makes lifelong learning attitudes worthwhile in a socio-economic context is the freedom of leisure and civil expression in this work-oriented world.

## Back to basics and beyond

Will global corporations be able to absorb the billions who are predicted to soon inhabit the Earth? Many would doubt it. The role of government in providing and promoting employment opportunities for the young without much formal education and for professionals seeking to advance their careers through continuing education and knowledge acquisition is and remains central to development. If mergers of the mega-transnational corporations continue, the corporations will be larger in terms of budgets and access to resources than most governments categorized as "developing." Indeed, mega-capital interests see these countries as underdeveloped. One example of this is in agriculture, where the former proviso of "agriculture on the road to industrialization" categorically did not work in Africa, as René Dumont had recognized back in the late 1950s. Today, I observe that, in contrast, *business is on the road to agriculture*, as food and agricultural interests seek to expand their "life industry" in developing countries. The advancement of agricultural businesses in developing countries has also resulted in changes regarding what agricultural research, education, and extension services should be about and how their systems should be developed. For example, new ideas about universities being involved in development, and not only in the academic, are making headway (Kibwika, 2006). Kibwika states categorically his conviction "that universities should play a dual role of academics and development" (p. 183). That role is precisely the one stressed in my paper on "Transforming post-secondary education and training by design: solutions for sub-Saharan Africa" (Rivera, 2006).

Lifelong *learning* is certainly a meaningful concept to anyone wanting to "get ahead," as well as to those who simply recognize that life is about learning. But it is lifelong *education* that constitutes the formal "instrument," and consists of the institutions and programs required to promote formal, in-service, and non-formal lifelong learning opportunities in society—more so in societies that recognize knowledge as an important aspect of economic development. While education and learning go together, to mix lifelong learning and lifelong education conceptually is a mistake. Such merging of terms particularly damages the encompassing purpose that lifelong learning denotes.

Increasingly, more and more people are gaining access to television and other instruments of telecommunications. Cellular phones, for example, are no longer a luxury of advanced societies and their capital cities, but are still limited as regards distribution and affordability in rural areas. Nonetheless, this rapidly changing reality already suggests that access to new technology means the advancement of new knowledge and that new knowledge provides the desire for, if not always the immediate possibility of, new and better livelihoods. While a practical approach and one goal for education, the question of what education is for "after," or in addition to, "livelihoods" is seldom considered.

Lifelong learning and the advancement of knowledge societies as concepts, and their advancement through educational institutions, are certainly central to development—for the rich, the middle class, and the poor. These concepts are changing the way we think about education policy and strategies, but not necessarily in the way some specialists would suggest (Field, 2000). It is not necessary, I would argue, to turn every concept into policy and strategy.

More to the point, lifelong learning is not just "a way of thinking about and structuring our society" (Drucker, 2003: p. 169). It is about learning throughout life. It seems to me that the long-term productive option for the Bank is to invest in institutions, programs, and facilitators for education and training. That, in my view, is the Bank's functional business. But that functional business should not suggest that functional education and training are the be-all and end-all of the process of lifelong learning.

Lifelong learning can serve as one of the conceptual premises for the Bank's promotion of education. But the concept demands systems, programs, and projects in the form of accessible and sustainable social instruments—that is, support for schools, for business in-service programs, and for non-formal educational services. The fundamental challenge is to promote and advance basic elementary and secondary knowledge, post-secondary training and higher education, and continuing and recurrent education through support for both public and private education institutions and programs.

If lifelong learning is, in a sense, "the queen" of education concepts, the concept of a knowledge society is, to continue the analogy, "the king." I say this knowing that the knowledge-society concept, when read closely, tends to promote primarily specialists and the professionals—what Drucker calls the "knowledge workers." It is a natural instinct in a sense to want to help those who are succeeding and motivated, just as extension agents generally prefer to work with progressive farmers. *Hard Tomatoes, Hard Times* (Hightower, 1973) is a treatise against this tendency to overlook and bypass the poor; nonetheless, it is a "natural" inclination.

The knowledge society, according to Drucker (1994), depends on "knowledge workers." They are, he claims, "the leading class" of workers. However, in making this statement Drucker recognizes that this fact of "class" is a possible problem. He states:

> This society, in which knowledge workers dominate, is in danger of a new class conflict: the conflict between the large minority of knowledge workers and the majority of people who will make their living through traditional ways, either by manual work, whether skilled or unskilled, or by services work, whether skilled or unskilled. The productivity of knowledge work, still abysmally low, will predictably become the *economic* challenge of the knowledge society. On it will depend the competitive position of every country, industry and institution within society. The productivity of the non- knowledge services worker will increasingly become the *social* challenge to the knowledge society. On it will depend the ability of the knowledge society to give decent incomes and with them dignity and status to non-knowledge people.
>
> (Drucker, 1994: 169)

The role of the Bank, in my view, is that, while recognizing the importance of Drucker's "knowledge workers" and their need, the Bank continues to concentrate on assisting the poor in low-income countries by generating "decent incomes and with them dignity and status." The first MDG discusses the reduction of poverty, but attention to employment for those trained and educated is equally demanding or else the brain drain from undeveloped countries will continue and the countries in need of development will once again become dependent on outside consultants.

Ultimately "lifelong education" and "the knowledge society" need to translate into lifelong educational opportunity *in* the knowledge society. Such an ideal befits the Bank, promoting modernity and progress via investment in every level of education and training in its effort to promote opportunities for lifelong work-oriented learning.

While the World Bank's view of lifelong learning as a "handmaiden of the market" is considered herein as a limitation on the full meaning and scope of the term "lifelong learning," there is no intention to suggest that the Bank does not rightly use education as an "instrument" to promote economic benefits to its borrowers.

Indeed, there is a need by the Bank to foster and budget for "workforce education" networks that promote and advance the education of adults, not just the traditional system of public/private "post-secondary education and training." We are determined by our metaphors and language. It is time to *think* of education as truly a lifelong activity with the educational content and purpose changing over time. Education is a lifelong activity, not always purposive or particularly meaningful, but education in the broadest sense is continually in process.

In the frame of its current ideological orientation, I argue that the Bank can best benefit from two investments: first, in the "bricks and mortar" side of education, and, second, in the promotion of work and career development through learning by practice, employing teachers who know how to be facilitators. There is public prestige in supporting the concept and the practice of lifelong learning and by encouraging the "knowledge for economic development" aspects of a knowledge society. These ideas also play a strategic role by pushing societies to recognize the importance of learning and knowledge to their economies, and to take note that the economies in economically advancing societies are increasingly based on knowledge acquisition and use.

In sum, the Bank's socio-economic purpose in promoting lifelong learning and knowledge-based economic systems seems straightforward. It is to educate and train adults to become productive members of the existing and potential workforce (preferably in the scope of a "Workforce Education System," including training for human resource development and institutional capacity). The second purpose is to organize pluralistic and integrated education systems—aimed at advancing knowledge by contributing to research and its dissemination, professional development, and market connections that contribute to growth and the reduction of poverty. These two purposes need to be clearly stated but in such a way as not to suggest that they encompass all lifelong learning pursuits.

The Bank will benefit from clarifying its lifelong learning goals as work- and market-oriented. If the Bank is successful in promoting public/private partnerships and a workforce orientation to development, then the Bank's position and purpose will be better appreciated, and its support and assistance in developing lifelong education opportunities will be understood as dedicated to the ideal of lifelong learning.

## Note

1    All too seldom is the task of human resource management (HRM) mentioned in organizing, educating, and motivating "human resources."

## References

Anderson, J.R., Feder, G. and Ganguly, S. (2006) "The rise and fall of Training and Visit extension: an Asian mini-drama with an African epilogue?," in A.W. Van den Ban and R.K. Samanta (eds) *Changing Roles of Agricultural Extension in Asian Nations*, New Delhi: B.R. Publishing Corporation, pp. 149–74. (An expanded version is available as World Bank Policy Working Paper Series 3928.)

Becker, G.S. (1975) *Human Capital: A theoretical and empirical analysis, with special reference to education*, Chicago, IL: Chicago University Press.

Clardy, A. (1992) *Vocationally-oriented Self-directed Learning Projects (VO SDLPs): An exploratory study of the types of VO SDLPs and the organizational and individual factors affecting their occurrence*, Ph.D. dissertation, College Park, MD: University of Maryland.

Cross, K.P. (1981) *Adults as Learners*, San Francisco: Jossey Bass.

Drucker, P.F. (1994) "The theory of the business," *Harvard Business Review* 72 (Sept/Oct): 95–104.

Drucker, P.F. (2003) *A Functioning Society: Selections from sixty-five years of writing on community, society and policy*, New Brunswick, NJ and London: Transaction Publishers.

Faure, E. (Chair) (1972) *Learning to Be: The world of education today and tomorrow*, Paris: UNESCO.

Field, J. (2000) *Lifelong Learning and the New Educational Order*, London: Trentham Books.

Goldman, M. (2005) *Imperial Nature*, New Haven, CT: Yale University Press.

Hightower, J. (1973) *Hard Tomatoes, Hard Times: The failure of the land grant college complex*, Agribusiness Accountability Project, Cambridge, MA: Schenkman Publishing.

Hinchliffe, G. (2006) "Plato and the love of learning," *Ethics and Education* 1(2): 117–31.

Holford, J. (2006) "The role of lifelong learning in building citizenship: European Union approaches in the light of British and colonial experience," *International Journal of Lifelong Education* 25(3) (May/June): 321–32.

Husèn, T. (1974) *The Learning Society: A collection of essays*, London: Meuthen.

International Conference on "Advancing Knowledge and the Knowledge Economy" (2005). Held at National Academy in Washington, DC. Available online at http://advancingknowledge.com, accessed November 2006.

Jarvis, P. and Holford, J. (2006) "Editorial: Measuring learning for citizenship," *International Journal of Lifelong Education* 25(5) (September/October): 445.

Jarvis, P., Holford, J., and Griffin, C. (2003) *The Theory and Practice of Learning*, London: RoutledgeFalmer.

Kibwika, P. (2006) *Learning to Make Change: Developing innovation competence for recreating the African university of the 21st century*, Wageningen, The Netherlands: Wageningen Academic Publishers.

Knowles, M. (1975) *Self-directed Learning: A guide for learners and teachers*, New York: Association Press.

Martin, I. (2003) "Adult education, lifelong learning and citizenship: some ifs and buts," *International Journal of Lifelong Education* 22(6): 556–80.

Mocker, W.D. and G.E. Spear (1982) *Lifelong Learning: Formal, nonformal and self directed*, Information Series no. 241 (Doc. No. ED 220–723), Columbus, OH: ERIC Clearinghouse on Adult, Career and Vocational Education.

Rivera, W.M. (2006) *Transforming Post-secondary Agricultural Education and Training by Design: Solutions for sub-Saharan Africa*, Washington, DC: World Bank.

Tough, A. (1971) *The Adult's Learning Projects*, Toronto: Ontario Institute for Studies in Education.

World Bank (1999) *A Proposal for a Comprehensive Development Framework*, Washington, DC: World Bank.

—— (2003) *Lifelong Learning in the Global Knowledge Economy: Challenges for developing countries*, Washington, DC: World Bank.

—— (2005) *Education Sector Strategy Update* (ESSU), Washington, DC: World Bank.

# 26

# The OECD and lifelong learning

*Tom Schuller*[1]

This chapter considers aspects of the Organization for Economic Cooperation and Development (OECD)'s role in the development of policy thinking on lifelong learning. I set out to do the following:

- provide an essentially descriptive background of the OECD itself, and specifically on the different roles and functions it discharges in the field of educational policy research;
- provide some historical perspective (not a full narrative) on the evolution of the OECD's approach to lifelong learning, reflecting both changes in its internal structures and developments in the external political climate that shapes its programme;
- identify a selection of key dimensions for assessing the effect of the OECD on thinking about lifelong learning.

## Background

As its name implies, the Organization for Economic Cooperation and Development was originally set up to promote economic growth. Initially it was confined to European countries rebuilding their economies after the Second World War with Marshall Fund support, but it came over time to include most of the industrialised democracies – the 'rich man's club' as it was known in those unreconstructed days – and currently is wrestling with how to accommodate emerging major economies such as Brazil and China. It remains primarily geared to economic growth as an overall objective, though the notion of growth is itself one that changes, notably to reflect environmental considerations.

The OECD has accumulated policy areas as well as members over the four and a half decades of its existence, so that it now includes directorates in such areas as energy and environment. Education has always been a part of the OECD portfolio, but its relationship to the core OECD business of economic development has changed over time. I shall address this in more detail later on; at this point it is enough to say that the initial approach to education was quite tightly tied to the emerging (in the 1960s) interest in human capital theory, but at the same time had an explicit commitment to social objectives. Later on, in the period of economic downturn that characterised the 1980s and some of the 1990s, the focus became somewhat more instrumental, giving priority to moves to solve structural change and the employment crisis, but there remained a range of programmes that gave variety to the educational mission. Measuring investment in education and analysing the returns to that investment remain core features of the OECD's educational work, but these activities range far more widely than this might suggest.

In 2002 education was taken out of the directorate of employment and social affairs and constituted as a separate directorate. The move can be seen as an indication of the priority given to education as a discrete policy area; or, alternatively, or indeed simultaneously, as a weakening of the link between education and labour market analysis that has been so characteristic of the OECD approach.

The OECD's role in educational policy thinking has been the subject of several accounts, or even critiques, from insiders and outsiders. George Papadopoulos (1994), a longstanding member of the OECD Secretariat and Deputy Director of Education, gives a detailed and not wholly uncritical historical account, tracing the evolution of educational work over the first three decades, up to 1990. Rinne *et al.* (2004), by contrast, speak as academic researchers from a country (Finland) that has consistently come top of the PISA rankings (see "External testing", p. 294) and may therefore be considered to have had its reputation strengthened as a result; they offer a critique of the OECD as an organisation with considerable (by implication, excessive) influence, operating within a neo-liberal paradigm. Martens and Balzer (2004) adopt a political science/governance approach to draw an interesting contrast between the OECD and the European Union, demonstrating how international policy work can have unintended consequences for its sponsors. Wolter *et al.* (2004) discuss one of CERI's (see next section) reviews of national educational research and development (England), and I have followed this with a broader account of this process in different countries (Schuller, 2006).

None of these accounts focuses specifically on lifelong learning. However, a collection of essays published in honour of Jarl Bengtsson, the Swede who led CERI for many years, addresses different aspects of lifelong learning. The essays are written by range of authors, some of them former or current OECD staff, some of them researchers who have worked as consultants (Istance *et al.*, 2002). I draw on some of these below; for the time being it is enough to observe that there is no single OECD paradigm: although the basic approach is one of promoting lifelong learning in a world of increasing global competition, there is a variety of views both on the definition of the current situation and on prescriptions for the research and policy agenda.

## OECD activities and their relevance to lifelong learning

The Directorate for Education consists of five programmes or divisions: Education and Training Policy Division (ETP); Centre for Educational Research and Innovation (CERI); Programme for International Student Assessment (PISA); Programme on Educational Building (PEB) and Programme on Institutional Management in Higher Education (IMHE) – (see www. oecd.org/edu). But, rather than give a bureaucratic description of each of these, I shall present different kinds of major activity that they variously engage in, and that have a link to lifelong learning.

### Reviews of educational policy

Because of their specific focus, OECD's *national reviews* can have a direct, visible causal effect on policy. These may be of a single country, more often of a sector rather than the whole education system. A recent example of this includes the review of higher education in Ireland (OECD, 2007a). Lifelong learning as such has only been the topic of a national review once, for Norway in 2001, but such reviews can and do refer to lifelong learning in relation to the particular sector; indeed, the role of higher education in lifelong learning was a significant focus in the Irish report.

Thematic reviews include a number of countries, rather than single country reviews whose outcomes will be of limited interest to the other Member countries. Recent thematic examples include one on tertiary education, with 14 countries (see www.oecd.org/edu/tertiary/review); and, most relevantly, one on adult learning, carried out in 17 countries (OECD, 2004c). A thematic review on lifelong learning in its overall sense would be an exciting if daunting prospect – but it would require the political commitment of countries to make it a priority.

Three points are worth making for those unfamiliar with the OECD review process. First, participation is voluntary. Countries are not obliged to take part in any of these reviews. They are part of a peer learning process, but Member countries do not try to force other countries into participating, nor does the Secretariat. Second, the expert examiners are chosen by the Secretariat in consultation with the country, to achieve an appropriate mix of expertise. Third, the outcomes of the reviews are recommendations. Again, there is no obligation on the country to act on these; their impact depends both on the quality of the analysis and on the domestic political climate. It is worth stressing that the impact may not be immediate; OECD reports may rather prepare the ground for medium-term policy reform. But the OECD is not a law-making body; hence its recommendations are less subject to negotiation and compromise, and can on occasion be quite forthright and controversial.

## External testing

The most well-known example of the OECD's evaluation work is the huge Programme for International Student Assessment, or PISA (OECD, 2004a). This is a direct test of the competences of 15-year-olds, carried out on a three-yearly cycle and now with more non-OECD countries participating than Member countries. The last test, in 2006, covered some 450,000 students in over 60 countries. The fact that the tests – focused on literacy, numeracy and IT competences – are direct (having been very carefully standardised across different countries and cultures), rather than proxies based on qualifications, gives PISA its extraordinary power. The PISA website attracts far more hits than any other OECD activity – somewhat to the chagrin of the mainstream economists – and its results attract huge headlines, especially in some countries, such as Germany.

The key relevance of the PISA activity to lifelong learning is the information it supplies about the foundation that young people have as they embark on their adult careers and lives (e.g. OECD, 2001d). In particular, it points to the major discrepancies in achievement within, as well as between, countries, and suggests some of the reasons for these, notably in the extent of premature tracking in the system and in the degree of autonomy given to schools.

Currently in preparation is another major exercise of a similar kind but with more direct relevance for lifelong learning and especially adult learning: the Programme for the International Assessment of Adult Competences (PIAAC). This is due to be launched in 2010, with the first results not coming on stream before 2012 – the efforts and lags involved in mounting cross-country comparative testing of this order are enormous. PIAAC will test the learning outcomes of adults of working age – defined as 15–64. It builds on previous international studies such as the International Adult Literacy Survey (IALS) (OECD, 2001a) and the Adult Literacy and

Life Skills Survey (ALL) (OECD, 2005a), but addresses the issues in a broader context and with the goal of providing information over time rather than on a cross-sectional basis. It will include not only literacy, numeracy and IT skills, but also data on non-economic outcomes such as health (see also OECD (2007b) for analysis of the links between education and social outcomes). PIAAC confronts several very difficult methodological issues that were not present for PISA, for instance to do with sampling appropriately across the age range and how to reach the respondents, who are as adults not compulsorily present in educational establishments.

PISA has been controversial at a number of levels, both technical and political (e.g. Prais, 2003), and PIAAC is likely to be also. One reason is of general political significance: PISA has in part had such an impact because its comparability meant that international league tables could be constructed, and these raised major outcries in some countries for which the ranking was considered to be a national embarrassment. There is no doubt that this opened up room for educational change in an almost unparalleled fashion. Equally, however, overemphasis on the league table itself can obscure the positive use of the results to improve performance, wherever a country may be ranked. This is an issue that would certainly impinge strongly on any attempt to produce international comparisons of lifelong learning: a good question for educational policy analysts is, would league tables of national performance on lifelong learning be helpful?

## Innovation and good practice

As its name implies, the Centre for Educational Research and Innovation (www.oecd.org/edu/ceri) has a particular focus on innovation. The innovation may be in policy or in practice, and includes new thinking in conceptual terms. Outstanding examples relevant to lifelong learning are the seminal report on recurrent education (OECD, 1973), of which more later, and the report on *The Well-being of Nations*, which introduced social capital into the lexicon of international educational policy (OECD, 2001b). CERI has a strong orientation towards futures thinking, aiming to identify issues that are only barely on the policy horizon and encouraging policy-makers and practitioners to engage in debates that broaden the range of possible future options (OECD, 2001c, 2006a).

A series of CERI activities that deal specifically with case studies of good practice runs under the title of *What Works*. Here a theme is chosen, and countries are invited to participate in the activity by identifying a small number of examples of good practice. These are then analysed using a common framework, with the goal of identifying common features and developing benchmarks for countries to use in promoting innovation internally. The 'sample' of countries and cases is not scientific in the strict sense; rather, an attempt is made to achieve a reasonable spread to illustrate different experiences around the common theme. A recent strengthening of the scientific basis has involved including literature reviews in different languages, embedding the different cases in a broader research base.

Two particular examples of *What Works* studies are particularly relevant to the theme of lifelong learning. The first was published in 2000 under the title *Motivating Students for Lifelong Learning* (OECD, 2000). It covered three case studies from each of eight countries, presenting formal and informal initiatives designed to appeal to marginal youth. The second, to be published in 2008, deals with the teaching, learning and (especially) assessment of adults with low basic skills. The main aim here is to peer into the black box of adult pedagogy in order to identify innovative approaches to assessing learning by this group of learners. A previous study (OECD, 2005b) drew heavily on Black and Wiliam's seminal study (1998) to show how beneficial formative assessment (continuous feedback) can be to lower secondary students. The overall conclusion was the need for a more careful policy balance between formative and summative assessments – a warning against over-reliance on high-stakes testing. In the case of adults the argument has an added dimension: continuing to stress the value of formative assessment while acknowledging that information on what adults have actually learnt in different programmes is a legitimate concern for policy-makers and practitioners alike.

## Lifelong learning: a narrative on development

The OECD played a significant, though not dominant, role in the emergence of lifelong learning as an exciting if not always clearly formulated policy concept or goal in the early 1970s. It formed part of a trio of international organisations that promoted the notion, each with its own emphasis (see Kallen, 2002). UNESCO's vision was promoted across the world by the Faure Report, whose breadth reflected the organisation's worldwide membership and general cultural remit (Faure, 1972). The OECD's line was more geared to economic development, but nevertheless with a very strong social dimension and particular emphasis on the inclusion of social disadvantage as an issue to be addressed. The so-called 'clarifying report', *Recurrent Education: A strategy for lifelong learning* (OECD, 1973), formed the basis for much policy debate over the next decade, with its radical call for a rethink of the way educational opportunities are distributed over the life course. This was not an extension of current provision, but an alternative pattern. Finally, the Council of Europe expressed itself largely within the UNESCO cultural domain, but with a more limited geographical range.

Several accounts have described how the original vision of a significantly different pattern of educational provision has been diluted over the decades by a mixture of inbuilt policy conservatism and harsher economic climate (e.g. Papadopolous, 2002). In particular, the idea that the expansion of educational systems should not mean the continuous extension of initial schooling but a better balance of opportunities over the life course has been effectively defeated as countries compete with each other to see how high a proportion of their youth cohorts they can enrol in higher education (Schuller *et al.*, 2002 ). Lifelong learning remains something that all OECD Member countries explicitly say they believe in. But the wry query of the 2003 publication, *Beyond Rhetoric? Adult learning policies and practices*, signals a partial acknowledgement that lifelong learning aspirations are honoured more verbally than in reality. So what are the key components of this somewhat paradoxical position?

First, there is a reasonable consensus that a *secure foundation* must be laid for every individual if lifelong learning is to have effective meaning for the population as a whole. A major recent study on pre-school education, published under the title *Starting Strong*, was careful to emphasise that effective policies on pre-school had to be seen in this context (OECD, 2006b). Without universal high-quality provision for very young children, lifelong learning for all is simply not a realistic prospect. The scope of debate and analysis on lifelong learning is therefore extended, and not only in the sense of covering all ages. For a further component of the *Starting Strong* analysis is the need for cross-sectoral provision that brings in health and social services. The evidence on the lasting effects of early childhood education, positive and negative, is sufficiently compelling.

Second, there is some recognition that the *school curriculum* should lay the foundations for lifelong learning. The PISA report referred to earlier addresses this directly. Countries may be able to boost their school performance very significantly, but the effect will not last if they are unable to change their school practices to ensure lasting competences such as learning to learn rather than knowledge implants that will have a shorter and shorter half-life. Korea is a potential example here: a country that has achieved a huge spurt in educational achievement at secondary level, and whose families spend enormous proportions of household income on education, but where the expansion risks falling short because the schooling is not designed to enable young students to keep learning autonomously.

Third, the roles of *technology and qualifications* or certification are increasingly interlinked, in a way that has not been foreseen or properly analysed. On the one hand, technologies are opening up learning opportunities that are time- and space-free, so that people of all ages can have access. CERI has recently published analyses of e-learning within higher education (OECD, 2005c) and more recently of the exciting trend towards Open Educational Resources, that is, digitalised materials placed on the web with free access to them (OECD, 2007c). Often – for example in the United States and Japan – it is highly prestigious universities that are doing this, either to boost further their reputation or as a way of meeting social goals (or a mixture of both). But access to the materials does not enable people to gain a qualification from these universities. The same is true of many other materials that are now publicly or commercially available. At the same time, many employment systems demand formal qualifications to a greater extent than before. This therefore raises the question of who will control the certification process, and how the relationship between learning and assessment will work, as technologies enabling freeing up and at least some labour markets press for formalisation.

Fourth, as you might expect, OECD pays some attention to the *financing* of lifelong learning. In the 1970s there was some prospect that paid educational leave might follow in the wake of paid holidays to become a standard feature of employment contracts, and a six-country study explored different legislative (as in France and Germany) or collective bargaining (as in Italy) arrangements (OECD, 1975). Since then the prospect of individual or collective rights to educational leave as such has receded. Instead we see exploration of systems of financing lifelong learning that focus on the complementary roles of different stakeholders in enabling such systems to be put in place, nationally, locally or occupationally, under the heading of 'co-financing' (OECD, 2004b). As with other educational policies, developing adequate tools for allocating costs and benefits fairly and efficiently is a key feature of OECD work.

Finally, the potential impact of *demographic trends* has yet to be properly assessed, although everyone is broadly aware of them. In some countries the contraction of the population is quite dramatic, with birth rates falling well below replacement. In Japan, for example, the population is projected to drop from around 120 million today to 105 million in 2025, with no tradition of immigration to counter this. The implications for institutions of post-compulsory education are considerable, but the most likely response at present seems to be to reduce capacity rather than increase opportunities for older people. The OECD has argued for training for older workers and for longer working careers as a component of combined employment and social security policies (OECD, 2006c); but there is little sign of any real adjustment within education systems to reflect these trends, despite the fact that they affect almost every Member country.

## Conclusions: a rough balance sheet

It would be tendentious to attempt to produce an overall evaluation of the OECD's work on lifelong learning, and anyway inappropriate for a serving member of the Secretariat to do so. But as a partial framework for judging progress in policy thinking it might be possible to propose a number of different dimensions, and append some comment (rather than evidence) on the OECD's contribution under them. The list of dimensions is not at all comprehensive.

## Does lifelong learning include initial schooling?

The 1973 Clarifying Report on recurrent education contained remarks on the reforms to schooling implied in its strategy, and based part of its rationale on how initial schooling itself could never properly address social inequalities. However, the main thrust was concerned with alternation of work, education and leisure in the adult (i.e. post-compulsory school) life course. The radical message of that approach arguably remains as valid as ever, even though the 'lockstep' of education–work–retirement – anyway never true for women – has crumbled into highly variegated work career patterns. The OECD's work has covered pre-school as a foundation for life, and the evidence on the performance of lower and upper secondary schools in laying the platform for future learning. Curricular issues tend to receive less attention. Given the remorseless prolongation of initial education in most countries, the relationship between schooling and lifelong learning remains a central issue.

## Efficiency of the distribution of educational opportunity over the life course

The OECD is much concerned with efficiency, that is, the best use of resources to achieve given ends, and rightly so. One of the most powerful arguments in favour of lifelong learning is that it allows a more efficient allocation of resources than a system that attempts to retain young people in formal education for as long as possible and then underperforms in providing subsequent opportunities. Here the OECD made the original case very powerfully, but has subsequently tended to treat adult learning as a necessary additional process rather than as part of an overall system.

The assumption is that extending initial education is inherently a positive move, for individual and system. Here there is a tension. For the individual, in a competitive labour market, getting an early advantage (or at least not being disadvantaged) is usually significant for most of the subsequent decades, at least in terms of earning power and employment security. Education is a positional good, and the benefits to those who attain the position remain strong. From the wider policy point of view, the position is less clear. There is strong evidence that economies benefit as a whole when qualification levels go up, and it seems that people at the lower end benefit more from this absolute gain than they lose from being at a relative disadvantage; so this suggests a positive sum game. On the other hand a more sophisticated approach would suggest that people learn best when motivated and the current system attempts to persuade too many young people to learn in contexts that do not motivate them, especially those without the cultural capital that might help them to make the necessary adjustment. Moreover, evidence from work bringing together neuro-scientific and educational research suggests that, while brains are more plastic (i.e. capable of developing over the life course) than is often assumed, the maturational period for young people is also longer, and it is therefore asking for trouble to attempt to institutionalise them in formal educational settings (OECD, 2007d).

## The equity argument

This is closely linked to the previous point, since those who fail early often come from relatively disadvantaged backgrounds. Here the OECD has, perhaps contrary to some popular belief, consistently argued for the need for equity in education and training. Some of this argument is phrased in cold economic terms, that is, economies and societies cannot afford to have a long tail of unskilled and marginal dependants. But this is inseparable from value positions as articulated by most Member countries, who wish also to address the problem of social justice and equal opportunity. Their urgency in this is not inversely related to their success in dealing with it (in other words, countries with big equity problems are not necessarily the ones most concerned to do something about it), but it is a strong common theme. The recently concluded thematic review on equity, though focusing on schools rather than lifelong learning, illustrates the point (see www.oecd.org/edu/equity/equityineducation).

## Labour market and demographic issues

Paid work remains a defining feature of most people's lives, for good and less good reasons. The quality of working lives shapes the nature of lifelong learning: in the access it provides to education and training opportunities, on and off the job; in the extent to which the job itself is suitably stimulating; and in the extent to which it pays sufficiently for people to afford to be customers in the growing market for lifelong learning. Assessing trends in all these areas is a key challenge, against a changing employment and demographic background. The OECD is arguably the major global provider of basic information on these issues, at least for its Member countries. It is strongest on the first set of issues, puts some emphasis on the third, but deals less with quality of work issues.

I have already indicated that few systems exhibit any serious engagement with the educational implications of the emergent aging of our societies. This dimension intersects with both of the previous ones, but with particular angles. On the efficiency side, there is a strong case for inter-sectoral coordination: can education play a part in maintaining health and independence among older people – and hence contribute to containing the additional welfare costs that older populations inevitably bring? On the equity side, as younger generations gain more and more access to higher education, and therefore higher qualifications, there is a risk they will crowd out older people who may have significant experience but not the up-to-date certificates.

## Statistics and indicators

The OECD's hallmark is the production of reliable and reasonably up-to-date statistics to aid policy-making and research. Figures on participation rates in all kinds of formal education are routinely gathered, now in great profusion: the best-selling *Education at a Glance*. Originally launched as a slim compendium of educational statistics, it is now a 450-page doorstop, still eagerly awaited as an annual publication. However, the further we get away from formal education, the less reliable and comprehensive the figures become. Capturing adult education generally in its various forms is a formidable challenge that has only been addressed very partially. This is, to some extent, inevitable, but it does hamper the building of an adequate knowledge base on lifelong learning.

Here the recommendations of Albert Tuijnman, a former OECD staff member, stand as key elements of any strategy for improving the knowledge base (Tuijnman, 2003):

- changing a front-loaded and input-oriented statistical system;
- covering life-wide learning: non-formal and informal;
- measuring cumulative learning across the lifespan;
- including a wide range of outcomes.

To these I would add the need to combine such quantitative information with qualitative studies and experimental designs, to give a full range of insights into the effectiveness and impact of lifelong learning.

## Note

1    This chapter is written in a personal capacity and does not engage the OECD in any of its views.

## References

Black, P. and Wiliam, D. (1998) 'Assessment and classroom Learning', *Assessment in Education: Principles, Policy and Practice* 5(1): 7–74.

Faure, E. (Chair) (1972) *Learning to Be*, Paris: UNESCO.

Istance, D., Schuetze, H. and Schuller, T. (eds) (2002) *International Perspectives on Lifelong Learning: From recurrent education to the knowledge society*, Buckingham: The Society for Research into Higher Education/Open University Press.

Kallen, D. (2002) 'Lifelong learning revisited', in D. Istance, H. Schuetze and T. Schuller (eds) *International Perspectives on Lifelong Learning: From recurrent education to the knowledge society*, Buckingham: The Society for Research into Higher Education/Open University Press, pp. 32–8.

Martens, K. and Balzer, C. (2004) 'Comparing governance of international organisations: the EU, the OECD and educational policy', TransState Working Papers, University of Bremen.

Organization for Economic Cooperation and Development (OECD) (1973) *Recurrent Education: A strategy for lifelong learning*, Paris: OECD.

—— (1975) *Educational Leave of Absence*, Paris: OECD.

—— (2000) *Motivating Students for Lifelong Learning*, Paris: OECD.

—— (2001a) *International Adult Literacy Survey* (IALS), Paris: OECD.

—— (2001b) *The Well-being of Nations*, Paris: OECD.

—— (2001c) *What Schools for the Future?*, Paris: OECD.

—— (2001d) *Knowledge and Skills for Life: First results from PISA 2000*, Paris: OECD.

—— (2003) *Beyond Rhetoric? Adult learning policies and practices*, Paris: OECD.

—— (2004a) Learning for Tomorrow's World: First results from PISA 2003, Paris: OECD.

—— (2004b) *Co-financing Lifelong Learning Towards a Systemic Approach*, Paris: OECD.

—— (2004c) *Promoting Adult Learning*, Paris: OECD.

—— (2005a) *Adult Literacy and Life Skills Survey* (ALL), Paris: OECD.

—— (2005b) *Formative Assessment: Improving learning in secondary classrooms*, Paris: OECD.

—— (2005c) *E-learning in Tertiary Education: Where do we stand?*, Paris: OECD.

—— (2006a) *Think Scenarios, Rethink Education*, Paris: OECD.

—— (2006b) *Starting Strong II: Early childhood education and care*, Paris: OECD.

—— (2006c) *Live Longer, Work Longer*, Paris: OECD.

—— (2007a) *Higher Education in Ireland*, Paris: OECD.

—— (2007b) *Understanding the Social Outcomes of Learning*, Paris: OECD.

—— (2007c) *Giving Knowledge for Free: The emergence of open educational resources*, Paris: OECD.

—— (2007d) *Understanding the Brain: The birth of a learning science*, Paris: OECD.

Papadopoulus, G. (1994) *Education: The OECD perspective 1960/1990*, Paris: OECD.

—— (2002) 'Lifelong learning and the changing policy environment', in D. Istance, H. Schuetze and T. Schuller (eds) *International Perspectives on Lifelong Learning: From recurrent education to the knowledge society*, Buckingham: The Society for Research into Higher Education/Open University Press, pp. 39–46.

Prais, S.J. (2003) 'Cautions on OECD's recent educational survey (PISA)', *Oxford Review of Education* 29(2): 139–63.

Rinne, R., Kallo, J. and Hokka, S. (2004) 'Too eager to comply? OECD education policies and the Finnish response', *European Educational Research Journal* 3(2): 454–85.

Schuller, T. (2006) 'International policy research: evidence from CERI/OECD', in J. Ozga (ed.) *Education Research and Policy: Steering the knowledge-based economy,* London: World Yearbook of Education, pp. 131–52.

——, Istance, D. and Schuetze, H. (2002) 'From recurrent education to the knowledge society', in D. Istance, H. Schuetze and T. Schuller (eds) *International Perspectives on Lifelong Learning: From recurrent education to the knowledge society,* Buckingham: The Society for Research into Higher Education/Open University Press, pp. 1–22.

Tuijnman, A. (2003) 'Measuring lifelong learning for the new economy', *Compare* 33(4): 471–82.

Wolter, S., Keiner, E., Palomba, D. and Lindblad, S. (2004) 'OECD examiners' report on educational research and development in England', *European Educational Research Journal* 3(2): 510–26.

# 27

# UNESCO's drive for lifelong learning

*Adama Ouane*

Lifelong learning is a continuous process, present in all cultures, societies and religions. The provision of lifelong learning opportunities over the entire life span is a sine qua non if communities, individuals and organizations are to be able to handle and make effective use of knowledge, skills, values and capacities and also to contribute to their creation and transformation. Often referred to as a 'master concept' and a 'guiding principle', the advent of lifelong education involved a reinterpretation of the notion of education as a whole. This meant integrating into an overall conception the partial insights and experiences gradually gained through the solution of specific educational problems. Lifelong learning takes many different complementary forms of a sequential as well as parallel nature. The individual is always at the hub of this process – all other components of the educational process should combine to develop his or her capacity for self-directed learning (Careli, cited in Dave, 1976: 9)

The idea of lifelong learning rests upon integrating learning and living both *vertically*, over an individual's whole life from birth to death, and *horizontally*, that is to say involving all aspects of a person's life – family, community, study, work and leisure. It is horizontal also in the sense of taking place within all learning systems – formal, non-formal and informal. Lifelong learning enables individuals to lead fulfilling lives, and to be able to understand themselves and their surroundings and the consequences of their actions. It helps them to be responsible not only for themselves, but for others as well, and to have the capacity to perform with ease and self-confidence the roles and functions demanded in different settings, so as to be able to live as a family member, a friend, a worker, an employee, an entrepreneur, a member of society, a citizen of a nation and ideally a world citizen.

The concept of lifelong learning is not new. The vision of learning from birth to death is an ancient one that is shared by many societies and religions. The term, however, gained currency following the growth in education after the Second World War. Permanent education and recurrent education were early manifestations of its conceptualization. It grew from concepts such as 'fundamental education', 'continuing education' and 'basic education'. UNESCO never equated these concepts with minimal education but saw them as fundamental to all learning and an essential part of further and lifelong education. Lifelong education was consolidated from the 1970s, and in the early 1990s the term was replaced by 'lifelong learning' or 'learning throughout life', as advocated by the Delors report (1996).

The roots of this concept, however, can be traced back to much earlier times. To give a few examples, Plato spoke in the *Republic* about *dia viou pedia* as the obligation of every citizen to learn for the ultimate good of the city and the community. For Yeaxlee (1929), education should be seen as a lifelong process, and he pointed out that lifelong education is reflected in the knowledge, experience, wisdom, harmony and self-realization manifested in the practical affairs of ordinary men and women. Along with Lindeman (1926), he provided an intellectual basis for a comprehensive understanding of education as a continuing aspect of a person's everyday life rather than merely a preparation for an unknown future. The whole of life is learning, therefore education can have no end (Lindeman, 1926: 4–5). John Dewey expressed the view that the trajectory of adult learning must begin with the education of children. 'To prepare him (the child) for future life means to give him command of himself . . . so that he will have the full and ready use of all of his capacities' (1966: 27).

The growth of adult education provision is opening the door to further learning for an increasingly large number of adults, and is giving a new dimension, meaning and value to the act of learning, which is becoming a means and an end as well as a lifelong and lifewide process. Paul Lengrand, who was in charge of lifelong education at UNESCO in the 1960s and 1970s, describes lifelong education as representing 'an effort to reconcile and harmonize different stages of training in such a manner that the individual is no longer in conflict with himself/herself' (Lengrand, cited in Dave, 1976: 35). In the 1970s, B. Suchodolsky pointed out:

> The great need for adult education could no longer be explained by the fact that many people had to make up for educational deficiencies of childhood and adolescence. Now the need for adult education is accounted for by the fact that in many relevant fields the kinds of learning skills required demand a certain maturity which is found only in adults. Thus the field of adult education manifests the value of education which permeates the whole course of life. Once education has become available to all, it will no longer be a factor in the formation of an elite and in the stabilization of its position. While retaining its value as a means of preparation for social and vocational tasks, education acquires a value of its own. It is no longer desirable as a means of advancement in society, or because of the financial benefits it brings, but as means of developing a need for and interest in cultural values, because it corresponds to the orientation of human liking and propensities, and because it makes life more colorful and more worthwhile. Thus education helps to intensify our awareness of the values of life and so creates one form of human happiness.
>
> (Dave, 1976: 63)

## UNESCO's drive for lifelong learning

Since its creation, UNESCO has focused on the right to education for all throughout life. It was the first international organization to develop the concept of continuing education, present already in the idea of 'fundamental education' defined as 'a campaign to raise educational standards both at level of children and adults' (UNESCO, 1947: 159).

When writing about the idea of evolutionary humanism, Julian Huxley, the first Director-General of UNESCO stated in 1957:

> this new vision is based upon the enlargement of knowledge, not only or even mainly in the natural sciences, but equally in the social sciences and the humanities. From these

303

bits and pieces of new knowledge, new realizations and new understandings, man is capable of forming a new picture of himself, of his place in nature, his relations with the rest of the universe, his role in the universal cosmic process – in other words, his destiny; and on that in turn, building new and more adequate beliefs . . . In becoming aware of his own destiny, man has become aware of the entire evolutionary process on his planet; the two are interlocked.

(Huxley, cited in Dave, 1976: 107)

One of the first definitions of lifelong education was that given by Paul Lengrand and R.H. Dave in a UNESCO report of 1970, in which they regarded lifelong education as:

[a] process of accomplishing personal, social and professional development throughout the lifespan of individuals, in order to enhance the quality of life of both individuals and their collectives. It is a comprehensive and unifying idea which includes formal, non-formal and informal learning for acquiring and enhancing enlightenment so as to attain the fullest possible development in different stages and domains of life.

(Dave, 1976: 34)

Suchodolsky, Dave and Lengrand, among others, argued that the meaning of education itself had to be understood in a new way. And as Lengrand pointed out:

Education is not an addendum to life imposed from outside. It is no more an asset to be gained than is culture. To use the language of philosophers, it lies not in the field of 'having' but in that of 'being'. The being in a state of 'becoming' at each different stage and in varying circumstances is the true subject-matter of education.

(Dave, 1976: 63–4)

These early definitions have two significant features. One is the way in which they are underpinned by humanistic values, and the second is their evolutionary nature. The standpoint of UNESCO and its Member States has always been that education is a process of development in human life closely connected with the humanistic values transmitted from Socrates down to Comenius and Dewey. The underlying assumption is that modern civilization has to lay foundations for sound values and to create the motivation for their full realization, and that this is possible only through education. According to this view, education is a value in itself and not merely a means of gaining higher social status or material advantages. Consequently education should aim at a more general human development.

If the educational process is to include all stages of life, its whole character will be fundamentally changed. Also the objective of each stage will change. The educational process will no longer be confined to school and book-learning and concerned with merely intellectual faculties. It will embrace the totality of human life, experience and activity. As Suchodolski, Lengrand and Dave agreed, it will promote maturity of feelings, power of imagination, strength of mind, curiosity and a sense of responsibility for one's words and actions in social contexts. Most of the above statements about lifelong education might not appear new. Now however, the attempt is being made by UNESCO to use this concept as a norm for educational practice and reform at national level and for the whole range of relevant groups and educational services.

## Contributing structures and institutional arrangements

UNESCO promoted lifelong education through a section at its HQ from the 1960s to the 1980s, with a particularly dedicated International Commission of eminent personalities, resulting both in the Edgar Faure report of 1972, *Learning to Be: The world of education today and tomorrow*, and the Jacques Delors report of 1996, *Learning: The treasure within*. Another organization playing a major role in promoting lifelong is the UNESCO Institute for Lifelong Learning (UIL), formally the UNESCO Institute for Education (UIE), located in Hamburg, Germany. Lifelong learning has been a particular focus of this Institute since 1972. Its activities include action research, training and capacity building, networking, and the sharing of experience so as to strengthen the foundations of lifelong learning and promote policies, concepts and practices to institutionalize lifelong learning worldwide. Over the past few decades the Institute has acquired a large store of knowledge and expertise on many different dimensions of the lifelong learning concept and its use as a guiding and organizing principle of educational reforms.

The concept of lifelong education was crystallized in the 1972 Faure report, which was considered to be a turning point and the start of an optimistic phase in international education policy. The architecture of the Faure report was organized around three concepts: the vertical integration, the horizontal integration and the democratization of education systems. (Holford *et al.*, 1998: 7). It was recognized that education was no longer the privilege of an elite, or a matter for one age group only; it should be *both universal and lifelong*. Essentially this meant moving to a humanistic, rights-based and holistic view of education. The Faure report proposes 21 guiding principles for the implementation of lifelong education.

The studies in the 1970s, undertaken particularly by R.H. Dave (as lead researcher and later Director of UIE), were concerned with conceptual characteristics including 'educability' (Dave, 1976), but also with curriculum issues, in particular self-direction, content and evaluation. His much-used book, *Foundations of Lifelong Education* (1976), provided guidelines for identifying and developing specific goals, content, methods, evaluation procedures, educational structure and so forth. It helped to open up the perspectives of lifelong education in order to obtain insights necessary for formulating educational policies, plans, structures and so on.

Under Dave, UIE carried out an exploratory study, *Curriculum Evaluation for Lifelong Education*, together with three national teams, from Japan, Sweden and Romania (Skager and Dave, 1977), which referred to the 21 guiding principles of the Faure report and arrived at a set of 20 concept characteristics of lifelong education, which describe such things as its meaning, function, goals and relationships. For example, lifelong education seeks to view education in its totality. It covers formal, non-formal and informal patterns of education and attempts to integrate and articulate all structures and stages of education along the vertical and horizontal dimensions. The study also defined three major prerequisites for realizing the goals of lifelong education: learning opportunity, motivation and educability. These goals include the full development of the individual's adaptive and creative functions, leading to the continuous improvement of the quality of personal and collective life (Dave, 1976: 35–6).

Already during this study the Swedish team discussed if it would be better to use the concept of lifelong learning instead of lifelong education. In the report the Swedish authors took the following position:

In this report we often use the term 'Lifelong Learning' and not 'Lifelong Education'. This is because we think that the word learning suggests the individual's own activity in connection with learning. Behind this lies the educational hypothesis: the individual himself is the only person who can be active in such a way that learning takes place.

(Skager and Dave, 1975: 9)

For Paul Lengrand:

> In any learning process the stress can no longer be laid on a necessarily limited and arbitrarily fixed content; it must bear upon the ability to understand, to assimilate and analyze, to put order into the knowledge acquired, to handle with ease the relationship between the abstract and the concrete, between the general and the particular, to relate and action, and to co-ordinate training and information. In a setting of Lifelong Education this is tantamount to equipping the human being with a method which will be at his disposal throughout the length of his intellectual and cultural journey.
>
> (1975: 55)

Lengrand related lifelong education to awareness of global issues that transcended particular human societies, such as human rights, justice and equality (Lengrand, 1975).

One of the most radical views of lifelong education was that of Ettore Gelpi. For him, lifelong education was 'fundamentally concerned with conceptualizing an alternative perspective on global education' (Gelpi, 1979). Replacing Paul Lengrand as Head of the Lifelong Education Section at UNESCO HQ, Gelpi wanted the organization to echo the call for deeper transformation in education, exemplified by Freire's radical pedagogy. He was not followed by the leadership of the Education Sector and almost single- handedly ran the unit without institutional support. He gained several followers, especially among young researchers outside the organization, and made a significant impact on many universities. His merit was to link the concept to the world of work and focus on the situation of the poorest and marginalized segments of the population (Gelpi, 1979).

The theme of lifelong education was also treated by the Club of Rome report of 1979, *No Limits to Learning* (Botkin *et al.*, 1979), upon which UNESCO had a great influence: innovative learning and anticipatory learning were the new focus and the new context, requiring individuals to be able to analyze and to transform new knowledge and information into creative problem-solving, through which they could develop responsible values and attitudes. A broad-based mobilization of the creative talent inherent in every human being was considered to be the only way to enable people to understand and adapt to changing conditions and to make progress in an increasingly complex world (Longworth, 2003).

## The change from lifelong education to lifelong learning

By the mid-1990s a clear preference had emerged for the term 'lifelong learning' rather than 'lifelong education'. There are differing views on the major distinction between these two concepts, but it is generally felt that 'lifelong education' reflects a view of education as a pre-scriptive and normative process, while 'lifelong learning' puts the emphasis on learner demand and individual choice.

The World Conference on Education for All (WCEFA, Jomtien, 1990) defined basic education as a foundation for lifelong learning and aimed at meeting the basic learning needs of all people. This conference clearly referred to the ultimate goal of lifelong learning and educational transformation. Its *Declaration* pointed out:

> basic learning needs comprise essential learning tools such as literacy, oral expression, numeracy and problem solving required by human beings to be able to survive, to develop their full capacities, to live and work in dignity, to participate fully in development, to improve the quality of their lives, to make informed decisions and to continue learning.

The WCEFA in Jomtien 'advocated an expanded vision of basic education. However this vision was not translated into practice over the 1990s in the aid-assisted countries in the South' (Torres, cited in Medel-Añonuevo, 2002: 4).

In the 1990s two important transformative shifts took place, both of them linked to the influence of UNESCO. The first was brought about through the publication of the above-mentioned Delors report, *Learning: The treasure within* (1996). The report was produced by the International Commission on Education for the 21st Century, set up by UNESCO and chaired by Jacques Delors. This was a continuation of the Faure report, but it also updated and adjusted the latter for the age of globalization and the new economy, while insisting on the retention of core values such as 'learning'. The Delors report recognized that lifelong learning is essential in order to equip human beings to live meaningful lives and meet whatever challenges they will face. This report defined four pillars of learning: learning to know, learning to do, learning to live together and learning to be. Another pillar could be added to these, namely learning to learn. This implies developing the ability to work out how new tasks can be tackled, to transfer competencies to new situations, to analyse problems, to put order into the knowledge acquired, to handle with ease the relationship between the abstract and the concrete, between the general and the particular, to relate knowledge and action, and to coordinate training and information (Lengrand, 1975: 55). As Lengrand had underlined much earlier, both individual and social competencies have to be acquired, consolidated and renewed. This involves transmission through various different educational institutions.

The Delors report, while acknowledging the changes in the world of work and the decisive influence of the market, still reflected UNESCO's rights-based, humanistic, transformative approach to learning, underlining the need for developing skills and attitudes that enable people to live in peace with each other despite religious and cultural differences, and linking learning with common human moral and ethical values. In other words this approach saw learning as being about more than just the acquisition of skills and competencies related to work, the economy and the market. This contrasts with the approach of the OECD, the EU and the World Bank, which tend to view lifelong learning as being primarily work- and economy-related. Even if they recognize wider goals of lifelong learning, such as creating active citizens, their main emphasis is on employability. The Delors approach also emphasized the importance of competencies and skills needed for lifelong learning itself, as well as the importance of knowledge in the context of the increasingly knowledge-based societies of the modern world.

The Delors report focused on *why* lifelong learning is important rather than *what* it is important for. The report urges us to 'rethink and update the concept of Lifelong Learning so as to reconcile three forces: competition, which provides incentives; cooperation, which gives strength, and solidarity, which unites'. It speaks of the foundational element of learning. We have to look further than that and speak about a foundational curriculum.

The Delors report also encouraged the three UNESCO educational Institutes – the Institute for Educational Planning (IIEP), the International Bureau of Education (IBE) and, in particular, the UIE – to commission action research and other studies that afford greater understanding of lifelong learning in action around the world.

Following the Faure report, the Delors report pointed out the urgency of embedding lifelong learning as educational principle in policies and programmes:

UNESCO has included Lifelong Learning in its medium term strategy from 1996 to 2001. At the reflective level it proposes:

- The fundamental right of every human being to learning throughout life.
- The adaptive integration of educational institutions into an overall framework of Lifelong Learning.

- An increase in the provision of self-directed learning which can be incorporated into the context of an individual's work and life. Connected with this is the creation of a world–wide network of open-learning centers through which people can both communicate and learn new skills and competencies.
- The development of learning societies in which institutional provision and life experience become sources of learning which enhance the individual's ability to cope with change.

(Norman Longworth, 2nd draft, Eus, France, 1998)

The second shift, in which UNESCO again played a pre-eminent role, was linked with the Fifth International Conference on Adult Education (CONFINTEA V), held in Hamburg in1997, which welcomed the concept of lifelong learning and sought to connect it with a strong obligation to achieve 'a learning society committed to social justice and general well-being'. It was emphasized that lifelong learning should be a necessary principle to guide educational policy makers everywhere and should not be the prerogative of a developed society. The CONFINTEA report pointed out:

> the objectives of youth and adult education, viewed as a lifelong learning process, are to develop the autonomy and the sense of responsibility of people and communities, to reinforce the capacity to deal with the transformations taking place in the economy, in culture and in society as a whole, and to promote co-existence, tolerance and the informed and creative participation of citizens in their communities; in short to enable people and communities to take control of their destiny and society in order to face the challenges ahead.

(UNESCO, 1997)

It was indicated that adult learning has grown in depth and scale.

Following the Delors report as well as the OECD and EU drives, CONFINTEA V as a UNESCO-led conference marked the triumph of the concept of 'adult learning' as the new paradigm, as against 'adult education'. As indicated in the *Hamburg Declaration* (UNESCO, 1997), adult education has grown in depth and scale and has become imperative at the workplace, at home and in the community, as men and women struggle to create new realities at every stage of life. Adult education plays an essential and distinct role in equipping women and men to respond productively to the constantly changing world and in providing learning that acknowledges the rights and responsibilities of the adult and the community. Adult education is both a consequence of active citizenship and a condition for full participation in society. The conference underlined the importance of social transformation and empowerment through the fundamental acquisition of skills, competencies and knowledge. UNESCO considers this humanistic approach to learning to be fundamental for the twenty-first century.

Subsequent initiatives, such as the Dakar Framework for Action (DFA) in 2000, the United Nations Literacy Decade, and the Decade of Education for Sustainable Development, have all stressed the importance of lifelong learning as a key to the twenty-first century.

The DFA (World Education Forum, April 2000) confirmed the *World Declaration on Education for All*, approved at Jomtien. It represents a collective commitment to achieve Education for All (EFA) by 2015, according to six goals set for the future:

(i)    expanding and improving comprehensive early childhood care and education, especially for the most vulnerable and disadvantaged children;

(ii) ensuring that by 2015 all children, particularly girls, children in difficult circumstances and those belonging to ethnic minorities, have access to and complete, free and compulsory primary education of good quality;

(iii) ensuring that the learning needs of all young people and adults are met through equitable access to appropriate learning and life-skills programmes;

(iv) achieving a 50 per cent improvement in levels of adult literacy by 2015, especially for women, and equitable access to basic and continuing education for all adults;

(v) eliminating gender disparities in primary and secondary education by 2005, and achieving gender equality in education by 2015, with a focus on ensuring girls full and equal access to and achievement in basic education of good quality;

(vi) improving all aspects of the quality of education and ensuring excellence of all so that recognized and measurable learning outcomes are achieved by all, especially in literacy, numeracy and essential life skills.

(UNESCO, 2000: n. 7)

With the resolution 51/116, the UN General Assembly proclaimed the United Nations Literacy Decade (UNLD) for the period 2003–12 as a contribution to the goal of EFA and decided that UNESCO should play a coordinating role in stimulating and catalysing the activities undertaken at international level within the framework of the Decade. This challenging task required UNESCO to promote the creation of a literate environment under the slogan 'Literacy as Freedom'. UNLD also endorses the expanded notion of literacy, which is not limited to the generic skills of reading, writing and calculating, but is instead a human right related to development. The definition of literacy may vary from one cultural and linguistic group to another, and may change over time. It cannot be encompassed by a one-off learning process occasion but only by lifelong learning.

The Literacy Decade presents the international community and UN Member States with an unparalleled opportunity to increase their efforts to meet the literacy and non-formal education (NFE) goals within EFA and the Millennium Development Goals. In particular, the Decade gives special attention to achieving a 50 per cent improvement in adult literacy by 2015 as well as equitable access to basic and continuing education for all adults (EFA goal 4). It also focuses on meeting the learning needs of those who are excluded from quality learning (EFA goal 6).

## UIE becomes UIL

A new momentum in UNESCO's drive for lifelong learning was the institutional transformation of the UNESCO Institute for Education into the UNESCO Institute for Lifelong Learning. In 2006 UIE became:

[a] fully fledged UNESCO institute specialized in literacy non-formal education and adult and lifelong learning in fulfillment of the mandate of UNESCO. It was decided that the UIL should focus on the following activities:

a) Strengthening adult and lifelong learning by working with and providing services in its areas of competence to UNESCO member states, to international and inter-governmental agencies, to NGOs, grassroots and community associations and to partners in civil societies and private sectors.

b) Fostering a holistic and integrated approach to Lifelong Learning based on awareness of different needs with special concern for the disadvantaged and marginalized.

c) Helping to build bridges and networks for cross-fertilization and sharing of knowledge, experience and tools in the areas of literacy, non formal eduction and adult and lifelong learning within and between nations, with special emphasis on least developed countries.

(UNESCO, 2006)

A whole programme cluster was set up exclusively devoted to lifelong learning. The overall objective of the lifelong learning cluster of UIL is to:

- promote knowledge partnerships within the expanding international community of lifelong learning;
- strengthen UIL further as an international centre and platform for advancing lifelong learning and multi-dimensional best practice research across the world;
- showcase leading innovations in the area of lifelong learning for active citizenship, workforce development and social integration;
- create more dynamic forums where research will be combined with practice, interfacing and informing one another;
- share ideas and research insights and promote dialogue and collaboration between regions and between countries;
- promote learning societies.

## Conclusion

While acknowledging the fact that economic issues are important, UNESCO upholds a holistic and integrative view of lifelong learning, giving emphasis to the social and humanistic dimensions, which are not quantifiable in economic terms, such as learning for critical thinking, learning for critical and active citizenship, and intercultural learning. Lifelong learning means looking at the human being as a whole, as well as looking at life in all its manifold aspects.

Adopting lifelong learning as a new paradigm for education and learning in the twenty-first century is not adopting a slogan or opting for an abstract 'edutopia'. It implies defining in each particular context, even for each individual learner or group of learners, the kind of learning content, modalities and goals that are called for.

Lifelong learning is only to be recommended if it is offered within a framework of liberal-democratic values, such as justice, independence and autonomy. It should also be underpinned by such values as respect for the traditions of indigenous peoples, for different religions and for the environment. Lifelong learning, in turn, can help to inculcate and cultivate these values. At the same time it can provide the conditions and capacities for genuine empowerment and inclusion. This necessitates working through both the formal and informal sectors in education, which is why there is a need for close cooperation between these sectors.

UNESCO has not created a uniform schema of lifelong learning. There cannot be a uniform implementation strategy that all countries can follow. There cannot be a 'common definition' of lifelong learning, because definitions vary not only over time but also between regions, countries and different fields of study. Cultural, linguistic and national diversity has to be kept in mind and be respected.

Practices will need to build upon specific national traditional and cultural heritages, and policies should be modified to suit particular conditions and needs. Even though the scope and content of strategies for lifelong learning may well be unique to the specific circumstances of countries, certain questions are pertinent to all, whether economically developed or developing (Husén, 1977).

There are, as we have seen, differing views concerning the aim of lifelong learning, when one compares the EU, the OECD, the World Bank and UNESCO. However, all four organizations share the view that learning is meant to be for all, that it should continue throughout life and that there is a need for strong cooperation between formal, non-formal and informal education. What is needed therefore is a synergy between these organizations, combining their respective strengths and competencies.

If lifelong learning includes all sectors of life and society, then its potential for transformation is far-reaching. It can help to alleviate poverty, ensure democracy, combat inequality and extremism, promote world peace, create a better balance between developed and developing countries, and encourage people to live decently as human and social beings in a harmonious society, understanding and respecting themselves and others, tolerating difference and diversity, and being always open to dialogue and new perspectives.

## References

Botkin, J.M., Elmandjra, M. and Malitza, M. (1979) *No Limits to Learning: Bridging the human gap*, Oxford: Pergamon Press.

Dave, R.H. (ed.) (1976) *Foundations of Lifelong Education*, Oxford: Pergamon Press (for UNESCO Institute for Education).

Delors, J. (Chair) (1996) *Learning: The treasure within*, Paris: UNESCO.

Dewey, J. (1966) *Selected Educational Writings* (ed. F.W. Garlath), London: Heinemann.

Faure, E. (Chair) (1972) *Learning to Be: The world of education today and Tomorrow*, Paris: UNESCO.

Gelpi, E. (1979) *A Future for Lifelong Education*, Manchester: Manchester University Press.

Holford, J., Jarvis, P. and Griffin, C. (1998) *International Perspectives on Lifelong Learning*, London: Routledge.

Husén, T. (1977) 'An agenda for the education of world citizens', *Prospects* 27: 201–5.

Lengrand, P. (1975) *An Introduction to Lifelong Education*, London: Croom Helm, and Paris: UNESCO.

Lindeman, E. (1926) *The Meaning of Adult Education*, New York: New York Republic.

Longworth, N. (1998) *Modern Approaches to Lifelong Learning, OECD, UNESCO, European Commission and Key Factors for Measuring and Monitoring Progress*, A preliminary discussion paper for international governmental organizations (IGOs) and Government, Paris: OECD.

—— (2003) *Lifelong Learning in Action: Transforming education in the 21st century*, London: Kogan Page.

Medel-Añonuevo, C. (2002) *Integrating Lifelong Learning Perspectives*, Hamburg: UIE.

Skager, R. and Dave, R.H. (1977) *Curriculum Evaluation for Lifelong Learning*, Oxford: Pergamon Press.

UNESCO (1947) *Fundamental Education: Common ground for all peoples: Report of a special committee to the Preparatory Commission of the United Nations Educational Scientific and Cultural Organization*, Paris: UNESCO.

—— (1997) *Fifth International Conference on Adult Education, Final Report, UNESCO Paris: Contributing to a more sustainable future: quality education, life skills and education for sustainable development*, Paris: UNESCO.

—— (2000) *Dakar Framework for Action*, Final Report of the World Education Forum, Dakar, 26–28 April, Paris: UNESCO.

—— (2005) *World Report Towards Knowledge Societies*, Paris: UNESCO.

—— (2006) 'Proposal to change the name of UIE to UIL', UNESCO Executive Board, 174th Session, 5 April, Paris: UNESCO.

Yeaxlee, B. (1929) *Lifelong Education: A sketch of the range and significance of the adult education movement*, London: Cassell.

# 28

# Learning for development
## The work of the Commonwealth of Learning

*John Daniel*

The Commonwealth of Learning (COL) is committed to promoting lifelong learning as a means of achieving development objectives. By contributing to the effective use of distance learning and information and communications technologies (ICTs) at all levels, COL helps countries apply educational technology to their own needs.

## What is COL?

The Commonwealth of Learning is a Commonwealth intergovernmental organisation created by the Heads of Government at their meeting in Vancouver in 1987. It has its own Board of Governors with representation from around the Commonwealth, a headquarters office in Vancouver and a unit in New Delhi, the Commonwealth Educational Media Centre for Asia. Our staff of 40 includes professionals who are recruited from throughout the Commonwealth and serve on rotation. COL is also supported by an extensive network of collaborators in all regions and we have a focal point – a main contact person – in each country.

COL's purpose is to help Commonwealth governments and institutions use a variety of technologies to improve and expand education, training and learning in support of development. We have a special focus on open and distance learning (ODL), because it has proven its cost-effectiveness in many countries. ODL provides economies of scale, country-wide geographical reach and flexibility. A special project that we are coordinating on behalf of Ministers is the Virtual University for Small States of the Commonwealth. The Ministers of Education conceived this idea at their conference in Canada in 2000 and endorsed a proposal three years later when they met in Edinburgh. Twenty-seven small states of the Commonwealth are now engaged in making this a reality.

COL's core budget comes from voluntary contributions from Member States. The six largest donors, with automatic seats on COL's Board of Governors, are Canada, India, New Zealand, Nigeria, South Africa and the United Kingdom. In the 2003–6 period we also had contributions from 27 other governments. Our aim is to have all Commonwealth countries contribute something – we believe that COL gives them good value.

While a basic principle of COL is that we are not a teaching institution, we raise extra-budgetary funds by helping international organisations with their staff development. We have been doing this for some time with the International Federation of Red Cross and Red Crescent Societies, the International Labour Organization (ILO), the Joint United Nations Programme on HIV/AIDS, the UN Refugee Agency, the World Bank and the World Health Organization (WHO). These eLearning courses focus on specific areas such as editorial skills and report writing.

## The impact of learning technologies

The Commonwealth Heads of Government formed COL 20 years ago to exploit the potential of learning technologies. Were they right about this potential? Has it justified their expectations? COL recently conducted a review of the use of learning technologies in four areas that makes a strong case for supporting the application of technology to learning.

### Higher education

A good example of the growth of technology-mediated learning over the past two decades is the multiplication of open universities in the Commonwealth. The number has grown from 10 in 1988 to 23 open universities today (2007) with an enrolment exceeding four million students. But open universities are only part of the story. Over these 20 years there has been a massive increase in the number of campus universities functioning in 'dual mode' – teaching at a distance as well as in classrooms. On a global scale, enrolment in higher education is growing beyond the most optimistic forecasts as developing countries recognise expanded higher education as the key to attaining developed country status.

### Teacher development

Teacher education at a distance is now a vibrant activity. The numbers being trained are impressive: hundreds of thousands in Africa and over one million in India. COL has contributed substantially to this trend by helping to increase capacity for distance learning in countries as diverse as The Gambia, India, Lesotho, Nigeria and Sri Lanka. Recently, COL worked with Zambia to formulate a strategy for using ODL and ICTs in both pre- and in-service teacher development. Teacher education administrators from all countries of the Commonwealth have received support through an annual COL-sponsored workshop series in Singapore. Some of COL's most recent work has focused on raising standards by developing Commonwealth quality assurance guidelines with partners in Asia and Africa.

### Open schooling

As countries strive towards achieving universal primary education, many more youngsters are finishing primary school. Sadly, most of them have little chance of getting into secondary school. There are simply not enough secondary schools or the trained teachers to staff them. Ministries of education are therefore turning to alternative means of secondary schooling. Open schooling uses high-quality self-instructional materials coupled with networks of local centres staffed with capable facilitators trained to support the learners. Recent successes in Asia and Africa show that open schooling is a feasible alternative to classroom education. It increases access to schooling in a timely, efficient and cost-effective manner and is especially good for reaching girls, women and other disadvantaged groups that have difficulty accessing conventional schooling on a full-time basis. For example, there are now some 1.5 million children enrolled in the open schooling system in school-level and technical/vocational training courses in India alone. COL has worked with India's National Institute for Open Schooling (NIOS) to update its production processes for quality learning materials and to extend awareness of the potential of open schooling in India. As a result, NIOS is now working with state governments to establish 14 state open schools across India.

### Non-formal learning

Finally, the basic development agenda of improving health and reducing poverty and hunger calls for learning on a massive scale, with the focus on improving livelihoods and fostering a healthy population. While the content of learning in these areas is necessarily very locality-specific, economies of scale have been achieved by sharing similar models for technology use and learner support. Improving livelihoods in rural areas is central to world poverty reduction. These livelihoods are mostly farming-dependent, and agricultural extension is still largely based on face-to-face communication and demonstration. However, since the Green Revolution of the 1960s, communications technology has also been applied to agricultural extension. Radio remains the most important medium for communicating with the rural populations of developing countries. This is particularly true in Africa where there were already 65 million radio receivers a decade ago. More recently, video has become an important medium for agricultural education, the basic principle being to empower agricultural extension officers by teaching them camera and video production skills for use at the local level. This supports government policies of crop diversification among small-plot farmers in response to changing patterns of trade.

These are just four examples of the growing role of distance learning – broadly defined – in development. The challenge for COL now is to build on these successes, a challenge we embraced in a comprehensive new plan.

## The three-year plan, 2006–9

COL's new three-year plan is called simply *Learning for Development*, because that is our business. Achieving the Millennium Development Goals (MDGs), not just in education but also in health and hunger, is basically a matter of mass learning. Conventional methods cannot cope with the scale of the learning challenge. COL helps countries use technology to increase the scope and scale of learning. The plan is based on the premise that creating sustainable livelihoods for billions of young people is the key development challenge. It is a diverse world and a diverse Commonwealth. However, contemporary technology can help us to complete the unfinished development agenda.

Feedback from the Commonwealth for this plan also underlined the development disaster that is HIV/AIDS, the importance of learning for women and the imperative of bridging the digital divide. COL also commissioned a formal external evaluation of our work in 2003–6. It told us that we should offer fewer programmes and continue them for longer; we must match government priorities with a programme focus, not a project focus; we must strengthen teamwork while taking full advantage of the tremendous skills and experience of our individual staff members; and we must always work in partnership. Our plan tries to do all those things.

We think of development as the combination of the MDGs, the Dakar Goals of Education for All and the Commonwealth values of peace, democracy, equality and good governance. This led us to divide our activities into three sectors: Education, Learning for Livelihoods and Human Environment. In our activities and initiatives we aim for one or more of four outcomes:

- The longer COL exists, the more we observe that successful use of technology for learning depends on laying down a foundation of policy.
- Much of COL's work is capacity building to help systems that involve technology-mediated learning to work better.
- We try to analyse our areas of work in terms of models. This helps us understand why something works and the ingredients of its success. It also helps in transferring the programme to a different country.
- Although we do not develop materials ourselves, we help institutions to produce them. COL then tries to get them used across the Commonwealth.

## Specific areas of focus

Those are the outputs and outcomes we aim for in each of our initiatives. To keep it simple we have five initiatives in each of the three programme sectors.

In Education, we offer help in:

- Quality Assurance;
- Teacher Development;
- Open or Alternative Schooling;
- Higher Education;
- eLearning for Education Sector development.

These are the areas to which governments attached most importance in our consultations with them.

Similarly, in the sector of Learning for Livelihoods we have five areas of endeavour:

- Learning and Skills for Livelihoods, where the aim is to find ways of translating learning as directly as possible into improved livelihoods.
- Our Rural and Peri-Urban Community Development Initiative, which is our successful programme for improving the prosperity of farmers.
- National and International Community Development refers particularly to working with the international organisations in the agriculture sector to extend our poverty reduction programme.
- Transnational Programmes, which are courses and materials whose use we facilitate around the Commonwealth. The best example is the Commonwealth Executive MBA and MPA programmes, developed in South Asia but now being adopted in Africa, the Caribbean and the South Pacific.
- The Virtual University for Small States of the Commonwealth (VUSSC) (see p. 316).

The final sector, which we shall develop further in the coming years, is Human Environment. The five initiatives are:

- Gender and Development;
- Health, Welfare and Community Development;
- Environmental Education;
- Good Governance and the Educational Use of Mass Media;
- ICTs.

All this is done with a budget that is tiny by any measure. However, governments seem convinced that they get great value from COL. Our fundamental strength is that Ministers like us and trust us. From their point of view, COL's assets are that we work for them, we have first-rate expertise in educational technology, we stress South–South cooperation, we focus on locally driven development and we have some proven models of development that work.

## The Virtual University for Small States of the Commonwealth

The Virtual University for Small States of the Commonwealth (VUSSC) is an important initiative in the Learning for Livelihoods sector. COL has secured funds for the development of VUSSC from two sources: the William and Flora Hewlett Foundation of the USA and the Commonwealth Fund for Technical Cooperation (CFTC). The CFTC has allocated £1 million over four years as part of its policy of supporting human resource development in the Commonwealth.

A major use of these funds has been to hold planning, organisational and course development meetings around the Commonwealth. Although much of the work of course development will take place online and at a distance, we believed that, to get the project going, people needed to meet. One thing we had to get right is the subjects on which courses and programmes will focus. There has been widespread agreement among the governments of small states that VUSSC should focus on skills and livelihood related courses.

A very important milestone in the development of VUSSC was the first course development meeting held in Mauritius in August 2006. It was quickly nicknamed the 'Boot Camp' because, for many participants, it was a basic training in working and collaborating online. Participants were introduced to the ICT components of VUSSC, open source software, Wikis and ePortfolios.

Participants at the Mauritius boot camp created content on Tourism and Hospitality and on Small Business Management – three times as much material as we expected in the time available. This course development work is continuing as participants contribute online from their offices at home. Participants picked up skills fast and are now providing buddy-training to their colleagues back in their countries. This illustrates what a useful tool VUSSC will be in bridging the digital divide.

COL became involved with VUSSC after the Conference of Commonwealth Education Ministers in Halifax, Canada in 2000 when Ministers asked COL to work up a proposal with them. Since then we have coordinated the initiative. We have put all our considerable expertise in educational technology at the disposal of the participants, we have assisted in building local capacity and we have obtained funds for the programme.

But it is important to understand what COL is not. COL is not a degree-awarding body. COL is not the Virtual University. Awards made as a result of VUSSC study will be made by institutions in the countries. We are working with them and the South African Qualifications

Authority to facilitate arrangements for credit transfer and recognition of qualifications. This is not COL's project; it is the Ministers' project. Ministries of Education have a crucial role in developing policy to fit national priorities; in liaising with other ministries where courses are of interest to them; in allocating people; and generally in supporting and monitoring the implementation of the programme.

The beneficial impact of VUSSC will depend very directly on the extent to which Ministers get their people engaged and have them take responsibility for it. VUSSC must develop in close collaboration with local institutions, which will have the responsibility for linking into the international teams developing the courses and then adapting and delivering them in appropriate ways in each country.

## Models of learning for development

Our Lifelong Learning for Farmers programme – L3 Farmers – is a successful example of learning for development in the area of Learning for Livelihoods. We are extremely proud of this initiative on Rural and Peri-Urban Community Development, which takes dead aim at the Poverty MDG. L3 Farmers began in India and is now being replicated in Sri Lanka and Africa.

The model, like most of our models, is simple but effective. We start at the grassroots and get the farmers to define their vision of a better future and the questions it raises. We then get the information providers (such as agricultural universities) to work together to answer those questions, using commercial ICT kiosks as an information channel. Then, banks and businesses get involved, attracted by the prospect of a more prosperous village.

In one village in Tamil Nadu, India, for example, the farmers decided that better dairying was the way to a more prosperous future. Their first question was how to tell a good milk cow from a poor one. The information providers came up with a checklist. Some of the village women, who had learned some web programming skills, converted the list into an instructional sequence on the ICT kiosk. This generated other learning needs, such as testing the quality of the milk, because the bank got a dairy company in the local town to guarantee regular purchases of good-quality milk. The banks then started loaning money.

Two years later, the results are good. Loans of $200,000 dollars have been made with a repayment rate of more than 100 per cent because some are repaid early. Hundreds more loans are in preparation. The farmers, 60 per cent of whom are women, are more prosperous and more empowered. Best of all, the model is spreading spontaneously from village to village without COL's involvement. We shall launch it in Sri Lanka very soon, and discussions are going on in several African countries.

In the Human Environment sector, COL has had success with our work in Health, Welfare and Community Development. Another simple model of learning for development – what we call Media Empowerment – is a contribution to tackling the three Health MDGs. It began in Africa but is now being adopted in Asia, the Pacific and the Caribbean. The model begins with a partnership with WHO. Local WHO offices identify effective local non-governmental organisations (NGOs). COL equips the NGO with a complete set of video recording and editing equipment, which costs less than $20,000, and then trains it intensively in its use. The NGO then shoots and edits videos on health matters, usually HIV, the stigma of AIDS, malaria or, soon, diabetes. These videos communicate very effectively because they are made by the people for the people. To reach the audience, the NGO often uses what we call village cinema: they go to a village at night, hang up a sheet between two trees, and project the video using a projector powered by a generator on the back of a pick-up truck.

In The Gambia, it is estimated that some 60 per cent of the total population have seen videos aimed at the prevention of HIV/AIDS and malaria. The government says they have had a substantial impact on reducing HIV transmission and increasing the number of people using insecticide-treated bed nets. It is effective and inexpensive. COL refreshes the equipment from time to time, but otherwise this is development without donors. This model has been successfully implemented in a dozen Commonwealth countries in all regions of the world.

## Moving forward

From COL's perspective, the increasing disparities between developing countries are a disturbing geopolitical trend. Fortunately, India (the Commonwealth's largest country) seems set to continue robust economic growth that will make major inroads into poverty reduction and generate extra resources to expand education and training in the coming years. But it is harder to be optimistic about the future of some of the Commonwealth's smaller states that are faced with one or more of the challenges of civil strife, fragile democracy, rising sea levels, high HIV infection rates, deteriorating natural environments and the collapse of traditional cash crops.

Nearly all developing countries, however, share the phenomenon of young population profiles, with median ages between 20 and 25 years. The pressure for more education, training and jobs for young people can only become more acute. This will intensify governments' interest in:

- developing alternative methods of education;
- making more effective links between schooling, training and livelihoods;
- encouraging private investment in education;
- establishing regulatory frameworks, especially at the tertiary level.

Two continuing trends will ensure that ICTs play an expanding role in the life of developing countries. Connectivity will continue to increase as countries adopt more liberal regulatory frameworks and telecom monopolies face more competition. Meanwhile, the price of electronic hardware continues to fall. The overall cost of software may also fall dramatically as the Free/Libre Open Source Software (FLOSS) movement continues to gain ground.

In economic terms, the communications revolution will have its greatest impact in the developing world through the spread of mobile telephony. Mobile phones will provide greater benefits to ordinary people than laptop computers will. At the same time, an easing of regulations may give a boost to community mass media (both radio and TV), which will have beneficial effects on development. The growth of eLearning will have a transformative effect on ODL that may be primarily semantic and harmful at first, but more profound and positive in the longer term.

Already, the growing use of eLearning as a synonym for ODL poses two challenges. First, the international development agencies often combine conservative views on educational methods with scepticism about the value of high-tech solutions in developing countries. Just when they have realised that mass ODL is the only way to scale up access to education beyond the primary level, the renaming of ODL as eLearning is unhelpful because it makes the activity sound more electronic than it really is – even in industrialised countries.

Second, the disappointing track record of 'pure' eLearning (i.e. online learning) in the industrialised world risks creating doubts about the effectiveness of ODL generally, just at a time when traditional mass ODL systems are beginning to have a major impact in developing countries. So far, online learning in the richer countries has rarely contributed either to open learning or to distance learning because many online enrolments are simply campus students seeking more flexible study timetables. Far from extending access and reducing costs, pure eLearning may, in such circumstances, actually curtail access for remote students and increase overall costs by adding new options for campus students without compensatory savings.

Nevertheless, COL must engage resolutely with eLearning because, in the longer term, it holds great promise for developing countries, as well as being a powerful symbol of the bridging of the digital divide. At present, the promise of eLearning lies less in the online delivery of materials than in the possibility of developing those materials through international online collaboration. COL has already done more than any other agency to foster the international sharing of ODL materials, but now – in the spirit of the FLOSS movement – it will be possible to create, distribute and adapt open educational resources much more easily. This will help to make VUSSC a vibrant reality that could serve as an example for larger states.

In this era of burgeoning information and communications media, COL is needed more than ever. Its role is to help countries and institutions make sense of the ICT revolution and use technology appropriate to their education and training systems and to expand learning generally.

COL has experience of a wide array of applications of technology to learning for many purposes and in diverse contexts. It has captured this experience in a number of models that help to identify the local factors necessary to ensure the success of any new activity that brings together people, institutions and technology. This allows countries to make judicious choices about learning for development.

# Part 6
## Social movements

# 29

# The role of non-governmental organisations and networks

*Alan Tuckett*

Wherever you look governments seem to have fallen out of love with adult learning. The World Bank has encouraged countries of the South to focus on securing universal primary education, failing to recognise that children who learn reading and writing in societies where none of the adults use those skills risk losing the skills rapidly once school is over; and failing to recognise, too, the key role of parents as partners in the educational process. Where the World Bank has led, bilateral and multilateral donors have all too often followed, narrowing the opportunities for adults to learn. Gone are the days when Nyerere could argue that, since Tanzania could not afford the luxury of waiting a generation for well-educated young people to emerge from schooling and transform the economy, it had better focus on teaching adults now.

A similar picture is to be found in much of the industrialised North. The pressures deriving from the growth of international trade, and increased competition, tempt governments to cut back on broad educational provision for adults, and to focus more and more effort on the preparation of labour market entrants. Where adult learning is supported, it is increasingly focused on utilitarian, work-related study, at the expense of public support for liberal education for active democracy.

These developments take place against a background of international policy initiatives that declaim the importance of lifelong learning. Throughout the 1990s United Nations (UN) conferences were held to address the key challenges facing the globe. At each event member states committed themselves publicly to implement jointly agreed agendas. From the environment conference in Rio de Janeiro in 1992, to the Cairo population conference in 1994, from the women's conference in Beijing in 1995, to the Education for All (EFA) conferences in Jomtien in 1990 and Dakar in 2000, each major world event identified roles for adult learning in improving the lot of the world's poor, and enriching the lives of all. That approach informed the UNESCO CONFINTEA World Conference on Adult Learning in Hamburg in 1997, and Jacques Delors' UNESCO study, *Learning: The treasure within* (1996). A striking feature of these UN conferences was the active engagement of civil society organisations in the process.

Again in the 1990s, a whole sequence of European Presidency conferences on dimensions of lifelong learning culminated in the European Union Lisbon memorandum on Lifelong Learning (EU, 2000). So far, at least, the warm words and promises made at international conferences have not been backed by sustained action in the majority of countries, and adult learning opportunities are, across the globe, under more pressure now than a decade ago, as governments juggle the competing demands of a variety of specific interests, and to remain solvent.

One key function of non-governmental organisations (NGOs) in general is to monitor gaps like this between what statutory bodies say and what they do – whether they are local, regional, national or transnational. A second key function is maintaining a steady commitment to the specific interest, whatever the focus of current policy. A third is to experiment and develop new forms of provision, and a fourth is to act as advocate, creating a momentum, often in alliance with other partners, to secure policy change to the advantage of the specific interest. In the current context all these tasks need to be undertaken to a high level of competence for the case for adult learning to be reasserted successfully in local and national practice and in the fiscal priorities of international funding agencies and major donors.

In this chapter I examine the effectiveness and impact of such interventions through an exploration of the work of the International Council for Adult Education (ICAE) at a global level, and the work of the National Institute of Adult Continuing Education (NIACE) in England and Wales – each of which seeks to influence policy made by governments and their agencies, and through a consideration of the emergence of the World Social Forum, as an alternative international space for people, rather than governments, to explore how best to learn from each other's experiences, and to develop convivial and democratic strategies for development.

## The International Council for Adult Education

The International Council for Adult Education (ICAE) was founded following the 1972 UN conference on adult education in Tokyo, to give a voice to NGOs working in adult education. It operated through regional associations – the largest and most dynamic of which were, perhaps, ASPBAE – the Asian South Pacific Bureau for Adult Education (which enjoyed active financial support from the Deutsche Volkshochschul Verband, DVV), CEEAL – Consejo de Educación de Adultos de América Latina, and EBAE, the European Bureau of Adult Education. The network had considerable success in securing funds from agencies in Scandinavia and Canada in particular and redistributing them to the countries of the South, and in developing transnational programmes on gender, sustainability and peace and conflict resolution. Like many organisations, however, the period following Budd Hall's charismatic leadership saw a decline in activity, and despite considerable impact on the conclusions of CONFINTEA, the Hamburg UN conference on adult learning, donors became uncertain about its priorities and effectiveness.

This diminution in activity led the Nordic funding agencies, who were substantially the largest supporters of ICAE, to cooperate in commissioning an evaluation of the work of the Council in 2000, which was undertaken by Arne Carlsen and Anette Svensson. Their report made major recommendations on the governance, programme and focus of the Council's work, which were overwhelmingly accepted by the Council at its World Assembly in Ocho Rios, Jamaica in 2001. Despite this, and in part as a result of the swing towards support for primary education fostered by the World Bank, ICAE's external funding reduced dramatically.

Nevertheless, the new Board of the Council, led by Paul Bélanger, elected President following his retirement from the UNESCO Institute for Education, and Celita Eccher, the Secretary General, set about regenerating the network. The Ocho Rios conference charged ICAE with concrete tasks to undertake. First among these was the preparation of a monitoring report, to scrutinise the actions taken by national governments to enact the agreements made at CONFINTEA, key elements of which had been reconfirmed at the EFA Conference in Dakar.

The CONFINTEA Agenda for the Future was built around a critical examination of ten key themes:

- adult learning and democracy: the challenges of the twenty-first century;
- improving the conditions and quality of adult learning;
- ensuring the universal right to literacy and basic education;
- adult learning, gender equality and equity, and the empowerment of women;
- adult learning and the changing world of work;
- adult learning in relation to environment, health and population;
- adult learning, culture, media and new information technologies;
- adult learning for all: the rights and aspirations of different groups;
- the economics of adult learning;
- enhancing international cooperation and solidarity.

The analysis adopted by the conference accepted that education had a vital enabling role to play across the range of social policy – impacting on the success of health policies and environmental initiatives as well as on the individual and communal development of learners. In designing a tool for monitoring how far governments had followed up on the commitments made at the conference, ICAE adopted a tool that focused on these themes, but subsuming finance and quality in its consideration of the other themes, and considering media and technology as subsets of promoting active citizenship. In addition, recognising the importance of the EFA conference at Dakar for adult education, ICAE added consideration of the two key EFA goals impacting on adult education.

The Council then sought to report in detail on developments in a representative sample of 20 countries, selected according to their placing on the Human Development Index (HDI), ranging from Japan (9th) to Senegal (145th) in the 2001 Human Development report. In the event, non-government partners in 17 countries contributed to the study. The HDI was chosen since it incorporates economics (gross domestic product), health (life expectancy) and education (literacy rates) – reflecting the Hamburg conclusion that adult learning impacts across the social policy agenda. The product of this work, *Agenda for the Future – Six Years Later: The ICAE report* (ICAE, 2003), was authoritative, and its conclusions powerful. It found, perhaps unsurprisingly, that governments had done most to address adults' opportunities in work-related adult learning. In literacy, the report found that 'although some countries made important efforts regarding their illiterate population, only one of them, Bolivia, made noticeable progress in terms of coverage'. On active citizenship, human rights and peace adult learning, the report's findings were bleak:

> Improvements have been documented in a minority of countries and in a few areas, but we cannot refrain ourselves from comparing these small improvements with the current cold reality of disrespect for human rights, of wars, of violations of international laws by international dominant forces and rampant discrimination.
>
> (ICAE, 2003: 4)

Overall, the report found little connection between a country's place on the HDI and its commitment to adult learning. Its impact at the UNESCO mid-term review on progress since CONFINTEA was dramatic, and contrasted strikingly with the poverty of paperwork from UNESCO itself. At a conference where a small minority of states sent official delegations, and where Sir John Daniel, the Assistant Director for Education at UNESCO, used his keynote address to tell adult educators that they were seen as 'boring, sanctimonious, backward-looking and parentalist' (2003), the international NGOs demonstrated a measured professional and dedicated determination to hold member states of UNESCO to account for the promises they had freely entered into. While no one can be contented with the gap between aspiration and practice in the field globally, ICAE can take considerable credit for the UNESCO decision to sustain the 12-year cycle of global adult education conferences, with CONFINTEA VI in Brazil in 2009. At that event, ICAE will have a key role as a recognised civil society partner in the work of the main conference.

A second dimension of ICAE's work following the Ocho Rios conference was borrowed from the experience of the transnational women's network, DAWN. DAWN had organised intensive residential training seminars in international advocacy work for young activists and emerging leaders, to great effect. ICAE adopted the model and, with the support of the Norwegian aid agency, the national Norwegian folk-high school association, and with a tutorial team drawn from each continent, ICAE ran the first of its annual advocacy training workshops, attracting 30 to 40 emerging and younger leaders to develop skills in representing the interests of adult learners, nationally and internationally. The graduates of this programme play an increasingly visible role in regional and global policy for advocacy, and thereby ensure that experience and skill in transnational work is not concentrated in too few hands.

The third innovation in ICAE's work seeks to overcome the difficulty that most adult learning organisations are poorly resourced, and that transnational cooperation and sharing of experience is expensive, and inevitably privileges those who can afford to travel. Using the internet, ICAE has supplemented its regular newsletters by mounting moderated virtual seminars in advance of major international conferences, to ensure that members across the world can help to shape the experience of events they cannot attend. This was used to powerful effect at the CONFINTEA mid-term review, where the findings of the seminar were published so that each delegate could benefit from the findings of such wide discussions, a process repeated at a global conference on poverty and adult learning hosted in Botswana.

These developments have revitalised the work of the Council at a time when its funding base was eroding, as its major donors shifted priorities away from adult learning, or from infra-structural agency support to local initiatives. Its resilience and imagination, and the remarkable dedication of its Uruguay-based secretariat have, fortunately, led to modest renewal of support in particular from Scandinavian donors, and from the resources of some members. However, the fragility of the finances are a constant challenge for an organisation whose representative tasks must always exceed the money available to undertake them.

There is, too, a tension in a federated body like ICAE, whose key members, the regions, are also reliant on a narrow and uncertain range of funding sources, that the success of one can be at the expense of the other. Once again ICAE has come out of a period of uncertainty about the balance of its responsibilities to support national and regional members, and to make an effective global case. While it remains more sure-footed in its relations with major networks such as the women's education alliances, REPEM in Latin America, and DAWN in Asia and Africa, nevertheless the success of the e-journal *Voices Rising*, and the practical benefits deriving from the International Academy for Lifelong Learning Advocates (IALLA), have established goodwill to overcome such tensions as persist.

## The National Institute of Adult Continuing Education

The National Institute of Adult Continuing Education (NIACE) attempts, at a national level, to parallel the work of ICAE in monitoring government policy, and helping to shape developments. It began life as the British Institute of Adult Education (BIAE) in 1921. BIAE itself was established as the British arm of an early and hopefully named World Association for Adult Education, with a membership of individuals committed to the field. In its first 20 years it demonstrated clearly the role voluntary associations can play in effective social innovation. Its committees and staff inspired, directly or indirectly, the establishment of an educational committee of the British Broadcasting Corporation (BBC), the founding of the British Film Institute (BFI), the establishment of the Arts Council, and the creation, during the Second World War, of the Army Bureau of Current Affairs (ABCA). These last two initiatives were the brainchildren of the Institute's Secretary, W.E. Williams, who first noticed an absence of public access to painting or sculpture in Northampton in the late 1930s, and set about changing this through the organisation of travelling exhibitions, backed by opportunities to find out about their context. The success of his Arts for the People initiative led on to the creation of a Council for the Encouragement of Music and the Arts, which became the Arts Council, with Williams as its first Director. Similarly, with the Army Bureau Williams argued, successively, that, if soldiers were to fight to preserve democracy, it would be as well if they knew something about it. Again, it was Williams who led the work of ABCA, on secondment from BIAE, commissioning short papers on topical issues as background for an hour a week's current affairs discussions.

This early period of innovation did not survive once the Institute had evolved into the National Institute of Adult Education (NIAE) in 1948, with the arrival of institutional members. Perhaps, too, the departure of such a powerfully innovative leader as Williams was followed by a period of consolidation. There was certainly a move away from the commitment to learning for social change that characterised the Institute's early years. During the 1940s and 1950s adult education in Britain became an arena for people to develop new leisure activities – with a dramatic growth in badminton and keep fit courses, and of classes in European languages, as the arrival of package holidays led more people to take foreign holidays.

The trigger for a change of direction came with the Russell report on adult education (1973), which identified key constituencies of adults with learning needs that current provision was failing to address. While the government failed to act on the recommendations, the field, led by the national institute, took the report's focus on disadvantaged groups as an agenda for a revitalised social purpose. From 1975, NIAE hosted the government-funded Adult Literacy Resource Agency (ALRA), created to support innovation in the teaching and learning of literacy at the time of a BBC campaign, 'On the Move', which stimulated thousands of adults to seek to improve reading and writing skills. Initiatives followed in women's education, in English for Speakers of Other Languages, and in work with adults with learning difficulties and disabilities.

The Institute's success with ALRA and its successor agencies led government to see it as a partner in later government initiatives, too. The REPLAN programme was supported from 1984–91 to offer educational opportunities to unemployed adults, and the Unit for the Development of Adult Continuing Education was supported from 1984 to 1992 to research and offer advice on adult learning issues of key importance to government. Both were impressive successes, yet they came at a price for the Institute, by now renamed NIACE, since the tension between the Institute's role as partner of government and its role as advocate for civil society organisations offering adult learning was substantially resolved by minimising those aspects of advocacy work that conflicted directly with government policy. Where such opposition was offered, it had the effect of ensuring that government support for national initiatives would be secured through discrete agencies administered by NIACE but directly accountable to government for policy.

Advocacy was reasserted as a central role in NIACE's work at the beginning of the 1990s, at a time when a government White Paper sought to end any public support for liberal adult education. The argument used in Parliament to justify this change was that there was no need to fund flower arranging on the taxes when what was needed was a focus on vocational education. Through the membership, NIACE found a Brixton florist, formerly a merchant banker, who had been to evening classes in flower arranging in Lambeth to prepare for his new job, and had employed half the people in the class in his shop. *The Independent* newspaper carried the story prominently, NIACE mobilised the National Federation of Women's Institutes, and the local education authority providers, generating more mail than the deeply unpopular poll tax. Within weeks, politicians were saying, 'Of course, flower arranging can lead to careers in floristry', and accepting that you cannot always tell the purpose of the student from the title of the course, and the government 'clarified' its position by abandoning the proposal.

The key lesson the Institute took from the campaign was that politicians were unaware of the great differences among adults taking courses, and of the complexity of their purposes in participating. It set about changing this through the vehicle of Adult Learners' Week – a festival designed to celebrate current adult learners in all their diversity, and to encourage others to emulate them. Once again it secured formidable partners in the enterprise. All the terrestrial television companies agreed to broadcast prime-time programming promoting adult learning during the week. The government department responsible for employment funded a free telephone helpline, which attracted 55,000 phone calls in a week, overwhelmingly from people who had not previously taken part in courses. By creating a permissive festival that anyone could use for their own initiatives, NIACE secured the partnership of thousands of local institutions. It was also successful in securing support from the European Social Fund.

Adult Learners' Week was a vehicle to demonstrate that the curriculum for adult learning begins with motivating and reaching adults. Few outside the workplace are obliged to take part. As the festival has grown over 16 years, the creativity of providers in developing new ways of reaching people has been impressive. Perhaps most memorable was the Merseyside initiative, Growing Old Disgracefully, where women who had denied themselves the full range of social expression earlier in their lives used the week for an extraordinary range of events. They sang opera from the top of an open double-decker bus, water-skied on the Mersey, abseiled down Council buildings, and far more besides. Learning at Work Day encouraged people to bring a daughter to the office or factory, to swap jobs and to share skills not normally used at work. This is adult learning as theatre. Harbans Bhola (1997) describes it as adult education as culture – where people demonstrate their passion for learning through public manifestations designed to change things – and as a complement to adult education as structure, the world of curricula, and registers, rules and regulations.

NIACE complemented the attention-seeking theatre of the week by ensuring that research was published, monitoring the impact of public adult learning policy. By representative sample surveys of the whole population, NIACE was able to keep a consistent focus on groups under-represented in current provision, as a challenge to politicians and policy makers alike. By engaging the All Party group for Adult and Lifelong Learning in support of the week, the Institute was able to secure a regular annual focus on the case for adult learning, and to identify sympathetic members of Parliament willing to speak on the issue in the legislature. Just as an earlier burst of creativity had led to the establishment of the Arts Council, the success of the Adult Learners' Week telephone helpline led to the creation of a permanent line, which is now embedded in the work of Ufi – formerly known as the University for Industry.

Adult Learners' Week attracted attention among non-government agencies and governments in other countries. The idea was borrowed and adapted (just as the UK initiative adapted a more modest programme of the US AAACE), and following CONFINTEA was adopted by UNESCO as an international week. It now takes place, in different forms in around 50 countries, and in the best form of conviviality organisers share experience and best practice on a regular basis. In the UK the week was significant in changing public attitudes towards adult learning, and in helping policy makers see the role mass media can have in stimulating participation among groups previously unengaged.

The cohort of learners who have been recognised through national and regional awards have, too, formed the nucleus of an adult learners' national forum stimulated by NIACE, and developed in Europe by its Scottish partner SALP (the Scottish Adult Learning Partnership). If NGOs were successful in securing a voice at global decision-making level at the CONFINTEA V event, the challenge is to secure a voice for learners' own organisations at the next world conference in Brazil in 2009.

Following the 1991 campaign to save publicly funded adult education, and the success of Adult Learners' Week, NIACE re-established an effective partnership as a critical friend of government. The Institute played an active role with each of the major political parties in developing lifelong learning policies, and co-managed major innovative programmes designed to develop community education initiatives in deprived communities. More recently, to reflect the effectiveness of NIACE's relations with government, it secured a voluntary sector compact with government that recognised the balance of risk in cooperative relationships between the state and voluntary bodies, by offering three-year security of funding, to deliver an agreed programme. Government recognised the benefit to be gained from NIACE's robust critique of public policy as a critical friend, and NIACE offered 'no surprises' – a guarantee that, when it disagreed publicly, or planned to campaign against proposals, it would inform government in advance. The Institute preserves independence by earning 90 per cent of its budget through trading activities (in research and development, consultancy, publications, conference and training services, and through information and advice services), yet secures through the compact regular consultation on issues affecting adult learning.

Preserving the confidence of members and government involves flexibility and a willingness to compromise in the short run, but to be intransigent about longer-term aims. It puts a premium on skills of communication, and engaging with the dominant discourse shaping public policy, to ensure that the interests of adult learners whose needs and interests are not well served by current arrangements are represented effectively. This does not guarantee that policies always serve adults' best interests as learners, but at least that decisions are taken in the full understanding of their impact on adults.

## World Social Forum

If much of the work of NIACE involves patient engagement with the dominant discourse of the day, an alternative strategy is perhaps best illustrated in the glorious flowering of the World Social Forum since 2001. The Forum was conceived, initially by a committee of Brazilian organisations, as:

> an open meeting place for reflective thinking, democratic debate of ideas, formulation of proposals, free exchange of experiences and interlinking for effective action, by groups and movements of civil society that are opposed to neo-liberalism, and are committed to building a planetary society directed towards fruitful relationships among Humankind and between it and the earth.
>
> (World Social Forum, 2001)

The first meeting of the Forum, at Porto Alegre in Brazil, was timed to coincide with the meeting of the World Economic Forum in Davos, where governments and corporate leaders meet annually, to offer rich alternatives to an economics that secures increasing profits for global corporations at the expense of the impoverishment of millions in the global South. The form of the Forum is in striking contrast to the organisation of many of its constituent members. The Forum does not seek to be a body representing world civil society. Indeed, as its Charter of Principles makes clear:

> The meetings of the World Social Forum do not deliberate on behalf of the World Social Forum as a body. No-one, therefore, will be authorized, on behalf of any of the editions of the Forum, to express positions claiming to be those of all its participants. The participants in the Forum shall not be called on to take decisions as a body, by vote or acclamation . . . it thus does not constitute a locus of power to be disputed by the participants in its meetings, nor does it constitute the only option for interrelation and action by the organizations and movements that participate in it.
>
> (World Social Forum, 2001)

Despite the conscious decision not to become an organisation, the Forum has grown into a powerful, dynamic site of learning and social intervention, linking organisations and movements that believe that 'another world is possible', and that we can create it together. The philosophy of the Forum's founders share much in common with the confidence of the Plebs League writer who argued that 'it will be a smart policeman who can arrest the spread of ideas'. The World Social Forum attracts hundreds of thousands of participants – landless peasants, women's organisations, literacy campaigns, trade unions, anti-war activists, environmental groups, development economists, aid agencies and adult educators alike rub shoulders in a cacophony of marches, seminars, workshops, street theatre and public lectures – reminding participants that the spaces for learning from one another, and imagining alternative ways of addressing common problems rely not solely on the agency of states or the mechanisms of the market, but upon the agency of people working cooperatively. The Forum, which has held global meetings in Asia and Africa as well as Latin America, and has spawned regional and national forums, is a vivid new manifestation of popular education, fundamentally committed to human rights, offering the energy generated in autonomous spaces. These spaces can be transformative for participants working day to day in very different contexts. As Gigi Francisco, the distinguished feminist put it:

> We are in the WSF to engage in liberative cultural translations of our visions and alternatives. We are here because we continually seek spaces and create moments, albeit briefly, to live out our individual self-consciousness because we could not find our authenticity in a world system that has been so constructed and structured on domination and hegemonic control. And we are here to contribute to the specific project of inter-linking differentiated struggles and resistances so that together we can each locate tactical and strategic trajectories for multidirectional critique, mass actions and alternatives.
>
> (2003: 91)

Many of the participants contributing to the work of the Forum return to a world of negotiating with government, or, for the educators, teaching structured programmes in classrooms, bringing back connections and ways of working that ensure that civil society has the resilience and imagination necessary to continue to struggle for societies where all adults are free and able to engage in creating a world better fitted to their aspirations and needs. In this sense the Forum is a giant adult education event in itself, providing the space for people to identify and explore solutions to problems they have in common.

The Forum represents a vibrant example of the way civil society can explore alternative forms and alternative solutions to those of the State. Much of their creativity may prefigure programmes later adopted, however timidly modified. This task is, for many working in liberal democracies, complementary to the kinds of negotiations and monitoring illustrated in the work of ICAE and NIACE, but for many working in contexts where the freedom of association is denied and the voices of civil society are silenced it will complement more explicitly political action. Almost 80 years ago, in the report of the UK government's Adult Education Committee of its Ministry of Reconstruction, the case for voluntary organisation was eloquently made:

> In a modern community voluntary organisation must always occupy a prominent place. The free association of individuals is a normal process in civilized society, and one which arises from the inevitable inadequacy of state and municipal organisation. It is not primarily a result of defective public organisation; it grows out of the existence of human needs which the State and municipality cannot satisfy. Voluntary organisations, whatever their purpose, are fundamentally similar in their nature, in that they unite for a defined end people with a common interest. There is, therefore, in a voluntary body a definite point of view, a common outlook, and a common purpose which give it a corporate spirit of its own.
>
> (Ministry of Reconstruction, 1919: 112)

If the role of governments and their agencies is to identify and promote the general interest, the key task of voluntary agencies in adult learning is to challenge governments to ensure that their conception of the general interest includes a commitment to the development of all adults, recognising the diversity of their needs and aspirations, and providing space for the realisation of their creativity and imagination, and their capacity to engage in and shape the development of wider society, to secure meaningful work, and to satisfy curiosity. Where governments and their agencies do not respond to that challenge, it is then the task of NGOs and civil society to create spaces where communities can seek to secure those goals for themselves.

## References

Bhola, H.S. (1997) 'Transnational forces and national realities of adult basic education and training', *Convergence* 30(2/3): 41–50.

Daniel, Sir J. (2003) 'Advocating adult education – and then what', *Adults Learning*, October, Leicester: NIACE.

Delors, J. (Chair) (1996) *Learning: The treasure within*, Paris: UNESCO.

European Union (EU) (2000) *A Memorandum on Lifelong Learning*, SEC (2000) 1832, Brussels: Commission of the European Union.

Francisco, G. (2003) 'Inaugural speech at the Women's Conference of the Asian Social Forum', 5 January 2003, Hyderabad, India.

International Council for Adult Education (ICAE) (2003) Agenda for the Future – Six Years Later: The ICAE report', Montevideo: ICAE.

Ministry of Reconstruction (1919) *Final Report* (of the Adult Education Committee chaired by Arthur L. Smith and commonly known as 'The 1919 Report'), Cmnd 321 (1919), London: HMSO.

World Social Forum (2001) *Charter of Principles*. Available online at www.forumsocialmundial.org.uk.

# 30

# The role of NGOs in adult education and capacity-building for development
## The case of *dvv international*

*Chris Duke and Heribert Hinzen*

## Introduction

This chapter examines the role of non-governmental organisations (NGOs) and their contributions to the field of adult education, taking as an example from the diverse range of international NGOs (INGOs) the case of what is now called *dvv international* in Germany, and referring to others in respect of their interconnectedness and collaboration. While acknowledging substantial growth and success the chapter looks also at obstacles and challenges. The growth of the third, non-governmental, or civil society sector alongside the public and private sectors is a major phenomenon of our time, one crucial to the development of adult education for lifelong learning.

The Third UNESCO World Conference on Adult Education in Tokyo in 1972 was a milestone in setting out complementary governmental and non-governmental roles and responsibilities for the development of adult education and of its professional bodies. It laid the foundations for a common understanding of policies, legislation, finances, organisation and administration, methods and materials, programmes, providers and staff training. Building on this, UNESCO agreed during its Nineteenth General Conference in Nairobi in 1976 to a *Recommendation on the Development of Adult Education*.

Key participants on governmental delegations in Tokyo felt that national and regional adult education associations, universities, and other organisations should cooperate more closely at an international level. Together with the UNESCO Secretariat they prepared the ground for the non-governmental International Council for Adult Education (ICAE), founded in 1973.

The German Adult Education Association, more precisely the Deutscher Volkshochschuly-Verband (German Association of Folk high schools), is better known by its abbreviation DVV. It is the national body of German regional associations, of which the local folk high schools are members. Founded in 1953, DVV has, since the early 1960s, taken a keen interest in international activities. Why and how does a national association invest itself so much, to the point of creating its own Institute, now *dvv international*, formerly the Institute for International Cooperation (IIZ/DVV), and at the same time get such high recognition and financial support that it can extend its professional services and advocacy work regionally and internationally to partners in many countries?

In 1994 a wide-ranging IIZ/DVV twenty-fifth anniversary commemorative publication considered such subjects as literacy and basic education, capacity-building, professionalisation, the emphasis on development and combating poverty, women's education and civil society. A collection of documents illustrated the close parallels between internationalism in DVV and the development of international adult education organisations, including the two-way influence between these. Other important documents looked back at DVV's international achievements (Hinzen, 1994).

## Adult education and lifelong learning, dialogue, cooperation and development – terms and concepts

Everyday experience shows the importance for Europe of international and global considerations alongside local, regional and national concerns. The two dimensions are intimately intertwined. What does the call to 'shape globalisation' mean, not just for the poorest of the poor but also for governments and civil society organisations? Adult education has also become increasingly important and complex, especially when seen and provided in terms of lifelong global learning. 'Development-oriented adult education as world domestic policy' is a call to take into account broader currents and social changes that have yet to receive adequate theoretical and practical attention.

### Adult education in lifelong learning

As a result of globalisation, technological change and the development of knowledge and information-based societies, there is a growing need for lifelong learning in developing countries, countries in transition and industrialised countries. Successful education systems are built on four equal pillars: school education, vocational training, universities and continuing education. Flexible transition between them is essential. Non-formal and out-of-school education and training programmes for young people and adults fulfil complementary functions. Adult education plays a key role in the process of lifelong learning by offering general, vocational, cultural and academic continuing education.

Lifelong learning covers the whole cradle-to-grave lifespan, whereas adult learning denotes the long period after youth. There is no convincing reason why learning should stop at a certain time. Lately a change of language, and to some extent a paradigm shift from education to learning, has become almost universal. The shift, prefigured from at least the time of the Faure report in 1972, and later deepened in 1996 in the Delors report on *Learning: The treasure within*, has brought forward new and different approaches. Some try to make learning more relevant, effective and better motivated by taking it into different settings and using new methods. Others reflect the understanding that learning is a shared property and a social process at levels above the individual. Hence the search for learning communities, cities, regions and countries, and for learning organisations, and even learning festivals. These have in common that the learner rather than an educational institution is at the centre, and that learning cannot be confined to traditional educational establishments, but occurs throughout society.

Educational institutions are still needed; the better they perform their function, the better for the learners. However, learners do increasingly access all kinds of information and communication technologies. Individualised or self-organised informal learning is often combined with face-to-face sessions within institutions. This calls for institutional and professional change, often requiring cooperation between ministries, universities, specialist organisations and NGOs.

## Education for all – lifelong and crucial for living

In April 2000 the World Education Forum in Dakar acknowledged that nearly 900 million young people and adults cannot read and write, with over 100 million children of school age deprived of the right to education. The year 2015 was the date declared for decisive advances to be made – halving the illiteracy rate, schooling for all children and equality of opportunities for girls and women.

Since then high-level committees and working groups have beavered away. Yearly General Monitoring Reports include substantial materials and discussions, most recently on early childhood, literacy, quality and gender, but it remains unclear where the necessary additional 15 billion euros are to come from. Demographic growth means that another 150 million school places have to be found for Africa, the Arab States and South Asia alone; at the same time the target is for around 90 million adults to become literate each year. It is obvious that the poor countries alone cannot succeed without support and funding from the donor community (Burnett *et al.*, 2005; Duke and Hinzen, 2006).

## Adult education and capacity development

In addition to non-formal and out-of-school education programmes for young people and adults, projects that secure participation in the social development of broad sections of the population, especially the poor, and that strengthen partners' capacity for self-help and help develop social institutions are essential to the long-term goal of poverty reduction. Institutional improvements for adult education in the areas of policy, legislation and funding, and professionalism in theory and practice are all crucial elements. They require cooperation from ministries, universities, specialist organisations, voluntary associations and NGOs.

According to a recent report (Federal Ministry of Economic Cooperation and Development, 2002) on the development policy of the German Federal Government:

> Education is both a human right and a key to solving many problems of human develop-
> ment: education is an indispensable requirement for reducing poverty . . . education is
> indispensable if more people and regions are to be able to make use of the increasing
> opportunities of globalization being opened up in the world economy and through the
> worldwide use of new technologies, and if they are to acquire the skills needed to shape
> the future in the direction of sustainable development.
>
> (p. 122; see also Hinzen and Schindele, 2005)

It is not only projects aimed at crisis and conflict prevention that require greater prominence in development work and in foreign policy on culture and education, but also those dealing with poverty, because of the close connections between the two.

## Dialogue between cultures – foundations for cooperation

In 1989, the General Conference of UNESCO declared 2001 the International Year of Dialogue between Civilisations. The UN General Assembly had stressed 'the importance of toleration in international relations and the significant role of dialogue plays as a means of reaching understanding, removing threats of peace and strengthening interaction and exchange among civilizations' and asked UNESCO to 'plan and implement appropriate cultural, educational and social programmes to promote the concept of dialogue among civilizations, including through organizing conferences and seminars and disseminating information and scholarly materials on the subject' (UNESCO, 1999: 67).

The need for dialogue between different cultures and religions has acquired new meaning as the appalling events of 11 September 2001 and their aftermath make plain. It became evident that more attention needs to be paid to analysis and future strategic planning in order to deal with the growing gulf between rich and poor exacerbated by globalisation. As former UN Secretary-General Kofi Annan's (2001) initiative *Crossing the Divide: Dialogue among civilizations* asks, 'can there be peace without justice?', and how can we appeal to people's consciences throughout the world so that they recognise that poverty is an issue wherever it appears?

A high-level conference in 2002 on Intercultural Dialogue mainly in the Mediterranean region ranged from economic and other forms of globalisation, and the image of Europe in the world, to dialogue between religions. In his opening address, European Union President Prodi said:

> The fault lines are also produced by political injustice, economic disparities, grinding poverty, a lack of future prospects – the consequences of uncontrolled globalisation that are perceived as cultural and political oppression . . . Dialogue is not something that takes place only elsewhere, beyond our borders; it has to start here, in Europe itself, in our inner cities, which are all too often the seedbeds of intolerance and prejudice.
>
> (2002: 5)

This dialogue also needs to address cultural globalisation. Mutual acceptance is called for, going well beyond economics.

## Adult education at all levels: recent decades and *dvv international*

Adult education is essentially a local concern in terms of need, demand and institutional provision. However, changes such as the growing importance of the new media now demand particular attention and adult education also has regional, national, transnational, European, international, global and, increasingly, intercultural dimensions.

### Folk high school roots and global perspectives

This notion of national and international is particularly true for the folk high schools (VHS) in Germany, though not equally for every school and branch. Here as elsewhere the international dimensions are changing over time. Some 1,000 VHS as local adult continuing education centres work through 3,600 branches in order to reach out to the German population. They are covered by adult education legislation, maintained by the local authorities, and work as associations, as part of the municipality structure, or as not-for-profit limited companies. They offer language courses, vocational retraining, political education, cultural and leisure time activities, and health and environmental education. They are popular, easy to access, open to all citizens, and relatively inexpensive. About ten million participants come to the centres each year. Some activities are more like community development, making them more than adult schools. At a regional level 16 Land Associations provide services for the VHS that form their membership. They are members of DVV, which acts as a national association representing local and regional interests.

Following the transfer of the German capital to Berlin, within DVV two units remain in Bonn: the national headquarters and *dvv international*. The major ministries dealing with Education, Development and Technology, and related institutions such as the German Vocational Training Institute, the German Institute for Adult Education and the German Institute for Development Policy, are still in Bonn under a special law. DVV is the single shareholder of telc GmbH (the European Language Certificates), and principal shareholder of the Adolf Grimme Institute (AGI), dealing with media and education.

What were the historical roots of the international involvements of the VHS and DVV? There were early encounters with British and American adult education. The Scandinavian countries also played a significant role after the Second World War, welcoming colleagues from VHS on placements in their establishments. Everything European was then linked to the very difficult post-war situation, and the goals of reconciliation between peoples, which, along with town twinning initiatives, called for educational and organisational action. A European Working Group had already been set up in DVV in 1961. Support from the Culture Department of the Foreign Office made it possible to plan and conduct information and professional exchanges with adult education partners in Europe and other industrialised countries worldwide. This also applied during the Cold War to many countries in the Eastern Bloc, laying the groundwork for the rapid expansion of cooperation in the early 1990s with the changes at that time.

DVV's African adult education contacts in Africa grew rapidly from the late 1950s, with decolonisation and the start of development assistance. German embassies in Africa sought support for literacy as part of this assistance. The newly established German Federal Ministry for Economic Cooperation and Development (BMZ) discussed this with DVV; government departments thought DVV well suited to conducting international adult education projects. The first courses for adult educators were held in Cameroon from the early 1960s, and the first one-year course to train African colleagues was held at the Göhrde residential VHS in 1963. Support began for the Central American Institute of Popular Education (ICECU) in Costa Rica, and in 1964 DVV became a founder member of the Asian South Pacific Bureau for Adult Education (ASPBAE). In 1965, the first course for Latin American adult educators was held at Rendsburg residential VHS.

Cooperation also grew in the 1960s with specialist bodies such as European Association for the Education of Adults (EAEA), UNESCO and the UNESCO Institute for Education (UIE) in Hamburg. In 1969, DVV set up the Department for Adult Education in Developing Countries to organise cooperation with partners in Africa, Asia and Latin America (Hinzen *et al.*, 1982). Guidelines for its work were committed to writing in 1973. They emphasised:

- the emancipatory importance of social and individual development;
- adult education as an important component of lifelong learning;
- the historical and cultural factors governing aim, content, forms and methods;
- the aim of enhancing professional quality through cooperation based on partnership;
- setting goals for the work in participatory cooperation with partners.

The first issue of the specialist journal *Adult Education and Development* appeared in the same year, initially planned as a bulletin in English, French and Spanish for former recipients of studentships.

## Consolidation and expansion in the 1970s and 1980s

Systematising relations with the BMZ was very important in this period, thanks in part to the Ministry's own capacity development and its ability to plan for long-term federal commitments over a number of years. Expansion in projects was accompanied by the development of the capacities and skills within the Department itself needed to plan and carry them out, and led by then Director Jakob Horn. Staff continuity and stability was important. In 1978, the Department was renamed the Department for International Cooperation of DVV.

Africa remained the continent where most projects took place, with projects and partners in Ethiopia, Somalia, Zaire, Zambia and Tanzania, often with support from offices run by DVV. This corresponded with priorities set for German development cooperation. In countries where partners wished and the resources allowed, DVV opened project offices with a staff member posted from Germany to develop work over the longer term with a wide range of partners in various fields. In other countries, projects were run with partners supported from headquarters in Bonn. Cooperation focused particularly on:

- initial and continuing training for adult educators;
- relevant teaching and learning materials and media;
- practice-oriented evaluation and research;
- institutional and material infrastructure;
- occupational and income-generating activities;
- recognition and protection through education policy.

Environmental education, health education and democratisation became important fields in which IIZ/DVV developed recognised expertise. Literacy and basic education were integral to almost every project.

In the early 1970s IIZ/DVV discussed with its partners how the initial and continuing training of professionals in the Ghörde residential college could be transferred in the short or medium term to the countries themselves. Some ten African universities strengthened their respective departments, developed diploma and certificate studies and received support in the form of studentships, advice and production of teaching materials, enabling them to train more than 200 students a year. Decades later, together with these universities, the Adult Education Department of the University of Botswana, the UIL (now Lifelong Learning) and *dvv international* started, in 2003, a series of African textbooks entitled *African Perspectives on Adult Learning* for university adult education courses. Within a few years, they became available throughout the continent as *Foundations of Adult Education in Africa*, *Research Methods for Adult Educators in Africa*, *The Social Context of Adult Learning in Africa* and *The Psychology of Adult Learning in Africa*.

Africa continued to dominate the work of the Department, and the bulk of resources were employed there. However, slow but steady growth in funding allowed expansion to other regions. Work in Asia began in the 1970s, starting in Kerala State and then in Rajasthan in India, with emphasis on literacy and basic education in the context of basic needs, environment and participation. ASPBAE, which had been in suspended animation since it was set up in the 1960s, came to life in the mid-1970s, initially with regional conferences and publications, later with country-specific activities, particularly in Thailand and Indonesia where the first World Bank adult education projects began. In China in 2003, ASPBAE and DVV celebrated and reflected on 25 years of project partnership (AED, 1981, 1989; Duke, 2003).

Meanwhile annual alternating four-week study tours in Germany by young colleagues from Africa and Asia enabled them to learn about the situation in Germany, not only about adult education and its institutions, and to inform themselves about the situation in their home countries, with the opportunity to find out how other DVV partners' projects were faring.

Colombia became a particular focus of work in Latin America, often with emphasis on occupational and income-generating activities. The Alfonso Lopez Centre became a substantial institution with a wide range of provision, now operating without *dvv international* support. A project office was set up in Bolivia to strengthen decentralised cooperation with individual Education Ministry centres locally. At this time the Latin American Council for Adult Education (CEAAL) was based in Chile. It was of great significance for adult education throughout the continent and is still associated with the name of Paulo Freire. Like ASPBAE, EAEA and the African Association for Literacy and Adult Education (now PAALAE), CEAAL functioned from 1976 as the regional arm of ICAE, which has, since 1973, supported non-governmental adult education organisations from its headquarters, first in Canada and then in Montevideo.

## Going global during the 1990s

During the 1990s new needs and opportunities for adult learning have occurred as a result of the political upheavals in Central and Eastern Europe. When these changes are combined with the declared aims of democratising societies and globalising markets they have had far-reaching and wide-ranging effects that have posed new fields of work for DVV.

The collapse of the socialist camp in Europe and of the Berlin Wall made it possible to bring together the VHS of East and West Germany. It also opened up new prospects for cooperation with partners in Eastern Europe, Central Asia and elsewhere, including new opportunities in Africa, Asia and Latin America, regions on which DVV had traditionally focused. With the end of the Soviet Union the situation changed radically for the socialists in power in Ethiopia, who had abolished the Empire in 1973. The former regime fell and Eritrea subsequently split away and fought a war of liberation that lasted decades. In Vietnam the *doi moi* – a variant of perestroika and glasnost – brought hopes of greater openness in the way socialism would be conducted in future, making space for NGOs to spring up; through their international connections it was possible to make contacts. In China the opening of the borders, frequently in the context of economic cooperation, led to new thinking about modernisation, which appeared impossible without the massive expansion of adult education. In South Africa the opponents of apartheid achieved a largely peaceful transition of power. This did not automatically remove the effects of discrimination; all areas of society, especially education, face a lengthy process of achieving greater equality of opportunity. In the Latin American countries, developments in Chile, Nicaragua and Guatemala must also be seen in the context of political changes and economic globalisation, coinciding with the celebration of 500 years of discovery or colonisation linked with the name of Columbus.

For DVV and its members many new initiatives followed. Thus the Land Association of VHS in Schleswig-Holstein and the Mannheim Evening Academy developed wide-ranging intensive dialogue with Chinese partners. DVV was able to open new project offices in Ethiopia and South Africa. In the Latin American countries cooperation started mainly with NGOs. In all these cases the focus was on learning from each other, capacity building and providing expertise, and on initial and in-service training, supplemented by the production of teaching and learning materials, research and evaluation. Topics included ecology and agriculture, democracy and participation, and income-related and occupational activities.

In some countries the changes were unfortunate and indeed disastrous. In Somalia not even international intervention could bring peace and end the civil war. In Burundi and Rwanda tribal vendettas led to deliberate genocide, with innumerable dead. DVV had been working there on and off for many years in both countries in the fields of literacy, vocational education and indeed in human rights and peace education; it had to close project offices and evacuate staff. Sierra Leone suffered successive military coups, persecutions and killings and DVV partners could barely continue with adult education, so cooperation had to be scaled down.

The end of the Cold War meant new opportunities to support adult education as a social institution, as part of development cooperation with funding from the BMZ, and for adult education as part of cultural policy abroad, with funding from the Foreign Office. IIZ/DVV took the opportunities that presented themselves. Studies in 1992 and 2001 set out the nature and content of cultural agreements between individual states and Germany, and practical undertakings agreed in the protocols of the Joint Cultural Committees. They showed (Muller, 2001):

- That adult education featured in 68 per cent of all cultural agreements, a 20 per cent increase over ten years.
- That the model agreement drawn up and used by the Foreign Office, which covers all sectors of education, has led to a somewhat more equal distribution.
- That the projects actually to be carried out had not kept pace with this rise in importance, featuring in only 49 per cent of protocols.
- That the cultural agreements and protocols with industrialised countries refer to adult education twice as often as those with developing countries.

These findings indirectly strengthen the thesis that the higher the level of economic, technological and other development of a society, the greater the need for ongoing continuing education. At the same time they show DVV as being unable to respond more to the demand for adult education in agreements and protocols with developing countries in Africa, Asia and Latin America, which still account for most of the cooperation.

VHS and DVV professional contacts with states in the Eastern Bloc during the Cold War paid dividends in terms of specialist knowledge and contacts. Civil society needed to be hugely expanded. Potential partner organisations and individual colleagues in the state sector and the universities were ready to take advantage of the new opportunities. The first developments took place in Hungary and Poland, with new project offices opening in Budapest in 1991, Warsaw in 1992, St Petersburg in 1993 and Bucharest in 1994, and cooperation without project offices in the three Baltic States and the Slovak and Czech Republics.

Adult education enjoyed new opportunities for cooperation in the mood of upheaval and opportunity after the collapse of socialism. The *dvv international* took soundings in Ethiopia, Angola, Vietnam, Kazakhstan and Cuba. Many new initiatives were launched with partners in all continents, as described by Michael Samlowski, Deputy-Director of *dvv international* (1993a, b). Early on in this phase of the Institute's development, Samlowski posed the question: 'Does the South end in the East?' He traced similarities, commonalities and differences in project work in the developing countries of Africa, Asia and Latin America on the one hand, and the countries in transition in Central and Eastern Europe on the other.

## Continuity and innovation since 2000

Comprehensive activity reports on the work of *dvv international* are made available to the public in a two-yearly sequence, serving at the same time the needs for the General Assembly of DVV (*dvv international* 2003/4, 2005/6). From the last one it can be followed that, early this decade, Institute projects in Europe were strategically realigned under three new headings:

- Cooperation with countries in the first round of EU expansion: bilateral cooperation to be continued, while regional initiatives addressed common aims and activities – education policy and legislation, cooperation in university courses, etc. The Institute has one or more partners in all countries. The Project Office in Warsaw was to assume a regional coordination role.

- Cooperation with countries in the Stability Pact for South Eastern Europe: support to create and expand adult education institutions, especially for initiatives aimed at cross-border, inter-ethnic regional networking contributing to sustainable development, integration of marginalised groups and democratisation of development with partners and/or project offices in all countries. A coordination scheme (EBiS, Adult Education in South Eastern Europe) to be set up, in which all eight countries and *dvv international* are represented. The Regional Office moving from Sofia in Bulgaria to Sarajevo in Bosnia and Herzegovina in 2007.
- Cooperation with the countries of the Commonwealth of Independent States (CIS), built up with partners in the Russian Federation, to be continued, through the project office in St Petersburg. In Ukraine, cooperation with the support of the VHS in Regen. In the southern Caucasus, a project office in Tbilisi from 2001 for Azerbaijan and Armenia through coordination centres in Baku and Yerevan. From 2001, a project office in Tashkent for initiatives in Uzbekistan and such neighbouring countries in Central Asia as Tadjikistan and Kirgistan.

Development in Central and Eastern Europe, taking in the Caucasus and the Central Asian states, thus took DVV deeper into Asia. Substantial efforts have been made to integrate these new Central Asian partners into the older Asian ASPBAE networks. In Africa, also working towards regionalisation, the project office in Cape Town has begun to look after partners in Angola, Botswana, Lesotho, Madagascar and Mozambique. The Conakry Project Office in Guinea is now also a direct point of contact for partners in Chad, Mali, Senegal and Sierra Leone. The same applies to Addis Ababa, which is responsible for Ethiopia, Uganda and Kenya as well as other initiatives in the region. In Latin America too there is work in the majority of countries, not only through the regional association CEAAL but also bilaterally. The emphasis is on intercultural education in Guatemala and Mexico. Women's education and gender work extends via the REPEM network (Red de Educacion Popular Entre Mujeres de America Latina y el Caribe) from Uruguay to all other countries. Vocational and income-related activities are strongly represented in Bolivia and Colombia, and partners are engaged in agriculture in Argentina and Chile.

For a short time additional funds were made available to combat extreme poverty with the approval of the Federal German Government of *Action Program 2015*, which provides a binding framework for all other policy areas. The November 2001 federal budget contained a separate heading for back-up funds to reduce extreme poverty. DVV submitted various applications to the Ministry for:

- support for non-formal basic education and income-oriented training in regions affected by poverty in Ethiopia;
- information and education about HIV/AIDS – initial and in-service training for community workers in South Africa;
- income-oriented craft training in selected urban and rural areas in Southern Caucasus;
- in-service training for multipliers to promote equal rights and representation for women in the Asia region;
- intercultural education in village communities with largely indigenous populations in Central America.

After 11 September 2001, BMZ funds from the Anti-Terrorism Package (ATP) were provided to strengthen projects for democratisation, reintegration of young former child soldiers and crisis prevention. The Foreign Office also made funds available for dialogue between Europe and Islam, used for Turkish–German cooperation in adult education, a field neglected despite the large number of Turks in Germany and Turkey's growing importance in Europe. There was intense DVV discussion about how to use these funds. If the nexus of 'poverty, exploitation, deprivation of rights, oppression and powerlessness' was the breeding ground for terrorist acts, then specific steps to strengthen projects should be taken in selected countries to improve people's general conditions and particular circumstances. Later, DVV projects funded from this special budget vote of BMZ included:

- education for peace and democracy;
- reintegration of refugees and ex-combatants in Sierra Leone;
- model income-generating vocational training projects in Central Asia;
- educational events providing intercultural and inter-religious dialogue between leading public figures in India;
- education for democracy and peace in regions of religious and ethnic disturbances in the Asia region;
- education and strengthening of citizens' groups and civil society initiatives in Colombia;
- threats to democracy – education for peace and human rights in the Latin American region.

At the home front in Germany, for almost 30 years IIZ/DVV could support VHS who had worked in development education (now renamed global learning). It is now generally accepted that this is important, especially with the increasingly harmful effects of globalisation. The BMZ has again increased resources for this type of work in VHS, including programmes for youth and younger adults as a special target group. The former series on *Volkshochschulen and the Theme of Africa, Asia and Latin America* gave way to a new title, *Global Learning in the Volkshochschulen*, still in German.

Two Institute projects supported through EU Socrates and Grundtvig programmes should expand work on intercultural and inter-religious issues: a two-year project on *Tolerance and Understanding – Our Muslim Neighbours* with several partners; and a network funded initially for three years on *Intercultural Learning in Europe*. A number of European partners participated; with extension by the EU for another three years this was enlarged to 25 partners in different countries. Two more projects were to be added from 2006 onwards: on cultural diversity, and on developing a tool kit for intercultural work (Schmidt-Behlau, 2004, 2006).

## Developments and structures for future cooperation

Despite often short-sighted and short-term projects and funding cycles, IIZ/DVV institutional management and organisational development improved.

### Finances and support

There has so far been no core institutional funding of *dvv international*. Everything is done on a project basis, with an administration fee. Since the 1960s, the most important funding body has been the BMZ; without its funding over the decades there would have been no such level of international work. The Foreign Office has lately reduced funding in some areas, and was strongly criticised for this by the International Board and the General Assembly. Other funds for individual projects come from the Federal Ministry of Education and Science (BMBF), and the Federal Government Press and Information Service (BPA).

Over the last 15 years, successful bids to various budget lines of the EU have funded other work of the Institute and its partners in Bulgaria, Georgia, Kirgistan, Russia and Uzbekistan. The World Bank funded a major literacy project in Guinea and a study and conference on livelihood and literacy as well as poverty reduction and adult education. Most recently, the Royal Netherlands Development Funding supported the Integrated Women Empowerment Program in Ethiopia. Most funds are spent on seminars and initial and continuing training, advice, evaluation and research, and on publications. These, together with equipment and materials, account for about half the budget. The institutions providing coordination, project offices and partners, including staff costs, are a major factor, these funds being used to provide professional and organisational support for the work. Administrative overheads from projects pay for the Institute in Bonn.

## Staff and the Advisory Board

In 2006, about 140 *dvv international* staff worked in a wide variety of functions, positions and places, about 25 of them in Bonn. More women were employed than men, and more people worked in administration than in positions with academic or pedagogical backgrounds. This excludes people working for partner institutions on joint projects paid out of project funds provided by *dvv international*.

Staff rotation means that senior staff do not work all the time at the headquarters in Bonn, but are also posted abroad, ideally five out of every ten years in Bonn and five abroad. The aim is to learn from recent developments on the ground while feeding in what has been learnt centrally and then in turn to bring project experience back to headquarters. At headquarters, responsibility for the entire Institute means there is an emphasis on management, staffing and finance, including government relations. Abroad, the sheer volume of project management produces a quite different situation.

The DVV articles of association state that: 'within the Association there shall be an Institute for International Cooperation (IIZ/DVV)', for which an Advisory Board shall be convened by the Board of Management and whose Director shall have special responsibility for this area of operations under the terms of Clause 30 of the Civil Code. This is important as it demonstrates the will of the Association to have the international dimension and projects well embedded, while allowing for strong relative autonomy to be efficient and competitive on a professional level. From the beginning of 2007, the abbreviation IIZ/DVV was replaced by the name *dvv international*.

The International Advisory Board stands between the DVV Board of Management and the Institute. It advises on the overall international perspectives of the Association and the Institute's policy and practice, work and projects. The Advisory Board makes recommendations in both directions, to the Board of Management on decisions and to the Institute on improvements in its work. In 2006 it called attention to the lower profile of adult education in foreign cultural policies.

## Information and communication

The journal *Adult Education and Development* continues to be directed principally at middle-level adult educators in Africa, Asia and Latin America, without losing sight of global issues of development cooperation or Europe as a region. Launched in three languages in 1973, it has reached a production level of about 25,000, with supplements at irregular intervals. The series *International Perspectives in Adult Education* allows the Institute to extend studies and documents arising out of its work to a wider public. A country monographs series began in 1992; in all 55 volumes have now appeared. The Institute website, set up in 1999, covers all major projects and partners in English, French, German and Spanish and carries links to the Institute's main partners and their websites.

It has been a challenge to promote debate on adult education as a part of learning throughout life, resulting in numerous declarations and documents, on, for example, poverty reduction and development, capacity-building, basic education and lifelong learning, enhancing international cooperation and solidarity, and university training of adult educators. The Institute was responsible for the thematic working paper and workshop on international cooperation of the Fifth UNESCO World Adult Education Conference (CONFINTEA V). A special issue of *Adult Education and Development* in English, French and Spanish contained all the thematic background papers, and was expanded to include a Declaration and Action Plan in several languages; 20,000 copies were distributed widely.

## Research and evaluation

Research and evaluation feature regularly without dominating. Almost 50 feasibility studies, formative or summative evaluations cover all continents and diverse thematic areas. Project-related research has included orality and literality – how writing down the previously oral literature of fables, fairy stories, songs and proverbs can contribute to literacy (this via a project in the 1980s of the People's Educational Association of Sierra Leone). In the late 1990s, research in Hungary on institutions in the continuing education market looked at 730 establishments involved in adult education, training and lifelong learning; more than 30 graduate students wrote their dissertations on this topic. In 2002 a major study for the World Bank on Skills and Literacy Training for Better Livelihoods provided an opportunity to look more thoroughly at how adults who cannot read and write learn skills important in their lives and work, a crucial consideration for the world's thousand million adult illiterates. During 2003, a research project reviewed university initial and continuing training courses in Central and South Eastern Europe, identifying the potential for cooperation and leading to a project called TEACH, which developed new modules for the teaching of adult educators at universities (see Duke, 2004; Fordham, 1997; Hinzen *et al.*, 2001; Knoll and Hinzen, 2005; Oxenham *et al.*, 2002, among others).

## Lobbying and collaboration

A statement of the International Advisory Board of DVV in 2001, *The Decline in the Importance of Education in Development Cooperation*, pointed out that education was receiving less funding via development cooperation than in the previous decade. This applied to school and out-of-school basic education and to higher education; vocational training was an exception, having been maintained as an element of economic support. The issue commanded attention: together with the German Agency for Technical Cooperation (GTZ), IIZ/DVV called for a committee on Education within Development Assistance to reverse the trend. This was set up with additional partners, such as the BMZ, the German UNESCO Commission (DUK), the German Bank for Reconstruction (KFW), the churches with their aid agencies, and members of the NGO Association for Development Policy (VENRO).

Cooperation has expanded within the Social Improvement Network (AGS). The separate BMZ budget heading introduced in the 1960s now covers support for organisations such as Workers' Welfare, Caritas, the Education Service of the German Trades Union Congress, the German Association of Cooperatives and Credit Unions, and the Kolping Society; these have

343

particular expertise in fields of social policy, trade union and cooperative activities. These organisations meet quarterly, together with the BMZ official responsible for the budget heading, and discuss prospects for future lobbying as well as current issues.

From the 1980s onwards the Institute took on much representation in and direct cooperation with regional and international organisations, notably with and for EAEA and ICAE. Advice is sought from the Institute by UNESCO in supporting the General Monitoring Report on Education for All (EFA), the Consultative Group preparing CONFINTEA VI, and the Expert Group of the UN Literacy Decade. The President of DVV, Professor Rita Süssmuth, who at that time was President of the Federal German Parliament, was elected President of CONFINTEA V in 1997. This political embedding as a professional NGO for international adult education appears positive from both sides.

## Conclusion: what next?

The increased pace of globalisation, together with calls, in the knowledge that the process cannot be reversed, for a globalisation that serves human needs, implies ever more work to be done. Some still hope that even the poorest of the poor will benefit from globalisation, and base their development policy on global structures; but a growing number believe that globalisation will be less the solution than the cause of further problems. These are not questions for economists and world social summits alone, whether convened at the highest levels of government or profiled as 'alternative'.

The internationalisation of life will surely lead to more international cooperation, ever more varied in political and regional terms in its aims and content, institutions and resources. It looks easy to distinguish between industrialised, threshold, transitional and developing countries and yet many developing countries have highly developed industries and productive technologies, while industrialised countries reveal growing new-found poverty. In all these fields, development-oriented adult education is of rising significance.

In Europe, cooperation within the EU may one day cease to be regarded as international, as EU education initiatives become increasingly important for national education authorities and voluntary associations. The general adoption since the mid-1990s of Lifelong Learning as *the* idea governing educational thinking and action in Europe is extraordinary. DVV will face ever more tasks in this field as a result of calls made on the VHS and their Land Associations because of migration and resettlement. These in turn depend on overall social developments, in Europe and worldwide. It will be a matter for continuing dialogue within DVV and with other institutions as to which of these tasks *dvv international* will need and be able to concentrate on.

In essence, three forms of cooperation can be distinguished and will presumably co-exist for some time to come, doubtless with much overlap and intermingling:

*   First, we can assume strong growth in the need for, and interest in, exchanges of information and experience, whether by means of the new information and communication technologies or face to face.
*   Second, project cooperation through joint programmes and networks will grow, mainly between countries having the greatest similarities in the structure of adult education and its degree of development. The main reason will be the benefits expected from learning from one another, although it will also reflect an obligation to work together across borders and transnationally, reflecting broader goals built into some projects as a prerequisite of participation.

- Third, alongside partnerships, mentoring will remain important to give support, chiefly in and with poorer countries that vary greatly in the way adult education has developed, and will require infrastructural as well as professional input.

It is timely to evaluate the innovatory elements of the ever-growing international cooperation of recent years and to learn from examples of good practice. Despite unquestionable trends towards universalisation and globalisation, carefully differentiated approaches are needed in different sectors and regions for viable forms of professionally planned cooperation and solidarity between partners. It also now appears beyond question that the voluntary, civil or non-governmental sector has a vital part to play, with its closer anchorage to and acceptance by poor people and local communities than the state and private sectors normally enjoy. This chapter has taken just one, albeit leading, exemplar of non-governmental endeavour, showing its links to sectors, elements and partners at all levels, and the growing interconnectedness of affairs that is a part of globalisation.

## References

*Adult Education and Development* (AED) (1981) 'Indonesia', *Adult Education and Development* 16.
—— (1989) 'Thailand', *Adult Education and Development* 33.
Annan, K. (ed.) (2001) *Crossing the Divide: Dialogue among civilizations*, South Orange, NJ: School of Diplomacy and International Relations, Seton Hall University.
Burnett, N. *et al.* (2005) *Literacy for Life: EFA Global Monitoring Report 2006*,
    Paris: UNESCO.
Delors, J. (Chair) (1996) *Learning: The treasure within*, Paris: UNESCO.
Duke, C. (2003) 'The year of the sheep: international cooperation for adult education', *Adult Education and Development* 60: 27–46.
—— (2004) 'From comparison to cooperation: partnership and diversity in the training and accreditation of adult educators by institutions of higher education: report of the conference', *International Perspectives in Adult Education* 44: 15–41.
—— and Hinzen, H. (2006) 'Basic and continuing adult education policies', *Adult Education and Development* 66: 131–61.
*dvv international* (2003/4) *Activity Report 2003/4*, Bonn: DVV.
—— (2005/6) *Activity Report 2005/6*, Bonn: DVV.
Faure, E. (Chair) (1972) *Learning to Be*, Paris: Librairie Fayard.
Federal Ministry of Economic Cooperation and Development (2002) *Elfter Berichdzur Entwicklungspolitik der Bundesregierung. Materialien 111*, Bonn: BMZ.
Fordham, P. (1997) *Training Adult Educators in African Universities: An evaluation of the scholarship programme of the Institute for International Cooperation of the German Adult Education Association*, Bonn: IIZ/DVV.
Hinzen, H. (ed.) (1994) '25 years, Institute for International Cooperation of the German Adult Education Association', *Adult Education and Development* 43: 1–448.
—— and Schindele, H. (eds) (2005) 'Capacity building and the training of adult educators', *International Perspectives in Adult Education* 52.
——, Horn, J., Leumer, W. and Niemann, R. (1982) 'The international cooperation of DVV in Africa, Asia and Latinamerica', *Adult Education and Development* 19: 299–310.
——, James, F.B., Sorie, J.M. and Sheikh Ahmed Tejan Tamu (eds) (2001) *Fishing in Rivers of Sierra Leone: Oral literature*, Freetown: PEA (People's Educational Association of Sierra Leone).
Knoll, J. and Hinzen, H. (eds) (2005) 'Academic study and professional training: new BA/MA courses and qualifications in adult education', *International Perspectives in Adult Education* 50.
Müller, G. (2001) 'Erwachsenenbildung: auswärtige Kulturpolitik und internationale Zusammenarbeit', *International Perspectives in Adult Education* 29.

Oxenham, J., Diallo, A.H., Katahoire, A.R., Petkova-Mwangi, A. and Sall, O. (2002) *Skills and Literacy Training for Better Livelihoods: A review of approaches and experiences: Africa region human development*, Working Paper Series, March, Washington: World Bank.

Prodi, R. (2002) 'Why dialogue is important', in *Brussels: Conference on Intercultural Dialogue, 20–21 March*, p. 5. Available online at www.europa.eu.int/comm/index_en.htm.

Samlowski, M. (ed.) (1993a) 'Partnership and solidarity in action: international cooperation activities of IIZ/DVV', *International Perspectives in Adult Education* 28.

—— (1993b) 'Does the South end in the East?', *Adult Education and Development* 40: 287–310.

Schmidt-Behlau, B. (ed.) (2004) 'Building bridges for dialogue and understanding: results from the EU-Socrates Project, *Tolerance and Understanding – Our Muslim Neighbours*', *International Perspectives in Adult Education* 47.

—— (ed.) (2006) 'Adult education embracing diversity, I: Snapshots from intercultural learning in Europe, and II: Developing strategies for mainstreaming intercultural learning based on needs and experiences', *International Perspectives in Adult Education* 53, nos. I and II.

UNESCO (1999) *Records of the General Conference, 30th Session*, vol. 1: *Resolutions*, 26 October–17 November, Paris: UNESCO.

## Websites

www.aspbae.org
www.dvv-international.de
www.dvv-vhs.de
www.eaea.org
www.icae.org.uy
www.sozialstruktur.org
www.teach.pl
www.telc.net
www.unesco.org/education
www.unesco.org/education/uie/confintea

# 31

# To change the world
## Adult learning and social movements

*Budd L. Hall*

As I sit writing this chapter in my home in Victoria, British Columbia, Canada; as you are reading this chapter, no matter where you are living, or what you are reading or thinking about; and as we go about our daily practice of looking after our families, doing domestic work, fulfilling employment requirements, writing, studying, travelling or speaking at conferences, there are others in the streets, writing blogs, sending press releases, making banners, stopping traffic or meeting about strategy to change the world. There are so many people engaged in this kind of activity that the *New York Times* of a few years ago referred to this vast collectivity as the 'third super power'. These persons, these activities, these intentions, these hopes and these educational strategies are part of social movements. Social movements are the names that we give to groups of us working together to change things.

We are feeling the results of the work of global and local social movements in our daily lives. Climate change has become a practical form of public policy, individual choice and international discourse as a result of the many global environmental movements. I declined to buy fruit yesterday in my corner market because I noted that it came all the way from South Africa and I did not want to support the carbon emissions that such long-distance travel requires. My son and daughter-in-law speak of the 100-mile diet, an educational strategy that calls on us to eat only those foods that can be found within 100 miles of our homes.

Shawn Grant of the Bay of Quinte, Tyendenaga First Nations was interviewed on national television and radio yesterday about Aboriginal Land Claims. It seems that there are nearly 1,000 unresolved land claims in some form of litigation and negotiation at this point in time in Canada. Shawn was suddenly able to get some visibility for the cause because he had been part of a group that blockaded the main railroad link between Toronto and Montreal. He and thousands of Canadians are calling for a day of action across the country in support of Aboriginal land claims. He and all those who support this call are part of a social movement for Aboriginal self-determination and justice for land claims.

Tony Blair was in Washington, DC on a farewell tour as he stepped down from his position as Prime Minister of Great Britain. His successor did not come to Washington, DC for a visit, and George Bush Jr was being described as the worst foreign policy president in the history of the United States. The Democratic Party in the United States has seized control of both houses of the legislative branch in response to an angry public that wants to end the war in

Iraq. Barack Obama has risen to prominence and other powerful political persons have been forced to curb their ways, albeit long after tragic loss of life with much more still to come because, among other things, of the impact of the diverse social movements for peace, justice and global fairness.

This chapter makes the case that it is precisely the learning and knowledge-generating capacities of social movements that account for much of the power that is claimed by these movements. Deepening our understanding of learning within the contexts of social movements is a contribution, however modest, to the achievement a larger historic project of a world we want.

## What is a social movement?

> It goes on one at a time
> It starts when you care
> To act, it starts when you do it again after
> They said no
> It starts when you say we and know what
> You mean, and each
> Day you mean one more.
>
> Marge Piercy, *The Low Road*

The poetic definition of Marge Piercy is, to my mind, the clearest and most easily communicated statement about how we understand a social movement. David Snow, Sarah Soule and Hanspeter Kriesi, in their Introduction to the *Blackwell Companion to Social Movements*, note:

> Social movements can be thought of as *collectivities acting with some degree of organization, and continuity outside of institutional or organizational channels for the purpose of challenging or defending extant authority, whether it is institutionally or culturally based, in the group, organization, society, culture or world order of which they are a part.*
>
> (2004: 11; italics in original)

Donatella Della Porta and Mario Diani have, in synthesizing an enormous variety of European and North American literature, noted that most social movement scholars share a concern with four characteristics of movements: 'informal interaction networks; . . . shared beliefs and solidarity; . . . collective action focusing on conflict; . . . use of protest' (1999: 14–15).

## What is social movement learning?

Social movement learning refers to: (1) learning by persons who are part of any social movement; and (2) learning by persons outside of a social movement as a result of the actions taken or simply by the existence of social movements (Hall and Clover, 2005: 584–9). Learning by persons who are part of a social movement often takes place in informal or incidental ways because of the stimulation and requirements of participation in a movement. When one becomes involved in a movement to counter homelessness, statistics about how many people are homeless or the impact of living without fixed shelter are learned quickly simply through interaction with others in the movement or through the literature of the movement or the movement's opponents. What we all know as facilitators of learning is that nothing is as powerful a stimulus to learning as the necessity to teach or inform others. The organizational or communicative mandate of all social movements is a necessarily educational concern. And, while much of the learning within social movements is informal or incidental in nature, organized or intentional learning also takes place as a direct result of educational activities organized within the movement itself.

There has been a variety of intellectuals, scholars and activists over the years, such as Vandana Shiva and Mahatma Gandhi of India, Julius Nyerere of Tanzania, Jimmy Tompkins and Moses Coady of Canada, Myles Horton and Jane Adams of the United States and Paulo Freire of Brazil, who have planted the seeds of social movement learning. Today these traditions are vibrant with activities of various kinds. Examples are *Padayatras* (footmarches) that an increasing number of social movements use as a mode of pedagogy in various parts of India. In Fiji, WANIMATE, a non-governmental organization with links to the University of the South Pacific, supports the exchange of women's traditional knowledge of herbal medicines. Worldwide, what John Gaventa of the Highlander Centre and the University of Sussex calls the 'housewife researchers' are generating knowledge about toxic dumping, depletion of forest resources, pollution of water and issues of environmental racism. In rural Nepal, the forest user groups are not only taking care of the forest, they are actually changing the context and scope of what we mean by forest, what their use is and who can use and protect the forest. In the poor neighbourhoods of Chicago, groups such as the Covenant Group are learning how to transform abandoned buildings into renewed and socially useful housing for the long-term residents. In northern Canada, the Cree of James Bay educated millions of people in Canada, the United States and elsewhere, through multiple non-formal educational paths, about the dangers of uncontrolled mega-hydroelectric projects.

The Canadian labour movement, as Jeffery Taylor's book on *Union Learning* (2001) illustrates, is one of the oldest and strongest movements in Canada. It has a rich and well-documented history of social movement learning (Taylor, 2001; Martin, 1995; Spencer, 1995, 2002). The literature describes the sophisticated range of internal educational provision about the histories of unions, the functions of collective bargaining and procedures of union-management life. It also documents some of social unionisms' educational work on such topics as the nature of capitalism and the challenges of major national and global social issues. The biography of the life of Muriel Duckworth of Nova Scotia sheds light, as does some of the writing of the late David Smith, on many of the ways in which peace activists have worked to create organized space for learning (Kerans, 1996; Smith, 1995). This writing draws our attention to the reasons why peace must be struggled for and includes examples of peace education approaches that have been used with the broader public. Ron Faris has written in earlier works about the educational aspects of the New Canada Movement, a rural social movement that rose for some time in the Ontario that had as its goal the creation of a 'new and better Canada' (1975: 17). The Antigonish movement is perhaps the best-known and best-documented social movement in adult education history (see Lotz and Welton (1997) and Welton (2001) for two recent treatments). James H. Morrison has documented the early moments of learning and the movements for better working conditions in the work camps of early English Canada through Frontier College (1989).

## The impact of social movements on learning in broader society

A most powerful form of social movement learning, and one often neglected in the literature, is the learning that takes place by persons who are not directly participating as members of a given social movement and by people outside of a given movement. Canadian men, for example, have learned much about gender and power relations as a result of the women's movements, not necessarily because we were part of the movements themselves. Our mothers, partners, daughters and friends created a learning environment where we *learned* in experiential ways as we negotiate/d our daily lives. The actions of social movements, be they large-scale media events, such as those that Greenpeace and other environmental groups have staged, or benefit concerts for victims of HIV/AIDS, or the creation of quilts by women to protest the building of an unwanted power station on Vancouver Island (Clover, 2003), create rich environments for learning by large numbers of the public.

## Social movement learning theorists

Given the extent to which Canadian adult education frames itself within a social movement or at least a social action or social change framework, one would think that social movement theorists themselves might have noticed us when developing their own theories! Such does not appear to be the case. A review of social movement theory reveals the invisibility of a discourse on learning and education. Indeed neither the word 'education' nor the word 'learning' appears in the index of the encyclopedic *Blackwell Companion* mentioned above.

In the absence of specific references to learning or education in the social movement literature, which ideas show the most promise as theoretical building blocks? Eyerman and Jamieson are unique among social movement scholars in their recognition of the creative and central role of learning processes in what they call *cognitive praxis*. Their thoughts were drawn first to the attention of adult educators by John Holford and have subsequently been referred to by others when seeking to theorize learning in social movements (Holford, 1995; Foley, 1999; Walters, 2005). Eyerman and Jamieson state that, 'There is something fundamental missing from the sociology of social movements' (1991: 45). North American social movement theory, they suggest, focuses on what movements do and how they do it and not on what its members think. Knowledge is seen to be largely outside the sociologists' areas of competence, according to them. Their own work is informed by the writings of Habermas (1987), Cohen (1985) and Melucci (1988). Eyerman and Jamieson suggest that it is, 'through tensions between different groups and organizations over defining and acting in that conceptual space that the (temporary) identity of a social movement is formed' (1991: 22). Through the notion of cognitive praxis, they emphasize the creative role of consciousness and cognition in all human action, individual and collective. They focus simultaneously on the process of articulating a movement identity (cognitive praxis), on the actors taking part in this process (movement intellectuals), and on the context of articulation (politics, cultures and institutions). What comes out of social movement action is neither predetermined nor completely self-willed; its meaning is derived from the context in which it is carried out and the understanding that actors bring to it and/or derive from it.

Melucci offers some useful concepts for further developing theories of social movement learning. Social movements make power visible. They challenge the dominant meaning systems or symbols of contemporary everyday life. The 'movements no longer operate as characters by signs . . . They do this in the sense that they translate their action into symbolic challenges that upset the dominant cultural codes' (1988: 249). Social movements contest for ownership of specific social or political problems in the eyes of the public, 'imposing their own interpretation on these' (Della Porta and Diani, 1999: 70) and, in cases when they are successful, actually change the way that we understand knowledge and the relations of power. The Clayquot Sound summer of protest over clear-cutting on Vancouver Island, for example, not only challenged forestry practices, but changed our understanding of the relations of the rest of nature to human community and industrial exploitation. This changed understanding, which we *learned*, and led eventually to public policy changes and legislation in British Columbia and to many innovations in areas of social forestry.

Mario Diani, among others, offers the notion of 'interpretive frames' as another way of understanding social movements that has value for a knowledge or learning agenda (1996: 1053–69). An interpretive frame is a generalized conceptual structure that allows one to make sense of daily lived experiences and locate actions within an understanding of the world. Social movements offer a variety of interpretive frames, alternative frames to the public in the contestation over meaning. Freire, of course, referred to speaking from the perspective of marginalized peasants as naming the world. The various namings of the world or interpretive frames, according to Della Porta and Diani, can be usefully categorized as 'antisystem frames, realignment frames, inclusion frames and revitalization frames', depending on their specifics (1999: 80).

The work of Michael Roth, a Canadian cognitive psychologist working from a broad educational pallet, provides a very promising body of empirically based work to examine (Lee and Roth, 2003; Roth *et al.*, 2005). He speaks of the articulation of individual and collective learning in what he calls 'free choice learning' within community social action projects. Drawing on Bakhtin, Lave, Vygotsky and others, he and colleagues with whom he writes note that 'collective learning fosters individual learning and vice versa, whereby individuals produce resources in action and as outcomes of their activities. These resources expand the action possibilities of the collective and thus constitute learning' (Boyer and Roth, 2005: 75).

Adult educators, not surprisingly, have been the major contributors to theorizing social movement learning. While much of the writing has been descriptive, documenting practices and sharing stories, there is a growing body of more analytic and theoretical writing that has surfaced over the past 15 years. Mathias Finger, the Swiss adult educator and ecologist, and José Manuel Asun, a colleague from Spain, see new social movements as the catalysts for personal transformation, and the environment within which transformation occurs (Finger and Asun, 2001). Social movements define the future topics of adult education. Learning within social movements, according to Finger, has a more powerful impact on society than does all of the learning that takes place in schools. Social movement learning is viewed within a framework of endogenous knowledge creation, not dissimilar to Eyerman and Jamieson's cognitive praxis notion. Learning is seen as a people's tool (a political dimension), a democratic right (learning by all) and as learning from the world (epistemological dimension). They contrast this with exogenous knowledge transmission, which understands education (rather than learning) as a tool for maintaining the status quo, a package *for* all, and *about* the world (Finger, 1989).

Griff Foley, of Australia, is often drawn on by Canadian adult educators as he directly addressed the informal learning that happens within social movements in his book, *Learning in Social Action* (1999). He notes that informal learning emerges from, as well as advances, social action by contributing to building alternative organizational forms, by making links between the spiritual and the political, by illuminating the power of a small group of committed people, and by showing how expertise can be brought in from outside. He notes, in the context of several diverse social movement settings—a Brazilian women's organization, an environmental campaign and an African liberation movement—that learning deepens in the process of taking action. He writes on the nature of learning and emancipatory struggle from an historical materialist theoretical framework: 'A critique of capitalism must be at the heart of emancipatory adult education theory' (1999: 138).

351

Shirley Walters' feminist explorations of learning and gender in the context of popular education on an international scale are particularly well known (Walters and Manicom, 1996). In the context of co-teaching a course on social movement learning with Shirley Walters, the author of this chapter gained some new insights on social movement learning that have since been partially reflected in a chapter in the Nesbit collection on *Adult Education and Social Class* (Walters, 2005: 63–71). Based on her experience within the South African anti-apartheid struggle, Walters makes the case that the form of social movement learning is in part determined by the material conditions of the class structures from where the social movement activists emerge. The white South African allies of the anti-apartheid struggle were able to produce sophisticated policy briefs and research papers, and to create a huge network of organizations. The forms of social movement learning within this class of activists involved workshops, retreats and the reading of theory from other parts of the world. For South African Blacks working, when they had jobs, at low-paying and insecure settings, or living long distances from the city centres in poor housing with poor transportation, the predominant form of social movement learning took place at the large rallies, the funerals and the demonstrations where masses of people were able to be present. Leaflets, handbills and speeches were the dominant forms of social movement learning.

John Holst, of the United States, has added a substantial critique of much of the recent social movement and civil society learning theorizing and issues a call to adult educators to return to a deeper reading of Gramscii within the body of Marx and Lenin's writings. He argues in his book, *Social Movements, Civil Society and Radical Adult Education* (2002), similarly to Foley, that there has been insufficient fidelity to socialist roots in the past several decades of social movement and civil society theorizing. 'A theory and practice,' he notes, 'of revolutionary or radical adult education must explore the pedagogical nature of the most widely adopted and successful form of revolutionary organization of the 20th century . . . the revolutionary party' (2002: 113). His work speaks less of the forms of social movement learning, but more to the focus. Attention to social movements and civil society structures, in the absence of clarity about the ultimate goal being the transfer of power from capital to the working people, is misplaced at best and at worst facilitates the very weakening of capitalist control over democratic practice that we seek as adult educators.

## Social movement actors as knowers, learners and teachers

Social movements deal with overlapping themes. Some are creating sustainable livelihoods, protecting biodiversity or making communities self-reliant on food and agriculture. Some others are seeking equity and respect for women and sexual preferences, or decolonizing body, birth, health and the sense of beauty from the overtly corporatized health industry and insurance companies. Some others are seeking land and other sources of life, such as forest, fresh air, biomass and water, for the direct producers and appropriate technologies in harvesting as well as enhancing them. While some demand cultural diversity, language and identity, some others try to achieve their goals through active civic participation as citizens. Knowledge produced among these groups reverberates throughout the life-world: informal market networks, cooperatives, movements to save a sacred grove, rituals, festivities, struggles to save and diversify seeds through communal networks, or movements to institute self-governance. We have tried to interpret these formations in various ways: as the civil society (Hall, 2000; Tandon, 1994), or as 'social majorities' (Esteva and Prakash, 1998), or as 'ecological ethnicities' (Parajuli, 1996).

These new generations of social movements are neither single issue nor based on, nor enveloped within, the larger narratives of nationalist struggles. Neither are they limited to seeking 'equal opportunity' within the state and/or the market. They have opened the Pandora's box of multi-issues and multi-actors. Most important is the fact that each actor is embodied in his/her own pragmatic action and symbolic meanings. While sharpening their own knowledge claims, there appear to be convergences and alliances across a diversity of social actors. One such example is the convergence between ecologists, women and other social justice activists (Clover, 1995; Gadgil and Guha, 1995; Guha and Martinez-Alier, 1997; Kothari and Parajuli, 1993), between indigenous peoples' concerns and ecologists (Gediks, 1993; Laduke 1992), between analysts of peasant traditions of knowledge and discourses of green revolution (Esteva, 1996; Marglin and Marglin, 1996) or bio-technology (Moser and Shiva, 1995; Visvanathan 1997).

The preliminary sense is that today's social movements are not a phenomenon taking place in isolation or narrowly limited to a single issue or actor; they seem to be cognizant of a variety of overlapping issues. For example, WINAMATE in Fiji is involved in the task of regenerating women's healing and herbal knowledge. Now it is inextricably linked with the redefinition of gender roles and a critical look at the pharmaceutical industry. The communities that are at the forefront of protecting forest in India and Nepal are finding that their success is inextricably linked with land ownership patterns and the rights of inheritance for women. Hence today's movements are radical, complex, visionary and inclusive of more different identities than any existing social movement theories have been able to capture (Hunter, 1995; Melucci, 1995).

In the Jharkhand region of India, people of diverse caste, class and tribe are envisioning a pan-Jharkhandi composite culture (Parajuli, 1996). This is the trend we have depicted throughout India. At India's national level too, there are attempts to bring together actors of a host of movements, such as peasants, fisherfolk, women, agricultural labourers and adivasis, so that they can form a broader yet cohesive voice in matters of development and politics. During the last decade, some of these attempts have given birth to larger umbrella organizations, such as *Bharat Jan Andolan* (Indian People's Movement), *Bharat Jan Vikas Andolan* (Indian Movement for People's Development) and *Stri Mukti Sammelan* (Women's Liberation Conferences). Mobilization and networks on specific issues such as displacement, minimum wages, employment guarantees, gender issues and tribal rights over forest are more common and frequent. Several other organized efforts are attempting to articulate people's alternatives to state politics (e.g. the Movement for Tribal Self-rule).

## The importance of social movement learning now

Attention to social movement learning is critical at this specific transformative moment in time. For us to be able to make the scale of changes that many of us feel are needed in our troubled world, we need to be able to move beyond the market as the primary driver of learning theory. We need to move beyond the a-contextual, de-genderized and de-racialized ideas about how learning takes place within individuals, whether child or adult. Our ability to deepen our understanding of social movements depends in part on our studying the hidden dimensions of social movement action—the learning dimensions. Attention to social movement learning will also add to our understanding of adult, popular, and transformative learning at a time when such attention is needed.

From the perspective of social movements, their leaderships and their constituents themselves, attention to the learning dimensions of their work has never been more needed. Real movement resources need to be devoted to the intentional structuring of learning opportunities for those within movements and those outside of movements to engage in. Reflection on the tacit skills being learnt by social movement activists is of critical use for strengthening the organizational base and capacity of movements.

## New utopian visions and practices are being created everywhere in profusion

Ulrich Beck has noted that 'The blueprints for alternative world views are carried about in the breast pockets, backpacks and hearts of social activists today' (1997: 23). These new blueprints are deep, elaborate, practical and even spiritual approaches to another world, where fairness and respect form the heart of human, and more than human, relationships.

Whether in the oral naming of our world by the Aboriginal People; or the documented practices of green economists; or the business successes of women's grassroots saving groups in Asia and Africa; or the community business incubators of Van City Credit Union; or the participatory budget of the city of Porto Alegre Brazil; or the thousands of groups building the world social movement; or the sustainable forestry of smallholder loggers in British Columbia; and in spite of the attempts of the global market forces to silence or render invisible other ways of being, our world, our imagination and our creativity have not been stopped. The anti-globalization and anti-capitalist movements are creating a powerful epistemic community where learning is accelerating. Attention to the power of learning and the power of knowledge-making in social movement contexts is a contribution that those interested in learning and the engagement of civil societies can make.

It seems apt to close this chapter in poetic form—a form that, like social movements themselves, is drawn from both our heads and our hearts.

## Learning to imagine

Education is about our relationships, our communities, our places of work,
Our bio-regions, our political structures, our planet and our universe.
It is about us.
It is about the kind of work we do.
But above all it is about the right to imagine.
To imagine a context where we are each respected for who we are;
To imagine a life of sufficiency and health;
To imagine that all our children could live without abuse;
To imagine that violence or the fear of violence in the lives of all women and
    children could decline;
To imagine that race would be a code for creativity and contribution rather than
    a filter that excludes;
To imagine relationships of harmony and rhythm with the earth;
To imagine that differences in ability could be cherished for the gifts they make
    possible;
To imagine that we have the courage to speak.

But to be able to move forward
Taking firm hold of or on the right to imagine,

We need to accept some quite simple and basic notions:
That things are not OK the way they are;
That we have the capacity to transform our lives;
That the current global economic machine is killing humans, all other forms of life
and puts the survival of the planet at risk;

That the ways in which we think constructs our lives;
That our lives, including our race, gender, sexual orientation, abilities, age, class and
relations with the earth, construct the ways in which we think;
That the seeds of a transformed world exists within our communities, our schools, our
social movements, our locations of resistance and even among those who hear or
read this poem.

## Conclusions

Adult educators seeking to really change the world, activists and social movement leaders seeking increased impact, and social movement theorists who seek to do more than describe need to pay particular attention in these early decades of the twenty-first century to the interaction of learning, social action, and the creation of the world that we want. The slogan of the World Social Forum is 'Another World is Possible'. Indeed it is. It is forming as you read/I write. You/we are part of it. Learning for resistance, understanding, survival, humor, transgression, displacement, hope and possibility lie at the centre of our times.

## References

Apprel-Marglin, F. and Parajuli, P. (1998) 'Geographies of difference and the resilience of ecological ethnicities', *Development* 41: 14–21.
Beck, U. (1997) *The Reinvention of Politics*, Cambridge: Polity Press.
Boyer, L. and Roth, M. (2005) 'Individual/collective dialectic of free-choice learning in a community-mapping project', *Environmental Education Review* 11(3): 75–91.
Clover, D. (1995) 'Gender, transformative learning and environmental action', *Gender and Education* 7(3): 243–58.
—— (ed.) (2003) *Global Perspectives in Environmental Adult Education*, New York: Peter Lang.
—— with Follan, S. and Hall, B. (2000) *The Nature of Learning: Environmental adult education*, 2nd edn, Toronto: Transformative Learning Centre.
Cohen, J.L. (1985) 'Strategy and identity: new theoretical paradigm and contemporary social movements', *Social Research* 52: 663–716.
Della Porta, D. and Diani, M. (1999) *Social Movements: An Introduction*, Oxford: Blackwell.
Diani, M. (1996) 'Linking mobilization frames and political opportunities: insights from regional populism in Italy', *American Sociological Review* 61: 1053–69.
Esteva, G. (1996) *Grassroots Postmodernism: Beyond human rights, the industrial self, the global economy*, New York: Peter Lang.
—— and Prakash, M.S. (1998) *Grassroots Post-Modernism: Remaking the soil of cultures*. London: Zed Books.
Eyerman, R. and Jamison, A. (1991) *Social Movements: A cognitive approach*, University Park, PA: Pennsylvania State University Press.
Faris, R. (1975) *The Passionate Educators*, Toronto: Peter Martin.
Finger, M. (1989) 'New social movements and their implications for adult education', *Adult Education Quarterly* 40(1): 15–22.

—— and Asun, J.M. (2001) *Adult Education at the Crossroads: Learning our way out*, London: Zed Books.

Foley, G. (1999) *Learning in Social Action: A contribution to understanding informal education*, London: Zed Books.

Gadgil, M. and Guha, R. (1995) *Ecology and Equity: The use and abuse of nature in contemporary India*, New Delhi: Penguin.

Gedicks, A. (1993) *New Resource Wars: Native and environmental struggles against multinational corporations*. Boston South End Press.

Guha, R. and Martinez-Alier, J. (1997) *Varieties of Environmentalism*, London: Earthscan.

Habermas, J. (1987) *The Theory of Communicative Action*, Cambridge: Polity Press.

Hall, B. (2000) 'Global civil society: theorizing a changing world', *Convergence* 32(12): 10–32.

—— and Clover, D. (2005) 'Social movement learning', in L. English (ed.) *International Encyclopedia of Adult Education*, London: Palgrave Macmillan, pp. 584–9.

Holford, J. (1995) 'Why social movements matter: adult education theory, cognitive praxis and the creation of knowledge', *Adult Education Quarterly* 45(2): 95–111.

Holst, J. (2002) *Social Movements, Civil Society and Radical Adult Education*, Westport, CT: Bergin and Garvey.

Hunter, A. (1995) 'Rethinking revolution in light of the new social movements', in M. Darnovsky, B. Epstein and R. Flacks (eds) *Cultural Politics and Social Movements*, Philadelphia: Temple University Press, pp. 345–78.

Kerans, M. (1996) *Murial Duckworth: A very active pacifist*, Halifax, Nova Scotia: Fernwood.

Kothari, S. and Parajuli, P. (1993) *No Nature Without Social Justice: A plea for cultural and ecological pluralism in India*, London: Zed Books.

Laduke, W. (1992) 'The political economy of radioactive colonialism', in M.A. James (ed.) *The State of Native America: Genocide, colonization and resistance*, Boston South End Press.

Lee, S. and Roth, M. (2003) 'Of transversals and hybrid spaces: science in the community', *Mind, Culture and Activity* 10, 120–42.

Lotz, J. and Welton, M.R. (1997) *Father Jimmy: Life and times of Jimmy Tompkins*, Wreck Cove, Nova Scotia: Bretton Books.

Marglin, F.A. and Marglin, S. (eds) (1996) *Decolonizing Knowledge: From development to dialogue*, Oxford: Clarendon Press.

Martin, D. (1995) *Thinking Union: Activism and education in Canada's labour movement*, Toronto: Between the Lines.

Melucci, A. (1988) 'Getting involved: identity and mobilization in social movements', in B. Klandermans, H. Kriesi and S. Tarrow (eds) *From Structure to Action*, Greenwich, CT: JAI Press.

—— (1995) 'The global planet an the internal planet: new frontiers for collective action and individual transformation', in M. Darnovsky, B. Epstein and R. Flacks (eds) *Cultural Politics and Social Movements*, Philadelphia: Temple University Press, pp. 322–46.

Morrison, J.H. (1989) *Camps and Classrooms: A pictorial history of Frontier College*, Toronto: Frontier College.

Moser, I. and Shiva, V. (eds) 1995 *Biopolitics: A feminist reader on biotechnology*, London: Zed Books.

Nesbit, T. (2005) *Class Concerns: Adult education and social class*, New Directions in Adult Education no. 106, San Francisco, CA: Jossey Bass.

Parajuli, P. (1996) 'Rethinking ethnicity: developmentalist hegemonies and emergent identities in India', *Identities: Global Studies in Culture and Power* 3(1–2): 15–59.

Piercy, M. (1980) *The Moon is Always Female*, New York: Alfred A. Knopf.

Roth, M., Hwang, S., Lee, Y.J. and Goulart, M.I.M. (2005) *Participation, Learning and Identity: Dialectical perspectives*, Berlin: Lehmanns Media.

Smith, D. (1995) *First Person Plural: A community development approach to social change*, Montreal Black Rose Books.

Snow, D.A., Soule, S.A. and Kriesi, H. (eds) (2004) *The Blackwell Companion to Social Movements*, Oxford: Blackwell.

Spencer, B. (1995) 'Old and new social movements as learning sites: greening labour unions and unionizing the greens', *Adult Education Quarterly* 46(1): 31–41.

—— (2002) *Unions and Learning in a Global Economy: International and comparative perspectives*, Toronto: TEP.

Tandon, R. (1994) *Citizens: Strengthening global civil society*, Washington, DC: CIVICUS.

Taylor, J. (2001) *Union Learning: Canadian labour education in the twentieth century*, Toronto: TEP.

Visvanathan, S. (1997) *Carnival for Science: Essays on science, technology and development*, Oxford: OUP.

Walters, S. (2005) 'Social movements, class and adult education', in T. Nesbit (ed.) *Class Concerns: Adult education and social class*, New Directions in Adult Education, no. 106, San Francisco, CA: Jossey-Bass, pp. 37–46.

—— and Manicom, L. (1996) *Gender in Popular Education: Methods for empowerment*, London: Zed Books.

Welton, M. (2001) *Little Mosie From the Margaree: A biography of Moses Michael Coady*, Toronto: TEP.

# 32

# International aid

*Cornelia Dragne and Budd L. Hall*

Adult education had been an international field of cooperation long before the creation of government international development funding bodies in the last half of the twentieth century. The early work of the Worker's Education Authority, for example, was spread throughout the industrialized world in the early twentieth century. The first World Conference on Adult Education was held in 1929 in England and had representatives from more than 50 countries, including countries of what we would now call the 'global South'. In many countries, the international development activities of non-governmental organizations (NGOs) and even universities pre-date the setting-up of the modern Official Development Assistance (ODA). For example, in 1948 the Oxford Extra-Mural Delegacy sent Lalage Bown and Paul Bertelsen to Ghana and Nigeria to work with the Universities of Ghana in Legon and the University of Ibadan on the establishment of extra-mural departments. The late J. Roby Kidd of Canada worked in both Jamaica and India in the early 1960s under the auspices of the Commonwealth Colombo Plan, establishing adult education departments in the universities in that part of the world.

By the 1960s most of the richer countries of the world had established some kind of international development governmental organizations. Depending on the history, tradition, focus and priorities of these various agencies, adult education may have been one of the types of activities that were supported. Historically, the Nordic countries and Germany have been the most generous in the funding of adult education activities in developing countries. This is not surprising, as these are countries with a long tradition in the field of adult education. Canada has had a mixed record of some remarkable early support, but a collapse of ODA support for adult education in more recent years. Even so, for programmes labelled as lifelong learning, Canada remains the main donor country.

This brief chapter cannot possibly do justice to the entire range of international aid for adult education. The largest proportion of funding by far for adult education activities, for example, passes through such NGOs as Action Aid in the UK, *dvv international* (German Association of Folk High Schools Institute, or the German Adult Education Association) and a wide variety of other NGOs based in both the North and the South. This chapter is based on an examination of ODA as provided to adult education. It is almost impossible to determine the actual flow of ODA to adult education as the breakdowns in the sources of this data are not detailed enough, so this is a very rough portrait on international aid and adult education.

# Trends in international aid in adult education

## *International policy context*

One point of departure for international development cooperation is the eight Millennium Development Goals (MDGs) that the world countries agreed upon at the Millennium Summit in 2000 in order to halve poverty and hunger by 2015. Another one, specific to education, is the Dakar Framework for Action (DFA), adopted in Senegal in 2000 by 164 countries, which outlines a strategy for achieving the goal of Education for All (EFA), which has been conceptualized as a human right.

These goals suggest that the focus of international development aid should be placed on primary and secondary education rather than on adult education; also that, in the field of adult education, funding should be channelled primarily towards two objectives: literacy and achieving gender equality. It should be mentioned, though, that late developments in the

---

### Two Millennium Development Goals (MDGs) refer to education

MDG 2: Achieve universal primary education

> Target 3: Ensure that, by 2015, children everywhere, boys and girls alike, will be able to complete a full course of primary schooling.

MDG 3: Promote gender equality and empower women

> Target 4: Eliminate gender disparity in primary and secondary education, preferably by 2005, and at *all levels of education* no later than 2015.

### Education for All (EFA) goals

1 Expanding and improving comprehensive early childhood care and education.

2 Free and compulsory primary education by 2015.

3 Ensuring that the learning needs of all *young people and adults* are met through equitable access to appropriate learning and *life-skills* programmes.

4 Achieving a 50 per cent improvement in levels of *adult literacy* by 2015, especially for women, and equitable access to *basic and continuing education for all adults*.

5 Eliminating gender disparities in primary and secondary education by 2005, and achieving gender equality in education by 2015, with a focus on ensuring girls' full and equal access to and achievement in basic education of good quality.

6 Improving all aspects of the quality of education and ensuring excellence of all so that recognized and measurable learning outcomes are achieved by all, especially in *literacy, numeracy and essential life skills*.

Source: UNESCO (2000, 2005)

---

discussion surrounding literacy expanded the field from the narrow concept of the capacity to read and write, and the wider interpretation implies a stronger focus on creating literate environments and learning societies and a lesser focus on eradicating illiteracy (Buchert, 2003).

The EFA and MDG goals have led to the establishment of several global strategic frameworks for collaborative action, such as:

- the UN Literacy Decade (UNLD), declared by the UN General Assembly for 2003–12 – this focuses on the needs of the 781 million youths and adults, particularly women and girls, who are still deprived of literacy;
- LIFE 2005–15 – UNESCO's Literacy Initiative for Empowerment, a country-led and country-specific process that will be implemented in 35 countries over a ten-year period (UIL, 2006);
- International Literacy Day;
- the UN Decade of Education for Sustainable Development.

## Trends in financing adult education

Data used for this analysis were extracted from the International Development Statistics (IDS) databases (the Development Assistance Committee (DAC) database on annual aggregates and the Creditor Reporting System (CRS) database on aid activities) and from the Accessible Information on Development Activities (AiDA), provided jointly by the Development Gateway Foundation, OECD-DAC, the World Bank and United Nations Development Programme (UNDP). In addition to these institutions, AiDA also draws from a wealth of data sources (United States Agency for International Development (USAID), MacArthur Foundation, Natural Resources Information System (NARSIS), etc.).

During the last decade and a half the ODA for education has had ups and downs, but overall it experienced important growth. Between 1990 and 2000, it increased by 51.89 per cent. Starting with 2001, it displays a spectacular growth, which culminates with the year 2004 (see Figure 32.1). At its peak, the total ODA for education was a bit short of USD10 billion (9.35 billion), almost four times the total funding in 1990.

Data suggest that ODA for education increased steadily from 2001 to 2004 and that the latter year represents an inflection point in the trend. However, since there are not yet available data for 2006 and 2007, it is hazardous to conclude that the decrease represents a new trend.

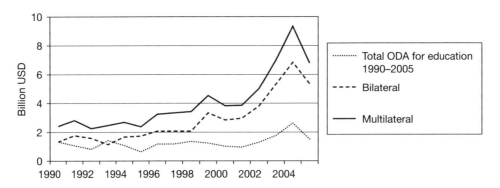

*Figure 32.1* ODA for education, 1990–2005.

Source: Compiled from data extracted from the OECD CRS database.

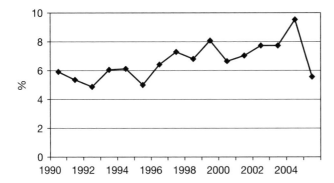

*Figure 32.2* Percentage ODA for education from total ODA.

Source: Compiled from data extracted from the OECD CRS database.

We should note that the values of ODA for 2003 and those for 2005 are comparable (6.96 billion and 6.88 billion respectively) and that the value for 2004 is much larger (9.35 billion). International development agencies, such as the Swedish International Development Cooperation Agency (SIDA), contend that the unusual increase in the funds for 2004 is attributable to the increase in the humanitarian aid component, due to the devastating tsunami in the Indian Ocean (SIDA, 2005). If we compare the values in 1990 with the one in 2004, we see that ODA for education had increased almost threefold. It may be concluded that the adoption of a common framework for action in the form of the MDGs and EFA in 2000 triggered indeed a real upwards trend in international aid for education in volume terms.

As a percentage from the total ODA (see Figure 32.2), the aid for education presents a more sinuous variation. The year 2005 saw a return to the 1990s, but the values vary roughly between 4 per cent and 10 per cent and tend to oscillate around 6 per cent.

Another evident trend is the fact that, in the last ten years, the bilateral component of the aid parallels the total evolution (increase), whereas the multilateral component tends to stagnate. Although the flow through traditional channels may have enlarged in terms of volume, as a percentage of the total it is in decline. However, this decline does not mean that all intermediary agencies have a lesser role to play than in the past. UNICEF, for example, started to become more active from 2000 and the funds channelled through the European Commission (EC) increased twofold, starting from 2003.

It is hard to know which country contributed most to education, because the multilateral component of ODA is not divided by individual donor country but rather by intergovernmental organization. Only the bilateral component is clearly attributable to individual countries. All the following considerations refer thus to the bilateral component only. Overall, for education as a whole, the top donor countries were Japan, the UK and the USA between 1990 and 1998; Germany was the top donor in 1999; and, from 2000 onwards, France (see Figure 32.3).

Between 2001 and 2005, Japan, Germany, the Netherlands, the UK, the USA and Canada have been important contributors. This is not a strict classification; for example, Japan's contribution more than doubled from approximately 6 per cent of the total ODA for education in 2001 to approximately 15 per cent in 2005, whereas Germany's contribution dropped from 16 per cent in 2004 to 8 per cent in 2005 (see Figure 32.3).

An analysis of the financing of adult education is impeded by the fact that there is no reference to adult or continuing education in official statistics on education assistance. Thus the authors

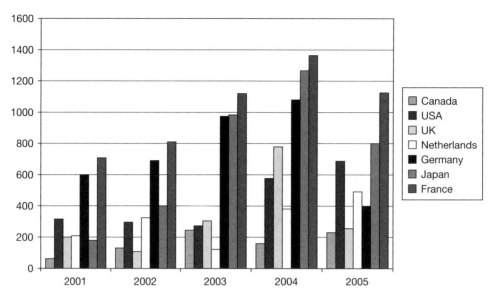

*Figure 32.3* ODA for education, 2001–5 (million USD).

Source: Compiled from data extracted from the OECD CRS database.

compiled the data on international aid in the field of adult education from the CRS destination sectors (purpose codes) that were considered by us as adult education activities (see Table 32.1). Another impediment is the fact that ODA, although the major component in financing adult education, it is not the only one. Other components are OA (official assistance for countries that are not on the ODA list) and private funds.

We can see that adult education is an important component of ODA, ranging from 22 per cent to 40 per cent of the total ODA for education. The most funded component is the strengthening of civil society. Without it, the percentage of adult education in the total ODA for education would range approximately between 10 per cent and 20 per cent. Although 2005 represents a drop in aid in volume terms, as a percentage from the total aid for education it represents a 3 per cent increase from 2004 (see Figure 32.4).

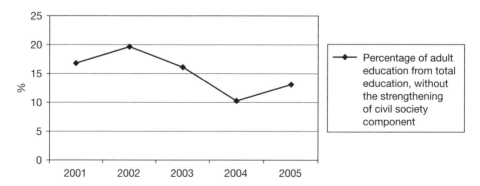

*Figure 32.4* Percentage of adult education from total education.

Source: Compiled from data extracted from the OECD CRS database.

*Table 32.1* ODA for adult education, 2001–5 (Million USD)

| Year | 2001 | 2002 | 2003 | 2004 | 2005 |
|---|---|---|---|---|---|
| *Basic life skills for youths and adults* | | | | | |
| Bilateral | 132.41885 | 160.5115 | 154.58901 | 170.05967 | 108.78592 |
| Multilateral | 46.496681 | 1.547393 | 17.860084 | 28.935561 | 13.948378 |
| | 178.9155 | 162.0589 | 172.4491 | 198.9952 | 122.7343 |
| *Strengthening civil society* | | | | | |
| Bilateral | 851.92712 | 700.79576 | 671.80603 | 1058.8617 | 1096.6484 |
| Multilateral | 37.670903 | 80.32628 | 130.59744 | 82.270933 | 211.04446 |
| | 889.598 | 781.122 | 802.4035 | 1141.133 | 1307.693 |
| *Educational research* | | | | | |
| Bilateral | 10.210007 | 7.201954 | 15.950757 | 6.343638 | 19.35931 |
| *Environmental education and training* | | | | | |
| Bilateral | 21.764553 | 21.442677 | 40.091273 | 81.406296 | 36.586688 |
| Multilateral | 2.426017 | – | – | 0.695739 | – |
| | 24.19057 | 21.44268 | 45.63325 | 82.10204 | 36.58669 |
| *Health education* | | | | | |
| Bilateral | 32.199565 | 41.080805 | 34.165099 | 38.82618 | 28.55361 |
| Multilateral | 4.219 | 9.852941 | 8.560283 | – | 14.896508 |
| | 36.41857 | 50.93375 | 42.72538 | 130.0777 | 43.45012 |
| *Promotion of development awareness* | | | | | |
| Bilateral | 85.463864 | 131.83153 | 374.70099 | 173.31945 | 208.82729 |
| Multilateral | 18.573883 | 21.527888 | 28.210771 | 31.034552 | 49.821924 |
| | 104.0377 | 153.3594 | 402.9118 | 204.354 | 258.6492 |
| *Teacher training* | | | | | |
| Bilateral | 48.844042 | 49.345645 | 93.11352 | 78.283436 | 113.29614 |
| Multilateral | 0.578834 | 20.161708 | 0.147687 | – | – |
| | 49.42288 | 69.50735 | 93.26121 | 78.28344 | 113.2961 |
| *Vocational training* | | | | | |
| Bilateral | 184.24218 | 188.05743 | 252.47413 | 242.05804 | 257.44781 |
| Multilateral | 67.435342 | 328.22071 | 102.54499 | 97.88384 | 49.198282 |
| | 251.6775 | 516.2781 | 355.0191 | 339.9419 | 306.6461 |
| *Total ODA* | 1544.471 | 1761.904 | 1924.812 | 2089.979 | 2208.415 |

Source: Compiled from data extracted from the OECD CRS database.

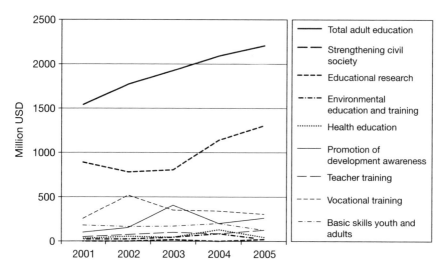

*Figure 32.5* ODA for adult education, 2001–5.

Source: Compiled from data extracted from the OECD CRS database.

Overall, funding for adult education increased steadily during 2001–5 by 30 per cent (see Figure 32.5). The increase is largely due to the increase in the number of programmes and projects directed towards strengthening democracy that has been manifest since 2003; each subsequent year the number of such projects increased twofold and between 2000 and 2005 their number increased by a factor of ten.

When it comes to aid directed specifically towards developing the basic life skills for youths and adults, data for the years 2001–5 (see Figure 32.6) suggests a clear preference of the donor

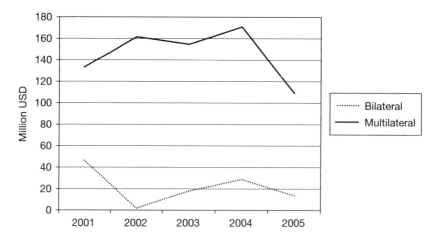

*Figure 32.6* ODA for basic life skills for youths and adults, 2001–5.

Source: Compiled from data extracted from the OECD CRS database.

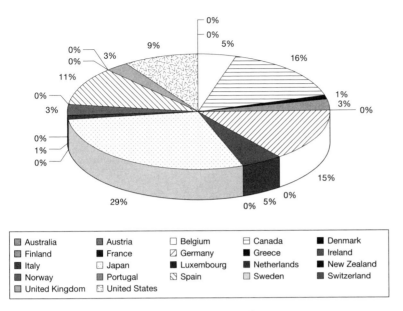

*Figure 32.7* ODA for basic skills for youths and adults, 2005.

Source: Compiled from data extracted from the OECD CRS database.

countries for working directly with the recipient state, which may mean that governments are being required to take more responsibility.

The main donor countries in this area between 2001–5 have been the USA, Germany and Japan. In 2001 and 2002, the USA was by far the largest contributor, accounting for around half of the total ODA. In 2005, the USA's contribution fell dramatically by an order of magnitude. Whereas in 2001, the USA contributed some USD81m to the ODA for adult education, representing approximately 61 per cent of the total, in 2005 it contributed only USD9.7m (approximately 9 per cent). In 2003 and in 2004, the major contributor became Germany, with approximately USD40m (26 per cent) and USD42.2m (25 per cent), while in 2005 its place was taken by Japan with some USD31m (29 per cent). Canada also became a major contributor in 2005, with USD17m. Figure 32.7 shows a distribution by country for the year 2005. The largest contributor is Japan, followed by Canada, Germany, Spain and the USA. Germany and Japan are also the main contributors when it comes to vocational training (see Figure 32.8). Data suggests that the UK has been a major donor to adult education overall, followed by Germany, Japan, Canada, the USA and Sweden.

An important loan directed to lifelong learning and training that is not accounted for in the above OECD data has been recently approved by the World Bank. From a total loan of USD877m to support infrastructure and social programmes in Argentina, USD200m will be directed towards developing job skills and improving employability for unemployed and poor workers in Argentina, through training and adult education (World Bank, 2007).

## Thematic components of adult education

The world of adult education is traditionally a fuzzy world (Torres, 2004). The fields of adult learning are not clearly defined in the supporting policies. Also, there is no total agreement in the world of international development on a common terminology. Old terms and new terms coexist in the statistical data, making the analysis even more difficult. However, although

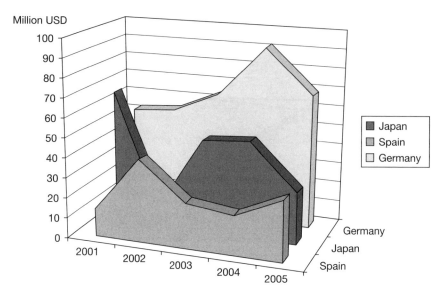

*Figure 32.8* Major ODA contributors to vocational training, 2001–5.

Source: Compiled from data extracted from the OECD CRS database.

different donor countries and agencies may use different terms and definitions, several domains of adult education become apparent:

- adult literacy;
- basic life skills;
- gender equality;
- health education;
- microfinance;
- vocational education.

Overlapping/parallel terminology contains: non-formal education (NFE), lifelong learning, continuing education, basic education (BE), basic learning needs (BLN), adult basic learning and education (ABLE) and open education.

### Challenges and progress

One important challenge in the field of financing adult education is in fact a challenge for educational researchers: to reach a consensual conceptual framework to orient action. An example of the importance of a solid conceptual foundation for action is in the field of literacy. There is a risk that literacy is understood as, and limited to, eradication of illiteracy. Limiting the aid to this purpose may deepen the divide between the South and the North at a time when adult education in the North is understood as the continuous adaptation of know-ledge and experience to sustain the establishment of knowledge societies under the impact of globalization (Buchert, 2003). Today the need to include IT skills in the definition of literacy is largely accepted. According to Torres (2004), 'cleaning the field, and agreeing on a common terminology, whenever possible, is essential for communicational and operational purposes, for the advancement of theory and research, and for international comparability' (p. 28). Another challenge stems from the difficulty of evaluating and reporting the results of past programmes. Finally, international development cooperation actors are faced with a lack of models for adult education policies and legislation, as well as recommendations, from which to draw (Hinzen, 2007).

Despite challenges, important progression has been made. One progress is the growth in funding in volume terms. Another is the tendency towards an integrative approach. The boundaries between thematic areas are increasingly blurring, in recognition of the need to treat adult education in a holistic manner. Today the world of international development prefers to see the interrelationships between areas of adult education, aiming more at creating learning communities. This integrative approach is in synch with theoretical developments, which tend to treat the subject of adult education within the lifelong learning context. The important growth in funding for civic adult education suggests a will to reorient education and learning towards social transformation and human development.

## Actors in the field of international development cooperation for adult education

### National efforts

### Sweden and SIDA

Sweden is a major donor country in the field of international development cooperation, being one of the five countries that met the UN target for ODA of 0.7 per cent of GNI (gross national income) (CCIC, 2006: 2). In 2006, Sweden allocated SEK15.9 billion for development cooperation and almost SEK24 billion in 2005 (SIDA, 2007). The drop in funding is mainly attributable to the humanitarian component. SIDA channels more than half of the total Swedish ODA; in 2006 it distributed 54 per cent of the total (SIDA, 2007). The education component of SIDA's total disbursements varies slightly around an average of 8 per cent. During 2005, SIDA provided SEK995m to education. Around half of the total disbursements go to primary education (54 per cent in 2005) (SIDA, 2006). SIDA's education cooperation is present in all developing regions of the world, but the bulk goes to Africa (46 per cent) and to Asia (31 per cent). Although the percentages vary slightly from year to year, there has been no major change in the education cooperation focus on regions. As recent trends, an increase in the aid for Asia (from 22 to 31 per cent) and a decrease in the disbursements for Africa (from 53 to 46 per cent) may be noted (SIDA, 2004, 2005, 2006).

In SIDA's funding statistics, adult education does not represent a stand-alone subsector, being divided between vocational education and adult/literacy education. There is also a subsector, general education, which may also encompass programmes that are in fact non-formal adult education. Among the two components, literacy represents 3–4 per cent (SEK 16.4–36.1) and vocational education represents 0.5–1 per cent (SEK3.2–6.7m) of the total SIDA education cooperation (2003–5). The main recipient for vocational education aid is the Commonwealth of Independent States (CIS) (ex-USSR).

In addition to bilateral programmes, SIDA supports the work of several global institutions: the International Council for Adult Education (ICAE), UNESCO's Child Protection Education, the Centre for Adult and Continuing Education (CACE), South Africa, and the UNESCO Institute for Lifelong Learning (UIL).

## The UK and DFID

The Department for International Development (DFID) of the UK government channels the major part of the UK aid effort. The UK uses several aggregation instruments for development assistance, the main being: DFID programme aid, the Gross Public Expenditure on Development (GPEX) and the net UK ODA. The GPEX shows development aid flows from all official UK sources, including the DFID programme. In 2005/6, the UK's GPEX amounted to £6,612m, an increase of 27 per cent from the previous year. Part of this increase reflects a large amount of debt relief to Nigeria (£1,435m). Excluding the debt relief, the GPEX increased by 10 per cent from the previous year. For 2005, the UK reported an ODA of £5,916m, placing it in third place as the largest DAC donor (provisional data). As a percentage of GNI though, UK ODA represents 0.47 per cent, which means the UK is below the 0.7 per cent UN target, which puts it in the eighth place.

From the total of £6,612m, £4,413m or 66 per cent was channelled through DFID, which in turn devoted over half of its funds (£2,504m or 57 per cent) to bilateral assistance and £1,674m (38 per cent) to multilateral organizations, the rest being administration costs.

Overall, the DFID programme increased by 51 per cent between 2001/2 and 2005/6 (see Figure 32.9). By region, the main beneficiary of the UK aid flow was Africa (45 per cent), followed by Asia (38 per cent).

According to data from AiDA, starting from 1996 the UK has financed almost 1,400 projects, 94 per cent of which were funded through DFID. Of these, 72 have been dedicated to education, 273 to building or strengthening civil society and democracy, 160 to health, 36 to industry and 24 to peace-building. Data from CRS for 2001–5 shows the UK to be the top donor in teacher training, strengthening civil society, health education and educational research, and one of the largest in environmental education.

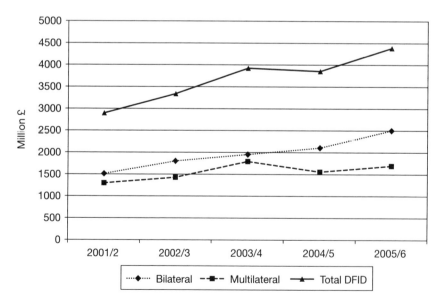

*Figure 32.9* DFID programme, 2001/2–2005/6.

Source: DFID (2007).

## Germany and DVV

In Germany, international development cooperation is coordinated at federal level by the Federal Ministry for Economic Cooperation and Development (the BMZ). The net German ODA for 2005 was €8.112m, or 0.36 per cent of GNI (BMZ, 2007a). According to BMZ's official site, in 2007 provision was made for €4.5 billion and the financing plan for 2005–9 provided for further increases (BMZ, 2007b). Germany has been the top donor country in vocational education for several years in a row and one of the top donors in educational research.

Germany's key actor in channelling its development cooperation funds towards adult education is the Institute for International Cooperation of the German Adult Education Association (IIZ/DVV, now known as *dvv international*). The Institute works with government and NGO partners and supports the major international networks in the field of adult education (ICAE and its regional partners). The foci of their work are: adult literacy, vocational training, women's education, environmental education and peace and human rights education, as well as the development of teaching and learning materials, institution- and capacity-building and the provision of training for adult education practitioners. The *dvv international* contends that its overall goal is that of global sustainable development and states that it identifies its work with the interests of the poorer sections of the population in its partner countries (*dvv international*, 2007).

## Canada and the Canadian International Development Agency

In the late 1970s, the Canadian International Development Agency (CIDA) created a funding window for international NGOs (INGOs). The thought was that some of the INGOs that were traditionally located in New York or Geneva might relocate to Canada. This funding mechanism provided the initial support for ICAE that was founded by the late Dr J. Roby Kidd in 1973. ICAE had its world headquarters in Canada from 1973 until 2002, when the headquarters was shifted to Montevideo, Uruguay. Between 1976 and 2000, CIDA invested around USD20m in adult education capacity-building and networking, funding not only ICAE but regional adult education organizations such as the Latin American Council for Adult Education, the Asia and South Pacific Bureau of Adult Education and the African Association for Literacy and Adult Education. And while funding to adult education in its more diffuse forms has continued, the direct support of adult education NGOs and much of the governmental support of adult education has nearly dried up. This resulted in the decision by ICAE to move the world headquarters to Uruguay. Canadian adult educators, Budd L. Hall and Paul Bélanger, remain active in the international arena, but official government support has nearly disappeared.

## *Intergovernmental organizations and agencies*

One of the challenges for adult education funding stems from linking policy, action and research. To bridge them, one of the most important actors is the UNESCO Institute for Lifelong Learning (UIL), which is a non-profit international research, training, information, documentation and publishing centre on literacy, non-formal education, adult and lifelong learning. UIL provides services to UNESCO's member states, to NGOs, to grassroots and community organizations, and to partners in civil society and in the private sector. UIL is based in Hamburg, Germany. We should also mention the World Bank and UNICEF as major conduits for funds towards adult learning.

369

## *Non-governmental organizations*

### The International Council for Adult Education

The International Council for Adult Education (ICAE) is the major global partnership of adult learners and adult educators and their organizations. ICAE's regional partners are:

- the Arab Network for Literacy and Adult Education (ANLAE);
- the Asian South Pacific Bureau of Adult Education (ASPBAE);
- the Caribbean Regional Council for Adult Education (CARCAE);
- the Latin American Council for Adult Education (CEAAL);
- the European Association for the Education of Adults (EAEA);
- the North-American Alliance for Popular and Adult Education (NAAPAE);
- the Pan-African Association for Literacy and Adult Education (PAALAE).

ICAE promotes lifelong learning as a necessary component for people to contribute creatively to their communities and to live in independent and democratic societies. It acts from the tenet that adult and lifelong learning is deeply linked to social, economic and political justice, equality of gender relations, living in harmony with the environment, respect for human rights, peace and recognition of cultural diversity.

### ActionAid

ActionAid is an international development agency that works with local partners in 42 countries. Their aims are to fight poverty and injustice. ActionAid International is member of over 100 alliances and networks. In the field of adult education, ActionAid is best known for its innovative approach called *Reflect*, which fuses the theories of Paulo Freire with participatory methodologies. In 2003, *Reflect* was awarded the UN International Literacy Prize in recognition of exceptional work in the fight against illiteracy, and it is now used by 350 organizations in 60 countries (ActionAid, 2006).

## Critical reflection

Our look at the world of international development cooperation for adult education today is sketchy and incomplete. For example, private funds that flow through foundations such as Rockefeller or MacArthur, or through the private sector, were unaccounted for; so too was the OA, or funds from countries other than the 22 DAC countries. Also, when comparing funds in 1990 with funds in 2005, we should adjust for inflation.

Even though sketchy, the picture lets us draw some conclusions:

- funding for adult education accounts for roughly a quarter of total education funds;
- since 2000, the bilateral component is increasingly larger than the multilateral component;
- strengthening civil society has prominence over all other thematic components; we should keep in mind though that not all projects within this area can be equated with civic education;
- educational research is the least funded component of education;
- the fuzziness between thematic areas may be attributable to an integrative policy approach that places adult education in the context of lifelong learning.

# References

ActionAid (2006) *Introducing ActionAid International.* Available online at www.actionaid.org/ (accesssed 8 October 2007).

Buchert, L. (2003) 'Financing adult education: constraints and opportunities', *Adult Education and Development* 60: 67–82.

Bundesministerium für wirtschaftliche Zusammenarbeit und Entwicklung (Federal Ministry for Economic Cooperation and Development) (BMZ) (2007a) *Net German ODA 2000–2005.* Available online at www.bmz.de/en/figures/ (accessed 10 October 2007).

—— (2007b) *Facts and Figures: Germany's contribution to development.* Available online at www.bmz.de/en/figures/ (accessed 10 October 2007).

Canadian Council for International Co-operation (CCIC) (2006) 'Artificial increases: debt relief pushes ODA to exceed the US$100 billion mark in 2005', in CCIC (eds) *The Reality of Aid: An independent review of poverty reduction and development assistance.* Available online at www.ccic.ca/e/docs/ (accessed 10 October 2007).

Department for International Development (DFID) (2007) *About DFID: Performance and expenditure: Statistics on international development 2006*, Section 1. Available online at www.dfid.gov.uk/pubs/ (accessed 11 October 2007).

*dvv international* (2007) *Adult Education – Development – Cooperation.* Available online at www.dvv-international.de/englisch/default.htm (accessed 10 October 2007).

Hinzen, H. (2007) 'Adult education: organisation and financing – background document' (electronic version), *Adult Education and Development* 68. Available online at www.dvv-international.de/englisch/default.htm (accessed 10 October 2007).

Swedish International Development Cooperation Agency (SIDA) (2004) *Facts and Figures 2003, Education Sector.* Available online at www.SIDA.org/ (accessed 15 October 2007).

—— (2005) *Facts and Figures 2004, Education Sector.* Available online at www.SIDA.org/ (accessed 10 October 2007).

—— (2006) *Facts and Figures 2005, Education Sector.* Available online at www.SIDA.org/ (accessed 10 October 2007).

—— (2007) *This is SIDA.* Available online at www.SIDA.org/ (accessed 10 October 2007).

Torres, R.M. (2004) 'Lifelong learning in the South: critical issues and opportunities for adult education, *SIDA Studies* 2: 1–172.

UNESCO (2000) *The Dakar Framework for Action. Education for All: Meeting our collective commitments*, Paper presented at the World Education Forum, Dakar, Senegal, 26–28 April, Paris: UNESCO.

—— (2005) *Millennium Development Goals (MDGs).* Available online at http://portal.unesco.org/education/ (accessed 18 October 2007).

UNESCO Institute for Lifelong Learning (UIL) (2006) *United Nations Literacy Decade (2003–2012).* Available online at www.unesco.org/uil/ (accessed 10 October 2007).

World Bank (2007) 'Argentina: World Bank approves US$877 million to support the country's development program', News Release 2007/497/LAC. Available online at http://econ.worldbank.org/ (accessed 8 October 2007).

# Part 7

## Perspectives on lifelong learning

# 33

# Financing lifelong learning

*Hans G. Schuetze*

After an initial discussion in the 1970s and early 1980s of how lifelong learning could be financed (see, for example, Stoikov, 1975; Levin and Schuetze, 1983; Schuetze and Istance, 1987), the theme was more or less dormant for a while. It was not taken up again until the late 1990s, when a number of economists started to plough the field again (for example, Timmermann 1996; Levin 1998; Oosterbeek 1998). The renewed interest was instigated by one of the international organizations that had been an early promoter of lifelong learning, the Organization for Economic Cooperation and Development (OECD), then called 'recurrent education' (OECD, 1973). At an OECD meeting in 1996, Ministers of Education requested the OECD secretariat to:

> identify the benefits of increased investment in lifelong learning, its implication for education and training policies in the effort to move towards a 'learning society' . . . how sharing the costs of such investments can be related more equitably to the benefits, [and] analyze how more investment for learning by all partners might be mobilized.
>
> (OECD, 1996: 24)

In compliance with this mandate, the OECD undertook a number of studies on the cost and financing of lifelong learning (OECD, 1997, 1999, 2000, 2001a, b, 2003, 2004 a, b). Roughly at the same time, the World Bank published a study on lifelong learning in the developing countries (World Bank, 2003), which spelled out principles and various models of financing lifelong learning. Parallel to that work, a number of expert papers were commissioned by both the OECD and the World Bank (in addition to the authors mentioned above, see Palacios, 2002), which described and analysed existing country models of financing various types of education and training. Contributing to this work at the international level were a number of national studies that looked into the issue of the financing of lifelong learning, among them the German Expert Commission on Financing Lifelong Learning (2004).[1]

The renewed interest in lifelong learning is at least in part due to the recognition that it might be the adequate strategy for the new 'knowledge-based economy' or, more generally, a 'knowledge-based society'. Partly, too, it is a reaction to the failures of the traditional 'front-end' education system with its relatively high non-completion rate and unclear pathways between education and work. This shortcoming entails dead-ends, detours and repetition for the learners, caused by a system that does not reflect more flexible and individualistic life patterns and styles or the changing realities of working life.

This chapter is structured as follows. First, I shall briefly discuss the main characteristics and models of lifelong learning: a necessary, if often overlooked, prerequisite for a discussion on financing ('financing what?'). In the second section, I shall briefly present and analyse the main financing systems that have been suggested for a lifelong learning system ('Financing how?'). In the final section, I shall discuss these models as to their suitability for attaining the objectives of lifelong learning.

## Financing what? Elements and models of lifelong learning

Lifelong learning is an umbrella concept that lends itself to many interpretations. Due to its ambiguity, the concept can be compared to a chameleon whose colours are changing according to its environment, thereby confusing the very concept (Jarvis, 2004). Thus, for industry leaders the term tends to mean more continuing training, for teachers more formal schooling, and for adult educators more adult education. As many ships sail under the banner of lifelong learning while charting different courses, it is useful to briefly review the main features and models.

### *Main features*

The concept of lifelong learning is based on three principles that break with the traditional notion of 'front-end' formal education: lifelong learning is lifelong, 'lifewide' and centred on 'learning' rather than on 'education'.

(1)   That lifelong learning should be lifelong is implied by the name: people should be enabled and encouraged to continue learning throughout their lives, not just in informal ways ('everyday learning'), but also through organized learning in formal and non-formal settings.[2] While lifelong learning importantly includes learning after formal schooling, the quality of education during the 'formative' years is considered as essential for the ability and motivation to engage in further learning later in life (Hargreaves, 2002).

The lifelong aspect of learning raises questions about the structures and interrelationships between different sectors of the educational system. While a lifelong learning system must allow and promote individual choice and smooth progression, and provide multiple access and exit points as well as clearly defined pathways for the passage from school to work and back from work to learning, present structures in many countries make lifelong learning very difficult, if not impossible.

(2)   Organized learning occurs not just in schools, colleges, universities and training institutions, but in a variety of forms and in many different settings, many of them outside the formal educational system. In a system of 'lifewide' learning the assessment and recognition of knowledge learned outside the formal education system become a fundamental necessity. This poses a major challenge to the established hierarchy and traditional validation of different kinds of knowledge, that is, both the places where, and the mode in which knowledge and know-how have been acquired.

If learning is to become 'lifewide', the organization, regulation and financing of learning activities no longer fall exclusively into the domain of ministers of education but also the

376

ministers of other government departments, such as culture, economic and social affairs, health and employment. Such a lifewide learning system requires a certain degree of consistency regarding policies, procedures and standards of the various agencies concerned, as well as efficient mechanisms of coordination. Nor is coordination required solely between public agencies. With much of non-formal learning occurring at the workplace and other places outside the formal education system, public and private policies and programmes need to be articulated and coordinated. Moreover, a lifelong learning system requires a comprehensive and reliable information system about learning possibilities (and their prerequisites and outcomes) as well as a system for the assessment and recognition of knowledge and know-how acquired outside the formal education system.

(3)   The third principle of lifelong learning, the change of perspective from 'education' and 'schooling' to 'learning', entails an even more radical departure from the present system than the former two features. The first consequence is the recognition that, in a system of lifelong learning, there is little room for prescribed and rigidly structured and sequenced curricula or programmes that apply to every individual belonging to the same age group. With the exception of the early years of formal learning, where a common structure and content seems useful, what is learned, and when, and where and how it is learned, should be determined, in principle, by learners themselves. This would make lifelong learning a menu à la carte instead of a fixed meal force-fed to all learners. Second, individuals have not only much more choice but also a greater responsibility for taking the initiative and making meaningful – and often difficult – choices among the various options open to them.

### *Principal models*

Looking more closely at the various interpretations of lifelong learning in the literature and policy reports, we can distinguish three basic models, envisioning and advocating different models of education and learning, of work and ultimately of society:

1   An emancipatory or social justice model that emphasizes equality of opportunity and life chances through education in an egalitarian society ('Lifelong learning for all').
2   A mixed state-market model in which lifelong learning is seen as an adequate learning system for the knowledge economy and society ('Lifelong learning for all who wish, and are able, to participate').
3   A human capital model where lifelong learning connotes continuous work-related training and skill development to meet the needs of the economy and employers for a qualified, flexible and adaptable workforce ('Lifelong learning for finding or keeping jobs in a changing labour market').

Behind these definitional differences stand concrete and diverging political agendas. The first is propagating lifelong learning for all, a normative and somewhat utopian[3] concept. The other two are more limited in scope, and the third particularly is most specific about which types of learning activities, namely work-related and job-specific, are included. The second model does not advocate a social agenda to be achieved by equal learning chances, rather it is designed to promote learning for a variety of purposes, and to eliminate or lower institutional barriers, for example through the use of modern information and communication technologies allowing distance education and learning, especially now through online learning. Unlike the first model, which achieves its objectives by targeting specific populations facing specific barriers, under the second model individuals are responsible for informing and availing themselves of learning opportunities.

The third model, nowadays the dominant one (see Schuetze, 2006), understands lifelong learning as a continuing training system appropriate for a knowledge-based economy in which a highly trained and adaptable (or 'flexible') workforce is seen as a principal prerequisite for industrial innovativeness and international competitiveness. In contrast to an earlier view, which understood initial and continuing vocational or professional training to be primarily a responsibility of industry, the human capital notion of lifelong learning sees individual workers as responsible for acquiring and updating their skills or for acquiring new qualifications in order to enhance their employability and career chances.

It follows from these differences in objective and scope that these models require different amounts of resources (see section 'Financing schemes' below) as well as different financing mechanisms for mobilizing resources and distributing them among the various stakeholders.

## Financing how?

As pointed out, lifelong learning is not just a special type of education, training or other learning activity, such as adult education or web-based learning, but covers various forms of formal and non-formal learning that are at present largely separate and operate in isolation from each other. This includes the way they are financed. Table 33.1 shows which principal activities are a constituent part of a lifelong learning system and by whom they are presently funded.

In a system of lifelong learning, the various activities, programmes, sectors and providers would need to be more clearly articulated in relation to each other. They also need a certain degree of coordination or integration to allow lifelong learners to navigate through the system without encountering unexpected roadblocks, major detours or dead ends that are the result of piecemeal sectoral or institutional policies and regulations.

A similar problem concerns the financing of lifelong learning activities. Presently, financing systems for the different learning activities at different places of learning vary a great deal, depending not only on the type of programme or institution, but also on who shoulders the costs. Is it feasible and does it make sense to consider replacing the present variation of financing mechanisms with a more coordinated or even a unified system, or are different schemes acceptable or preferable, provided they are in line with the objectives of lifelong learning? (see 'Financing lifelong learning: criteria and suitability', p. 384).

### How much money is needed, and who should pay?

In light of the goals that lifelong learning is supposed to meet, the problem of financing does not solely concern the analysis of different financing modes. It is also a question of how many additional resources might be needed and how they can be found. In other words, 'financing' does not only entail the question of how resources should best be spent in order to reach the goals and desired outcomes of lifelong learning, but also how these resources may be mobilized.

How many additional resources are required in order to move towards a (lifelong) learning society? For a number of reasons (see OECD, 1999, 2000; World Bank, 2003) estimates are very difficult to make in the abstract and therefore tend to vary greatly. Many analysts argue that important savings will be made by greater efficiency through a more coordinated system that will offset some of the additional costs. But even they agree that substantive additional resources will be needed if the comprehensive model of lifelong learning for all is to be

*Table 33.1* Formal and non-formal learning activities and their financing

| Types of non-formal education and training | Funders/financing instruments | Types of formal education and training | Funders/financing instruments |
|---|---|---|---|
| Voluntary sector-based | Member and user fees, state subsidies | Pre-school | State |
| Community-based | Local taxes and user fees, state subsidies | Compulsory schooling:<br>• primary<br>• lower secondary<br>• upper secondary | State<br>State and/or private households |
| Workplace-based | Employers and/or parafiscal funds | Post-secondary education/training:<br>• college<br>• university<br>• private | State and/or private households |
| Organized individual | Individual households | • training institutes<br>Continuing education/training | Private households<br>Private households, employers |

- articulation
- coordination
- integration

implemented. How much is needed will depend on several factors, one being the existing educational attainment and levels of literacy of the adult population.[4]

One problem of estimating the volume of resources needed is that costs are more easily calculated than benefits against which these costs can be offset. That is true both for overall system and individual costs, even if statistics show clearly that there are economic benefits from greater amounts of schooling. Thus, for example, individuals with higher levels of education have higher employment rates, higher average rates and a high internal rate of return – benefits that have stayed relatively constant even when more people have participated in more schooling and advanced education (OECD, 2007). Likewise, calculations based on data from industrialized countries show that one additional year of education for the whole population of working age will mean a 1 per cent gain in the rate of growth and a 3 to 6 per cent increase in GDP (OECD, 2006). If these calculations are correct, it would appear that investments in more education for more people will yield benefits that will easily pay for them.

The question then is who pays, or should pay. This question can be answered in two ways: the individual who benefits should pay, or the one who can pay should pay. In the heyday of the welfare state there was an assumption that the state should pay for much (most) formal education and companies respectively for vocational training, since they were seen to be 'able to pay'. More recently, most policy makers seem to agree that, with the notable exception of initial (school) education and special programmes for minority populations and special groups under-represented in education, the distribution of costs should better reflect the benefits and beneficiaries of education and learning.

In principle, there are four parties ('economic subjects') that could be required to pay for education and learning, either separately paying for all the costs or sharing the costs with others ('co-financing'): individual learners or their families, single organizations or private companies, collective groups or the state.

As can be seen from Table 33.2, the majority of financing systems for lifelong learning are so-called 'mixed' or 'co-financing' models. That makes economic sense under the (s)he-who-benefits-should-pay principle: except in rare circumstances, benefits from learning do not only accrue to one of the parties but to several. For example, a person engaging in and graduating from advanced education or training is very likely to earn a higher income than someone without education beyond school. At the same time, the company employing that person will gain in terms of productivity or quality of its goods or services, while the state will enjoy higher tax revenues. While all three parties benefit, they also share in the cost of the individual's education: tuition fees and forgone or reduced income in case of the student, the company through granting release time and (partial) reimbursement of tuition, and the state through assuming the investment costs and operational expenditures of public educational institutions.

## *Financing schemes*

Several basic schemes can be distinguished, ranging from individual funding and single-purpose to more comprehensive models (see Table 33.2). Most of these schemes do not cover the whole gamut of learning activities that fall under a comprehensive lifelong learning concept. In fact none of them includes the early years of learning (kindergarten to the end of compulsory education), which is nonetheless, as was mentioned above, a very important part of a system of lifelong learning. Nor do all schemes cover all the costs incurred by learners, both the direct ones such as tuition and the indirect costs such as the cost of living of learners when they are not, because of their learning, in (full-time) employment ('opportunity costs'). In other words, the schemes vary widely with respect to their comprehensiveness in terms of the range of learning opportunities they cover. While some support only specific activities, or target specific groups (e.g. labour-market training for the unemployed, or language education for immigrants), others provide a single financing system for all lifelong learning activities.

There is a multitude of financing mechanisms, often under country-specific names or with country-specific particularities, that are being used for financing learning. The list in Table 33.2 is by no means complete; rather, it contains some of the better known 'prototypes'. There are other proposals being discussed, for example human capital contracts, some of which are being tested or implemented on a small scale (for an overview see Palacios, 2002).

Although most of the prototype schemes imply co-financing, it is useful to classify them by way of identifying the primary bearer of the cost. In this way we can distinguish schemes that are primarily financed by the individual learner, by employers or jointly by workers and employers, and by the state.

## Learner financing

The first group comprises different mechanisms of learner self-financing, which include different types of loans, such as traditional mortgage-type, government-supported and income-contingent loans, as well as individual learning accounts. The rationale that individuals should finance their own learning is based on the assumption that they are the main beneficiaries of it. A second assumption is that individuals who do not have the means can and will borrow money from the banks and repay their debts from the higher income they can expect as the

*Table 33.2* Financing models for lifelong learning and their coverage

| Characteristics of financing schemes | Scope | Costs covered | |
|---|---|---|---|
| | | Direct [a] | Indirect [b] |
| **1 *Self-funding by learner*** | | | |
| Funding from past, present or future income; possible co-financing through tax scheme | Multi-purpose | All | All |
| *Income-contingent student loans* | | | |
| Risk reduction through deferred financing, contingent on earning an income above a certain level | Single-purpose; higher education | Tuition, all or some | None |
| *Individual learning accounts* | | | |
| Tax-friendly individual savings for the purpose of increasing vocational skills, augmented by contributions by employer and the state | Single-purpose; work-related skill training | All or some | None |
| *Individual drawing rights* | | | |
| Comprehensive transfer system of extending social security to cover all non-work activities | Multi-purpose; integrated | None | All |
| **2 *(Single) employer funding*** | | | |
| Financing of on-the-job-training, professional continuing education | Single-purpose; work-related up-skilling | All or some | All |
| *Paid educational leave* | | | |
| External short-term courses/programmes during paid work time | Multi-thematic: general, civic, vocational | None | All |
| *Collective bargaining agreements* | | | |
| Up-skilling training for workers | Single-purpose vocational | All or some | All or some |
| **3 *Collective or parafiscal funding*** | | | |
| Funding from employers' and workers' contributions and public subsidies administered through autonomous public bodies | Single-purpose; labour market training | All or some | All or some |
| *Levy-grant schemes* | | | |
| General or industry-specific system for collecting levies from non-training companies and distributing grants to increase training | Single-purpose; labour market training | | |
| **4 *State funding*** | | | |
| Institutional funding; grants to needy individuals, or special groups (unemployed, minorities, immigrants) | Single-purpose | All or some | Some |
| *Taxation* | | | |
| Tax deductions, tax credit, tax-sheltered savings for learning-related expenditure | Multi-purpose | All or some | Some |
| *Individual entitlements (vouchers)* | | | |
| Public funding given to students/learners instead of to institutions, covering fees | Single-purpose | All or some | None |

Notes:
a   Primarily the cost of tuition, but also books or tools, and transportation.
b   Living costs during full-time education learning if learner is not receiving income from (full-time) work.

result of their learning. This second assumption, however, is questionable since, first, banks will not lend money for learning, except against sufficient collateral security, due to the higher risk of human capital investments, and, second, learners, and especially those from low-income backgrounds, are also risk averse and shy away from indebting themselves, especially for the purpose of education.

This is the reason why loan programmes for low-income learners are supported by the state in the form of default guarantees to the lender and subsidies for the interest to be paid by the borrower. This is relatively common for loans to post-secondary students in formal programmes leading to recognized qualifications; however, guaranteed loan schemes for older learners who learn outside the formal education system are much less frequent.

Income-contingent loans are designed to decrease the risk for borrowers (learners) since they will be required to repay the loan only if and when their income reaches a certain level. This idea on which the Australian Higher Education Contribution System (HECS) system is based has been emulated by several other countries seeking to shift public funding, or parts thereof, for post-secondary education from educational institutions to more learner-centred forms of support.

Individual Learning Accounts (ILAs) or, alternatively, 'training' or 'development accounts', are another financing model for post-secondary education and training. They have been implemented in some countries, in most cases on a trial basis, with the objective of giving the individuals more personal choice and ownership in their learning, and hence increasing motivation for investing in it. These special purpose accounts provide learners with money to pay for their learning activities, mainly for tuition fees. In all cases where such accounts exist or are being discussed, eligible learning activities are confined to participation in programmes related to skill or competency development (Schuetze, 2007). ILAs were hailed 'as a means of putting flesh to the bones of the lifelong learning vision' (OECD, 2001a: 122). If the eligibility for such learning accounts, or the size of government contributions to them, depend on the socio-economic background of the individuals, learning accounts 'are part of a general class of policies aimed at individuals, especially from a population that traditionally has not participated in such activities, to increase their asset holdings and, with that, their "stake-holding"' (p. 122) in their own learning.

Individual drawing rights are another way in which individuals can support themselves during (full-time) periods of learning through taking out 'drawing rights' from their personal lifetime account (Rehn, 1983). This scheme, by far the most extensive one, would cover the essential parts of the costs of (post-compulsory) learning activities over a person's lifetime, namely income maintenance. Funded by contributions from the individuals themselves, but also their employers and the state, drawing rights are not limited to education or learning, but provide a

> single comprehensive system for financing all periods of voluntary or age-determined non-work that would [not only] replace the present systems of financing youth education, [and] adult studies [but also] vacations, old age retirement and other leisure periods that need income maintenance [such as] sabbaticals, long service leave and temporary retirement.
>
> (Rehn, 1983: 70)

Because the scheme is built on the idea of an individual account, it resembles the ILAs. Drawing rights are, however, quite different with regard to their objective and scope as they provide income maintenance for *all* types of non-work activities.

The second and third categories include various forms of employer-financed schemes, including training at or through the enterprise, and paid educational leave. Collective (or parafiscal) funds, paid for either by employers alone, jointly by employers and workers, or by a tripartite arrangement where the state is also co-financing, belong in this category also.

## Single-employer funding

Single-employer funding covers continuing training and retraining for work-related learning activities of an employer's own workers: these activities range from on-the-job training to short external courses for various work-related purposes, such as technical updating and management training. They take place mostly during paid working time, and tuition costs are usually paid for by the company. Except when obliged by law or collective bargaining, this type of funding will not absorb costs incurred by workers for learning activities pursued during non-work time and not directly work-related.

One example of a legal obligation is paid educational leave, which, in some countries, gives workers the right to paid leave, mostly no more than for five days a year, to pursue education of their choosing that takes place outside the company on company time. Touted in the 1970s as a major instrument of lifelong learning, but strongly resisted by employers, paid educational leave has not lived up to the expectations of its proponents (unions) and has therefore remained insignificant (see Schuetze, 1996). Also, some collective bargaining agreements contain qualification clauses that stipulate that employers must pay for training that is in their interest. In most cases, however, that does not give the workers an individual right to training.

## Parafiscal (collective) funding

Collective funds, financed by contributions from employers and workers, and in some systems topped up by public funding, are designed to cover labour market training (workplace-related skill development) but usually not general education. Such collective funds exist in several countries and are either the result of legislation or of collective bargaining agreements. Examples are the parafiscal funds for labour market training as they exist in Germany, Austria and the Scandinavian countries. A special case is the levy-grant schemes for training. One example of industry-specific levy-grant schemes would be the ones administered by the (now defunct) Industrial Training Boards in the UK, such as in the construction and roofing trades. Another is the French system of continuing training, whereby companies are obliged to spend a certain percentage of their wage payroll on recognized training activities, failing which they will have to pay a levy in the amount of the non-met training obligation. Funds thus collected will be used for training schools or educational institutions providing continuing education and training (Merle and Lichtenberg, 2001).

## State funding

The fourth category consists of financing mechanisms that are primarily funded by the state, even if they may imply some kind of co-financing from individuals or enterprises (the fact that individuals as taxpayers are the ultimate source of most state funding is not discussed here). State financing for education and training, even after market mechanisms of funding have increased investments from other sources, still covers by far the largest share of overall funding for learning, at least learning taking place in the formal sector.[5]

Direct funding covers the whole or, in countries in which public institutions charge student fees, the bulk of the cost of public institutions, both capita and recurrent costs. It also can take the form of grants to needy students or special groups (for example the unemployed, minorities or immigrants) and individual entitlements for individuals. Such individual entitlements (vouchers) are distributed in some jurisdictions to increase individual (parents') choice. In most cases entitlements cover tuition costs (fees), but not indirect costs (Levin, 1998). Individual learners (or their families) therefore contribute to their learning by assuming other cost items from their own sources. Income maintenance schemes for special populations is an example for state indirect funding, for example for war veterans and their families, high school drop-outs and immigrants while they undergo education or training.

## Financing lifelong learning: criteria and suitability

Besides organizational and infrastructural changes to the present, highly segmented system of learning, financing is a crucial instrument for putting the concept of lifelong learning into practice. A number of the schemes listed in Table 33.2 already exist in some countries, even if sometimes only at an experimental stage. In spite of this, solid evidence on the effects of these schemes is mostly missing, either because there are no systematic and rigorous evaluations or because such evaluations are very limited in scope. In this section, we shall look into a number of criteria to assess the suitability of these schemes for lifelong learning and briefly discuss the financing schemes in light of them.

### *The three models*

Before doing this, a short analysis is in order to see what the three different models of lifelong learning mean to the financing debate. In which way do the human capital level and the open society models require different mechanisms of financing?

The 'mixed state-market model' reflects the current situation in most (developed) countries: uneven access to, and uneven participation in, learning, based primarily on socio-economic background. Although the state pays for public education as well as some special programmes for those under-served by the public system, state intervention is patchy and normally starts too late, that is, after students have dropped out from school. The market has nothing to offer that would help these poor learners or drop-outs since they are normally too poor to pay or to borrow money from the capital market. Moreover, some forms of state financing discriminate against the economically disadvantaged, especially tax credits or reductions that are available only for those families that do have a taxable income.

Regarding the 'human capital model' of lifelong learning, enterprises generally provide training, or are paying for training primarily for workers who are already well educated and trained, not for those who lack general education and are unskilled. Moreover, workers in smaller firms and those not in regular employment, for example shift and part-time workers, are disadvantaged with regard to training compared to workers in larger firms and those with regular work contracts. While labour market training paid for by collective or parafiscal funds targets the unemployed and those threatened by unemployment, remedial education and basic training under their auspices is often short-term only, relatively specific and, overall, not efficient.

This brief assessment suggests that many would-be learners are left behind by the current system. Therefore, lifelong learning for all will have to provide assistance to those who are not served, or not served well, by the two other regimes. For providing lifelong learning opportunities to all, it is not sufficient to target adults who are not participating in continuing education or training. As it has been well established by numerous research studies, individual motivation to engage in learning beyond compulsory schooling, as well the capacity for learning successfully, depends on a number of other factors, especially the learner's socio-economic background, their endowment with cultural and social capital, and the quality of their early childhood and primary education experience. If it is here that the foundations for lifelong learning are laid, then assistance to individuals who are lacking this background must start as early as kindergarten and primary school and continue through secondary school and beyond. As market-based financing is not available for these forms of early learning, it is the public (state and local community) and private charities that will have to bear the costs of such programmes.

## Criteria for financing lifelong learning

A number of different criteria have been suggested for assessing the various financing systems that are in line with the multiple objectives lifelong learning is expected to realize. It is fairly obvious that providing incentives and financial assistance for high school drop-outs and illiterate adults will need different mechanisms from motivating highly educated professionals to engage in continuing professional education. What, then, are the criteria by which financing systems or schemes are to be assessed as to their suitability for lifelong learning?

Logically and most importantly, financing schemes seem suitable for lifelong learning if they have the effect of making learning possible over the entire lifetime and enabling and encouraging individuals to avail themselves of various learning opportunities throughout that lifetime.

For making lifelong learning possible, that is, accessible and affordable for all, there are some additional criteria. The World Bank (2003) stipulates that learners should be responsible for their own learning; governments should promote equity; and financing schemes should promote efficiency in education and labour markets. The OECD (1996, 2004b) emphasizes that costs of investments in learning should (1) be shared and (2) be more equitably related to the benefits. Also financing schemes should (3) mobilize more investment for learning by all partners. Timmermann (1996) thinks it important that lifelong learning financing schemes should foster integration or coordination of currently segregated sectoral activities, such as general and academic studies on the one hand and vocational training on the other.

As was just pointed out, a particular requirement for a policy of lifelong learning for *all* is to convince groups and individuals from low-education family backgrounds and others under-represented in formal education to complete compulsory school and hence lay the foundation for further learning later in life. While this is a crucial prerequisite, they must also be convinced to engage in learning activities beyond school. As individuals from such backgrounds and their families are often poor, they are particularly averse to financial risks and debt. Especially with this group in mind, financing schemes must try to reduce the fear of prospective learners who often expect that returns to learning will be low, even if they complete their studies or training.

Together these criteria form a challenging list of principles and conditions that financing schemes can be compared against. Table 33.3 summarizes the assessment of how the various financing schemes reflect the above criteria.

The upshot of this summary assessment is that there is no comprehensive financing system that would cover all learning abilities over an individual's lifetime. This is true even for the individual drawing rights model, since it covers, as do the other schemes, only the post-compulsory portion of people's learning activities. Also, drawing rights would only provide income maintenance for periods of (full-time learning), while direct costs would not be covered. All other mechanisms apply only to one sector or one type of activity.

Table 33.3 Suitability of financing schemes for lifelong learning

| Financing schemes/criteria | Allowing/encouraging lifelong learning | Making learners responsible for their learning | Promoting equity | Promoting efficiency | Sharing costs | Mobilizing additional resources | Promoting coordination/integration | Reducing risk |
|---|---|---|---|---|---|---|---|---|
| 1 *Self-funding by learner* | N | Y | NN | N | N | U | N | NN |
| Income contingent student loans | U | Y | Y | Y | N | Y | NN | YY |
| Individual learning accounts | (Y) | Y | (Y) | (Y) | Y | (YY) | NN | (Y) |
| Individual drawing rights | YY | Y | N | (Y) | Y | Y | U | U |
| 2 *(Single) employer funding* | (Y) | N | N | Y | (Y) | Y | NN | N |
| Paid educational leave | YY | Y | Y | ? | Y | Y | NN | Y |
| Collective bargaining agreements | (Y) | (Y) | N | (Y) | U | Y | NN | Y |
| 3 *Collective or parafiscal funding* | Y | Y | Y | ? | Y | Y | N | Y |
| Levy–grant schemes | Y | Y | Y | (Y) | Y | Y | N | Y |
| 4 *State funding* | (Y) | (U) | Y | ? | Y | ? | N | Y |
| Taxation | YY | Y | NN | N | Y | Y | N | (Y) |
| Individual entitlements (vouchers) | (YY) | (Y) | (Y) | ? | Y | (Y) | N | N |

Notes:

YY   Strong positive correlation.

Y   Positive correlation.

?   Correlation unclear.

NC   No correlation.

N   Negative correlation.

NN   Strong negative correlation.

( )   Brackets indicate a possible correlator, depending on the design of the scheme.

Would a more articulated financing system be possible? To combine these different mechanisms into one overall system would be very difficult indeed, even if it were just for the different parts of the formal (education and training) system. It would appear to be outright impossible if learning activities in the non-formal sector were to be included. Would it be desirable? Certainly, greater coherence and consistency of the existing financing schemes would be important. The question is here if such a 'seamless web' of financing for learning throughout life can be woven without a major administrative regulation process and agency – a bureaucratic nightmare to inspire a Kafka novel.

Clearly a summary assessment of the various schemes of financing lifelong learning is unsatisfactory, especially since they have different features depending on their exact design. While models can be easily discussed and acclaimed in abstract, the mode of their translation into actual policy and their implementation are crucial.

One recent example is the spectacular failure of the ILA scheme in the UK. While the programme was praised initially for its bold vision and success, it had to be shut down abruptly a short time later because of its poor design, as well as the lack of adequate management and monitoring arrangements. Moreover and equally importantly, ILAs were poorly coordinated, if at all, with other existing schemes for financing adult learning activities as well as with other social transfers (see Schuetze, 2007).

The major challenge consists of integrating new financial mechanisms into the existing system in order to eliminate the one-way streets and cul-de-sacs that are still characteristic of the wide variety of existing education and learning programmes. That does not necessarily mean that a grand master plan is required that replaces all other financial mechanisms for education and organized learning. Rather, for a new scheme of financing lifelong learning to be efficient, it must be articulated and coordinated with presently existing mechanisms.

## Conclusion

Lifelong learning is still an elusive concept, yet is an idea whose time clearly has come. In spite of major differences in the way it is interpreted and propagated, there seems to be a general consensus that lifelong learning is the answer to several problems with the existing system of education and training, as well as the major instrument of enhancing the even more elusive learning or knowledge-based society.

To make more (organized) learning possible for more people over their lifetimes requires more resources. It also requires new ways of financing more and new learning activities. A learner-based model of lifelong learning emphasizes the importance of responsibility by individuals for investing in their further learning and in the freedom of choice in what, when and how they learn. This emphasis on freedom of choice is closely linked to a more general move towards a market-based system of education and training, and to 'consumer' choice among different 'education service' providers and non-formal learning opportunities. In the course of this shift, which reflects the progressive move from a welfare state model to a market model, governments, which in the past have provided and financed the great bulk of formal education and training activities, are now advocating individual choice and requiring private investments.

Whether or not existing schemes should be replaced by an integrated system for all formal learning, and whether a unified single system is desirable and feasible, is debatable. Yet clearly the existing patchwork of largely uncoordinated schemes for different sectors and learning activities is inefficient, especially with regard to lifelong learners and new types of learning. The overview of financing schemes, existing or proposed, shows that there is so far little interest in, and no discernible trend towards, more coordinated approaches. Given the costly experience with ILAs in the UK and with other well-intended but inefficient schemes elsewhere, the time might have come to change that.

## Notes

1  Two other international organizations, UNESCO and the European Commission, which had also propagated lifelong learning as the learning system of the future (Delors, 1996; EC, 2000), did not seriously engage in any analytical work on cost and financing issues.
2  'Formal' settings comprise the education system, i.e. schools, colleges, universities, whereas 'non-formal' settings are other places outside the formal sector where organized learning takes place (e.g. the workplace, museums, community centres, trade unions, sports clubs). By contrast, 'informal' learning is learning that takes place anywhere, yet in an unplanned, unorganized and mostly incidental manner. This informal 'everyday learning' is not included in the discussion of the organization and financing of lifelong learning.
3  In the sense of 'a reachable goal, even if not yet realized' (see Bloch, 1986).
4  It is clear that this indicator puts developing countries at a disadvantage compared to developed countries with a well-established formal system and that more resources would be needed to bring poorer countries up to the standard of richer ones – a gap that tends to widen rather than to narrow (see, e.g., Walter, 2005).
5  Opportunity costs of individual learners are not being taken into account here.

## References

Bloch, E. (1986) *The Principle of Hope*, Cambridge, MA: MIT Press.
Delors, J. (Chair) (1996) *Learning: The treasure within*, Paris: UNESCO.
European Commission (EC) (2000) *A Memorandum on Lifelong Learning*, Brussels: European Commission.
Expert Commission on Financing Lifelong Learning (2004) *Financing Lifelong Learning: The way to the future*, final report, Bielefeld: Bertelsmann Verlag.
Hargreaves, D.H. (2002) 'Effective schooling for lifelong learning', in D. Istance, H.G. Schuetze and T. Schuller (eds) *International Perspectives of Lifelong Learning: From recurrent education to the knowledge society*, Buckingham: Open University Press, pp. 49–62.
Jarvis, P. (2004) *Adult Education and Lifelong Learning: Theory and practice*, 3rd edn, London and New York: RoutledgeFalmer.
Levin, H.M. (1998) 'Financing a system for lifelong learning', *Education Economics* 6(3): 201–18.
—— and Schuetze, H.G. (eds) (1983) *Financing Recurrent Education: Strategies for increasing employment, job opportunities, and productivity*, Beverly Hills, CA: Sage.
Merle, V. and Lichtenberg, Y. (2001) 'Formation et éducation tout au long de la vie, 1971–2001: Deux reformes, un même défi (Lifelong learning 1971–2001: two reforms, same challenge)', *Formation Emploi* 76: 169–90.
Oosterbeek, H. (1998) 'Innovative ways to finance education and their relation to lifelong learning', *Education Economics* 6(3): 201–18.
Organization for Economic Cooperation and Development (OECD) (1973) *Recurrent Education: A strategy for lifelong learning*, Paris: OECD.
—— (1996) *Lifelong Learning for All*, Paris: OECD.
—— (1997) 'Lifelong investment in human capital', in Organization for Economic Cooperation and Development (eds) *Education Policy Analysis*, Paris: OECD, pp. 29–43.

—— (1999) 'Resources for lifelong learning: what might be needed and how might it be funded?', in Organization for Economic Cooperation and Development (eds) *Education Policy Analysis*, Paris: OECD, pp. 7–26.

—— (2000) *Where are the Resources for Lifelong Learning?*, Paris: OECD.

—— (2001a) *Economics and Finance of Lifelong Learning*, Paris: OECD.

—— (2001b) 'Lifelong learning for all: policy directions', in Organization for Economic Cooperation and Development (eds) *Education Policy Analysis*, Paris: OECD, pp. 9–42.

—— (2003) 'Strategies in sustainable investment in adult lifelong learning', in Organization for Economic Cooperation and Development (eds) *Education Policy Analysis*, Paris: OECD, pp. 79–102.

—— (2004a) 'Taxation and lifelong learning', in Organization for Economic Cooperation and Development (eds) *Education Policy Analysis*, Paris: OECD, pp. 99–126.

—— (2004b) *Co-financing Lifelong Learning: Towards a systemic approach*, Paris: OECD.

—— (2006) *Education at a Glance*, Paris: OECD.

—— (2007) *Education at a Glance*, Paris: OECD.

Palacios, M. (2002) 'Options for financing lifelong learning', World Bank Policy Research Working Paper 2994. Available online at http://siteresources.worldbank.org/ (accessed 1 October 2005).

Rehn, G. (1983) 'Individual frawing tights', in H. Levin and H.G. Schuetze (eds) *Financing Recurrent Education: Strategies for increasing employment, job opportunities, and productivity*, Beverly Hills, CA: Sage.

Schuetze, H.G. (1996) 'Paid educational leave through legislation and collective bargaining', in A. Tuijnman (ed.) *International Encyclopedia of Adult Education and Training*, Oxford: Pergamon, pp. 303–7.

—— (2006) 'International concepts and agendas of lifelong learning', *Compare* 36(3): 289–306.

—— (2007) 'Individual learning accounts and other models of financing lifelong learning', *International Journal of Lifelong Learning* 26(1): 5–23.

—— and Istance, D. (1987) *Recurrent Education Revisited: Modes of participation and financing*, Stockholm: Almquist & Wicksell International.

Stoikov, V. (1975) *The Economics of Recurrent Education and Training*, Geneva: International Labour Office.

Timmermann, D. (1996) 'Lifelong education: financing mechanisms', in A. Tuijnman (ed.) *International Encyclopedia of Adult Education and Training*, Oxford: Pergamon, pp. 300–3.

Walter, S. (2005) 'South Africa's Learning Cape aspirations: The idea of a learning region and the use of indicators in a middle-income country', in C. Duke, M. Osborne and B. Wilson (eds) *Rebalancing the Social and Economic: Learning, partnership and space*, Leicester: NIACE, pp. 126–42.

Williams, G. (2000) 'Paying for lifelong learning: problems and possibilities', in A. Hodgson (ed.) *Policies, Politics and the Future of Lifelong Learning*, London: Kogan Page, pp. 69–83.

World Bank (2003) *Lifelong Learning in the Global Knowledge Economy: Challenge for developing countries*, Washington, DC: World Bank. Available online at http://siteresources.worldbank.org/ (accessed 1 March 2004).

# 34

# Lifelong learning and philosophy

*Kenneth Wain*

## Relations and clarifications

The relation between lifelong learning and philosophy goes back to the beginnings in the 1970s, when the lifelong education movement was the driving force behind the theoretical development of a politics of lifelong education within UNESCO, which had officially adopted lifelong education as the master-concept for its initiatives in the field of education. The philosopher in the movement was Bogdan Suchodolski, who opened one of his contributions to the subject by observing that the concept of lifelong education is old and reference to it could be found 'in the cultures of ancient China, India, Greece, in the early Christian culture, in humanism, and in the neo-humanism developing in the beginning of the nineteenth century' (1976: 58). In a later contribution, Suchodolski named Comenius as the first to write a treatise on it entitled *Pampaedia*, in which Comenius gave a detailed description of the educational tasks for the different phases of life, starting from 'schooling for newborns' and achieving their completion with 'schooling for death' (1979: 36). Comenius also set out his programme's goals: 'fighting against those who "wished to govern in darkness" – a struggle seeking to make all people more human'. Suchodolski identifies this humanizing of the world as 'also the major task of lifelong education' (1979: 39) lying at its heart 'the vital modern hope that the future will belong to educated people and not to dictatorships pretending to know best how and where to lead the people' (1979: 39). In short, consistently with the movement's outlook, Suchodolski ties lifelong education with a humanistic programme and sees his task as a philosopher as that of articulating that programme and spelling out the political conditions under which it is possible.

A few clarifications are necessary at this point. First, lifelong learning and lifelong education are not the same thing, though they are commonly confused. Second, the justificatory argument for lifelong learning was, and still is today, not political but pragmatic: the need to respond to a world changing fast thanks to rapid technological development. Accelerating change brings instability and risk – economic, political and social – conditions endemic to our societies today (Giddens 1991; Beck, 1994), and hence personal and social disorientation. A period of compulsory schooling preparing people for life is not enough to meet the challenge; learning must be for life for everyone – hence the movement's call to institutionalize lifelong education.

Third, the call for lifelong education was often linked with the expansion and extension of adult learning facilities so that it was commonly, and wrongly, taken as another name for adult education and training, and the same remains true today with respect to lifelong learning. Fourth, when Suchodolski wrote, and the lifelong education movement militated for its political programme, the world was very different politically and economically from how it is now. It was split into enemy ideological camps by the Cold War. The European Union (EU) was in a fledgling state, simply an economic union. Today's global and European reality is different; the Cold War is over, and the former Communist and Fascist countries are in the EU. Fifth, the fashionable expression today is 'lifelong learning' not 'lifelong education'.

This last-mentioned distinction is important. 'Learning', unlike 'education', is a normatively neutral, permissive word. Like Dewey's notion of 'growth' (1938, 1966) it can apply to an inexhaustible variety of processes and activities occurring in different ways with different intentions and outcomes. Dewey, correctly in my view, identified as the modern philosopher precursor of the lifelong education movement (Cross-Durant, 1984; Wain, 1984; Snook, 2001), defined education as open-ended growth; the openness to more learning being what distinguishes any particular learning process as educative. For Dewey, non-educative learning was learning that led into a cul-de-sac. The philosopers working in the new discipline of philosophy of education in the post-Second World War years, however, were unhappy with this 'working' definition as too hazy and ambiguous. They wanted a substantive definition instead; one incorporating values that could serve as aims for teachers and curricula to achieve. They wanted its outcome to be defined in the characteristics of the 'educated person', whose mark would be rational autonomy. The countless articles addressing the question, 'What is education?', at the time culminated in the conclusion that education is an unavoidably 'contestable concept' and could not be unambiguously pinned down. This same reason has been given today to explain why the expression lifelong learning is preferred to lifelong education (Eurydice European Unit, 2000). Indeed, there were countless complaints about the notoriously slippery nature of the latter concept even in its heyday (Cropley, 1979: 8).

But this explanation, like that putting it down to 'a change of fashion', seems politically naive because this shift to lifelong learning in the language of today's policy-making is reflected in a very different political agenda from that which inspired Suchodolski and the lifelong education movement (Griffin, 1999; Wain, 2001; Gustavsson, 2002; Wain, 2006). Some concerns, namely those with the cultivation of democratic citizenship and social cohesion, remain common, but the main thrust of the former is different. The agenda of the lifelong education movement, whose manifesto was the Faure report of 1972 *Learning to Be*, promoted a participative democracy and a humanist education project. Suchodolski described 'alienation' as the biggest obstacle to lifelong education in the contemporary world because it attacks the most crucial condition for education to take place – motivation. The problem of social cohesion for him was with industrialization and urbanization, which 'destroyed the structures of "neighbourly solidarity", led to the disintegration of traditional family ties and social links, and produced the restlessness and superficiality characteristic of mass civilization' (1976: 83). Suchodolski described alienation in terms of Marcuse's concept of the 'one-dimensional man' (1976: 74) and spoke of it in the workplace, and of 'cultural alienation', where culture is either elitist or completely commercialized as a mass culture. Against the one-dimensional society he held up the utopian hope of an education-centred society.

Today's discourse of lifelong learning, on the other hand (in the European context at least), is about economic competitiveness in the global market and employability in the workplace and its main political concern is with political apathy and societies growing increasingly multicultural and multi-ethnic. In this context, though the political targets of social cohesion and citizenship are nominally the same, the agenda for lifelong learning policies is very different from that of the movement. Suchodolski regarded finding a way out of the 'labyrinth' of alienation as 'one justification for advocating a "learning society"' (1976: 83) or 'education-centred society'.

The 'learning society' – a society that mobilizes its resources for learning – was a key component of the lifelong education movement's language. In the movement's reconceptualization of education as a lifelong process, it displaced the school as the new strategic focus for theory, with schooling being redefined as one element in the learning society with the specific role of preparing the individual for membership of such a society. One essential requirement, in this respect, was the quality of being a self-directed learner; of being capable, freely and intelligently, to use the resources of the learning society rather than mindlessly follow a learning programme for all; of being a 'one-dimensional man'. But the realization that it could as well be a closed totalitarian learning society as an open democratic one was largely why the movement took so many pains to emphasize its interest in an active democracy.

The notion of the learning society also features in the more recent lifelong learning literature, giving rise to a vast amount of theoretical writing on the subject. More recently, however, it has fallen out of favour with the policy makers who have replaced it with a new notion – that of the knowledge-based society and economy. Moreover, today's societies are information societies, whatever else they may be, and Asher Deleon, not long after, pointed to the fallacy of thinking that 'more information and improved communication facilities mean more and better education', or that 'the use of communication facilities and electronic "gadgets"' necessarily means more efficient education (1984: 32). This is a view echoed in more recent times by Hendrick van der Zee, who points to the danger of an information society 'in which the pressure from technology and the economy is so great that people, the users of information, feel defeated. If we don't take action,' he continues, not an 'education-centred' but 'an inhuman, highly technocratic society lies ahead of us (see, for example, Martin 1988 and Roszak 1986)' (van der Zee, 1996: 164).

## Conceptual matters

There was a time, especially in the middle and early period of the lifelong education movement, when the literature was charged with being too 'philosophical'. This was because of its tendency, probably because of its home at UNESCO, to address the human condition, 'man' in general, and to be utopian (particularly in its projections about the learning society) and internationalist. The Faure report, in fact, set the tone for this kind of writing. The 'philosophical' approach was, however, abandoned by a second, post-Faure, strand of writers, of which Ettore Gelpi was the most prominent, and which was pragmatic and more interested in the theoretical input of the social sciences and in doing comparative work than in philosophizing about 'man' and the future of humanity and education (Ireland, 1978). This second wave also abandoned any interest in the notion of the learning society on the grounds that it was theorized on the model of economically advanced Western societies and held no appeal for activists in so-called third world countries. More than that, it encouraged these activists to regard lifelong education itself and its active promotion among them as a hegemonic project by the Western countries to gain more political control over them.

Dewey's own philosophical approach to the idea of lifelong education (an expression he never actually used), was not, in effect, utopian, though Dewey was also a humanist. Like Marx, who referred to creativity as our 'species-being', in fact, in the opening pages of *Democracy and*

*Education* in 1916, he identified a human vocation to be creative, to want to change the world, not just adapt to it, and this vocation, he believed, is replicated politically in a democracy that he understood not primarily as a set of institutions but as a form of life. Favourably disposed to change, which he regarded as its life-blood, Dewey conceived of democracy as dynamic and experimental, a form of life marked by active communication between its members. He described his democratic learning society (though he didn't use the expression itself and spoke rather of a 'public' (1997)) in these minimal terms, just as he described education in minimal terms, as a place where learners would grow each in her or his own way. For Dewey the job of philosophers is not to define the aims of education but to describe the conditions for open-ended growth, and an experimental democratic environment best fitted this purpose for him. He thus emphasized the importance of learning from experience, or informal learning as we now call it. In so doing he preceded the lifelong education writers who distinguished three levels of learning as relevant to education; the 'formal' teacher-directed and institutional kind typical of schooling, the 'informal' and unintended or experiential (what is learned from the environment), and the 'non-formal' kind where there is intention to learn but the learning is not teacher-directed. Dewey's use of 'informal' covered the 'non-formal' also, but the distinction of the two is important and established today. For the lifelong education writers the inclusion of informal learning was important because it enabled them to complement the notion of lifelong learning with that of lifewide learning in the broadest technical definition (maximalist, as they called it) of the learning society as one that values all three kinds of learning. It also laid them open to the criticism, however, that they thereby rendered the word 'education' meaningless (a criticism made against Dewey), and has justified using the expression 'lifelong learning' instead of lifelong education.

Kenneth Lawson made the argument in a perceptive article, which he described as 'a conceptual exploration of the idea of "lifelong education"' in the UNESCO literature, which 'appear(s) to present the most coherent developed view of the subject' (1982: 98). While he lauded the concept as an attempt 'to enhance the status of education by presenting a policy which puts education at the centre of society', he suggested that another not including the word 'education' would define that policy better, since education cannot stand for a programme of undifferentiated learning such as theirs (1982: 99). It is 'of significance' in this respect, he observed, 'that "lifelong learning" is sometimes used as a synonym for "lifelong education"' (1982: 100). The humanistic lifelong education writers' attempt to solve 'the tension between man and society by making "education" a non-evaluative concept,' he held, does not work (1982: 102). It could work if we described education along Dewey's lines as indeterminate growth. But Lawson does not think Dewey's notion of growth is coherent. For education, he says, we need a notion not of indeterminate growth but of development, and 'for an individual to "develop" we imply that the change is in a desirable direction' (1982: 102). He thus concludes that the lifelong education writers should, if they retain the term 'education', redefine it 'as planned, intentional preparation', or if they retain informal learning use another expression instead, such as 'lifelong learning'(1982: 103). He thus provides us with another non-political argument for shedding the normatively loaded lifelong education in favour of the undifferentiated lifelong learning. But doing this raises the question of the future of the word 'education', and whether it is not one we can do away with altogether.

A conclusion of this kind would, of course, raise the problem for philosophers of education to justify the need for something called the philosophy of education. It would not prevent philosophers from taking an interest in schooling as the locus for enculturation or upbringing, and it may encourage them to look beyond at the other learning regimes of the society, the other places where learning occurs, and at the society itself as a learning society, but it would be a truly revolutionary move. The early, pre-1980s, analytic philosophers of education, coinciding with their early interest in teachers' education, restricted the interest of their subject to schooling – to the practices of teachers, to the curriculum and to school policy-making. They wanted their product to be philosophically respectable and professionally useful for practising teachers, they adopted analytic philosophy because it was the dominant school of philosophy in the Anglo-Saxon world then, and they had no doubt that the proper object of schooling is education. For different reasons, analytic philosophy has lost its hegemony since, but their programme and understanding has remained largely intact (Blake *et al.*, 2003; Carr, 2005). Indeed, although it continues to refer to itself as the philosophy of education, the current discipline would more appropriately be called the philosophy of schooling were it not for this assumption it continues to harbour that education is the proper object of schooling and educating the primary task of teachers – an assumption that is contested, as John White (1982) realized early on, by the notion of lifelong education.

This is not to say that the philosophers of education of the time, inspired as they were by liberal principles, identified education with schooling. They did not. R.S. Peters, the major figure in the United Kingdom in those early pioneering days, defined education as a never-ending voyage (he thus articulated, if in very different terms, the idea of open-ended growth expressed by Dewey). But White showed the contradiction that lay inherent in his views! I worked on lifelong education as the subject for my Ph.D. thesis with the University of London in Peters' department, under White's supervision in the early 1980s. The subject had not yet featured in any of the published work in the philosophy of education in the English-speaking world until then. Rewritten as a book, the thesis was eventually published in 1987 with the title *Philosophy of Lifelong Education*. In it I drew attention to the current lack of interest in the literature on lifelong education by philosophers of education in their bias towards schooling and proposed a post-analytic paradigm for the philosophy of education responding to the maximalist mode of re-articulating education as a lifelong process. In this new paradigm I conceived of a re-described panorama for education theory made up of competing education research projects with different 'ideological cores' (an idea taken from Kevin Harris (1979) and freely modelled on the work of the philosopher of science Imre Lakatos (1980)) and with lifelong learning strategies in their 'operational belt', which I defended on the usual pragmatic grounds that these alone are relevant to the contemporary world of change.

But resistance to lifelong education came early, before I had finished my thesis even, in the shape of White's book *The Aims of Education Restated* (1982), where he discussed lifelong education in a chapter devoted to the idea of 'The educated man', an idea central also to Peters' thinking 'If education is to be reconceptualised as a "lifelong process" and not as something belonging only to youth,' White argued, 'then we may as well drop the concept of the educated man: there is no line to be crossed; the journey goes on for ever' (1982: 130–1). The problem had not occurred to Peters! In any case, White did not, in my view, give good reasons for worrying about the future of the notion of the educated 'man' or person, which has, in fact, now disappeared. His other concern was that the idea of lifelong education clashed with that of education defined as 'upbringing', a 'preparation for life'. Upbringing, he argued, whether we want to call it 'education' or not (and this, he said, was not important) is both necessary for children and non-voluntary. Lifelong education 'or "education as a way of life"', on the other hand, must be voluntary, and this is the difference (1982: 132).

We have a case here, however, where, despite what White says, distinctions are important. The argument, education is about upbringing, upbringing is about compulsion therefore education cannot be lifelong, at least in a society that embraces liberal values, leads to the conclusion that lifelong education is a misnomer and cannot be of interest to philosophers of education. If the first premise is denied, however, and upbringing and education are separated as different but continuous processes rather than united into one, the second following the first, then upbringing belongs to childhood and schooling, and education to adulthood. This is a Rortyan (1990) solution, which I endorse. Upbringing, which is about learning the truth as one's society sees it, goes with schooling, and education goes with freedom. Rorty defines it as self-creation and sees its place in the non-vocational university. White agrees that 'to become free, he [the educated man] must pass through a period of compulsory education (in the up-bringing sense)' (1982: 132). But he seeks to conflate the two together and makes schools the place of their joint occurrence, though he perceives the difficulty with this approach when, while insisting that we should regard schooling as a preparation for life, he concedes that educatedness, the general quality of being educated (which he defines as having a coherent life-plan), may not be achieved by the time one leaves school – that it may not be achievable before, say, the age of 30, and for some maybe not ever. He concludes from this that the cut-off point when educatedness is achieved must remained blurred, but insists that one cannot continue to compel the individual to persist until one has reached it, so that becoming educated must always remain optional. This is true, but his argument breaks the connection between education as upbringing that he started with. On the other hand, he is right to insist that in the Western liberal understanding of the word, which I endorse, education is not something that can be forced on people whether at school or 'lifelong'. What separating education from upbringing implies is that education must be conceived, in some sense, as self-education, and this suggestion would enjoy the support of a number of philsophers along a wide spectrum of thinking from Nietzsche, to Dewey, to Alasdair MacIntyre.

## The pragmatic argument remade

Charles Bailey (1988) who reviewed *Philosophy of Education* for the *Journal of Philosophy of Education*, argued, among other things, that the pragmatic argument from relevance fails to make a persuasive case for lifelong education. He questioned the assumption that lifelong learning is the logical response to conditions of accelerating change and suggested two possible alternatives to it: (1) a programme that encouraged and faciliated resistance to rapid change on the argument that such rapid change is harmful to persons; and (2) a programme that encouraged and facilitated the development of rationally critical judgement of change on the argument that change should be more significantly under human control (1988: 122). His point was that, by itself, the pragmatic argument could signify a mindless support for change, a programme of uncritical adaptation to it, that 'relevance will not help us judge between these different programmes', and that what any educational programme requires for its justification is deeper normative reasons (1988: 123). Bailey suggested that a Kantian argument – that we have a duty to educate ourselves for life, and to help others with their self-education – could be a deeper, normative justification of lifelong education, a suggestion I discussed in a subsequent reply to the review (Wain, 1991). In any case, the pragmatic argument for lifelong learning does not stand alone in my book. It should be understood within the rationale of an education research project with an 'operational belt' (lifelong learning strategies) *guided by* an 'ideological' core (the project's understanding of 'education', humanistic, liberal, etc.). The point that lifelong learning should not be accepted uncritically as an unmitigated good simply because it seems to follow from the argument for survival in a rapidly changing world has been echoed by different critics recently, but it was never my position. The writers of the lifelong education movement themselves pointed to the different purposes to which lifelong learning policies could be put – repressive and one-dimensional or open and pluralistic – and worried about it.

Philosophers of education who have repeated Bailey's scepticism about 'lifelong learning' more recently, and often, are Nigel Blake *et al*. For instance, remarking on the opening statement in the British Government's Green Paper *The Learning Age* that 'In an era of change the only thing certain is change itself', they say that such statements are usually followed with something about the importance of managing change; so that one of 'the nostrums' of our time is that since 'all is in flux substance can be ignored and more power given to managers immediately' (2000: 2). In an earlier book, *Thinking Again* (Blake *et al*., 1998), commenting on a particular literacy programme, they remark sarcastically that 'Perhaps if children are reading to learn they are hurrying to leave reading in favour of some other business altogether: in order to become members of the Learning Society for example, accumulating useful skills and having them accredited' (1998: 49). In the same book they complain with respect to open learning, which, they say, 'claims a key role in the learning society', that it is promoted 'as a kind of educational panacea', but that it involves a 'technologized conception of teaching and learning, shaped significantly by psychology and information technology (IT)' (1998: 157). In their more recent introduction to *The Blackwell Guide to the Philosophy of Education* (Blake *et al*., 2003), they comment that philosophers have learnt in the recent past that educational practice 'does not need theory in quite the way it was once thought to', but that theory flourishes nevertheless because of 'the new educational pragmatism', the dichotomies of the new managerialism, of performativity, for which 'The personal delight of Lifelong Learning is often proposed as the solvent' (2003: 8). In short, Blake *et al*. perceive lifelong learning as tied to a managerialist agenda, interested predominantly in skills-based learning, and obsessed with measuring competencies.

The criticism is commonplace today and not inaccurate when addressed to the current dominant discourse of lifelong learning, but not to the argument for lifelong learning as such. The authors seem to recognize this when they write 'Lifelong Learning' in capital letters. By 'the argument for lifelong learning as such' I mean the pragmatic argument that lifelong learning strategies are forced on us by the conditions of rapid change that we live in. I think that argument is still persuasive. My argument is that lifelong learning is a key phenomenon of the postmodern world just as mass schooling was of the modern world, and that today's philosophers of education need to work with and within that reality; that the appropriate response to the dominant discourse in lifelong learning is not to criticize and then ignore it but to engage with it. Indeed, Blake *et al*. themselves suggest how; by creating a counter-discourse to respond to its threat to 'drain(ing) practice of normative validity', thus protecting 'the autonomy of education as a practice' (2003: 8). Inspired by 'the poststructuralist movement', involving 'deconstructionism in particular' (2003: 9), they conceive this kind of theorizing 'not as legitimation for principles and actions but as a form of deeper reflection on the nature and implications of the very educational enterprise' (2003: 8). What the pragmatic argument would suggest in this respect is that this counter-discourse be a counter-discourse about education re-conceptualized as lifelong, with the implication that its interest would extend beyond schooling to the learning society. Unlike the lifelong education movement's, the counter-discourse would be utopian but in a Derridean, deconstructive, sense. On the other hand, the follow-up book to *Philosophy of Lifelong Education* I projected was to construct a utopian social democrat learning society.

More about that later. Meanwhile, the situation with the philosophy of education today is that, though the hegemonic dominance of the analytic paradigm is largely broken and other influences, particularly Continental, have grown, analytic philosophy remains a powerful force, probably the most powerful, within the discipline, and philosophers of education of all descriptions still retain the original prejudice towards schooling and the practice of teachers as their central concern. Though the world may have changed radically in the last two decades, nothing has changed in the philosophy of education in this respect since *Philosophy of Lifelong Education* was published. Walter Feinberg is typical of a conservative view shared by most philosophers that the philosophy of education is 'institutional philosophy', a 'reflection on the aims of actual organizations and the practices of established institutions that are involved in some official or semi-official way in educating people' (1995: 27). But there are other dissenters besides myself. One is David Aspin. Working in tandem with Judith Chapman, Aspin wrote a book about 'providing young people with a good start to their lifelong learning through the agencies of school and community' (Chapman and Aspin, 1997: 3), in line with the lifelong education movement's programme to redefine schooling within the perspective of lifelong learning. That programme gave prominence to the 'self-directed learner' as the product of schooling so redefined. Chapman and Aspin refer to the notion just once. They begin the book with an examination of the notion of 'lifelong learning for all', drawing on the earlier debate around my book (Wain, 1987) and Richard Bagnall (1990) and Bailey's (1988) contributions to it. Bagnall, whose interest in lifelong learning has continued since, criticized the maximalist account of lifelong education (i.e. the one culminating in a learning society and incorporating informal learning) I supported as illiberal, and my representation of a world of competing and incommensurable education research projects as relativist and regressive. Both Bailey and Bagnall were influenced by the current liberal philosophy of education. At the time I replied to Bagnall's criticism by defending the maximalist programme (Wain, 1993), but I have moved away from it since, not because of Bagnall's criticism but because of my encounter with poststructuralism, which eventually produced *The Learning Society in a Postmodern World* in 2004 instead of the intended sequel to *Philosophy of Lifelong Education* referred to at the end of the previous section.

More recently, Aspin has produced and edited a two-volume *International Handbook of Lifelong Learning* (2001) together with Chapman and with Michael Hatton and Yukiko Sawano. Section 1 of the first volume, which he edited alone, was about 'Lifelong learning: conceptual, philosophical and values issues'. It included an introductory chapter written by himself and Chapman entitled 'Towards a philosophy of lifelong learning' and other chapters written by Richard Bagnall, Robin Barrow and Patrick Keeny, Penny Enslin, Shirley Pendlebury and Mary Tjattas, Paul Hager, John Halliday, Mal Leicester and Stella Parker, James Marshall, Stuart Ranson, Glenn Rikowski and Michael Strain, Ivan Snook, Robin Usher, and myself. Several of these writers, of course, are well-established philosophers of education, and one sees the same strategy at work here as that used by the early pioneers of the philosophy of education to promote their new discipline when they invited established philosophers to contribute to their edited volumes (a strategy that seems not to have worked much in their case).

Many of these contributions are as critical of the contemporary lifelong learning discourse as Blake *et al*. Richard Bagnall, for instance, measures it against 'progressive sentiments' he detects in the earlier discourse, and concludes that the contemporary discourse 'is largely ignorant of these sentiments and non-reflective of them', and that 'it constructs learning entirely in the service of its contribution to the consumerist, economically centred culture of advanced capitalist production, consumption and exchange'. In this landscape, he concludes, 'learning and education have become commodified, as have learners themselves' (2001: 46). In an earlier article (Bagnall, 2000) he had described the contemporary lifelong learning discourse as the product of economic determinism. But the negative criticism of the contemporary discourse is not universal. While acknowledging that technological determinism lies at the heart of contemporary lifelong learning policies, Colin Griffin locates the concepts of lifelong learning that the policy literature projects also 'as a social democratic response to the crisis of the welfare state . . . or as an integral part of the neo-liberal critique' (1999: 332). He reads this social democratic agenda into the UNESCO and OECD approaches to lifelong education and reads the insistence in the EU's documents on democratic citizenship and social cohesion as fundamental objects of lifelong learning policies, and as continuous with it. This insistence on democratic citizenship and social cohesion is, in fact, the other side of the contemporary lifelong learning agenda that critics of its managerialist thrust tend to ignore. With some justification, it must be owned, since it is much the weaker, more subdued, side. It has, however, encouraged the sort of theorizing of social democratic accounts of the learning society that put these concerns in a position of competing priority on the lifelong learning agenda.

## The learning society

What both Bagnall and Griffin point to is politically richer conceptions of lifelong learning in the literature itself to which a counter-discourse to the contemporary could make recourse. Aspin and Chapman themselves, however, do not see the job of philosophy as that of re-articulating the discourse of lifelong learning on different political lines. In their joint contribution to the section they see the main tasks of philosophy in relation to lifelong learning as: (1) 'a rigorous analysis and elucidation of those concepts, criteria and categories that are embedded and embodied in any lifelong learning undertaking, together with an examination of the presuppositions underlining them (the kind of activity described by Strawson (1958) as "descriptive metaphysics"; see also Trigg (1973))'; and (2) pointing to the implications of such analysis, 'to settle what ought logically to follow from it with respect to putting on programmes of lifelong learning', that is, 'ensuring that the theory/ies embodied in these programmes will be the temporary best theory that fits the phenomena and helps us to answer the problems at the time when we look at them' (Aspin *et al.*, 2001: 5). Echoing Bagnall's charge of 'relativism', and his concern with the 'almost totalitarian character' of the maximalist learning society', they contrasted this 'problem solving' approach with my theoretical approach in *Philosophy of Lifelong Education* (p. 5) and with Bagnall's own 'plea for lifelong learning to be seen as a species of liberal education generally' (p. 15).

Thus, though they regard the learning society as the end-point to which lifelong learning policies and strategies would contribute (p. 21), the notion is not central to their approach to lifelong learning. They object to its openness to utopian and millennarian approaches. The current reality is that, though it featured in the EU's lifelong learning policy discourse of the 1990s, the notion has fallen out of fashion since, replaced by the very different notion of a 'knowledge-based economy and society', a notion that, in turn, accords better with the discourse's performativist agenda. So, perhaps, creating a utopian counter-discourse of a learning society (which is what any counter-discourse must, by its very nature, be), such as I had contemplated after writing *Philosophy of Lifelong Education*, is required to oppose this trend!

Such a project is, in fact, the subject of Stewart Ranson, Glenn Rikowski and Michael Strain's article in Aspin *et al.*'s book. Its object is to 'outline an alternative approach to lifelong learning in a learning democracy' (Ranson *et al.*, 2001: 135). Ranson has elsewhere, alone and in collaboration with others, theorized a 'learning democracy' that encourages and recaptures 'an active public domain . . . a public and an educated public that has the capacity to participate actively as citizens in the shaping of a learning society and polity', using Kant and MacIntyre as his points of reference (1994: 102). My own intention had been to construct a similar theory using my model of an education research project, and I also had read MacIntyre on the educated public. In *The Learning Society in a Postmodern World* (2004) under poststructuralist influence, however, as I wrote earlier, I was persuaded to dispense with grand theories and with the idea of constructing a learning society. My influence, however, was not Derrida but Foucault. Reading Foucault (1991) suggested to me that, instead of thinking of the learning society as an utopian project, one could think of our present societies as already learning societies, and presented me with the not implausible hypothesis that our contemporary postmodern societies are obsessed with discipline rather than education. Taken with Baudrillard's (1983) complementary hypothesis that they are also obsessed with spectacle, producing mass societies, the project of an educated public seems unrealizable to me and self-creation the more credible way of preserving education.

# References

Aspin, David, Chapman, Judith, Hatton, Michael and Sawano, Yukiko (eds) (2001) *International Handbook of Lifelong Learning*, Dordrecht: Kluwer Academic Publishers.

Bagnall, Richard G. (1990) 'Lifelong education: the institutionalisation of an illiberal and regressive ideology?', *Educational Philosophy and Theory* 22: 1–7.

—— (2000) 'Lifelong learning and the limitations of economic determinism', *International Journal of Lifelong Education* 19(1) (January/February): 20–35.

—— (2001) 'Locating lifelong learning and education in contemporary currents of thought and culture', in David Aspin, Judith Chapman, Michael Hatton and Yukiko Sawano (eds) *International Handbook of Lifelong Learning, Part 1*, Dordrecht: Kluwer Academic Publishers, pp. 35–52.

Bailey, Charles (1988) 'Lifelong education and liberal education', *Journal of Philosophy of Education* 22(1): 121–6.

Baudrillard, Jean (1983) *In the Shadow of the Silent Majorities*, New York: Semiotext(e).

Beck, Ulrich (1994) *Risk Society: Towards a New Modernity*, London: Sage.

Blake, Nigel, Smith, Richard and Standish, Paul (2000) *The Universities We Need*, London: Kogan Page.

——, Smeyers, Paul, Smith, Richard and Standish, Paul (1998) *Thinking Again: Education after Postmodernism*, Westport, CT: Bergin and Garvey.

——, Smeyers, Paul, Smith, Richard and Standish, Paul (eds) (2003) *The Blackwell Guide to the Philosophy of Education*, Oxford: Blackwell.

Carr, Wilfred (ed.) (2005) *The RoutledgeFalmer Reader in the Philosophy of Education*, London and New York: RoutledgeFalmer.

Chapman, Judith and Aspin, David (1997) *The School, the Community and Lifelong Learning*, London: Cassell.

Cropley, Arthur J. (1979) 'Lifelong education: issues and questions', in Arthur J. Cropley (ed.) *Lifelong Education: A stocktaking*, Hamburg: UIE Monographs 8, pp. 8–22.

Cross-Durant, Angela (1984) 'Lifelong education in the writings of John Dewey', *International Journal of Lifelong Education* 3(2): 115–25.

Deleon, Asher (1984) 'Some thoughts regarding education versus communication', in Kenneth Wain (ed.) *Lifelong Education and Participation*, Malta: The University of Malta Press, pp. 30–7.

Dewey, John (1938) *Experience and Education*, New York: Macmillan.

—— (1966) *Democracy and Education*, New York: Macmillan.

—— (1997) *The Public and Its Problems*, Athens: Swallow Press/Ohio University Press.

Eurydice European Unit (2000) *Lifelong Learning: The contribution of education systems in the Member States of the European Union*, Brussels: Eurydice European Unit.

Faure, Edgar (Chair) (1972) *Learning to Be*, London: Harrap.

Feinberg, Walter (1995) 'The discourse of philosophy of education', in Wendy Kohli (ed.) *Critical Conversations in the Philosophy of Education*, New York and London: Routledge, pp. 24–33.

Foucault, Michel (1991) *Discipline and Punish: The birth of the prison*, London: Penguin Books.

Giddens, Anthony (1991) *Modernity and Self-Identity: Self and society in the late modern age*, Oxford: Polity Press.

Griffin, Colin (1999) 'Lifelong learning and social democracy', *International Journal of Lifelong Education* 18(5) (September/October): 329–42.

Gustavsson, Bernt (2002) 'What do we mean by lifelong learning and knowledge?', *International Journal of Lifelong Education* 21(1) (January/February): 13–23.

Harris, Kevin (1979) *Education and Knowledge*, London: Routledge and Kegan Paul.

Ireland, Timothy (1978) *Gelpi's View of Lifelong Education*, Manchester: Manchester University Press.

Lakatos, Imre (1980) *The Methodology of Scientific Research Programmes*, Cambridge: Cambridge University Press.

Lawson, Kenneth (1982) 'Lifelong education: concept or policy?', *International Journal of Lifelong Education* 1(2): 97–108.

Ranson, Stewart (1994) *Towards the Learning Society*, London: Cassell.

——, Rikowski, Glenn and Strain, Michael (2001) 'Lifelong learning for a learning democracy', in David Aspin, Judith Chapman, Michael Hatton and Yukiko Sawano (eds) *International Handbook of Lifelong Learning*, Dordrecht: Kluwer Academic Publishers, pp. 135–54.

Rorty, Richard (1990) 'Education without dogma', *Dialogue* 2: 44–7.

Snook, Ivan (2001) 'Lifelong education: some Deweyan themes', in David Aspin, Judith Chapman, Michael Hatton and Yukiko Sawano (eds) *International Handbook of Lifelong Learning Part 1*, Dordrecht: Kluwer Academic Publishers, pp. 155–64.

Suchodolski, Bogdan (1976) 'Lifelong education: some philosophical aspects', in R.H. Dave (ed.) *Foundations of Lifelong Education*, Oxford: Pergamon Press/Hamburg: UNESCO Institute for Education.

—— (1979) 'Lifelong education at the crossroads' in Arthur J. Cropley (ed.) *Lifelong Education: A stocktaking*, Hamburg: UIE Monographs 8, pp. 34–49.

van der Zee, Hendrik (1996) 'The learning society', in Peter Raggatt, Richard Edwards and Nick Small (eds) *The Learning Society: Challenges and trends*, London and New York: Routledge/Open University Press, pp. 162–83.

Wain, Kenneth (1984) 'Lifelong education: a Deweyan challenge', *Journal of Philosophy of Education* 18(2): 257–64.

—— (1987) *Philosophy of Lifelong Education*, Kent, NSW: Croom Helm.

—— (1991) 'Lifelong education: a duty to oneself?', *Journal of Philosophy of Education* 25(2): 273–8.

—— (1993) 'Lifelong education: illiberal and repressive?', *Educational Philosophy and Theory* 25(1): 58–70.

—— (2001) 'Lifelong learning: small adjustment or paradigm shift?', in David Aspin, Judith Chapman, Michael Hatton and Yukiko Sawano (eds) *International Handbook of Lifelong Learning, Part 1*, Dordrecht: Kluwer Academic Publishers, pp. 183–98.

—— (2004) *The Learning Society in a Postmodern World*, New York: Peter Lang.

—— (2006) 'The future of education . . . and its philosophy', in Padraig Hogan, Kenneth Wain and Joseph Giordmaina (eds) *International Network of Philosophers of Education Conference Proceedings*, August 2006, Malta, pp. 29–41.

White, John (1982) *The Aims of Education Restated*, London: Routledge.

# 35

# Lifelong learning as a psychological process

*Knud Illeris*

From a psychological point of view learning can be defined as 'any process that for living beings leads to a durable change of capacity and is not caused by oblivion, biological maturing or ageing' (Illeris, 2007). For humans this process is ongoing throughout life, whether it be intentional or incidental. In order to examine what this means in relation to the slogan of life-long learning it will be useful to start by observing some of the most important characteristics of the very complex process of human learning. After this the question will be how human learning potential can be used and what is specific and important in different phases of the life course.

## Some basic features of human learning

First of all, it is important to observe that human learning always consists of two very different processes, which are usually going on simultaneously and in an integrated way and therefore also are experienced as one and the same thing. On the one hand, learning is an external interaction process between the individual and his or her social and material environment. On the other hand, the impressions and influences that the individual receives from this interaction must be elaborated and internalised by an internal process of acquisition. Only if both of these processes are active will there be any learning (Illeris, 2007).

However, the criteria of the two processes are very different. The interaction process, on the one hand, is by nature social, cultural and societal; it is dependent on when and where it is taking place: what can be learned today is, for instance, to a great extent marked by modern technology that did not exist just a few decades ago. The acquisition process, on the other hand, is by nature individual and psychological; it is dependent on the immense and highly differentiated capacities of the human brain as developed over millions of years as part of our species' adaptation to environmental conditions: the human capacity for learning is characterised by the processes of language, thinking and consciousness, whereas other species may have sharper senses or better physical resources of strength and suppleness (see, for example, Solms and Turnbull, 2002).

Another important aspect of learning is that the acquisition process always includes both an incentive and a content dimension. The incentive is the mobilisation of the necessary mental energy for the process to take place – it is what we usually talk about as motivation. The content is about what is learned – it is impossible to speak about learning without speaking about something that is learned.

In schooling and education, learning content is usually conceived as knowledge and skills, but it can also be such properties as understanding, insight, meaning, attitudes, methods, viewpoints, culture, qualifications, competencies, etc. It is, however, important to realise that the incentives – emotion, motivation and volition – are not only driving forces, but also an integrated part of the learning processes and outcomes. If something is learned in an active and positive mode the learning will be easier to recall and apply in a broad range of different situations. But if the learning process has been reluctant or disengaged the learning result is obsessed with negative feelings and needs some kind of surmounting to be reactivated.

It is also important to be aware that the acquisition is always an integration of new impact into structures that have been developed by prior learning processes (this is the Piagetian view, which was strongly emphasised by Ausuble (1968)). This is in direct opposition to the traditional understanding of learning as a transfer of knowledge and skills. There is no such simple transfer, but a joining together in which the existing mental schemata are just as important as the new impact. And as the existing schemata are always individual structures – no two individuals have learned exactly the same during their life course – the learning result is also always a specific individual creation.

In addition, there are many different types of learning. Learning typologies can be set up from many perspectives, but it is significant that all the more advanced typologies in some way make a main distinction between what may be termed as additive and restructuring learning (e.g. Piaget, 1952 [1936]; Flavell, 1963; Rogers, 1969; Bateson, 1972; Engeström, 1987; Argyris, 1992). By additive learning is meant the usual everyday event of adding new elements to the already developed mental structures. This is generally easy, not very demanding, and we are doing it all the time, whenever we meet something new that is worth remembering. Restructuring learning, on the other hand, is demanding, because we have to break down and reorganise our patterns of behaviour or understanding in order to include some new elements that cannot fit into the existing structures. It is a way of learning that we can use when we meet impressions or situations that we cannot immediately grasp or cope with. But we only make the effort if the new is something that we experience as important or interesting to us. If not, we rather tend to reject it or distort it so that it is in accordance with the already established patterns or notions.

This leads us to the last general point on learning that will be mentioned here: that human beings in the overwhelmingly complex existence of today are not equipped to take in all the learning possibilities they are faced with. Our mental capacity, however magnificent it may seem, is not able to match the versatile and ever changing cultural and societal developments of the latest centuries. So we all have to develop ways of defence and resistance in order to avoid a lot of possible learning. Just think of how much you generally remember from half an hour's TV news! (Illeris, 2007).

## Learning through the life course

Seen from the point of view of learning, it seems to be adequate to operate using four main phases of life (Illeris, 2003a, 2007):

- *Childhood* lasts from birth to the onset of puberty, which occurs these days around the age of 11–13 (previously it was at a later point).
- *Youth* lasts from puberty until the preconditions for a more or less stable identity are established, typically through relatively permanent relationships with partners and work, or perhaps a consciousness of not wanting to enter into such relationships. It is a characteristic of present-day society that the period of youth is longer than it has ever previously been, and has a very fluid transition to adulthood.
- *Adulthood* lasts from the end of the youth period until the 'life turn' – a concept that implies that the end of life has been perceived on the distant horizon, and the person is beginning to accept this and relate to it.
- *Mature adulthood* lasts until death or, in terms of learning, perhaps only until mental weakness begins to take hold to a considerable extent.

In the following, the main characteristics of learning motivation in each of these four life ages will be examined and described in more detail.

### Learning in childhood is uncensored and confident

The overall characteristic of children's learning is that, in line with their development, they are absorbed in capturing the world by which they see themselves surrounded and of which they are a part. In child psychology there are comprehensive descriptions of the many different facets and stages in this capturing process, including, for example, Freud's division into phases, Erikson's development ages and Piaget's stages theory. Here only certain overriding factors that determine some of the general conditions for the process will be pointed out.

In learning terms, it is naturally important that cognitive learning capacity develops gradually throughout childhood. It is also important that children basically expect to be guided by adults as to what and how they should learn. As babies their only connection with the surrounding world is through the mother and other adults, and the first 'capture' involves establishing the separation between themselves and the surrounding world (e.g. Stern, 1985). The child is from the start subject to the control of adults and can only gradually free itself from it.

In childcare institutions and in the early years at school, children are still obliged to unfold and develop within a framework set by adults. They must of necessity accept this as a basic condition, even though naturally they can resist when they feel that they are being restricted or they are unable to understand what is going on – and this resistance is also a highly significant factor in development and learning. However, children are typically ready to accept explanations that tell them that learning something may be good or important for them later even if they cannot grasp it right now.

Nevertheless, the development of our late-modern society has brought about certain trends for change that apply to some of these basic factors affecting learning in childhood. In general, cultural liberation gives children plenty of opportunities for activities, relations and impulses that previously lay beyond their reach, while at the same time, the disintegration of traditions and norms weakens or removes a number of fixed points and structures from which children could previously take their bearings. Like young people and adults, children today perceive a number of potential choices from an early age – of which some are real and many others are only apparent – while previously there was a much higher degree of certainty (e.g. Giddens, 1991).

The mass media play a special role here. More than parents or other adults, they give children the opportunity to experience – or often almost force on to them – a mass of impulses, including such things as catastrophes, violence and sex; experiences to which they have not previously had access, and which can have strong emotional influences on them. Also, introducing these things in advance of the formation of personal experience makes it more complicated for children to later acquire their own experiences in these spheres.

Another important factor is that developments in some spheres of society can happen so fast that adults have difficulty keeping up, while children can leap, so to speak, straight into the development at its present stage, which in some areas such as information technology makes some of them able to overtake adults.

From a learning perspective, it is generally important to remember that childhood as a life age is basically influenced by the huge acquisition process of integrating and relating to the whole of the complex material, social and societal environment. This requires a broad spectrum of protracted constructive processes that the child is disposed to carry out, trusting in adults and being supported by them. Childhood is typically a period of primarily gentle, gradual and stable additive learning processes, even though these processes have tended to become more complex and contradictory. Examples of the processes that are gone through are motor and linguistic development, acquisition of symbol management (including reading, writing and arithmetic), and knowledge of the surrounding world and its rules, structures and means of function.

In connection with these processes, there also occur a number of reconstructions, mainly directed towards getting the acquisition process back on track again when it has gone astray, but also more complex in the spheres connected to identity development, including the development of gender roles (Illeris, 2007).

## Learning in youth is searching and identity building

Youth has not always been perceived as a life age in its own right. Historically, the concept of youth developed together with capitalism and industrialisation. In the beginning, the concept of youth was limited to a few years, but gradually it became a longer period and the notion of youth increasingly spread beyond the middle classes. The period of youth has from the start been linked with a particular need for socially necessary learning and personal development. With Erik Erikson's book, *Identity, Youth and Crises* (1968), the conception of youth took the direction typical for the interpretation today, which is that youth is primarily a period for a more or less crisis-determined development of a personal identity or self-comprehension.

However, with the development of late modernity, recent decades have seen a further expansion of the youthful period, so today it may often extend far into the twenties. In addition, youth has become very much idealised – and commercialised – as the age of freedom and happiness with no responsibilities, while at the same time, the personal and societal problems that attach to youth seem to be steadily increasing. The essence of this development, particularly as seen from a learning perspective, is that the demands on the formation of identity have undergone an explosive growth in line with cultural liberation – there is a lot of 'identity work' that young people have to do, as well as getting through their education, forming relationships with a partner, finding their place in society and so on.

Previously there was family affiliation, a gender role, class attachment and usually also an attachment to a particular profession, as well as a mass of given values and norms that the young person was expected to take on, perhaps through a somewhat rebellious process. Now all this is disintegrating or becoming redundant, and the young person must find his or her own way through personal choices. It is not only about education, career, partner and home; also lifestyle, personal identity and a lot of preferences and attitudes must be chosen. Development in these areas has been overwhelming, and young people currently have to struggle with new, untried processes, the conditions of which change almost from day to day – new educational opportunities, new consumer opportunities, new communication systems and new lifestyle offers make themselves felt in an almost chaotic confusion; everything seems possible, and yet young people perceive countless limitations, for many opportunities are completely inaccessible for the vast majority – only very few can become actors, TV hosts, designers or sporting heroes (see Simonsen, 2000).

Earlier it was generally accepted that human beings were cognitively fully developed from about the onset of puberty. But today it seems clear that, throughout the period of youth, new possibilities can be developed for thinking dialectically, making use of practical logic, recognising what one knows (meta-cognition) and mastering critical reflection. Modern brain research has most recently shown that the working memory – the brain centre that precisely stands for such advanced cognitive functions – is only fully developed at the end of the teenage years. It is thus only during the period of youth that, together with all the other changes that take place during these years, we acquire our full cognitive capacity (Brookfield, 2000).

In terms of learning, the first part of the youth period is in the more developed countries still subject to compulsory education, and later one should go through some youth education and, as a rule, also some further education of a more vocational nature. However, all learning in the youth period is very much oriented towards the formation of identity and can only be understood in this light. This leads to a contradictory relationship with a lot of problems. Often young people react more or less reluctantly to academic subject requirements, which for the most part are forced upon them, and which they may find outdated, while the representatives of the system attempt to keep their concentration on academic work, which they themselves are trained in, are committed to and are under an obligation to uphold.

The most important things for young people to learn today are to be able to orient themselves, to be able to make choices that can be answered for, to keep up with everything, not to waste their lives on the wrong thing, and to be able to decline in the many situations where a choice has to be made. Society and employers also demand maturity, independence, responsibility and so on. The best security for the future seems not to be learning a subject on what are perceived as traditional premises, but to be ready to change and take hold of what is relevant in many different situations. Uncertainty cannot be countered by stability, but only by being open, flexible and constantly oriented to learning.

Youth is also the period in which to learn how to deal with gender and sexual relations. For both genders this is closely linked with the personal identity process – and here as in education it is most often the formation of identity that is given priority: young people today are often more absorbed in reflecting themselves in their partners than they are in the partners themselves.

There is so much to be learned in the period of youth: academically, emotionally, socially, societally and, most of all, in terms of identity. Whereas childhood is a time for constructive additive learning, youth is a period for major reconstructions and transformations in which, one by one, profound changes are made to the knowledge structures and the emotional patterns. And the reflexivity that is so characteristic of late modernity, where it is always the individual's relationship to him- or herself that is the focal point of learning, unfolds without doubt most dramatically in the years of youth as an essential yet enormously taxing tool for the identity process (Illeris, 2003b).

## Learning in adulthood is selective and goal oriented

The beginning of the adult period may typically be marked by external events such as starting a family or finishing education. There are no decisively new cognitive opportunities; what happens in terms of learning and consciousness is that the person fully takes on the management of, and responsibility for, his or her own life, with this normally occurring gradually as a long process throughout the years of youth and into adulthood.

In general adulthood has traditionally been marked by a kind of ambition that implies a striving to realise more or less clear life aims relating to family, career, interests or something else – but in late modernity this representation is also on its way to being overlaid by the continual societal changes, the unpredictability of the future, the conditioning of the market mechanism and the unending succession of apparent choices.

Many factors that were in earlier times already marked out for the individual have now become things to be decided on again and again. It is no longer possible to make your choice of life course once and for all when young, and then expect to spend the rest of your life accomplishing it. Whereas, once a large number of factors were given, based on gender or class affiliations, for example, all now appears to be redundant (Giddens, 1991). The fact that this is only how it appears can be seen from statistics showing that the large majority of people, now just as previously, live their lives in the way that their gender and social background has prepared them for. However, this does not influence the perception that now this is something people choose themselves, something for which they are responsible, and thus for which they have only themselves to blame if it turns out to be unsatisfactory.

With the earlier, firmer structures, the individual could use his or her years of youth to develop an identity, or at least a sort of draft identity, that would be of help in governing future learning. In career terms, school and education would have provided for the acquisition of a groundwork that was regarded as feasible for the rest of that person's life, so that whatever was needed later could generally be gained through practice learning at work and maybe a few additional courses. In life also, it was necessary to keep up with any developments, but this did not go too fast for people to manage to acquire the requisite learning as they went along. Thus, for the vast majority of people, learning in adulthood was fairly manageable and predominantly additive in nature, with its most characteristic aspect probably being the development of a system of defence mechanisms that could screen out any new impulses that were too insistent, thus ensuring stability and self-respect.

Becoming an adult formally in our society means coming of age and so taking responsibility for one's own life and actions. This happens legally by the age of 18, but from a psychological perspective it is actually a process, and it is characteristic that this process has become longer and longer, to such an extent that today it is most often accomplished well into a person's twenties or perhaps never. Late-modern society's promotion of youth also makes it difficult to let it go.

In the field of learning this goes hand in hand with the continual extension of the average time spent in education. Today, after the compulsory school years, a majority go on to further courses for many years before the end of the preliminary period of education. In addition to this, adult education programmes have been greatly developed, and correspondingly young people's expectations today are for recurrent or lifelong education; they can hardly imagine that they could 'stick' in the same job all their lives.

However, it is basically characteristic that adults learn what they want to learn, and have very little inclination to acquire something they do not want, that is, something they do not perceive as meaningful for their own life goals, of which they are aware in varying degrees of clarity (Illeris, 2006). As a consequence of this, rather than having various more or less unconnected learning motives, adults have more coherent strategies relating to goals that are normally fairly clear and known to the individual.

This approach to education is, however, far from always in accordance with the way adult education is organised. In principle, adult education is nearly always voluntary. Nevertheless, very many participants in adult education today have been indirectly forced to take part in programmes, and many even feel they have been 'placed' there by different counselling bodies. It is experienced as particularly contradictory when one feels that one is an adult and would like to manage one's own life. Adult education is at present a strange mixture of old ideals concerning public enlightenment and modern vocational orientation and economically oriented targeting (Illeris, 2003c).

With the pace of change and need for reorganisation in the late-modern period, the phrase 'lifelong learning' primarily implies a need to be constantly prepared for reorganisation. This can be hard enough for young people, but for those who first became caught up in this development as adults, the challenge of reorganisation is even harder. The stability, self-assurance and professional pride that were crucial qualifications for many a few years ago now seem like burdensome encumbrances. Where before there was stability, there now has to be flexibility, and if there is to be any hope of survival in the job market, the defence mechanisms of stability must very quickly be replaced with service-mindedness and readiness for change.

Societal demands that adults must learn on a far greater scale and in a totally different way than previously are inescapable on every level. It is primarily a demand for a mental reorganisation and personal development, but there may also be technical or academic demands, for example, typically in connection with information technology developments. All these demands are for profound restructuring processes of a reflexive nature – and that is something many adults will not spontaneously accept.

At the same time, however, there are still many participants in adult education who are there of their own free will because they wish to or need to learn something specific – and in some cases also for more social reasons. On this basis it might be expected that these adults would themselves take responsibility for the learning that the course is providing. However, ordinary conceptions and experiences of education often get in the way of this. Even though the institutions, the teachers and the participants might say and believe otherwise, everyone in the education situation obstinately expects that the responsibility will lie with the teacher. It is, after all, the teacher who knows what has got to be learned.

The situation is paradoxical, for while these adult participants have a tendency to behave like pupils, they have a very hard time accepting the lack of authority the traditional pupil role entails. They get bored and become resistant in a more or less conscious way – but nevertheless they will not themselves take on the responsibility, for that is actually far more demanding. The conflict can only be resolved by effectively making a conscious break with the prevailing roles as pupils and teachers at school. And as a rule it is the teacher who has to take the initiative and insist on it. It is normally only when the participants realise that they truly can take responsibility and use the teacher as a support for their own learning that the picture alters, and after that the way is clear for the learning to become goal-directed, effective, transcendent and libidinal, as is characteristic of adult learning outside, which is not institutionalised (Illeris, 2004).

However, there is much to suggest that the conditions described here stand in the way of complete changes. The 'new youth' of late modernity, who have in recent years turned youth education upside down, are well on their way to making their entry into adult education as the 'new adults' (Simonsen, 2000).

## Learning in mature adulthood is exclusive and conclusive

'The age of maturity', 'the third age' or 'second adulthood' are all terms for the phase of life that for most people in modern society lies between the so-called 'life turn' and actual old age, and can well last a period of 20 years or more.

The life turn is a psychological phenomenon concerning the perception and acknowledgement that the remaining time in your life is not unlimited. It is, however, most often external events that bring about and mark the life turn – typical examples are the children leaving home, losing a job, taking early retirement or being given reduced hours; it can also be a divorce or the death of a loved one, and for women the menopause may play a part in the situation.

In contrast to the first age of adulthood, the mature age is characteristically not dominated by the same form of purposefulness – the goals being reached for do not have the same existential nature as having a family, raising children, or work and career. As far as they are able – and the mature age is for many today a period with certain personal and financial abilities – people spend their time on things they perceive as quality activities, such as cultural or social activities, or helping others, their partner, if they have one, their children, their grandchildren or disadvantaged groups that they are involved with.

In this context there may often be important elements of learning, both formal education and less formal processes of development and change, characterised by being something absolutely personally chosen, because it is experienced as important or interesting, or perhaps has the nature of something one needs to prove to oneself and to others that one is well capable of but simply has not had the opportunity to do previously (Jarvis, 2001).

However, it must be remembered that this only applies to relatively privileged mature adults. Many people have more than enough to do just getting by practically and financially, and have neither the opportunity nor the reserves to look towards the self-actualisation or learning in which those in more favourable positions increasingly get involved. The new wave of learning and education for mature adults is for the time being mainly a middle-class phenomenon.

Cognitively there may be a trend towards learning beginning to happen more slowly if it concerns new areas the person is not very committed to, but this does not normally apply when it concerns things he or she is interested in, and for which he or she has good presuppositions and experiences. The usual popular notion that elderly people are worse at learning things can thus be seen to relate only to the fact that they can be slower in learning something new – which people are often not particularly interested in acquiring. People are satisfied with their own interests and experiences, and if the new matter is not connected to that it can make it more difficult to mobilise mental energy.

It is something else, of course, if it is a case of dementia or other diseases – but it is still worth noting that, even when such disability occurs, there would seem to be a tendency for it not to directly affect the areas where one has special competence and which one has maintained, and where the brain therefore has been 'kept in good condition' (Goldberg, 2005).

## Three general lines of development in lifelong learning

It is important to stress that the described typical background attitudes to learning in various life ages are current attitudes, for the details of life ages are to a great extent determined by history, culture and society, and can alter rapidly. It has become clear, for example, how late modernity has influenced learning today, particularly in childhood and youth, but also increasingly in adulthood.

Nevertheless, there are also a number of important common links running through the life ages that are more general and that, to a certain extent, run across changing circumstances. From the descriptions previously given, three closely linked long lines of development of this kind can be pointed out:

- First, a gradual liberation occurs throughout the life ages for the individual in relation to the external determination of learning. Whereas learning in childhood is framed in an interaction between biological maturing and external influences, in youth it is characterised to a great extent by young people's fight to have a say in things and, partly through this, construct their identity. In first adulthood, people move towards learning what they themselves think is important, but to a great extent this is determined by their external conditions. It is only in mature adulthood that external determinations move into the background for those people who have the opportunities and the resources to liberate themselves.
- In close interaction with this gradual liberation of learning from its external bondage, there also typically occurs an individuation, that is, learning increasingly directs itself towards the development of an individual person and is determined by personal needs and interests. Again it is a development that first takes off properly in the period of youth, but which only has a full impact in mature adulthood.
- Finally, there also occurs a gradual development of responsibility for learning that is closely connected with the two other developments and so follows the same pattern.

In modern society, it seems very clear that it should be both a condition and a goal for society to strive to organise itself along the lines of these developments and to support them. However, learning is not only an individual process and education can also have perspectives other than supporting personal development and the provision of qualifications for individuals, which the late modern individualisation trend so clearly puts in central position. Society wants something from us, and individualisation goes hand in hand with equally strong measures that seek to control our learning.

# References

Argyris, Chris (1992) *On Organizational Learning*, Cambridge, MA: Blackwell.

Ausuble, David P. (1968) *Educational Psychology: A cognitive view*, New York: Holt, Rinehart and Winston.

Bateson, Gregory (1972) *Steps to an Ecology of Mind*, San Francisco, CA: Chandler.

Brookfield, Stephen D. (2000) 'Adult cognition as a dimension of lifelong learning', in John Field and Mal Leicester (eds) *Lifelong Learning: Education across the Lifespan*, London: RoutledgeFalmer, pp. 89–101.

Engeström, Yrjö (1987) *Learning by Expanding: An activity-theoretical approach to developmental research*, Helsinki: Orienta-Kunsultit.

Erikson, Erik H. (1968) *Identity, Youth and Crises*, New York: Norton.

Flavell, John H. (1963) *The Developmental Psychology of Jean Piaget*, New York: Van Nostrand.

Giddens, Anthony (1991) *Modernity and Self-identity*, Cambridge: Polity Press.

Goldberg, Elkhonon (2005) *The Wisdom Paradox*, New York: Simon and Schuster.

Illeris, Knud (2003a) 'Learning changes through life', *Lifelong Learning in Europe* 8(1): 51–60.

—— (2003b) 'Learning, identity and self orientation in youth', *Young – Nordic Journal of Youth Research* 11(4): 357–76.

—— (2003c) 'Adult education as experienced by the learners', *International Journal of Lifelong Education* 22(1): 13–23.

—— (2004) *Adult Education and Adult Learning*, Malabar, FL: Krieger Publishing.

—— (2006) 'What is special about adult learning?', in Peter Sutherland and Jim Crowther (eds) *Lifelong Learning: Concepts and contexts*, London: Routledge, pp. 15–23.

—— (2007) *How We Learn: An introduction to learning and non-learning in school and beyond*, London: Routledge.

Jarvis, Peter (2001) *Learning in Later Life*, London: Kogan Page.

Piaget, Jean (1952 [1936]) *The Origins of Intelligence in Children*, New York: International Universities Press.

Rogers, Carl R. (1969) *Freedom to Learn*, Columbus, OH: Charles E. Merrill.

Simonsen, Birgitte (2000) 'New young people, new forms of consciousness, new educational methods', in Knud Illeris (ed.) *Adult Education in the Perspective of the Learners*, Copenhagen: Roskilde University Press, pp. 137–56.

Solms, Mark and Turnbull, Oliver (2002) *The Brain and the Inner World*, New York: Other Press.

Stern, Daniel N. (1985) *The Interpersonal World of the Infant*, New York: Basic Books.

# 36

# Lifelong learning
## Between humanism and global capitalism

*Kjell Rubenson*

The last 40 years have left us with two competing paradigms of lifelong learning, the UNESCO and OECD worldviews. UNESCO and OECD paradigms can be seen as the two halves of a Janus[1] face that together express the ambiguous nature of lifelong learning (Rubenson, 2006). With UNESCO promoting a vague idea of a humanistic-inspired paradigm of lifelong learning, today's national policy debates are almost exclusively driven by the OECD's economistic paradigm of lifelong learning and with the European Union as its prophet. It is from this perspective that this chapter sets out to analyse how the OECD interpretation of lifelong learning became the taken-for-granted 'rule of ideas'. This chapter also scrutinises the political project of lifelong learning and explores the possibilities for establishing a more balanced relationship between the two competing ideas of lifelong learning.

## The OECD's hegemonic influence on the lifelong learning agenda

In order to establish the history of current hegemonic policies and to provide insight into the conditions under which the idea was shaped and won out against competing worldviews, we have to look for a 'first mover situation' (Dostal, 2004: 444).

The dominant OECD discourse on lifelong learning belongs to what has been labelled the second generation of thoughts on the concept (Rubenson, 1999). It is preceded by a failed attempt by the OECD to launch recurrent education as a planning principle in the early 1970s and UNESCO's significant work on defining and promoting its version of lifelong learning at around the same time. The idea of recurrent education quickly faded and will not be further addressed here (see Rubenson, 2006 for a discussion) but UNESCO came to play an important role in the struggle over agenda setting.

The Faure Commission is often given credit for initiating the UNESCO programme on lifelong learning. While it is true that the Faure report (1972) resulted in lifelong education becoming the official position of UNESCO, it should be noted that this was an idea that UNESCO staff had engaged with during the entire 1960s. The concept had surfaced already at the UNESCO International Conference on Adult Education in Montreal in 1960 and the

411

follow-up meeting in 1965 contains a concrete proposal for the implementation of 'l'éducation permanente' (Lengrand, 1965, cited in Hasan, 1999: 52). Further, Paul Lengrand, active within UNESCO, had already published *An Introduction to Lifelong Education* (Lengrand, 1970).

The Faure Commission pointed to the unsettling impact of modernisation processes on daily life. The challenge for education was: 'to help man to develop a scientific frame of mind in order to promote the sciences without becoming enslaved by them' (Faure, 1972: xxvii). Another concern was that the system reflected a bygone era characterised by strict hierarchies in society and schools. Improving the prospect of equal opportunity was defined as a major challenge. The Commission acknowledged that a system built for the education of children and youth would not be well suited to respond to the growing demand for adult education. While not endorsing Illich's drastic de-schooling idea, the Commission found present structures of education to be redundant and, in response, promoted the need for lifelong learning and the idea of lifelong education.

It fell on the UNESCO Institute of Education to concretise the Faure Commission's inspiring but vague ideas on lifelong education. The following decade saw a series of reports from the Institute with titles like *Lifelong Learning: A stocktaking* (Cropley, 1978), *Lifelong Education and the Training of Teachers* (Cropley and Dave, 1978), *Foundations of Lifelong Education* (Dave, 1976) and *Towards a System of Lifelong Education: Some practical considerations* (Cropley, 1980). These contributions primarily explored two topics: the foundations of lifelong education, and pedagogical and curriculum aspects. The foundational debate was situated within a humanistic tradition, arguing that lifelong education would promote a better society and quality of life and allow people to adapt to and control change. The concept was one of personal development; the catchwords became that people were 'making themselves' rather than 'being made'. Individuals were expected to work towards achieving the central goals of democracy and humanism, and the total development of self, through self-evaluation, self-awareness and self-directed learning. An important issue in the analysis was how a 'system of lifelong learning' could reduce educational gaps in society. It was stressed that:

> A crucial weakness in the structure of society is an absence of political will, not only towards the democratization of education but also towards the democratization of society. Consequently, the existing social relations of production provide a major obstacle to the true realization of lifelong learning – indeed lifelong learning will become a new arena for social struggle because it will require a classless societ.
>
> (Vinkour, 1976: 362)

The second stream of work, which, strangely enough, does not attempt to build on the foundational explorations, discussed curriculum, pedagogical directions and teacher education. It is an interesting mixture of traditional adult education arguments and curriculum theory. Further, it is also characterised by a strong criticism of the traditional school, which is to be blamed for all ills. What is striking about this literature is the total absence of any reference to the vibrant work done within the new sociology of education that had made it clear that education and teaching processes should be preferably understood in a political structural perspective. The absence of any such links made UNESCO's work highly idealistic. As Wain (1986) concludes, the practical questions never really got answered and the discussion remained at the level of vague ideas. It is therefore no surprise that the UNESCO agenda for lifelong learning never became the dominant mode of thinking in policy circles and came to have little or more often no effect on national educational policy. Third world countries regarded lifelong education as a luxury of the developed world and the latter took no notice of the idea. Issues such as equality, democratisation and human development were not those ideas that came to inform the educational discourse in the industrialised countries. The 1970s saw the beginning of a different politico-economic paradigm – neo-liberalism – that was driven by a different ideology with different goals and dreams. The lack of impact of the UNESCO model has to be understood in the context of where it was located in respect to the three major institutional arrangements in society: state, market and civil society. The UNESCO tradition was strongly anchored in civil society and the adult education community, from which it had originated, while the state showed little interest in the UNESCO principle of lifelong learning and the market remained oblivious to the idea.

Instead it was the OECD's discourse on lifelong learning that came to comprise the raison d'être of lifelong learning in the industrialised world. This perspective, which will be discussed in more detail in the next section, had its origin in the market and became something of a 'New Jerusalem' for Ministries of Education and Labour. It should be noted that the 1980s had seen slow economic growth, rising public deficits, increasing unemployment and increased uncertainty on how to handle the rapid changes caused by new information technologies. This was now an era of global capitalism, characterised by increased economic competition and rapid advances in information technology. A neo-liberal framework had replaced the Keynesian creed. Educational policy was shaped by severe limitations on public expenditures, a general suspicion of state and public institutions, and a belief in the efficiency of free-market forces. The new discourse was pushed by leading industrialists such as The European Round Table of Industrialists (ERT) who put pressure on government to keep the public sector under check and increase labour market flexibility. Education is another area where the ERT tried to influence government policy. The main complaint was that the education system did not produce the human resources needed in industry. In order to remedy the problem, ERT recommended three major changes to the system: first, greater involvement of industrialists in public education; second, that higher education be more related to the world of work; and, third, the development of lifelong learning as an instrument for keeping up with technological change and maintaining competitiveness (ERT, 1989; Nyberg, 2000).

It was in this context that, at the end of the 1980s, the OECD again turned its attention to education as the generator of economic growth. As a response to the new economic and political context, the OECD's 1989 report, *Education and the Economy in a Changing Society*, stressed the need to adopt a human resources perspective within the context of lifelong learning. The report noted that national differences in economic performance could increasingly be attributed to varying degrees of educational effectiveness and a country's learning capabilities. The report pointed out that '"education" is becoming less clearly distinct from that which is "the economy"' (OECD, 1989: 19), and that '"Education and the economy" has become a catch-phrase for a vague but urgent dissatisfaction with the status quo' (p. 17). The OECD's new position on lifelong learning was further elaborated and presented in the report *Lifelong Learning for All* (OECD, 1996), prepared for the 1996 Council of Ministers meeting. Reflecting the new economic reality driving the return of the concept, the 1996 ministerial declaration on lifelong learning was a joint communiqué with the OECD ministers of labour. The 1989 and 1996 OECD reports quickly became a bible not only for ministers of education but also for their colleagues holding labour portfolios. In fact it is difficult to find any policy document where educational policy is not discussed in the context of the challenges and threats of global competition and new technologies and where lifelong learning is not being 'sold' as part of the solution.

In Gramscian terms, the argument is that the OECD achieved hegemony over the lifelong learning discourse through its capacity to manufacture a broad consensus that becomes the 'common sense' of society. Its hegemony rests on the organisation's capacity to set policy agendas that become taken-for-granted 'rules of ideas', which have come to govern national policy actors' approaches to educational reforms (see, for example, Adamson, 1980; Boggs, 1976). It is the unique combination of being a semi-autonomous think-tank capable of sophisticated long-term planning while also being a part of an international civil service and a shared state apparatus (Dostal, 2004) that has positioned the OECD to gain hegemony over the educational agenda. The OECD's long-term ability to gain control over the lifelong learning discourse and influence national policy agendas rests mainly on two pillars: bureau-shaping strategies focusing on hegemony over knowledge management (Dunleavy, 1991, cited in Dostal, 2004: 443) and an extensive interface between national bureaucracies and their counterparts at the OECD (Dostal, 2004; Henry *et al.*, 2001; Rinne *et al.*, 2004; Vickers, 1994). In competition with UNESCO, the OECD's capacity to authoritatively provide comparative expert knowledge has afforded the organisation a discursive advantage. As an example of how the organisation uses the knowledge management instrument, I would like to point to the OECD's proposed Program for the International Assessment of Adult Competencies (PIAAC) with the purpose of providing the statistical and analytical basis needed to address policy issues such as the types of skills most in need, the extent to which there are mismatches between available skills and economic and social requirements, and the mechanisms through which skills are acquired and lost (Com/Delsa/EDUC, 2005).

In doing so, PIAAC could facilitate policy development in Ministries of Education and Labour in numerous and in some instances unique ways. For example, among other issues, PIAAC will enable countries to assess: how their education and training systems perform in the production of key competencies; the effects this has on their labour markets, social development and long-term macro-economic performance; and which policies and institutional settings are associated with success in bringing about efficient school-to-work transitions, enhancing the labour market situation of adults at risk of socio-economic distress, and enabling learning throughout the life-cycle (Com/Delsa/EDUC, 2005: 6).

If PIAAC were to be implemented, it would allow the OECD to more seamlessly extend its overriding economic discourse into its lifelong education agenda and further, at the national level, a strengthening of the ties between Ministries of Labour and Education.

## The OECD discourse and the political project on lifelong learning

Over the last decade there have been intensive debates in the social sciences of the implications of globalisation and the declining role of the nation state. Rejecting 'methodological nationalism' and embracing the idea of transnational governance (Cox, 2005) does not imply that the nation state has disappeared, but stresses the point that national policies are increasingly impacted by 'the transnational networks that link policy making from country to country' (p. 144). Consequently the OECD's discourse on lifelong learning functions as a policy lesson for national policy makers. It is therefore of interest to look a bit closer at the content of the policy learning that is being encouraged.

As referred to above, the OECD's interest in lifelong learning grows out of the analysis of the economic crises of the 1980s and has later been fuelled by the organisation's research on the knowledge economy and knowledge society. With regard to the so-called knowledge economy, the OECD grounded its analyses on findings from economists who argued that technological change functions as a mediating factor promoting demand for education that in turn promotes technological change and ultimately results in productivity gains (Rubenson, 2004). Thus, education must be viewed not only as an investment but also as a factor of production (Welch, 1970: 41). Welch and others highlighted the role of education in developing the workers' innovative capacity and adaptability to new technology. The following quote from the declaration of the 1999 G8 summit meeting typifies how well the main message of the lesson has been learned:

> Adaptability, employability and the management of change will be the primary challenges for our societies in the coming century. Mobility between jobs, cultures and communities will be essential. And the passport to mobility will be education and lifelong learning for everyone.
>
> (G8 Communiqué Cologne, 1999: 3)

There are four central elements in the OECD's message on lifelong learning. First, there is a call for a Copernican shift from a narrow focus on higher and upper-secondary education and workplace-based continuing training to the broader perspective of lifelong learning. 'Ministers agreed to focus on how to make learning a process extending from early age through retirement, and occurring in schools, the workplace and many other settings' (OECD, 1996: 3). Increasing engagement in various forms of non-formal education discussions on how these activities should be recognised is seen as resulting in pressure on the formal educational system to issue some form of accreditation. Further, the Education Ministers' communiqué, 'Making lifelong learning a reality for all', points out that recognising informal learning requires improved mechanisms for assessing and recognising skills and competencies (OECD, 1996).

Second, true to the principle of lifelong learning, the OECD saw the formative years to be of crucial importance, and pre-primary and formal education stay very much in the frame. Thus, while the concept of lifelong learning has come to be used more or less as a synonym for adult learning, at least, for example, in the Anglo-Saxon countries, the original concept clearly includes all forms and stages of education. Third, the concern for a rapid and continuous transformation of working life meant that adult education and training for the first time became a central policy issue (OECD, 1989, 1995, 1996). After more or less having neglected adult education for close to 40 years, it was a noticeable event when, at the end of 1998, the OECD Educational Committee launched its thematic review of adult learning (OECD, 2003). The initiative was a follow-up to the 1996 decision by OECD educational ministers to make 'lifelong learning for all' the key educational goal in member countries (OECD, 1996).

Fourth, the various recommendations for reforms across the entire educational system are shaped by labour market concerns. Schools and universities are told to improve their responsiveness to labour market needs (OECD, 1989, 1996). 'The need for a more adequate introduction to jobs, careers, and the world of work in schools and familiarization with and command of information technologies' is being stressed (OECD, 1989: 30). According to the OECD, initial education should foster the capacity of learning to learn and for continuous learning in order to promote flexibility in the labour market (Papadopoulos, 1994). Turning to adult learning, the classic distinctions between firm-specific and general training were blurred as firms are urged to recognise the importance of continuous ongoing education for workers. Further, welfare-to-work considerations became a central issue. In this context adult education and training are seen as part of an active labour market policy aimed at getting the growing number of unemployed people off welfare and into the labour market.

The OECD's concept of lifelong learning has been severely criticised by adult education scholars who object to its economistic outlook and see it as an expression of the dominant

415

neo-liberal paradigm (see, for example, Bagnall, 2000; Field, 2000; Martin, 2003; Olssen, 2006; Rubenson, 1999). There is ample evidence to support this position. Already in the mid-1970s the OECD had abandoned the reigning Keynesian position that had guided its earlier work and became an advocate of neo-liberal informed supply-side labour market reforms (Keohane, 1978, cited in Dostal, 2004: 447). The OECD's approach to lifelong learning was formed around its understanding of the changing structure of the labour market as outlined in the Job Study report (OECD, 1994, 1995). Here, the OECD was recommending what has come to be labelled a low-skills approach to the knowledge economy (Brown *et al.*, 2001; Wong and McBride, 2003). This strategy assumes a bifurcated labour market and argues for job creation in the private sector in two streams – skilled, high-wage jobs and low-wage jobs. The latter would provide employment for the large group of low-skilled unemployed workers (Cruikshank, 2002). Similarly there would be two streams of training, one for high-skill jobs and another for the low-skill sector. The latter would be focused on getting the clients 'job ready' and would promote short welfare-to-work programmes. This position has been widely accepted and, as Crouch *et al.* (1999: 5) point out, for many political parties, encouragement of education seems to have been a way of getting out of certain welfare commitments while at the same time offering governments opportunities for constructive and positive action. Welfare and social assistance get linked to willingness to take any work, and readiness to undertake some form of labour market training programme to enhance employability prospects.

The emphasis on learning rather than education as promoted in the conceptualisation of lifelong learning is well suited for a neo-liberal agenda. The heightened emphasis on the individual's responsibility for his or her own learning is closely embedded in a changing understanding and articulation of the very concept of lifelong learning and signals a move away from a preoccupation with education to a focus on learning (Griffin, 1999; Rubenson, 1999). As Tuijnman and Broström astutely observe:

> The emphasis on 'learning' rather than 'education' is highly significant because it reduces the traditional preoccupation with structures and institutions and instead focuses on the individual . . . the realisation of lifelong learning depends to a large degree on the capacity and motivation of individuals to take care of their own learning.
>
> (2002: 103)

It becomes the responsibility of persons to make adequate provisions for the creation and preservation of their own human capital (Marginson, 1997). This value system of individualisation is embedded in a new ethics that is based on the principle of duty to oneself (Beck and Beck-Gernsheim, 2002: 38). Failure in the labour market is increasingly seen to be an outcome of an individual's decision with regard to education and training (Holzer, 1996). Thus, under neo-liberal globalisation, acquisition of skills and competencies has become the social rationalisation for accepting unequal opportunities, poverty and inequalities (Bourdieu, 1998).

Towards the end of the 1990s, policy makers had started to come to the insight that, while the new economy holds the promise of increased productivity and an improved standard of living, it also introduces a new set of transitions and adjustment challenges for society, industry and individuals. If not met, these challenges could increase the permanent exclusion or marginalisation of segments of the population and exacerbate socio-economic divisions. These concerns in combination with electoral changes have, according to some political scientists, shifted the policy agenda in the direction of 'inclusive liberalism' (see, for example, Craig and Porter, 2005; Mahon and McBride, in press). Mahon and McBride argue that, while 'inclusive liberalism' shares certain features with neo-liberalism such as acceptance of trade and investment liberalisation, commitment to non-inflationary growth and fiscal conservatism, a supply-side 'activation' approach to employment, the embrace of flexibility in labour markets, and acceptance of inequality, it differs in other important aspects. The differences can be found in 'inclusive liberalism's emphasis on the idea of investing in people who demonstrate that they are willing to take responsibility for their own development and providing more incentives and 'carrots rather than sticks' within a supply-side approach. As the authors point out, it is presently difficult to judge whether or not what we see are minor adjustments to neo-liberalism or if something more fundamental has occurred. The former is the conclusion reached by Craig and Porter, who note that policies in 'third way' governments, while giving more attention to the poor, fall well short of social liberalism (2005: 233). Similarly, Ryner (2002) claims that policies of 'third way' governments, although advocating an understanding of the good society that promotes a balance between state, market and civil society, reflect the hegemonic influence of neo-liberal thinking on left-leaning governments.

The influence of 'inclusive liberalism' is also reflected in a changing rhetoric around lifelong learning. Thus, it should be noted that the 1996 report on lifelong learning was entitled *Lifelong Learning for All*, while the 1989 report contained no such reference. The shift in rhetoric is particularly noticeable in European Commission (EC) documents. *A Memorandum on Lifelong Learning* (EC, 2000), reflecting on decisions taken at the 2000 Lisbon European Council, departs from the assumption that contemporary social and economic change are interrelated and stresses that there are two equally important aims for lifelong learning: promoting active citizenship and promoting employability. It states:

> [The] EU must set an example for the world and show that it is possible both to achieve dynamic economic growth and to strengthen social cohesion. Lifelong learning is an essential policy for the development of citizenship, social cohesion and employment.
>
> (p. 4)

Recognising market failures, and growing concerns about large groups not participating fully in social and economic life, the 'soft' version of the economistic paradigm can be read as a shift in balance between the three institutional arrangements. The market still has a central role, but the responsibilities of the individual and the state are also visible. The language is one of shared responsibilities. However, a closer reading of the text might lead one to be more sceptical of what looks to be a major shift in the public discourse on lifelong learning. Despite repeated references to the involvement of all three institutional arrangements, what stands out in recent policy documents is the stress on the responsibility of the individuals for their own learning – something that is underscored time after time. Recognising that the member states in the EU are responsible for their education and training systems, the 2000 document – as well as later ones – points out that these systems are dependent upon the input and commitment of a wide range of actors from all walks of social and economic life. However, with special emphasis on the individual, the EC document goes on to state: 'and not the least upon the efforts of individuals themselves, who, in the last instance, are responsible for pursuing their own learning' (EC, 2000: 4).

The special narrowness in approaching the states' responsibility for lifelong learning for all, as presented by the EC, may be understood as 'inclusive liberalism' in the sense that it does invoke a form of inclusiveness. But it also has strong neo-liberal features. This can be further exemplified with reference to the conclusion from the OECD's review of adult learning policies and practices in 17 countries, which provides an in-depth analysis of factors found to contribute to increased participation (OECD, 2005a). The adult learning thematic review was launched

417

with an overall goal to contribute towards making lifelong learning a reality for all and to increase employability among the low skilled (OECD, 2005a). The purpose was to better understand factors affecting adults' access to and participation in education and training so as to enhance policies and approaches to increase incentives for adults to undertake learning. The purpose of the project clearly had an inclusiveness agenda constructed around employability and low skills. The final report highlights several crucial conditions for reaching the participation of low-skilled adults. An overall conclusion is that governments can play a useful role by: (1) creating the structural preconditions for raising the benefits of adult learning; (2) promoting well-designed co-financing arrangements; (3) improving delivery and quality control; and (4) ensuring policy coordination and coherence. These recommendations may at a first glance sound as though there has been a shift back to Keynesianism. However, the OECD finds that, because of non-conclusive evidence about the overall quantitative impact of market failures, adult learning policy ought to primarily focus on schemes with large leverage potential. The OECD therefore concludes: 'Regulatory and institutional arrangements that are conducive to enhancing investments by firms and individuals, while limiting public financing, are key within this type of strategy' (2005a: 11). This message is textbook neo-liberalism and shows that not only is the perspective on inclusiveness set within a narrow parameter, employability, but that the policy agenda continues to be constructed within a neo-liberal framework. This is particularly remarkable as, despite the claim for evidence-based policy making, I find OECD's conclusion to be diametrically contrary to the policy lesson that can be drawn from the available statistics on participation in adult learning that have been collected as part of the OECD's indicators programme on adult literacy (see OECD, 2000, 2005a, b).

## Potentials for moving towards the other side of the Janus face

The discussion started with the observation that there are two distinct paradigms of lifelong learning: a vaguely visible humanistic-inspired paradigm and an economistic idea that has been driving the political project on lifelong learning. The final section will briefly consider the possibilities for a hegemonic shift resulting in a more even balance between the two halves of the Janus face. Such a discussion should not be exclusively situated in a normative-utopian position on what lifelong learning ought to be, but forged around a link between normative ideals and what can be learned from research on how lifelong learning is formed and operates in contemporary society (see Rothstein, 2005). Thus, the issue becomes what present research can tell us about the conditions and possibilities for a praxis that takes the utopian notion seriously and embraces the emancipatory ambition of lifelong learning.

The first observation is drawn from studies on participation in adult learning and speaks to the importance of the nation state also in times of transnational governance. Research on participation in adult learning shows that there appears to be a Matthew Effect operating in most societies (that is, the ones who already have get more and those who do not have get less) (Desjardins et al., 2006). This can be explained by how 'the long arm of the family' mediates opportunities for adult learning. The long arm of the family refers to the well-documented relationship between social background, educational attainment and position in the labour market, which affects adults' subjective readiness to participate, as well as actual opportunities for improving their knowledge and skills. Later in the lifecycle the long arm of the family is extended through adult life via what can be called 'the long arm of the job'. The latter refers to the way the labour market structure, and more generally the nature of occupations and production, have a strong influence on the distribution of adult learning. The comparative findings on participation suggest that, while the long arm of the family and the job will always be present the level of inequality varies substantially between countries (OECD, 2000, 2005b). Further, there are substantial differences in participation rates between countries at comparable stages in the modernisation process and with quite similar economies. The patterns of inequality in adult learning mirror broader structural inequalities in society and reflect its particular welfare state regime (Rubenson, 2006).

What has made the UNESCO half of the Janus face more visible under the rationale of the Nordic welfare state regime reflects the division between the exercise of economic power and the exercise of political power, that is, between markets and politics. In the economic sphere, the main power resource is control over capital assets and the principal beneficiary is the capitalist class. This is not the case in the political sphere, where power comes from the strength of numbers mobilised through the democratic process (Korpi, 1983). This favours large collectives such as organised labour. The capitalist class is by far the most powerful actor in society, due to control of the means of production, but labour also has potential access to political resources 'which can allow it to implement social reform and alter distributional inequalities to a significant degree' (Olsen and O'Connor, 1998: 8). Thus, Korpi suggests 'that the extent of bias in functioning of the state can vary considerably as a reflection of the distribution of power resources in these societies and thus politics can be expected to matter, e.g. for the distributive processes in society' (1998: 54). Korpi sees institutionalised power struggles between markets and politics reflected in the development of citizenship and the welfare state. Korpi (1983) also maintains that the difference in power resources in a society between major collectives or classes, particularly capital and organised labour, regulates the distribution of life chances, social consciousness and conflicts on the labour market, and, I would add, lifelong learning.

Similarly, changes in power tend to be reflected in changes in social institutions and their modus operandi. The stronger the labour movement the more developed will the welfare state become. In this respect the weakening of working-class organisations in most countries, particularly large trade unions that have been the core organisations striving for class identification, consciousness, solidarity and political behaviour among the workers, makes a shift in lifelong learning in the direction of the UNESCO ideal problematic. Like post-Fordist production, politics tends to become specialised and issue-centred in its response to a population that is increasingly being differentiated by educational attainment and skills, gender, generation, ethnicity and sexual preferences (Pakulski, 2004: 148). With the individualisation processes gaining in strength, Beck and Beck-Gernsheim believe that the traditional class society will become insignificant beside an individualised society of employees (2002: 30).

From what has been said above, it will be difficult for the labour movement, and it is not very likely that the collective strength of labour will be able to assemble the necessary political force to fulfil Esping-Andersen's suggestion that, under a knowledge economy and knowledge society the accent of social citizenship might move from a 'preoccupation with income maintenance towards a menu of rights to lifelong learning and qualification' (1996: 260).

Instead it might be contradictions within capitalism itself that provide some hope that inclusive liberalism will move in the direction of lifelong learning for all. I am basing this statement on the observation that organisations like the OECD have started to notice that the Nordic countries are doing exceedingly well under the knowledge economy. The revisited job study report, *Boosting Jobs and Incomes: Policy lessons from reassessing the OECD jobs strategy* (OECD, 2006), notes that the Nordic model provides a viable alternative to the neo-liberal economic model. Although the changes to welfare policies in the Nordic countries during the last decade have received criticism from supporters of the traditional Nordic welfare state regime, the present labour market strategy provides a clear alternative to the dominant neo-liberal labour market strategy. Thus, this model, which assumes a major involvement by the state to provide economic security and a broad arrangement of educational opportunities appropriate to a high-skills equilibrium, can deliver the labour force flexibility demanded by globalised capitalism while providing security and opportunities for the individual citizen. The likelihood for a broader political acceptance of the Nordic model of stimulating flexibility in the labour market through heavy state intervention in training in countries favouring a more neo-liberal oriented approach may be argued from a neo-Marxist position. This position states that the state has relative autonomy and is not directly controlled by the capitalist classes. The democratic capitalist state is an institutionalised form of political power that operates to achieve and guarantee the collective interests of all members of a class society dominated by capital (Offe, 1984). For Offe, three conditions guide the institutional operation of the state. First, that the state does not directly organise production; in a liberal democracy this is outside its direct control. Second, as the state is dependent for its taxation revenue on successful capital accumulation, it is in the interest of state officials to assure a healthy capital accumulation. Third, in order to legitimate its roles, including its role in the capitalist mode of production, the state needs democratic legitimisation. The state must try to avoid legitimisation crises that can threaten long-term capital accumulation. According to Poulantzas (1978), the autonomy of the state allows it to adopt measures serving the subordinate classes if these are found to be politically unavoidable or necessary for promoting the long-term interests of capital. Offe's point is that state institutions, although not directly controlled by the interests of the capitalist class will, through their dependence on capital accumulation, generate policies that tend to guarantee and enhance these very interests. The promotion of lifelong learning for all can, in this perspective, be seen as a way of protecting capitalism from itself. While a development in this direction is a far cry from the humanistic ideals espoused under the UNESCO paradigm of lifelong learning, it holds out some hope for a change, although perhaps only partially, for making the other side of the Janus face visible in the praxis of lifelong learning.

## Note

1    Janus, the Roman god, with the two faces pointing in opposite directions, has come to symbolise ambiguity. The idea for using this metaphor in the context of lifelong learning comes from Hartman, who applies it to the context of popular adult education (2004).

## References

Adamson, W.L. (1980) *Hegemony and Revolution: A study of Antonio Gramsci's political and cultural theory*, Berkeley, CA: University of California Press.

Bagnall, R. (2000) 'Lifelong learning and the limitation of economic determinism', *International Journal of Lifelong Education* 19(1): 20–35.

Beck, U. and Beck-Gernsheim, E. (2002) *Individualization*, London: Sage.

Boggs, C. (1976) *Gramsci's Marxism*, London: Pluto Press.

Bourdieu, P. (1998) *Acts of Resistance: Against the tyranny of the market*, New York: New Press.

Brown, P., Green, A. and Lauder, H. (2001) *High Skills: Globalization, competitiveness and skill formation*, Oxford: Oxford University Press.

Com/Delsa/EDUC (2005) *International Assessment of Adult Competences: Proposed strategy*, 24 October, Paris: OECD.

Cox, R. (2005) 'Global perestroika', in R. Wilkinson (ed.) *The Global Governance Reader*, New York: Routledge, pp. 175–83.

Craig, D. and Porter, D. (2005) 'The third way and the third world: poverty reduction and social inclusion strategies in the rise of 'inclusive' liberalism', *Review of International Political Economy* 12(2): 226–63.

Cropley, A.J. (1978) *Lifelong Learning: A stocktaking*, Hamburg: UNESCO.

—— (1980) (ed.) *Towards a System of Lifelong Education*, Oxford: Pergamon Press.

—— and Dave, R.H. (1978) *Lifelong Education and the Training of Teachers*, Hamburg: UNESCO.

Crouch, C., Feingold, D. and Saco, M. (1999) *Are Skills the Answer? The political economy of skill creation in industrial countries*, New York: Oxford University Press.

Cruikshank, J. (2002) 'Lifelong learning or re-training for life: scapegoating the worker', in *Proceedings of the 21st Annual Conference of the Canadian Association for the Study of Adult Education*, May 30–June 1, 2002, pp. 54–9.

Dave, R.H. (ed.) (1976) *Foundations of Lifelong Learning*, Oxford: Pergamon Press.

Desjardins, R., Rubenson, K. and Milana, M. (2006) *Unequal Chances to Participate in Adult Learning: International perspectives*, IIEP Fundamentals of Educational Planning Series 83, Paris: UNESCO.

Dostal, J.M. (2004) 'Campaigning on expertise: how the OECD framed EU welfare and labour market policies – and why success could trigger failure', *Journal of European Public Policy* 11(3): 440–60.

Dunleavy, P. (1991) *Democracy, Bureaucracy, and Public Choice*, New York: Harvester.

European Round Table of Industrialists (ERT) (1989) *Education and European Competence: ERT study on education and training in Europe*. Available online at www.eric.ed.gov/ (accessed 22 April 2007).

Esping-Andersen, G. (1996) 'Positive-sum solutions in a world of trade offs?', in G. Esping-Andersen (ed.) *Welfare States in Transition: National adaptations in global economies*, Oxford: Pergamon Press, pp. 256–67.

European Commission (EC) (2000) *A Memorandum on Lifelong Learning*, Luxembourg: Office for Official Publications of the European Commission.

Faure, E. (Chair) (1972) *Learning to Be*, Paris: UNESCO.

Field, J. (2000) 'Governing the ungovernable: why lifelong learning policies promise so much yet deliver so little', *Educational Management and Administration* 28(3): 249–61.

G8 Communiqué Cologne (1999) Available online at www.g8.utoronto.ca/summit/1999koln/finalcom.htm (accessed 3 February 2007).

Griffin, C. (1999) 'Lifelong learning and social democracy', *International Journal of Lifelong Education* 18(4): 329–42.

Hartman, P. (2004) 'Bildningens Janusansikte: Tankar kring folkbildningens praktisk-estetisak studier', in J. Stenøien, A. Laginder, K. Rubenson and S. Tøsse (eds) *Utfordring for voksnes læring*, Linköping: Mimer, pp. 186–99.

Hasan, A. (1999) 'Lifelong learning: implications for education policy', in A. Tuijnman and T. Schuller (eds) *Lifelong Learning Policy and Research*, London: Portland Press.

Henry, M., Lingard, B., Rizvi, F. and Taylor, S. (2001) *The OECD, Globalisation and Education Policy*, Oxford: Pergamon.

Holzer, H. (1996) *What Employers Want*, New York: Russell Sage Foundation.

Korpi, W. (1983) *The Democratic Class Struggle*, London: Routledge and Kegan Paul.

—— (1998) 'Power resources approach vs action and conflict: on causal and intentional explanations in the study of power', in J.S. O'Connor and G.M. Olsen (eds) *Power Resources Theory and the Welfare State*, Toronto: University of Toronto Press, pp. 37–69.

Lengrand, P. (1970) *An Introduction to Lifelong Education*, Paris: UNESCO.

Mahon, R. and McBride, S. (in press) 'The OECD and transnational governance: an introduction', in R. Mahon and S. McBride (eds) *OECD and Transnational Governance*, Toronto: University of Toronto Press.

Marginson, S. (1997) *Markets in Education*, St Leonards, NSW: Allen & Unwin.

Martin, I. (2003) 'Adult education: lifelong learning and citizenship: some ifs and buts', *International Journal of Lifelong Learning* 22(6): 566–79.

Nyberg, M. (2000) *The Hidden Agenda of the European Union*. Available online at www.mikael nyberg.nu/english/engart03.html (accessed 3 February 2007).

Organization for Economic Cooperation and Development (OECD) (1989) *Education and the Economy in a Changing Society*, Paris: OECD.

421

—— (1994) *The OECD Jobs Study: Facts, analysis, strategies*, Paris: OECD.

—— (1995) *The OECD Jobs Study: Implementing the strategy*, Paris: OECD.

—— (1996) *Lifelong Learning for All*, Paris: OECD.

—— (2000) *Literacy in the Information Age*, Paris: OECD.

—— (2003) *Beyond Rhetoric: Adult learning policies and practices*, Paris: OECD.

—— (2005a) *Promoting Adult Learning*, Paris: OECD.

—— (2005b) *Learning a Living: First results of the Adult Literacy and Life Skills Survey*, Paris/Ottawa: OECD/Statistics Canada.

—— (2006) *Boosting Jobs and Incomes: Policy lessons from reassessing the OECD Jobs Strategy*, Paris: OECD.

Offe, C. (1984) *Contradictions of the Welfare State*, London: Heinemann.

Olsen, G.M. and O'Connor, J.S. (1998) 'Understanding the welfare state: power resources theory and its critics', in J.S. O'Connor and G.M. Olsen (eds) *Power Resources Theory and the Welfare State*, Toronto: University of Toronto Press, pp. 3–33.

Olssen, M. (2006) 'Understanding the mechanisms of neoliberal control: lifelong learning, flexibility and knowledge capitalism', *International Journal of Lifelong Education* 25(3): 213–30.

Pakulski, J. (2004) 'Class paradigm and politics', in T.N. Clark and S.M. Lipset (eds) *The Breakdown of Class Politics: A debate on post-industrial stratification*, Baltimore, MD: Johns Hopkins University Press, pp. 286–337.

Papadopoulos, G. (1994) *Education 1960–1990: The OECD perspective*, Paris: OECD.

Poulantzas, N. (1978) *State, Power, Socialism*, London: New Left Books.

Rinne, R., Kallo, J. and Hokka, S. (2004) 'Too eager to comply? OECD education policies and the Finnish response', *European Educational Research Journal* 3(2): 454–85.

Rothstein, B. (2005) *Social Traps and the Problem of Trust*, Cambridge: Cambridge University Press.

Rubenson, K. (1999) 'Adult education and training: the poor cousin: an analysis of OECD reviews of national polices for education', *Scottish Journal of Adult Education* 5(2): 5–32.

—— (2004) 'Lifelong learning: a critical assessment of the political project', in P. Alheit, R. Becker-Schmidt, T. Gitz Johansen, L. Ploug, H. Salling Oleson and K. Rubenson (eds) *Shaping an Emerging Reality: Researching lifelong learning*, Copenhagen: Roskilde University Press, pp. 28–47.

—— (2006) 'The Nordic model of lifelong learning', *Compare: A Journal of Comparative Education* 36(3): 327–41.

Ryner, M.J. (2002) *Capitalism Restructuring: Globalisation and the third way*, London: Routledge.

Tuijnman, A. and Broström, A.-K. (2002) 'Changing notions of lifelong education and lifelong learning', *International Review of Education* 48(1/2): 92–110.

Vickers, M. (1994) 'Cross-national exchange, the OECD, and Australian education policy', *Knowledge & Policy* 7(1): 25–47.

Vinkour, A. (1976) 'Economic analysis of lifelong learning', in R.H. Dave (ed.) *Foundations of Lifelong Education*, Oxford: Pergamon Press.

Wain, K. (1986) *Philosophy of Lifelong Education*, London: Croom Helm.

Welch, F. (1970) 'Education in production, *Journal of Political Economy* 78(1): 35–59.

Wong, L. and McBride, S. (2003) 'Youth employment programs in British Columbia: taking the high road or the low road?', in M.G. Cohen (ed.) *Training the Excluded for Work: Access and equity for women, immigrants, First Nations, youth and people with low income*, Vancouver: UBC Press, pp. 230–44.

# 37

# Feminist perspectives in lifelong learning

*Julia Preece*

Feminist critiques of lifelong learning have emerged relatively recently. Yet feminist *adult education* literature is well established (Barr, 1999; Hayes and Flannery, 2000; hooks, 1994; Thompson, 1980, to name but a few). Their work is pertinent to lifelong learning discussions and this chapter will draw on both sources to explain some of the contemporary issues surrounding lifelong learning for women. A less recognised feminist issue for lifelong learning is the policy divide between countries in the global North and global South. The chapter will also offer some insights in relation to the latter point. I will start with a brief explanation of feminisms and the feminist agenda – the common concerns and the different approaches to addressing them. Then a selective literature review of the gendered nature of dominant lifelong learning discourses discusses concepts of autonomy, learning and work, citizenship, pedagogies and the 'North'–'South' divide. A concluding section offers some ideas for more gender-sensitive approaches to learning for all.

## Feminisms

Feminism is a perspective – or way of seeing the world. While there are many positions within feminism, they share a common goal – to explain societal behaviour through a gender lens. Gender refers to the social roles that are attributed differentially to men and women as a result of culturally, socially and institutionally internalised values. These distinctions intersect with race, class, ethnicity, disability, sexual orientation and culture. Different feminisms pay attention to one or more of these aspects, often through theoretical positions such as liberalism, Marxism, psychological positions, post-structuralism or post-colonialism. The feminist lens enables writers and educators to explore the extent to which lifelong learning discourses, policies, structures and provision are gendered. This means recognising women's experiences of learning in relation to teaching (pedagogy), curriculum, interpersonal relationships, training opportunities, locations of learning, ways of knowing and so on. Feminism, therefore, is a political position – which aims to privilege the marginalised voice. While gender (and women in particular) is the primary focus, the issues raised are pertinent to most marginalised social groups and individuals since the emphasis is on moving beyond the dominant voice to recognise diversity. Much of the feminist literature is therefore relevant to wider concerns about dominant lifelong learning discourses.

Feminisms are not static. They are variously described but a common way of categorising them is as follows.

## Liberal feminisms

Liberal feminisms are generally associated with a concern over equal, democratic, rights with men within existing social structures. Their emphasis is on campaigning for a level playing field of access within a legal framework. The focus is on challenging women's invisibility and marginalisation of women's experiences and arguing for the equal right of men and women to jobs, choices and decision making through democratic processes. In lifelong learning situations this would mean ensuring, for example, that both men and women are entitled to go on the same training courses and men and women are allowed to study computers or science. The main critique of liberal feminisms is that this position tends to see women as a unitary category and pays less attention to the structural causes of women's oppression. So the focus is on changing women's status in society rather than challenging the nature of the social order (Hayes and Flannery, 2000).

## Radical and socialist feminisms

Radical and socialist feminisms challenge the unitary (all-embracing) category of 'woman'. They identify the specific historical role of male domination over women. They do this in two ways. On the one hand, radical feminists have tried to raise the profile of women's marginalisation by emphasising the biological and psychological differences between men and women. So, for example, women are seen as having particular characteristics that are associated with nurturing, intuition and caring; men are associated with aggression and objectivity. A learning programme on management, therefore, should emphasise the equal importance of being both nurturing and objective. It can also recognise the role of experience in producing knowledge. On the other hand, socialist feminism brings in an awareness of differences between women but primarily explores the ways in which gender is socially, rather than biologically, constructed throughout history. The concept of 'difference', for socialist feminists, recognises the impact of race, class and (more recently) disability on how women are differently marginalised or oppressed. Socialist feminists often use Marxist concepts of production, capitalism and class to explain gender oppression. Socialist feminists, therefore, are interested in challenging the way the education system itself promotes middle-class, male-dominated values about knowledge. Hayes and Flannery (2000) bracket these arguments under 'structural theories'. One criticism of these positions is that they tend to portray women as victims of oppression and fail to analyse the power relations that help to explain how women can challenge their experiences.

## Post-structuralist feminisms

The postmodernist or post-structuralist debate shifts the focus of difference on to the relationship between language and power, and the concept of discourse as a manifestation of power relations through behaviour, texts, communication systems and institutional and societal structures. This analysis explores how women (and therefore other social groups) are positioned in different ways as a result of constantly shifting identities and meanings – in particular, how individuals are caught between acting as knowing 'subjects' and acting unconsciously as individuals who are socially conditioned (Jones, 1997). This enables us to identify different interest groups and different forms of oppression across all groups. As the analysis is based on understanding power relationships, it also enables us to see how individuals might act as their own agents of power and challenge normative assumptions and expectations for themselves. Through this analysis we can see how masculinities are formed and how they help to shape men's behaviour towards women (Mac an Ghaill, 1994; Whitehead, 2000). Post-structuralism recognises that experience constantly changes according to context and allows for an analysis of the complexity of intersections between language, agency and resistance. So gender is seen as a system of 'social relations that are continually renegotiated' (Hayes and Flannery, 2000: 15). Post-structuralist analyses have exposed gendered behaviours in classrooms between teachers and learners and deconstructed texts that describe apparently gender-neutral learning policies. Unitary truths or representations of reality for lifelong learning are exposed as being partial, fragmented and often silencing women's truths or realities.

Critiques of post-structuralism include a concern that the emphasis on fragmentation and difference makes it difficult to claim a shared agenda for change. For people in formerly colonised countries, the whole concept of feminism is still problematic, because the dominant voices in these debates continue to come from Western, white people. And since the dominant voices are still labelling and naming difference, there is an imbalance in what is being heard and whose knowledge actually counts. So, while women of colour (such as hooks, 1991; Ntseane 1999) do acknowledge the role of post-structuralism in raising issues of difference and complexity, they have also sought to claim their own definitions that represent more accurately the experiences and priorities of women in more relevant socio-political contexts. These feminisms are categorised here as post-colonial feminisms (Chilisa and Preece, 2005).

## Post-colonial feminisms

In formerly colonised countries, a core argument is that the experience of colonialism is a central experience of both men and women. Gender should therefore be recognised as one aspect of oppression that is embedded in the experience of colonialism and racial discrimination in formerly colonised countries. The second argument is that culture should be seen as dynamic. It should therefore be possible to challenge oppressive cultural practices in relation to gender without rejecting one's culture per se. Both men and women are encouraged to work together for positive change. Mohanty (1991: 11) points to the fundamental difference for women of colour being: 'the contrast between a singular focus on gender as a basis for equal rights, and a focus on gender in relation to race and/or class as part of a broader liberation struggle' (cited in Chilisa and Preece, 2005: 215). Mohanty further elaborates on how Western discourses have both distorted and made invisible 'third world' women:

> A homogeneous notion of the image of women is assumed, which in turn, produces the image of an 'average third world woman.' This average third world woman leads an essentially truncated life based on her feminine gender (read: sexually constrained) and her being 'third world' (read: ignorant, poor, uneducated, tradition-bound, domestic, family-oriented, victimised etc.). This, I suggest, is in contrast to the (implicit) self-representation of Western women as educated, as modern, as having control over their own bodies and sexualities, and the freedom to make their own decisions.
>
> (Mohanty, 1991: 56)

So post-colonial feminisms problematise Western feminisms, present alternative feminisms that reflect their life experiences and include the ongoing struggle against colonial interference, racisms and the micro-politics of work, home and family (Mohanty, 1991: 20–1). Recent literature on behalf of such countries reflects this concern in their critique of lifelong learning discourses that promote basic education for the 'South' but argue for a more elaborate, continuous lifelong learning concept for the 'North' (Preece, 2006; Torres, 2003).

Post-structuralist and post-colonialist feminist literature is the most likely to problematise lifelong learning discourses in terms of pedagogies, recognition of women's spaces, and key concepts in lifelong learning texts such as 'autonomy', 'independence', 'employability', 'citizenship' and the 'self-directed learner'.

## Feminist critiques of lifelong learning

The primarily economistic discourse for lifelong learning is constructed as a seamless resource for all ages, premised on flexibility, choice and employability. Institutional structures and systems have adjusted their provision to cater for part- and full-time learners and compete in the lifelong learning market place where individuals can purchase courses to suit their autonomous and independent lifestyles. The marketability of lifelong learning is that it makes you more employable and increases your earning power. The dominant policy formulations of lifelong learning's vocationalist, skills-based agenda have been critiqued for their narrowness of purpose (Edwards, 1997; Field, 2002) and especially for their undermining of the traditional social development domains of adult education discourses (Rogers, 2006a). The feminist literature exposes these concerns, too, but through a gender lens.

Leathwood and Francis' (2006) collection of 'critical feminist engagements' challenges the ways men and women are constructed as spouses, parents and workers to fit into the dominant model for lifelong learning. In particular they profile the invisible spaces of women's learning (such as the family and community) and question the gender-neutral assumption that women's qualifications translate into equitable earnings and salaried jobs or other financial rewards (Blackmore, 2006). Moreover, the enforced relationship between lifelong learning, individualism and independence does not reflect the reality of most women's lives, which are concerned with interdependence and interrelationships with other family members, multi-tasking, and juggling home, work and care responsibilities. Blackmore (2006), for instance, argues that the lifelong learning discourse that promotes flexibility and mobility contradicts family and social relations of intimacy, which are more concerned with concepts of belonging, place and sense of security. While men also interact with families and home, research shows that the balance of these interactions and the impact of family on all forms of decision making is significantly weighted towards women (Preece and Edirisingha, 2001). So there is a disjunction between lifelong learning, ostensibly presented as gender neutral, and the gender-specific lives of men and women. These issues also intersect with the life experiences of people with disabilities, social class, culture and ethnicity. A closer examination of selected features of the dominant lifelong learning discourses helps to expose its hegemonic agenda of equality.

### Autonomy and independence

Leathwood (2006) and Brine (2006) both highlight the focus in European and UK policy on constructing the lifelong learner as autonomous and independent – in binary opposition to pathological notions of dependence. Yet women's lives are far more likely to be constrained by care commitments. Furthermore, when choices of where to work are made it is usually the woman who follows the male partner's career, at the expense of her own, or it is she who makes sacrifices by prioritising her family (dependency) rather than career (independence) needs (Preece and Edirisingha, 2001).

Hayes and Flannery (2000) argue that the notion of individuality is culturally specific and competitive individual achievement is not a universal value. Leathwood (2006: 48) elaborates that the dependence/independence dichotomy 'disguises the interdependencies of social relations, denigrates those who need support and assumes a self unencumbered by domestic and caring responsibilities with sufficient material and other resources and capitals to maintain the myth of independence'.

She cites a Vietnamese woman's reaction to the concept of individuality within her collectivist culture that emphasises interdependent aspects of the self: 'There is no such thing as I . . . we define ourselves in a relationship' (2006a: 613). This sense of the collective also resonates with African societies encapsulated in the proverb, 'It takes a village to raise a child', and where people defer to their wider family before making decisions about themselves or their children (Chilisa and Preece, 2005).

The economistic model of a learner as an individual customer is therefore gendered and Westernised and based on the archetypal economic man who is free to make rational objective choices 'unburdened by social and material considerations' of domestic responsibilities or self-doubt (Leathwood, 2006a: 615). Autonomy is achieved by rejecting the emotional self. Yet women, she argues, often tend to draw on different forms of reason. Their focus of decision making is often premised on a 'morality of rights' or commitments, whereas men claim to be able to develop abstract rules and judgement unfettered by the ethic of care and responsibility, so that women are 'associated with relationship and connection rather than distance and individuation' (p. 616).

Blackmore (2006) further highlights that the discourse of independence also assumes there is a linear model of a learner who moves from dependence to independence. But for most women families constantly intersect at different levels and stages to influence the balance of family interdependence. The basic premise of the autonomous and independent lifelong learner, therefore, ignores the reality of many women's lives and denigrates other forms of relationships as inferior. When disability and ethnicity or culture are added to the equation, we can see that autonomy and independence are relative terms. There are similar concerns with the way education is marketed as a primarily economistic resource.

### Work-based learning and link with earning

Blackmore (2006) points out that, when learners are constructed as earner learners – self managing, independent, self reliant, this reinforces the notion that needing support is a deficiency. Yet this is a human capital version of learning that neglects the influence of social capital (family and community ties, networks and reciprocal arrangements) on people's lives with its invisible social infrastructures and power relations to contradict such a simplistic notion of learner autonomy.

Hayes and Flannery (2000) raise several concerns about lifelong learning's dominant learner-earner discourses. For women there is not a direct link between the two. Work-related learning opportunities primarily benefit men. For instance, family responsibilities make it difficult for women to train outside working hours; training is usually offered to full-time, higher-level management posts, yet women dominate the part-time labour market where there are fewer opportunities for formal training (Howell *et al.*, 2002). This is linked to a perception that women's jobs require less skill, with no recognition of the skills and knowledge acquired in the home that could be translated into waged work opportunities. On top of this, fewer women than men belong to trade unions where collective bargaining for training takes place. Field (2002) and Thompson (2007) support the statistical evidence that more men than women are training in the workplace and that the expansion of lifelong learning is in the workplace rather than community or elsewhere.

When work-based training does take place, the experience is problematic. For instance Howell *et al.* (2002) studied women's experiences of work-based training in team work. The findings suggest that the women's preferred ways of knowing, thinking and behaving were disregarded so that the only acceptable voice was identified as 'cheerful, adaptable, supportive', which denied them the opportunity to criticise or complain or argue for new opportunities for their own progression (p. 119). Dissent or critique was attributed to psychological or attitudinal problems:

> Several informants felt strongly that management wished to cast off their desire for continuity, their rooting of working life and personal experience, their sense of self, and a connection to others, all characteristics traditionally described as feminine (Fenwick 1998b). The women felt the training courses were attempting to erase or belittle many of the things they valued about their jobs.
>
> (Howell *et al.*, 2002: 120)

The issue that women must either be moulded into a masculine version of humanity or remain excluded translates into other domains for learning.

Brine (1999) points out that the learner-earner emphasis ignores the unwaged worker – who is more likely to be a woman – focusing on economic growth rather than social development, while Leathwood (2006), citing Morely (2001), suggests that the employability discourses need to talk about employer-ability – so employers 'become attuned to issues of inequality' (p.49). And, of course, despite demographic trends for an aging society, the focus of policies on learner-earners ignores older learners (Kammler, 2006).

Blackmore (2006) claims that, when policy discourses do pay attention to those who are out of work, it is with the aim of updating the skills of the unemployed in order to thereby reduce welfare costs. She argues that the outcomes and competency focus of skill training is at the expense of programmes that cater for young mothers (needing a crèche) or disability (needing extra support) because these do not fit the autonomy and independence agenda for learners. The end result is that boys get longer-term training, apprenticeships and full-time employment while girls (and often migrants and people with disabilities) fall into the casual work trap with fewer training opportunities. Blackmore also demonstrates that women historically invest more of their own money in training costs (since their work is less frequently employer supported), but because of lower wages they take longer to repay loans.

Blackmore further argues that the privatisation of labour means that paid work is now often undertaken from the home. This affects women more than men so that the blurred boundaries between work and home simply result in extended work hours and more commitments for women. Family responsibilities are not shared out equally. The lifelong learning discourse ignores the complexity of these public/private issues.

## Citizenship and public spaces for learning

Although the second strand of lifelong learning policy is associated with engendering citizenship and its associated responsibilities, there is a long tradition of feminist research that demonstrates that spaces commonly dominated by women, such as the home, family and many community activities, are given less or no status in terms of citizenship activity (Lister, 1997; Porter, 2001; Preece, 2002). Indeed the role of the family in fostering values for responsible citizenship is well argued by these writers. Yet Elliott (2000) points out that unpaid work – whether in the home or community – has no citizenship status. So notions of citizenship are also gendered, favouring a particular kind of activity associated with certain public spaces. Vogel (1991), Lister (1997) and others point to a number of anomalies in the characteristics that define citizenship in a male image, even where women's tasks may be quite similar. Vogel reveals, for example, that a primary feature of citizenship was defined by the man's capacity to bear arms – but also to perform a soldier's services to the community, contributing to the common good, such as working in hospitals. Vogel points out that this is: 'nothing but what women do anyway' (1991: 69). For ethnic minorities in the UK, citizenship status is equally contradictory. So in terms of legislation in relation to citizen rights, we see the coexistence of anti-racist legislation and racist immigration laws (Yuval Davis, 1997). Citizenship status, therefore, is a contested concept – with implications for how people act as citizens and how they learn to become active citizens.

## Pedagogies and knowledge

Issues to do with pedagogy in relation to lifelong learning have been visible by their absence. The emphasis on outcomes and targets has detracted from consideration of how people prefer to learn and with very little reference to the adult education literature on teaching or knowledge production (Rogers, 2006; Thompson, 2007; Zukas and Malcolm, 2002), in spite of the fact that the majority of targeted lifelong learners are adults. This omission necessarily avoids the extensive literature on emancipatory learning (Freire, Mezirow), critical thinking (Brookfield) and feminist pedagogies (for a summary of this literature see Preece and Griffin, 2006). Space prevents an elaborate discussion of these issues but a brief summary follows.

Tisdell (1998) links the range of feminisms with different approaches to pedagogy, but emphasises that there are four major themes in the literature: the construction of knowledge, voice, authority and positionality. One of the most well-known expositions of women's ways of knowing comes from research conducted by Belenky et al. (1986), where women were able to identify different ways of constructing knowledge. This is summarised in Hayes and Flannery (2000) as: subjective knowing (knowing in relation to oneself), connected knowing (knowing in relation to others, recognising others personal experience, using your experience to understand the other person) and procedural knowledge (separate knowing).

A critique of Belenky et al. (1986) has been that their findings did not focus on the larger social and political mechanisms that affect what kind of knowledge is recognised (Hayes and Flannery, 2000). So one aspect to feminist pedagogy is to reinstate, for example, the representation of women who have been erased from the legitimised knowledge of public literature. An example of this comes from Mirza (2006), who highlights how Indian suffragettes have never been spoken of in the history of the women's suffragette movement. The feminist educational project is to 'excavate such erasure and expose a counter memory to tell a different truth' (p. 139). In other words, the classroom and its curriculum are not politically neutral. The classroom should be a space where the unproblematical is problematised. Learners are encouraged to look beyond the limitations of their current situation with a view to building a better world.

Other writers, such as Hill Collins (1990), talk about knowledge for black women in terms of 'motherwit' and 'wisdom'. Many of these forms of knowledge privilege experiential understanding and intuition, intermeshed with emotion as a means of reinforcing or affirming truth and reality. Pedagogical styles that encourage this kind of learning and knowledge creation include sharing stories and feelings and confronting those storytellers with a view to raising

429

consciousness and affecting social change (hooks, 1994). Such teaching explicitly rejects the notion that emotions interfere with applying logic or gaining an accurate understanding. Indeed recognition of emotions and their impact enables us to highlight contradictions in seemingly objective knowledge. This can be done partly by recognising our positionality in terms of class, race, disability or other social category, both as teacher and learner, and by working with these positions within a shared critique of our experiences and understandings. Through this degree of openness we enable the marginalised to have an equal voice and demonstrate their authority in producing legitimate knowledge.

The problem for feminist perspectives on lifelong learning is that its discourse is so gender neutral that notions of different truths or knowledges, and even ways in which people prefer to learn, are submerged and simply not addressed.

## Women and the economically poor countries

A significant example of how women's voices are silenced in wider public policy debates for lifelong learning is evident in the campaign by women from economically poor countries, or formerly colonised nations, for a broader understanding of gender-based needs that would extend beyond the current internationally designated minimum targets for girls education (Preece, 2007).

There have been a number of international events where women's agendas for development (including education) have been ratified. For instance, the UN World Conference on Women in Beijing in 1995 produced the Beijing Declaration and Programme for Action (PFA), identifying education as one of 12 critical areas of concern for women. The PFA education goals were supported by the Dakar World Education Forum in 2000, which produced four educational targets relevant to women's education. CEDAW, the UN Convention on the Elimination of all forms of Discrimination Against Women, ensured agreement from 173 countries in 2003 that educational provision should extend beyond primary education, and included measures to compensate women's livelihood and care needs so that they have equitable and relevant learning opportunities.

These targets and agreements, however, were superseded by the Millennium Development Goals (MDGs), which produced far fewer women-focused agendas – in spite of recognition that poverty is highly gendered and poor women are also the least educated. The MDGs ignore the complexity of structural, attitudinal and legal constraints for women in their rather general targets for universal primary education and poverty reduction. The only explicit reference to women's empowerment is subsumed under the goal to eliminate gender disparity in primary and secondary education. Adult education is not a development goal at all. The result has been that few country strategic plans have highlighted gender-specific indicators for poverty reduction and women's literacy needs are poorly recognised (Preece, 2007).

## Conclusions and suggestions for a feminist lifelong learning agenda

This chapter has highlighted that the largely gender-neutral discourse of lifelong learning has submerged women's issues without taking account of the spaces in which women operate, or the complexity of women's lives in relation to dominant notions of learning-for-earning and the autonomous, independent learner. The recent history of womens' efforts to influence international agendas for those who are most disadvantaged in terms of education demonstrates the extent to which women's agendas continue to be silenced. A core feature of women's empowerment has been through critical education, yet this aspect of lifelong learning is the least represented in the lifelong learning literature, partly because its vocabulary does not reflect the dominant marketisation or vocationalism trends.

Lest this list of issues becomes a mere tirade on current lifelong learning policies, we must see how the feminist project can contribute to reforming lifelong learning for both social and human capital.

The first priority is to recognise that there is a worthwhile feminist agenda at all. Perhaps we should start with Tett's assertion that: 'if learners are positioned as experienced and knowledgeable social actors then they become active players, rather than passive recipients of education' (2006: 103). This means addressing the notion of autonomy from a different angle. Instead of treating learners as customers, we can regard them as agents of change and thus create space for critical thinking to facilitate change.

A core concern for feminist critical thinkers is that gender (and race, class, disability, etc.) are structural and embedded within relationships of power. Learning projects that challenge learners to critique embedded practices could provide momentum for revisiting policies so they take account of women's spaces and the family–work balance of people's interdependent lives. This means recognising the (economic and social) value of pursuing learning in different social contexts and revisiting pedagogies that legitimise only certain forms of knowledge.

Perhaps this could be achieved by government commissions that research lifelong learning and training issues that marginalise or ignore women's work spaces – with attention to the spaces occupied by different groups according to race, culture or disability. Then attention to how those spaces interface with legal, social, economic or other constraints could facilitate pedagogical projects that invite critical analysis of how women and men are positioned in societies and who has access to what in terms of relationships, responsibilities, materials and systems of participation. A primary means of ensuring women's voices are heard is to create spaces for them to speak on their terms, recognising and accepting that their experiences are part of knowledge, truth and reality. Examples of such learning are documented in isolated projects (Tett, 2006, for example) and for different objectives (see, for instance, Preece *et al.*, 2007). The trick in critiquing those projects is to then turn them into policy dialogues.

## References

Barr, J. (1999) *Liberating Knowledge: Feminism and Adult Education*, Leicester: NIACE.

Belenky, M.F., Clinchy, B.M., Goldberger, N.R. and Tarule, J.M. (1986) *Women's Ways of Knowing*, New York: Basic Books.

Blackmore, J. (2006) 'Unprotected participation in lifelong learning and the politics of hope', in C. Leathwood and B. Francis (eds) *Gender and Lifelong Learning*, London: Routledge, pp. 9–26.

Brine, J. (1999) *Undereducating Women: Globalising inequality*, Buckingham: Open University Press.

—— (2006) 'Locating the learner within EU policy', in C. Leathwood and B. Francis (eds) *Gender and Lifelong Learning*, London: Routledge, pp. 27–39.

Chilisa, B. and Preece, J. (2005) *Research Methods for Adult Educators in Africa*, Capetown: Pearson Education.

Edwards, R. (1997) *Changing Places? Flexibility, lifelong learning and a learning society*, London: Routledge.

Elliott, J. (2000) 'The challenge of lifelong learning as a means of extending citizenship for women', *Studies in the Education of Adults* 32(1): 6–21.

Field, J. (2002) *Lifelong Learning and the New Educational Order*, Stoke on Trent: Trentham Books.

Hayes, E. and Flannery, D. (2000) *Women as Learners: The significance of gender in adult learning*, San Francisco, CA: Jossey Bass.

Hill Collins, P. (1990) *Black Feminist Thought*, London: Routledge.

hooks, b. (1991) *Yearning: Race, gender and cultural politics*, London: Turnaround.

—— (1994) *Teaching to Transgress*, London: Routledge.

Howell, S.L., Carter, V.K. and Schied, F.M. (2002) 'Gender and women's experience at work', *Adult Education Quarterly* 52: 112.

Jones, A. (1997) 'Teaching poststructuralist feminist theory in education: student resistances, *Gender and Education* 9(3): 261–9.

Kammler, B. (2006) 'Older women as lifelong learners', in C. Leathwood and B. Francis (eds) *Gender and Lifelong Learning*, London: Routledge, pp. 153–63.

Leathwood, C. (2006) 'Gendered constructions of lifelong learning and the learner in the UK policy context', in C. Leathwood and B. Francis (eds) *Gender and Lifelong Learning*, London: Routledge, pp. 40–54.

—— (2006a) 'Gender, equity and the discourse of the independent learner in higher education', *Higher Education* 52: 611–33.

—— and Francis, B. (eds) (2006) *Gender and Lifelong Learning*, London: Routledge.

Lister, R. (1997) *Citizenship: Feminist perspectives*, Basingstoke: Macmillan.

Mac an Ghaill, M. (1994) *The Making of Men*, Milton Keynes: Open University Press.

Mirza, H.S. (2006) 'The in/visible journey', in C. Leathwood and B. Francis (eds) *Gender and Lifelong Learning*, London: Routledge, pp. 137–52.

Mohanty, C.T. (1991) 'Under western eyes: feminist scholarship and colonial discourses', in C.T. Mohanty, A. Russo and L. Torres (eds) *Third World Women and the Politics of Feminism*, Bloomington and Indianapolis, IN: Indiana University Press, pp. 51–80.

Ntseane, P.G. (1999) 'Botswana rural women's transition to urban business success', unpublished Ph.D. thesis, University of Georgia.

Porter, E. (2001) 'Interdependence, parenting and responsible citizenship', *Journal of Gender Studies* 10(1): 5–15.

Preece, J. (2002) 'Feminist perspectives on the learning of citizenship and governance', *Compare* 32(1): 21–33.

—— (2006) 'Beyond the learning society, the learning world?', *International Journal of Lifelong Education* 25(3): 307–20.

—— (2007) 'Women's education in the south', in A. Tuckett (ed.) *Participation and the Pursuit of Equality*, Leicester: NIACE, pp. 47–64.

—— and Edirisingha, P. (2001) 'Learning to be an active citizen: a gender perspective', *Sociale Interventie* 10(4): 37–46.

—— and Griffin, C. (2006) 'Radical and feminist pedagogies', in P. Jarvis (ed.) *The Theory and Practice of Teaching*, 2nd edn, London: Routledge.

——, van der Veen, R. and Raditloaneng, W.N. (eds) (2007) *Adult Education and Poverty Reduction: Issues for policy, research and practice*, Gaborone: Lentswe La Lesedi.

Rogers, A. (2006) 'Lifelong learning and the absence of gender', *International Journal of Educational Development* 26: 189–208.

—— (2006a) 'Escaping the slums or changing the slums? Lifelong learning and social transformation', *International Journal of Lifelong Education* 25(2): 125–37.

Tett, L. (2006) 'Community education', in C. Leathwood and B. Francis (eds) *Gender and Lifelong Learning*, London: Routledge, pp. 97–107.

Thompson, J. (ed.) (1980) *Adult Education for a Change*, London: Hutchinson.

—— (2007) 'Time to use the F word', in A. Tuckett (ed.) *Participation and the Pursuit of Equality*, Leicester: NIACE, pp. 33–47.

Tisdell, E.J. (1998) 'Poststructural feminist pedagogies: the possibilities and limitations of feminist emancipatory adult learning theory and practice', *Adult Education Quarterly* 48(3): 139–56.

Torres, M. (2003) 'Lifelong learning: a new momentum and a new opportunity for adult basic learning and education (ABLE) in the South, *Adult Education and Development*, Supplement 60: 239.

Vogel, U. (1991) 'Is citizenship gender-specific?', in U. Vogel and M. Morgan, *The Frontiers of Citizenship*, Basingstoke: Macmillan, pp. 58–85.

Whitehead, S.M. (2002) *Men and Masculinities: Key themes and new directions*, Cambridge: Polity.

Yuval Davis, N. (1997) *Gender and Nation*, London: Sage.

Zukas, M. and Malcolm, J. (2002) 'Pedagogies for lifelong learning: building bridges or building walls?', in R. Harrison, F. Reeve, A. Hanson and J. Clarke (eds) *Supporting Lifelong Learning, vol. 1: Perspectives on learning*, London: RoutledgeFalmer, pp. 203–18.

# 38

# Lifelong learning and religion

*Peter Jarvis*

In this chapter I will argue that learning is an aspect of the human condition and that religion is a reflection of this condition, so that we all have the potential to acquire a spiritual dimension to our questions of human existence. I want to argue that each theological statement, from whatever organised religion or none, is a response to a human question – in this sense, it is a learning process. Whether the response is correct, or not, is another matter, but I want to show that, in the very process of learning, there is a wider dimension than we usually see in the textbooks. It is, however, important from the outset to clarify our terms and to contextualise the argument and so the first part of this chapter sets the scene. Thereafter, the following section examines a number of aspects of our human experience from which we can learn but not discover empirical answers.

## Setting the scene

While the terms 'religion' and 'the spiritual' are separate concepts, they are frequently used in an interchangeable manner, so I shall start by exploring the definition of religion. There is a number of ways to define religion in the most general rather than in confessional terms, two of which predominate    what might be called functionalist and existential definitions.

The functionalist definition of religion is epitomised by Émile Durkheim:

> A religion is a unified system of beliefs and practices relative to sacred things, that is to say, things set apart and forbidden – beliefs and practices which unite into one single moral community called a Church, all those who adhere to them.
>
> (1915: 47)

This functionalist definition has come in for considerable criticism in recent years for many reasons, but mainly because functionalism has itself been under attack; for example, functionalist definitions only include those elements of the phenomenon that perform the functions specified in the definition. From the beginning of the Enlightenment, the scene was set for a decline in certain forms of religion as Western society endeavoured to build its own 'city of man' (Manent,

1998). This has certainly resulted in some decline in some forms of institutionalised religion in the West, but what we are actually seeing in contemporary society is that religion is at the heart of many agendas, from those of George Bush and other forms of fundamentalism, to the Christian efforts to overcome poverty in Africa and the Muslim efforts to halt Westernisation in the Middle East. Nevertheless, this is a definition that faith communities can accept.

However, there is another way of approaching religion and this can be seen in the work of Max Weber (see Gerth and Wright Mills, 1948: 267–359), where religion is treated as an existential phenomenon. In many ways this approach is epitomised by such writers as Berger, who suggests that 'religion is a human enterprise by which a sacred cosmos is constructed' (1967: 26). Kolakowski also adopted a similar existentialist perspective when he suggested that religion is 'the awareness of human insufficiency, it is lived in the admission of weakness' (1982: 194, cited in Bauman, 1998: 58). There is a problem with this latter type of approach that is typified by a 'god of the gaps' philosophy, but if we accept that the human condition is one in which we will never have empirical answers for all our questions, although we might try to find rational ones, then we can see that such a problem is misplaced. This might be seen to be part of the postmodern agenda, yet we might claim with Milbank that not only is there

> no 'purely human' space which stands disclosed once we are free of the burden of religious illusion . . . [but] a more important consideration may be that there is no purely *secular* space, outside of constitutive opposition of this term to that of 'the sacred'.
>
> (1992: 37)

Basically, religion, according to existentialist approaches, is any coherent set of answers to the questions that cause us ultimate concern. This definition suggests that all human beings are potentially religious, even if they are not committed believers of any creed, but such a definition does give rise to the conceptual problem of the spiritual.

The *Concise Oxford Dictionary* (1996) offers four similar definitions of the spiritual:

- of or concerning the spirit as opposed to matter;
- concerned with sacred or religious things, holy, divine, inspired (the spiritual life, spiritual songs);
- (of the mind, etc.) refined, sensitive, not concerned with the material;
- (of a relationship, etc.) concerned with the soul or spirit, etc., not with external reality (his spiritual home).

While all of these definitions seek to capture the idea of the spiritual, they actually omit the precise element that concerns us here, which is its relationship to personal knowledge. In this sense, spiritual knowledge is knowledge that cannot be proven by empirical scientific methods but may be legitimated through both rational argument and pragmatic lifestyle. This perspective is almost captured by the *Dictionary*'s definition of the term spirit: 'the intelligent non-physical part of a person'. One implication of this approach to the spiritual is that many so-called New Age spiritualities (see Woodhead and Heelas, 2000: 110–68) can be included within it, although the emphasis on rational argument and pragmatic lifestyle also excludes some of them.

This meaning of 'spiritual' is individual and captures not only knowledge but also attitudes, beliefs and ethical values, and it is not only cognitive but also emotive (Otto, 1927), so there is a sense in which it also captures the idea of human volition and reflects our subjective identity: it is individualistic and subjective and overlaps with the concept of religion. But such approaches to religion as Berger's (1967) can incorporate both an individual spiritual and a social – a public and a private – understanding of religion. And as only certain forms of traditional institutionalised religion – public religion – have apparently declined, although even this is debatable (see Bernstein, 2005: 95–119), the emphasis on spirituality is a clear demonstration of the significance of the private in postmodern society and also the fact that so-called material and scientific claims do not provide answers to many questions life raises for most individuals, so that the so-called secular space has actually been occupied by humanist, even spiritual, answers.

While there has been some apparent decline in institutionalised religious belief in parts of the West, it is clear that individual religiosity (spirituality) is very common, but institutionalised belief systems are still very common and, therefore, there is a sense in which we see the individual quest for meaning being pursued through lifelong learning and certain sets of institutionalised answers being offered by the established religions, as this chapter demonstrates.

Religion, private or public, ultimately begins with the person and the person's response to the questions of human living – it is existential. In precisely the same way, human learning is an existential phenomenon in which learning is seen as the process by which individuals give or are given an explanation of the disjunctural experiences (those in which the current level of understanding does not allow a taken-for-granted response to a current experience) of everyday life. In this way they are learned explanations, transformations of any individual experience into knowledge and so on. Experiences occur in two different ways: primary experiences occur through the senses and secondary experiences are cognitive. They both occur at the intersection of individuals' inner life-worlds with the wider social or empirical world and when they are unable to take the external world for granted and act in an almost unthinking manner. It is this that I have called 'disjuncture' and it is the point at which learning begins. This can occur at any stage in the lifespan, although young children probably experience more disjunctural situations, especially primary ones, than do older persons for whom the majority of experiences may be cognitive.

Lifelong learning is:

The combination of processes throughout a life time whereby the whole person – body (genetic, physical and biological) and mind (knowledge, skills, attitudes, values, emotions, beliefs and senses) – experiences social situations, the perceived content of which is then transformed cognitively, emotively or practically (or through any combination) and integrated into the individual person's biography resulting in a continually changing (or more experienced) person.

(Jarvis, 2006: 134)

In a sense, we are dealing with the human condition, which is one that cannot be fully understood by rational thought or empirical/scientific research – but a part of that condition is that it demands answers to the questions that arise from existence itself. In this sense, it can be argued that curiosity is innate – all children, for instance, go through a period of asking the question 'Why?' An aspect of the human condition is that we are not born with answers to the questions of our existence and so, as part of our humanity, we seek to discover them – some of them may be empirical and provable while other questions have no empirical answers, but ones that may well be rational and pragmatic. Thus, we want to differentiate between those questions that have empirical or potentially empirical explanations and those that may never have empirical answers, which we want to call spiritual. Here I concede that this is not a clearly demarcated division, but a very fuzzy one, so that disputes may arise at this point as to whether some answers should be included in the one or the other side of the hypothetical line; but what is clear is that there are 'answers' on both sides of the line! In all cases we learn from the experiences of our human condition and that some elements of the process of learning can give rise to spiritual answers as well as scientific ones.

But within the learning society learning is also institutionalised and it may defined as:

> Every opportunity made available by any social institution for, and every process by which, an individual can acquire knowledge, skills, attitudes, values, emotions, beliefs and senses within global society.

> (Jarvis, 2007: 99)

Both of these definitions refer to different approaches to lifelong learning, which may be conceptualised as a combination of learning and recurrent education. Learning is always personal but some of the opportunities to learn are provided by social institutions, such as the state, employers and voluntary organisations – such as the faith communities. The religious communities, like other organisations, also run continuing education training courses for both their professional employees and their voluntary workers. In addition, many faith communities run programmes to teach their members how they should respond to the exigencies and complexities of daily life. In many of the faiths these programmes are quite extensive – ranging from public meetings (even to preaching in public worship) to evening courses and individual instruction; many local churches, mosques, synagogues and other places of worship organise these programmes. However, the intention of this chapter is not to examine the nature of these courses or the level of participation but to look at the spiritual dimensions of learning itself.

## The spiritual dimensions of human learning

In this section I want to explore the idea of human learning itself, disjuncture and experience, and aspects of reflection, meaning and self-identity.

### Human learning

It is almost impossible to conceptualise a human being who has never learned since learning epitomises our humanity and, in a similar manner, it is as impossible to think of a time when the human being stops learning. Learning is intrinsic to our humanity – it is world-forming (Heidegger, cited in Agamben, 2002: 51), but, as Luckmann (1967) suggests, when we do transcend our biological nature then a religious experience occurs. In this sense our learning is religious. But this raises another question – if we continue to grow and develop as a result of our lifelong learning, then humanity is an unfinished project and so we are confronted with an unanswerable question when we ask: What is the end of our learning? What then is the end of our humanity? Why are we here? Are we here just to keep on learning? No answer, secular or sacred, can provide a satisfying response to these questions, so if we ask them we are confronted with the unanswerable: a void that reflects the human condition itself. This 'nothingness' points us beyond the scientific and empirical to perhaps a spiritual space, but once it has done this we can learn little more about the unfathomable mystery of human learning itself.

### Disjuncture and experience

Our lives comprise a series of experiences made up in such a way that our biography appears as continuous experience added to by each unique episode of learning that we call an experience. But each of these unique episodes begins with the same type of question that we posed in the previous paragraph: Why has this occurred? How do I do this? What does this mean? And so on. It can be cognitive, emotional or a combination of the two: it is this that I call disjuncture. While we learn to live with our ultimate disjunctural questions we are frequently confronted with less ultimate ones that stimulate our learning or that leave us in a state of having learned once again that we do not know all the answers to our questions. Consequently, we can see that it is disjuncture itself that drives learning – it is emptiness and void that underlie our need to learn, for our learning is the continuous attempt to establish harmony between our experience and our understanding of the world. In this sense, it reflects our need to discover answers that enable us to live in harmony with both our environment and with ourselves. But we sometimes feel the need to reach out beyond our taken-for-granted, beyond our everyday, since there are still more things to learn and to do – for a paradox of our responding to our disjunctural experiences is that we are immediately confronted with new disjunctures – for life is a journey to we know not where.

Experience is a problematic concept since we have both primary and secondary experiences – primary ones are sense experiences and secondary ones are cognitive. Each of the five senses (sight, smell, sound, taste and touch) can be the start of a learning experience. Children seek to give meaning to their sense experiences and we might wonder why they do this since no fact or artefact has intrinsic meaning, but, as I have pointed out already, the very process of human learning is an element of the human condition in which we endeavour to give meaning to the apparently meaninglessness. Children give names to the artefacts with which they play, which are the names approved by our culture, but it is these sense experiences that can take us beyond the cognitive to the emotional: What a gorgeous sound! How beautiful is this scene! What a tranquil moment! And so on. In these situations the experience is disjunctural because the beauty, tranquillity, etc. take us outside of our taken-for-granted world and we are confronted with the extraordinary – something that has no meaning or explanation in itself but is something so extraordinary that we want to hang on to it for as long as we can – a magic moment – yet, paradoxically, we know that we can give no empirical meaning to it.

It is experience itself that was James's (1960) starting point for religious experience – 'individual men in their solitude'. What James is saying here is that these experiences occur to the individual, not that meaning is given to them in isolation from previous knowledge, and we do not have to be a mystic isolated in the desert somewhere to have them but we do need the time to concentrate upon the mysteries of the experience, a process that Crawford (2005) referred to as 'attentive experiencing'.

However, there is another aspect of experience and that is what is usually called religious, or numinous, experience – awe, wonder and the experience of beauty. How do we make meaning/learn from this experience? Ricoeur (1995: 48–55), I think, accurately describes the way in which we learn from the senses in general and especially from these religious-type experiences that theologians call numinous. He makes five points and these are similar to the learning process that I have described in the second chapter of this book:

- the 'numinous' element of the sacred is not first of all something to do with language;
- following Eliade, this is hierophantic – that is, while we cannot describe the numinous element as such, we can at least describe how it manifests itself – this I have already done;
- the sacred may also reveal itself in significant behaviour – although this is only one modality of the numinous and it may have been my intense concentration, my contemplative nature, and so on that could be described as behavioural;
- the sacred is dramatic;
- each of these elements points to a logic of meaning – to signify something other than itself.

These five points describe precisely what happens when we learn from our senses (see Chapter 2, this volume) – what we may describe as a phenomenology of manifestation, about which Ricoeur concludes by claiming that 'in the sacred universe the capacity for saying is founded on the capacity of the cosmos to signify something other than itself' (1995: 54). In his study, Ricoeur goes on to discuss a hermeneutic of proclamation but this takes us in a different direction to the one underlying this chapter. It is, however, to the second point in Ricoeur's discussion that we need to return – we cannot describe it, but we can describe how it manifests itself to us. But any description that I might give to this experience is already clothed in a language and a culture into which I have been socialised and this moves us on to Ricoeur's final point: each of these elements point to a logic of meaning and so the meaning that I might give the experience is almost certainly bound to reflect my own life-world and my previous experiences. But the process may be one of meaning-making, meaning-taking or meaning-transforming.

This is a function of language – but it is through language that my description of this event becomes a secondary experience for those who either hear me describing it or read the words of the chapter. This is the nature of secondary experience and it is secondary experience from which we learn most things. Consequently, it is now important to look at the nature of learning itself – something that we can already see has a number of different processes. We learn though both the body and the mind – it is the whole person who learns and who learns from the whole of the experience. In this sense learning is both an existential phenomenon and an experiential one – it relates to our existence and is lifelong, and religious experience is a learning experience inasmuch as it points us to the potentiality of meaning.

### Reflection

It is here that attentive experiencing becomes contemplation – a form of reflective learning that I have discussed in all my models of learning from the very first (Jarvis, 1987). But that reflection need not be the cold rational learning of modernity; it might well be wonder at the mystery of the experience (Otto, 1927), the admiration, even the worshipful attitude, of the believer. Reflective learning can take the learners outside themselves, providing that they have the time to think about their experience – a point that Crawford (2005) makes very strongly. Through reflection we learn, but our answers might merely reveal that the world in which we are learning is itself a mystery that is slowly being uncovered by science, but that beauty, awe and wonder are emotions that can take us beyond the scientific to make us aware of the non-material dimensions of human existence.

### Meaning

Learning is a process of meaning-making, but writers such as Mezirow (1991) regard it as a process of transforming meaning, while I regard learning as a process of transforming experience and giving it meaning, as well as transforming meaning into new meaning. The search for meaning is a paradoxical experience (Jarvis, 1992) – from the moment we discover a meaning it leads to new questions, and so on. As soon as we begin the endeavour we realise that there is no intrinsic meaning to existence itself and that we have to give it meaning – something that has been recognised from time immemorial. In the Judaeo-Christian creation myth, recorded just a few hundred years before the beginning of the Christian era, Adam gave names to the animals, or to interpret the myth humankind gave meaning to the world. Every meaning that we produce gives rise to further questions about Being itself for, like learning, the human condition is always a journey that appears to have no end. Additionally, new members

439

of any faith community need not have had a specifically religious experience so long as they accept the meaning system that they are taught by the community; this system can change in dialogue with other systems of meaning without reference to any primary experience, and interestingly enough this is precisely what Mezirow (1991: 12–13) regards as learning. He writes that 'Learning may be understood as the process of using a prior interpretation to construe a new or a revised interpretation of the meaning of one's experience in order to guide a future action' (p. 12).

Meaning is transient and a matter of belief since there is no empirical answer to the question of meaning itself.

### Self-identity

The outcome of every learning experience is that it is incorporated into our identities: through our learning we are creating our biographies. We are continually becoming – we are existential beings; but what we are becoming and why we are becoming remain the problematics of existence itself. Our identity is neither an empirical nor a scientific phenomenon – it is not intrinsic to our body but is constructed as a result of our being and acting and from our learning. Indeed, we become selves but Chalmers (1996), among other philosophers, concludes that the selves that we have are not merely psychological selves residing in the brain, but that there is a metaphysical self that occurs beyond it. Significantly, once we enter the debate about the brain and the mind, some of the more 'scientific' theories of learning, such as behaviourism and information processing, need considerably more discussion. To be able to claim an identity is to make a spiritual statement, for 'I' have become myself as a result of my learning.

Among the four aims of lifelong learning in the European Commission (2001) policy document is that of fulfilling our human potential: one that is rarely discussed in depth since the word 'potential' is itself a problem. Potential seems to suggest that there is an innate set of abilities that can be drawn out from us as we learn, but it is a restrictive concept. But the nature of our humanity is potentiality itself (Agamben, 1990: 42). If we can keep on learning we can transcend totality, in Levinas' sense, and he argues that, in relationship with others, which is the beginning of religion, we can learn to reach towards infinity:

> To approach the other in conversation is to welcome his expression, in which at each instance he overflows the idea a thought would carry away with it. It is therefore to *receive* from the Other beyond the capacity of the I which means exactly: to have the idea of infinity. But this also means: to be taught. The relation with the Other, or Conversation, is a non-allergic relation; but in as much as it is welcomed this conversation is teaching (enseignement). Teaching is not reducible to maieutics; it comes from the exterior and brings me more than I contain. In its non-violent transitivity the very epiphany of the face is produced.
>
> (1991[1969]: 51; italics in original)

Thus, in a learning relationship we can transcend ourselves and reach towards infinity.

## Conclusion

Lifelong learning is more than the change of behaviour or the transformation of meaning as a result of experience: it is the transformation of the experience itself and maybe also its meaning throughout the lifespan. Lifelong learning is fundamental to human living and being: it is becoming itself and thus it points us to a mystery that is Being itself and so it is a religious or spiritual process.

## References

Agamben, G. (1990) *The Coming Community*, Minneapolis, MN: University of Minneapolis Press.

—— (2002) *The Open*, Stanford, CA: Stanford University Press.

Bauman, Z. (1998) 'Post-modern religion?', in P. Heelas (ed.) *Religion, Modernity and Post-Modernity*, Oxford: Blackwell, p. 58.

Berger, P. (1967) *The Social Reality of Religion*, London: Faber and Faber.

Bernstein, R. (2005) *The Abuse of Evil*, Cambridge: Polity.

Berry. P. and Wernick, A. (eds) *Shadow of Spirit: Post-modernism and religion*, London: Routledge.

Chalmers, D. (1996) *The Conscious Mind*, Oxford: Oxford University Press.

*Concise Oxford Dictionary* (1996) Oxford: Oxford University Press (CD-ROM).

Crawford, J. (2005) *Spiritually Engaged Knowledge*, Aldershot: Ashgate.

Durkheim, E. (1915) *The Elementary Forms of Religious Life*, London: George Allen and Unwin.

European Commission (2001) *Making a European Area of Lifelong Learning a Reality*, COM (2001) 678 final, Brussels: European Commission.

Gerth, H. and Wright Mills, C. (1948) *From Max Weber*, London: Routledge and KeganPaul.

Heidegger, M. (1962) *Being and Time*, New York: Harper and Row.

James, W. (1960) *Varieties of Religious Experience*, London: Fontana.

Jarvis, P. (1987) *Adult Learning in the Social Context*, London: Croom Helm.

—— (1992) *Paradoxes of Learning*, San Francisco, CA: Jossey-Bass.

—— (2006) *Towards a Comprehensive Theory of Human Learning*, London: Routledge.

—— (2007) *Globalisation, Lifelong Learning and the Learning Society: Sociological perspectives*, London: Routledge.

Kolakowski, L. (1982) *Religion: If there is no God . . . On God, the Devil, sin and other worries of the so-called philosophy of religion*, London: Fontana.

Levinas, E. (1991[1969]) *Totality and Infinity*, AH Dordrecht: Kluwer.

Luckmann, T. (1967) *Invisible Religion*, London: Macmillan.

Manent, P. (1998) *The City of Man*, Princeton, NJ: Princeton University Press.

Mezirow, J. (1991) *Transformative Dimensions of Adult Learning*, San Francisco, CA: Jossey-Bass.

Milbank, J. (1992) 'The post-modern agenda', in P. Berry and A. Wernick (eds) *Shadow of Spirit: Post-modernism and religion*, London: Routledge, p. 37.

Otto, R. (1927) *The Idea of the Holy*, Harmondsworth: Penguin.

Ricoeur, P. (1995) *Figuring the Sacred*, Minneapolis, MN: Fortress Press.

Woodhead, L. and Heelas, P. (eds) (2000) *Religion in Modern Times*, Oxford: Blackwell.

# Part 8
## Geographical dimensions

# 39

# Lifelong learning in Africa

## Michael Omolewa

Lifelong learning is not a novel idea in Africa. Indeed, many scholars have posited that it was deeply embedded within African culture and epistemology long before our peoples came into contact with colonialism (Nabudere, 2007: 20; Mugo, 1999: 213). Colonialism in part dictated what kind of change was needed in the new contexts in which our peoples found themselves. Long before then, Africans recognised learning as the process of engagingly actively with experience. They understood that learning was a necessity if they were to make sense of the world. They knew and adopted the idea that learning generally involves a deliberate effort that must be made in order to acquire (and increase) skills, knowledge or understanding, and strengthen values, interests and attitudes. They realised that, thus equipped, they would possess an immense capacity for reflecting and engaging in action to improve their personal development and that of their communities. It was expected that effective learning would lead to change, development and a desire to learn more. Africans knew that the critical areas in which they could increase participation in learning processes involved:

- discovering – and sharing – new knowledge on how to stimulate the demand for learning;
- creating new opportunities for, and awareness of, formal, non-formal and informal learning;
- providing access to resources that empower learners;
- extending the campaign's influence and presence as a powerful advocate for learning.

These various areas must be addressed within the concept of lifelong learning. This concept has been interpreted in a variety of ways. The European Commission (EC) sees the concept of lifelong learning as 'all learning activity undertaken throughout life, with the aim of improving knowledge, skills and competencies, within a personal, civic, social and/or employment related perspective' (EC, 2001: 1).

Jarvis (2001) observes that lifelong learning aims to transform, takes place throughout life and is the process whereby human beings create and transform experiences into knowledge, skills, attitudes, beliefs, values, senses and emotions. It attempts to put learning at the 'heart of humanity'. This approach means that lifelong learning enables students and adult learners to learn at different times, in different ways and for different purposes at various stages of their lives and careers (Nabudere, 2003).

Promoting lifelong learning in Africa involves many things. It entails the creation of literate societies, and the valuing of local knowledge, talent and wisdom. It also involves promoting learning within formal, informal and non-formal settings, and profiting as much as possible from the new information and communication technologies that are the fruit of globalisation. Lifelong learning is the sum of all learning activity undertaken throughout life. It is a deliberate progression throughout the life of an individual, whereby individuals continuously review and upgrade their knowledge and skills in order to meet challenges posed by an ever changing society. It encompasses learning through involvement in such areas as sports, cultural activities, hobbies, recreation and volunteer activities. The places in which learning activities are conducted are equally diverse.

The lifelong learning ethos stipulates that learning must be flexible, backed by clear information and advice, and supported by the state, employers and individuals. Learning should lead to qualifications that can easily be understood by all, are achievable in manageable steps, are relevant to the skill needs of the local economy and are equivalent to general qualifications. The concept of lifelong learning reflects the fact that, in the midst of change, we must continuously update the skills of the workforce and better equip people to manage their own future. Lifelong learning is particularly concerned with improving access to learning opportunities and encouraging people to take greater responsibility for their own learning.

Lifelong learning is now the guiding principle for policy strategies concerned with objectives ranging from a nation's economic well-being and competitiveness to its people's sense of personal fulfilment and social cohesion. It is widely assumed that lifelong learning is essential for everyone and must therefore be made available to all (OECD, 1996). Moreover, the concept applies to all peoples and nations regardless of their level of development. It is, therefore, increasingly receiving the support of governments, funding bodies and international organisations, with a view to boosting cultural and human capital so that it is on a par with other countries (Jary and Thomas, 1999).

In the light of the above, this chapter examines the concept of lifelong learning in the context of globalisation. It provides an overview of the origins and scope of lifelong learning in Africa, using its historical and philosophical dimensions as points of discourse. The chapter highlights the contexts and varieties of lifelong learning, including formal, informal and non-formal, as well as work and societal contexts. In the main, the chapter pursues the subject of the development of a learning society in Africa in view of the pervasive influence of globalisation. It discusses the various gains, challenges and frustrations of the Africans while exploring strategies for the promotion of an informed lifelong learning ethos in Africa. The thesis of this chapter is that such a promotion requires the invaluable contribution of ways of thinking, talents and initiatives unique to Africa, as well as its wisdom, wit and ways.

## Lifelong learning in the context of globalisation

Today, learning to learn, learning for the purposes of problem solving, learning in order to achieve critical understanding and anticipatory learning are all prerequisites for facing the new challenges brought about by globalisation (Nabudere, 2003). This demonstrates that globalisation has generated a number of processes and outcomes that mean that the learning of skills and competencies is of paramount importance in people's lives. Globalisation affects learning and everything else besides. The fields of business and finance are becoming more global. Practice is becoming more standardised, while provisions aimed at meeting the demands of the people are becoming increasingly internationalised. People are becoming more mobile. Hence, there are as many explanations of the meaning and purpose of globalisation as there are ideologies and critics discussing the concept.

However, key to the concept of globalisation is the removal of barriers hindering trade and interaction across international borders. Issues of language commonality, a near return to Babel, new purchasing patterns and new global cultural possibilities are just a few of the trends observed. However, if we must dispense with barriers, there remains a need to determine the extent to which barrier removal is equitable across countries and cultures. In his observations on the effects of change on society, Giddens (1991) has noted a 're-organisation of time and space' and an opening up of social existence that results in a certain level of social injustice. Contemporary societies, in the view of Beck (1994) and others, are risk societies.

Within the context of globalisation, the role of lifelong learning is to mitigate the effects of the subsequent social and political exclusion that may affect many people. Its role is also to ensure a parity of systems, enhance trends compatibility and, in some instances, enable system users and workers to relate appropriately to new social trends and patterns. Attempts to separate globalisation from internationalisation have been at best tenuous, as they are the two sides of the same coin (Adekanmbi, 2000). However, the driving forces of globalisation are strong, and to respond to it we must first recognise what it entails. There is a need to understand its significance for the purposes of educational planning and policies, and to develop an appropriate response after identifying its implications for lifelong learning. Globalisation requires appropriate responses in the form of lifelong learning initiatives.

## Overview, origins and scope of lifelong learning in Africa

Before Muslim Arab missionaries and Western explorers and missionaries started to arrive in Africa in the eleventh and fifteenth centuries respectively, there were no schools and education systems as we know them. Nonetheless, the need for community learning, starting in childhood and continuing through adolescence, youth, middle and old age, was already clearly recognised and implemented, albeit in a rather informal sense.

Nabudere (2007: 20) has quoted Mugo (1999: 213) as having categorically stated that learning and culturalisation in African societies were accepted as continuous and ongoing processes that took place from birth until death, in which the family unit, extended family, village and entire community participated. This system of extended and collective participation in learning by both adults and children was accompanied throughout by professionals who taught specialised knowledge and skills, and its conceptual and methodological framework proved highly practical – especially as a means of inculcating a cultural ethos – as well as being part and parcel of the much-cherished African cultural experience (Nabudere, 2007: 21; Higgs, 2002: 27; Avoseh, 2000: 1–2; Obidi, 1995: 369–83).

Traditional African education is based on two fundamental principles: learning through action and peer-group learning. The process involves the whole of life. The basic tools are the culture and language of the people. Msimuko (1987) observes that, apart from being a lifelong process, traditional education is broad in both scope and function, as well as in the means that it employs. It is collective in nature, a cooperative and voluntary venture (Omolewa et al., 1998). The curriculum according to Msimuko includes history, social skills, rural education, language, music and dance, sex education, religious education, recreation and technical education. The individual is socialised through the family. This family is larger than its modern-day equivalent: it is an extended family of blood relatives and female spouses. The individual also has a place, and a position within this larger family. Socialising is partly individualistic and partly collective.

447

Learning takes place through social, cultural and economic activities in the course of which different age groups, the different genders and the collective play distinctive roles in accordance with their status (Nabudere, 2003).

In African society, traditional life decreed that, after a day's work, children, youth and adults would organise themselves into groups to carry out a series of learning activities by the light of the moon. The adults, for example, would focus on acquiring knowledge that would enable community development, with the traditional head acting as a facilitator. The younger adults, coordinated by a chosen elder, would engage children and young people with folklore, proverbs, stories, riddles and jokes. Folklore, which is rich in content, used lively stories to impart values such as honesty and diplomacy, while stories of great leaders, successful rulers and warriors were relayed to the children not for the purposes of knowledge alone, but also to influence their life pattern. This perhaps informed the statement credited to Babs Fafunwa in Omolewa (1981) that 'if by intellect we mean the ability to integrate experience and if by intellectualisation we mean the ability to reason abstractly, traditional African education provided a forum for intellectual growth and development'.

Traditional education, which forms the basis for character training, is found across Africa. In Nigeria, parents versed in any vocation would encourage their children to adopt it as a profession. Omolewa traced the practice of naming children after their parents' vocation. Thus, names such as Odeyemi, Ayangbemi, Ifabunmi and Agbesola symbolise parents' belief that vocations and deities were instrumental in the birth of their children. The offspring of parents who believed strongly in Ifa (the god of divination) bear names like Ifayemi or Ifabunmi (the god of divination has blessed me), while the children of blacksmiths or hunters might be named Ogundele (Ogun, the god of iron has come home) and so on. The tradition of lifelong learning in Africa was well understood by all as everyone knew when to begin, where to go to learn at a particular age, why and how they should go about it and what the final goal of learning was. The contexts varied and were relatively broad. Fortunately, Africans were clear as to what lifelong learning meant and where it was heading.

Traditional African communities valued recreation and leisure. Dancing remains a constant means of conveying history. For example, during the inter-tribal wars, generals went to war with their drummers, whose eulogies invariably encouraged them to perform brilliantly at the war front. Such dances, associated with historical occasions, such as wars, festivals or the reigns of great rulers, are today considered historical artefacts. Such dances are now only staged in order to remember the past. Distance education, traced in the West to the use of greeting cards, has been in use for much longer in Africa. Drums speak the language of their localities, communicating information from one location to another. Again, messages were sent through what is called 'aroko', a symbolic message that can only be understood by the respondent. The bearer served merely to convey the message, much as a postman delivers letters.

Lifelong learning in traditional Africa responded to the general quest for harmonious co-existence, peace and improved quality of life. The destiny of man was an important issue for the traditional African, and steps were taken to ensure that lifelong learning responded adequately to the need for everyone to achieve a position in the spiritual realm.

For most African communities, the process of lifelong learning was supported by initiation schools, initiation rites, transitional rites and, more importantly, institutions of cultural learning such as the Kgotla (meeting places) in Botswana, and the village square meetings that are still held today by Igbos of modern-day eastern Nigeria. Effective use was made of the apprenticeship system through informed institutions and methodologies. To all intents and purposes, it was clear that Africans identified the need to motivate everyone to want to learn. The main goal at that time was not to push people into acquiring qualifications for the sheer sake of it. Rather,

Africans were motivated to learn in order to acquire relevant knowledge, skills, attitudes, aptitudes and values that would help them to lead long, self-employed, valuable and active lives as participants in the process of individual and community development. Learning was broad-based, effective, enjoyable, challenging and equitable from the foundation stage right up to old age and beyond. In essence, the foundation of lifelong learning practices and programmes reflected the challenges with which people were faced.

For Africans, powers of reasoning had to be developed and cultivated at a very early stage in life, and built upon as one got older through incipient community learning systems that were flexible, limitless, cheap and reliable. There was a need to respond rationally to the challenges facing Africans as a people in terms of their continuous search for new knowledge, skills, values, interests, aptitudes and attitudes. There was also a need for active involvement in the processes of governance and people's economic, socio-cultural, political and spiritual development. In addition, African lifelong learning responded to the need for peace, freedom, plurality and diversity, and the generation of a sense of pragmatism, practicality, urgency and change.

The world of work was yet another force to which lifelong learning responded in Africa. There was a dire need to provide each person with the kinds of knowledge, attitudes, skills and values that would enable him or her to perform effectively in a chosen profession, vocation or trade. Such professions, vocations and trades maintained our communities, and people had to learn to perform well in order to sustain our very existence.

The scope of lifelong learning in traditional and modern Africa placed a strong emphasis on the personal development and fulfilment of the individual as a prerequisite for community and societal development. To achieve this, lifelong learning was organised to provide the knowledge, skills and attitudes needed for individual development in a creative way.

The scope of lifelong learning in Africa also encompassed economic growth. Emphasis was placed on a strong, adaptable, openly competitive and responsive economy that was usually self-sufficient. For example, no one was allowed to be unemployed. Everyone was expected to contribute to the progress of the economy by engaging in a wide range of activities that helped to sustain African livelihoods. From the moment they entered adulthood, Africans were expected to choose to specialise in a profession, vocation or trade to which they would devote their time, energy and resources in order to achieve the goals of economic progress and development. Ideally, they should attain perfection in whatever fields they had chosen to specialise in. This was how they responded to the division of labour concept even as they learned how to share things with one another.

Literature additionally informs us that the scope of lifelong learning also extended to the active participation of individuals in the process of governance. Although this scope is restricted in African nations that are under military regimes or dictatorships, the fact is that lifelong learning, as provided for in educational policies in Botswana, Nigeria and South Africa, deliberately promotes active citizenship to ensure that people are free to contribute ideas to the development of parliamentary acts and policies. They are also free to demand some measure of accountability from political leaders.

## Lifelong learning and the creation of literate societies in Africa

Lifelong learning in traditional African societies relied largely on informal and non-formal structures and systems that were relatively difficult to regulate, monitor or evaluate. It also relied on visual and oral literacy and all the inadequacies and challenges inherent therein. In a globalised world, however, Africa cannot continue to rely on ancient practices, no matter how efficient they may once have been.

In the context of globalisation, information and communication technologies (ICTs) play a dominant role. Illiterate societies cannot promote or apply ICTs. As a result, modern African nations have embraced the planning and implementation of elaborate literacy programmes for the adult population and Universal Basic Education (UBE) for children. Success stories have been recorded across the continent. For example, Oduaran (2006: 4) reports that Botswana had achieved a literacy rate of 81 per cent by the year 2003.

For Africa, change and, indeed, continuous and rapid change, is imminent. African nations are consequently expected to keep planning for lifelong learning programmes that would enable their peoples to acquire the new knowledge, skills, attitudes, aptitudes, values and interests that are considered vital for life. They are expected to give pride of place to informal, formal and non-formal learning systems. Research and scholarship in the area of indigenous knowledge systems is currently returning to prominence. Thus, there is a move towards exploring the 'lost treasures' embedded in our traditional learning practices.

Though some have questioned the feasibility of a 'learning society', there is a belief that skills can be picked up at any stage in life, in contrast to the more restrictive and pessimistic vision that skills are only developed through a process of formal learning (Jary and Thomas, 1999). The creation of literate and learning societies in Africa is based on the premise that new needs, interests and challenges must push us to ensure that everyone has access to learning on a continuous basis and that all available cultural, informal, formal and non-formal learning institutions are being used. The seemingly ambitious goal of making everyone learn continuously throughout life is matched by the volume and quality of learning programmes and institutions that are provided by our governments. Current developments in Botswana, Namibia, Lesotho, Swaziland, South Africa, Uganda, Kenya, Egypt, Libya, Gabon, Nigeria, Ghana or Togo show that the focus and vision underlying lifelong learning measures are the same, even when obvious variations in political commitment, actual capital outlays and support systems are taken into account (Oduaran, 2006).

Our nations must adopt this focus as our peoples strive to position themselves as effective and efficient competitors in the globalised economy, and as we respond to other societal forces such as the explosion of knowledge and technology, robotics, automation, changes in relationships, cultural diversity, increasing leisure time, migration, and climatic and environmental changes, to name just a few.

## Post literacy initiatives: cases and thrusts

Establishing a link between post literacy education and people's day-to-day lives is a major task. Such a link is important, not only in order to overcome an unwillingness or lack of interest on the part of learners, but also as a practical necessity and prerequisite for lifelong learning. Quoting the apartheid-era Minister of Education and Training in South Africa, Soliar said that:

> adult literacy programmes should fit in with the existing school programmes on the one hand, and programmes for continuing education on the other hand. Any literacy programme, which is divorced from the normal school system, can only lead to frustration.
>
> (2001: 15)

One of the responses that Buuba offers to the question 'why is the promotion of literacy such an important educational challenge for Senegal?' is that:

The democratisation process in Senegal requires a greater number of citizens who have access to the information sources and are able to choose their leaders and their representatives in the country's institutional bodies. Likewise, a high demand for transparency, equity and the control of the elected people requires literate people. Moreover the adjustment policies, restructuring and decentralization requires adequate qualified labour force in the country. The lack of State commitment along the breakaway from the tutorship system requires the empowerment of peasants. The emergence of new social agents, including women with their numerous economic initiatives, requires new skills that can be inculcated only by literacy and basic education. Thus, development can only be done through literacy.

(2001: 28)

In turn, Omolewa (2001) reiterated the importance of literacy for Nigerians, noting that Nigeria's democracy is yet to have a strong root. This can only happen if the level of literacy improves. Illiterate people cannot read manifestos, and therefore cannot follow promises made by political parties. There is a wide communication gap between the government and the masses. If this situation persists, illiteracy can lead to the misinterpretation and misrepresentation of government policies. This means, in part, that lifelong learning strongly rooted in adult basic education is central to the move towards more democratic participation in the process of governance in Africa.

UNESCO (1997) corroborates that adult literacy is not a transient phase that prepares one for the rest of life. Instead, it is part of an individual's and a group's constant development and evolution throughout a life cycle. This involves adopting an approach in which people make use of increasing numbers of educational opportunities to acquire the skills they need in order to take more effective control of their lives, ranging from basic skills, such as literacy and numeracy, to more complex ones, such as data processing. In his *Call to Action for American Education in the 21st Century*, Clinton (1997) said that 'learning must last a lifetime, and all our people must have the chance to learn new skills. Basic literacy and adult education are more important than ever for adults as well as children'.

In the advancement of post literacy, it is parenting issues that take centre stage. These include family involvement in helping children with homework and activities that promote children's first experience of education. Employers also recognise that it is important to foster family involvement at this stage. Interactive exercises and structured discussion groups aim to give parents the understanding, confidence and skills they need to become positively involved in their children's education. All of these measures constitute a post-literacy programme, otherwise known as continuing education. It is for this reason that lifelong learning, as outlined in the UNESCO report of the Delors Commission (Delors, 1996), focusing on the human rights situation of indigenous peoples, is divided into four pillars. These are:

- Learning to be: the right of self-identification and self-definition.
- Learning to know: the right to self-knowledge.
- Learning to do: the right to self-development.
- Learning to live together: the right to self-determination.

Viewed from a historical perspective, as long as Africans are still denied their human rights, the right to self-definition and self-identification are paramount. The same applies to Africans'

451

right to learn in their own languages. The obvious link between post-literacy and lifelong learning was to preoccupy African delegates at the Dakar 1997 meeting, which was held in order to prepare the African position for presentation at the 1997 Hamburg Conference on Adult Learning. African representatives took with them to the Hamburg Conference a demand for an integrated, self-training adult education system that would lead to sustainable development and contribute towards the establishment of knowledge, skills and attitudes. This is in line with critical or reflective literacy, both of which come into play at the level of post-literacy learning (Aderinoye, 1997). The goal was for all to be involved in the planning of learning at any given stage in life, according to the needs of the individual and his or her desire to learn. The four pillars of lifelong learning thus adopted by UNESCO highlight the four different phases in life that should be addressed.

As regards the methods of delivery, these must be flexible and innovative. Such methods would include distance learning, which enables everyone to be reached regardless of time and location. Then there is the indigenous AFFRELA method, which is a fusion of three distinct methods: AF represents the African traditional method, which is a return to the roots, FRE represents Freire's participatory structure and conscientisation, and LA is the adoption of the Laubach method of literacy (each one teach one (EOTO)). The three methods fused into one have proven an effective means of mobilising, recruiting and retaining learners. A further technique is Real Literacy Materials (RLM), developed by Alan Rogers, which focuses on using real materials available in the learner's environment as opposed to primers. The literacy shops or drop-in centres promoted and used by the University Village Association (UNIVA) focus on buyers and sellers in market places. Here, the shopkeeper has already received some training as an adult-turned-literacy vendor, and encourages literates to assist non-literates, while also motivating non-literates to return home and seek the support of a literate with the aim of improving their literacy skills (Aderinoye and Rogers, 2003). The delivery method could also include elements of REFLECT, the Regenerated Freirean Literacy through Empowerment Community Technique (Omolewa, 2001).

As a result of the various innovative methods, each individual will benefit from some of the elements of modern thought that are woven into lifelong learning. Africans cherish their cultures, traditions, religions, languages, values, beliefs, customs, ideas, folklore, mores, laws, taboos, music, riddles, legends, myths and proverbs, to mention just a few (Fasokun, 2000). Hence, in traditional African societies, music could be used to transmit messages, ideas and emotion. It could be used to maintain law and order and to convey historical information. Its content, lyrics, form, mood, style, etc. are very useful for transmitting information from one generation to another (Fasokun, 2000).

Efforts should be made to ensure that each individual continues to acquire skills and training that will enhance his or her development throughout life and beyond, for learning not only prepares us for the good things in life, but also for the hereafter. In any scheme of learning throughout life, learning in adulthood must play an essential role. It is thus that post-literacy, continuing education or work-based literacy are all vehicles of development, self-realisation, and of self-definition and determination.

## Lifelong learning initiatives at the workplace

The need for and the pursuit of lifelong learning at the workplace is underscored by the factors of career mobility, workforce changes over the years, the need to prevent knowledge from becoming obsolete and the growing irrelevance of age restrictions at the workplace that can probably be credited to high standards of living. In some parts of Europe, it is becoming increasingly likely that it will no longer be the norm to retire at a specific age, thus enabling older adults to remain married to their jobs until death. Such a move has implications both for the training of the older adults in question and the development of new work paradigms. In some settings, there is a call for university degrees to be accompanied by some form of maintenance contract, due to the fact that such degrees may not be able to serve the individual fully over a longer period of time (Guiton, 1999). Yet, at another level, Jarvis (2001) has noted the continuing rebuttal of claims that it is a myth that workers are being made redundant at 45. He also reports on increasing volunteering, mentoring and the involvement of older people in research activities. At another level, the role of universities is gradually changing as they become more open to developing short courses aimed at addressing educational deficiencies. Distance and conventional learning systems within universities are also experiencing mergers, and the expectation is that the days of distance education as an activity that is distinct and separate from known traditional practices may soon be over (Moran and Myringer, 1999).

Africa's dilemma here is obvious. While the rest of the world is trying out new frameworks of practice, older adults on the continent are still struggling to ensure that retirement benefits are paid and learn the new rules of survival to carry them through their remaining years. Welfare benefits, old-age pensions and social services for the elderly are all things that developed countries take for granted and that are virtually non-existent in Africa, at least in terms of formal governmental provisions. Provisions for old age must be arranged by children, concerned family members and, in some cases, religious organisations. In some cases, older people have been known to resort to begging on the streets out of desperation. Consequently, what Africa has lacked over the years, reflected in gaps in literacy provisions, underscored by continually growing demands for distance education and compounded by a near absence of adequate legislative lifelong learning plans, may yet push Africa backwards. Notably, this is taking place in the same global context in which postmodernist debates have become common discourse. The development of new lifelong learning policies to mitigate the effects of absent post-work provisions for older adults is thus a vital means of addressing the problems highlighted above.

Technology has a critical role to play in lifelong learning. The reasons behind the push for new technologies in lifelong learning are obvious. Across the globe, learners have become very mobile, needs are constantly evolving and office space is no longer static. These changes have generated a need to receive education on the move. The technologies of discourse, social relations and structured living have changed. The technologies that are being used for social interaction and communication are identical to those being used to promote educational access. As a rule, the statistics pertaining to technological possibilities in Africa give a good indication of a number of gaps that still have to be bridged. Writing in the *FID Review*, Adam (1999) observed that telephone communication in Africa is problematic, with about 75 per cent of Africans having never made a telephone call.

The applications of these ICTs would dramatically increase Africa's ability to propagate and promote its vision, mores, values, ethics, ethos and cultural aesthetics internationally. Nabudere (2003) observes that the development of information and communication technologies helped to:

- provide topical information;
- promote non-formal education;
- provide a two-way communication;
- create conditions for interactive learning;
- provide motivation;

453

- facilitate group decisions;
- enable planning and design;
- create conditions for data supply;
- provide the basis for monitoring;
- ensure financial control.

The important thing is that the content of what we want to transmit to others must reflect Africa's reality, not the reality of other peoples' visions of Africa, which are imported through imposed donor policies and programmes about Africa. At the same time, this African reality must reflect the general humanistic traditions in education that enable Africa to be linked to other humanistic learning systems and ideas (Nabudere, 2003).

The growth of new technologies and their application in the field of pedagogy has led to an increased awareness of the availability of learning wherever, whenever, however and for whatever reasons. This is emphasised by the pedagogical possibilities inherent in the new technologies. However, Africa has experienced growing pains and the attempt to provide existing educational initiatives with technological input has proven problematic. Although mobile telephony has experienced some level of rural and urban success, the same cannot be said of pedagogical applications in tune with global trends. The sources of frustration have been local and global, as well as social and pedagogical, and have been further compounded by a number of perceived unfair trade practices. With regard to communication and transport, for example, has Africa been bearing the brunt of costs incurred in the North for the same services? How then should Africa respond to the pursuit of lifelong learning in order to meet local needs? How can Africa address lifelong learning adequately despite the intercontinental gaps that are obvious on an international scale and the need for some degree of parity to be established? The answers may lie in the following propositions.

First, Africa must realign its educational plans by accepting lifelong learning as a paradigm worth reassessing. Africa's traditional educational ethos has never had a problem with lifelong learning; rather, the difficulty lies in the imbalance and unhappy marriage between new educational mores and traditional values. This was never an ideal union and the educational planning that emerged from it was to be viewed as a bastard son from the outset. Second, the continent's policies on technology should be sufficiently comprehensive to combine the expectations of the informal with the formal and non-formal within a framework that provides clear plans and policies that can easily be understood and implemented. Third, African countries must re-examine the structures of social support that enabled lifelong learning to function in traditional societies. It is the cushioning effect of such support that allows a viable lifelong learning agenda to thrive.

## Developing a learning society in Africa

Notions of the learning society have gained considerable currency in policy debates in a number of countries since the appearance of *Learning to Be*. If learning involves all of one's life, in the sense of both time-span and diversity, and all of society, including its social and economic as well as its educational resources, then we must go even further than the necessary overhaul of 'educational systems' in order to attain the status of a learning society (Faure, 1972). Husén (1986) argued that it would be necessary for states to become 'learning societies', in which knowledge and information lay at the heart of their activities.

A learning society is an educated society, committed to active citizenship, liberal democracy and equal opportunities. This enables lifelong learning to be supported within the social policy frameworks of post–Second World War democracies. A learning society is a learning market, enabling institutions to provide services for individuals in order to assure the competitiveness of the economy. This in turn enables lifelong learning to be supported within the economic policy framework adopted by many governments since the mid-1970s. The aim is to establish a market in learning opportunities to meet individuals' and employers' demands for updated skills and competences.

There is a need for Africans to embrace a learning society in which learners adopt a learning approach to life, drawing on a wide range of resources to enable them to support their ways of life. This enables lifelong learning to be supported for individuals living in the present-day context to which policy must respond. A learning society embraces learning throughout life. All individuals are entitled to plan and choose relevant quality learning and manage their own learning. Employers become learning organisations and support individuals in achieving their goals. The entitlement to learning does not expire once a certain age is reached.

The strategy that must be adopted in order to become an effective learning society prizes learning processes and dynamics over and above immediate outcomes. It seeks to create networks and social interactions related to the production and dissemination of the twin instruments of learning: information and knowledge. Dissemination is a crucial means of encouraging further participation and reducing the perception of risk, thereby enabling new dynamic processes to be generated. It is important to publicise information about useful best practices – both local and international – that highlights achievements as well as lessons learned.

The past has shown us that, for individuals to choose their learning well, they needed information that suited their individual needs. They needed to know what previous learning was required. They needed to know who the suppliers were and how successful they were. They needed to know about modes of learning, including the times of the sessions and the materials required. They needed to know about learning support, including access to peers. Furthermore, of course, they also needed to know about funding. Adults had to be offered access to advice, guidance and technological systems. New and more flexible provisions had to be established. All this led to a need for a nationwide accessible adult guidance system that would build confident learners.

How can we change people's attitudes while at the same time transforming their actions? Foundation learning required a curriculum with a stronger focus on work. This should be general requirement for all and not just those who have been deemed non-academic. In the past, key skills truly were the key; their importance overshadowed individual subjects because they helped learners to learn and to create a learning environment. Career path planning skills would lead to learning-to-learn skills and to changes in learning methods. To support these learners, we would have to invest more in initial and in-service training for teachers, and train careers teachers to adopt a new perspective. Learning and life management would be inextricably bound together. Employers will be instrumental in bringing about a learning society. In the words of Mary Lord, speaking at the TEC Lifelong Learning Conference:

> If we want them to make their firms learning organisations, we must provide some guidelines. We should define clearly what such an organisation should be like – or at least provide a definition of a starting point. We should emphasise the benefits that have been demonstrated through research. This would be the key element in a campaign for promoting learning organisations.
>
> (Lord, 1997)

Today there is much talk of the learning organisation, the knowledge economy and the like. The 'learning society' is an aspect of this movement to look beyond formal educational environments and to locate learning not only as a quality pertaining to the individual, but also as an element of a larger system. If it is now the world's responsibility to view lifelong learning as the principal means of improving citizens' lives, Africa's duty must be to continue to revamp the tradition it laid down so long ago. This is one reason that Nabudere (2007: 21) has continuously demanded the establishment of a Pan-African University that can provide the mechanisms and strategies that will afford everyone, especially adult learners, the opportunity of gaining easy access to formal institutions of learning – and effectively remove the divide between informal, non-formal and formal education in line with our traditions and cultures. The kind of lifelong learning that could enable Africa to develop rapidly would unite the University and the communities in the recognition of needs-related learning outcomes through a collaborative process of research and discourse that extends beyond the framework of formal systems of learning.

## Conclusion

Lifelong learning in Africa should take place through a continuously supportive process of ongoing learning that motivates and enables individuals to acquire and apply the knowledge, values, skills and critical understanding required to respond confidently and creatively to the challenges of a changing social, political and economic environment.

Africa's evolution towards lifelong learning will require the dynamic interplay of a series of success factors: leadership, broad-based participation, experimentation, the measurement of results and systematising experiences. To establish a comprehensive system of lifelong learning, aspects of economic competitiveness, social welfare, cultural enrichment and improved social services must be provided by and for its principal stakeholders. Such a system therefore entails the participation of all sectors, so that all interests are well represented, without any particular social, economic or political segment of the population extending their hegemony over the rest.

Lifelong learning in Africa implies an attitude that welcomes change and favours flexibility and innovation over rigidity and the fear of making mistakes. Furthermore, initiative must be encouraged, errors must be used as learning tools, reward must prevail over punishment, and professional merit must be valued over personal connections. The emphasis on lifelong learning is well placed given the rapidly changing pace of the technological, social, economic and political realities of the modern world. This rapid change has led to globalisation, which now dictates the pace of almost everything else in the human community, including learning.

Although the concept of lifelong learning is best understood as a philosophical and a policy device, it has a lifewide dimension, referring not only to formal education provided in institutions but also to non-formal learning at work and informal learning occurring at home and in daily life (Tuijnman, 2002). It is therefore imperative that we ensure that the emphasis of lifelong learning is placed on learning rather than education in order to reduce its preoccupation with social structures and enable a focus on individual demands from time to time. For Africa to derive maximum benefit from the adoption of this concept as a framework for its education policies, it must continue to value and evaluate its past achievements and then begin to apply all the available ICTs, especially the community-based telecentres of learning as proposed by Nabudere (2002: 1–10). For the overall goal to be achieved, Africa will require a profound commitment to lifelong learning on the part of its leaders and the people themselves.

# References

Adam, Lishan (1999) 'Connectivity and access for communication and publishing in Africa', *FID Review* 1(2/3): 133–44.

Adekanmbi, Gbolagade (2000) 'Review [of] higher education through open and distance learning', *Open Learning* 1(1): 207–10.

Aderinoye, Rachid (1997) *Literacy Education in Nigeria*, Ibadan: University of Ibadan Publishing House.

—— and Rogers, Alan (2003) 'The intervention of the literacy shop at Bodija Market, Ibadan in the promotion of literacy in Nigeria', *Journal of Latin America on Literacy* 6: 37–42.

Avoseh, Mejai B.M. (2000) *Learning to be Active Citizens: Lessons from African Pedagogy*, paper presented at the International Conference on Lifelong Learning, Higher Education and Active Citizenship, University of the Western Cape, Cape Town, South Africa, 10–12 October.

Beck, Ulrich (1994) *Risk Society: Towards a new modernity*, London: Sage.

Buuba, Babacar Diop (2001) *Adult Literacy Policy and Practice in Senegal*, London: Sage, pp. 27–74.

Clinton, Bill (1997) *A Call to Action for American Education in the 21st Century*, Washington, DC: Department of Education.

Delors, Jacques (Chair) (1996) *Learning: The Treasure Within*, Paris: UNESCO.

European Commission (EC) (2001) *Making a European Area of Lifelong Learning a Reality*, COM (2001) 678 final, Brussels: Commission of the European Communities.

Fasokun, Thomas O. (2000) 'Towards the creation of lifelong learning culture in Africa', in Gillian Youngs, Toshio Ohsako *et al.* (eds) *Creative and Inclusive Strategies for Lifelong Learning: Report of International Roundtable*, Hamburg: UNESCO Institute for Education, 27–29 November.

Faure, Edgar (Chair) (1972) *Learning to Be*, Paris: UNESCO.

Giddens, Anthony (1991) *Modernity and Self-Identity: Self and society in the late modern age*, Oxford: Polity Press.

Guiton, Patrick (1999) 'Professional reflective practice and lifelong learning', in K. Harry (ed.) *Higher Education through Open and Distance Learning*, London: Routledge, pp. 48–56.

Higgs, Philip (2002) 'Indigenous knowledge and African philosophy: an educational perspective, *Indilinga – African Journal of Indigenous Knowledge Systems* 1: 27–35.

Husèn, Torsten (1986) *The Learning Society Revisited*, Oxford: Pergamon.

Jarvis, Peter (ed.) (2001) *The Age of Learning: Education and the knowledge society*, London: Kogan Page.

Jary, David and Thomas, Liz (1999) 'Editorial: Widening participation and lifelong learning', *Widening Participation and Lifelong Learning* 1(1): 3–7.

Lord, Mary (1997) Speech delivered at the TEC Lifelong Learning Conference at the Stakis Hotel, Norwich, 6 May. Available online at www.lifelonglearning.co.uk/conf97/conf3.htm (accessed 9 February 2007).

Moran, Louise and Myringer, Brittmarie (1999) 'Flexible learning and university change', in K. Harry (ed.) *Higher Education through Open and Distance Learning*, London: Routledge, pp. 57–71.

Msimuko, Arthur K. (1987) 'Traditional education in pre-colonial Zambia', *Adult Education and Development* 29 (October): 21–31.

Mugo, Micere Githae (1999) 'African culture in education for sustainable development', in William Makgoba Malegapuru (ed.) *African Renaissance: The New Struggle*, Cape Town: Mafube Publishing.

Nabudere, Dani W. (2002) *How New Technologies Can Be Used for Learning in Pastoral Communities in Africa*, paper presented at the World Social Summit, Porto Alegre, Brazil, February.

—— (2003) *How New Information Technologies Can Be Used to Advance Learning in Agro-Pastoral Communities in Africa*. Available online at www.friendspartners.org/ (accessed 9 February 2007).

—— (2007) *Towards the Establishment of a Pan-African University: A strategic concept paper*. Available online at www.sarpn.org.za/documents/ (accessed 9 February 2007).

Obidi, Samuel S. (1995) 'Skills acquisition through indigenous apprenticeship: a case study of the Yoruba blacksmith in Nigeria', *Comparative Education* 31(3): 369–83.

Oduaran, Akpovire (2006) *Literacy for Sustainable Development in Botswana: A 21st century perspective*, keynote address given on the occasion of the commemoration of National and International Literacy Day, Goodhope, Botswana, 8 September.

Omolewa, Michael (1981) *Adult Education Practice in Nigeria*, Ibadan: Evans Brothers (Nigeria).

—— (2001) *Challenges of Education in Nigeria*, university lecture, Ibadan: Ibadan University Press.

——, Adeola, O.A., Adekanmbi, G., Avoseh, M.B.M. and Braimoh, D. (1998) *Literacy, Traditions and Progress: Recruitment and retention in a rural literacy programme*, Hamburg: UNESCO Institute for Education.

Organization for Economic Cooperation and Development (OECD) (1996) *Lifelong Learning for All*, Paris: OECD.

Soliar, Deena (2001) 'Adult literacy policy and practice in South Africa', in Ila Patel (ed.) *Learning Opportunities For All*, New Delhi: ASPBAE and ILSS, ICAE, pp. 1–26.

Tuijnman, Albert (2002) 'Measuring lifelong learning for the new economy', in *Lifelong Learning and the Building of Human and Social Capital*, BAICE Conference, Centre for Comparative Education Research, The School of Continuing Education, University of Nottingham, 6–8 September.

UNESCO (1997) *CONFINTEA*, Hamburg: UNESCO.

# 40

# The lifelong learning system in Asia
## Emerging trends and issues[1]

*Soonghee Han*

Lifelong learning inhabits two worlds that co-exist: 'life-world' and 'system', if I may apply Habermas's concept. In the world of life-world, learning by nature is private and personal. It takes care of the living spirit and inner self. Lifelong learning discourse in this world deals with various kinds of education and learning that give meaning of life and spirit to the whole career of human beings. In the world of system, lifelong learning expands the territory of the exchange value of learning to the global capitalism and its changing labor market system. The lifelong learning system that this article is dealing with refers to the latter dimension.

Lifelong learning as a system is a global phenomenon. It is 'global' in a sense that global world standards have significant influences on local initiatives in defining the shape of education systems. The learning economy that 'knowledge capitalism' created becomes the most important instrument with a particular mode of production and reproduction (Burton-Jones, 1999). 'Lifelong learning' as a system, in this context, stands at the very centre of the structural transition from capital-based economy to knowledge-based economy.

The Asian economy has just moved towards this direction. It is very important to consider that Asia is the world's largest continent, with enormous economic potentiality, where almost four billion people, or more than 60 per cent, of the world's current population live, and also the largest nominal gross domestic product (GDP) of all continents when measured in purchasing power parity (PPP). The task of this chapter is to unravel the characteristics of lifelong learning practice and theory in East and Southeast Asia. Among the many countries in these regions, I selected seven countries – China, Japan, Korea, Hong Kong, Singapore, Thailand, and the Philippines – all of which are almost or already into the development stage of being newly industrialized countries (NICs). In this chapter, I am going to show what the lifelong learning system means in the Asian context and how it has been recently established. Especially, I am going to focus on the changes before and after the Asian Economic Crisis of 1997–8. While experiencing economic crises in various stages in the 1990s, each country accelerated the transformation of traditional adult continuing education towards an evolutionary model of lifelong learning in which schooling and indigenous adult education were merged to formulate a new type of national learning system.

# Lifelong learning emerging as a system

## *A scenario*

The lifelong learning discourse incessantly invents new codes of education system that challenge the old educational order of schools and universities in Asia as well as in other regions. As Rinne noted, 'the principle of lifelong learning challenges many of the principles of the older school system' (1998: 117–18). It changes the ways in which borders of education are placed, learning activities are selected and organized, and the learning outcomes are produced and exchanged in the labour market. The learning market, combined with labour market, produces particular modes of learning society or a new platform of lifelong learning practices, in which the foundation of public education is seriously undermined. In so doing, as Schuetze nicely puts it, lifelong learning changes its focus from a somewhat idealist reform model to a human capital based model, and 'this shift from welfare state to market rule is a main plank of the dominant neo-liberal agenda' (2006: 302). The role of traditional schools as academic fortresses, including education providers, learning resources, definition of qualifications, etc., is being reformulated to maximize the degree of exchange and accumulation to fit into the capital forms.

To put it simply, while education in the life-world is non-formal by nature, education as 'system' has begun with a part of formal initial education. Education and learning as part of a social system try to adapt the dominant code of social reproduction and expand their territory as do the living creatures in the wilderness, continuously. So schooling expands the new territories in two dimensions: its 'lifelong' dimension expands parts of initial education into adult continuing education and integrates them into a continuous learning sequence, while its 'lifewide' dimension extends the realm of the education system beyond the formal, and absorbs the non-formal and informal areas in an integrated space of a socially manageable learning system (see Figure 40.1).

When the frame of lifelong learning was adapted into a nationwide educational reform process, the following key aspects accompanied it:

- The knowledge economy and newly established employment contract rituals require new modes of education and labour market training, in which entrepreneurs criticize traditional schools and urge them to reform.
- The terminology of 'lifelong learning' is becoming popular among the business sector, which gradually supersedes the old way of educational classifications and systematic conceptualization.
- At a state level, legal foundations and administrative government structures are invented to support the rationality of the practice. The notion of human resource development takes the central position in the lifelong learning system.
- In lifelong learning, educational demand rapidly increases towards higher education, both formal and non-formal, or as part of initial or continuing education. Most of the increase is owed to private universities that sensitively interconnect with the professional labour market.
- In lifewide learning, formal and non-formal initial education are interlocking and overlapping, thus influencing each other, to create new credit recognition and qualification systems such as the National Qualification Framework (NQF).
- In turn, school is under serious pressure to transform; for example, the Organization for Economic Cooperation and Development (OECD)'s scenarios for the future of schooling by expansion and fusion. The subject-based school curriculum and qualification systems are significantly under criticism from the competence-based approach.

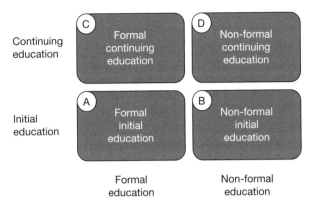

*Figure 40.1* Lifelong learning matrix 1.

- The whole processes are progressed under the global knowledge capitalism that requires neo-liberal market policies to accept the core principle of lifelong learning and adult continuing education. While the states contribute to legal foundation and administrative bodies, the roles of employers and individuals are increasing under the global learning market in decision making and financing.
- The prior labour market policies that used to be a part of the public sector are destructured and restructured under the neo-liberal lifelong learning policy. Also, adult education provision increasingly is seen as a strategic investment. In this context, private education providers began to play the key roles in most countries.

## Looking at the realities of Asia

### Seven countries

East Asian history has witnessed the influence of China on its neighbouring countries in a variety of dimensions. In particular, China, Korea and Japan have long shared a cultural heritage, in which the influence of Chinese characters is fundamental, even though Korea and Japan already had their own oral language and invented alphabets. Of course, Hong Kong and Singapore are a part of Chinese heritage combined with British colonial experience. Southeast Asian countries are somewhat differentiated in cultural heritage.

In terms of economic structure, Thailand, the Philippines and China are rapidly changing the economic structure from agriculture-oriented to manufacture-oriented. While China and Thailand rely extremely upon foreign direct investment (FDI), the Philippines are suffering from a lack of it because of the political unrest. Table 40.1 is composed of several different sources of information: the Human Development Index (HDI) (United Nations Development Program) of 2001, GDP data of 1999, and UNESCO enrolment data of 2000. Some data were not available and have been adapted from different years.

### The learning ecosystem of the countries

The lifelong learning system constructs its architecture upon the foundation of the formal education system. As Brennan indicated, non-formal education is closely related to formal

461

Table 40.1 The economic and educational structure of the chosen countries

| Country | World ranking (2001) | HDI value (2001) | GDP in sectors (1999) | | | Education index (2001) | Enrolment by ISCED level (2000) | | | |
| | | | Agriculture | Industry | Service | | ISCED 1 | ISCED 2 | ISCED 3 | ISCED 5 & 6 |
| --- | --- | --- | --- | --- | --- | --- | --- | --- | --- | --- |
| Japan | 9 | 0.928 | 2.0 | 35.0 | 63.0 | 0.93 | 101 | 103 | 101 | 47 |
| Korea | 27 | 0.875 | 5.6 | 41.4 | 53.0 | 0.95 | 98 | 95 | 100 | 73 |
| Hong Kong | 24 | 0.88 | 0.1 | 14.3 | 85.6 | 0.83 | 106 | 95 | 67** | 30> |
| Singapore | 26 | 0.876 | 0.0 | 30.0 | 70.0 | 0.87 | 103** | 92** | 39** | 20** |
| Thailand | 66 | 0.757 | 13.0 | 40.0 | 47.0 | 0.84 | 95 | 70* | 54* | 34* |
| Philippines | 70 | 0.749 | 20.0 | 32.0 | 48.0# | 0.91 | 113* | 81* | 65* | 31* |
| China | 87 | 0.718 | 14.7 | 52.3 | 33.0 | 0.8 | 118* | 84 | 39 | 8 |

Notes: # data of 1998; * data of 2001; ** data of 1991; > data of 2003. ISCED stands for International Standard Classification of Education.

Sources: HDI (UNDP) (2001); GDP data (-999); UNESCO enrolment data (2000).

education in various ways and reflects its shadow of it (1997: 187). Several characteristics can be drawn from the basic features of formal education.

First, Korea and Japan satisfy most demands for primary, secondary and tertiary education through formal education. Especially, higher education in Korea (73 per cent in 2000) absorbs the demands for higher continuing education. It is, nevertheless, partly 'diploma disease' that is the most serious problem in the learning ecosystem. As Alberici (1998) noted paradoxically, the future of lifelong education lies in a fundamental renewal of the role and function of 'formal' educational systems, in order to eradicate the diploma disease symptoms. Non-formal education in this context plays a less crucial role in complementing the lack of formal initial education. The expected role of lifelong learning will be how to diversify the directions of school-centred learning needs to go beyond the boundaries.

Second, differently from Japan and Korea, all the other countries control, intentionally or unintentionally, enrolment at ISCED 3 level, which produces a more direct and central role for non-formal education system in the lifelong parameter. The Philippines and Thailand depend on the community learning centres under the Non-formal Education Department, while Singapore and Hong Kong are using vocational training centres to embrace the demands. The colonial legacy, in part, should be one of the significant considerations in setting conditions for creating the national lifelong learning system. In Singapore and Hong Kong, the chances for regular schooling and higher education were strictly confined to the legacy of British colonialism and they had to find alternative ways to cater for the shortage for knowledge-intensive industries. It was not until the year 1988 that the Hong Kong government changed the basic policy orientation of higher education, under which the previously elite-oriented universities and polytechnics embraced more of the mass population in the realm of higher education opportunity, but this, in fact, still seems to be struggling to find ways of doing so. The long history of Spanish colonialization of the Philippines, which reflects the Latin American situation and social movements from the grassroots, cannot be underestimated when considering the future development of education systems in the Philippines.

Third, the rapid increase in the demand for higher education is a key issue, especially for the private universities. Korea already had more than 80 per cent of the private colleges and universities. The surplus universities in Korea and Japan are under structural adjustment in order to accept more adult continuing learners. Singapore and China, for different reasons, keep to a strictly elitist hierarchy in educational stratification, which is now turning in the other direction by employing private higher education systems. China is one of the most rapidly growing countries in the higher education sector since the user-fee policy was adopted (3 per cent in 1991 to 20 per cent in 2005). In Hong Kong and Singapore, the contrast between the elitist academic track and the mass non-formal vocational track can characterize the major feature of the lifelong learning system architecture. Polytechnics and Institutes of Technical Education (ITEs) are targeting the population who are trying to obtain post-secondary diplomas in vocational areas, and some upward social mobility.

While initial and formal education were the result of global transplantation adopting a universal code of typical schooling, such as the academic credit award system and the equivalent learning outcome recognition system (Boli *et al.*, 1985), non-formal and adult education are rather different: they have their own local authenticity and tradition. Most of all, they have a long historical context of adult education, non-formal education and community education regardless of the universal code of the formal school system. Non-formal education before the discourse of lifelong learning was the battleground of ideological contestations mostly driven by non-governmental organizations (NGOs) using political and social movement activism. For example, the political democratization movements and labour unionism in Korea, Japan, Thailand and the Philippines fertilized the soil of the indigenous learning ecosystem.

In fact, non-formal education in this region has historically unique and authentic terminologies. Since the early twentieth centuries, Korea, Japan and China shared the presupposition that education can consist of three domains: school education, social education and family education. Among them, the terminology of 'social education' was adapted by the social reformists to bring modernity with along with the political consciousness of the grassroots. While China officially coined the term worker-peasant education, instead of social education, under Mao's communist regime, Korea and Japan still used it. Since 1985 China began to apply the new concept of 'adult education' with the 'economic open door' policy and double-digit real GDP growth accompanied the first wave of FDI into China, and non-state enterprises started to develop, which needed to reform the former worker-peasant education into a new form of adult education (Makino, 2001). In Hong Kong and Singapore, with their British heritage, the term adult education was mostly used to refer to adult basic education and vocational technical education. The notion of non-formal education in Southeast Asian Countries such as Thailand and the Philippines comes under the influence of UNESCO's Education for All (EFA) project.

However, while non-formal education in most countries pertains to an emancipatory and collective identity, the newly emerging post-industrial global capitalism, with the support of a knowledge-based economy, tries to fully leverage lifelong learning for maximizing the value of knowledge workers as well as for minimizing the discontent of the unemployed who are continuously expelled from the labour market (Holford et al., 1998). Considering that the public foundation of vocational training and professional continuing education was relatively less developed and mostly privatized, the simple replacement of the non-formal tradition with new neo-liberal lifelong learning practice constitutes a serious ecological change in the realm of learning in this region. For example, vocational training in Japan and Korea has been mostly dependent upon the internal labour market, in that further education and training of employees were taken care of by the firms. With the increasing FDI, countries like China, Thailand or the Philippines, where the new workforces are primarily in short supply, will easily rely on the private training business sector for low-skill workers. In lifelong learning embarked on under a market-oriented human resource development concept with the banner of knowledge workers' self-directed learning, motivation turns out to be the obligation of learners themselves rather than that of the providers or employers, for the beneficiaries of the earned outcome that the learning produced became recognized to be the learners themselves. According to Daswani:

> In many countries in the region, the basic philosophy of adult education is based on economic development. Consequently, most programmes emphasise skill, technical and vocational training . . . Most adult education programmed tend to be measured against the formal school requirements. Indeed, many programmes prescribe formal school equivalence for evaluation of adult education programme. This formal school syndrome often constricts the non-formal character of adult education and tends to turn these programmes into poor copies of formal school courses.
>
> (2002: 47)

## The Asian Economic Crisis and the lifelong learning front line

### The impact of the Asian Economic Crisis

During the past few decades, third world education has developed significantly in formal as well as non-formal areas. However, the prevailing global conservatism since the 1980s gave

*Table 40.2* Gross national product growth rates of selected Asian countries

| Country | 1970 | 1980 | 1990 | 1996 | 1997 | 1998 |
|---|---|---|---|---|---|---|
| Japan | 10.76 | 2.66 | 5.05 | 5.32 | 1.61 | −2.66 |
| Korea, Rep. | 7.20 | −3.92 | 9.53 | 6.70 | 4.81 | −6.64 |
| Hong Kong | 9.51 | 10.37 | 3.40 | 4.49 | 5.26 | −5.13 |
| Singapore | 12.64 | 6.33 | 8.85 | 8.40 | 9.02 | 1.49 |
| Thailand | 9.62 | 5.34 | 11.22 | 5.02 | −1.10 | −7.69 |
| Philippines | 2.75 | 4.63 | 3.79 | 7.24 | 5.30 | 0.07 |
| China | 19.4 | 7.80 | 3.80 | 9.60 | 8.80 | 7.80 |

Source: World Bank, *Social Development Index*, 2000.

Asia as well as other third world continents serious challenges in cutting back the foundations of economic development and the welfare system. This period of austerity and restructuring caused a slow-down in educational expansion, and has sometimes led to a reverse trend. Diminishing national and regional resources have also contributed to a decline in the quality of educational opportunities by forcing a reallocation to more short-term needs. Structural adjustment programmes imposed by World Bank and the International Monetary Fund (IMF) drastically forced developing countries to draw resources away from public expenditure, especially from education (Atchoarena and Hite, 2001: 201).

As seen in Table 40.2, the years 1997–8 were a nightmare to most of the Asian countries. In these fiscal years, most Asian countries suffered from a negative economic growth rate. Although not negative in numbers, so to speak, Singapore and the Philippines also experienced a drastic drop in the GDP growth rate. While Western Europe and especially North America enjoyed unprecedented economic prosperity, the Asian economy in this decade, or specifically in this period, was bombarded. Education and other social welfare domains formed the first group of victims.

It is an irony that lifelong learning gained significant attention at that very moment and in its aftermath. The key phenomenon was a high unemployment rate and the subsequent need for economic structural adjustment. The transition from industrial to information or knowledge economy became an urgent issue. The crisis led the IMF and the World Bank to intervene in national policies not only in economic but also social dimensions, especially education policies.

Two severe issues were put to the decision makers: the drastic increase of uncontrollable structural unemployment and the urgent need to restructure the national economy to cope with the global challenge. One of the needs was nationwide retraining plans so that excluded workers could re-enter the labour market. The other need was changing the focus of the previous labour-intensive manufacturing sector towards a labour-efficient, if not yet knowledge-intensive, service sector.

The discourse of lifelong learning attracted the policy makers. Interestingly, Europe had already promoted Lifelong Learning Year in 1996, with the two important global documents, the Delors Report from UNESCO and the Education for All Report from the OECD in the same year. The newly invited lifelong learning discourses were indeed waiting for a moment to be implemented in practice, and the global economic crisis gave them this chance.

## *Responses in the realm of lifelong learning*

In fact, most of the Asian countries in this period had to face the significant necessity of economic restructuring, which also had to accompany education reform and labour market reconditioning. In one sense, the discourse of lifelong learning was merely political propaganda to turn the responsibility for the economic crisis towards the educational scapegoats. However, the reality was even more brutal and the consecutive sudden bankruptcies of major companies and massive unemployment pushed the landscape of education systems towards adopting anything new, if not exactly lifelong learning.

Korea was one of the gravest victims of the crisis, and the experience accelerated the speed of its education reform. The Lifelong Education Law was enacted in 1999 and in the same year the new Minister of Education initiated the structural transformation of the Ministry of Education, which was later changed to the Ministry of Education and Human Resource Development (MOEHRD), intending to integrate lifelong learning into the framework of national human resource development.

Although with some time gap, Japan had also experienced, about a decade before, what Korea suffered in 1997–8 . From 1988 Japan fell into the 'long-term depression' or 'lost ten years', a down-turn of the 'bubble economy' from the middle of 1980s that lasted until 2002. Significant reformations of lifelong learning happened in that period of time. During that decade, the Japanese lifetime employment system was undermined and the tradition of in-house training for employees lost ground. Since the collapse of the system, occupational skills development had been left outside the remit of companies. The concept of lifelong learning was focused in this respect, while the term 'social education' was still used for adult liberal education. During that period, several significant changes in the legal and administrative systems of education occurred, including: (1) The Social Education Bureau changed its title to the Lifelong Learning Bureau and (2) in 1990 the Lifelong Learning Promotion Law was enacted.

The response of the two city-nations, Singapore and Hong Kong, was somewhat controversial. The impact on Singapore was not small, even if not severe. In 1998, like other Asian countries, Singapore vigorously changed the Ministry of Labour to the Ministry of Manpower, and the following year the well-known lifelong learning policy called 'Manpower 21' was announced. As Kumar mentioned:

> Singapore's approach to lifelong learning is pragmatic and rational. It is one of the economic drivers used by policy makers to enhance Singapore's competitiveness and is viewed as an antidote against unemployment. With the emergence of a more integrated and interdependent global economy, the premium placed on ideas and continuous learning becomes critical to an individual, organization and the country.
>
> (2004: 559)

Even though the year of 1997 was a nightmare for Hong Kong, there were no particular changes directly related to the challenge. In fact, Hong Kong had to suffer the Asian crisis as soon as it was handed over to Mainland China. According to Kennedy (2004), the handover government hardly handled it aiming for a soft landing, and lifelong learning in this context was deployed for mitigating the pressing political dissent raised against the government:

> However, to view recent Hong Kong education policy just in terms of an apparent convergence with global trends would be to neglect the ways in which the discourse of lifelong learning has been tactically deployed to serve local political agendas . . . an

executive-led administration to demonstrate 'performance legitimacy' – through major policy reforms – in the absence of (democratic) political legitimacy. It is against this political background that the strategic deployment of a 'lifelong learning' discourse needs to be seen.

(2004: 589)

Thailand had also experienced the most severe consequences of the 1997 Crisis along with Korea. In 1999, the same year in which the Korean government passed the Lifelong Education Law, the Thai government also passed a new National Education Act, which reformulated the education system as lifewide as well as lifelong. It was lifewide because not only the Ministry of Education but also other training activities, either formal or non-formal, under other ministries were involved in weaving the national fabric of the educational system with credit and diplomas. It was also lifelong because the law encompassed pre-primary up to adult continuing education in one framework. Along with the policy change:

> In 1999 the Thai Government passed The National Education Act under which 'education' was defined as the learning process for personal and social development, through the imparting of knowledge, practice, training, transmission of culture, enhancement of academic progress, and building a body of knowledge by creating a learning environment and society with available factors conducive to continuous lifelong learning.
>
> (Somtrakook, 2002: 33)

China also experienced a serious challenge, although it was relatively less directly touched by the Asian Crisis, since at that time Chinese foreign currency policy was not market-led. However, China was urged to cool the overheating economy's GDP growth rate and create a 'soft landing' for the economy. From 14 per cent in 1992, it constantly decreased to 7.1 per cent in 1999. In this respect it was the right time for China to make structural adjustments in the education sector, and the notion of lifelong learning, in touch with the fast economic changes, was put forward in this respect. Directly after the Asian Crisis, the Chinese Ministry of Education issued the document *Education Promoting Action Towards the 21st Century* (1999), which brought forward the concept of 'constructing a lifelong learning system in a knowledge-based society'. It also prescribed that 'China would establish a lifelong learning system by 2010 to develop a qualified workforce for the National Knowledge Creative Project and for the modernization of the country' (Wang *et al.*, 2006).

The Philippines was a little bit different in its dealing with the impact of Crisis. Compared with other countries, the Philippines had a relatively weak formal education system. According to the Philippine National Development Plan for Children (PNDPC), among six-year-olds, 95.26 per cent will be enrolled in Grade 1 but only 69.51 per cent of them will complete Grade 6. The number will further dwindle to 66.24 per cent in high school and, eventually, only 45.02 per cent will graduate from high school. Survey figures for 1990 reveal that 17 per cent or 2 million school-age children were outside the formal school system. A large number of the 2.8 million illiterate people in 1990 were children who were not enrolled in schools. The situation was not much improved. An interesting change was seen in the amended Basic Education Act of 2001, which covers elementary, secondary and non-formal education. In this Act, the role of formal and non-formal education systems share a partnership; for example, Section 3(c) states, 'The purposes and objectives of this Act are to make schools and learning centres the most important vehicle for the teaching and learning of national values'; hereby 'learning centre' means a physical space to house learning resources and facilities of a learning programme for out-of-school youth and adults (Section 4(h)).

In sum, the global economic environmental changes look to stimulate the new enactment or amendment of education legal systems for the foundation of lifelong learning systems. Korea and Japan had explicit laws embracing the concept of lifelong learning, while Thailand enacted the new National Education Act, which, in fact, covered the idea and practice of lifelong learning as a whole. China, although not having a separate law, also put lifelong education at the forefront of the National Education Law. The small city nations of Hong Kong and Singapore raised national strategic banners as policy bandwagons, such as 'Manpower 21' (Singapore) and 'Education Blueprint' (Hong Kong), instead of establishing independent lifelong learning legislation. Meanwhile, the Philippines still rely heavily on restricted local networks of non-formal education.

Also, school policy that was mostly under the sole control of the Ministry of Education was urged to be interlinked with labour market policy, in which interministrial cooperation was observed to broaden the focus from formal education to also encompass non-formal and informal education and its relationship with labour-related ministries in Japan, Singapore and Hong Kong. Thailand, Hong Kong, Singapore, Japan and Korea explicitly adapted new policies to deal with efficient and effective human resource development and its management. Under the auspices of the Lifelong Learning Promotion Law, the Japanese Ministry of Education, Culture and Science began to work with the Ministry of Trade and Industry. Singapore and Hong Kong had already established partnerships between the Ministries of Education and Manpower (in Singapore), and the Education and Labour Departments (in Hong Kong). In Korea, although not allied with the Ministry of Labour, the Ministry of Education itself was transformed into the Ministry of Education and Human Resource Development to cope with new demands.

If NGOs and NPOs were the major partners for previous non-formal education practice, working with government literacy campaigns and self-help learning centres, now the new circumstances brought the private education business sector into an important partnership with lifelong learning or human resource development. Private education institutions, which in many cases apply distance learning as a major means of knowledge delivery, appeared and gradually acquired a dominant position in Hong Kong, Korea, Singapore and Japan. Especially, new private higher education institutions with or without accreditations began to play a key role in increasing higher education enrolments everywhere, especially in China, Thailand, the Philippines and Korea.

## Conclusion

In this chapter, recent lifelong learning system-building in seven selected Asian countries has been traced in the context of the Asian economic crisis in the 1990s and their response to it. In this chapter I examined two aspects: global universalism and local authenticism. In the global dimension, I found that drastic challenges to economic foundations provided a unanimous crucial momentum to implement the discourse of lifelong learning, if neo-liberal, with strong governmental support. I also found in the local dimension that lifelong learning in the life-world, in which was embedded the authentic mode of local living, was seriously colonized by the dominance of lifelong learning discourse. More than ever, formal education systems with signal effect on the labour market continuously expand education markets beyond school and universities towards the realm of non-formal and adult continuing education. However, I am suspicious of who the real beneficiaries are. What happened to the 'education in the life-world' that cannot be transformed into market values and the collective memories of community empowerment and popular education in particular?

## Note

This chapter is a revision of an article previously published in 2007, namely Han, S. (2007) 'Asian lifelong learning: a task revisited', *Asia Pacific Education Review* 8: 343–55.

## References

Alberici, A. (1998) 'Towards the learning society', in J. Holford, P. Jarvis and C. Griffin (eds) *International Perspective on Lifelong Learning*, London: Kogan Page.

Atchoarena, D. and Hite, S. (2001) 'Lifelong learning policies in low development context: an African perspective', in D. Aspin, S. Chapman, M. Hatton and Y. Sawano (eds) *International Handbook of Lifelong Learning*, London: Kluwer Academic Publishers, pp. 201–28.

Boli, J., Ramirez, F.O. and Meyer, J.W. (1985) 'Explaining the origins and expansion of mass education', *Comparative Education Review* 29(2):145–70.

Brennan, B. (1997) 'Reconceptualizing non-formal education', *International Journal of Lifelong Education* 16(3): 185–200.

Burton-Jones, A. (999) *Knowledge Capitalism: Business, work, and learning in the new economy*, Oxford: Oxford University Press.

Daswani, C.J. (2002) 'Evolution of adult learning in the Asian region,' in M. Singh (ed.) *Institutionalising Lifelong Learning*, Hamburg: UNESCO Institute for Education, pp. 43–8.

Holford, J., Jarvis, P. and Griffin, C. (eds) (1998) *International Perspectives on Lifelong Learning*, London: Kogan Page.

Kennedy, P. (2004) 'The politics of "lifelong learning" in post-1997 Hong Kong', *International Journal of Lifelong Education* 23(6): 589–624.

Kumar, P. (2004) 'Lifelong learning in Singapore: where are we now?', *International Journal of Lifelong Education* 23(6): 559–68.

Makino, A. (2001) 'Trends in and objectives of adult higher education in China', in D. Aspin, J. Chapman, M. Hatton and Y. Sawano (eds) *International Handbook of Lifelong Learning*, London: Kluwer Academic Publishers, pp. 285–316.

Organization for Economic Cooperation and Development (OECD) (2004) *The Schooling Scenarios: Background OECD papers*, International Schooling for Tomorrow Forum, Toronto, June 6–8.

Rinne, R. (1998) 'From labour to learn: the limits of labour society and the possibilities of learning society', *International Journal of Lifelong Education* 17(2): 108–20.

Schuetze, H.G. (2006) 'International concepts and agendas of lifelong learning', *Compare* 36(3): 289–306.

Somtrakool, K. (2002) 'Lifelong learning for a modern learning society', in C. Medel-Añonuevo (ed.) *Integrating Lifelong Learning Perspectives*, Paris: UNESCO, pp. 111–16.

Wang, A., Song, G. and Kang, F. (2006) 'Promoting a lifelong learning society in China: the attempts by Tsinghua University', *Higher Education Management and Policy* 18(2): 1–16.

# 41

# The changing face of adult education in Australia[1]

## Mark Tennant and Roger Morris

It is very difficult to describe briefly and simply the history and current provision of adult education in Australia. This is partly due to the constitutional arrangements in Australia, which is a federation made up of six states and two territories: a federation in which the principal responsibility for education, including adult education, remains with the states and territories. The best and most complete way to describe adult education in Australia would be to write eight separate accounts. Nevertheless there are commonalities among the states that have been forged by a common history, a common set of issues and a common federal government that is increasingly intent on establishing a national approach to education and training.

In recent years there have been two principal drivers for a national approach to education: an economic concern for Australia to develop a more highly skilled and adaptable workforce if it is to compete effectively in global markets; and a social concern with providing opportunities for an increasingly diverse population. Education is more than ever seen as an instrument of government economic and social policy and as having the potential to transform the economic and social fabric of Australian life. Contemporary adult education in Australia needs to be understood within this context and thus seen as part of a range of changes that are occurring in education: increasing school retention rates; mass participation in higher education; the development of a more open education and training 'market' with a range of providers; increasing links between different educational sectors; a growing emphasis on vocational outcomes; more flexible pathways of learning and routes to skill formation; and a growing emphasis on quality, accountability and common standards.

## The scope of adult education

Arguably, at a global level, the term 'adult education' is becoming outmoded, and this is also true in Australia. Partly this is the result of adult education being successful, in the sense that there are more opportunities for adult learning across the lifespan than ever before. Adult education, reconceived as 'adult learning' or 'lifelong learning', is thus ubiquitous, and no longer recognisable as a separate entity, as a separate 'sector' of education, or as a social movement, as it once was. Indeed the professional association representing adult education in Australia is now called Adult Learning Australia, instead of the Australian Association of Adult Education, as it once was. This is testimony to a shift in concern with adult learning, wherever it occurs: in the workplace, in vocational education and training, and in higher education. In the higher education sector, for example, the majority of commencing students are now adults, which is very different from the situation in the middle of the twentieth century (41 per cent of commencing students are now aged 25 or over and 62 per cent are over 20 years of age (DEST, 2005)).

Ironically, adult education is most recognisable when it is a marginal activity: when it is anti-establishment, anti-vested interests, anti-status quo and for the underprivileged and dispossessed either directly – through education for direct action, or indirectly – through a utopian vision of education for a democratic egalitarian society. When adult education becomes institutionalised and mainstreamed as it has in Australia and elsewhere, by definition, it loses these revered qualities – it becomes co-opted and compromised to serve the interests of the state and the corporations who benefit from globalisation. On this logic adult education can never achieve its goals – it evaporates as a movement once its agenda is institutionalised.

But of course this is only part of the story because, in addition to the lofty ideals of participative democracy and social justice, adult education has also been long concerned with workforce preparation, economic competitiveness and even national pride. While it is no doubt true that the majority of adult learning is no longer identified as 'adult education' (e.g. adults learning in the workplace or adults studying at university), it is also true that there remains a great deal of provision that is labelled and recognised by all participants as 'adult education'. As such, it is important to understand the antecedents of what counts as 'adult education' today.

## The origins and development of Australian adult education

The earliest attempts at adult education in the Australian colonies were the missionary activities directed at 'reforming' the convicts (Australia was first settled as a penal colony) and at 'saving' the Aborigines. These attempts have been described as high-minded, wrong-headed and almost completely unsuccessful. Within a decade of the foundation of the original institutes in Scotland, the first mechanics' institutes were operating in Australia. Though they may not have completely met their proponents' high expectations, they were a powerful force for adult education and popular culture in the nineteenth-century colonies. Right from the beginnings of public education, colonial elementary schools offered night classes for undereducated adults.

From the 1870s, as local industry grew and public infrastructure was laid down, technical education was established and began to grow, first as part of the wider mechanics' institute movement. By the 1890s, Australian universities had established, on the British model, Extension Boards and were offering extensive programmes of extra-mural classes. Other, more uniquely Australian, forms of university adult education were also evolving at this time. These forms, designed to overcome the problem of distance and to meet popular egalitarian norms, included the late afternoon part-time class for the working adult and correspondence courses of study for the rural dweller.

As the labour movement grew and strengthened, education in political and industrial matters became an important component of informal adult education. The first formal involvement of the trade union movement in adult education came with the formation of the various state Workers' Education Associations (WEAs) under the auspices of the local trades and labour councils and the local universities. The WEA model soon became the standard model for the provision of 'official' adult education in Australia. During the Second World War, the AAES

(Australian Army Education Service) provided a useful example of what a well-resourced comprehensive adult education service could accomplish.

After the war and, in the spirit of post-war reconstruction, there was a renewed interest in adult education and what it could achieve. Some state boards were established to manage adult education. The growth of post-war immigration led to the establishment of the Adult Migrant Education Service (AMES) to provide instruction in the English language. The adult night public schools were revamped as Evening Colleges, providing general education and leisure-time activities for adult learners. As the baby boom developed and suburbia spread, the parent education movement grew, providing an interesting new dimension to the adult education mix. In 1964, a UNESCO regional seminar on adult education was held in Australia. Out of this seminar grew ASPBAE (the Asian South Pacific Bureau of Adult Education). As the 1960s proceeded, formal higher educational opportunities for adults continued to expand as Australia pioneered many initiatives in mature age entry to higher education institutions. As a result of this trend, traditional university non-credit adult education came to be increasingly under question.

The 1970s was a very lively decade in which Australian society changed direction. The new Labor government was strongly reformist in nature and nowhere were the possibilities for change more apparent than in education. For adult education, the more significant of these changes were the strong development of a new community-grounded adult education and a complete renovation and repositioning of technical education, which hereafter was to be called TAFE (Technical and Further Education). AMES became more localised and responsive to learner needs. Control of the Evening Colleges passed from the state educational bureaucracy to local community management. The Neighbourhood Houses and Learning Centres movement emerged as an offshoot of the broader women's movement. In 1975, the Trade Union Training Authority (TUTA) was established as a federally funded statutory authority to provide, promote and coordinate trade union education. At about the same time the independent community controlled Aboriginal education movement, as exemplified by Tranby Aboriginal College, emerged as a powerful force in building indigenous self-determination. There was also at this time an increasing interest in the initial preparation and continuing professional development of adult educators and a number of university and college-based courses of study were established.

Thus, from about the mid-1980s, a critical mass of issues – regarding lifelong learning, re-training, re-skilling, second chance learning, access and equity – came together to create a very positive climate for adult education. Increasingly, government came to see adult education as a fourth sector of education, which could be used to achieve important governmental priorities. However, such government recognition was not without its drawbacks. In particular, over the last 20 years or so, adult education can be construed as part of a broader government agenda to establish an 'education market' in which a range of education providers compete for both government and private funds. The adult education sector was also drawn into offering many more formally accredited courses leading to qualification under the National Qualifications Framework.

Today, adult education comprises a range of formal and non-formal (non-award) educational programmes for adults provided by educational institutions, industry, commerce, government departments, welfare agencies, professional associations, community-based organisations and voluntary groups. It addresses identifiable national priorities, such as increased levels of literacy, the formation of adaptable and multi-skilled workers, the creation of an equitable multicultural society, and the promotion of public debate and awareness of key social issues in areas such as civic education, health, indigenous rights and the environment. It includes basic education, community development, workplace learning, literacy, English as a Second Language (ESL), liberal and general education, public education and indigenous education.

## The policy framework for adult education

Over much of its history, adult education in Australia has operated without the benefit of formal legislative foundation or overt policy. Governments have seemed to believe that adult education was a good idea as long the demand on public funds was small. Up until about 25 years ago, public policy was informed by what has been called the 'Great Tradition' view of adult education as exemplified by Whitelock in his book *The Great Tradition: A history of adult education in Australia* (1974). He emphasised the continuity in the Australian context of the nineteenth-century English educational idea – the ideal of the 'liberally educated person', the 'cultured adult' – as the ultimate outcome of successful adult education. Of course such education is not necessarily devoid of important social and other purposes, but there is a strong insistence that the major purpose must be a liberal one and that adult education should be non-vocational and non-credit. Advocates of this point of view like to separate adult education as a specific form of educational provision from 'the education of adults', which simply comprises all educational activities undertaken by adults.

We argue that this point of view presents an incomplete picture of the history of adult education in Australia. Further, that this incomplete picture retarded the development of a body of Australian adult education scholarly literature firmly rooted in local practices. In particular, the great tradition view failed to give due emphasis to the more working-class, more radical, more indigenous and more practical aspects of that development. Australian adult education, as it developed, was more than just a remote branch of British adult education, just as Australians were more than 'Austral Britons'. It was not merely English adult education with better weather.

Nevertheless the view persisted, largely because many academic staff in university adult and continuing education (usually referred to as ACE) departments held on to the English liberal tradition. These university-based adult educators stressed the similarities and continuities with the 'mother country' and overlooked important local initiatives and developments. Today this situation has changed quite dramatically and much broader definitions of adult education prevail.

Australia does not have a lifelong learning policy as such. Instead there have been a number of national enquiries and consultations with catchy but somewhat demeaning titles, which have had little direct impact on policy or funding (e.g. 'Come in Cinderella', 1991; 'Beyond Cinderella: towards a learning society', 1997; and 'You can too', 2003). In 2002 all states and territories endorsed a 'Ministerial Declaration on Adult and Community Education', which emphasised the importance of learning in building community capacity and the importance of ACE as a pathway to further education and training for 'second chance' learners. But the major thrust has been, not with the ACE sector as such, but with adult learning in the context of the range of education available.

In more recent years, economic and social issues have come together in such a way as to prompt a closer governmental involvement in adult education, broadly defined. There have been a number of reports on post-compulsory education and the economy. All of these have addressed the need for a fundamental rethinking of the education and training system. The overarching idea to emerge from these reports was that education, training and work should fit together better so that the acquisition of useful knowledge and skill, no matter where it occurred, would be encouraged, recognised and rewarded.

Throughout the education system there is now more scope for having learning recognised wherever it occurs: in schools, in Technical and Further Education colleges, through workplace training, and through private and community-based education providers. Indeed, the level of participation by Australian adults in education and training is very high (Karmel, 2004: 18). A recent international study places Australia in the second highest grouping of nations (of four groupings) in terms of overall participation rates in adult education and training (Desjardins *et al.*, 2006). The participation rate for Australians over 40 is 6 per cent – well above the average for OECD countries. The next highest are the UK at 5 per cent, Sweden at 3.3 per cent and New Zealand at 2.9 per cent (DEST, 2003).

Studies have shown that almost 80 per cent of Australian adults have participated in adult education activities at some time in their life. It is also reported that each year about 25 per cent of all adults (about three million) participate in some form of further education or training. About half of all adult education classes taken each year are employer-provided or work-related. Women make greater use of the community providers than men – 75 per cent as opposed to 25 per cent (McIntyre and Crombie, 1995). However, men are more likely than women to participate in courses run by employers or related to work. Men and women make about equal use of courses provided by formal educational institutions.

A full range of providers, from private teachers, through voluntary associations, community groups and social movements, to statutory authorities and government departments, carries out the actual delivery of adult education. Generally the nature of the provision determines the degree of public funding provided. Labour market programmes, some other forms of vocational education and training (VET), many second chance and other access programmes are funded by government. General adult education, leisure learning and hobby programmes are usually offered on a full-fee user pays basis. The state or territory agency with responsibility for adult education maintains control through its management of the quality assurance processes that determine the distribution of the limited funding that the government provides to meet basic infrastructure costs and the needs of its target groups. Thus, through the expenditure of quite small amounts of money, the agency can generate a considerable amount of adult education, the direct costs of which are largely borne by the learner.

Traditionally, in Australia, people have entered the vocation of adult educator from some other occupation, often, at least initially, in a part-time or voluntary capacity. Many hold long-standing occupational qualifications, which are usually regarded as adequate for their new role. Often the volunteers and/or part-timers do not possess any relevant formal qualifications. However, about 20 universities provide courses of professional education leading to formal awards for the educators of adults – ranging in level from the undergraduate diploma to the doctorate – involving almost 4,000 students and about 150 full-time equivalent academics. In the past, the study of adult education at the university level in Australia has been overly dependent on the work of British and North American scholars. Today, this situation has begun to change as graduate study grows and local research and scholarly writing increase.

## Current provision

There are key providers who have been a sustained part of the adult education landscape for many years: the Evening Colleges, Community Adult Education Centres, Neighbourhood Houses, the Colleges and Institutes of Technical and Further Education, the universities with their continuing education divisions or extra mural programmes, the WEA and the large providers such as the Council of Adult Education in the state of Victoria. The issues too seem to persist: the paucity of government funding for general adult education and for programmes addressing areas of social need, the ongoing debate about the identity of the 'sector', the tension between vocational and 'non-vocational' provision, the tension between volunteerism and professionalisation, and the fight for recognition beyond the mere marginal status in Australian education.

In many ways the narrowness of the 'great tradition' has now given way to a narrow and economically driven version of adult education and training. Despite this, there have been significant initiatives that have grown from local communities concerned with the learning needs of their residents. Examples of such initiatives can be found in a number of partnerships and pathways projects; the concept of the 'learning community'; and activities designed to better involve older men as learners.

In Australia, ACE providers have in recent years been greatly impressed by the potential that working together in partnership offers to amplify their ability to assist learners to find and traverse individual pathways to further learning and development. One such example is the long-term and very successful project conducted by the Local Community Services Association (LCSA) in conjunction with a range of local ACE providers to meet the learning needs of various target groups, such as women returning to paid work, Aboriginal Australians, recent immigrants, the disabled and the long-term unemployed. The results of this project have been reported as follows:

> Over the course of the various partnership projects, mutual understanding between and among the partners grew and the profile of the work done by both within the local community was raised. Most partners reported that they had enhanced their ability to provide appropriate learning opportunities and pathways for marginalised groups. Almost all participants were positive about their experiences with the program. Most participants had identified further steps on individual learning and development pathways. Many had already enrolled in further education and training. Some had even secured paid employment.
>
> (Rooney, 2003: 15–16)

Recent Australian studies have reinforced the importance of the role that the community, as well as the workplace, can play in facilitating and validating adult learning. Community activity, as well as paid work, generates much non-formal and informal learning. The value and currency of this learning, though it may not be endorsed by the formal qualifications system, has important social, community and economic associations, dimensions and values. In many rural communities with limited access to more formal and structured education opportunities, such informal and non-formal learning are likely to be of even greater significance: hence the important negative impact of social exclusion on ongoing adult learning. There is a growing realisation across Australia that there need to be local initiatives to build real community learning as the bedrock foundation for the development of Australia as an inclusive lifelong learning society. There is evidence of this thrust in many local government areas: Albury-Wodonga Learning Community; the Mawson Lakes Learning Community; Hume Global Learning Village; Yarra Ranges Learning Communities; Marion and Salisbury in South Australia; and Lithgow, the Learning City in NSW (see Henderson et al., 2000, for further descriptions).

A wholly Australian phenomenon is the 'sheds movement', which has developed over the last ten years or so. It takes its name from the 'working sheds' evident in many Australian households and predominantly used by men. Today there are over 150 such men's sheds. A diverse range of providers sponsor these sheds, including health care, aged care, churches, war veterans, Aboriginals, and adult and community education organisations. Research by Golding (2006) has demonstrated that, while their origins may be diverse, the sheds can and do provide for older men a space where they can feel at ease and learn by doing, while 'working' with other men. As a group such men have historically been excluded from adult education. As children they had typically received less education and had worked long and hard in manual occupations. Over their lives these men have constructed much of their personal meaning and identity through their work. Now that their working lives are over, participating in the activities of the shed can provide a means for maintaining their identities and a source of new meanings, of social connections and of a continuing capacity to learn and grow.

It is not surprising, given Australia's vast spaces and history of distance education, that many providers have utilised the capabilities of the internet. The Australian government has established an education portal (www.education.gov.au/goved/go/pid/190), which provides an access point for a variety of online courses in the different sectors of education, including ACE. Among the resources in the ACE sector is the Ngapartji Ngapartji Language Course (http://ninti. ngapartji.org). The course is described as follows:

> This online Pitjantjatjara language course enables young Pitjantjatjara speakers from the Alice Springs region to become language tutors through the content that they are making for this site. Language lessons are based on films, radio, flash animation and photography. Each lesson is accompanied by a vocabulary sheet and the lesson content is supplemented by a range of other Pitjantjatjara archival material; songs from the Pitjantjatjara choir, films from the early days of Pitjantjatjara Yankunytjatjara Media (PY Media) and more.
>
> Young Pitjantjatjara speakers, with support from their elders and BighART artists, become Pitjantjatjara language tutors . . . As well as the films, radio, flash animation and photography based language material BighART are exploring mobile phone and podcasting delivery of content.

This is certainly uniquely Australian with its dual focus on indigenous community-building and distance education using the resources of the internet to overcome, ironically, the isolation of the city from rural life. A further glimpse into the community-based nature of this initiative is gained through the promotional material:

> Your tax deductible donation to Ngapartji Ngapartji gives you access to the world's cheapest online language and culture site! This money goes directly to the day to day running of this $1.7m project, which we are hard at work fundraising to be able to create. This income enables us to fuel our old landcruiser, buy tape stock, keep the fridge full, buy crowbars, pay everyone, buy shoes for the cast when we tour and many more crucial costs of running a long term community based project like this.

Other examples of internet-based cooperative arrangements include ACENET and Australian Correspondence Schools (ACS). ACENET is a cooperative of nine ACE providers operating in Victoria. Their website provides details of online courses currently available through ACENET institutions. ACS provide more than 300 vocationally oriented online or correspondence courses in areas such as health and fitness, information technology, business management, agriculture, and hospitality and tourism.

## Directions for the future

The current public rhetoric that surrounds education and training in Australia may present a very upbeat view of the potential for learning throughout life. But the average Australian could be excused for being a little cynical about its actual intent, given recent policies and initiatives (Seddon, 2001). For some of those involved in the public policy arena, lifelong learning for most adults seems to mean only a narrow and rather restricted version of lifelong VET.

Lifelong learning has been largely co-opted by the economic rationalists and is currently being largely redefined in rather narrow instrumentalist terms. As Boshier (2000) wrote, lifelong education, as a concept, always has been seen as lifewide as well as lifelong. It was about the total person not just the employee. It was concerned to democratise education and the wider society so as to eventually create a truly educative learning society for all. However, this 'newer' conception of lifelong learning, as many politicians and bureaucrats see it and use it, is not concerned with the emancipatory project or social justice. Rather, lifelong learning seeks to render invisible very real social conditions and relationships and seems to be directed at creating better lifelong servants of the system. Some, following Bowles and Gintis (1976), would even argue that the success of such individualisation and privatisation is crucial to the survival of contemporary capitalism.

McIntyre (2005) outlines quite nicely some of the needed directions for adult education to recapture some of its original intent as a vehicle for a learning society:

1   There is a need for national policy leadership to give coherence to efforts to promote adult learning.
2   There is a need for an ecological perspective on adult learning, emphasising strategies to facilitate learning in workplaces and communities.
3   There is a need for adult learning to be understood in relation to broad social policy.
4   There is a need for 'learning communities' to be a key focus of provision, especially the formation of partnerships of educational providers, community agencies, local government and employers.

Despite this increasing cynicism, there are still some promising signs. As Saulwick (2001) has argued, Australians, at the personal and local level, are still prepared to be helpful and cooperative. Indeed, there is a growing interest in and concern for local community life and development. Many Australians continue to participate in local activities and organisations. They pitch in and help in times of bushfire, drought and flood and they respond favourably to many community-wide initiatives, such as the Aboriginal Reconciliation initiative and the recent appeal to aid the victims of the Indian Ocean tsunami. Perhaps it is now time to build constructively upon this very real sense of community. The idea of the 'community' as a significant organising principle has long been a feature of adult education as a field of study and as a field of practice. It is an idea that has appeared and reappeared over the years. It is a force that has energised many practical initiatives in the field of practice. But unfortunately it is an idea whose true potential has never been fully realised (Brown, 2000).

The story of adult education, in Australia as elsewhere, has been characterised by a fight for formal recognition. Such recognition (albeit as 'adult learning') has now largely been achieved. The issue is unlikely to be problematic in the future as the boundaries between the sectors of education become ever more fluid and the funding for education is diversified. Lifelong learning will become an increasing reality for many. But there will always remain those who are without access to quality education during the adult years. As ever, it will be these adults that adult education will seek to reach, to include and to empower.

## Note

1    Parts of this chapter have been taken from earlier publications, namely Tennant (2005), Tennant and Morris (2001) and Tennant and Morris (2006).

## References

Boshier, R. (2000) 'Running to win: the contest between lifelong learning and education in Canada', *New Zealand Journal of Adult Learning* 28(2) (November): 6–28.

Bowles, S. and Gintis, H. (1976) *Schooling in Capitalist America: Educational reform and contradictions of economic life*, New York: Basic Books.

Brown, T. (2000) 'Lifelong learning in the community', *Australian Journal of Adult Learning* 40(1) (April): 10–26.

Desjardins, R. Rubenson, K. and Milana, M. (2006) *Unequal Chances to Participate in Adult Learning: International perspectives*, Paris: UNESCO International Institute for Educational Planning.

Department of Education, Science and Training (DEST) (2003) *You Can Too: Adult learning in Australia*, a consultation paper, Canberra: DEST.

—— (2005) *DEST Statistical Publications*, Canberra: DEST.

Golding, B. (2006) 'Shedding light on new spaces for older men in Australia', *Quest* (Newsletter of Adult Learning Australia), 1 (Autumn): 18–20.

Henderson, L., Castles, R., McGrath, M. and Brown, T. (2000) *Learning Around Town: Learning communities in Australia*, Canberra: Adult Learning Australia.

Karmel, P. (2004) *Australia's Approach to Lifelong Learning*, UNESCO International Expert Meeting on TVET, Bonn: NCVER.

McIntyre, J. (2005) *Adult Learning and Australia's Ageing Population*, a policy briefing paper, Canberra: Adult Learning Australia.

—— and Crombie, A. (1995) *Who Are Australia's Adult Learners? Report on ABS population survey monitor data collected for the Australian Association of Adult & Community Education*, Canberra: AAACE.

Rooney, D. (2003) *Partnerships in ACE: Final report to the Board, Adult & Community Education*, Sydney: Local Community Services Association.

Saulwick, J. (2001) 'By-election was a test of trust which all failed', *Sydney Morning Herald*, 16 July.

Seddon, T. (2001) 'Lifelong learning, social capital and capacity building: individualising the politics of social cooperation', in T. Brown (ed.) *Commentaries on Adult Learning*, Canberra: Adult Learning Australia, pp. 14–16.

Tennant, M. (2005) 'Adult and continuing education: continuities and discontinuities', *International Journal of Lifelong Education* 24(6): 525–33.

—— and Morris, R. (2001) 'Adult education in Australia: shifting identities', *International Journal of Lifelong Education* 20(1): 44–54.

—— and —— (2006) 'Adult education in Australia', in *Papers d'Educació de Persones Adultes*, Barcelona: AEPA, pp. 13–16.

Whitelock, D. (1974) *The Great Tradition: A history of adult education in Australia*, Brisbane: University of Queensland Press.

# 42

# Lifelong learning policy development in Europe

*Janos Szigeti Toth*

This chapter summarises the development of lifelong learning policy in Europe, focusing on the policy development of a key sector, namely adult education, and emphasising the activities of one of the most influential decision-making bodies: the European Commission (EC). The period covered starts with the *Memorandum on Lifelong Learning* in 2000 and finishes with the *Action Plan on Adult Learning* in 2007, both issued by the Commission of the European Union (EU). Dispensing with deep analyses, the study considered its task as giving to the readers – who have only a basic knowledge of community-level policy development in Europe – a summary. This chapter mostly relies on this study, produced by the European Association for the Education of Adults (EAEA) and entitled *Adult Education Trends and Issues in Europe* (2006), and its partnership, which has been one of fresh exploration of adult learning in the context of lifelong learning.

## European systems of lifelong learning

Kjell Rubenson (2000) draws a distinction between two generations of lifelong learning, both with different meanings and which have developed in different contexts. The idea of lifelong learning was first introduced over 30 years ago by UNESCO. Over a short period, lifelong learning, closely related to ideas on recurrent education from the OECD and 'éducation permanente' from the Council of Europe, made a great impact on the debate on educational policy. The idea was grounded in a humanistic tradition and linked to the expectation of a better society and higher quality of life. However, these ideas did not come to fruition in concrete educational policies.

At the risk of oversimplification, we can say that the term 'lifelong learning' was transformed from idealism and suffered reductionism in its second iteration. There is, though, something to be gained from both generations of the concept. Economic reality cannot be disregarded, but lifelong learning is also important for the development of democracy and from a humanistic educational perspective. The more integrated approach of the third generation of the concept is related to the fact that a concrete programme for its implementation was developed from 2000 onwards.

The EC (2000) has since launched a programme called the Lisbon Strategy, which states that the Union must become the most competitive and dynamic knowledge-based economy in the world, capable of sustainable economic growth with more and better jobs and greater social cohesion. To achieve this ambitious goal, Heads of States and Governments asked for 'not only a radical transformation of the European economy, but also a challenging programme for the modernisation of social welfare and education systems'. In 2002, they went on to say that, by 2010, Europe should be the world leader in terms of the quality of its education and training systems.

In November 2000, based on the conclusions of the 1996 European Year of Lifelong Learning and subsequent experience gained at European and national levels, the Commission issued *A Memorandum on Lifelong Learning* (EC, 2000). This formed the basis for a Europe-wide consultation, organised as closely with the citizens as possible, in accordance with the Commission's aim of reforming European governance. The Member States and candidate countries each conducted their own inclusive and wide-ranging consultations involving relevant national bodies. Based on these the Commission issued the plan of action entitled *Communication from the Commission – Making a European Area of Lifelong Learning a Reality* in November 2001 (EC, 2001).

## Six key messages of the memorandum

It will be useful to briefly introduce the key messages of the Memorandum, as these principle guidelines will be valid pillars in the long run. Politicians, educational experts, practitioners and researchers will come back to these themes and keep them on the agenda:

- New basic skills for all – Objective: To guarantee universal and continuing access to learning for gaining and renewing the skills needed for sustained participation in the knowledge society. This means lifelong learning is about combating social exclusion and promoting active citizenship.
- More investment in human resources – Objective: To visibly raise levels of investment in human resources in order to give priority to Europe's most important asset – its people. This message expresses that lifelong learning is about investing money and investing time in learning.
- Innovation in teaching and learning – Objective: To develop effective teaching and learning methods and contexts for the continuum of lifelong and lifewide learning. Lifelong learning is about new innovations and structures.
- Valuing learning – Objective: To significantly improve the ways in which learning participation and outcomes are understood and appreciated, particularly non-formal and informal learning. Lifelong learning is about valuing all kinds and forms of learning, and the new roles of the different actors in the field of lifelong learning.
- Rethinking guidance and counselling – Objective: To ensure that everyone can easily access good-quality information and advice about learning opportunities throughout Europe and throughout their lives. Lifelong learning is about supporting the learner.
- Bringing learning closer to home – Objective: To provide lifelong learning opportunities as close to learners as possible, in their own communities and supported through information and technology (ICT)-based facilities wherever appropriate. Lifelong learning is about providing opportunities for everybody to learn.

## *The main elements of an integrated approach*

A regularly recurring term used in all kinds of documents dealing with lifelong learning has been the 'integrated approach'. What is behind this special term 'integrated approach for lifelong learning'?

- Putting the learner at the centre.
- Consonance between mutually supporting objectives, such as personal fulfilment, active citizenship, social inclusion and employability/adaptability.
- A coherent and comprehensive lifelong learning strategy.
- Interlinked development programmes.

Putting the learner at the centre means taking into consideration the value of all forms of learning: formal, non-formal and informal. The document of the Communication used a new definition of lifelong learning: all learning activity undertaken throughout life, with the aim of improving knowledge, skills and competencies within a personal, civic, social and/or employment-related perspective.

After the consultation process, an overall consensus can be surmised around the following four broad and mutually supporting objectives: personal fulfilment, active citizenship, social inclusion and employability/adaptability. Keeping an interlinked balance among these priorities has attracted the most debate in the Member States recently.

Coherent and comprehensive lifelong learning strategies mean links to other policy measures. In concrete terms, this means that the Member States must develop and implement coherent and comprehensive strategies for lifelong learning. This requires concerted action initiated at a European level, in accordance with agreed priorities. In a wider sense it means consonance with other policy measures such as:

- The reconstruction of the whole educational and training systems put down in the working programme on the Concrete Future Objectives of Education and Training Systems.
- The European Employment Strategy, featuring a horizontal objective for lifelong learning, and specific guidelines that focus on the employment and labour market-related aspects of lifelong learning.
- The European Social Agenda, which aims to reduce inequalities and promote social cohesion, including through lifelong learning.
- The Skills and Mobility Action Plan, aiming to ensure that European labour markets are open and accessible to all.
- The e-Learning initiative, part of the e-Europe Action Plan, seeking to promote a digital culture and wider use of ICT in education and training.
- The White Paper on Youth, providing the Union with a framework for cooperation in the field of youth policy, focusing on participation of young people, their education, employment and social inclusion.
- The European Research Area in relation to the Communication on a mobility strategy for this area. An important component of this strategy for developing human capital could be fostering trans-European networks for knowledge and science.

While each of these strands has its own specificity and objectives, taken together they contribute to the realisation of a European area of lifelong learning. To facilitate this development, education and training will be brought together within a framework of lifelong learning, in synergy with the relevant elements of the other processes, strategies and plans.

The EU started a set of educational and training development programmes in the period 1995–2000 – Socrates, Leonardo da Vinci II and Youth. Lifelong learning became a guiding principle for the new EU education, training and youth action programmes, coming into effect in 2000. The funded activities – networks and partnerships, pilot projects and action research, exchange and mobility activities, EU sources of reference – were therefore prime tools for developing the European dimension of lifelong learning.

Following several evaluation studies and public consultations on the achievements and experiences of the 2000–6 education programmes, the concept of a new Integrated Action Programme 2007–13 in the field of lifelong learning was approved. This comprises sectoral programmes on school education (Comenius), higher education (Erasmus), vocational training (Leonardo da Vinci) and adult education (Grundtvig), and is completed by transversal measures and an additional Jean Monnet programme focusing on European integration.

## Working programme on the concrete future objectives of education and training systems

Following the conclusions of the Heads of State and Governments in Lisbon 2000, and their endorsement of the common objectives for education and training in Europe in Barcelona, 2002 (EC, 2006a) and Council Resolution (EC, 2002), a radically new process of cooperation was launched in this area, with the overall objective of making education and training systems in Europe a worldwide point of reference in terms of quality by 2010. From 2002 the Concrete Objective Work Programme[1] became the main means of implementing lifelong learning development in Europe. The programme has set three main aims:

- to improve the quality and effectiveness of EU education and training systems;
- to ensure that they are accessible to all;
- to open up education and training to the wider world.

## Open method of coordination

While respecting the breakdown of responsibilities envisaged in the treaties, this method provides a new cooperation framework for the Member States with a view to the convergence of national policies and the attainment of certain objectives shared by everyone. It is based essentially on the Open Method of Coordination (http://europa.eu/scadplus/glossary/open_method_coordination_en.htm), which consists of these main elements:

- jointly identifying and defining the objectives to be attained;
- commonly defined yardsticks (statistics, indicators) enabling Member States to know where they stand and to assess progress towards the objectives set;
- comparative cooperation tools to stimulate innovation, and the quality and relevance of teaching and training programmes (dissemination of best practice, pilot projects, etc.).

## Indicators and benchmarks

The Council set five European benchmarks in 2003 for the improvement of education and training systems in Europe by 2010:[2]

- an EU average rate of no more than 10 per cent early schools leavers;
- the total number of graduates in mathematics, science and technology in the EU should increase by at least 15 per cent by 2010, while at the same time gender imbalance should decrease;

- at least 85 per cent of 22-year-olds in the EU should have completed upper secondary education;
- the percentage of low-achieving 15-year-olds in literacy should have decreased by at least 20 per cent compared to the year 2000;
- the average EU level of participation in lifelong learning should be at least 12.5 per cent of the adult working age population (25–64 age group).

## Maastrich Communiqué on vocational education and training (VET)

In the framework of the overall Lisbon Strategy, the Copenhagen Declaration by ministers of the Member States on the development of vocational education and training (VET) was launched in 2002.[3] In 2004 the ministers responsible for VET in 32 countries and the European social partners agreed to strengthen their further cooperation with a view to modernising their VET system in order that Europe become the most competitive economy.

The document, known as the Maastricht Communiqué and issued in 2004, emphasises that the necessary reforms and investment should be focused particularly on:

- the image and attractiveness of the vocational route for employers and individuals, in order to increase participation in VET;
- achieving high levels of quality and innovation in VET systems in order to benefit all learners and make European VET globally competitive;
- linking VET with labour market requirements in the knowledge economy for a highly skilled workforce, and especially, due to the major impact of demographic change, the upgrading and competence development of older workers;
- the needs of the low-skilled and disadvantaged groups for the purpose of achieving social cohesion and increasing labour market participation.

## Working groups on the concrete objectives

During the process of the Open Method of Coordination, a number of expert working groups were set up in which representatives of the ministries, social partners and European-level stakeholders of 32 countries are taking part. Most of them have published their reports on the work of 2002–3.

## Education and training of teachers and trainers

The Council/Commission first Joint Interim Report, *Education & Training 2010* (2004), set the overall strategic direction for the work programme in 2005–6.[4] It identified priority levers for future action that should be given priority, and also requested the incorporation of actions at European level relating to vocational education and training (priorities and follow-up to the Maastricht Communiqué), lifelong learning (follow-up to the Council Resolution) and mobility (implementation of the Mobility Recommendation and Action Plan).

## Shifting the focus to the adult learning element of the lifelong learning policy

On the coat-tails of these policy documents, more and more technical tools and guides were produced in order to be able to more accurately measure the results of all kinds of learning.[5]

Producing new tenders and studies in the field is a clear signal to eliminate gaps in the data and common understanding of the importance of adult learning in the whole of lifelong learning policy.[6]

## Legislation, financial systems and related policy issues

Although adult education is more institutionalised and firmly structured in the northern and western nations of Europe, legislation relating to adult learning in this region is not the norm. Some countries, or states within a federal country, do have laws, such as some German Länder. In the southern and eastern countries various different bodies and social structures tend to supply the impetus, and adult learning often takes place in work or other social settings, rather than in specific institutions. These facts lead to a major problem, namely that adult education (especially informal and non-formal) lacks a visible face and is often perceived as being part of another field.

However, regulations on informal/non-formal adult education do exist. They tend to fall into the following four categories:

- regulations offering public financial support to providers of adult education;
- regulations establishing individual entitlements to educational leave;
- regulations offering financial incentives to learners to take part in education;
- regulations establishing a framework for the recognition of prior, non-formal and informal learning.

The first type is supply-based and is more common in countries with a well-developed institutional structure of adult education. This kind of support for adult education is diminishing, losing ground to the other three types, which target the individual learner and seek to promote demand rather than supply. Most countries have established regulations in at least one of these three.

Regulations establishing entitlements to educational leave may have different financial implications for either the employee taking the leave or the employer. Normally the learner decides which course to attend. Usually at least a certain degree of job relevance of the learning is required, or only courses that have been formally recognised by the state for this purpose may be chosen.

Financial incentives to motivate learners to engage in learning, such as co-financing schemes, are more readily found in the vocational field.

## Adult education in lifelong learning strategies

Some of the major issues on which policy debates focus are as follows:

- *Funding*: one of the most integral areas in policy formation on lifelong learning and one of the most contentious.
- *Stimulating demand*: especially to increase the demand for adult learning among groups most at risk, such as immigrants, older people, deprived younger people, the disabled, and those with low levels of education.
- *Flexible supply*: the flipside of stimulation of demand, placing the learner at the centre of educational offers. This includes catering for the individual needs of learners and making learning easily accessible especially for disadvantaged groups.

- *Disadvantaged groups*: Focusing on their inclusion in the process of adult learning. There are two main connected issues: raising the participation in adult learning of groups at risk through measures that stimulate demand and motivation, facilitating access to learning; or providing tailored supply and raising the skill level of low-qualified adults to ensure at least a given minimum level of knowledge and skills.

The 2002 Conference on Adult Education in Sofia called attention to the huge number of difficulties in the sphere of adult education:

> many countries do not have the policies, frameworks and structures required to advance Adult Education. Requirements include new legislation, adequate financial support, appropriate institutional structures, effective administrative systems, quality frameworks and the conditions required to support effective partnerships and lobbying.
>
> (Medel-Añonuevo, 2003: 191)

## Trends in participation – access and social inclusion – barriers, data and expectations

The first question that begs to be asked is who participates in adult learning? Such a question provides some challenging answers, essentially along the lines that those who need the most get the least. Despite recognition of the benefits of education and training to groups and individuals at risk of social exclusion, there is strong and consistent evidence that the participation of disadvantaged groups in all kinds of adult education (formal, informal and non-formal) continues to be lower than that of other groups (EU, 2003).

According to one of the latest studies conducted by Eurostat (Figure 42.1), participation rates vary depending on the type of learning. Participation in non-formal learning is four times higher than in formal learning.

For the 25 EU countries we find:

- Participation in formal adult education by previous educational attainment (percentages):
     Low   1.4          Medium   5.2          High   8.5.

- Participation in non-formal adult education by previous educational attainment (percentages):
     Low   6.5          Medium   16.4          High   30.9.

- Participation in enformal adult education by previous educational attainment (percentages):
     Low   18.4          Medium   34.1          High   55.2.

## Quality and development in adult education

Quality management models have been introduced into adult education organisations in many countries, most, such as ISO and EFQM, adopted from the business sector. Many institutions are unable to cope with the administrative workload that such quality assurance models bring.[7]

The second level is the learner level, where the main concern is how to assess and document learning outcomes. Some initiatives are under way to develop tools that will help to recognise quality in informal and non-formal learning.[8]

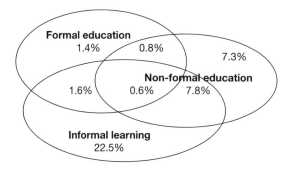

**Not in education, training or learning: 58%**

*Source:* Eurostat LFS, Ad hoc module on lifelong learning 2003
Target population: 25–64 years old

*Figure 42.1* Percentage of population 25–64 years old, involved in education and training.

Source: Eurostat LFS, Ad hoc module on lifelong learning 2003.

The third quality assurance level is at system level. How does quality assessment figure in legislation? In some countries dedicated institutes or expert bodies support the development and monitoring of adult education and learning (EC, 2000a, 2002a, 2004) – some are government-appointed, such as the Finnish Adult Education Council; some are NGOs, such as the National Institute of Adult Continuing Education (England and Wales), the German Institute for Adult Education, and the Slovenian Institute for Adult Education.

## Recognising and validating other forms of learning

### Current developments and problems

A growing body of professionals can see benefits in developing different kinds of recognition arrangements for different purposes, and there is commitment and creativity in developing new practices. However, there are also problems including lack of awareness, lack of guidance and training, lack of funding, lack of provision and, in some countries, legal barriers as well.

The recognition of non-formal and informal learning is part of a larger debate about the knowledge society and lifelong learning. It is also part of political and interministerial discussions at national and European level. There is no simple agreed definition. It includes a wide range of policies and practices in different settings, sectors and countries.

Overlying the diversity of institutional practice is a wide range of needs, purposes and aspirations from the individual's perspective, including:

- developing self-confidence, self-awareness and/or self-evaluation skills;
- verifying appropriate practice in voluntary work;
- making explicit learning from work placements, exchanges and social action;
- entering or re-entering employment;
- entering formal training or non-formal learning opportunities;
- making progress or getting promoted at work;
- obtaining part or all of a formal qualification;
- transferring qualifications gained in other contexts at other times;
- accumulating skills, part-qualifications and competences into a coherent package.

## Basic skills and key competencies: emerging issues

Until the mid-1990s, the traditional approach towards basic skills in Europe was generally narrow. Lack of basic skills was identified as a literacy problem; the successful completion of basic schooling implied possession of reading, writing and numeracy skills, which were mainly treated as a part of initial education.

The International Adult Literacy Survey (OECD, 1997, 2000; EC, 2006a) presented evidence of the nature and magnitude of literacy gaps in the OECD countries. Europe has some 72 million low-skilled workers – one third of the labour force. It has been estimated that, by 2010, only 15 per cent of newly created jobs will be for those with low skills demanding only basic schooling, while 50 per cent of such new jobs will require tertiary level qualifications.

The 2004 report of the basic skills working group, and the proposal on the key competencies for lifelong learning set out concrete recommendations and focused on how to approach the problem at a policy level. Also, NGOs have started European-level work in basic skills development, an example of which is the European Civil Society Platform on Lifelong Learning project run by the EAEA. The fact that the EAEA chose basic skills and key competencies as the subjects of the Grundtvig Award in 2004 is also an example of this. As is the Grundtvig project, entitled *Promoting Social Inclusion Through Basic Skills Learning*, which formulated and tested working tools to promote key competencies at regional and local levels, with contributions by eight countries.

## Active citizenship and adult learning

Learning active citizenship is part of the fight against discrimination that should embrace all citizens and underline the importance of the citizenship dimension, and bring into force an anti-racism directive. The knowledge economy also needs citizenship skills, including private and public services, consumers as well as employees. Renewed governance of adult learning institutes contributes to the citizenship skills of their clients.

## Local learning centres, partnerships and decentralisation

Local learning centres (LLCs) and local learning partnerships (LLPs) are important for adult learning. In rural corners of each country we find many of the same features of accumulating disadvantage. Many people feel isolated from the rest of the world, they have not heard of lifelong learning and may still live in a different place and time today. However, rural local learning centres are poor by comparison with those in urban areas. Linking local community and local learning to national and global processes is one key to sustainable development, to which adult learning can contribute massively.

Learning cities and regions are promoted from the viewpoint of the knowledge economy, regional competitiveness and innovative and sustainable economic development (OECD, 2001). It is insufficient simply to improve individual learning. Individual learning must be translated into organisational learning with significant economic growth benefit.

## The training and development of adult education personnel

There is little data and few studies available to sketch the state of this profession and its development at national or European level. Six *activity fields* can be identified that are important for the professional development of adult education:[9] teaching, management, counselling and

guidance, media, programme planning, and support. For some their relevance for adult education has developed only recently. These fields are differently shaped in the different European
countries, and are changing at different speeds.

## Latest developments

### *A new policy document issued on adult learning: Action Plan on Adult Learning: It is never too late to learn, 2006*

On 23 October 2006, the European Commission adopted a Communication calling on the
Member States to promote adult learning in Europe. The pressures of demographic change
mean that adult learning must be placed firmly on the political agenda. However, with some
exceptions, the implementation of adult learning remains weak. The participation of adults in
'lifelong learning' activities varies widely across the EU and is still unsatisfactory in many Member
States. Adult learning has not yet gained the recognition it deserves in terms of visibility, policy
prioritisation and resources (EC, 2006b).

### *Action Plan on Adult Learning, 2007*

The EC is urging Member States to have an efficient adult learning system, which is more
effectively integrated into their national lifelong learning strategies. To aid this process, the EC
issued a Communication entitled *Action Plan on Adult Learning* in 2007.

The *Action Plan*, which has been produced in concert with the Member States, will consider
the following five key challenges in adult learning:

- *Lift the barriers to participation.* Adult participation in education and training remains limited
  and imbalanced, with those with the lowest levels of initial education, older people, people
  in rural areas and the disabled being the least likely to participate. Member States should
  introduce high-quality guidance and information systems, as well as targeted financial
  incentives for individuals and support for local partnerships.
- *Ensure the quality of adult learning.* Poor-quality provision leads to poor-quality learning
  outcomes. To ensure the quality of adult learning special attention has to be paid to the
  various dimensions of quality with a special attention to staff development, quality assurance
  mechanisms and methods and materials.
- *Introduce systems that recognise and validate learning outcomes.* These are essential to motivate
  adults to participate in lifelong learning. Member States are invited to link these systems
  to their National Qualification Frameworks, within the context of the European
  Qualification Framework.
- *Invest in the aging population and migrants.* Member States should invest in older people and
  migrants, through education and training that matches the needs of the learner, while raising
  awareness about the important role of migrants and older people in European society and
  economy. In particular, immigration can be seen as a partial counterbalance to an aging
  population and to skills shortages in certain sectors, and adult learning has a key role to
  play to support the integration of migrants into society and the economy.
- *Be in a position to measure progress.* Reliable data, with appropriate indicators and benchmarks,
  are essential for evidence-based policy-making. Unfortunately, data availability in adult
  learning is limited, not least because providers often operate outside the public sector.

The quality and comparability of data must continue to be improved. More analysis and monitoring is needed of the benefits of adult learning and the barriers to its uptake. If relevant data remain unavailable, Member States should consider commissioning new data collection or surveys.

## Notes

1   Detailed work programme on the follow-up of the objectives of education and training systems in Europe, *Work Programme of the Education Council in cooperation with the Commission* (February 2002); http://europa.eu/.

2   Council conclusions, 2003; http://ec.europa.eu. See more on indicators, benchmarks: http://ec.europa.eu/education/policies/2010/back_indi_en.html.

3   Maastricht Communiqué on the Future Priorities of Enhanced European Cooperation in Vocational Education and Training (VET), *European Ministers of Vocational Education and Training, European Social Partners and European Commission*, review of the Copenhagen Declaration of 30 November 2002 (December 2004), http://ec.europa.eu/education/news/ip/docs/maastricht_com_en.pdf.
    –   Achieving the Lisbon goal: the contribution of VET, *Final report to the European Commission* (November 2004), Study prepared for the European Commission in preparation for the conference 'Strengthening European cooperation in VET: The way forward', Maastricht, 2004. See http://ec.europa.eu/education/policies/2010/studies/maastricht_en.pdf.

4   First interim report 2004, http://ec.europa.eu/education/policies/2010/doc/jir_council_final.pdf.
    –   Strategies for lifelong learning. See more on national planning and reporting: http://ec.europa.eu/education/policies/2010/111_en.html.

5   Measuring progress in education and training (Statistics, indicators and benchmarks). Progress towards the Lisbon Objectives in Education and Training – Report based on indicators and benchmarks 2006 Report (Annual Report, May 2006) *Commission Staff Working Paper detailed analysis of progress (Annex)*, http://ec.europa.eu/education/policies/2010/doc/progressreport06.pdf.
    –   Key data on education in Europe 2005, *Joint publication Eurydice/Eurostat* (July 2005), http://www.eurydice.org/Doc_intermediaires/indicators/en/frameset_key_data.html.
    –   New indicators in education and training, *Council Conclusions* (May 2005), http://eur-lex.europa.eu/LexUriServ/site/en/oj/2005/c_141/c_14120050610en00070008.pdf.
    –   Reference Levels of European Average Performance in Education and Training (Benchmarks), *Council Conclusions* (May 2003), http://ec.europa.eu/education/policies/2010/doc/after-council-meeting_en.pdf.
    –   European benchmarks in education and training: follow-up to the Lisbon European Council, *Communication from the Commission* (November 2002), http://ec.europa/eu/education/policies/2010/doc/bench_ed_trai_en.pdf.

6   Report studies funded by the Commission: http://ec.europa.eu/education/doc/reports/index_en.html.
    –   Adult education trends and issues, 2006 Study made by the group coordinated by the European Association for Education of Adults (EAEA).
    –   Study on Adult Education Providers.
    –   The National Institute of Adult Continuing Education (NIACE) December 2006 Contract number DG EAC 21/05.
    –   See: Adult learning practitioners in Europe (ALPINE), A study of the current situation, trends and issues, Draft Inception Report. This study has been financed by DG Education and Culture, Project number: B3276 Leiden, 12 February 2007.

7   This has been reconfirmed by current European projects on the issue, such as the still running Leonardo da Vinci project, 'Managing Quality of Adult Education in Europe', www.managingquality.lv/12partners.html.

8    Inventory at www.ecotec.com/europeaninventory/.
9    There are number of key development projects implemented:
     – Teaching Adult Educators in Continuing and Higher Education, www.teach.pl/.
     – AGADE – 'A Good Adult Educator in Europe', www.nordvux.net.
     – The EMAE Project, Developing and Implementing a Multinational Master's Programme in
     Adult Education, Regina Egetenmeyer, Susanne Lattke, www.die-bonn.de/doks/egetenmeyer
     0701.pdf.

## References

European Association of Education of Adults (2006) *Adult Education Trends and Issues in Europe*, Helsinki: EAEA.

European Community (2000) Lisbon European Council. Available online at 222.europarl.europa.eu/ summits/lis1_en.htm (accessed March 2008).

European Commission (EC) (2000) *A Memorandum on Lifelong Learning: Commission staff working paper*, 30 October, SEC (2000) 1832, Brussels: Commission of the European Union. Available online at ec.europa.eu/education/policies/111/life/memoen.pdf (accessed March 2008).

—— (2000a) *European Report on the Quality of School Education*, Brussels: Commission of the European Union.

—— (2001) *Making a European Area of Lifelong Learning a Reality*, Communication for the Commission, November. Available online at http://ec.europa.eu/education/policies/lll/life/communication/ com_en.pdf (accessed March 2008).

—— (2002) *Lifelong Learning*, Council Resolution, June. Available online at http://europa.eu/ (accessed March 2008).

—— (2002a) *European Report on Quality indicators of Lifelong Learning: 15 quality indicators*, Brussels: Commission of the European Union.

—— (2004) *Fundamentals of a 'Common Quality Assurance Framework' (CQAF) for VET in Europe*, Brussels: Commission of the European Union.

—— (2006a) *Progress Towards the Lisbon Objectives in Education and Training: Report based on indicators and benchmarks – 2006*, SEC (2006) 639, 16 May, Brussels: Commission of the European Union.

—— (2006b) *Action Plan on Adult learning: It is never too late to learn*, Communication from the Commission to the Council, The European Parliament, the European Economic and Social Committee and the Committee of the Regions. Available online at http://ec.europa.eu/education/policies/adult/ com558_en.pdf (accessed March 2008).

—— (2006c) *The Integrated Lifelong Learning Programme, 2007–13*. Available online at http://ec.europa. eu/education/programmes/newprog/doc/presentation_en.pdf (accessed 22 June 2008). This programme has been decided by the European Parliament and of the Council, No. 1720/2006/EC.

—— (2007) *Action Plan on Adult Learning: It is always a good time to learn*, available online at http://eurlex. europa.eu/LexUriserv.do?uri=com:2007:0558:FIN:EN:PDF (accessed 22 June 2008).

European Union (2003) *Labour force survey*, available online at http://circa.europe.eu/irc/dsis/employment/ info/data/eu_lfs/index.htm (accessed 22 June 2008).

Medel-Añonuevo, C. (ed.) (2003) 'Sofia conference call to action', in *Lifelong Learning Discourses in Europe*, Hamburg: UIE.

Organization for Economic Cooperation and Development (OECD) (1997) *Literacy Skills for the Knowledge Society: Further results from the International Adult Literacy Survey*, Paris: OECD.

—— (2000) *Literacy in the Information Age: Final report of the International Adult Literacy Survey*, Paris: OECD.

—— (2001) *Cities and Regions in the New Learning Economy: Education and Skills*, Paris: OECD.

Rubenson, K. (2000) *Lifelong Learning and Lifewide Learning*, Stockholm: The National Agency for Education.

# 43

# Lifelong learning on the Indian subcontinent

## Policies, programmes and progress

*C.P.S. Chauhan*

The Indian subcontinent is a large part of Asia on the Indian tectonic plate. In addition to the islands of Sri Lanka and the Maldives, it consists of countries on the continental crust – India, Pakistan, Bangladesh, Nepal and Bhutan. It is surrounded by three bodies of water: the Indian Ocean, the Arabian Sea and the Bay of Bengal. Historically known as *Hindustan* during the medieval period, it is called a subcontinent because it has certain distinctive geographical and political features. Among the countries included in this region, India has the largest land area and population, followed by Pakistan, Bangladesh, Nepal and Bhutan, in that order. The estimated population of this region is 1,450 million – about 22.50 per cent of the total population of the world (Malayala Manorama, 2007). The countries of this region share certain common problems, such as high population growth, acute poverty, low levels of literacy and slow economic development. The objective of this chapter is to discuss the progress and status of lifelong education in this region with a specific focus on India.

## The concept of lifelong education

The world is now heading towards the era of the knowledge-based economy, which has placed new demands on citizens for acquiring more skills and knowledge to ensure effective functioning in daily life. This requires a new model of education that encompasses learning throughout life – a model of lifelong learning. A lifelong learning framework covers formal learning (schools, training institutions and universities), non-formal learning (on-the-job and household training) and informal learning (skills learned through social interaction and experience). It allows people to access learning opportunities as they need (World Bank, 2003). Success in the knowledge economy requires mastering new competencies and skills, including basic academic skills, such as literacy, numeracy, oracy, foreign language skills, basic mathematics and science, and the ability to use information technology in everyday activities. The core elements of the process concern universal access to educational facilities for all children and adults both inside and outside the formal system, diversification of learning materials to suit the needs of a variety of learners, and development of learners' personal motivation, attitudes and abilities required for self-learning. The major strategies to achieve this goal are: universalization of elementary education for all children aged 6–14 years, eradication of illiteracy through adult and non-formal approaches, and development of open and distance learning systems at school and higher education levels. These aspects of the overall process of lifelong learning in the context of the Indian subcontinent, with a major focus on India, are discussed in the sections that follow.

## India

India is the largest democracy in the world, with about 1,135 million people (2007 estimate), who constitute 78 per cent of the total population of the subcontinent and 17 per cent of that of the world. According to 2001 Census, of about 300 million adult illiterates in the country, 64 per cent were women. According to a recent World Bank report (CIOL Network, 2005), India is 'one of the world's largest economies' and has made 'enormous strides in its economic and social development in the past two decades'. The report further states that India 'can do much more to leverage its strengths in today's knowledge-based global economy' and 'can increase its productivity and the well-being of its population by making more effective use of knowledge'. Indian society has accepted lifelong learning as the most viable tool to harness knowledge for the development and realization of its dream to become a major knowledge power in near future. In order to fulfil the constitutional obligation of achieving the goal of universalisation of elementary education (UEE) by 1960 under Article 45, the Government of India undertook a massive expansion of schooling facilities immediately after achieving independence in 1947. However, the task could not be accomplished even after 47 years of the target date, though considerable progress has been made.

In the year 1986, the Government launched the National Policy on Education (NPE), which was revised in 1992, and which made several significant proposals for elementary education. In view of the prevailing circumstances, the government realized that the formal system of education alone could not serve the purpose of UEE and decided to strengthen and expand the non-formal education (NFE) scheme for out-of-school children, not only as a supplement, but also as a substitute for formal schooling. However, the performance of NFE programmes was found to be sluggish and unsatisfactory when it was reviewed in 1994. The NPE also mooted the idea of micro-planning, which formed a strategy aimed at a 'family-wise and child-wise design of action' to ensure that every child attends school or an NFE centre regularly, progresses at his or her own pace, and completes at least five years of schooling within the specified time. A World Bank-financed District Primary Education Programme (DPEP) was also launched in 1993 – 4 as a part of the micro-planning strategy, which envisaged that a 'district' would be the unit of planning for UEE instead of a state, and specific plans would be developed by the state governments as 'projects' with specific activities and targets, depending on the specific needs and possibilities in the selected districts.

In the year 2000, the Government launched another massive programme known as Sarva Shiksha Abhiyan (SSA) meaning 'Education for All Campaign', aimed at providing, by 2010, elementary education of eight years to all children aged 6–14 years. The SSA has a central objective of mobilizing all resources – human, financial and institutional, necessary for achieving the goal of UEE. The Government reiterated its determination to achieve the goal of UEE and social justice by passing the '86th Constitutional Amendment Act 2002', thereby making free and compulsory elementary education a 'fundamental right' of every child in the 6–14 age group. Under the provisions of this amendment (Article 21A), the Government 'shall provide free and compulsory education to all children of the age of six to fourteen years in such a manner as the State may, by law, determine'. Further, by rewording the earlier Article 45, the

Government promises to 'endeavor to provide Early Childhood Care and Education (ECCE) for all children until they complete the age of six years'. Along with this, the Government has also introduced a new 'Fundamental Duty' through Article 51A (k) for every citizen 'who is a parent or guardian, to provide opportunities for education to his child or, as the case may be, ward between the age of six and fourteen years'.

By following these policies significant progress has been made in the direction of UEE during the last six decades since independence. According to a recent survey by the National Institute of Educational Planning and Administration (NIEPA, 2006), primary schooling facilities (classes I–V) are now available to 87 per cent of rural habitations within a radius of one kilometre, 78 per cent of the rural habitations are served by upper primary schooling facilities within a radius of three kilometres, and about 18 per cent of rural habitations have upper primary schools within them. Enrolment in elementary schools for children aged 6–14 years has increased from only 23 million in 1951 to over 156 million in 2005, the reported gross enrolment ratio (GER) being about 98 per cent at primary stage. The enrolment of girls has grown faster than that of boys both at primary and upper primary stages and constitutes about 47 per cent of the total enrolment in all elementary classes. The overall situation at present is that, out of the total projected population of 194 million in the age group 6–14 years, about 59 million are not enrolled in school at all. Moreover, the disparities based on region, caste, gender and the rural–urban dichotomy still persist. There are reasons to believe that, keeping in view the progress achieved during the last five years (2000–5), India may not be able to achieve the goal of UEE by 2010 as targeted in SSA.

The status of literacy programmes was reviewed in 1978 and the government made a policy statement regarding education of about 100 million adults, mainly in the age group 15–35 years, and a massive programme called the National Adult Education Programme (NAEP) was launched, which emphasized the correlation between working, living and learning. In order to supplement the efforts under UEE and adult education, the Government implemented NFE, which was supposed to be only a complementary system to formal education in 1979–80 with a view to supporting the formal school system in providing education for all children up to the age of 14 years, especially the school drop-outs. Selected universities/colleges were also provided with financial assistance to set up Centres of Adult and Continuing Education in order to promote lifelong and continuing education in the surrounding areas through the NFE mode. Through experiences, the government realized that centre-based programmes such as the existing NAEP and NFE would not provide desirable results in achieving the goal of the eradication of illiteracy within the shortest possible time. The need to plan some more effective programmes was felt.

As a part of the implementation of the National Policy on Education (NPE) 1986, an ambitious programme called the National Literacy Mission (NLM), aimed at achieving a sustainable threshold level of 75 per cent literacy by 2007, was launched. The basic idea underlying the NLM was to tackle the problem of illiteracy by pooling all possible resources – human and material, and by using scientific and technological knowledge so as to increase efficiency and obtain concrete results. It had a time-bound target of imparting functional literacy to 80 million illiterate adults in the age group 15–35 years by 1995 (Government of India, 1988). The NLM was based on people's participation and the mass mobilization of resources. Students were involved in the Mass Programme of Functional Literacy (MPFL), in which a student volunteer would teach an adult for 150 hours spread over a four-month period under the 'Each One Teach One' campaign. The strategy of the mass mobilization of various government and non-government agencies was named the Total Literacy Campaign (TLC), which required all concerned to join hands for the common goal of achieving full literacy in a specified area within a specified time limit. The first TLC was launched successfully in the Ernakulum district of Kerala state in January 1989, and in a period of one year set a record by bringing together voluntary agencies and all sections of society, and making the whole district literate by February 1990. Subsequently, it became a recognized approach of the Government. The cumulative number of literacy volunteers mobilized for TLC campaigns exceeded 10 million, which is the largest ever civil and military mobilization in the history of India.

Post-literacy and continuing education form integral components of NLM. Jan Shikshan Nilayams (JSNs), meaning 'People's Learning Centres', meant for sustaining the literacy levels of those who have been made literate through TLCs or otherwise, were started in selected districts and are still fully operational. Each JSN caters for the needs of five villages of about 5,000 people and provides for a library, a reading room, a forum for discussion, evening classes for the upgrading of skills, etc. These JSNs also offer simple and short-term training programmes in agriculture, animal husbandry and veterinary science, soil management and other similar fields. The literacy rate in India was only 5.35 per cent in 1901, which increased to 18.33 per cent by 1951 and to about 43.6 per cent in 1981. According to the 2001 Census, the figure has gone up to about 65 per cent – nearly 76 per cent for males and 54 per cent for females. Moreover, there are wide disparities and variations in literacy rates based on caste, religion, region, creed and gender. The literacy rate was 44 per cent in rural areas and 75 per cent in urban areas. Keeping in view the annual population growth rate of 18 million, the total population of India in 2007 may be estimated to be about 1,135 million and estimated literacy may be about 74 per cent. It appeared that the NLM target of achieving 75 per cent threshold literacy by 2005, was likely to be realized by the end of 2007, and that full literacy may be achieved by the 2011 Census.

During the later half of the twentieth century, part-time, open and distance learning (ODL) approaches revolutionized the process of lifelong learning, not only in India, but also in other developed and developing countries. The inherent flexibility and openness in the new system received ready recognition from prospective learners who had missed the opportunity to continue their studies because of compelling circumstances. The concept of ODL has been adopted in India at school as well as at college and university levels. Although the Government has a constitutional responsibility to provide free and compulsory elementary education for all children till they reach the age of 14, yet many children remain deprived of this provision for various socio-economic reasons. This led to the introduction of ODL also at the school level through print media and postal services.

The first correspondence education school was established at Bhopal in 1965 and the process accelerated with some other states also implementing the scheme. The International Council of Correspondence Education (ICCE) discussed the issues underlying this system in its World Conference, held in New Delhi in 1974. Subsequently, in 1979, the Open School was established at Delhi, now known as the National Institute of Open Schooling (NIOS), with its functions extended to providing education in the academic as well as professional areas, and playing a leading role in the development of a network of open schools in the country. The annual enrolment of students at NIOS increased from only about 40,900 in 1990–1 to over 0.7 million by 2001–2. There are about 1,370 accredited institutions spread over the length and the breadth of the country. In addition, there are 426 institutions offering vocational courses through the open learning system. This is a great achievement. The NIOS also has study centres outside India in such places as Dubai, Abu Dhabi and Muscat in the Middle East. The Commonwealth of Learning (COL) has conferred an Award of Excellence on the NIOS for its remarkable contribution in the area of distance education at the school level.

On the recommendation of a high-power expert committee, the first initiative towards ODL at the higher education level was the establishment of the School of Correspondence Courses and Continuing Education by the University of Delhi in 1962. The syllabus, examinations and university degrees were the same for regular and correspondence students. The examination results convinced the public and the Government that the experiment was fairly successful, and, subsequently, other universities felt encouraged and started correspondence courses in various disciplines. At present, India has two types of ODL institutions: (1) Correspondence Course Institutions (CCIs) (also called dual-mode institutions) functioning under the conventional universities, which initially used print media as the main vehicle for the delivery of study materials with some use of radio and television programmes; and (2) newly established open universities, which design their programmes by using modern technologies and approach the learners through multimedia technology using computers, satellites and the internet.

In 1982, the state government of Andhra Pradesh established the Andhra Pradesh Open University (APOU) – the first open university in India, which started functioning in 1983. At the national level, on the recommendation of a high-power committee, the Indira Gandhi National Open University (IGNOU) was set up by an Act of Parliament in 1985. Thereafter, some other state governments acted promptly to establish state open universities and the process still continues. At present, in addition to IGNOU, there are 13 state open universities and 126 dual-mode universities/institutions offering over 425 academic programmes and 3,800 courses through a network of 105 regional centres and 4,200 study centres. In 1971, when the system of correspondence education was in its infancy, only 48,000 students, constituting 2.32 per cent of the total enrolment in higher education, were enrolled in the correspondence stream. The enrolment of learners in the ODL system is about 2.8 million, which constitutes 25 per cent of the total enrolment of about 11 million in higher education. The IGNOU alone accounts for about 50 per cent of the enrolment in all ODL higher education institutions in the country. The large majority of those enrolled at ODL institutions are women and young people from socially and economically deprived groups. The IGNOU also encompasses the Distance Education Council (DEC), a national-level apex body for ODL institutions and a statutory authority under the IGNOU Act responsible for the promotion, coordination and maintenance of standards of open and distance education systems in the country.

The programmes of the IGNOU are telecast daily on the National Channel of Doordarshan (Indian television network). Interactive radio phone-in counselling is also popular, and is aired from 21 All India Radio (AIR) stations throughout the length and breadth of the country. The university also develops programmes for Gyandarshan, an educational TV channel. Socially relevant programmes on the environment, forest management, human rights, HIV/AIDS awareness, and food and nutrition are also being introduced at the IGNOU. It is being proposed that ODL institutions attached to the conventional universities should be upgraded to the level of open universities. The long-term objective is to have at least 30 open universities in the country in the near future – one in each state.

## Pakistan

In Pakistan also, it is the state's constitutional responsibility to provide free primary education of five years to all children, but school attendance is not compulsory. In the 2002–3 school year, 68 per cent of primary school-aged children were enrolled in school. While the enrolment rate was high for boys, less than half of girls attended school. There were 163,000 primary schools, of which merely 25 per cent served girls. Most of the schooling facilities are concentrated in the Punjab and Sind provinces. The situation is especially alarming in rural areas due to some sociocultural obstacles (Latif, 2005). From 1976 to 2001 the number of primary schools doubled, but so did the population. The high level of population growth continues to hamper educational development in the country. One of the most deplorable aspects is that, in some places, particularly northern tribal areas, the education of girls is strictly prohibited on religious grounds. The situation is the most critical in North Western Frontier Province (NWFP) and Baluchistan, where the female literacy rate stands between 3 and 8 per cent. Poverty is also a big hurdle in girls' education. According to available reports, about 18 per cent of Pakistani children work for wages to support their families. Even though there is a lack of concern on the part of the Government to promote girls' education, some religious groups, political parties and NGOs are working actively to do so despite all barriers.

One notable aspect of education in Pakistan (and also in Bangladesh) is the system of Islamic schools called 'madrassahs', which operate out of the control of the state. The Pakistani government released reports that suggested that, in 1998, only about 150,000 students actually attended madrassahs. This system is most prominent in NWFP and Baluchistan where the government system is the weakest.

Pakistan has one of the lowest literacy rates in the world. The education policy of 1998 accorded high priority to educating out-of-school children and young people through NFE and participatory methods with the aim of achieving a literacy rate of 55 per cent by 2003 and 70 per cent by 2010 (Bines and Morris, 2000). But, according to the Economic Survey of Pakistan (2001–2), only 50.5% of adult Pakistanis could become literate – 63 per cent male and 38 per cent female. The rural and urban literacy rates were 39 per cent and 70 per cent respectively. Although the media have played an effective role in convincing people to send their daughters to schools, the situation remains critical in the villages and small towns where almost 70 per cent of the country's population resides.

The ODL system is also being used as an effective tool for adult and lifelong education in Pakistan. The Allama Iqbal Open University (AIOU) at Islamabad was established in 1974 as an institution of non-formal and distance learning to: (1) provide educational facilities to employed persons and women; (2) provide education for the masses; (3) organize training courses for prospective teachers; and (4) to conduct examinations for the award of degrees and certificates to successful examinees. The AIOU provides a wide range of academic and technical courses in teacher education, technical education, business and commerce, humanities, social sciences, language and literature, and religious education.

## Bangladesh

The situation in Bangladesh is similar to that in Pakistan, but enrolment data in the primary schools show some positive trends, including a rise in female enrolment. The estimated net enrolment ratio in primary schools, according to official statistics, is 89 per cent of the age cohort with 49 per cent for girls (*Encyclopedia of Modern Asia*, 2001–6). But, the quality of education is reported to be poor due to a shortage of teachers, high student–teacher ratios, inadequately trained teachers, lack of proper learning materials, and poorly equipped laboratories. Madrassahs, the Islamic religious schools, are significant in number. The school-age population at the end of the twentieth century expanded at the rate of roughly one million each year, putting enormous pressure on the entire school system. About 27 per cent of girls of the relevant age group in 2000 were reported to be out of school. However, the non-governmental organizations took up the challenge of opening and running primary schools in areas where government schools did not exist. The most famous are those run by the Bangladesh Rural Academy Council, which established around 30,000 schools in rural areas that were not under the government's administrative and financial management.

The overall education arena is underdeveloped. The literacy rate is 56 per cent (2000 estimate) to 63 per cent for male citizens and 49 per cent for females. There is a significant disparity between female and male literacy rates. Along with primary education, adult literacy and NFE are being emphasized to achieve the goal of the eradication of illiteracy from the country. It was targeted that the country would be illiteracy-free by the year 2005. Government statistics on educational attainments suggest some optimism. According to the Fifth Five Year Plan (1997–2002), the overall literacy rate was 58 per cent and was increasing at the rate of 7 per cent per decade. Reviews of major non-formal projects have indicated that a large proportion of learners do not achieve a functionally useful and sustainable level of literacy skills. To compensate for this deficiency, post-literacy and continuing education (PLCE) programmes were conducted during the period 2001–5 (Ahmad and Lohani, 2001).

The Bangladesh Open University (BOU) was established by Act of Parliament in October 1992 on the basis of findings of a series of studies conducted by the Overseas Development Agency (ODA) of the UK, the Asian Development Bank (ADB) and a firm of Indian consultants. Bangladesh had already established the Bangladesh Institute of Distance Education (BIDE), which provided instruction through the distance mode to offer a Bachelor of Education degree to teachers. Under the BOU Act, BIDE became a part of the new University. The BOU offers courses at school and college levels to those who wish to continue higher studies or improve their vocational and professional skills.

## Nepal and Bhutan

Both Nepal and Bhutan are small independent Asian countries located in the foothills of the Himalayas, between China and India. Education is a high priority area for both as an instrument of socio-economic development. In Nepal, there has been a dramatic expansion of educational facilities during the past 50 years. Beginning from only 300 schools with about 10,000 students in 1951, there are now 26,000 schools (including higher secondary) enrolling 6.4 million students and employing more than 150,000 teachers (Wikipedia, 2006). However, disparities based on factors such as gender, ethnicity, location and economic class are yet to be eliminated. The shortage of resources has always been a problem in education, causing the achievement of the universal goal of Education for All to still be a challenge for the country. Literacy rates are low: according to a recent estimate, the overall adult (15+) literacy of the country is reported to be 53.7 per cent, up from about 11 per cent in 1952. The figures for male and female sections of the society are 65.1 per cent and 42.5 per cent respectively (Government of Nepal, 2006).

Bhutan had the system of monastic education as a part of its national culture for a long time until the introduction of modern education in the 1960s to address the basic educational needs and develop the human resources required for the socio-economic development of the country. Within a period of four decades, the government has been able to expand the modern education system from about 11 schools in 1961 to over 400 schools in 2004 (Government of Bhutan, 2004). During the same period, enrolment increased from 400 students in all levels of formal education and NFE centres to over 155,200 by April 2004. The literacy rate in Bhutan is reported to be about 47.3–61.1 per cent for male citizens and 33.6 per cent for females (2001).

Both Bhutan and Nepal are among the poorest countries in Asia and have a geographically decentralized higher education system that is suited to their geographical situations. Internet access is almost non-existent, excepting some urban clusters. The use of technology is costly and limited to elite families. The quality and the value of education in the ODL mode is rated as poor by most students, teachers, administrators, employers and the public at large (Rennie and Mason, 2007). The largest university in Nepal is Tribhuvan University, located at Kathmandu and having affiliated colleges spread over a large area of the country. Most of these colleges offer courses in education, humanities and management. Recently, there has been limited use of ODL, largely for the training of teachers in rural areas, but an interest in having an open university is being expressed. In Nepal, the aim has been to provide training for those teachers who have no teaching qualifications, and to offer professional updating for those who wish to continue their studies while working. Tribhuvan University started a one-year distance-taught B.Ed. programme in 2001 using print materials plus some face-to-face workshops, and is currently planning to use some distance learning processes in all their programmes as a way of spreading understanding and acceptance of the method. The University is also a partner in a network of Asian universities trialling networked videoconferencing, especially for science and technology subjects.

Bhutan also has only one university – The Royal University of Bhutan, which is a much newer institution and is conducting a more cautious appraisal of the role of technology to support their form of distributed learning within the university network. The use of ODL in education is almost non-existent due to limited advancement in technology. In both countries there is a strong tradition of face-to-face teaching, usually with long tutor–student contact hours.

## Tasks ahead

The analysis in the previous sections indicates that different countries in the Indian subcontinent are at different stages as far as progress in lifelong and continuing education is concerned. The most serious problem in the subcontinent is that of rapid population growth, specifically among weaker sections and some religious segments. During the decade 1991–2001, the annual growth rate of the population in India was 1.9 per cent, while that in Pakistan was 3.1 per cent, as against 1.4 per cent in the whole world. India, Pakistan and Bangladesh are among the seven most populous countries of the world. Education, as a tool of social change and enlightenment, has to be effectively utilized to contain this problem because the progress of UEE and adult education are closely linked to it. All the countries of the region should formulate a common population policy.

India is moving ahead in UEE, the eradication of illiteracy and continuing education, but some retarding factors have to be contained effectively. Although elementary schooling facilities have expanded several-fold, 59 million eligible children are still reported to be deprived of basic education. More than 5 per cent of the population is still unserved by primary schooling facilities, the situation being worse in rural areas. The incidence of heavy drop-out of children enrolled in schools, which is more than 40 per cent up to class VIII, is being taken seriously by the Government. Schemes such as the provision of mid-day meals have shown some positive results, but seem to be only short-term measures.

*Table 43.1* Literacy rates of the countries on the subcontinent (percentages)

| Country | All persons | Male | Female | Estimate year |
| --- | --- | --- | --- | --- |
| India | 65.38 | 75.85 | 54.16 | 2001 |
| Pakistan | 50.5 | 63.0 | 38.0 | 2002 |
| Bangladesh | 56.0 | 63.0 | 49.0 | 2000 |
| Nepal | 53.7 | 65.1 | 42.5 | 2001 |
| Bhutan | 47.3 | 61.1 | 33.6 | 2000 |

Source: Compiled by the author from various sources.

The comparative picture of literacy in various countries in this region is presented in Table 43.1. The figures show that the situation in India is better than in other countries in the region. As per the latest available data, the indications are that the overall literacy rate in India has touched the magic figure of 75 per cent (2007 estimate), which is a threshold value for rapid socio-economic advancement. However, efforts have to be intensified to bridge the gap between literacy levels of advantaged and deprived sections of the society, including women. It is expected that the report of the 2011 Census will record the literacy rate as nearing 80 per cent at an all-India level, with about 90 per cent for male citizens and 70 per cent for females.

The literacy rate in Pakistan is among the lowest in the world. Recently, the Government has launched an adult literacy plan as a part of National Plan of Action (NPA), which has envisaged an increase in the overall literacy rate from the present 50 per cent to 86 per cent by 2015 in three phases, minimizing the rural–urban differences and eliminating the gender disparity. For this purpose, one of the significant plans would be the opening of 270,000 literacy centres by 2005, with the active involvement of the private sector. Some 1,500 non-formal schools for girls and women are functioning in rural areas (Latif, 2005). Education development would be linked with poverty alleviation by providing training to the young in income-generating vocational skills.

The governments of other countries in the region should also make specific attempts to enhance literacy among their peoples. Special attention has to be paid to the education of girls. It is reported that many children of school age work for wages in the factories, mines, kilns, construction industry and agriculture, most of them being from poor homes. Because of poverty, women and girls have to work in their own family's vocation or outside in order to supplement the family income. In Pakistan, young children, especially girls, work as domestic helps in large cities. Bangladesh, Nepal and Bhutan have to make concerted efforts on both fronts – UEE and adult literacy. The progress so far shows that these countries also, like Pakistan, may not be able to achieve the goal of EFA by 2015. Therefore, on the one hand, both formal and non-formal modes of education need to be augmented for enhancing intake capacity and, on the other hand, family welfare programmes should be popularized, especially among the poor and the disadvantaged, in order to control population growth. Some educationally backward sections of society link the question of population control to their religious faiths due to the lack of proper education. It is a common belief worldwide that lifelong learning programmes can be used to meet the learning needs of all, both within and outside school systems, by using distance-learning technologies to expand access to and the quality of formal education and lifelong training programmes. In order to keep pace with the rest of the world, the countries of the Indian subcontinent should address the problem of lifelong education in three dimensions – expansion of facilities, modernization of instructional process and provision of increased financial resources.

With increasing demand for education at all levels it is becoming increasingly difficult for governments to provide the requisite facilities of formal, non-formal and continuing education for all who deserve and desire it. Due to the lack of adequate financial resources, governments are unable to expand the formal systems of education beyond certain limits. Experience all over the world suggests that the privatization of education on a large scale can be a viable solution to this problem. The private sector may play a significant role in financing courses for which personal returns are high, for example professional and technical courses. Governments may finance programmes, such as basic education and literacy, for which social returns are high. The process has already begun. The use of technology can also make the educative process more efficient and ensure wider coverage; thus, the distance education mode should be expanded and the multimedia approach should be adopted. India has already established a network of open schools and open universities. As discussed earlier, 25 per cent of total enrolment in tertiary education is in the ODL system. The government has planned to double the number of open universities in the country so as to divert 50 per cent of the total enrolment at tertiary level into distance education institutions. Pakistan and Bangladesh also have open universities, but the system has to be expanded and modernized. Nepal and Bhutan are yet to accept the ODL system as an alternative to formal face-to-face learning.

Resource crunch is a common phenomenon in the countries of the subcontinent. While India spends about 4 per cent of its GNP on education, Pakistan and Bangladesh spend only 1.8 per cent and 1.3 per cent respectively. The expenditure on education in Nepal is still lower. All the countries of the Indian subcontinent must raise their educational expenditure to at least 6 per cent of the GNP as soon as possible, if the strategies for effective lifelong education are to be planned and implemented. For this purpose, various financing measures, such as graduate taxes, study loans and subsidies may be considered as options. During the financial year 2007–8, the Government of India has levied a 3 per cent education levy on every taxpayer in order to enhance the education budget. The governments of other countries in the subcontinent may also consider such options.

## References

Ahmad, M. and Lohani, S. (2001) *NFE in Bangladesh: Synthesis of experience and future direction*, Dhaka: Directorate of Non-formal education.

Bines, H. and Morris, C. (2000) *Literacy, Livelihood and Poverty Alleviation in Pakistan*, paper presented at the Department of International Development Conference 'Literacy for Livelihoods', Nepal, 4–6 December.

CIOL Network (2005) *India Poised for Higher Growth in Knowledge Economy*, CIOL News, CyberMedia On-Line, June 29. Available online at www.ciol.com/news (accessed 4 March 2007).

*Encyclopedia of Modern Asia* (2001–6) 'Bangladesh: education system', in *Encyclopedia of Modern Asia*, Berkshire Hills, MA: Macmillan Reference.

Government of Bhutan (2004) *Education System in Bhutan*, Thimphu: Ministry of Education, Education and General Statistics.

Government of India (1988) *National Literacy Mission* (NLM), New Delhi: Ministry of Human Resource Development (MHRD).

Government of Nepal (2006) *Education in Nepal*, Ministry of Education and Sports. Available online at www.moe.gov.np (accessed 13 April 2008).

Latif, A. (2005) *Alarming Situation of Education in Pakistan*, Karachi: Pakistan Press Foundation. Available online at www.unesco.org/education/ (accessed 13 April 2008).

Malayala Manorama (2007) *Manorama Yearbook*, Kottayam, India: Malayala Manorama Press.

National Institute of Educational Planning and Administration (NIEPA) (2006) *Elementary Education in India: Analytical report*, New Delhi: Ministry of Human Resource Development.

Rennie, F. and Mason, R. (2007) 'The development of distributed learning techniques in Bhutan and Nepal', *International Review of Research in Open and Distance Learning* 8(1). Available online at www.irrodl.org/index.php/irrodl/article/viewFile/339/775 (accessed 13 April 2008).

Wikipedia (2006) 'Education in Bangladesh', in *Wikipedia* – the free encyclopedia, licensed under the GNU free documentation license. Available online at http://en.wikipedia.org/wiki/Education_in_ Nepal (accessed 13 April 2008).

World Bank (2003) 'Lifelong learning in the global knowledge economy', *TechKnowLogia* 5(1) (January–March). Available online at www.techknowlogia.org (accessed 13 April 2008).

# 44

# Lifelong education in South America
## Toward a distant horizon[1]

*Candido Gomes, Clélia Capanema and Jacira Câmara*

Education from birth to death is still part of a distant horizon in South America. A subcontinent with sharp social and economic contrasts, it ranges from sophisticated postmodern islands to somewhat pre-modern communities that did not take part in the Industrial Revolution (see Kliksberg, 2003). Even though South America has progressed economically in the past decades, and is included as one of the greatest economies in the world, GNP-wise, its main characteristic is still inequality. That is why, in view of the variations among countries and within each country, the allocation of public funds tends to contemplate, first, the education of children, adolescents and young people and, later, remedial adult education for those who did not have access to or success in education at the appropriate age. It is well known that remedial adult education is placed second in the educational system (Clark, 1978), due to the social groups it serves and to its less conventional nature. Between those competing objectives, that is, regular education and remedial adult education, lifelong education, in the terms of the Hamburg Declaration (CONFINTEA V, 1997) is still something of a utopia. In fact, it is largely an unarticulated area, composed of a high number of heterogeneous experiences reaching diverse populations. Statistics on numerous programs and projects, including remedial adult education, tend to be underestimated, since they do not include part of this complex labyrinth. Lifelong learning includes a wide array of choices, such as distance courses; extension university projects; non-formal technical and vocational education and training (TVET), offered by NGOs and unions; and support and parallel courses. A relevant number of these courses and programs are located outside the educational system and, since they depend only on non-educational authorities, they are still quite unknown. In general, third-sector initiatives and private education for profit predominate, so that many students must pay fully or partially for the courses, thus establishing a socio-economic selection. The positive side is that many of these projects would not have flourished if they had been under state hyper-regulation. However, beside elitist segments, broad lifelong learning sectors have less prestige, for their certificates do not bear the legitimacy conferred by public bureaucracy. As a result, lower prestige programs and projects are prone to be underfunded or to have unsteady resources, though such instability may even make them more responsive and cost-effective than traditional programs.

It is important to point out that adult education, as remedial schooling, may also play the role of lifelong learning. Repetition, drop-out, and high opportunity and direct costs make it difficult for people to enter and to remain at school. Also, they may enroll in adult education at different times of their lives, often starting school, getting a grade, interrupting their studies, and returning later. Undergraduate programs have a significant proportion of older students. College graduates often take some years to pursue a master's or doctoral degree. These comings and goings contribute not only to deepening their knowledge but also to updating it.

It is important to notice that, in this first decade of the millennium, South America is going through great changes, with the rise to power of leftist parties and center-left alliances in many countries, so that the stated educational policies can change quickly. Of course, the establishment of those policies is another matter; it depends on resources, on established bureaucratic structures and on management capability. Anyway, as one statesman has said, politics change like the clouds in the sky, and no one can risk accurate predictions. Unequivocal disappointment with economic growth can be perceived, for it does not lead to a significant decrease in poverty. Very much the other way around, the perception is that the advancement in globalization has contributed to making income concentration worse. As a result, there are social and ethnic repressed needs that arise in the power systems and to which several governments respond with relative success in the short term. It is hard to foresee, however, for how long and how they will be able to do it in a framework of apparent revision of neo-liberal policies. Nevertheless, the importance of education remains highlighted, whatever the political-ideological framework. However, as we say in Brazil, education is a sector of much discourse and few resources. Since school is associated with the expectation of upward social mobility, political discourse keeps hopes high with a lot of the population, bypassing painful structural changes in the sector.

## Some highlights

Since a thorough view of the situation is not possible, this chapter highlights several small, medium-sized, and large countries with regard to population, economy, and territory. Several of the smaller countries are restricted to remedial education and isolated projects. An expected statistical trend is that registration, in remedial adult education, is proportionately larger in medium-sized countries with lower schooling levels. For example, in Chile, one of the countries with the best educational indicators, enrollment in remedial adult education corresponded to 4 percent of the regular education enrollment in 2005. In Paraguay, in 2006, the proportion was 9.3 percent (UNESCO, 2005).

### *Argentina*

Starting with Argentina, we must say that this country has a historical tradition of attention to education, since the nineteenth century. Hence, it has relatively high educational indicators, even if it has critical problems that challenge adult education, both as remedial education and as lifelong learning. One such problem is the group of adolescents from 15 to 17 years of age who drop out of the system without completing mandatory schooling and thus tend to become socially excluded. Another problem is that of young people from 14 to 18 years of age, who do not study or work and who form about one fifth of the total. To face these problems, several projects have been carried out in past years, for, even with economic recovery, the vulnerable population groups are many in number.

One of the projects, Learning Teaching, put into action 10,000 students in their final years of middle school and teacher training institutes, to give assistance to 50,000 students, so that they would remain in school and improve their learning. Another project, articulated between the Ministry of Education and other ministries, focuses on continued education for men and women who are heads of families, from literacy to the end of middle school. Training programs in TVET strengthen the links between education and jobs, to promote the social inclusion of such population groups. Still, a national program of professional training was established, in addition to another for vocational training and social integration that targets the young people and adults who neither study nor work—people with different skills, and the population in penitentiary institutions. In order to decrease the need for remedial adult education, scholarships have been granted to students between 13 and 19 years of age who are in a condition of destitution or poverty. Likewise, the distribution of textbooks for regular secondary school and adult education has been expanded. Also, a system to support children and young people who dropped out of school has been created, with neighborhood education committees, the development of alternative educational strategies organized by the local community and school, management of schools associated with social organizations, and training and subsidies for teachers and people from the communities, in order to support local projects of social inclusion.

In turn, the Federal Network for Continued Faculty Development is an articulated system of training institutions, in which technical teaching assistance is disseminated. It gathers together the National Ministries of Education and the provincial ones, based on accredited institutions of teacher education.

In view of the institutional and economic crisis of 2001, priorities became initial literacy and the basic learning of language and mathematics. With economic recovery, the array of actions has been expanded. One can state that, from the legislative and practical points of view, in Argentina, as well as in South America as a whole, educators make up one of the groups most benefited by lifelong learning actions, in spite of the fact that this is, sometimes, sporadic, non-systematic, and doubtfully effective. Distance education and blended courses have been an important resource for continued training in teaching, mainly in countries that are more privileged with new technologies of information and communication.

## *Bolivia*

Bolivia, one of the richest countries in the world in natural resources, especially gas, and, at the same time, one of the poorest countries in South America, is going through great political-party transformations toward the left. Having a large Indian population, and also people of Indian descent, Bolivia's educational reform of 1995 was already concerned with "unity and diversity" and with the people's participation. The members of urban and rural communities have the right and the capability to become organized agents, whose action will affect the economic, social, and educational development of their districts. Education must be addressed to large national majorities; it must be intercultural and respectful of the country's several ethnic groups' identities. The former is organized into three components: adult, permanent, and special.

To demonstrate the significance of interculturalism, the current law proposes to "decolonize" education, building a "plurinational" educational system to encourage ample popular participation. Adult education consists of two years of basic education, two years of vocational education, and two years working in the world of production. As new technologies of education and communication (NTEC) are used in educational community telecenters, the gathering of students, faculty members, and the community is encouraged, mainly in the rural areas. The national Educational Portal is an electronic space used by teachers, students, and the community.

## *Brazil*

In Brazil, the educational boom is clear in the statistics, frequently underestimated regarding the identification of multiple partnership arrangements in adult education and lifelong learning in general, involving the third sector and community, and private, for-profit initiatives. Based on the 2000 Census and other data, that year, there were at least 72.3 million students in all areas, from a total population of 169.8 million, that is, 42.6 percent. In the TVET Census, enrollment of at least 6.8 percent of the economically active population was recorded. However, this is the tip of the iceberg, to which a wide diversity of short- and medium-term courses of the Ministry of Labor, in agreements with the labor unions, the third sector, and other entities, must be added. In addition to the action of the Ministry of Labor, Brazil relies on the so-called S-system, a para-state system of professional training, created in World War II, which inspired several similar organizations in South America. Its main source of financing is a quasi-tax on the payroll, destined to a system for each economic sector. In 2000, it had a total enrollment of at least 16.2 million adult students, 7.7 million of whom were enrolled in updating courses (Manfredi, 2002).

The SESI Worker Education program, part of that system, assisted over one million adults in literacy training and in primary and secondary education over the past five years. Such a number can only be reached by way of different partnerships, with UNESCO, companies, governments on all levels, and NGOs. To meet the workers' needs and possibilities, the program offers a broad array of courses, combining in-class and distance training. It is the clear recognition, mainly by employers, that general education is the foundation needed to improve productivity.

In its turn, the S-system organization dedicated to the rural sector integrates TVET with social promotion, bearing in mind the conditions of the Brazilian rural society, whose social indicators are below the average. The underlying concept is that productivity depends on general education and on the preparation of the society for better living standards and treatment of the environment (see Gomes and Câmara, 2004).

Among the countless second-opportunity education projects are MOVA and Veredas, offered by NGOs with different partnerships. According to Paulo Freire's philosophy, these projects value the culture of communities and often employ teachers from those communities, who know their students and their reality. Another program, Solidary Literacy, has focused on the areas with lower levels of human development, being in charge of over two million literate students 15 years old or over. Having become literate, participants then have access to adult education and occupational training programs sponsored by the Ministry of Labor. It is equally important to mention the university extension programs, especially the confessional, community, and public programs that focus on lifelong learning specifically for the elderly. They represent a growing challenge for the country, since their numbers tend to grow steadily, with the extension of longevity, while birth and fertility rates are decreasing. In many cases, the total number of people who benefit from these programs is more than twice the number of regular students enrolled in those university programs (Gomes, 2002).

In addition, we must add the countless lifelong learning programs and initiatives for educators in the three levels of government (federal, state, and municipal) and in higher education institutions. And we should highlight the Pro-training (Proformação), distance training for non-graduated teachers, of the Ministry of Education. Therefore, there are networks with multiple forms and capacity of reaching even smaller numbers of students, but their quality and effectiveness, very often, are their weak spots.

## Colombia

Among several activities, Colombia, a country considered to be medium-sized, has programs focused on vulnerable groups, such as Indians, scattered rural populations, refugees from civil conflicts, and handicapped people. Flexible methodologies are used, including distance education, tutorial assistance, and accelerated learning. The traditional division of the curriculum into yearly grades, in these cases, was substituted for structured curriculum units, that is, the cycles were integrated in order to consider the differences in learning paces. An important lesson, especially from Argentina and Colombia, is that it is not good to expand access indiscriminately, but to focus on different needs and population groups, although flexibly.

Ongoing faculty training associated with career progress, as in most of South America, is under the responsibility of a committee in each territorial entity. In view of the existing priorities, the committee signs agreements with educational institutions. A promising initiative in this field involved the Caldas digital literacy website to make the adoption of new information and communication technologies easier. Results were significant in terms of the development of awareness and the training of teachers, as expressed by the broad utilization of the educational website, which had 9,000 daily visits one year after its creation. Other South American countries, such as Venezuela, have also created educational websites with a broad scope of resources for teachers. However, the digital divide in the continent remains a serious obstacle, even in regions with a relatively high level of development.

## Ecuador

Ecuador has a small territory and population, but it is an oil exporter that is going through great leftist political changes. Just as in Bolivia and in other countries, the Indian ethnic groups, in the lower strata of society since colonization, play an increasingly more active role in the country, demanding multiculturalism or interculturalism. Adult education has developed in the context of popular, permanent education, and the courses can be in-class or distance. In the latter case, as was to be expected, educational work does not follow a pre-established schedule or a calendar, in order to adjust to the students' capabilities, to the climate, and to the demands of agricultural cycles and of the respective localities. Rural education and the education of ethnical-linguistic minorities deal with the less socially privileged population groups. One of the persistent problems is the offer of education in Spanish, with teachers who often ignore their students' idiom and cultural standards. Hence, the government develops national and regional literacy programs, permanent popular education programs, and intercultural education programs.

## Paraguay

Paraguay is a smaller country, with about half the population speaking the Guarani Indian language as its first language and the other half speaking Spanish, thus requiring bilingual education. Among its relevant experiences, there are five literacy and basic education programs for young people and adults:

- Reinvigorating the education of the population 15 years old and above. For that purpose, a pedagogical, curriculum, and teacher training superstructure has been organized.
- Distance literacy for young people and adults living in areas of difficult access. The professionals must have qualified training to work with adults.

- Distance training for teachers who hold only the teacher certificate at the secondary education level.
- The Active School, which aims at integrating the students' parents in the schools' education activities, seeking better quality education.
- In the area of new information and communication technologies, the country has not only encouraged distance education, including lifelong learning, but has also created a program for the renovation of technological resources. An educational website is dedicated to the public in general, to students, teachers, and parents, and also offers online courses. Several programs aim at the teachers' permanent teaching education and at raising their schooling level.

## Peru

Peru is also a medium-sized country, regarding territory, population, and economy, the seat of one of the greatest pre-Colombian empires. Hence, both in the Andes chain of mountains and on the coastline, there are many groups of Indians, thus making the country multiethnic and multilingual. These are the groups in which there is a concentration of illiteracy and underschooling. That is exactly why, during recent history, several literacy programs have been carried out for those of the population 15 years old and over. The legislation establishes that the literacy certificates give automatic access to the second grade of primary education. Where there is a lack of schools and adult primary education, post-literacy programs are offered, which are very important for the consolidation of the skills developed. Adult primary and secondary education is offered both in school form and in non-school form. In the latter case, in the non-school programs and the independent study programs, students receive teacher orientation, but they are not forced to attend classes, showing up for exams in a given group. People who have stopped studying for two or more years can take placement tests to be able to go on studying. In addition, adult education and community and environmental education promote, acknowledge, and value learning in the civil society.

## A Chilean case

Chile is a medium-sized country, with relatively high economic and social indicators and an internationalized economy. Even so, its social inequalities and income concentration are serious, as is characteristic of Latin America and the Caribbean. Despite progress in regular education, especially regarding access and efficiency, the country has sought to recover the time wasted in the field of adult education, which received less attention from public policies. The differences in quality among public, subsidized, and private schools constitute a glaring issue, which has mobilized society in favor of educational reform.

Lack of educational opportunities and failure feed adult education. Hence, there is a contrast between the demands of a globalized economy and the level of underschooling, mainly in the socially less privileged groups. The changes in the economy and in society have led to the social rise of part of the population, but also to unemployment, especially of youth, and to a descending social mobility. In order to face the double challenge of raising schooling and professional qualification, an innovative project was conceived of—*Chile Qualifies (workers)*, which is deserving of special mention. One of the project's innovations is that it is the result of the articulation among the Ministries of Education, Economy, Labor, and Social Welfare, with World Bank funding since 2002 (Chile, 2005; International Labour Organization, n.d.). This joining of ministries is particularly difficult to achieve, since traditional bureaucracies contribute to keep public policies compartmentalized, very frequently with a superposition of means for identical ends and, consequently, a waste of resources. That is why the permanent education and qualification system proposes to offer its contribution to the country's productive development and to the improvement of opportunities in people's lives.

For that to occur, it associates adult general education with TVET, promoting progress in one and the other, both vertically and horizontally, keeping bridges between the levels of general education and TVET. Hence, there are different entrances to and exits from the same training levels. A student can conclude one stage in general education and then take the TVET course at the corresponding level, or do both stages simultaneously, at his or her own pace. Then he or she can go ahead in general education and progress a few steps in TVET, improving labor opportunities. Its main beneficiaries are: (1) the economically active population's poorest sectors, which need improvement in both their educational and occupational requirements; (2) young people and workers who will benefit from middle school and college technical training; and (3) the economically active population in general. Once the Chilean economy is strongly based on foreign trade and on the country's insertion into the large world economic networks, competitiveness depends on permanently improving the workers' skills. At the same time, social inequalities must be decreased, parts of the population must be incorporated into the modern economy, and those who have been excluded from it, due to underschooling, obsolescence of skills, and so on, must be reintegrated.

The program is divided into five activities:

- adult education for completing secondary education;
- improvement of work capability;
- improvement of technical education;
- certification of work competencies, including the use of previous work experience;
- information and guidance about the job market. This last activity leads to improvement in transparency, stimulating initiative, in the sense of identifying and seeking appropriate opportunities for work and study.

Several initiatives considered successful can be taken into account: the involvement of faculty by way of consultation on educational reform and the curriculum; the development of primary and secondary education programs; faculty training by means of the participation of the national universities and of scholarships abroad; and the construction of the National Evaluation and Certification System. Educational offerings are modular, and the curriculum is based on competencies. Simultaneously, the project has progressed in defining competency standards, validating them with representatives from the world of production and institutionalizing a system of competency certification by law. Such standards are the basis for student evaluation and, to a certain measure, evaluation of the project.

Therefore, to articulate a technical training system, where the units acted independently, three key principles were adopted:

- capability at work, as an organizational axis, so as to ensure communication between training and the world of production;
- the acknowledgement of the validity of the different alternatives available in technical training, such as work experience, systematic study time, or attendance at a technical school or on a specific training course;
- the differentiation and articulation of training levels (training in the occupations of adult basic education, medium-level technician, higher-level technician, and engineering).

Hence, the system achieves flexibility, including the creation of various training itineraries, through which workers can travel, between training and qualification periods, as they deem necessary, since they have a general base of competencies. This base serves to increase and accelerate the economically active population's capability of adjustment to changes in labor, in order to update skills and make occupational mobility easier.

Moving away from the traditional compartmentalization of bureaucracies, the program establishes networks, coordinating the productive, academic, and educational sectors' efforts, in order to meet labor needs. The Chilean government offers funding to these networks for three years, for them to construct regional and interregional communication. For example, in the capital, educational and entrepreneurial institutions make up a network involving the financial, telecommunications, and civil construction sectors. In the extreme south, in Patagonia, tourism was the sector chosen, given the special interest in nature.

The role of the state is that of development agent, with a subsidiary function to finance services contracted by means of a subvention to each student and minimal curriculum contents. There is still a subvention by results. Up to 2005, the program reached 64,300 effective beneficiaries, corresponding to an increase of 97.6 percent since 2002. The average cost per student was estimated at 101 pesos for that year.

The difficulties, however, are manifold when they focus on socially less gifted populations. An evaluation has revealed obstacles such as weak adult education, as a function of the students' heterogeneous profile, low self-esteem, lack of study habits, and little motivation. The summative evaluation of the project results, as well as the policies of a government presided over by a socialist woman, will possibly guide future routes.

## Concluding remarks

Lifelong learning is present in the South American reality, but it is still a dream for the majority of the population. Rival objectives lead to a hierarchy in which regular schooling has greater priority, followed by remedial education and, finally, lifelong learning. This does not mean that the legislation and the publications on the topic underestimate it: for decades, there have been enlightened provisions and statements that reconceptualize adult education from the lifelong perspective. Nevertheless, according to historical tradition, it is difficult to apply what is prescribed in the real world.

It is necessary to stress that, amid a lack of resources and often low government priority, adult education is re-functionalized by way of students constantly entering and leaving the formal system at different ages, thus contributing to its updating. This means that formal education needs to consider the rich experience background of mature students. Goals, curricula, and evaluation are to be appropriate to diversified needs.

In general, what can work towards amplifying and improving lifelong learning in South America are some essential points:

- state-oriented policies toward the constitution of intersectoral networks, with significant community participation;
- the broadening of the adult education concept provided by the Hamburg Declaration, meaning holistic lifelong learning, covering all aspects of life and comprising cultural, social, and economic activities, that is, an education meaningful to life and a meaningful life with education. In other words, education does not sustain itself alone; it is part of a larger fabric, whose threads make each other mutually stronger;

- attention to quality requirements as a means to avoid second-class education status for lifelong learning;
- active interaction between education and its cultural context, providing books and public libraries as a means to extend the effects of education throughout life;
- clear public, integrated policies for adult education, in order to improve access, efficiency, quality, and equity;
- provision of well-defined and relatively stable sources of funding;
- and, finally, since the increase in financial resources does not necessarily bring better educational results, ethical and technically competent management of public and private monies.

The lessons from the South American experiences point out some measures that do not work: mass campaigns, short-term projects, restricted literacy training and schooling, neglect of cultural features, narrow approaches in general, confusion between social inclusion and homogenization, unarticulated efforts, and segmented and/or overlapping social policies. The omnipotent state, supposedly capable of providing every kind of service alone, has proved to be an anachronistic model, whereas the minimal state has demonstrated itself to be a failure in this subcontinent for its absenteeism and malfunctioning of the "invisible hand."

As is suggested by the Chilean case, the educational gap between developed and developing countries can become wider, as time and space limits force them into quick educational and social changes, in a world increasingly more interdependent. If lifelong learning lags behind, put off by the more urgent needs of regular education and remedial adult education, the educational divide may become more serious in view of the society and of the economy of knowledge. This social and economic gap, within each country and between countries, is not good for anyone; very much the other way around, it becomes increasingly more destructive, the closer we are to each other, whether we want it or not. For example, illegal immigration to developed countries will not be forcefully prevented forever. Even more so, predatory development will make the Earth increasingly smaller for a growing population, with increasingly expanded inequalities. The current climatic problems are evidence of that. The elites in the developing and developed countries cannot put themselves in an illusive perspective, like that of Queen Marie Antoinette, on her Versailles "island," amid full-fledged revolution. Acting as soon as possible is avoiding unnecessary suffering. This is the hope that shines as a beacon.

## Note

1    We are grateful to Fabiano Duarte de Carvalho, Flávio Gonçalves da Rocha Castro, and Pedro Leite Carvalho for their assistance with our research.

## References

Clark, Burton (1978) "Adaptação das organizações e valores precários (Organizations adaptation and precarious values)," in Amitai Etzioni (ed.) *Organizações complexas* (*Complex Organizations*), São Paulo: Atlas, pp. 161–8.

Chile Ministério de Educación (2005) *Revista de Educación* 318 (issue on Chile Califica), Santiago: Ministério de Educación.

Gomes, Candido (2002) *Lifelong Learning in Brazil*, Paper presented at the United Nations Interagency Strategic Group Meeting on Lifelong Learning, Hamburg, Brasília: UNESCO-Brazil.

—— with Câmara, Jacira (2004) *Training for Rural Development in Brazil: SENAR*, Paris: FAO and UNESCO International Institute for Educational Planning.

International Labour Organization (ILO) (n.d.) *Jóvenes, formación y empleo* (*Youths, Education and Employment*), Centro Interamericano de Investigación y Documentación sobre Formación Profesional—CINTERFOR. Available online at www.cinterfor.org.uv/spanish/amprof/cinterfor/temas/youth/esp/observa/chi/chi_califica.htm (accessed October 16, 2006).

Kliksberg, Bernardo (2003) *Por uma economia com face mais humana* (*Toward an Economy with a More Humane Face*), Brasília: UNESCO.

Manfredi, Silvia (2002) *Educação professional no Brasil* (*Vocational Education in Brazil*), São Paulo: Cortez.

UNESCO (2005) *La educación de jóvenes y adultos in América Latina y el Caribe: hacia um estado del arte* (*Youth and Adult Education in Latin América and the Caribbean: A state of the art*), Santiago: UNESCO.

# 45

# Lifelong learning in the United States

*Arthur L. Wilson*

In broad strokes, lifelong learning in the US at various times has been understood as essential to fulfilling individual human development, to enabling citizen participation in democratic states, to training contributors to the economy, to emancipating and transforming individuals and/or society, and sometimes all these together. It might seem then that lifelong learning in its growing ubiquity is either bereft of any real meaning and therefore of little use or over-surplused with so many meanings that it is subject to whoever wants to do whatever with it. Given its now considerable history in several formulations spanning most of the decades of the last century, however, the tautological but almost always agreed to definition of lifelong learning as learning throughout the lifespan is, as Field phrased it, "beautifully simple" (2006: 1). Or is it? What sense can we make of an idea that can be put to so many uses yet presents itself as so self-evident?

The task here is to examine lifelong learning in the United States. Right at the beginning I want to say that the rhetorical thematics just described as associated with lifelong learning and lifelong education have remained remarkably consistent for decades in the US. The significant shift, however, has been in ideological construction and impact rather than rhetorical difference—that is, similar language has come to mean different things. Specifically, I will make three seemingly paradoxical observations about the concept of lifelong learning in the US: that it is and has been generally a presumption necessary to the theory and practice of adult education but one beyond need of criticism or reconstruction; that it rarely has been an object of serious inquiry; and that, despite the mounting debates about lifelong learning occurring elsewhere, the question of lifelong learning seems to have disappeared in the US, or perhaps better said, never really risen to prominence.

To present these observations I will briefly review the generally accorded history of lifelong learning that emerges early in the twentieth century, to its robust assertions in the 1960s and 1970s, to the morphing of "education" into "learning" in the 1990s, to the ensuing co-optations of lifelong learning as a policy vehicle for advancing the neoliberal human capital interests of developed countries and multinational corporations. Necessarily such a review will focus more on general trends in policy thought as well as some of the different movements in academic appraisals of and advocacy for lifelong learning. Necessarily quiescent are the voices of the many who in one way or another "provide" opportunities/demands for lifelong learning, for it seems we know much more about lifelong learners than we do about lifelong learning providers (Edwards, 1997; Field, 2006). A final word on perspective: it is quite apparent that generally the term "lifelong learning" has come to be the preferred term since the 1990s. Field (2006) tends to see lifelong learning as the penultimate term because of its complex insinuation into and contribution to convoluted social, political, economic modern times (whether "late," "hyper," or "post" being of course open to much debate). That is useful contextualizing, but here I tend to favor Boshier's (2005) assessment that *lifelong education* needs to be seen as one ideological construct discursively culminating in/from the Faure Report (1972), but that subsequently *lifelong learning* has ideologically transcended the original construct to represent a constitutive production of an oppressive hegemonic regime that promotes the exploitation of workers/learners in the greater interests of capital. So, following on from Boshier (2005) and Edwards (1997), I see lifelong learning operating discursively to produce different regimes of truth (Foucault, 1980) that enable its active participation in what would sometimes seem contradictory interests and intentions. As Boshier (2005) illustrates (see also Fairclough, 1992), a discursive analysis enables questions of political economy in addition to the traditional functionalist analyses of lifelong learning's relationships to humanism, emancipation, and citizenship. I will not try to sort that out too historically in the US except to say that Boshier's clear parsing is preceded in the US by the largely undifferentiated and routinely synonymous use of the two terms as far back as the 1920s (with both often being employed as synonyms for "adult education").

## A grand narrative?

Grand narratives of course have been out of favor for some time now. That does not mean that they do not exist to ideologically shape the way people make sense of things. As Foucault (1973) would say, despite the plethora of varied statements, there often is a formulating structure of similar meaning. Depending upon how one unpacks them, the several lifelong learning philosophic, programmatic, and normative intentions (individual development, active citizenry, contributory worker reform or transformation) that intertwine significantly over the decades vary less than might be supposed. I will briefly review a general historical accounting of such intentions as background for the American situation.

There are numerous accounts of lifelong education/learning that definitely vary in emphases, nuances, ideology, and sometimes even "facts" (e.g. Bélanger, 1997; Boshier, 2005; Field, 2006; Holford and Jarvis, 2000; Jarvis, 2006; Youngman, 1998) but that vary considerably less in what they have to say about the course of lifelong learning/education over the decades. A rough outline of a history of lifelong learning/education gleaned from such sources might read something like this. While the 1960s and 1970s are routinely pointed to as the halcyon days of lifelong education, with the high-water mark by most accounts being the Faure Report (1972), historically the concepts of lifelong learning and lifelong education were "at work" in adult education much earlier. That earlier appearance is usually linked with the "intellectual ferment" (Fields, 2006: 12) surrounding post-World War I issues such as workers' rights and women's suffrage. Then the accounts generally leap to that intellectually strident time of the student movements of the late 1960s, during which much criticism was leveled at all levels of education. The accounts typically celebrate the efforts of UNESCO, through the aegis of the Faure Report, to imagine and employ a thoroughly lifespanning system of educational organizations and opportunities for adults. This humanist effort in and around UNESCO saw an emerging counter-discourse in the 1970s beginning to be promoted by the Organization for Economic Cooperation and Development (OECD) as an interest in and focus on the development of human capital. Then silence descends: "For much of the 1980s, the international and intergovernmental bodies found relatively little to say on the topic" (Field, 2006: 15). Bélanger (1997) attributes the silence to the fading in the 1970s of the unprecedented post-World War II economic expansion and looming economic turmoil, such as the oil crisis, rising unemployment, and inflation. Further, "the global vision of lifelong learning of the early seventies gave very little space to . . . the emerging new social movements . . . striving for the acknowledgement of difference" (p. viii). As corollary, Bélanger suggests, the vision of a universal lifelong education collapsed under its own grand narrative, which became increasingly suspect as a product of modernity. Then lifelong learning "returns" in the 1990s with the turning of "education" to "learning," by which lifelong learning contributed a key policy ingredient to governmental and intergovernmental organizations' efforts to promote competitiveness and economic growth: "when subjected to closer inspection, much of the policy interest in lifelong learning has in fact been preoccupied with a rather narrow agenda, namely the development of a more productive and efficient workforce" (Field, 2006: 3). Field argues that, whereas this economic interpretation significantly colors the burgeoning of lifelong learning at the millennium, there is a much broader story to tell, which he does in detail. I do not disagree. But Boshier more trenchantly cites the presumably innocuous linguistic shift of education to learning as an ideologically discursive manifestation that produces a new regime of truth signifying the need for humans to adapt to the needs of the global economy as well as "an attempt to shift responsibility for education from governments to individuals" (2005: 373). This is much in contrast to, and I suggest more critically precise than, the typically flaccid policy exhortations of governmental and intergovernmental agencies about the utility of lifelong learning and banal claims such as that of the Commission of the European Communities' *Memorandum on Lifelong Learning* that lifelong learning "must accompany a successful transition to a knowledge-based economy and society" by "promoting active citizenship and promoting employability" (2000: 3, 5).

It is not so much that difference resides in and among the various themes constituting lifelong learning/education over the decades as from whence the major ideological heft comes: the major shift is from humanist/progressive interests in human development to neoliberal interests in flexible workers for capital accumulation. While building ever since the neoconservative beginnings in the Reagan–Thatcher years (note the early work of the OECD), it is in the 1990s that the full blossom of the new capitalism begins to wreak its havoc over so much of the world, while continuing the upward spiral of its benefits for those fortunate enough to compete or privilege their way into its vanguard. Of the many indicators of the general ideological shift from socially conscious upwardly mobile class interests to the social, political, and economic oligarchies now orchestrating many developed nations over the last generation or so, one of keen interest to educators is this wholesale shift from "education" to "learning" that became prominent in the 1990s. As to adult education, Boshier (2005) gets this quite right, I think. Long challenging adult educators to pay more heed to the Faure Report (e.g. Boshier, 1997), Boshier (2005) repeats Faure's (1972) recommendation for lifelong education to consist of "a more pluralistic and accessible array of opportunities for education throughout the life-cycle" (2005: 374). Boshier argues that providing such an array requires not a "tinkering" but "a complete overhaul of entire educational systems," and that lifelong education was a "master concept for educational reform" (p. 375; following on, I might suggest that it is within such a reformist/transformationalist stance that some American adult educators, although not its middle-class mainstream, historically have tried to define the practical, organizational, and policy work of adult educators as educators). In contrast to the vision of Faure, Boshier delivers a paint-peeling depiction of neoliberal lifelong learning as "less emancipatory" orientations that

514

render invisible any obligation on educators to address social conditions. Predatory capitalism is unproblematized. Lifelong learning is nested in an ideology of vocationalism. Learning is for acquiring skills that enable the learner . . . to help the employer compete in the global economy . . . It avoids hard choices by putting learning on the open market. If the learner as consumer does not take advantage . . . it is their own fault . . . Learning is an individual activity.

(p. 375)

And, I would add, individuals not needing educators, as the prescient warnings of some (e.g. Edwards, 1997; Finger and Asun, 2001; Usher *et al.*, 1997) become increasingly true. So Field's (2006) "silent explosion" of adult learning has a devastating corollary with adult educators losing what little foothold they had on the educational terrain. If one were to care about such, the real practical importance and consequence of this seemingly innocuous and innocent shift from lifelong education to lifelong learning is that learners become unmoored from educators located in specific delivery systems to drift "freely" in the open market and subject to the demands of unfettered capitalism (Boshier, 2005). Let's see where the US might fit in this grand narrative.

## A US narrative

Right from the beginning of American efforts to organize adult education in the 1920s were the questions of professionalization, subject matter, and learners: who were they, what were they going to learn, and who would teach them (Wilson, 1993). Lifelong education/learning solved many of these questions and provided the ideological justification as well as programmatic necessity of a whole additional system of education that was not simply a continuation of that already in place for children—and hence, of course, the need for adult educators. Initial efforts to conceptualize and put into practice things like individual adult development and citizen participation emanated from a developmental progressivism drawn from John Dewey via Eduard Lindeman's sometimes nearly verbatim appropriations. The American emphasis from the beginning of the twentieth century was on a lifetime of learning for individual development with "good" citizenship as consequence. Lindeman was absolutely adamant that learning was a lifelong process:

A fresh hope is astir . . . the call to a new kind of education with its initial assumption affirming that *education is life* . . . the whole of life is learning . . . education can have no endings. This new venture is called *adult education*.

(1926: 4–5; italics in original)

In one of the first major theoretical statements—and one of the most repeatedly cited sources of theoretical inspiration for generations to come—there was a conflation of lifelong learning with lifelong education. And either and both were essential for individual development and active democratic citizenry (Lindeman believed adult education was sullied if in any way connected to vocationalism). But none of that development and participation mattered if the final focus was not on social transformation:

Orthodox education may be a preparation for life but adult education is an agitating instrumentality for changing life . . . Adult education will become an agency of progress if its short term goal of self-improvement can be made compatible with a long-time, experimental but resolute policy of changing the social order.

(pp. 104–5)

These major American understandings of lifelong education and lifelong learning emerge early and are the major conceptual and practical understandings from the 1930s to the 1980s that dominated both the practice of adult education and the study of it in the US. Thus the premise of lifelong learning/education gets set early and remains taken for granted from then on. The "beautifully simple" idea becomes the justification for the professional construction of adult education and thus becomes beyond question itself.

Lindeman's immigrant socialism, which tinged Dewey's progressivism with tones of radical social change, was soon muted, however. While there are many reasons for the moderation, Lyman Bryson (1936) begins to take the fierce edge off Lindeman's call to social action by saying that "the characteristic of a better society will be the more generous provision of opportunity for self-improvement" (1936: 8) because adult educators now knew then that "a person should attempt to learn what he [sic] needs when he needs it, and that age should be considered an unimportant factor" (1936: 9). By the 1950s, because of the growing interest in and research about adult development and the rise of Maslowian and Rogerian theory and research, a strong humanist dimension, already always there in the thought and practice of adult education, gets wedded with the progressive experiential roots. No more telling of this ideological packaging of thought is the ascendancy in the 1970s of Malcolm Knowles's borrowing of andragogy from its European origins. Knowles's reconstruction is essentially Lindeman's position on lifelong learning (sans the radical social critique) with Bryson's self-development in the forefront, all combined with many practical insights from his own career as a program administrator. Knowles's introduction of andragogy depended centrally upon lifelong learning and has dramatically shaped the intellectual perspective of American adult education ever since. But the ideological structure supporting the successful advent of andragogy in the 1970s was already well established by the 1950s (Wilson and Cervero, 1997). Consider Knowles's often overlooked *Informal Adult Education* (1950). Within it are clearly contained early programmatic thoughts that would define themselves later as andragogy, with a stronger democratic emphasis than that which would characterize his later efforts. With its presence certified in the late 1920s by Thorndike's initial studies of adult learning, lifelong learning became and remained a central and logically necessary premise to the progressive-humanist-andragogy regime of thought in American academic adult education, certainly from the 1950s through the 1980s (see Brunner *et al.*, 1959; Knowles, 1950, 1970; Jensen *et al.*, 1964). As Boshier (e.g. 1997, 2005) is wont to remind us, academic adult educators tend to overlook the significance of the 1972 Faure Report. One way to gauge its significance is to examine how closely its principles, practices, and recommendations for lifelong education parallel the state of theory in American adult education in the 1960s and 1970s. Although the report might be thought idealistic by some (Boshier, 2005), its tenets and prescriptions closely aligned with what passed for the normative and intellectual center of American academic adult education. It would appear of no small coincidence or consequence that Mondale's unfunded Lifelong Learning Act appeared in the 1976.

This package of thought coalesces in the 1950s and comes to dominate graduate training (and still does largely today) until the infusion of Jürgen Habermas's thinking through the work of Jack Mezirow's transformational theory in the 1980s. With the shift from andragogy, a fundamentally humanist-progressive orientation centered on individual experience and development, to transformational theory, a fundamentally critical humanist development theory centered on critical rationalist thought (not that much of an ideological shift), a growing number of adult educators in the US academy began to recreate (some argued, return to) a space in the study of adult education for a more radical transformationist stance that made space for the class, gender, race, sexual orientation, and diaspora interests that have come to fill the pages of the *AERC Proceedings* in the past decade and a half.

One consequence of the displacement of andragogy by transformational theory beginning in the 1980s was a social critique challenging the benign optimism inherent in progressivism/ humanism for an always improving future. As the critical margins gained presence in American adult education research and theory practice, the very question of progressive foundations was at least implicitly critiqued on the grounds suggested earlier by Bélanger (1997): how could we continue to believe in an ever improving society when it was so obvious that so much inequality and oppression needed attention? That is not to say that the progressive-humanist-andragogy regime was not interested in democratic practice and social equality, for they certainly were (see Knowles, 1950, and the 1948, 1960, 1970 American Handbooks). But it is to say that the critical intellectual frame of analysis that emerges in the 1980s has a different theory of society upon which it bases its criticality. Nor is this to say that the progressive/humanist foundations of much American adult education intellectual capital are still not prominent today. I dare say that the dominant ethos of most American adult education graduate programs, as indeed nearly any practitioner regardless of whether they are even aware of being an adult educator, is still the one of a "helping profession" founded on caring. But as a minor collision of regimes of truth, the critical turn in the 1980s and 1990s never seemed to raise any questions about the field's foundational belief in lifelong learning. I doubt there is a graduate program in the US today whose foundation course does not celebrate the field's long attachment to and support of lifelong learning. But I also see little intellectual engagement with the idea given its central role in providing justification for the very idea of adult education in the US.

By the 1990s the typically undifferentiated invocation of lifelong education/learning, which routinely configures in greater or lesser degrees a concatenation of individual development, vocationalism, citizenry, and various ranges of reform/transformation, clearly still has a presence in American understandings of adult education, at least in terms of graduate professional and academic training. One would have expected, with the continued success of the Conservative Restoration in the US through Bush I and Bush II, a similar paralleling of lifelong educational policy to that of other neoliberal governments. But there are no comparable White Papers in the US in the 1990s like those appearing in European policy debates, even though many American academics were aware of and even attended the UNESCO conference in Hamburg in 1997. Even in subsequent "transatlantic dialogues" between various adult education research conferences, the subject and debates about lifelong learning were clearly of importance among participants; but there seems relatively little participation by Americans on the topic of lifelong learning itself. A search of the premier American journal, the *Adult Education Quarterly*, reveals hundreds of invocations of "lifelong learning," appearing regularly since the 1950s, but little sustained engagement with the concept. The small spate of theoretical writings appearing in the *Quarterly* over the last decade or so are nearly all from non-American contributors (e.g. Edwards and Usher, 2001; Glastra *et al.*, 2004; Hake, 1999), contributing to the debates as they are occurring in the British Isles and on the Continent, not in the US. Nor do I think it an accident that the authors of the lifelong learning and learning society chapter in the American 2000 Handbook (Holford and Jarvis, 2000) were English. An electronic search of the US Department of Education, a cabinet level ministry, invoked over 500 references to lifelong learning (admittedly many of obscure or non-existent connection). The few substantive references refer to very traditional educational components of early and middle twentieth-century American policy on lifelong learning, such as adult literacy, citizenship education, vocational education, English as a Second Language, public libraries and reading, and so on. There are a few position papers, although nothing on American lifelong learning since the 1990s, and those that are are about lifelong learning in other countries or the role of the OECD in promoting lifelong education. The motto of the Department of Education is "promoting educational excellence for all Americans," seemingly a promising stance, but the bulk of the lifelong learning references are about the current administration's kindergarten through twelfth-year public schooling "No Child Left Behind" policy, a policy of accelerated standardized testing for compliance measures. The Secretary of Education testified about lifelong learning to Congress on April 15, 2005 that "we need to have courage to change the way we do business. This change starts with public education. No government program available at age 20 can make up for a poor education from ages 5–18" (Spelling, 2005). It would seem all is too quiet on this front.

## End of story?

Lifelong learning is still a very active constituent voice in America; it has reached a level of currency far exceeding any other term for the education and learning of adults. In the US in the 1960s, despite several decades of confirming research, the idea that adults could indeed learn throughout their lifespans was still largely a novelty to the general public, government policy makers, and corporate organizations, whereas now few would contest that civil, market, and government sectors routinely now depend upon lifelong learning. Similarly, from the very beginnings of the profession of adult education in the US, there has been a professional goal to make the idea of adult education as ubiquitous as is the notion of children's education. From the perspective of creating a recognized adult education profession, that has never happened in the US. The numbers who consciously conceive of themselves as practitioners or scholars are far exceeded by those who simply do adult education without so naming themselves under some other institutional or professional guise. Lifelong learning, however, as a presumably self-evident concept, is routinely bandied about as if there is no possibility of misunderstanding. A generation ago it was described as "enlightened common sense" (Darkenwald and Merriam, 1982: 3). Perhaps that is so. But the 500 questionably connected references to lifelong learning in the US Government's department and the hundreds more in the *Adult Education Quarterly* would suggest otherwise. Can they all mean the same thing? Is Field right when he describes lifelong learning as "beautifully simple"? As the term has grown in ubiquity it correspondingly seems to have lost much interest to those in the US who might stand to benefit the most from promoting it.

There are likely many reasons for a diminished presence of discourses on lifelong learning in the US. Field argues that "while policy debate has tended to focus largely on the economic dimensions of lifelong learning, most academic and theoretical debate has presented lifelong learning overwhelmingly as emancipatory" (2006: 18). As I indicated earlier, one might assume such in the US, as the critical emancipatory project of transformational learning has come to prominence in American intellectual efforts, yet it apparently has done so without any real focus on lifelong learning per se. Perhaps Merriam and Brockett (1997) are right when they suggest that lifelong learning is really an "international" term that is too broad a concept for what Americans think of as adult education. Maybe that is why the policy rhetoric of agencies like the European Commission never seemed to light the same fire in the US in the 1990s. There certainly is no end of multinational capitalists promoting the need for flexible workers in a knowledge economy but the White Papers and Congressional legislative efforts never materialized in the US. Although I have now given up such alarmist practices, until recently I continued to warn graduate students to expect such. Another possibility is that, in the US over the last 20 years or so, many adult education graduate programs have "added on" or converted to human resource and/or training and development programs. One way to think of these conversions is that, in order to survive in increasingly corporatizing higher education economies in the US, adult educators have renamed and reprogrammed themselves to more directly serve the interests of capital. More in line with the discursive analysis here would be Boshier's (2005) argument that lifelong learning has been captured by the neoliberal agenda of privatizing everything; lifelong learning is now a significant pillar of a regime of oppression in which governments are excused from their historically important social contracts as more and more policy and resources are allocated to the production of capital.

Field (2006: 4) argues for "holding on to the concept of lifelong learning" because the "silent explosion in lifelong learning is only partly driven by economic changes." True enough, but we cannot minimize the ascendancy of the political economy of lifelong learning in the era of "turbo capitalism" (Finger and Asun, 2001) and its undermining of the classic normative and political intentions of lifelong learning (Boshier, 2005). Field further argues that "whatever the weaknesses . . . something new is underway. Lifelong learning is not a myth, mish-mash, a fashion or a discourse" (2006: 4) and points to the "need to understand critically what policy-makers are doing" because lifelong learning "is now a mechanism for exclusion and control" (p. 5). Exclusion and control are precisely the issue. I am not saying anything not said before in saying that the classic rhetoric of lifelong learning has been reproduced to a new ideological agenda. So, lifelong learning is not a myth or a fashion but it just as clearly is a mish-mash and definitely a discourse with real consequences for people's lives. If life is about learning, it always has been so. Lifelong learning is not a new phenomenon at all, but our ideological use and interpretations have changed and the change is ominous. Lifelong learning has been co-opted to further the neoliberal agenda—it is being used to produce and concentrate capital and it is being done through the consent of the governed. That is what is new and our interests in using it to various ends, whether humanistic, transformational, or hegemonic, need fierce focus. Is it worth keeping as a "linguistic reach" for an "intellectual forum" to "engage in debate over something that matters" (Field, 2006: 6)? Yes, if we adult educators are going to question the practices of oppression—which raises the next question, so eloquently put by Richard Edwards (1997), and that is, where on this "moorland" do we as educators stand? Have we "failed to engage with the complexities" of our practices "on the assumption of the inherent worth and good intentions" (p. 21) of that work? As Edwards points out, there is irony in raising such questions from within the academy, like biting the hand that feeds us. But, as I suggest, if we have lost control of this discourse, then we have lost control of our practice—or perhaps just simply forgotten this ever-so-important arena for the work of adult educators, as the Americans seem to have.

## References

Bélanger, P. (1997) "Keynote: the astonishing return of lifelong learning," in National Institute for Educational Research in Japan and UNESCO Institute for Education (eds) *Comparative Studies on Lifelong Learning Policies*, Tokyo: Research Department of Lifelong Learning, National Institute for Educational Research of Japan, pp. vii–xii..

Boshier, R. (1997) "Edgar Faure after 25 years: down but not out," in J. Holford, C. Griffen, and P. Jarvis (eds) *Lifelong Learning: Reality, rhetoric and public policy*, Guildford: University of Surrey, Department of Educational Studies, pp. 44–9.

—— (2005) "Lifelong learning," in L. English (ed.) *International Encyclopedia of Adult Education*, Basingstoke: Palgrave Macmillan, pp. 373–8.

Brunner, E., Wilder, D., Kirchner, C., and Newberry, J. (1959) *An Overview of Adult Education Research*, Chicago, IL: Adult Education Association of the USA.

Bryson, L. (1936) *Adult Education*, New York: American.

Commission of the European Communities (2000) *Commission Staff Working Paper: A memorandum on lifelong learning*, Brussels: Commission of the European Communities.

Darkenwald, G. and Merriam, S. (1982) *Adult Education: Foundations of practice*, New York: Harper and Row.

Edwards, R. (1997) *Changing Places? Flexibility, lifelong learning, and a learning society*, London: Routledge.

—— and Usher, R. (2001) "Lifelong learning: a postmodern condition of education?," *Adult Education Quarterly* 51(4): 273–87.

Fairclough, N. (1992) *Discourse and Social Change*, Cambridge: Polity.

Faure, E. (Chair) (1972) *Learning to Be*, Paris: UNESCO.

Field, J. (2006) *Lifelong Learning and the New Educational Order*, 2nd revised edn, Stoke on Kent: Trentham.

Finger, M. and Asun, J. (2001) *Adult Education at the Crossroads: Learning our way out*, London: Zed Books.

Foucault, M. (1973) *The Birth of the Clinic: An archaeology of medical perception* (trans. A.M. Sheridan Smith), New York: Pantheon.

—— (1980) *Power/Knowledge: Selected interviews and other writings, 1972–1977*, New York: Pantheon.

Glastra, F., Hake, B., and Schedler, P. (2004) "Lifelong learning as transitional learning," *Adult Education Quarterly* 54(4): 291–307.

Hake, B. (1999) "Lifelong learning in late modernity: the challenges to society, organizations, and individuals," *Adult Education Quarterly* 49(2): 79–90.

Holford, J. and Jarvis, P. (2000) "The learning society," in A. Wilson and E. Hayes (eds) *Handbook of Adult and Continuing Education*, San Francisco, CA: Jossey-Bass, pp. 643–59.

Jarvis, P. (2006) *Towards a Comprehensive Theory of Learning: Lifelong learning and the learning society*, vol. 1, London: Routledge.

Jensen, G., Liveright, A., and Hallenbeck, W. (1964) *Adult Education: Outlines of an emerging field of university study*, Chicago, IL: Adult Education Association of the USA.

Knowles, M. (1950) *Informal Adult Education: A guide for administrators, leaders, and teachers*, New York: American Association for Adult Education.

—— (1970) *The Modern Practice of Adult Education: Andragogy versus pedagogy*, New York: American Association for Adult Education.

Lindeman, E. (1926) *The Meaning of Adult Education*, New York: New Republic.

Merriam, S. and Brockett, R. (1997) *The Profession and Practice of Adult Education*, San Francisco, CA: Jossey-Bass.

Spelling, M. (2005) *Secretary Spelling Testifies on Lifelong Learning: Part I: Improving high schools*. Available online at www.ed.gov/news/newsletters/extracredit/2005/04/0415.html (accessed April 3, 2007).

Usher, R., Bryant, I., and Johnston, R. (1997) *Adult Education and the Postmodern Challenge: Learning beyond the limits*, London: Routledge.

Wilson, A. (1993) "The common concern: controlling the professionalization of adult education," *Adult Education Quarterly* 44(1): 1–16.

—— and Cervero, R. (1997) "The song remains the same: the selective tradition of technical rationality in adult education planning theory," *International Journal of Lifelong Education* 16(2): 84–108.

Youngman, F. (1998) "Old dogs and new tricks? Lifelong education for all—the challeng facing adult education in Botswana," Inaugural Lecture delivered at the University of Botswana, April 8, 1998. National Institute of Development Research (NIR), no. 15, University of Botswana.

# Index